Praise for *Unnatural Law*

Humankind is undergoing an unprecedented and
totally unsustainable growth in numbers, technology,
consumption, and economic demand. Environmental
degradation is a direct consequence. Without a
fundamental understanding of our utter dependence
on nature for our physical, social, economic, and
spiritual sustenance and health, we become predators
embarked on a suicidal path.

Environmentalists have long pressed for better
legislation – tougher laws, harsher penalties, more
enforcement. David Boyd's monumental work reveals
the fatal weakness of the patchwork quilt of legislation that results because laws are invariably cobbled
together when environmental crises are encountered
rather than attempting to avoid such crises in advance.

Boyd's analysis is exhaustive and the comparison
with other countries, especially Sweden, is quite
revealing of our weaknesses. There is a vast opportunity for improvement, but only after Boyd's critique
has been fully digested and understood. He reminds
us that as biological creatures, we require clean air,
water, soil, energy, and biodiversity and once that is
acknowledged, the path of legislation is obvious: to
protect those needs for all life above anything else.
That would be legislation for genuine sustainability.

*David T. Suzuki, Chair of the David Suzuki Foundation, and
an award-winning scientist, environmentalist, and broadcaster*

David Boyd's magisterial work takes the often technical and dry subject of environmental law to its proper realm to show what really happens on the ground, in the water, and the air – and why. He presents a clear diagnosis and compelling prescription for Canada's appalling environmental record. Here, finally, is a well-written, comprehensive, and proactive strategy to overcome the false dichotomy of economic and environmental imperatives. In the post-Kyoto world, *Unnatural Law* gives us a roadmap to a sustainable future.

> *Michael M'Gonigle, Professor of Law, holding the Eco-Research Chair in Environmental Law and Policy at the University of Victoria, and a co-founder of Greenpeace International*

This book is a must-read for all Canadians concerned about our natural resources. They will be shocked to learn that our environmental laws and policies do little to protect the public interest.

> *David Schindler, Killam Memorial Professor of Ecology, University of Alberta*

Unnatural Law offers an outstanding contribution to the environment law and policy field through a comprehensive and critical review of the Canadian legal and political institutions and processes governing natural resource management and environmental protection.

> *David VanderZwaag, Professor of Law, Dalhousie University*

UNNATURAL LAW
Rethinking Canadian Environmental Law and Policy

DAVID R. BOYD

With a Foreword by Thomas R. Berger

A volume in
the Law and Society
series

UBCPress · Vancouver · Toronto

09 08 07 06 05 04 03   5 4 3 2 1

Printed in Canada on acid-free paper that is 100% post-consumer recycled, processed chlorine-free, and printed with vegetable-based, low-VOC inks.

National Library of Canada Cataloguing in Publication Data

Boyd, David R., (David Richard)
    Unnatural law : rethinking Canadian environmental law
    and policy / David R. Boyd.

    (Law & society series)
    Includes bibliographical references and index.
    ISBN 0-7748-1048-3 (bound). – ISBN 0-7748-1049-1 (pbk.)

    1. Environmental law – Canada. 2. Environmental policy –
Canada. I. Title. II. Series: Law and society series (Vancouver,
B.C.)

KE3619.B69 2003   344.71'046   C2003-910981-X
KF3775.ZA2B69 2003

Canadä

UBC Press gratefully acknowledges the financial support for our publishing program of the Government of Canada through the Book Publishing Industry Development Program (BPIDP), and of the Canada Council for the Arts, and the British Columbia Arts Council.

This book has been published with the help of a grant from the Canadian Federation for the Humanities and Social Sciences, through the Aid to Scholarly Publications Programme, using funds provided by the Social Sciences and Humanities Research Council of Canada, and with the help of the K.D. Srivastava Fund.

Set in Arrus and News Gothic by Artegraphica Design
Text design: Irma Rodriguez
Printed in Canada by Friesens
Copy editor: Sarah Wight
Proofreader: Deborah Kerr
Indexer: Christine Jacobs

UBC Press
The University of British Columbia
2029 West Mall
Vancouver, BC V6T 1Z2
604-822-5959 / Fax: 604-822-6083
www.ubcpress.ca

This book is dedicated
to the environmental lawyers who inspired me
to follow in their footsteps –
Harvey Locke, Wendy Francis,
Greg McDade, Stewart Elgie, Doug Chapman,
Mark Haddock, Kate Smallwood, Elizabeth May,
and Tom Berger.

Today, legal regimes
are being rapidly outdistanced by the accelerating pace
and expanding scale of impacts on the environmental
base of development. Human laws must be reformulated
to keep human activities in harmony with the unchanging
and universal laws of nature.

World Commission on Environment and Development, 1987

When I was in space
looking down on our magnificent blue and brown planet
Earth, I realized how truly unique Canada is. This country,
with its fresh water, soil, atmosphere, and various types
of climate, may well be the salvation of the whole planet.

Roberta Bondar, Canadian astronaut, 2000

Contents

PART TWO: DIAGNOSIS

PART THREE: PRESCRIPTION

Foreword

Disputes about the environment are often carried on at the top of our voices. Industry can always find reasons to justify its undertakings. Environmentalists can always find reasons to challenge industry's motives. One side regards its activities as essential to progress and economic well-being, the other feels a solemn duty to oppose industrial development that it regards as degrading the natural world.

Disputes over water, climate change, pesticides, parks, and a multitude of other subjects occupy us and preoccupy us. As they should. For in the twenty-first century these issues will loom ever larger. Especially, perhaps, for Canadians. We are a prosperous, educated people, with stewardship of a northern land mass that reaches from the Atlantic to the Pacific to the Arctic.

But we often do not speak with any real knowledge of the environmental regime already in place in Canada. For that regime may be required to be enforced, or improved, or reconsidered altogether. David Boyd in this book gives us a complete account of that regime – federally and provincially – as it applies to water, air, land and resources, and flora and fauna. If that were all that he had done in this book, it would be a notable achievement.

But he has gone on to provide a powerful analysis of the weaknesses of our environmental regime. His underlying concern is that current rates of consumption of energy and resources together with population growth lead necessarily toward environmental degradation, and that our legal regime, since it does not address these causes, has a limited ameliorative effect. It addresses only the symptoms. David Boyd has given us a road map in which the underlying issues are considered. And he has reminded us that we are not only citizens of Canada but also citizens of the world.

Can we alter our environmental regime so as to come to grips with these root causes? Only if we do so can we create a model of sustainability. And this means a reconsideration of the idea of unceasing growth.

David Boyd has examined our condition, given us a diagnosis, and written a prescription for a sustainable future. The doctor is in.

Thomas R. Berger, O.C., Q.C.

Preface

This book has three purposes: to provide an accurate assessment of the effectiveness of Canadian environmental laws and policies; to examine the reasons for Canada's progress (or lack thereof) in untangling the Gordian knot of environmental challenges; and perhaps most important, to provide some constructive guidance on the changes to laws and policies needed for Canada to become a global leader in the quest for a sustainable future. Accordingly, the book has three parts – an examination, a diagnosis, and a prescription – like the three stages a doctor goes through when a patient comes in for a check-up.

Part One, the examination, begins with an assessment of Canada's overall environmental record and identifies a gap between Canadian values and Canadian actions on a range of key environmental issues. Part One then examines the Canadian laws and policies, both federal and provincial, that are intended to protect water, air, land, and biodiversity. A concerted effort is made to go beyond analyzing the strengths and weaknesses of laws and policies *on paper*, to explore the vital question of *on-the-ground effectiveness*. Too often, environmental laws are viewed in an analytical vacuum, without reference to their consequences in the real world. Are Canadian governments creating effective environmental laws and policies? Are these laws and policies being implemented and enforced? Are health and environmental objectives being met? The balance of evidence will show that despite a handful of success stories, Canada's overall performance is poorer than that of other industrialized nations.

Part Two, the diagnosis, analyzes the reasons for Canada's mixed environmental record. Why do some environmental laws and policies result in significant improvements while others fail to produce progress? What are the obstacles to improving Canada's environmental laws and policies, and more important, Canada's environmental performance? Part Two concludes with a discussion of the critical, yet often unacknowledged, importance of addressing the root causes of environmental degradation.

Because of the overwhelming evidence that current legal approaches are inadequate for achieving sustainability, Part Three, the prescription, offers new directions for Canadian laws and policies. Part Three also outlines a range of practical solutions for addressing the excessive consumption of energy and resources that is at the heart of Canada's environmental problems. How can Canada apply the lessons from its environmental successes to its unresolved problems? How can Canada adapt the approaches that have led to superior progress toward sustainability in other northern industrialized nations? How can Canada redesign its laws and policies to reflect, respect, and incorporate the laws of nature? How can we reduce consumption while continuing to improve our quality of life?

It would be presumptuous to suggest that this book provides a complete blueprint of how Canada can achieve a sustainable future. The challenges we face are so formidable that American author Kai Lee argues that "sustainability is not a condition likely to be attained on earth as we know it. Rather it is more like freedom and justice, a direction in which we strive."[1] On the contrary, sustainability is more than a lofty ideal or a direction in which we strive; it is an ecological, social, and economic imperative. The very survival of humanity depends on achieving sustainability, and changes to laws and policies will play a crucial role in determining whether our efforts are successful.

Acknowledgments

I am indebted to Joel Solomon, Carol Newell, the Endswell Foundation, Christine Lee, Patrick Johnston, the Walter and Duncan Gordon Foundation, Dr. Michael M'Gonigle, Randy Schmidt, Wesley Pue, and UBC Press for supporting this book.

My heartfelt gratitude for invaluable advice, encouragement, and friendship is owed to Dr. Scott Harrison, Dr. Scott Wallace, Ben Parfitt, Kate Smallwood, and Jerry DeMarco. My appreciation also goes out to Rachel Plotkin and Rumon Carter for valuable research assistance on several chapters. I would like to thank Holly Keller-Brohman and Sarah Wight for the wisdom of their editorial advice.

Most importantly, writing this book would not have been possible without the extraordinary love, patience, and good humour of Margot Venton.

Acronyms

AAC	allowable annual cut
CBA	Canadian Bar Association
CCCE	Canadian Council of Chief Executives
CCME	Canadian Council of Ministers of the Environment
CEAA	*Canadian Environmental Assessment Act*
CEC	Commission for Environmental Cooperation
CEPA	*Canadian Environmental Protection Act*
CFC	chlorofluorocarbon
CFSA	*Crown Forest Sustainability Act*
COSEWIC	Committee on the Status of Endangered Wildlife in Canada
DFO	Department of Fisheries and Oceans
EA	environmental assessment
EPA	Environmental Protection Agency (US)
EU	European Union
GDP	gross domestic product
GPI	Genuine Progress Index
GST	Goods and Services Tax
HCFC	hydrochlorofluorocarbon
HFC	hydrofluorocarbon
IJC	International Joint Commission
IMF	International Monetary Fund
IPCC	Intergovernmental Panel on Climate Change
IPM	integrated pest management
ISEW	Index of Sustainable Economic Welfare
MAI	Multilateral Agreement on Investment
MMT	methylcyclopentadienyl manganese tricarbonyl
NAFTA	North American Free Trade Agreement
NPRI	National Pollutant Release Inventory

NRTEE	National Round Table on the Environment and the Economy
ODA	official development assistance
OECD	Organization for Economic Cooperation and Development
PCB	polychlorinated biphenyl
PCPA	*Pest Control Products Act*
PMRA	Pest Management Regulatory Agency
POP	persistent organic pollutant
UN	United Nations
VOC	volatile organic compound
WHO	World Health Organization
WMO	World Meteorological Organization
WTO	World Trade Organization

PART ONE

Examination

A careful investigation of the condition of a subject
to determine its health or fitness.

A solitary "wildlife tree," with a "do not disturb" sign nailed to its trunk, is left standing in a clearcut (overleaf) in a forest near Desolation Sound on BC's Sunshine Coast. Photographs by Todd Korol.

1 Canada's Environmental Record

Canada's environmental record is among the best in
the world.
Environment Canada, 1996

Canada is viewed as a world leader in sustainability.
*Ralph Goodale, Canada's Minister of Natural Resources,
1997-2000*

Canada's reputation far exceeds our track record, and
it has begun to fray, badly.
David Suzuki

Far too often, the government is not keeping the
promises it makes both to Canadians and the world.
*Brian Emmett, Canada's Commissioner on the Environment
and Sustainable Development, 1996-2000*

Is Canada an environmental leader or an environmental laggard? Are Canadians carefully safeguarding our natural legacy so that it is passed on, altered
but not degraded, to future generations? Or are we, despite our best inten-
tions, fraying the fabric of this natural legacy, passing on a land that is less
natural, less clean, less healthy, less diverse, and less awe-inspiring? In the
global picture, is Canada contributing to solving such environmental challenges as climate change, depletion of the ozone layer, and the loss of biological diversity, or are we exacerbating these problems?

Canada is one of the wealthiest nations on Earth in terms of our natural
heritage. Canada is blessed with countless rivers and lakes, sprawling forests,
thousands of kilometres of coastline along three great oceans, extensive wilderness areas, and abundant wildlife. From a natural resource perspective,
Canada is again gifted – endowed with plentiful fresh water, energy, minerals,

timber, fisheries, and farmland. Canadians enjoy spectacular beauty in all regions of the country, from maritime seascapes to big sky prairies, from mountain grandeur to the painter's palette of the Canadian Shield and the subtle splendour of the Arctic.

Canada's Environmental Ethic

In a vast, geographically and culturally diverse country like Canada, there are very few points on which the overwhelming majority of people agree. Somewhat surprisingly, a passion for the environment is one of those rare subjects of societal convergence. As a people, Canadians define themselves in terms of their natural heritage. Canada's national and provincial flags, coats of arms, and currency reflect Canadian landscapes and wildlife. A recent study found that the only two symbols embraced by all segments of the Canadian population are the natural environment and medicare. Similarly, Ian Angus, in his book *A Border Within*, searched Canada for common bonds and identified two unifying Canadian values: multiculturalism and a love of nature.[1]

The deep-rooted connection between individual Canadians and the natural world is demonstrated by the following statistics:

- 98 percent of Canadians view nature in all its variety as essential to human survival.
- 90 percent of Canadians consider time spent in natural areas as children very important.
- 85 percent of Canadians participate regularly in nature-related activities such as hiking, bird-watching, and fishing.
- 82 percent of Canadians say nature has very important spiritual qualities for them personally.[2]

This love of nature translates into a strong environmental ethic. According to public opinion polls, Canadians are among the most staunchly pro-environment people on the planet. Eight out of ten Canadians believe that environmental protection should be given priority over economic growth. This is the highest proportion of support for environmental protection in the thirty countries surveyed by the research firm Environics International.[3] Two studies found that nine out of ten Canadians feel either "a great deal of concern" or "a fair amount of concern" about the state of the environment, and that nine out of ten Canadians rate it as one of their top concerns.[4] Neil Nevitte, in his book *The Decline of Deference*, tracks values across a span of decades and concludes that environmental protection is becoming part of Canada's fundamental moral belief system.[5] Given that Canadians appear to be among the most environmentally conscientious people in the world, the question is obvious: Are Canadians walking the walk of environmental responsibility or just talking the talk?

Conflicting Perspectives on Canada's Environmental Record

Canada's performance on protecting the environment is the subject of lively debate. On one side, environmental groups are relentlessly critical and negative. Their mantra is that both Canadian and global environments are deteriorating rapidly, and that ecological collapse is imminent if dramatic changes are not made. Environmental groups have published reports attacking Canada for failing to protect biological diversity, mismanaging forests, failing to address climate change, failing to protect children's health, failing to protect drinking water, allowing destructive mining practices, flawed environmental assessment processes, and outdated pesticide laws.[6] Canada's foremost environmental spokesperson, renowned broadcaster and scientist David Suzuki, warned in 1990 that if society didn't turn things around in the next decade, "civilization as we know it will cease to exist."[7] Most Canadians lean toward this pessimism, with 82 percent professing in 1999 that they were "currently upset about threats to nature in Canada."[8] Scientists and environmental experts forecast further declines in environmental quality in the next ten to fifteen years, both in Canada and globally.[9]

On the other side of the debate, government and industry insist that environmental conditions are improving. Canadian governments, both federal and provincial, promote Canada as a world leader on environmental issues including forest management, clean mining practices, safe drinking water, pesticide regulation, environmental assessment, and achieving sustainable development.[10] The Fraser Institute calculated that environmental quality in Canada improved by 17 percent between 1980 and 2002 (excluding so-called secondary factors such as climate change, ozone depletion, and the loss of biodiversity).[11] According to the Fraser Institute, "Canadians can be proud of all we have accomplished to reduce pollution and protect our environment."[12]

Is Canada headed toward ecological disaster? Or, having peered over the precipice, is Canada now pulling back from the brink and moving toward a sustainable future? While facts can be marshalled to support both sides of this argument, neither of these extremes presents an accurate picture of Canada's environmental record. Environmentalists sometimes exaggerate the extent of problems and are reluctant to recognize progress, while government and industry tend to downplay environmental problems and exaggerate their successes. As is often the case in public policy debates, the truth is somewhere in the middle.

Canada's Environmental Performance

What are the straight goods, the facts, about Canada's environmental performance? A recent analysis conducted by the University of Victoria's Eco-Research Chair in Environmental Law and Policy examines twenty-five key environmental indictors in ten broad categories: air, water, energy, waste, climate change, ozone depletion, agriculture, transportation, biological diversity, and miscellaneous issues.[13] The analysis is based entirely on information gathered, verified, and published biannually by the Organization for Economic Co-operation and Development (OECD). The OECD includes the G7 nations (Canada, the United States, Japan, Germany, France, Great Britain, and Italy), Mexico, Korea, Australia, New Zealand, and nineteen other European nations.[14] Canada's environmental record is compared with the twenty-eight other industrialized nations in the OECD at the time of the study to put our record in context and to determine whether Canada is a leader or a laggard. Canada's performance is also tracked over two decades to accurately determine whether it is improving or worsening.

In the University of Victoria study, Canada's overall ranking is second last, better only than the United States (see Table 1). Canada is not among the five best countries on any of the twenty-five indicators and is among the five worst countries on seventeen of them. Canada is among the three worst countries in the OECD on nine indicators: emissions of greenhouse gases, sulphur dioxide, carbon monoxide, and volatile organic compounds; consumption of water and energy; energy efficiency; volume of timber logged; and generation of nuclear waste. Canada's economy is among the dirtiest and least efficient in the industrialized world, in that we generate much more pollution and use much more energy to produce a given amount of economic output than other OECD countries. For example, Canada uses 33 percent more energy per unit of gross domestic product (GDP) than the United States. Canada's performance on most of the environmental indicators continues to worsen, with increasing water and energy consumption, increases in nuclear and hazardous waste, higher greenhouse gas emissions, higher numbers of endangered species, declining fish populations, higher commercial fertilizer use, more livestock, more timber logged, more motor vehicles, more kilometres travelled by road, and less official development assistance (funds used to promote sustainable development in poor countries).

On a brighter note, two reasons for optimism emerge from the study. First, on ten indicators, Canada's record is improving. Substantial progress has been

Table 1

Canada's environmental ranking, compared to other OECD nations

Environmental indicator	Canada's OECD ranking	
	Per capita	Total
Air pollution		
Sulphur oxides (kilograms)	27th out of 28	27th out of 28
Nitrogen oxides (kilograms)	25th out of 28	25th out of 28
Volatile organic compounds (kilograms)	25th out of 26	25th out of 26
Carbon monoxide (kilograms)	26th out of 27	25th out of 27

▶

◀ **Table 1**

Environmental indicator	Canada's OECD ranking	
	Per capita	Total
Climate change		
Greenhouse gas emissions (tonnes of CO_2)	27th out of 29	25th out of 29
Ozone depletion		
Consumption of ozone-depleting substances (kilograms)	13th out of 16	13th out of 16
Water		
Water consumption (cubic metres)	28th out of 29	26th out of 29
Municipal sewage treatment (% of population served)	N/A	9th out of 28
Energy use		
Energy consumption (tonnes of oil equivalent)	27th out of 29	26th out of 29
Energy efficiency (tonnes of oil equivalent/ US$1000 GDP)	N/A	28th out of 29
Waste		
Municipal waste (kilograms)	18th out of 29	18th out of 29
Recycling (% of glass and paper recycled)	N/A	23rd out of 27
Hazardous waste (kilograms)	24th out of 27	23rd out of 27
Nuclear waste (kilograms)	28th out of 28	27th out of 28
Agriculture		
Pesticide use (tonnes of active ingredients)	22nd out of 28	18th out of 28
Fertilizer use (tonnes)	25th out of 28	25th out of 28
Livestock (number of cattle, sheep, goats, and pigs)	16th out of 28	17th out of 28
Biodiversity		
Species at risk (number of species designated)	N/A	7th out of 29
Protected areas (% of land designated)	N/A	13th out of 29
Fisheries (amount caught, kilograms)	20th out of 28	20th out of 28
Forests (volume of forest logged, in cubic metres)	27th out of 29	28th out of 29
Transportation		
Road vehicles (number)	25th out of 29	22nd out of 29
Distance travelled (kilometres)	26th out of 29	24th out of 29
Miscellaneous		
Population (% growth/total population)	26th out of 29	18th out of 29
Official development assistance (% of GDP)	N/A	11th out of 20

Note: Higher ranking (e.g., 1st) for better performance, lower ranking (e.g., 28th) for worse performance.
Source: Boyd (2001a).

made in reducing various kinds of air pollution, improving sewage treatment, reducing municipal waste, increasing recycling, reducing the use of ozone-depleting substances, and creating more protected areas. Modest progress has been made in increasing energy efficiency. There are other issues, not covered by the OECD data, where Canada has also made commendable progress, such as reducing lead emissions and curtailing some forms of water pollution (e.g., releases of dioxins and furans from pulp and paper mills, and chemical discharges from petroleum refineries). Second, the superior progress of other industrialized nations proves that Canada's shortcomings are not due to an absence of viable, practical solutions. Answers to our environmental challenges exist and are being successfully implemented elsewhere, most notably Europe. Sweden, for example, is a northern nation with many similarities to Canada. But on twenty-three out of the twenty-five environmental indicators examined in the OECD comparison, Sweden outperforms Canada.[15]

Other Independent Assessments of Canada's Environmental Record

The University of Victoria's study demonstrates that Canada is more accurately described as an environmental straggler than as a star. This assessment of Canada's environmental performance is confirmed by the conclusions of several other respected organizations. In 2000 the World Economic Forum singled out Canada for criticism of our dismal record on energy efficiency (worst among eighteen high-income countries). Canada also trailed many of our industrial competitors on the effectiveness of environmental regulations covering air pollution, water pollution, toxic waste, chemical waste, and genetically modified organisms.[16]

The OECD is also highly critical of Canada's environmental record. An OECD report published in 2000 attacked Canada for its "over-use of water," "intensive exploitation of nonrenewable resources," subsidies to polluters, inefficient use of energy, lack of action to address climate change, unsustainable use of natural resources, and unwarranted reliance on voluntary agreements in lieu of enforcing environmental laws.[17] The OECD later noted that on environmental issues Canada has "a tendency to talk rather than act."[18] A 1995 assessment of Canada's environmental performance by the OECD had been equally critical, pointing out many areas where Canada was performing poorly.[19]

In 2002 Redefining Progress investigated the ecological footprints of 146 nations. The ecological footprint is an innovative tool that measures the area of land required to produce the resources and absorb the waste needed to sustain an individual at a particular standard of living. Canada placed third in the world, with only the United States and United Arab Emirates having larger footprints, that is, greater per capita impacts on the environment. The study estimated that each Canadian had an ecological footprint of 8.8 hectares. In other words, it takes 8.8 hectares of ecologically productive land to generate the resources and assimilate the wastes of the average Canadian. On a global basis, at today's population of 6.1 billion people, there are approximately 1.7 hectares of productive land available per person, or less than one-fifth of the amount used by Canadians.[20]

More than sixty audits by Canada's commissioner of the environment and sustainable development and the auditor general identify weaknesses in the federal government's efforts to protect the environment. In 1998 the commissioner criticized the government's lack of action on climate change and protecting biological diversity. In 1999 the commissioner emphasized the gap between the government's commitments and its actions, particularly in the area of pesticides and toxic chemicals. In 2000 the commissioner focused on "persistent problems with the federal government's management of key issues like climate change, toxic substances and biodiversity" and a failure to adequately safeguard Canadians from the health risks posed by smog. In 2001 the commissioner warned that "the continuing rise in Canada's greenhouse gas emissions places the country on a path that is far from sustainable" and expressed alarm about Canada's failure to protect and restore the Great Lakes. In 2002 the commissioner concluded, "Our audit findings this year make me more concerned than ever about the environmental, social and economic legacy we are leaving our children – we are burdening them with a growing sustainable development deficit."[21] Canada's auditor general has published audits critical of Canadian fisheries management, unacknowledged liabilities from contaminated sites, inadequate control of the transportation of hazardous waste, and the federal government's failure to complete and protect the national parks system.[22]

A comprehensive study published in 2001 by the International Development Research Centre, in cooperation with the United Nations, the World Conservation Union, and the Food and Agriculture Organization, ranks Canada very highly on overall quality of life but poorly on environmental sustainability. Canada tied Switzerland for seventh place out of 180 nations on overall quality of life. However, based on an examination of fifty-one environmental indicators, Canada ranked ninety-fourth out of 180 nations.[23]

More positive news can be found in the World Economic Forum's Environmental Sustainability Index, a complex rating system "aimed at measuring long-term environmental prospects." The index assesses a nation's *potential* to achieve a sustainable future, not a nation's current performance. Canada ranks fourth out of 142 nations, a testament to our wealth of natural resources, large area, small population, effective health care system, well-educated public, and strong democratic freedoms.[24]

The foregoing evidence makes the basic facts about Canada's environmental record relatively clear. The good news is that on a number of important environmental issues, Canada's performance is improving, and that Canada has tremendous potential for further progress toward sustainability. The bad news is that Canada is faring poorly in comparison to the rest of the industrialized world in terms of protecting our environment, and that Canada's record, on the majority of environmental indicators, is getting worse.

Great Expectations, Poor Performance

The values expressed by Canadians dramatically diverge from our performance, as a nation, on environmental issues. This is true not only in terms of the contradiction between our strong environmental ethic, described earlier, and our overall performance, but also on a range of specific issues and concerns. A public opinion poll conducted in 2000 found that 99 percent of Canadians believe reducing air pollution is important.[25] Yet according to the OECD, Canada ranks among the worst industrialized nations in causing air pollution.[26] The same poll found that 97 percent of Canadians believe it is important to reduce the amount of pesticides in our food, water, and soil. Yet Canada stands alone among OECD countries in failing to collect reliable data on the use of pesticides.[27] Ninety-four percent of Canadians polled think Canada should meet its international obligations on climate change. Yet Canada has broken all of its promises to reduce greenhouse gas emissions and is among the three worst OECD nations on this issue.[28]

The list of contradictions goes on and on. Ensuring clean air and water is viewed as more important than personal tax cuts by over 80 percent of Canadians and more important than corporate tax cuts by over 90 percent of Canadians.[29] Yet in December 2000 Canadians reelected a federal government and an official opposition whose top priorities include personal and corporate tax cuts but not environmental protection. Ninety-seven percent of Canadians want the federal government to pass a strong law to protect endangered species and their habitats.[30] Yet after promising to do so in 1992, the federal government dragged its heels for a decade before passing a law that many critics, including those within the government, deride as weak (see Chapter 5.2). Canadians believe that Canada's number-one priority in foreign affairs – ahead of peace, exports, and foreign aid – should be protecting the environment.[31] Most Canadians (62 percent) are concerned that international trade agreements lead to lower environmental standards.[32] Yet the federal government continues to pursue further trade liberalization, such as the Free Trade Agreement of the Americas and the General Agreement on Trade in Services, without due regard for the environmental consequences.[33]

The Legal System's Role in Environmental Protection

Why is there such a striking gap between the environmental values of Canadians and our environmental performance? Why are greenhouse gas emissions still soaring, numbers of endangered species still rising, consumption of energy and water still growing, and production of hazardous and nuclear waste increasing? On the other hand, how has Canada made strides in reducing the use of ozone-depleting substances and decreasing releases of certain toxic chemicals like dioxins and furans?

The legal system is central to the answers to these difficult questions. In a constitutional democracy, the legal system is the mechanism through which the values of the people are expressed and our beliefs acted upon. The legal system defines and balances the rights and responsibilities of citizens, businesses, and government, mediating the struggle between defenders of the status quo and advocates of change. Canada's legal system, for the purposes of this book, will be defined broadly to include the institutions and processes that make laws, apply or enforce laws, and interpret laws. These activities are carried out by the legislative (Parliament), executive (cabinet and the bureaucracy), and judicial (courts and other tribunals) branches of government.[34]

Law refers to a body of rules that govern the activities of individuals, governments, and corporations, rules that are enforced by a sovereign authority. From an environmental perspective, laws establish rules governing our rights to use natural resources and our responsibilities in protecting nature. Canada has many laws, regulations, policies, and institutions intended to protect the environment, at the federal, provincial, and local levels. Most were created in the last three decades, as the need to protect the environment from human despoliation became increasingly clear. Unwritten laws, in the form of social norms and customs, have a complementary role to play in achieving environmental progress. For example, the change in attitudes toward smoking in recent decades, combined with increasingly strict regulations, has significantly diminished smoking in public places.

The authority to enact laws to address environmental problems is defined by Canada's *Constitution Act, 1867,* which divides power between the federal and provincial governments. Although responsibility for the environment is not specifically assigned to either level of government, each has areas of jurisdiction with environmental consequences. The federal government has clear powers over fisheries, international trade, nuclear power, and criminal law, plus broad responsibility for matters of national and international concern. The provinces have jurisdiction over natural resources, property, municipal governments, local and private matters, and most Crown land within their boundaries. Municipal governments are created by provincial governments, and their jurisdiction is limited to areas explicitly identified in provincial legislation. Aboriginal governments have authority by virtue of constitutionally protected rights and powers defined in treaties. Any law that is inconsistent with Canada's Constitution, such as a law passed by a level of government lacking constitutional authority in that subject area, can be struck down by the courts. The uncertainty about constitutional responsibility for environmental protection is one of the most controversial aspects of Canadian environmental law and policy.[35]

Chapters 2 through 5 examine the laws, regulations, and policies intended to conserve and protect water, air, land, and biological diversity in Canada. These chapters also assess the international context of Canada's environmental laws and policies, including the influence of international environmental and trade agreements. The entire range of laws and policies employed by different levels of government – federal, provincial, local, and Aboriginal – to address environmental problems is evaluated.

2 Water

> Water will become Canada's foremost ecological crisis
> early in this century.
>
> *David Schindler, Killam Memorial Professor of Ecology*

Two-thirds of a person's weight is water. Life on Earth would be impossible without it. Water is one of the primary environmental concerns of Canadians, as well as an important element of our culture, history, and national identity. From Inuit kayaks, Aboriginal canoes, and the voyageurs, to Group of Seven paintings, novels by Michael Ondaatje, Margaret Atwood, and David Adams Richards, and summers in cottage country, water is at the heart of Canada. Despite our trademark modesty, we are stewards of six great lakes – Ontario, Huron, Erie, Superior, Great Slave, and Great Bear. Rivers like the Fraser, Tatshenshini, Mackenzie, Saskatchewan, Red, Bow, Don, Ottawa, St. Lawrence, Saguenay, and Miramichi are the arteries of our nation, both symbolically and ecologically. Yet recurring problems with drinking water, from Walkerton, Ontario, to North Battleford, Saskatchewan, make Canadians leery of turning on the tap. Stories about toxic chemicals polluting everything from groundwater to remote northern lakes garner headlines and burden our collective conscience. A stream of proposals to export massive volumes of fresh water also strikes a chord in our national psyche, inflaming passions from coast to coast.

According to conventional wisdom, Canada is endowed with a tremendous abundance of fresh water, more than any other nation on the planet. During the recent brouhaha about water exports, various media sources reported that Canada is home to two-thirds of the world's fresh water supply.[1] As is so often the case, conventional wisdom is detached from reality. An objective assessment of the state of water in Canada brings good news and bad news. Canada has 20 percent of the world's fresh water, but much of that is nonrenewable "fossil water" left over from the melting of the continental ice sheets, or else is tied up in glaciers and inaccessible groundwater. Canada's share of the global supply of *renewable* fresh water is much more modest, in the range of 6 to 9 percent, placing us behind Brazil, the former Soviet Union, and China.[2] Still, Canada's relatively small population means that on a per capita basis we have a huge amount of renewable fresh water: 99,000 cubic metres per person per year. This puts us well ahead of countries like the United States (9,277 cubic metres per person per year) or France (3,408), and light years ahead of water-stressed countries like Israel (389) or Kuwait (95).[3]

Canadians use about 1,600 cubic metres (1.6 million litres) of water per person per year for residential, agricultural, and industrial purposes.[4] This amounts to slightly less than 2 percent of the renewable fresh water in our country. When water used for hydroelectric power generation is included, Canada uses roughly 6 percent of its annual renewable water supply. World-wide, humans use as much as 50 percent of the renewable fresh water supply, placing Canada far below the global average.[5] We are, relatively speaking, water wealthy. That is the good news.

However, just as Canada's overall economic wealth masks the fact that some Canadians live in poverty, our overall water wealth masks the fact that some regions of the country face water shortages. One reason is that more than 60 percent of Canada's renewable water supply flows north into the Arctic Ocean and Hudson Bay, while more than 90 percent of our population lives in southern Canada.[6] Water is in particularly short supply on the Prairies and in the BC interior.[7] Between 1994 and 1999, 26 percent of Canadian municipalities reported problems with water availability, including such seemingly wet locales as Vancouver and Victoria.[8] The water in the Great Lakes is fully committed to existing uses.[9] In reality then, Canada is blessed with plentiful *though not unlimited* water.

The bad news is that the prevailing myth of Canada's endless water supply leads Canadians to take this invaluable substance for granted. Here are a few examples of our abuse of water:

- Hundreds of billions of litres of raw or minimally treated sewage are dumped into our water every year.[10]
- Companies annually discharge more than 20 million kilograms of toxic chemicals into rivers, lakes, and streams and inject 135 million kilograms of toxic chemicals underground, where groundwater may be contaminated.[11]
- Livestock operations (especially factory farms) produce 132 billion kilograms of manure annually, threatening water with coliform bacteria and nitrates.[12]
- Canadians are second in the world in water use per person, behind Americans.[13]
- Canada diverts more water from one river basin to another than any other nation in the world.[14]

- There were more than 2,800 beach closures due to polluted water in the Great Lakes region between 1992 and 1995.[15]
- Canada has drained, filled, paved, and polluted most of our wetlands, resulting in the loss of 65 percent of Atlantic coastal marshes, 70 percent of southern Ontario wetlands, 71 percent of Prairie wetlands, and 80 percent of the Fraser River delta.[16]
- Pesticide residues (most commonly atrazine and aldicarb) are frequently found in Canadians' water supply.[17]

The cumulative effect of these abuses is that Canada faces significant water quality problems throughout the country as well as regional water quantity concerns. Add stresses such as climate change, ozone depletion, acid rain, and other forms of airborne pollution, and it is easy to understand why David Schindler, Canada's preeminent water scientist, warns of "the degradation of Canadian freshwater on a scale hitherto unimaginable."[18] Ironically, the federal government went to great lengths in the 1980s to develop a comprehensive national water policy, commissioning dozens of expert reports and holding hearings across Canada. The 1987 Federal Water Policy provided a comprehensive blueprint for addressing Canadian water problems, but the majority of its recommendations were never implemented.[19]

Four of the most prominent water issues facing Canadians in the twenty-first century are drinking water, water pollution, water use and conservation, and bulk water exports. These issues are obviously interconnected, but from a law and policy perspective it is necessary to examine each separately because our legal system treats them separately. Do Canadian laws and policies adequately safeguard our drinking water? Address the threats posed by water pollution? Ensure conservation and wise use of our water? Prevent the export of vast quantities of water? Unfortunately, the Canadian legal system's approach to water issues is heavily influenced by the enduring myth of endless water, as the following analysis will demonstrate. As a result, our laws and policies generally fail to provide the level of water security sought by Canadians.

2.1 DRINKING WATER

> You can be sure that municipally treated water is safe, palatable and nutritious, no matter where you live or travel in Canada.
>
> *Health Canada (1993),*
> The Undiluted Truth about Drinking Water

> We should never be complacent about drinking water safety.
>
> *The Hon. Mr. Justice O'Connor,*
> *Commissioner of the Walkerton Inquiry*

Canadian complacency about the safety of our drinking water was shattered in May 2000, when a deadly strain of *E. coli* bacteria contaminated the water in Walkerton, Ontario, causing seven deaths and thousands of illnesses. Was Walkerton merely an anomaly, the unlikely product of a series of individual human errors and tragic coincidences? Or was Walkerton the tip of the iceberg, a warning that current laws, policies, and practices do not adequately protect drinking water in Canada? Consider the following:

- Thousands of residents of North Battleford, Saskatchewan, Collingwood and Kitchener, Ontario, and Kelowna and Cranbrook, British Columbia, became violently ill, and in a few cases died, because of waterborne disease outbreaks in the past decade.[1]
- Hundreds of Canadian communities are under long-term or permanent boil-water advisories (meaning water from the tap is unsafe to drink unless boiled first).[2]
- More than 20 percent of the water systems in Aboriginal communities contain excessive levels of fecal coliforms, lead, arsenic, nitrates, and trihalomethanes.[3]

- Out of 423 treated water samples from across Canada examined by Health Canada, 18.2 percent contained giardia, which causes "beaver fever," and 3.6 percent contained cryptosporidium, as these pathogens are resistant to chlorination.[4]
- A 1994 report from Ontario's auditor general found that 120 of the province's 490 water treatment plants either failed to meet provincial guidelines or didn't conduct tests to see whether the guidelines were met.[5]
- British Columbia has the highest levels of waterborne disease in Canada – especially giardia, cryptosporidium, and toxoplasmosis – with twenty-seven outbreaks of waterborne disease in the last eighteen years.[6]
- A 1993 study by Agriculture Canada and Health Canada found that about 40 percent of 1,300 rural wells in Ontario had unacceptable levels of at least one of the chemical and microbiological contaminants surveyed.[7]
- Scientists are increasingly concerned about the presence of algal toxins in drinking water on the Prairies.[8]
- A report card on drinking water in Canada, published in 2001, warned that "in the absence of a comprehensive, cross-country approach to protecting drinking water, more tragedies almost certainly await us."[9]

This list paints a bleak picture of drinking water problems in Canada at the beginning of the twenty-first century. However, Canada's drinking water woes must be seen in perspective. Canadians enjoy one of the lowest rates of serious waterborne diseases in the world: cholera, dysentery, and typhoid are virtually unknown in Canada today.[10] In contrast, in developing countries at least one billion people lack access to safe drinking water and more than two billion people lack access to safe sanitation for disposing of human waste.[11] The most recent estimate from the United Nations is that twenty-five thousand people die daily because of poor water quality.[12] On average, a child dies every fifteen seconds from drinking contaminated water.[13] These deeply disturbing statistics indicate that Canadian drinking water provides a relatively low level of risk. Within Canada, however, there are disturbing exceptions to this generalization, as illustrated by Walkerton, North Battleford, and Aboriginal communities. In addition, medical experts believe that Canadians are more likely to suffer from *chronic* health problems such as cancer, dementia, and infertility as a result of contaminated water than *acute* problems such as the infectious diseases that affect people in developing countries.[14]

Laws and Policies Required to Protect Drinking Water
Understanding the problems that afflict Canadian drinking water requires an analysis of the laws, policies, and institutions responsible for providing safe drinking water. In response to recent problems, comprehensive reports on improving drinking water laws, policies, and systems have been published by

the Walkerton Inquiry, the North Battleford Commission of Inquiry, the Canadian Environmental Law Association, the Sierra Legal Defence Fund, and, in British Columbia, by the auditor general, the provincial health officer, and the Drinking Water Review Panel.[15] According to these expert reports, an effective system to ensure safe drinking water must include:

1   protecting water at the source
2   water treatment, including filtration and disinfection
3   a well-designed and well-operated distribution system
4   comprehensive testing of drinking water
5   public notification and reporting of water quality problems
6   adequate resources to operate water systems and enforce the law.

The tragic events of Walkerton triggered a wave of regulatory changes, not just in Ontario but across Canada.[16] To what extent do the laws, regulations, policies, and institutions responsible for protecting and providing Canadian drinking water systems fulfill these six key requirements?

Protecting Water Sources

The most important step in providing safe drinking water is protecting water sources from contamination. According to David Schindler, "Only comprehensive approaches to the conservation and management of the catchments that supply drinking water can prevent major water problems."[17] Three-quarters of Canadians receive water from municipal systems supplied by rivers, lakes, and reservoirs, while the remaining 25 percent rely on groundwater for their domestic water needs. Industrial pollution, farming, ranching, logging, mining, sewage disposal, waste disposal, and urban sprawl can contaminate these water sources.

The most secure option for a community seeking to control activities that affect their water is to own their watershed. Ownership enables a community to decide what activities, if any, will be permitted. Saint John began purchasing land in its watersheds in the 1800s and continues to do so today.[18] Victoria has owned its watershed lands since the early twentieth century. Vancouver holds 999-year leases (tantamount to ownership) for the three watersheds that supply the city's water.[19] Several other BC communities have long-term leases for their water supply areas, including Enderby, Vernon, and Fernie. In addition to the obvious environmental benefits, protecting water sources can pay economic dividends. Purchasing land, in the long term, may be less expensive than building new or expanded filtration and disinfection plants. British Columbia's auditor general estimated that if the hundred municipalities in the province that neither own their watersheds nor use filtration had to build filtration plants, the total capital cost would be about $700 million and annual operating costs would approach $30 million.[20] New York City is spending hundreds of millions of dollars to purchase land and conservation easements in its watersheds instead of spending billions of dollars to build new filtration plants.[21] At the present time, Canadian communities that own land in their watersheds are the exception rather than the rule, as these lands are predominantly provincially or privately owned.

A second way to protect watersheds that supply drinking water is through laws specifically intended to protect watersheds or groundwater areas.[22] Under these laws, provincial governments may restrict the types of land-use activities allowed within watersheds. All of these laws are discretionary, not mandatory, meaning that the decision about whether or not to protect a watershed rests with a politician or bureaucrat. For example, regulations passed pursuant to New Brunswick's *Clean Water Act* enable the minister of environment to protect lands adjacent to watercourses in community watersheds and lands used as groundwater sources.[23] As of early 2003, thirty municipalities in New Brunswick enjoyed some level of protection for their drinking water sources. Because the law gives the minister the *discretion* to protect watersheds, rather than imposing a *duty* to do so, he or she cannot be compelled to act by concerned citizens. New Brunswick, to its credit, has gone further than any other Canadian province in designating watersheds for protection and imposing limitations on land use. In provinces without specific laws to protect drinking water sources, watersheds may be protected under laws used to designate parks and other protected areas, but in practice this happens infrequently and raises other problems, such as managing threats to water quality from tourism and recreation activities.

Nunavut and the Northwest Territories have potentially useful regulations allowing their chief medical health officers to stop any activity that poses a threat to drinking water.[24] Similarly, British Columbia's *Drinking Water Protection Act* provides drinking water officers with broad powers to prohibit any activity that poses a significant risk to drinking water.[25] Even if an activity, such as logging, has the appropriate permits under laws governing forestry, BC's drinking water officers have the legal authority to stop the activity. Of course these broad powers will be effective in protecting drinking water sources only if they are used. While it is too early to pass judgment, it is essential to note that in all three cases (Northwest Territories, Nunavut, and BC) the power to stop or prohibit an activity is entirely discretionary, not mandatory. Again, the consequence of the discretionary wording of these laws is that even if there is a serious threat to drinking water, the government has no obligation to act, nor can it be legally compelled to act.

As a general rule, the sources of drinking water for most Canadians are either poorly protected or not protected at all from the activities most likely to cause water contamination. Communities are often powerless to protect their drinking water because provincial governments regulate the land-use activities that pose risks of local water contamination. For example, residents

of the Slocan Valley and other BC communities fought logging in their community watersheds for decades to no avail, despite landslides, siltation, protests, and lawsuits.[26] Although a 1999 report by the BC auditor general
concluded that the province "is not adequately protecting drinking water sources
from human related impacts," the province's new *Drinking Water Protection Act*
offers few assurances of improvement over the status quo.[27] However, local
and municipal governments are becoming more assertive in the use of their
power to make bylaws in order to protect drinking water sources that are
within their jurisdiction.[28] Overall, Canada's legal system offers few effective
tools for citizens seeking to protect the source of their drinking water, although Ontario promises to introduce source protection legislation (as recommended by the Walkerton Inquiry).

Water Treatment
Weak protection for water sources increases the importance of water treatment, the second element of providing safe drinking water. Water treatment is
a two-step process involving filtration and disinfection. Passing water through
a filter eliminates organic materials, sediments, and some pathogens, such as
giardia and cryptosporidium, which are not effectively treated by chlorination. Filtration is therefore vital for all surface-water sources of drinking water.
Only three provinces currently require filtration by law (Alberta and, in the
aftermath of the Walkerton disaster, Ontario and Quebec), meaning seven
provinces and three territories fail to require filtration. Some individual communities in the provinces and territories without mandatory filtration provide
filtration on a voluntary basis, but these communities are exceptions to the
rule.[29]

Disinfection involves adding chemicals to water to destroy harmful microorganisms. Health experts describe disinfection as a basic necessity of good
drinking water management. Laws in most provinces and territories require
mandatory disinfection, except in Prince Edward Island, New Brunswick,
Newfoundland and Labrador, and the Yukon. Chlorine is the dominant dis-
infectant used in water treatment in Canada, with chloramine and ozone used
in some municipalities. However, chlorine causes trouble of its own. There are
growing concerns that consuming chlorine leads to long-term health problems
including bladder cancer and developmental abnormalities.[30] In some circumstances, chlorine combines with organic material in the water to form
trihalomethanes, a group of by-products that also poses a health threat.[31] These
disinfection problems reinforce the fundamental importance of protecting water
sources, because cleaner water can be treated with less chlorine.

Safe Distribution Systems
The third aspect of comprehensive drinking water protection is a safe distribution system that does not allow the disinfected water to be contaminated en

route to the consumer. Canada's drinking water infrastructure is widely ac-knowledged to be deteriorating, largely because inadequate resources have been allocated to repairing, upgrading, and replacing treatment and distribu-tion facilities. Estimates of the cost of addressing the Canadian water infra-structure problem range from $16.5 billion to $100 billion.[32]

A safe distribution system cannot be built from unsafe materials. Conse-quently, the federal government introduced the *Drinking Water Materials Safety Act* in 1996.[33] The proposed law would have established legally binding na-tional standards for construction and plumbing devices used in water delivery systems. For example, although lead pipes are no longer used in new water systems in Canada because of health concerns, lead continues to be used to repair water pipes and is present in many older water systems. An investiga-tion by CBC's *Marketplace* program found lead levels in excess of national guidelines in 30 percent of the homes examined in Saint John, Toronto, Ham-ilton, Winnipeg, and Vancouver.[34] The proposed *Drinking Water Materials Safety Act* could have prohibited all uses of lead in drinking water systems. However, an early federal election in 1997 prevented the passage of the law and it has never been reintroduced.

Competent, trained personnel are another integral element of a safe distri-bution system. The lack of well-trained water system operators was a promi-nent factor in the chain of events that led to the Walkerton disaster.[35] As a result, some provinces are beginning to amend laws to require the use of certi-fied operators in drinking water systems. Ontario's new *Safe Drinking Water Act* also establishes a legal standard of care that municipalities must meet.[36] How-ever, the majority of provinces still do not require training or certification.

Comprehensive Testing

Comprehensive water testing is the fourth element of ensuring safe drinking water. Testing enables water contamination to be identified, communicated to the public, and remedied before people become ill. Although the federal gov-ernment publishes the Guidelines for Canadian Drinking Water Quality, prov-inces and territories set the legal requirements (if any) for testing. Developed by Health Canada, the guidelines address more than eighty microbial, chemi-cal, and physical contaminants and seventy-eight natural and artificial radio-active contaminants.[37] Here is a subtle but absolutely crucial legal point. Guidelines and standards, although seemingly similar, are as different as day and night. Guidelines are voluntary, nonbinding, and evidently, given the drink-ing water problems across Canada, ineffective. Health Canada admits that its Guidelines for Canadian Drinking Water Quality are unenforceable.[38] Stand-ards, in contrast, are legally binding and enforceable. Canada's commissioner of the environment and sustainable development pointed out in 2001 that "unlike the U.S. and the European Union, Canada does not have nationally enforceable standards for drinking water."[39]

Why should anyone but lawyers care about the distinction between guidelines and standards? Because having soft guidelines instead of hard standards means citizens have limited remedies when drinking water is not safe. Guidelines reduce accountability and responsibility. Guidelines are interpreted as goals to be aspired toward, whereas standards provide certainty because they must be met. For example, the Capital Regional District in British Columbia, which provides drinking water to Victoria and neighbouring communities, explains that the Health Canada guidelines "are used *almost* as compulsory criteria that must be met *if possible*" (emphasis added).[40] A report by Saskatchewan's Environment Ministry admits that a substantial number of communities are violating the federal guidelines. However, the ministry argues against replacing guidelines with enforceable standards because "the public may perceive greater risk if there is non-compliance with a standard rather than exceedance of an objective [i.e., a guideline]. This would not promote public confidence in programs for protection of public health."[41] In other words, objectives and guidelines serve to limit public concerns about drinking water quality, while standards might, when violated, arouse public concern. Canadians would never tolerate guidelines to protect them from crime, or guidelines to ensure airplanes are properly maintained, so it seems incongruous that guidelines are used to protect something as important as drinking water.

Some provinces, to their credit, have made the federal water quality guidelines legally binding by incorporating them into provincial laws and regulations. For example, Quebec incorporates most of Health Canada's guidelines as binding standards in its legislation. Alberta, Nova Scotia, Ontario (as of 2001, after Walkerton), and Saskatchewan (as of 2002, after North Battleford) also have relatively strong water quality testing regulations. However, the extent of water testing varies dramatically from province to province. Newfoundland and Labrador and Prince Edward Island have no mandatory testing requirements at all. British Columbia requires testing for only three of 158 contaminants identified in the guidelines.[42]

Moreover, in some cases the federal guidelines are much weaker than comparable standards in the United States. For example, the Canadian guideline for trichloroethylene, an industrial solvent, is ten times higher than the legal maximum in the United States. The Canadian guideline was established in 1986, before research confirmed that trichloroethylene causes cancer. Trichloroethylene has been found in the drinking water of more than a million Canadians, yet many provinces have no standards at all for this chemical.[43]

Public Notice and Information

The fifth key element of a safe drinking water system is insuring that the public is promptly and fully informed about water quality problems. However, most Canadian provinces and territories have no legal requirement that the public be informed of known water quality problems.[44] This cavalier approach to protecting public health was another contributing factor in the Walkerton debacle, where authorities knew of problems plaguing the community's water system for months without notifying the public or taking remedial action.[45] In many provinces, the only legal requirement is that testing laboratories must report water quality problems to water system operators or to provincial health or environment officials. Quebec, British Columbia, Saskatchewan, and Ontario (beginning in 2001) are the only provinces with mandatory legal requirements to inform the public of water quality problems. Post-Walkerton, Ontario will also require the publication of quarterly "right-to-know" reports summarizing the results of water quality testing.[46] Saskatchewan's new regulations also require annual reports on drinking water quality.[47] Some individual municipalities, like Calgary, provide annual reports on drinking water quality but these reports are prepared voluntarily and by only a handful of Canadian communities.[48]

Adequate Resources

The sixth characteristic of systems to ensure safe drinking water is that significant financial resources are required to operate, maintain, and upgrade water treatment systems. Adequate budgets are also necessary to monitor and enforce drinking water laws and regulations. The myriad problems facing drinking water in Canada make it clear that more resources are needed for infrastructure and enforcement. However, during the 1990s provincial governments across Canada made unprecedented cuts to the budgets of environmental departments, ranging from 30 percent to 65 percent (see Chapter 8).

In Ontario, the cutbacks contributed to the Walkerton disaster in two important ways. First, although the Ministry of Environment was aware that the Walkerton drinking water system was experiencing difficulty, the ministry lacked the resources to adequately monitor the problem or ensure that remedial steps were taken. Second, the ministry cut water testing, resulting in the privatization of this essential service. When the private firm testing Walkerton's water discovered contaminated samples, it failed to notify either health authorities or the Ministry of Environment. Private laboratories had no legal duty to report adverse water tests to either the Ministry of Environment or provincial health authorities. Instead, there were voluntary guidelines. Commissioner Dennis O'Connor found that "matters as important to water safety and public health should have been covered by regulations which, unlike guidelines, are legally binding." However, O'Connor noted that in the antiregulatory environment created by the Ontario government and its Red Tape Commission, the idea of an additional regulation would have been a "non-starter."[49]

There are legitimate concerns that events like the Walkerton water tragedy could occur in other provinces. The agenda of cutbacks, deregulation, and privatization is not unique to Ontario. A similar sequence of events in North Battleford led to contamination of the city's water supply and widespread illness. The commission of inquiry into North Battleford's water troubles concluded that economics, rather than a concern for public health, dictated Saskatchewan's drinking water policies.[30] British Columbia is also putting drinking water at risk by pursuing policies similar to those implemented in Ontario, including even deeper cuts to environmental protection budgets, a similar Red Tape Task Force, and an intention to "minimize [the] provincial role in water utility regulation."[51]

Major spending will be required to improve the quality of drinking water in Canada and ensure that proper safeguards and monitoring are in place. British Columbia estimates that it may have to spend $1 billion to ensure safe drinking water for its residents.[52] Quebec is spending $600 million to implement new drinking water standards.[53] Ontario will have to invest up to $800 million and then spend up to an additional $250 million annually to provide drinking water with an acceptable level of risk.[54]

The Adequacy of Canadian Laws to Protect Drinking Water

The preceding analysis shows that legal protection for drinking water in Canada varies considerably from province to province and from community to community. As is the case for virtually every environmental issue facing Canada, part of the problem is that the responsibility for providing safe drinking water is fractured among many different jurisdictions – federal, provincial, and municipal – and between different agencies within each level of government. Federally, Health Canada is responsible for the voluntary Guidelines for Canadian Drinking Water Quality. Provincial governments provide laws and policies governing land use, water treatment, and testing. Local governments operate water treatment systems and distribute water to citizens and businesses. The consequent inconsistent hodge-podge of laws, regulations, standards, and guidelines results in uneven and sometimes inadequate drinking water quality in Canadian communities.

Canadians are well aware of the problems facing drinking water and have been demanding effective, legally enforceable national standards for decades. Back in 1982 environmental lawyers argued that "a *Safe Drinking Water Act* for Canada and the provinces is long overdue."[55] In 1990 the federal government, under Prime Minister Brian Mulroney, pledged to introduce a *Drinking Water Safety Act*. The proposed law would have created "mandatory" drinking water quality standards in order "to help reduce illness attributed to hazardous drinking water."[56] The promise of the Mulroney government was never fulfilled. Over a decade later, Canada still has no national law or mandatory national standards to ensure safe drinking water.

Indeed, prospects for attaining such legal protection at the federal level appear to be dim. The current Canadian government claims that it lacks the constitutional power to ensure national protection for drinking water, because water is an area of provincial responsibility.[57] This constitutional jurisdiction argument does not hold water. Safe drinking water legislation could be justi-fied on a number of constitutional grounds, as the Mulroney government evidently understood when it promised to enact the *Drinking Water Safety Act* in 1990. Similarly, the Chrétien government introduced but did not pass the *Drinking Water Materials Safety Act* in 1996.[58] The federal government enacts national standards for bottled water under the *Food and Drug Act*. How can the federal government have the power to regulate bottled water but not tap wa-ter? This obvious inconsistency led Senator Jerry Grafstein to introduce a law in 2001 to add drinking water from a community water system to the list of products governed by the *Food and Drug Act*.[59] Senator Grafstein's proposed law was not passed.

In the aftermath of the Walkerton disaster, provinces and territories scram-bled to improve laws and policies governing drinking water. Ontario, Quebec, Manitoba, Saskatchewan, and British Columbia strengthened laws and regu-lations. Improvements in other provinces are in progress. The Yukon is work-ing on drinking water legislation.[60] These regulatory changes are a step in the right direction, but fail to address source protection and the fundamental is-sue of uneven legal protection for drinking water across Canada. None of these provinces fulfill all of the recommendations made by the Walkerton Inquiry.

Many Canadians believe, incorrectly, that they have a right to clean, safe water. While this right may exist at a philosophical level, it does not exist under Canadian law. There is no such right provided in Canada's Constitution, the *Charter of Rights and Freedoms*, or in the common law. As a judge in the BC Supreme Court recently ruled in a lawsuit where citizens sought unsuccess-fully to halt logging activities in their watershed, "There is not before me an established case for the concept of a right to clean water."[61]

Canadians consume approximately a billion litres of bottled water each year. However, bottled water is a less-than-perfect solution, because it is expensive, energy-intensive, and can be contaminated.[62] Health Canada also warns that improperly maintained home water filtration devices can result in bacteria levels two thousand times higher than levels in unfiltered water.[63]

The Law Governing Drinking Water in the United States

Unlike Canada, which provided weak and inconsistent legal protection for Canadian drinking water, the United States passed the *Safe Drinking Water Act* in 1974, providing strong legal protection for American drinking water in all fifty states. The law sets minimum national standards (which individual states must meet or beat), requires public notification of any health threats or water quality problems, offers opportunities to participate in water use decisions, and allows citizens to assist the government in enforcing the law. The *Safe Drinking Water Act* was strengthened in 1996 to require all community water providers to send an annual report on water quality to local residents, provide enhanced opportunities for public involvement, and place increased emphasis on protecting the sources of local drinking water.[64] The Environmental Protection Agency (EPA) says it will cost US$22 billion annually to operate water systems in compliance with the new standards.[65] Canadian environmental lawyers look at the *Safe Drinking Water Act* with envy, claiming that it "sets the standard for regulated protection of drinking water, surpassing Canada in several important respects."[66] The Sierra Legal Defence Fund's 2001 report card on drinking water in Canada even refers to the "United States of Safe Water."[67] New Jersey, a heavily industrialized state, has not had an outbreak of waterborne disease from a public drinking water supply since passing its own drinking water legislation in 1983.[68]

However, it would be a mistake to blindly emulate the American system. A closer examination reveals that the United States is by no means free of serious drinking water problems. The EPA warns that "threats to drinking water quality and quantity are increasing."[69] Published estimates of the number of Americans stricken by waterborne illnesses annually range from 400,000 to 27 million.[70] The Centers for Disease Control and Prevention estimate nine hundred deaths per year due to contaminated water.[71] Other indications that the American regulatory system falls short of the panacea described by Canadian environmental lawyers include:

- Fifty-three million Americans drink tap water polluted with lead, fecal bacteria, or other harmful substances despite the *Safe Drinking Water Act*.[72]
- 4,769 out of 55,000 community water systems in the United States reported a violation of one or more drinking water health standards in 1996.[73]
- The Department of Agriculture reports that fifty-four million Americans relying on groundwater are at risk from pesticides, mainly atrazine and aldicarb.[74]
- More than seven hundred communities with over ten million residents faced boil-water advisories in recent years.[75]
- A cryptosporidium outbreak in Milwaukee resulted in 400,000 people becoming ill, 4,000 people being hospitalized, and 50 to 100 deaths.[76]
- The EPA estimates that repairs and upgrades to the American drinking water infrastructure will cost US$138 billion.[77]

Considerably stronger legal protection for water in the United States vis-à-vis Canada has not yet translated into superior water quality. The Achilles heel in the American system is at the critical first stage – protecting the sources of drinking water from contamination threats. In the United States, protecting sources of drinking water is more challenging because private land ownership is much more extensive than in Canada, industrial contamination is more widespread, and there is a higher overall degree of development.

Conclusion

Access to safe drinking water should not depend on which province or community a Canadian lives in, but that is the current reality. Instead of strong national standards to ensure drinking water quality, Canada has a moth-eaten patchwork quilt of voluntary national guidelines, inconsistent provincial standards, and crumbling municipal infrastructure that, in some cases, fails to adequately reduce the risks of acute and chronic waterborne disease. In the aftermath of Walkerton and North Battleford, several provinces strengthened drinking water laws, but binding *national* standards remain absent. The claim made by Ontario's environment minister, Chris Stockwell, that the new *Safe Drinking Water Act* is the "toughest legislation in the world," is not borne out by the facts.[78]

Acute drinking water problems affect only a small minority of Canadians – most notably Aboriginal people, a few small municipalities, and some rural populations. For these people, whose drinking water is currently unsafe, immediate remedial action is required and should be a national priority. For the majority of Canadians, whose drinking water is relatively safe, steps could still be taken to reduce the risks of contamination. Although drinking water will never be risk-free, the legal regime to protect water sources, ensure adequate treatment, maintain effective infrastructure, implement rigorous testing, and keep the public informed could be improved substantially. Canada needs to devote significantly more resources (money, expertise, and political attention) to maintaining and improving its drinking water systems. The allocation of $600 million, in the 2003 federal budget, to improve drinking water quality in Aboriginal communities is a step in the right direction. Again, protecting the sources of drinking water is of paramount importance. Fortunately Canada enjoys a remarkably high degree of public land ownership, which should reduce the complexity and cost of source protection.

Last but not least, it is important to situate Canada's drinking water problems in a global context. While we must become better stewards of our own drinking water, Canada also has a moral obligation to provide more assistance to developing nations, where more than a billion people lack access to safe drinking water. This is not to suggest that Canada should begin shipping tankers full of water to Bangladesh, sub-Saharan Africa, and other water-stressed regions. However, Canada should be providing extensive financial and technical assistance to developing nations to support locally appropriate water solutions and other aspects of sustainable development (see Chapter 14).

2.2 WATER POLLUTION

Canada's record on water pollution is mixed. We have made great progress in reducing some forms of water pollution, limited progress on other forms, and in some cases are moving backward. Most of the success stories involve point source water pollution – discharges of effluent from readily identifiable sources such as pulp and paper mills, petroleum refineries, and metal mining operations. Between 1994 and 1999, according to the National Pollutant Release Inventory, the total volume of toxic chemicals dumped into Canadian surface waters by industry fell by 63 percent.[1] This decline is mainly attributable to regulations governing pulp and paper mills and the prosecution of a Quebec company that was pumping prodigious quantities of chemicals into the St. Lawrence River. Notorious problem areas including the Great Lakes, the Fraser River, and the St. Lawrence River have improved modestly. With respect to discharges of municipal sewage effluent, there has also been progress, but many Canadian communities still discharge raw or inadequately treated sewage into water.

On the negative side, Canada faces significant water pollution from nonpoint sources, such as agricultural runoff (containing pesticides, fertilizers, and animal waste), urban runoff, and airborne deposits of toxic chemicals. Contrary to conventional wisdom, greater volumes of water pollution now come from nonpoint sources than from point sources. As well, scientists are particularly concerned about persistent organic pollutants (e.g., PCBs and DDT), endocrine disruptors (hormone-mimicking chemicals), and heavy metals (e.g., lead, mercury, and cadmium), because of the magnitude and longevity of their health and environmental effects.

It is difficult to generalize about water quality in Canada because there has never been a comprehensive national analysis.[2] To the contrary, in recent years the level of water quality monitoring has dropped dramatically. For example, British Columbia used to monitor water quality in 124 water bodies but now monitors only 16.[3] Despite incomplete information, Environment Canada observes that "water pollution problems do exist in many parts of the country

... usually in association with industrial, agricultural or mining activities or human sewage" and "groundwater contamination is also recognized as a widespread and growing concern."[4] Despite progress in reducing some forms of industrial pollution over the past three decades, there are still many indications that Canada faces major water pollution challenges, including:

- Canadian industry discharges more than 20 million kilograms of toxic chemicals directly into surface water annually, including 120,000 kilograms of carcinogenic substances (including arsenic, formaldehyde, benzene, and mercury).[5]
- Factory farming poses a serious contamination threat, with livestock generating 4,000 kilograms of animal waste per Canadian annually.[6]
- Lakes, glaciers, and snowfields in remote national parks and northern areas suffer from toxic contamination.[7]
- Acid runoff from dozens of abandoned mines is damaging aquatic ecosystems.[8]
- Thousands of square kilometres of marine areas are closed to shellfish harvesting because of pollution concerns.[9]
- Extensive areas, including the Great Lakes, are subject to health advisories warning that eating fish can cause birth defects and other serious problems.[10]

These daunting facts suggest that Canada has a long way to go before we can be satisfied with our overall water quality.

The Regulation of Water Pollution in Canada

Canada has dozens of federal and provincial laws and regulations addressing water pollution.[11] At the federal level, the two most important laws are the *Fisheries Act* and the *Canadian Environmental Protection Act, 1999*. The *Fisheries Act* prohibits the deposit of "deleterious" substances into waters frequented by fish. The *Canadian Environmental Protection Act, 1999* regulates toxic substances and ocean dumping. Ontario and New Brunswick have separate laws for water pollution, while the other provinces and territories rely on general pollution laws covering air, land, and water. Although the specific wording varies from one law to the next, the basic approach of all Canadian water pollution laws is the same. First, there is a broad prohibition on all pollution. For example, British Columbia's *Waste Management Act* states:

> 3(4). Subject to subsection (5), a person must not introduce waste into the environment in such a manner or quantity as to cause pollution.

Problems, however, are caused by broad exceptions to these blanket prohibitions. Subsection 3(5) of the *Waste Management Act* provides thirteen exceptions, that is, situations in which pollution is allowed. The exceptions range from burning leaves and foliage for agricultural purposes to air contaminants from retail food outlets. The broadest exception allows pollution as long as it is in accordance with a permit.[12] This is one of the fatal flaws of Canada's legal regime governing pollution. It is perfectly legal for an individual or business to pollute, as long as they have a permit and pollute within the limits of that permit.

The process for granting pollution permits is also flawed. Both federal and provincial governments have nonbinding water quality guidelines (analogous to the Guidelines for Canadian Drinking Water Quality) that establish the maximum allowable concentration of substances in water for particular uses (e.g., recreation or agriculture) and in particular locations.[13] These guidelines are used by government agencies in private negotiations with individual polluters to set the terms of pollution permits. This private negotiation process is secretive in nature and susceptible to lobbying pressure, job blackmail, and threats of leaving the jurisdiction, resulting in suboptimal levels of environmental protection.[14]

Another major problem is caused by the fact that most permits authorizing water pollution are based on either:

- maximum concentrations of a pollutant per unit of effluent, e.g., x milligrams of mercury per litre;[15] or
- a maximum quantity of a pollutant per unit of production, e.g., x kilograms of suspended solids per tonne of pulp.[16]

It is vital to understand that under this "dilution is the solution" approach, there is no limit to the *total* amount of pollution discharged into water.[17] If the volume of effluent or the amount of production increases, so does the authorized, legal amount of pollution. For example, because permissible levels of pollution from pulp mills depend on their production volumes, the more pulp they produce, the more they are allowed to pollute. As far back as the 1985 Federal Inquiry into Water Policy, experts asserted that the Canadian regulatory system's emphasis on discharge quality instead of ambient water quality (i.e., the state of the water body being polluted) was ill-conceived.[18] The goal of the current system is to ensure that effluent is not "acutely toxic," measured by tests that generally immerse rainbow trout in effluent for ninety-six hours to see if they die.[19] While this acute toxicity approach is relatively simple, it ignores long-term and cumulative effects, both of which are of great importance to human and environmental health.

Only recently have lawmakers begun to recognize the importance of imposing limits on the total quantity of pollution emitted (from both individual sources and all sources combined). For example, overall limits successfully reduced the production and consumption of ozone-depleting chemicals and emissions of sulphur dioxide (see Chapters 3.1 and 3.3). However, imposing total limits on individual pollutants remains the exception, rather than the rule.

Calls for a more ecological approach, requiring a shift toward pollution *prevention*, date back to the early 1970s but have gone largely unanswered.[20] Pollution prevention means using laws, policies, and incentives to reduce or eliminate various pollutants, rather than merely limiting releases to certain levels. Newer Canadian environmental laws and policies, such as Nova Scotia's *Environment Act* and the *Canadian Environmental Protection Act, 1999*, incorporate the concepts of pollution prevention and source reduction but largely through voluntary programs rather than regulatory requirements.[21] Although promising in theory, these programs have not yet significantly reduced water pollution in Canada.[22] The following sections examine the effectiveness of the Canadian legal framework in addressing water pollution from a range of point and nonpoint sources.

Point Source Water Pollution

It is worth reiterating that substantial progress has been made in reducing some forms of water pollution. How has this progress been achieved? In some of these success stories water pollution problems in particular ecosystems were targeted, while in other cases specific industries were the focus of clean-up efforts.

Ecosystem-Based Initiatives

Ecosystem-based initiatives were undertaken in areas of Canada with significant water pollution problems. These programs include the Great Lakes Initiative, St. Lawrence Vision 2000, the Fraser River Action Plan, the Atlantic Coastal Action Program, and Alberta's Northern Rivers Ecosystem Initiative. These joint federal-provincial programs focus public and political concern on the challenges facing these water bodies, supply much-needed resources, and fund valuable scientific research.

The Great Lakes

During the 1960s and 1970s, pollution in the Great Lakes was causing eutrophication and algae explosions that harmed fish and other aquatic species. When the source of the problem was identified as too much phosphorous entering the system, Canada and the United States signed the 1972 *Great Lakes Water Quality Agreement* and took swift regulatory action.[23] Canada passed regulations limiting phosphorous concentrations in laundry detergents and requiring modifications to municipal sewage treatment facilities.[24] By the mid-1980s, phosphorous deposits were less than half of their 1972 level and that particular problem was largely solved.[25]

Today, the main water concern in the Great Lakes involves toxic chemicals: directly discharged into the lakes, accumulated in sediments at the bottom of the lakes, and deposited from the air. Point source discharges have largely been addressed but nonpoint source discharges continue to rise.[26] Of forty-four Regional Areas of Concern targeted for clean-up, only one has met all targets for improvement and delisting.[27] According to the International Joint Commission (IJC), "despite significant improvements in water quality during the past two decades, current concentrations of polychlorinated biphenyls (PCBs) in Great Lakes water are still about 100 times higher than the water quality criteria under the Great Lakes Initiative."[28] The estimated cost of cleaning up the Great Lakes is between US$100 and $500 billion.[29] Governments have been reluctant to provide the necessary resources. In 1994, the federal government unveiled a $125 million, six-year plan for the Great Lakes, but subsequent budget cuts meant that less than 12 percent of the promised funding was provided.[30]

The Fraser River

The Fraser River Action Plan (FRAP) was a six-year, $100 million program to restore the health of British Columbia's troubled Fraser River watershed. The FRAP led to some significant improvements in targeted industrial sectors, such as the pulp and paper industry.[31] However, at the end of the program the Department of Fisheries and Oceans concluded that "the Fraser River is only slightly cleaner than it was before FRAP," because far more resources are required to restore and protect the watershed.[32]

The St. Lawrence River

The St. Lawrence Action Plan (later known as St. Lawrence Vision 2000) provides an interesting illustration of the problems associated with focusing on point source pollution. In 1988, the plan targeted fifty of the worst industrial polluters along the river for a 90 percent reduction in the volume of toxic effluent they discharged into Quebec's St. Lawrence and Saguenay Rivers. Although the plan was widely regarded as successful because the goal of 90 percent reduction was nearly met, the fifty polluters were responsible for only 10 percent of the overall toxic pollution entering the river.[33] In other words, the plan addressed just one-tenth of the St. Lawrence River's pollution problem. Nonpoint sources, which contributed the majority of the pollution load, were largely overlooked. In summary, although these regional programs deserve credit for adopting an ecosystem-based approach, the lack of sufficient resources and the failure to address nonpoint sources of water pollution limited their effectiveness.

Industrial Point Source Water Pollution

Reducing industrial water pollution has been a major government priority in recent years, with the implementation of both new regulations and voluntary programs. In some industrial sectors, such as petroleum refining, mining and smelting, and wood products, significant reductions were achieved. The greatest gains occurred in those sectors subject to regulations rather than voluntary guidelines. For example, between 1980 and 1994, petroleum refineries reduced discharges of phenols by 74 percent, oil and grease by 72 percent, sulphides by 71 percent, ammonia nitrogen by 65 percent, and total suspended matter by 57 percent. This progress was in direct response to federal regulations passed under the *Fisheries Act*.[34] Similarly, the mining and smelting industry decreased releases of pollutants to water: arsenic by 85 percent, cadmium by 86 percent, cyanide by 94 percent, copper by 75 percent, lead by 78 percent, mercury by 93 percent, nickel by 88 percent, and zinc by 87 percent.[35] These decreases were spurred by regulations passed pursuant to the federal *Fisheries Act* and by the listing of lead, mercury, and cadmium as "toxic" substances requiring control under the *Canadian Environmental Protection Act*.[36] In British Columbia, the aquatic discharge of toxic chemicals used as wood preservatives by the lumber industry declined by 90 percent.[37] The impetus for this reduction in water pollution was a provincial regulation passed in 1990, combined with federal enforcement actions financed by the Fraser River Action Plan.[38]

The Pulp and Paper Industry: A Case Study

For a long time the pulp and paper industry was regarded as one of the worst water polluters in Canada. While efforts to reduce water pollution from the industry have been ongoing for decades, the first federal regulation targeting pulp and paper mills, passed in 1971, applied only to *new* mills. As a result, there was no incentive to upgrade the pollution control technology at older pulp and paper mills. By 1990 the regulation covered only 11 out of approximately 150 mills in Canada.[39] Due to new scientific evidence about the environmental damage caused by mill pollution, pressure from groups like Greenpeace, and increasing public concern, improved federal regulations came into effect in 1992.[40] At around the same time, some provinces also enacted regulations aimed at pulp and paper mills.[41] Although the industry was given advance notice of the proposed regulations in order to make the necessary investments in new equipment, many companies dragged their heels and successfully lobbied for extensions of deadlines.[42] The penalties for violating the new federal regulations are potentially very high: up to $1 million per day and jail sentences up to three years. Enforcement agencies promised to rigorously enforce the new regulations.[43]

In response to the strengthening of federal and provincial regulations, the industry tried to reduce its water pollution. Pulp and paper mills cut total suspended solids by 80 percent and biological oxygen demand by 95 percent between 1980 and 1997, and decreased discharges of dioxins and furans by 99 percent since 1988.[44] These improvements are directly related to regulations under the *Canadian Environmental Protection Act*, the *Fisheries Act*, and

various provincial pollution laws. Federal regulations call for the virtual elimination of dioxins and furans.[45] British Columbia's regulations for pulp and
paper mill effluent were stricter than the federal regulations until weakened in
2002.[46] Critics maintain that a superior regulatory approach would focus less
on specific substances and more on broader, longer-term prevention.[47]

Despite the advances in recent years, the pulp and paper industry still discharges close to two million kilograms of toxic chemicals into Canadian waters every year.[48] Effluent from mills continues to harm fish and aquatic
ecosystems.[49] Progress has been hampered by the failure of both the federal
and provincial governments to consistently enforce the new regulations. A
report based on information obtained from Environment Canada found over
3,000 documented violations of federal laws by eastern Canadian pulp mills
in recent years but only seven prosecutions. These figures included 1,700 violations by pulp mills in Quebec, where there were *zero* prosecutions.[50] This
remarkable failure to enforce the law can be traced to a harmonization agreement between the federal government and the province of Quebec, in which
Ottawa passed responsibility for enforcing environmental laws to Quebec. The
inescapable conclusion is that, pursuant to this harmonization agreement,
both levels of government turned a blind eye to Quebec pulp mills that broke
the law. One exception to the lax enforcement in eastern Canada was the
prosecution of Newfoundland's Corner Brook Pulp and Paper in 1996 for
violating the *Fisheries Act*. This case resulted in one of the stiffest sentences in
Canadian environmental law history, including a $500,000 fine and $250,000
in additional court-ordered payments to college environmental programs and
habitat restoration.[51]

In contrast, federal authorities in British Columbia used funds from the
Fraser River Action Plan to mount an aggressive inspection and enforcement
campaign.[52] As a result, according to Environment Canada, "all mills [in BC]
demonstrated a high degree of compliance" with the new regulations.[53] Unlike
the situation in Quebec, no harmonization agreement between BC and Canada
transfers responsibility for policing pulp mills to the province. The stark contrast between the two provinces provides compelling evidence that regulations alone will not protect the environment and emphasizes the need for a
strong federal role in environmental law enforcement. Unfortunately, experts
assert that "Environment Canada has persisted in singling out its water programs for cuts which are much more severe than for the department as a whole.
Gains which took years to achieve are quickly being eroded."[54]

The federal government's inability to enforce environmental laws is exacerbated by the inability or unwillingness of provincial governments to pick up
the slack. Data obtained under Ontario's Freedom of Information legislation
revealed that the number of known water pollution offences tripled between
1996 and 1998, from just over 1,000 to more than 3,300.[55] Fewer than ten
companies were charged for breaking the law during this period, yet many

major corporations listed had been breaking the law for at least five consecutive years, including Inco Ltd., Ethyl Canada, Domtar Inc., and Petro-Canada.[56] A fairly clear pattern emerges from the foregoing examples of progress in reducing water pollution from point sources. First, most of the progress has occurred in addressing pollution from industrial activities at a limited number of large facilities. Second, in each case the progress has followed the enactment of strong regulations by federal or provincial governments. Third, the extent of progress depends upon active enforcement of these regulations.

Water Pollution from Municipal Sewage

It may surprise many Canadians that seven of the country's ten worst polluters, by volume of toxic chemicals dumped into water in Canada's National Pollutant Release Inventory, are not industrial factories but municipal sewage treatment plants.[57] Sewage treatment plants also regularly dominate the "worst polluter" lists available from provincial governments in British Columbia and Ontario.

Canada has made progress on the issue of sewage treatment, but given this nation's wealth, our overall performance still leaves much to be desired. The percentage of Canadians served by some form of public sewage treatment facility increased from 64 percent to 78 percent between 1980 and 1997. There are three levels of sewage treatment. Primary treatment involves the removal of large solids, sediment, and organic matter by using screens, filters, and settling chambers. Secondary treatment involves biological processes using bacteria and other microorganisms to process waste. Tertiary treatment uses a variety of processes to remove additional nutrients, toxic compounds, salts, acids, and metals. However, only 40 percent of Canadians are served by tertiary treatment, the most effective form of treatment, compared to over 70 percent of the population in Germany, Denmark, Sweden, Finland, and Switzerland.[58] Over ninety Canadian municipalities, including Victoria, Halifax, and St. John's, still discharge raw, untreated sewage into water bodies.[59] Less than half of Atlantic Canada's population is served by sewage treatment.[60] Even in cities with sewage treatment systems, "wastewater bypasses sewage treatment during heavy rainfalls, combining with storm water in sewer outflows" because of a widespread flawed engineering design.[61] To make matters worse, this wastewater contains hundreds of chemicals, grease, paint thinner, and other industrial waste. Thousands of litres of raw or minimally treated sewage per Canadian are still dumped into Canada's rivers, lakes, and oceans annually.[62]

Wastewater effluent from municipalities frequently violates the section of the federal *Fisheries Act* that prohibits depositing a deleterious substance into fish-bearing waters: repeated tests have proven that sewage effluent is acutely lethal to fish.[63] However, charges are rarely laid against municipalities, which, like foreign diplomats, seem to be immune from prosecution. In 1996 and

1997 there were nearly one hundred violations by municipal sewage treatment facilities in Ontario.[64] No charges were laid. During the same period municipal sewage treatment plants in BC broke the law seventy-six times.[65] Again, no charges were laid. Efforts by citizen groups to prosecute municipal governments for breaking the law have been repeatedly stonewalled.[66] With no threat of enforcement, most municipal politicians have insufficient incentive to allocate scarce financial resources to upgrading sewage treatment facilities.

On a positive note, Calgary's outstanding municipal sewage treatment system, which receives accolades from environmental groups, proves that it is economically and technologically possible to build and operate a system that does not pollute.[67] Canada's ongoing problems with municipal sewage are not due to inadequate laws or regulations. The fault lies in governments' refusal to enforce existing pollution laws; the failure to spend the money necessary to upgrade sewage treatment facilities; and the entrenchment of a flawed sewer design that mixes industrial effluent with household waste and combines wastewater sewers with storm sewers.

Nonpoint Source Water Pollution

Most experts and scientists now believe that current water quality problems are largely caused by nonpoint source pollution. According to the Union of Concerned Scientists, "Industrial and municipal point sources represent only a small fraction (10 percent-20 percent) of all sources of water pollution. The runoff of fertilizers and pesticides from agriculture, animal wastes from livestock, and urban sources are far more important."[68] Although Canada has made progress in reducing water pollution from point sources, water pollution from urban and agricultural runoff, the deposition of airborne contaminants, and other nonpoint sources continues to flummox our legal system.[69] Data are limited, while monitoring and enforcement are prohibitively expensive. The conventional command-and-control, end-of-the-pipe approach to water pollution is overwhelmed by the enormous number of "pipes," some of which emanate from outside Canada. Ontario's Walkerton tragedy exemplifies the dangers of nonpoint source water pollution: the water supply was contaminated by animal waste.[70] Several examples will illustrate the difficulty in using a traditional command-and-control approach to regulate nonpoint sources of water pollution.

Agricultural Runoff

The three main contaminants contained in agricultural runoff are pesticides, fertilizers, and animal waste. These substances may enter the water system directly (e.g., aerial application of pesticides), indirectly (e.g., through leaching after being spread on fields), or accidentally (e.g., through the rupturing of a manure lagoon). Nonpoint source pollution from agricultural operations presents a daunting challenge to regulators. Keeping tabs on Canada's hundreds of thousands of farmers is far beyond current regulatory capacity. Because the regulation of pesticides is dealt with in Chapter 4.1, the focus here will be on animal waste from livestock operations.

In Canada, there are more than thirteen million cattle, eleven million pigs, half a million horses and mules, and close to a million sheep and goats.[71] In Ontario and Quebec alone, livestock produce a volume of manure equal to the sewage from 100 million people.[72] While manure can be used beneficially as a natural fertilizer, it can also contaminate water with nitrate, phosphorous, and coliform bacteria.[73] The auditor general of Quebec "found excess manure spreading [from livestock operations] to be the leading source of non-point source pollution" in that province.[74] Between 1988 and 1998, there were 274 manure spills in Ontario, including 53 spills that killed fish. Up to one in three Canadian livestock farmers stores liquid manure in unlined lagoons, risking contamination of both surface water and groundwater.[75]

In recent decades small-scale farm operations have given way to industrial livestock operations (often referred to as factory farms). In Canada between 1961 and 1996, the average number of cows per farm rose 147 percent, the number of hogs per farm rose 2,451 percent, and the number of chickens per farm rose 1,610 percent.[76] With the proliferation of industrial-sized livestock operations comes an unprecedented volume of animal waste. Ontario's environmental commissioner concludes, "Environmental laws created when small operations were the norm may not address the associated environmental risks that come with more intensive farm operations."[77] Although Canada spends billions of dollars to treat human sewage, the far greater volumes of animal manure produced receive no treatment at all.

In some provinces pollution laws provide specific *exemptions* for animal waste. For example, Ontario's *Environmental Protection Act* exempts animal waste from provisions prohibiting the release of contaminants and requiring the reporting of spills.[78] Most provinces have "right-to-farm" laws protecting farms from nuisance lawsuits filed by neighbours.[79] On the other hand, New Brunswick, Manitoba, Saskatchewan, Alberta, and Quebec have implemented specific regulations for livestock manure management.[80] Ontario recently passed a law to govern waste generated by industrial livestock operations.[81] However, given the logistical challenges involved and limited enforcement resources, these rules may not be enforced. In response to a citizen complaint alleging that Canada is failing to enforce pollution laws against industrial hog farms in Quebec, the Commission for Environmental Cooperation found evidence of nonenforcement. The CEC recommended a formal investigation but environment ministers from Canada, the United States, and Mexico vetoed the recommendation.[82] Other provinces continue to rely on unenforceable voluntary guidelines in their efforts to control animal waste.

Urban Runoff

One of the most notorious symbols of water pollution is the *Exxon Valdez*, the oil tanker that ran aground off Alaska in 1989, spilling about forty million litres of oil into the ocean. Pictures of oil-choked sea otters and birds distressed people in Canada and around the world. Billions of dollars were spent on cleaning up the mess. Fortunately, an environmental disaster like the *Exxon Valdez* occurs only rarely. Yet Canadians dump and spill the equivalent of *seven Exxon Valdez* tankers of used motor oil into Canadian waterways *every year*.[83] Even in 1989, despite the magnitude of the *Exxon Valdez* disaster, oil spills from tanker accidents accounted for only 2 percent of total oil released into the North American environment.[84]

When precipitation falls, oil and grease wash off roads and into waterways, along with road salt, contaminants from motor vehicle exhaust, chemicals used on lawns and gardens, and other harmful substances, causing serious damage to aquatic ecosystems throughout Canada.[85] Experts believe that existing laws and policies are unable to solve the problem and that solutions will require "more sophisticated policies and programs than the traditional 'command and control' model of legislation."[86] A whole new approach to planning and managing cities, called "smart growth," offers a promising multi-faceted solution to the problem of urban runoff.[87]

Airborne Water Pollution

Airborne pollution has a major impact on water. Although largely invisible, "Airborne pollutants have caused acidification of lakes and contaminated food webs to the point where in many areas, concentrations of pesticides, polychlorinated biphenyls (PCBs), mercury, and other persistent organic chemicals in fishes are high enough to require that human consumption be restricted."[88] Chemicals and heavy metals can travel long distances by air before contaminating water bodies, and Canadian waters continue to be contaminated by pesticides and other toxic chemicals no longer used in Canada.[89] The fact that pollutants travel from one medium to another (e.g., from air to water and vice versa) reinforces the need for a holistic approach to regulating pollution. Otherwise, tough water regulations may perversely cause an increase in air pollution.[90]

Contrary to the Fraser Institute's claim that acid rain is good for the environment, acid rain is a prime example of the negative ecological consequences of air pollution for aquatic ecosystems.[91] Scientific evidence establishes that by the mid-1980s, as many as ten thousand lakes in eastern Canada were uninhabitable by fish. In Nova Scotia, one-third of available Atlantic salmon habitat has been lost to acidification since the 1950s.[92] Scientists explain that the long-range transport of air pollution means that purely national responses are insufficient.[93] International efforts to control air pollution are essential. Canada's role in developing international solutions, and our legal system's success in addressing some types of air pollution, including the emissions that cause acid rain, are examined in greater detail in Chapter 3.3.

Toxic Water Pollution

As noted earlier, health experts and scientists are particularly concerned about substances that are persistent, bioaccumulate, and are toxic at low levels of exposure. Persistent substances degrade very slowly or cannot be broken down at all; they may remain in the aquatic environment for extremely long periods of time. Bioaccumulative substances increase in concentration as they move up the food chain. The damage caused by these substances, such as PCBs, some pesticides, and heavy metals, either is irreversible or requires decades or centuries to repair. An entire class of chemicals, known as endocrine disruptors, may be damaging to reproductive systems, immune systems, and intelligence at very low levels of exposure in both humans and wildlife.[94] Canada is not moving expeditiously to eliminate hormone-disrupting chemicals despite the IJC's conclusion that "there is sufficient evidence now to infer a real risk of serious impacts to humans."[95]

Both point and nonpoint sources cause toxic water pollution. The conventional approach to regulating these substances, end-of-the-pipe dilution, fails because these substances have no safe level. These chemicals, such as the pesticide atrazine, can cause damage at levels measured in parts per billion. The only sound solution, as recognized by Canada and the United States in the *Great Lakes Water Quality Agreement*, is to eliminate anthropogenic discharges of these substances. The *Canadian Environmental Protection Act, 1999 (CEPA)* is intended to govern the elimination of particularly harmful toxic substances. *CEPA* incorporates progressive ecological principles like ecosystem management, pollution prevention, and the precautionary principle.[96]

Under *CEPA* the ministers of health and environment must screen substances to determine whether they pose a risk to human health or the environment. If a substance meets the criteria for designation as toxic, then the federal government has the authority to regulate the substance from cradle to grave, that is, from production through disposal. Once a substance is designated as toxic, *CEPA* places a legal duty on the federal government to design control measures within two years and implement those measures within another eighteen months.[97] If a toxic substance is persistent, bioaccumulates, and is capable of long-range transport, then *CEPA* requires that steps be taken for the "virtual elimination" of the substance.[98] On paper, *CEPA* appears to provide a sound system for regulating toxic substances.

However, Canada is handicapped by the limited scientific knowledge about toxic chemicals.[99] Scientists estimate that there are more than 110,000 chemicals in use globally, many of which are either rare or totally unknown in nature.[100] Approximately 1,000 new chemicals are added annually.[101] The United States lists over 70,000 chemicals under the *Toxic Substances Control Act*.

According to one estimate, we have sufficient information for safety assessments of only 7 percent of the chemicals we release into the air, 34 percent of the chemicals released to water, and 3 percent of all chemicals used in large volumes.[102] As the OECD notes, "New toxic chemicals continue to challenge the ingenuity of pollution control authorities."[103]

The effectiveness of *CEPA* is also impaired by the extremely slow screening process for potentially toxic substances. Over 350 persistent toxic chemical compounds were found in the Great Lakes prior to 1990. Yet as of 2001, only 52 substances were formally designated as toxic under *CEPA*.[104] Although *CEPA* endorses the precautionary principle in theory, in practice toxic chemicals are allowed to be used in Canada until there is conclusive scientific evidence of their health or environmental impacts. More information on the regulation of toxic substances can be found in Chapters 3.3 and 4.1.

The Regulation of Water Pollution in the United States

The United States has a much more comprehensive approach to water pollution than Canada, dating back to the enactment of the *Clean Water Act* in 1972. Driven by the ambitious legislative goal of making all American waters fit for swimming and fishing, the *Act* provides Americans with many legal tools for protecting water that do not exist in Canada.[105] For example, the *Act* requires governments to set "Total Maximum Daily Loads" which impose limits on *overall* pollution of a watershed and require across-the-board reductions from all sources in order to meet water quality standards. The *Act* enables the US government to set legally binding national standards for pollution abatement technology, water quality, and health. No comparable legal standards exist in Canada. Pursuant to the *Act,* the United States also created the Nonpoint Source Management Program, whereby the federal government funds state and tribal activities to reduce nonpoint source pollution.[106] No similar program exists in Canada. The *Act,* like many American environmental laws, also allows citizens to bring civil actions against any person or corporation that violates the *Act* or against the government for failing to carry out its duties under the *Act.*[107] Again, this tool is absent in Canada. The *Act* requires virtually all municipalities to install secondary sewage treatment and provides federal grants to states to facilitate this effort.

Despite the apparent strength of the *Clean Water Act,* reports from the General Accounting Office and the EPA reveal that:

- 49 percent of American drinking water sources were partially or significantly affected by contaminants.
- 65 percent of US watersheds were subject to advisories urging no fish consumption, 28 percent were subject to advisories recommending limited fish consumption, and only 7 percent had no advisories about fish consumption.

- Millions of fish are killed by pollution annually.
- 2,500 beaches are closed each year due to contamination.
- Only 15 percent of US watersheds received a good water quality rating, while 59 percent were subject to either minor or serious water quality problems, and insufficient data were available for the remaining 26 percent.[108]

According to the Toxics Release Inventory (the American equivalent of Canada's National Pollutant Release Inventory), industry discharged over 100 million kilograms of chemicals into US surface waters in 1998.[109] Although on paper it is a strong and innovative law, the *Clean Water Act* has failed to stem the flow of water pollution in the United States. Experts attribute the failure to a combination of inadequate knowledge, inadequate resources, lack of enforcement, and most critically, a lack of social and political will.[110]

Conclusion

It is encouraging that substantial progress has been made in reducing water pollution from some point sources. However, it is disturbing that Canadian water quality continues to face major challenges from industrial, municipal, individual, agricultural, and international contamination. Canada's experience over the past thirty years demonstrates that clear regulations can achieve progress in reducing point source water pollution as long as the law is enforced. Considerably more resources need to be dedicated to enforcement, and procedural obstacles need to be dismantled so that the public can enforce the law where the government lacks either the resources or the political will.

Finally, current Canadian approaches are evidently incapable of addressing the growing problem posed by nonpoint sources of water pollution. Nonpoint source pollution is like the Internet: widely dispersed, international in scope, and difficult to regulate using conventional thinking. Environmental lawyers Paul Muldoon and Marcia Valiante pointed out a decade ago that "one of the major deficiencies in Canadian environmental protection and management activities is the lack of comprehensive non-point source controls."[111] Despite this warning, little progress has been made in reducing nonpoint sources of water pollution. Unless Canada adds some new and innovative tools to our legal system's tool-kit to address water contamination from agricultural runoff, urban runoff, and airborne pollution, more disasters like Walkerton are almost inevitable. The question is not if more water sources will be contaminated, but when.

2.3 WATER USE AND CONSERVATION

Canadians are prodigious users of water, second in the world behind Americans in per capita water withdrawals (meaning water removed from rivers, lakes, and groundwater reservoirs).[1] Daily, Canada withdraws 4,400 litres of water per person, most of which is used for thermal power generation, industry, and agriculture. On a per capita basis, Canada withdraws twice as much water as France, three times as much as Germany, five times as much as Sweden, and more than eight times as much as Denmark.[2] These figures do not include water used for hydroelectric power generation (because water is not withdrawn from the aquatic ecosystem), or Canada's record would be even worse. In total, Canada withdraws roughly 2 percent of our annual renewable

Table 2

Renewable fresh water used annually by OECD countries

Country	Water use as a % of water supply	Country	Water use as a % of water supply
Iceland	0.1	United Kingdom	14.6
New Zealand	0.6	Turkey	15.2
Norway	0.7	Czech Republic	15.6
Sweden	1.5	Denmark	15.7
Canada	**1.7**	Mexico	17.4
Finland	2.2	Poland	18.7
Ireland	2.6	United States	19.9
Austria	2.7	Japan	20.8
Luxembourg	3.4	France	23.9
Australia	4.3	Germany	24.4
Switzerland	4.9	Italy	32.2
Netherlands	4.9	Korea	35.6
Hungary	5.0	Spain	36.8
Portugal	11.9	Belgium	42.5
Greece	12.1		

Source: OECD (1999b, 72).

water supply, far less than most countries, given that the global average exceeds 25 percent (see Table 2). However, Canadian water use is concentrated in the southernmost parts of the country. According to Environment Canada, the fresh water in southern Canada is often heavily used and often overly stressed.[3]

Between 1980 and 1997 total water withdrawals in Canada increased 26 percent. In contrast, during the same period total water withdrawals in the United States fell 5 percent, despite major economic growth and a large population increase. Many European nations also achieved large gains in water efficiency between 1980 and 1997, with total water withdrawals falling 52 percent in the Netherlands, 34 percent in Finland, 34 percent in Sweden, 31 percent in the United Kingdom, and 20 percent in Denmark.[4] The fact that Canadian water use continues to grow when our industrial peers are achieving reductions suggests that there are systemic obstacles to water conservation in Canada. This chapter examines laws and policies governing water use and water conservation in an effort to explain Canada's poor record.

The Use of Water in Canada

Where is all of this water being used? Canadian water withdrawals, totaling 47.3 billion cubic metres in 1997, can be broken down as follows:[5]

Thermal power generation	63 percent
Manufacturing	16 percent
Municipal	11 percent
Agricultural	9 percent
Mining	1 percent

Thermal Power Generation

Thermal power generation accounts for almost two-thirds of Canada's water withdrawals. Power stations relying on nuclear energy or fossil fuels use large amounts of water for cooling purposes. The water is often returned to its source at much higher temperatures, which can have negative environmental consequences, particularly today when climate change is already warming waters to the detriment of species like salmon. In other countries, power stations are required to recycle the water they use for cooling, resulting in major reductions in water withdrawals at minimal cost (or even with cost savings).[6]

Manufacturing

Certain kinds of manufacturing also use large volumes of water. For example, it takes 70,000 litres of water to make one tonne of paper and 86,300 litres of water to make one tonne of steel. To make a car requires over 250,000 litres of water, while manufacturing a desktop computer requires over 33,000 litres. The pulp and paper industry (38 percent), steel and iron industry (22 percent), and chemical industry (21 percent), account for over 80 percent of the water used by Canada's manufacturing sector.[7]

Municipal Use

On an individual basis, Canadians use 343 litres of water per day for household purposes – almost twice as much as Europeans do – mostly in bathrooms.[8] The average Canadian household uses about 500,000 litres per year, and Environment Canada estimates that "at least half of this is unnecessary."[9] The main culprits are inefficient toilets, leaking or inefficient faucets, and wasteful activities like watering lawns and washing cars. Moreover, all of the water used for household purposes in Canada, from flushing toilets to washing cars, meets guidelines intended for drinking water quality. This is obviously inefficient, and points to a systemwide design flaw. Similarly, all of the water that leaves residences via the sewer system is treated as wastewater that must be disposed of because it poses a health threat and has no use. In countries with more advanced water conservation systems, a substantial portion of this so-called wastewater is reclaimed for other purposes, such as irrigation.

Agricultural Use

The agricultural sector uses water mainly for irrigation. Conventional irrigation technology is inefficient, with much of the water lost to evaporation and only a small proportion reaching the roots of crops where it is needed. Seventy percent of Canada's irrigated land is in Alberta, one of the few areas in Canada that suffers from a modest degree of water scarcity. The controversial Oldman Dam in southern Alberta was built to provide water for farmers, despite protracted litigation and an environmental assessment recommending that the project not proceed.[10] In British Columbia's Okanagan Valley, also a water-stressed region, irrigation for fruit orchards and other agricultural endeavours has damaged the environment. Fish habitat in three-quarters of the streams flowing into Okanagan Lake was destroyed by water withdrawals for irrigation.[11]

Hydroelectric Power Generation

Water used to generate hydroelectricity is not included in water use statistics because the water is never actually withdrawn from rivers. However, the construction and operation of hydroelectric power generating facilities has major effects on aquatic ecosystems.[12] There are more than 650 large dams in Canada, of which more than 80 percent are for electric power generation. These dams flood more than twenty thousand square kilometres of land and make Canada a world leader in hydroelectric power generation.[13] Hydroelectric projects divert more than 4 percent of Canada's total annual water flow, compared to less than 2 percent for all other water uses combined.

The Environmental Impacts of Water Use

The environmental impacts of water withdrawals upon aquatic ecosystems are well known. Lower water levels can damage habitat and cause increased temperatures (during summer), and increased freezing (during winter). These changes (compounded by other factors like climate change) have potentially significant consequences for fish, animals, and plants. For example, Pacific salmon are particularly sensitive to high temperatures, which may prevent them from successfully spawning. In addition, the more water withdrawn from an aquatic system, the lower the system's capacity to dilute and assimilate pollutants. Other environmental effects may include changes to river deltas, estuaries, and the flow of nutrients to the ocean.[14]

Hydroelectric operations also have environmental consequences. Reservoirs formed by flooding increase evaporation, raise temperatures downstream, trap silt and nutrients and may release a toxic form of mercury, rendering fish unsuitable for human consumption (with disproportionate effects on Aboriginal people eating traditional diets). Dams block the movement of migratory fish and kill fish as water passes through power-generating turbines. Altered stream flows destroy habitat, affect river deltas, increase turbidity, damage estuaries, harm fish, and eliminate wetlands. Recent studies also suggest that reservoirs created by flooding for hydroelectric projects may be a significant source of greenhouse gas emissions, contributing to climate change.[15]

Laws and Policies Governing Water Use in Canada

> Canada is behind other countries in providing consistent codes, guidelines, regulations, and policies affecting water use efficiency.
>
> *Canadian Council of Ministers of the Environment, 1994*

Federal Government

Few federal laws directly address water use because this is mainly an area of provincial jurisdiction under Canada's *Constitution Act, 1867*. However, Ottawa has jurisdiction in the fields of fisheries, navigation, and boundary waters, creating three potentially important exceptions to this general rule.

Under the *Fisheries Act,* the federal government has the power, but not the duty, to order dam operators to ensure that there is adequate water downstream to protect fish.[16] In practice, this power is seldom used, because the federal government wants to avoid confrontations with provinces over natural resource issues. In the rare cases where the Department of Fisheries and Oceans has ordered increased water flows, protracted lawsuits have ensued.[17] In court, the federal government argues that its fisheries power authorizes intervention to ensure minimum flows for fish. Dam operators, such as BC Hydro or Alcan

Inc., respond that provinces have jurisdiction over hydroelectric power developments under section 92A (1)(c) of the *Constitution Act, 1867*. Although courts have upheld the federal government's authority to regulate flows to protect fish, Ottawa remains reluctant to take actions that provinces regard as interfering in their business.

Ottawa's refusal to fulfill its responsibility to protect fisheries from the damaging impacts of hydroelectric facilities resulted in a submission to the Commission for Environmental Cooperation (CEC) by a number of Canadian citizens' groups. The submission alleged that Canada was failing to enforce the *Fisheries Act* against BC Hydro. (The CEC is a watchdog established as part of the environmental side agreement to NAFTA.) The investigation by the CEC concluded that Canada's policy is failing to protect fish habitat.[18] Unfortunately, the CEC's powers are limited to fact-finding and do not provide for sanctions or even recommendations.

The second potential angle for federal involvement in water use management is that projects affecting fisheries or navigation may trigger the federal environmental assessment process. Again, however, the federal government is reluctant to play a prominent role in what are often perceived as provincial projects such as mines or dams. Lawsuits by concerned citizens, environmental groups, and Aboriginal people were necessary to force the federal government to fulfill its legal duty to assess hydroelectric projects such as Alberta's Oldman Dam, Saskatchewan's Rafferty-Alameda Dam, and Quebec's proposed Great Whale project.[19] Apart from these rare instances, there is little evidence that federal environmental assessments have a significant effect in addressing water use in Canada (see Chapter 4.3).

The third avenue for federal involvement in managing water use is through its jurisdiction over boundary waters. Since the time of the 1909 *International Boundary Waters Treaty* with the United States, Ottawa has played a major role in issues involving the Great Lakes.[20] Canada and the United States signed the *Great Lakes Water Quality Agreement* in 1972 and since that time have been attempting to reduce human stresses on the lakes. Concerns about water uses and withdrawals from the Great Lakes were the subject of a special study by the International Joint Commission in 2000, leading the federal government to prohibit large-scale transfers or diversions of boundary waters.[21] However, the majority of water used in Canada comes from internal waters rather than international or boundary waters. Internal waters are primarily within provincial jurisdiction.

Provincial and Territorial Governments
Provincial and territorial laws governing water use in Canada vary considerably but produce similar results.[22] Ownership of water is vested on behalf of the public in provincial and territorial governments, which issue licences to individuals and corporations for the use of water. Canada's water laws "are

heavily biased toward the individual's [or corporation's] right to withdraw water for private gain and against the public's common interest in leaving water 'instream' to maintain fisheries, recreational values, and the integrity of ecosystems."[23] In western Canada, water rights are allocated on a first-come, first-served basis. In eastern Canada, water rights are based on property ownership, meaning property owners enjoy riparian rights to use adjoining waters. In the northern territories, water rights are based on a hierarchy of public purposes established by statute. None of these outdated systems evolved with water conservation in mind, largely because of the myth of Canada's endless water supply. To the contrary, "the law does little to encourage the efficient use of water" because of the "use it or lose it" principle and the inability to transfer water rights.[24] The "use it or lose it" principle means that a person with a water licence must use the water or face the reduction or loss of the licence. Similarly, the inability to transfer or sell licences means there is no incentive to conserve water (which could then be sold to other users or the government).

For more than a century, the idea that aquatic ecosystems are, in a sense, "water users" escaped the notice of Canadian lawmakers.[25] Only in recent years have environmental considerations become relevant for water licensing decisions in some provinces. British Columbia introduced the *Fish Protection Act* in 1997, breaking new ground by requiring the water comptroller to consider water *quality* and water *quantity* when making decisions about water licences for designated sensitive streams. The *Act* also contains unprecedented provisions requiring licence holders to reduce water withdrawals during periods of drought if the survival of fish is threatened.[26] Other provinces, such as Alberta, are beginning to take similar steps, although most water rights in southern Canada have already been allocated without considering ecosystem needs or conservation. Alberta is a leader in allowing water licensees to sell or trade surplus water, which encourages conservation.[27] Efforts to reallocate water rights to meet society's changing needs are hampered by inflexible regulatory systems in most provinces.[28]

Water Prices

A critical element of Canadian water policy, contributing to overconsumption, is the price of water. Prices for water are set provincially or regionally for industrial and agricultural users, and locally for municipal water users. Canadians enjoy the cheapest water prices in the industrialized world, and Canada has been repeatedly chastised by the OECD for our profligate, heavily subsidized use of water, and our refusal to charge prices that reflect, at a minimum, the costs of water supply infrastructure. In an unusual departure from its generally conservative language, the OECD describes Canadian water as "cheaper than dirt."[29] Canadian households pay from $0.20 to $0.60 per thousand litres of water, or from 0.02 to 0.06 cents per litre.[30] In other words, Canadians pay more for one can of pop, one beer, or one cup of coffee than they pay for

Table 3

Municipal water prices, including water and sewage services

Country	US$/1,000 litres	Country	US$/1,000 litres
Canada	**$0.70**	Australia	$1.64
Hungary	$0.82	Germany	$1.69
Italy	$0.84	Japan	$2.10
Luxembourg	$1.01	Belgium	$2.18
Austria	$1.05	Sweden	$2.60
Spain	$1.07	Finland	$2.76
Greece	$1.14	France	$3.11
United States	$1.25	United Kingdom	$3.11
Switzerland	$1.29	Netherlands	$3.16
Turkey	$1.51	Denmark	$3.18

Source: OECD (1999d, 38).

a thousand litres of treated drinking water. On average, Canadians pay half as much as Europeans for water and use twice as much water (see Table 3).[31]

The method used for pricing water in Canada also contributes to high levels of water use. Fifty-six percent of Canadian utilities charge a flat rate for water, meaning consumers pay the same amount regardless of how much they use. Another 13 percent of Canadian utilities charge a declining block rate, which means the more consumers use, the lower the price per unit becomes (like a bulk discount).[32] In contrast, almost all European countries employ water pricing systems where prices are progressively higher on higher volumes. The European philosophy is that a certain level of water is required to meet basic human needs and water above that level is a luxury. Recent changes in Denmark raised water prices to US$4.18 per thousand litres, almost six times the average Canadian price.[33] Many studies confirm that price increases result in significantly lower household water consumption.[34] Water prices in Canada are gradually creeping upward, increasing 2.9 percent per year from 1986 to 1996, but remain the lowest in the OECD.[35]

Making matters even worse is the fact that only 57 percent of Canadian households have their water usage metered.[36] In major cities like Vancouver and Montreal, the figure is less than 1 percent.[37] In contrast, all households are metered in most OECD countries.[38] Studies show that per capita water consumption in Canada is, on average, 50 percent higher in areas where consumers are charged a flat rate than where they are metered.[39] Given the low level of metering, the extensive use of flat rate pricing, and the rock-bottom prices, the Canadian Council of Ministers of the Environment (CCME) concludes, "Pricing policies in most municipalities actually discourage efficient use of water."[40]

The underpricing causes an environmental and economic domino effect. First, cheap water contributes to our profligate overconsumption. Overconsumption spurs the construction and expansion of dams and reservoirs, strains water treatment and delivery infrastructure, increases stress on aquatic ecosystems, and places pressure on dwindling groundwater supplies. High levels of water use also create huge volumes of wastewater that require larger, more expensive sewage treatment plants. Underpricing also means that less revenue is generated. As a result, water infrastructure in Canada is, in the words of Environment Canada, in a state of "severe deterioration."[41] At least 13 percent of the water withdrawn for municipal use is lost to leakage, and in cities with particularly decrepit systems, such as Montreal, the waste can be upward of 35 percent.[42]

The Canadian Water and Wastewater Association says that Canada needs to spend $27 billion for water treatment and distribution infrastructure and another $61 billion to upgrade sewers and wastewater treatment. Environment Canada estimates that repairing Canada's municipal water supply and waste treatment systems could cost up to $100 billion.[43] The municipal water system in Canada costs at least $4.5 billion per year to maintain and operate, while water fees generate only $3.3 billion in annual revenues.[44] This gap is worsening as stronger standards for drinking water are implemented: governments will have to invest in better facilities, more comprehensive testing, and certified operators. For example, Quebec announced new spending of $600 million in 2001 to implement its improved drinking water regulations.[45] The OECD and the Canadian Council of Ministers of the Environment concur that Canada's municipal water systems are unsustainable under current approaches to pricing.[46]

The price of water paid by industrial, agricultural, and commercial users in Canada is even lower than municipal water prices. The OECD reports that for industrial water users, Canada charges "very low" prices, "there are no incentives to use water efficiently and all user demands are met, regardless of their water-using practices."[47] Water licence fees paid to provinces are "only sufficient to recover the administrative costs of the system," meaning that water is more or less given away free.[48] For example, British Columbia charges companies that are bottling publicly owned water $8.50 for 1,659,290 litres, or 0.00051 cents per litre.[49] Coca-Cola uses water purchased at extremely low prices from various Canadian municipalities for its Dasani bottled water, which is then sold for roughly a thousand times the price of tap water.[50] Canada's farmers either use groundwater, which is free, or pay what the OECD describes as "heavily subsidised rates," with subsidies of up to 90 percent. Canada, along with New Zealand and Portugal, has the lowest agricultural water prices among the twenty-nine OECD nations.[51]

In a promising development, Ontario passed a law in 2002 authorizing municipalities to recover the full costs of providing water, including the costs of source protection as well as treatment and distribution. British Columbia's Drinking Water Review Panel also called for full-cost pricing.[52]

Canadian Water Conservation Laws and Policies

> Water conservation is still in the early days of
> development.
>
> *BC Ministry of Environment, Land and Parks, 1998*

The federal government plays a minor role in Canadian water conservation efforts, although it participated with provincial and local governments in the development of Canada's *National Action Plan to Encourage Water Use Efficiency* in 1994. To its credit, the federal government is taking steps to reduce its own consumption through its Greening Government Operations program. Federal departments and agencies are implementing water efficiency measures such as auditing, installing meters, and retrofitting wasteful equipment. Environment Canada sponsors research on water conservation and engages in public education and awareness campaigns. Canada has no national tax on water, unlike many European nations that charge value-added tax on water use. By taxing water use at the national level, European countries encourage conservation and efficiency. Progressive water taxes (i.e., rates that increase as water use increases) protect the poor and raise revenues for reinvestment in European water systems.[53]

Water conservation in Canada, for the most part, is handled by provincial and local governments (municipalities, regional districts, and so on). Although many promising water conservation initiatives are under way in Canada, they are sporadic rather than systemic.[54] It is increasingly obvious that the focus of water management must be redirected from the supply side to the demand side. The basic elements of demand management include metering, volume-based pricing, education, water audits (for leak detection and repair at the system level and to identify wasteful practices at the user level), water-efficiency labelling (analogous to energy-efficiency labelling on appliances), and changes to building and plumbing codes.

Several provinces have made minor modifications to building codes to address water conservation. British Columbia and Ontario, for example, now require all new construction to install low-flow fixtures (toilets, faucets, and showerheads) under their plumbing codes.[55] Local governments in other provinces have passed similar bylaws. BC's *Municipal Sewage Regulations* break new ground by allowing the use of reclaimed (i.e., recycled) water.[56] The level of metering in Canada, although relatively low, is increasing. Many local governments have enacted sprinkling bylaws, restricting times for watering lawns and gardens. Some neighbourhoods in Victoria decreased water use by 30 percent to 50 percent during the dry summer of 2001 through the use of conservation measures.[57]

According to Environment Canada, conservation measures can achieve the same results as expanding municipal water infrastructure for as little as one-fifteenth of the cost.[58] Local governments are beginning to appreciate the economic and environmental benefits of demand management. Cochrane (Alberta) deferred a multimillion-dollar pipeline to import water by giving away toilet dams, low-flow showerheads, and faucet aerators. Port Elgin (Ontario) avoided a $5.5 million expansion of its water treatment plant by spending $550,000 to install 2,400 residential water meters and implementing an intensive conservation program.[59] Similarly, Winnipeg estimates that a 5 percent decrease in per capita water use would enable the city to defer, for thirteen years, the construction of new facilities costing $350 million.[60]

It should be emphasized that municipal water use accounts for only 11 percent of Canadian water withdrawals. Significant conservation efforts are also necessary in the power generation, agricultural, and industrial sectors. Current laws and policies are often barriers to innovation and new technologies. As mentioned earlier, Canadian laws require that wastewater be treated as a "bad" substance requiring disposal. Yet in other countries, wastewater is viewed as a potentially valuable resource. In water-poor Israel, 70 percent of the nation's wastewater is treated and reused for irrigation, with multiple benefits. Water use for agriculture also can be reduced with drip irrigation, another conservation innovation developed in Israel.[61]

Economics dictates that as the price of water and wastewater treatment rises, recycling water becomes more cost-effective. Canada's rock-bottom water prices mean that water is recycled less than in the United States.[62] Thermal power-generating facilities, which account for two-thirds of Canadian water withdrawals, are prime candidates for water recycling. The city of Waterloo passed an innovative bylaw in 1990 that made it illegal to discharge water into the sewer system that had been used only once for cooling purposes. This mandatory recycling law led some companies to reduce water use by more than 60 percent within a year.[63] The Canadian pulp and paper industry claims to have reduced its water use per tonne of output by 45 percent between 1980 and 1999.[64] If this claim is accurate, it represents a significant and commendable improvement by the largest water user in Canadian manufacturing. Some experts estimate that "with technologies available today, farmers could cut their water needs from 10 percent to 50 percent, industries by 40 percent to 50 percent and cities by one-third, with no sacrifice to economic output or quality of life."[65] Others suggest that overall efficiency savings could be even higher, in the range of 40 to 90 percent.[66] Gains of this magnitude will not be achieved without significant changes to laws and policies governing water use and conservation.

Conclusion

A decade ago, experts concluded that "public policy in Canada has exhibited an almost total disregard for the potential uses of economics in carrying out the tasks of water management."[67] Despite this warning, Canada has moved at a snail's pace in implementing pricing reforms, conservation programs, and efficiency measures. Canada's current water laws and policies are producing the lowest municipal, agricultural, and industrial water prices, the lowest rates of metering, the lowest fees for water pollution, and the lowest rates of industrial water recycling in the OECD. Blinded by an unshakeable faith in a never-ending supply of fresh water, Canadian governments at all levels have focused almost exclusively on increasing the water supply rather than on reducing demand. Our water laws and policies continue to reflect this archaic approach despite mounting evidence of environmental and economic costs. Given the success of other nations, including the United States, in reducing water use, it should be relatively easy to reduce industrial, agricultural, and municipal water consumption through economic reforms, incentives, regulations, and public education.

The greater challenge for Canada will be to reduce the environmental effects of hydroelectric power generation, the leading use of water in this country. Laws intended to mitigate these impacts are not being enforced. Canada suffers from the misperception that hydroelectricity is environmentally benign because it produces little pollution. In fact, the construction of hydroelectric megaprojects has caused extensive environmental damage and wreaked havoc on many Aboriginal people. The operation of dams and reservoirs continues to harm aquatic ecosystems. Canada depends on hydroelectricity, however, not only for a significant percentage of our domestic energy needs, but also for large export revenues generated by selling power to the United States.

In terms of the big picture, Canada has *relatively* abundant amounts of fresh water. We face more serious problems with water quality than water quantity. As the Inquiry on Federal Water Policy concluded, "With few exceptions, Canada's water problems are not related to inadequate supply at all, but to degraded water quality and to disrupted flow regimes."[68] Still, Canada must come to terms with the fundamental fact that our supply of fresh water is not endless. Our water laws and policies must evolve to reflect the ecological realities of limited water supplies, limited capacity to absorb pollutants, and the needs of aquatic ecosystems.

2.4 WATER EXPORTS

> Every day millions of kilowatt hours flow downhill
> and out to sea. What a waste.
> *Robert Bourassa, Premier of Quebec, 1970-6, 1986-93*

The world is embroiled in an unprecedented and worsening water crisis. Water consumption by humans has quadrupled in the past fifty years.[1] At least forty nations, with a combined population of 500 million, are already experiencing severe water stress, defined as using more than 40 percent of their available supply of fresh, renewable water. By 2025 severe water stress is expected to affect between 2.4 and 3.2 billion people (depending on the rate of population growth in affected countries).[2] The vice-president of the World Bank and chairman of the World Water Commission anticipate that "the wars of the twenty-first century will be fought over water."[3]

More than 97 percent of the Earth's water is salt water. Of the less than 3 percent of water that is fresh, 99.7 percent is inaccessible, locked up in polar icecaps, snowfields, glaciers, and deep rock. As a result, fresh water is a rare and valuable resource. As noted earlier, Canadians enjoy almost 100,000 cubic metres of renewable fresh water per capita annually. Canada uses 1,600 cubic metres per person each year, or less than 2 percent of its available supply. Some nations in the Middle East, Asia, and Africa use more than 100 percent of their available renewable water supply, meaning they either import water, mine groundwater, or use desalination to produce fresh water. Table 4 provides the annual renewable water supply (cubic metres per capita) for fifteen countries in 1995 and their projected supply in 2025, given present trends.

Given the water shortages faced by other regions of the world, Canada's water has attracted global attention, sparking an impassioned national debate about bulk water exports. The reaction ranges from hysterical warnings about environmental disaster and the loss of Canadian sovereignty to starry-eyed dreams of vast fortunes to be made. Media reports raise "the spectre of massive

Table 4

Annual renewable water supply (cubic metres per capita) for fifteen countries in 1995 and 2025

Country	1995	2025 (projected)
Canada	98,667	79,731
Congo	320,864	144,771
China	2,295	1,891
Egypt	936	607
France	3,408	3,279
India	2,244	1,567
Israel	389	270
Kuwait	95	55
Libya	111	47
Norway	90,489	84,084
Pakistan	3,435	1,740
Saudi Arabia	249	107
Singapore	180	142
South Africa	1,206	698
United States	9,277	7,453

Source: de Villiers (1999, 367-73).

exports of water sucking the country dry."[4] On one hand, Canada's former ambassador to the United States, Raymond Chrétien, said, "Water is sacrosanct for Canadians. The idea of exporting water in bulk shipments is anathema."[5] The Council of Canadians warns, "They're coming to take our water ... right now. Canada's water – our water – is under terrible threat."[6] On the other hand, *National Post* columnist Terence Corcoran urges Canada to "turn on the tap" and use the Organization of Petroleum Exporting Countries (OPEC) as a model in an "attempt to cartelize the world supply of water and drive the price up." Corcoran predicts that "by the year 2010, Canada will be exporting large quantities of water to the United States, and more by tanker to parched nations all over the globe."[7] Provincial politicians bemoan the "waste" of river water "spilling into the ocean."[8]

Important Facts about Bulk Water Exports
The inflammatory and polarized rhetoric about water exports obscures some important facts. First, Canada *already* exports water in bulk to the United States via pipeline and truck and has licensed bulk export via marine tanker. Current bulk water export licences from British Columbia to the United States include:[9]

Alpine Glacier Water, Inc.	marine transport	246,549,600 litres/year
Greater Vancouver Water District	pipeline	1,161,503,000 litres/year
Clearly Canadian Ltd.	tanker truck	26,700,272 litres/year

Water is also exported by pipeline from Manitoba to North Dakota, from New Brunswick to Maine, and from Alberta to Montana to supply American communities near the border.[10] On a larger scale, we are also exploiting huge quantities of Canadian water in order to export hydroelectric power to the United States.

Second, total demand for water in the United States and many other countries is declining. Between 1980 and 1997, total American water use fell 5 percent, while European nations saw total water use decreases of up to 50 percent.[11] These countries have demonstrated that reducing demand through conservation is much less expensive (economically and environmentally) than increasing supply. Third, water flowing into the ocean from rivers is by no means wasted. Environmental concerns about bulk water exports include the impacts of reduced flows on fish, wildlife, and plants, the potential introduction of non-native species, and damage to estuaries and coastal regions.[12] Scientists also worry about the cumulative effects of bulk water removals in combination with pollution, global warming, and ozone depletion.[13] These concerns are exacerbated by our lack of knowledge about the complexity of aquatic ecosystems. As the International Joint Commission concluded in its study of potential bulk water exports from the Great Lakes, "It is difficult to quantify with any degree of precision the ecological impacts" of various human water uses.[14]

Fourth, while some experts claim that there are no markets or that shipping water is too expensive, these assertions are ill-conceived.[15] Assertions that a given use of natural resources is not economical are frequently proven wrong. Bulk water exports are, in fact, economically viable; Korea and Taiwan both import water via tanker.[16] Nations in the Middle East, like Saudi Arabia, get significant proportions of their water through the process of desalination, which may be more expensive than tanker imports.[17] A Canadian company called Global Water Corporation hopes to export water to China from Alaska. Alaskan law allows the removal of water that is surplus to state and environmental needs.[18] Fifth, proposed bulk water exports from Canada are not intended to alleviate suffering in water-stressed nations. The hundreds of millions of people who lack access to adequate supplies of clean water and the governments of these impoverished nations are generally far too poor to pay for large quantities of imported water.[19]

Proposals to Export Water, in Bulk, from Canada

Plans to remove water from Canada in large quantities have bubbled to the surface repeatedly for decades, dating back to two megaprojects conceived in the 1960s. The GRAND (Great Recycling and Northern Development) Canal was a scheme to divert water from twenty rivers flowing into James Bay in northern Quebec. Dams, dikes, and canals would send this water south to the Great Lakes and beyond into the United States. NAWAPA (North American

Water and Power Alliance) was an even more ambitious plan to dam dozens of rivers in British Columbia, the Yukon, and the Northwest Territories and use the Rocky Mountain trench as a massive storage reservoir eight hundred kilometres long.[20] While corporate interests continue to describe these megaprojects as "potentially awesome catalysts of economic and environmental change," they face huge legal, environmental, economic, and social obstacles.[21] As a result, both Environment Canada and the IJC believe that the era of large dam construction in Canada is over.[22]

Proposals for water exports morphed into a different form in the 1990s, with plans for bulk removals via tanker ship moving to the fore. In 1991 a BC company, Snowcap Waters Ltd., its American partner, Sun Belt Water Inc., and about a dozen other corporations sought to export water from British Columbia. After granting a licence to Snowcap, the BC government was flooded by public opposition, leading to the imposition of a moratorium on large-scale exports. In 1995, the province passed the *Water Protection Act,* prohibiting new licences for the bulk export of water. Snowcap's licence was cancelled. Dreams of blue gold were turned, by law, into fool's gold. Or so it seemed.

Snowcap and Sun Belt sued the provincial government. Snowcap, the Canadian company that had been issued a licence, settled out of court for $335,000. The BC government could not reach a settlement with Sun Belt, which sought roughly $700 million in compensation. In 1997, on a preliminary motion, the BC Supreme Court ruled that Sun Belt's legal challenge had "little likelihood of success."[23] Sun Belt abandoned the Canadian court system but its chief executive officer, Jack Lindsey, boasted that "Canadian courts cannot block me, cannot slow me down."[24] Lindsey was referring to the North American Free Trade Agreement (NAFTA), Chapter 11 of which gives corporations from the United States and Mexico the right to sue Canada and have the case determined by international arbitration, thus circumventing the Canadian judicial system. In the fall of 1998 Sun Belt filed a NAFTA claim for $15.75 billion in damages, alleging that BC's ban on bulk water exports violated its investment rights.

Sun Belt's Notice of Intent to Submit a Claim to Arbitration refers to secrets, bribes, payoffs, private investigators, insider trading, anti-American premiers, biased courts, and rogue governments violating their own laws.[25] Whether Sun Belt's claim has merit is a subject of debate among lawyers in Canada. In an independent legal opinion, McCarthy Tétrault, one of Canada's leading law firms, concludes, "It is our view that Sun Belt has a good arguable case under the fair and equitable treatment guarantee of NAFTA."[26] In contrast, trade lawyer Barry Appleton, who has successfully represented American corporations in NAFTA complaints against Canada, describes Sun Belt's case as "ludicrous."[27] The current status of the case is unknown, due to the fact that NAFTA proceedings take place behind closed doors, hidden from public scrutiny.

In 1998 two new proposals to export bulk water brought the issue back to a boil. The Ontario Ministry of Environment issued a five-year permit to the Nova Group allowing the withdrawal, by tanker, of up to 600 million litres of water per year from Lake Superior for shipment to Asia. The quantity sounds huge but according to Marq de Villiers, author of *Water*, "600 million litres is the amount of water that flows into the St. Lawrence River every minute."[28] Vancouver already exports twice that volume of water to Point Roberts, in the state of Washington. In response to vocal public opposition, the Ontario government quickly cancelled Nova's permit.

Soon after the Nova debacle, the McCurdy Group sought approval to export from 50 to 100 billion litres a year from Gisborne Lake in Newfoundland. The McCurdy proposal is one hundred times the size of the Nova project, yet involves a much smaller lake. McCurdy's plan was to ship the water by supertanker to the oil-rich, water-poor Middle East. Optimistic Newfoundlanders compared the economic potential of Gisborne Lake to the Hibernia offshore oilfields, noting that the price of bottled water is higher than the price of gasoline. In reality, Canadian royalties on water are so low that little government revenue is generated.[29] After Newfoundland announced that the McCurdy proposal had cleared provincial environmental assessment hurdles, public opposition intensified. Premier Brian Tobin pulled the plug on McCurdy's proposal in 1999. However, Tobin's successor, Premier Roger Grimes, announced in 2001 that he supported McCurdy's plan to export water in bulk from Gisborne Lake.[30]

Canadian Laws and Policies Governing Bulk Water Exports
The seemingly endless debate about bulk water is due to the broken promises of Canadian governments about dealing with the issue. Back in 1985 the Inquiry on Federal Water Policy recommended that the government of Canada enact legislation to address the issue of large-scale water exports.[31] In 1987, Environment Minister Tom McMillan said, "The federal government emphatically opposes large-scale exports of our water." The 1987 Federal Water Policy stated that Ottawa would "take all possible measures within the limits of its constitutional authority to prohibit the export of Canadian water by interbasin diversions."[32] Prime Minister Brian Mulroney's Conservative government introduced the *Canada Water Preservation Act* in 1988 to "prohibit large scale exports or diversions for the export of water." The proposed law died on the order paper when the 1988 election was called and was never resurrected by subsequent governments.[33]

During the NAFTA negotiations there was a storm of controversy about whether the deal applied to Canadian water. The Progressive Conservative government claimed that Canada's water was exempt, but in hindsight it clearly misled the public. Neither Pat Carney, Canada's trade minister at the time, nor a senior policy advisor could identify any provision in the text of the agreement to support such a claim.[34] As the leader of the opposition, Jean Chrétien argued that water should be excluded from the deal. Yet as prime minister, Chrétien signed NAFTA – without an exemption for water.

The Nova and McCurdy export proposals forced the federal government to finally take action on bulk water exports. In general, provincial governments in Canada reject any federal actions that could be construed as interference with the development of provincial natural resources. But when confronted by public opposition to the Nova and McCurdy bulk water export proposals, provincial governments in both Ontario and Newfoundland claimed that the final decision was up to Ottawa. Ontario environment minister Norm Sterling said that "the primary responsibility for laws governing export remains clearly in the federal domain." Newfoundland environment minister Oliver Langdon maintained McCurdy's Gisborne Lake proposal could not proceed "without federal consent."[35]

Federal environment minister David Anderson told Newfoundland and Ontario that the federal government had no jurisdiction to make decisions about provincial resources. Although this position reflects the federal government's long-standing tradition of denying that it has the constitutional ability to address issues involving provincial resources, it lacks legal merit. According to legal experts, from a constitutional perspective, "Parliament can pass laws regulating the export of water from Canada" pursuant to its power over international trade, just as the federal government regulates energy exports (from provincial natural resources) under the *National Energy Board Act*.[36]

Instead of passing a law to ban or limit bulk water exports, the federal government responded to the Nova and McCurdy proposals with a three-pronged strategy:

1   asking the International Joint Commission (IJC) to investigate the impacts of exporting water from the Great Lakes
2   amending the *International Boundary Water Treaty Act* to prohibit bulk water removals from boundary watersheds (principally the Great Lakes)
3   persuading the provincial governments to pass legislation prohibiting large-scale diversions of water.

The IJC conducted an extensive study and recommended a moratorium on bulk water exports. It concluded that governments "should not permit any new proposal for removal of water from the Great Lakes Basin to proceed unless the proponent can demonstrate that the removal would not endanger the integrity of the ecosystem."[37] The federal government fulfilled its promise to amend the *International Boundary Water Treaty Act* to prohibit large-scale exports or diversions of waters along Canada's international borders.[38]

The provinces grumbled about the federal government's strategy but for the most part moved to introduce new legislation. British Columbia already had the *Water Protection Act* in place, banning large-scale exports and diversions. Ontario, Newfoundland and Labrador, Alberta, Manitoba, Nova Scotia, Prince Edward Island, and Saskatchewan made it unlawful either to export water in bulk or to engage in large-scale water diversions. Quebec initially balked but eventually passed its own *Water Resources Preservation Act*.[39] New Brunswick is the only province without a law banning bulk water exports.

Strengths and Weaknesses of Canada's Laws and Policies on Water Exports

Instead of a single national law addressing Canadian concerns about large-scale water diversions and exports, Canada has the *International Boundary Water Treaty Act,* nine different provincial laws, and one provincial gap. This multiplicity of laws causes all kinds of problems. First, there are major irregularities among the provincial laws. For example, Quebec's law has a loophole allowing bulk water export if the water is used to produce electric power.[40] The laws in Alberta, Manitoba, and Nova Scotia have loopholes allowing the provincial cabinet or legislature to make exceptions to the rules banning bulk water exports.[41] Alberta recently passed a special act to approve a licence for the transfer of water between two water basins within the province.[42] Some of the new provincial laws prohibit transfers of water between watersheds, while others focus on banning the removal of water from the province.

The second problem is that provincial laws prohibiting water exports may be unconstitutional. Although regulating water use is primarily a provincial responsibility, regulating international trade is a matter of federal jurisdiction under Canada's *Constitution Act, 1867*.[43] This concern is particularly applicable to the provinces whose legislation emphasizes prohibiting exports (a trade focus) instead of preventing diversions from water basins (an environmental focus). The third flaw in the present approach is that any province may decide to change its mind. As noted earlier, Newfoundland and Labrador premier Roger Grimes supports bulk water exports.

Does NAFTA Apply to Bulk Water Exports from Canada?

The biggest problem facing Canadian laws and policies governing bulk water exports is NAFTA. As mentioned earlier, there is considerable controversy over the extent to which NAFTA applies to water. NAFTA applies to all "goods." Is water a good? The federal government argues that NAFTA does not apply to Canadian water (except bottled water) because water in its natural state is not a good.[44] Ottawa relies on a joint statement issued by the governments of Canada, the United States, and Mexico in 1993, claiming that their intention was that NAFTA not include water.[45] The federal government also points to a section in the Canadian law passed to implement NAFTA, which states that nothing in the free trade agreement applies to water in its natural state.[46] The joint statement and the Canadian law raise a puzzling question: why not put an exemption for water in the text of the trade agreement? Canada negotiated specific exemptions from NAFTA's trade rules for exports of raw logs and unprocessed fish, which are in the text of the agreement. Why not water? An exemption for water in the text of NAFTA itself would be legally binding and enforceable. As it stands, the consensus among lawyers outside government is that neither the joint statement nor the Canadian law is legally binding or enforceable with respect to prohibiting water exports.

A legal opinion prepared for the Council of Canadians argues, based on international trade law and court decisions from the United States and Europe, that water *is* a good and therefore covered by NAFTA.[47] The Council of Canadians position is that as soon as water is traded (i.e., sold) between Canada and the United States, NAFTA applies. The US government's position is also that, once it is traded, water becomes a good and is fully covered by NAFTA.[48] For the record, NAFTA defines "goods" as "domestic products as these are understood in the *General Agreement on Tariffs and Trade* or such goods as the Parties may agree."[49] The *General Agreement on Tariffs and Trade* (GATT) contains the following tariff item for water:

> 22.01 waters, including natural or artificial waters and aerated waters, not containing added sugar or other sweetening matter nor flavouring; ice and snow.[50]

An explanatory note in the GATT states that this tariff item includes "ordinary natural water of all kinds (other than sea water). Such water remains in this heading whether or not it is clarified or purified." Basing his arguments on these provisions, Barry Appleton writes in his book *Navigating NAFTA*, "one must conclude that natural water will be treated as a good under the NAFTA, even when it is in its natural state."[51] It therefore seems highly likely, though not certain, that Canadian water is a good covered by NAFTA. As noted earlier, Canada already exports significant quantities of water, in bulk, to the United States. At a minimum, there is a substantial *risk* that NAFTA applies to Canadian water.

Errors, exaggerations, and deliberate omissions by all sides have plagued the debate about NAFTA's impact on Canadian water exports, making it difficult to separate fact from fiction. There are five main questions about NAFTA's ramifications for Canadian water and water policy.

Can Canada Ban Bulk Water Exports?

The first question is whether NAFTA affects Canada's ability to pass a law banning or limiting water exports. The federal government claims that it could not ban water exports because NAFTA does not allow export bans or restrictions.[52] On the other hand, the Council of Canadians urges the federal government to "enact legislation prohibiting large-scale water exports from

Canada." Both of these positions are flawed. NAFTA does prohibit Canada from banning or restricting water exports.[53] However, the federal government fails to mention the legitimate exceptions available to justify such restrictions. These exceptions specifically include laws that are necessary to protect health or the environment.[54]

The problem with the total ban on bulk water exports sought by the Council of Canadians is that such a ban would almost certainly be too broad to qualify for such an exception (a fact that even the Council's legal advisor concedes). International decisions have ruled that these exceptions must "only be used to the extent necessary and in proportion to the objective being served."[55] Thus the provincial laws prohibiting all water diversions and exports are also susceptible to NAFTA challenges, because they could be interpreted as out of proportion with the objective of environmental protection. The bottom line is that NAFTA constrains but does not eliminate Canada's ability to ban or restrict water exports. Any ban or limitation imposed by Canada or the provinces must have a legitimate health or environmental objective and must be "in proportion" to those objectives.

National Treatment for American and Mexican Corporations

The second controversial aspect of NAFTA involves national treatment, the requirement that American and Mexican corporations must be given the same rights as Canadian companies.[56] Narrowly interpreted, as per the federal government, national treatment is not problematic because if neither Canadian nor foreign corporations can export water in bulk, they are treated equally, there is no discrimination, and no NAFTA issue arises. A broader interpretation of national treatment, favoured by the Council of Canadians, is that American companies must be given the same access to water resources as Canadian companies. According to the Council's argument, an American corporation seeking water for agricultural, industrial, or municipal purposes would be entitled to take water regardless of whether its customers were in Canada or the United States. Both the narrow and broad interpretations have some merit. Neither can be conclusively described as right or wrong until a dispute about water exports arises and a NAFTA arbitration panel makes a ruling.

Can Canada Turn Off the Tap?

Another controversial element of NAFTA is the proportionality provision, Article 315, commonly described as "once the tap is turned on, it cannot be turned off." The proportionality provision in NAFTA means that once Canada starts exporting water, which we already have, we cannot reduce exports unless we also reduce domestic consumption by the same proportion. The assertion that "as long as there is a drop of water left we can never end water exports" is unnecessarily alarmist.[57] The reality of Canada's huge water supply, declining American demand for water, and the extremely low volume of Canadian water exports at this time makes proportionality a minimal threat in the foreseeable future.

In contrast, NAFTA's proportionality mechanism could be deeply problematic in the context of Canadian energy exports to the United States because the level of energy exports is already significant. Canada cannot reduce electricity exports to the United States without reducing domestic consumption, even if Canada's objective is to take better care of aquatic ecosystems harmed by the operation of dams. As well, Canadian supplies of oil and gas are limited (by definition, as nonrenewable resources) but are currently exported to the United States in large quantities.[58] Canada could not reduce oil and gas exports to reduce greenhouse gas emissions without reducing domestic consumption by an equivalent amount. Current levels of oil and gas exports have a much larger environmental impact than current or foreseeable levels of water exports.

Can Canada Enact Environmental Laws to Protect Water?

A fourth contentious aspect of NAFTA involves the extent to which the free trade agreement precludes Canada from passing environmental laws to protect water. The Council of Canadians claims that as soon as water is exported from Canada, NAFTA applies and "American corporations will have the actual legal right to come in and buy as much of our lake water as they want – *without restriction*."[59] The federal government argues that NAFTA does not affect the ability of Canadian governments to protect the environment. NAFTA is not as black and white as either the Council of Canadians or the federal government suggest. As noted previously, Canada already exports water to the United States and there is no indication that American companies are rushing to buy large volumes of Canadian water, let alone doing so without restriction.

The reality is that Canadian governments can still pass environmental laws, but subject to two limitations imposed by NAFTA.[60] First, laws must be carefully tailored to achieve environmental objectives while *minimizing* any restrictions on trade. A series of decisions by the World Trade Organization has attacked environmental laws for being overly broad and failing to use the "least trade-restrictive" approach.[61] Second, laws must be carefully drafted to avoid expropriating the investment of American corporations. Both "expropriation" and "investment" are so broadly defined under NAFTA that a huge range of government activities could potentially "expropriate" an "investment."[62] These two constraints influenced the federal government's attempt to address the issue of water exports by focusing on the *environmental* concerns associated with diverting water from one watershed to another, instead of taking a *trade* approach that focused on limiting exports. The latter focus would have been more vulnerable to American challenges.

NAFTA's Chapter 11: The Investor-State Dispute Settlement Mechanism

Perhaps the most important part of NAFTA from the perspective of threats to Canadian water, and environmental law generally, is Chapter 11, covering investment and investor-state dispute settlement. Chapter 11 offers investors extensive protection from government regulation and an unprecedented mechanism for resolving complaints about government actions. Whereas most of NAFTA deals with trade and is limited to "goods," Chapter 11 deals with investment and has a broader scope. Thus Chapter 11 applies to foreign water investments regardless of whether water is determined to be a good for the purposes of the trade provisions of NAFTA. The federal government acknowledges that Chapter 11 applies to investments in water.[63]

Article 1110 of NAFTA protects investors against expropriation or "any measure or measures having equivalent effect." This goes far further than any Canadian expropriation law, thereby placing a broader range of government actions at risk of being challenged. Barry Appleton maintains, "Preventing a contract from taking place can also be an expropriation in some circumstances."[64] Would denying an American corporation a water licence for bulk export purposes violate Article 1110? What rights would an American corporation with a valid water licence for a pulp mill in Canada have if the corporation decided that it wanted to export the water instead of using it for the mill? Again, these questions cannot yet be answered definitively because NAFTA's language is ambiguous, and, as yet, no trade panel has considered these issues.

NAFTA's investor-state dispute mechanism is unprecedented in that it allows foreign investors (predominantly corporations) to bypass the Canadian legal system and challenge our government through binding international arbitration. Historically, in international law, only governments were given access to dispute resolution mechanisms. NAFTA's Chapter 11 process is completely private, precluding public participation or media coverage, and is guided by international arbitration rules, not the principles and precedents of Canadian law. Contrary to popular belief, NAFTA arbitration tribunals do not have the power to strike down laws that violate NAFTA, but they can require governments to pay compensation to affected investors, which can be millions or even billions of dollars. The prospect of paying these huge sums may coerce governments into repealing laws or refusing to pass certain laws in the first place (see Chapter 9).

Summary of NAFTA's Implications for Canadian Water

In summary, it is impossible to state with certainty the extent of the risk that NAFTA poses to Canadian water because of ambiguities in the text of the agreement and the unpredictable nature of international arbitration panels (which, unlike Canadian courts, are not bound by precedents). The Canadian government is reluctant to admit that NAFTA has dictated Canadian water policy, yet the conclusion is inescapable. In 1990 legal experts agreed that "the federal government's ability to prohibit direct exports of water from Canada is not in doubt."[65] In 1993 NAFTA changed the rules. A law like the *Canada Water Preservation Act,* proposed in 1988 but not enacted, could violate Canada's NAFTA obligations. Despite the federal government's attempt to tiptoe around NAFTA with its three-pronged approach to prohibiting large-scale diversions, the free trade agreement still places Canadian fresh water at risk. The only ways to eliminate the threat posed by NAFTA are for Canada to withdraw from the agreement (a highly improbable scenario) or negotiate a specific exemption for water (as was done for raw logs and unprocessed fish). In the meantime, the outcome of Sun Belt's case may provide the first glimpse of the magnitude of the risks that NAFTA poses to Canadian water and to Canadian taxpayers.

Conclusion

In the late 1990s, the perceived threat of water exports fuelled the passage of new environmental laws to protect Canadian water and watersheds. Most Canadian governments adopted an ecological approach to water exports, focused on preventing large diversions, and embraced the concept that water is more than a mere commodity. For a nation that has diverted more water from one river basin to another than any country on Earth, this represents significant progress. However, NAFTA threatens to undermine the effectiveness of the new laws intended to protect Canadian water. Despite government claims to the contrary, NAFTA unquestionably restricts Canada's ability to manage our fresh water, although not to the dramatic extent suggested by some critics. Other trade agreements, such as the Free Trade Agreement of the Americas and the General Agreement on Trade in Services, may exacerbate the risks to Canadian water.[66]

Will Canadian water exports increase in the future? In 1998 Prime Minister Chrétien said, "I will not allow any large water exports to take place as long as I am prime minister."[67] In 2001 Chrétien reversed his position, equivocated, and then reversed himself again.[68] US president George W. Bush threw fuel on the fire by urging Canada to export water via pipeline to the American southwest.[69] The only safe prediction about the prospect of increasing bulk water exports from Canada is that the issue will continue to stir Canadian passions well into the future.

The final crucial point is that concerns about bulk water exports need to be put in perspective. At this time, these concerns are largely speculative, while hydroelectric projects, other water uses, and energy exports are *already* having a major impact on Canadian ecosystems. Given that major diversions like NAWAPA and GRAND are highly unlikely, the only foreseeable water exports from Canada are via tanker. The volumes of water that could physically and economically be removed by tanker from Canada cannot begin to rival the volumes of water already diverted to produce hydroelectricity.[70] Current bulk water export proposals would use up to 1 percent of the flow of affected rivers, while existing hydroelectric operations often divert more than 30 percent, and in some cases over 80 percent, of river flows. The existing environmental impacts caused by electricity and energy exports to the United States dwarf the potential impacts of foreseeable bulk water exports. Water experts J.C. Day and Frank Quinn conclude that "we have been deceived by our preoccupation with conventional water exports" when attention should have been focused on the damaging use of water by producers of hydroelectricity.[71]

3 Air

Air quality in Canada has improved dramatically.
Laura Jones, Fraser Institute, 2000

Smog worst in Ontario history
Globe and Mail *headline, 2002*

Water and clean air are consistently the top two environmental concerns of Canadians.[1] While there has been great public consternation about the deaths caused by tainted drinking water in Walkerton, many more Canadians suffer health problems, and in some cases die, because of air pollution. Estimates vary, with the David Suzuki Foundation asserting that air pollution causes sixteen thousand premature deaths annually, and the federal government using a figure of five thousand deaths. Provincial medical associations place the figure somewhere in the middle.[2] They agree, however, that air pollution costs Canada billions of dollars annually in health care.

The three main air pollution issues are the depletion of the ozone layer, climate change, and the regional impacts of air pollution. Ozone depletion and climate change are vitally important international atmospheric problems. As Environment Canada points out, "For the first time in the history of the planet, human beings have precipitated a major geophysical disturbance on a global scale."[3] The potential ramifications of ozone depletion and climate change are catastrophic from environmental, economic, health, cultural, and social perspectives. As an industrialized nation, Canada's contribution to these two problems has been disproportionately large relative to our small population. Canada's Arctic is also, for complex scientific reasons, particularly vulnerable to the effects of ozone depletion and climate change.

Yet Canada's reactions to these two global problems, despite their similarities, could not be more different. Both ozone depletion and climate change spurred negotiations leading to international legal agreements that required nations to take domestic actions. On the issue of ozone depletion Canada is recognized as a world leader, and our domestic actions have lived up to our international commitments. With respect to climate change, Canada is regarded as a rogue state, sabotaging international negotiations and violating our obligations under environmental treaties. Canadian laws and policies successfully addressed the threat posed by ozone-depleting chemicals but have barely begun to tackle the challenge of reducing the greenhouse gas emissions that cause global warming.

Regional air quality is the third major air pollution issue. Acid rain, smog, particulate matter, and other air pollutants cause widespread health and environmental damage. In some parts of Canada, air pollution from the United States is a major factor, meaning that Canada cannot solve its air quality woes unless the Americans reduce air pollution. For example, more than half of the acid rain that damages Canadian lakes, forests, and fisheries is American in origin.[4] Other parts of Canada are affected by the long-range transport of pollutants such as pesticides and PCBs. Activities thousands of kilometres away, involving substances banned in Canada, poison the arctic food chain, posing a dire threat to ecosystems and Aboriginal people. For example, levels of persistent organic pollutants are five to ten times higher in the breast milk of Inuit women than in women from southern Canada.[5]

Canadians cannot simply blame their air quality problems on others. Industrial and municipal sources in Canada discharge over 100 million kilograms of toxic substances into the air every year, including over 13 million kilograms of carcinogenic pollutants.[6] Transportation, agriculture, and residential emissions add millions more kilograms of air pollutants. Canadian emissions of greenhouse gases, sulphur dioxide, nitrogen oxides, volatile organic compounds, and carbon monoxide are among the highest in the OECD. In fact, Canada ranks among the worst five nations in the OECD regardless of whether total emissions, per capita emissions, or emissions per unit of GDP are being measured.[7] The province of Ontario is one of the highest air polluters among all jurisdictions in Canada and the United States.[8]

The news is not all bad. With regard to some forms of air pollution, substantial progress has been made since the 1970s. Sulphur dioxide emissions, a component of acid rain, are down roughly 50 percent in eastern Canada.[9] The use of ozone-depleting substances in Canada is down by 95 percent.[10] Levels of lead in the air are dramatically reduced.[11] Despite our progress, however, Canada continues to have one of the worst air pollution records of all the industrialized nations.[12] What laws and policies account for Canada's successes in reducing some types of air pollution? Why have laws and policies intended to similarly reduce greenhouse gas emissions, smog, and other pollutants been inadequate? The following sections answer these questions and explain Canada's mixed results in achieving clean air.

> The "boundless" blue sky which gives us breath and
> protects us is but an infinitesimally thin film. How
> dangerous it is to threaten even the smallest part of
> this gossamer covering, this conserver of life.
> *Vladimir Shatalov, Russian cosmonaut*

Ozone depletion is a global atmospheric environmental problem that rose to prominence in the late twentieth century. The world's swift response to this unprecedented challenge is a powerful yet largely unrecognized reason for environmental optimism. Scientists discovered the problem, the public became concerned, politicians negotiated an international treaty, and the treaty was repeatedly strengthened. Nations, both rich and poor, took concrete steps to address the problem. While the ozone layer has not yet recovered, the requisite legal tools are in place to ensure that the problem of ozone depletion will be solved. Canada's prominent role in advocating, negotiating, and implementing effective steps to protect the ozone layer merits careful examination as a successful model of environmental problem solving.

The Science of Ozone Depletion

The stratospheric ozone layer is like a protective shield, a natural sunscreen for the planet. The ozone layer blocks out most of the harmful form of ultraviolet radiation, known as UV-B, emanating from the sun. Life on Earth would be impossible without this shield. Although ozone occurs throughout the atmosphere, it is concentrated in the stratosphere, eighteen to thirty-five kilometres above the Earth's surface. The thickness of the ozone layer varies seasonally and geographically, but historically the amount of ozone was in a dynamic balance, as the ozone naturally produced in the stratosphere offset the amount destroyed by natural causes.[1]

Ozone depletion refers to the destruction of the ozone layer by human-made chemicals such as chlorofluorocarbons (CFCs), hydrochlorofluorocarbons (HCFCs), halons, carbon tetrachloride, methyl chloroform, and methyl bromide. These chemicals are used, or were used, in refrigeration and air conditioning equipment, aerosol sprays, fire extinguishers, foamed plastics, industrial processes, and pesticides. Chemical reactions involving the bromine and chlorine molecules in these substances destroy ozone by breaking it down. Because of their unique chemical properties, a single molecule of chlorine or bromine is capable of destroying hundreds of thousands of ozone molecules. Although there are natural sources of chlorine and bromine (e.g., volcanic eruptions), studies by the World Meteorological Organization (WMO) indicate that 82 percent of the chlorine entering the stratosphere in recent years is from human activities.[2] Chlorine levels in the atmosphere are now six times historic levels.[3]

Because of a number of meteorological factors, ozone depletion is greatest in the Antarctic and Arctic regions during spring, where thinning has reduced the ozone layer by up to 80 percent and 45 percent, respectively, in recent years. Overall, the ozone layer has thinned by approximately 5 percent over midlatitude regions and 11 percent in polar regions.[4] Ozone depletion results in higher levels of UV-B radiation reaching the Earth's surface. According to Environment Canada, "Measurements show that globally averaged ground-level UV-B radiation rose 10 percent from 1986 to 1996."[5] The current increases in UV-B radiation range between 4 percent in the Northern Hemisphere midlatitudes in the summer/fall; 6 percent in the Southern Hemisphere midlatitudes year-round; 7 percent in the Northern Hemisphere midlatitudes in the winter/spring; 22 percent in the Arctic in the spring; and 130 percent in the Antarctic in the spring.[6]

The Health and Environmental Effects of Ozone Depletion

Higher levels of UV-B radiation could cause extensive damage to both the environment and human health.[7] Potential health impacts include sunburn, skin cancer, eye cataracts, and reduced efficiency of the human immune system. A medical study found "alarming increases" in skin cancer between 1973 and 1987.[8] According to the World Health Organization (WHO), there are 2 million nonmelanoma skin cancers and 200,000 malignant melanomas globally each year. The WHO predicts that a 10 percent decrease in stratospheric ozone would cause an additional 300,000 nonmelanoma and 4,500 melanoma skin cancers annually. Eye cataracts make 12 to 15 million people blind annually, worldwide. The WHO estimates that each 1 percent decrease in stratospheric ozone will increase cataracts by 0.5 percent.[9] In other words, an additional 600,000 to 750,000 people will suffer from cataracts annually for every 1 percent decline in the ozone layer.

Ozone depletion also affects the environment. UV-B radiation damages aquatic ecosystems, particularly phytoplankton and zooplankton. These tiny plants and animals, living in the surface layers of lakes and oceans, are the foundation of many food chains. Other aquatic organisms that are particularly sensitive to UV-B radiation include sea urchins, corals, amphibians, macroalgae, and seagrasses. Studies show that increased exposure to UV-B radiation has adverse impacts on plant growth, photosynthesis, and disease resistance, resulting in reduced crop yields. The environmental effects of ozone depletion also interact with other stresses such as climate change and pollution to produce cumulative impacts on living organisms and ecosystems.[10]

Because of our northern location, Canada is one of the countries most at risk from ozone depletion. Between 1969 and 1992 there was a threefold increase in melanoma cancer rates in Canada, partially due to ozone depletion. In 1997, according to the federal auditor general, 61,000 Canadians developed skin cancer, of whom 3,200 will be afflicted with malignant melanoma, resulting in 660 deaths.[11] Canada's arctic ecosystems are particularly vulnerable. According to the WMO, "Polar marine ecosystems, where ozone related UV-B increases are the greatest, are expected to be the oceanic ecosystems most influenced by ozone depletion."[12]

The Evolution of International Concern about Ozone-Depleting Substances

CFCs, the main ozone-depleting substances, were synthesized decades ago and for many years were believed to be safe, stable, nontoxic, nonflammable, and inexpensive – almost "miracle chemicals" – with many uses including spray propellants, refrigerants, foam-blowing agents, solvents, and cleaning fluids.[13] Canadians in the 1970s were unwittingly dependent on CFCs at home, at work, and in their vehicles as CFCs were used to cool their cars and offices, package their food, and manufacture their computer and electronic equipment. However, in 1974 two scientists, Sherwood Rowland and Mario Molina, released a groundbreaking and controversial study suggesting that chlorine from decomposing CFCs could lead to the depletion of stratospheric ozone.[14] The study was met with widespread skepticism, particularly from the industries that manufactured or used CFCs. However, during the late 1970s and 1980s scientific evidence accumulated to support the assertion that these chemicals were in fact eroding the stratospheric ozone layer and endangering life on Earth.

As a result of this evidence, Canada was one of the first countries, along with Sweden, Norway, and the United States, to ban the use of CFCs as propellants in a range of consumer items (e.g., hair spray, antiperspirants, and deodorants) in the late 1970s.[15] This early action thrust Canada into the role of an international leader on ozone depletion and lent moral suasion to Canadian efforts to persuade other nations to follow our lead. Amidst growing public concern, international negotiations resulted in the 1985 *Vienna Convention on the Protection of the Ozone Layer*, a preliminary agreement to monitor scientific developments, cooperate in research, and meet again in two years. Canada was the first nation to ratify the *Vienna Convention*, but the agreement contained no provisions requiring the reduction or elimination of ozone-depleting substances.[16] Shortly thereafter, scientists discovered that the springtime ozone layer over Antarctica had decreased by up to 50 percent since the late 1970s. This thinning was dramatically but not accurately described as a "hole" in the ozone.[17]

Motivated by the new information about the Antarctic ozone "hole" and high levels of public concern, Canada hosted and was at the forefront of talks culminating in the *Montreal Protocol on Substances That Deplete the Ozone Layer* in 1987. At the time the *Montreal Protocol* was negotiated, scientists were still uncertain about the process of ozone depletion, the rate of the ozone layer's deterioration, and the extent of the health and environmental impacts. However, nations agreed to implement the precautionary principle, meaning that "where there are threats of serious or irreversible damage, lack of full scientific certainty should not be used as a reason for postponing measures to prevent environmental degradation."[18] As a result, the *Montreal Protocol* established a concrete schedule for industrialized countries to halve CFC consumption by 1999 and freeze halon consumption levels at 1986 levels by 1992.

Developing countries were given a ten-year grace period to meet these targets because historically most ozone-depleting substances were produced, consumed, and released by the industrialized countries. The grace period enabled developing nations to benefit from new technologies transferred from industrialized nations. The *Montreal Protocol* also established a multilateral fund to sponsor research into substitutes for CFCs and to subsidize developing countries in their efforts to phase out ozone-depleting substances.

Overcoming Obstacles to Protecting the Ozone Layer

The binding and ambitious targets in the *Montreal Protocol* were negotiated despite opposition from the chemical industry. Led by CFC manufacturers, the industry made three main arguments against taking concrete steps to protect the ozone layer. The first argument attacked the science behind ozone depletion, claiming there was "no concrete evidence" that synthetic chemicals were causing ozone depletion.[19] The second argument was based on economics. A 1990 study estimated that CFC production and use in the United States alone involved five thousand companies employing 700,000 people and producing goods and services worth US$28 billion.[20] The industry-sponsored Alliance for Responsible CFC Policy "maintained that CFCs were unique and irreplaceable, and that their elimination would result in devastating impacts on the quality of modern lifestyles as well as on national economies."[21] Similarly, a book published by Canada's Fraser Institute suggested that cutting back on the use of CFCs would probably require "large sacrifices on the part of everyone."[22]

The third industry argument was that banning CFCs would annually cause twenty to forty million deaths because of the "collapse of refrigeration" and five million additional children's deaths because refrigerated vaccines would not be available for immunization.[23] A book published by the Fraser Institute suggested, "More people would die from food poisoning as a consequence of inadequate refrigeration than would die from depleting ozone."[24]

Then in 1988 the WMO's Ozone Trends Panel produced the so-called smoking gun, scientific evidence confirming beyond a reasonable doubt that CFCs and other human-made substances were responsible for ozone depletion. Within a week of the WMO report, DuPont, one of the world's largest manufacturers of CFCs, announced it would phase out the chemicals completely.[25]

As the scientific evidence of ozone depletion grew more compelling, the international community recognized the need to act even more swiftly. In 1990 a follow-up meeting in London resulted in amendments to the *Montreal Protocol* to accelerate the elimination of CFCs and halons and add methyl chloroform and carbon tetrachloride to the list of substances to be abolished. Subsequent meetings in Copenhagen (1992), Vienna (1995), and Beijing (1999) further compressed the elimination schedule while adding more chemicals (HCFCs, hydrobromofluorocarbons [HBFCs], and methyl bromide) to the list of substances targeted for elimination. In 1995 Rowland and Molina were awarded the Nobel Prize for their groundbreaking research establishing the connection between manmade chemicals and depletion of stratospheric ozone. The *Montreal Protocol* has been ratified by more than 175 nations. Ratification means that a nation is legally bound by an international agreement, whereas simply signing an agreement, without ratification, may be only a symbolic gesture and is not legally binding.

Canada: International Leadership, National Action

As mentioned earlier, Canada was one of the first nations to ban the use of CFCs as a propellant in consumer products and one of the first nations to ratify the *Vienna Convention*. Canada then set and strengthened domestic targets for eliminating the production or use of ozone-depleting substances based on the *Montreal Protocol* and the subsequent London, Copenhagen, Vienna, and Beijing adjustments, as follows:

- elimination of halons by 1994
- elimination of carbon tetrachloride by 1995
- elimination of CFCs by 1996
- elimination of methyl chloroform by 1996
- elimination of HBFCs by 1996
- elimination of methyl bromide by 2005
- elimination of HCFCs by 2020.

In many cases Canada's domestic targets were even more ambitious than required by our international commitments. Working cooperatively, the federal and provincial governments passed strong, effective laws and regulations. The first federal regulations were passed in 1989 under the auspices of the *Canadian Environmental Protection Act*. These binding rules placed strict, mandatory limits on the manufacture, use, sale, import, and export of ozone-depleting substances. These regulations also imposed strict record-keeping and reporting requirements on users of ozone-depleting substances. The federal regulations were amended in 1990, 1991, 1994, 1995, 1998, and 2000 to address more ozone-depleting substances, accelerate the schedule for elimination of certain substances, close loopholes, and streamline reporting requirements. As a result, Canada's current *Ozone Depleting Substances Regulations* fulfill our obligations for all substances covered by the *Montreal Protocol* and the subsequent adjustments.[26]

The federal regulations are comprehensive and well drafted, with loopholes only for essential uses, such as allowing CFCs to be used in inhalers for asthma. To qualify as an essential purpose, the use of a controlled substance must be "necessary for health and safety" or "critical for the good functioning of society." As well, there must be "no technically or economically feasible alternatives or substitutes."[27] Efforts are continuing in an attempt to find viable substitutes for the remaining essential uses.

Two ozone-depleting substances are not yet eliminated in Canada: methyl bromide and HCFCs. Methyl bromide, used in agriculture, is to be eliminated by 2005 while HCFCs, a CFC substitute, can no longer be used after 2020. To accelerate the phasing out of these substances, Canada implemented an experimental permit trading program, which allocated consumption quotas to users of methyl bromide and HCFCs based on historic levels of use. Users with access to more affordable alternatives can sell their quotas to other users.[28] The environmental end result is the same, as the chemicals are gradually phased out, but from an economic perspective, the trading system provides partial financing of alternatives (to users who sell their quota) and results in the use of least-cost alternatives and substitutes.[29] In effect, the program allows government to set reduction targets and then use free market principles to minimize the costs of achieving those targets. A similar program for sulphur dioxide emissions was a highly successful component of the American effort to reduce acid rain.[30]

The provinces passed laws complementing the federal regulations by dealing with other sources of ozone-depleting substances, such as the large quantities of CFCs that remain in use in air conditioners, refrigeration units, and fire-fighting equipment. All provinces and territories, with the exception of the Northwest Territories and Nunavut, have enacted extensive, legally binding rules to prevent the release of CFCs into the environment as well as regulating the recovery, recycling, and disposal of ozone-depleting substances. For example,

Ontario amended its *Environmental Protection Act* to deal specifically with ozone-depleting substances and passed the *Ozone Depleting Substances General Regulation* to complement the federal regulations.[31] The Northwest Territories created a set of guidelines (weaker than regulations because they are not legally binding) while the new government in Nunavut has not yet addressed ozone depletion.[32]

Like the federal regulations, most of the provincial regulations are also strong. The most recent version of British Columbia's ozone regulations uses the mandatory phrase "must not" twenty-three times and the positive obligation "must" another sixteen times in controlling the release, recovery, and recycling of ozone-depleting substances.[33] This mandatory language is much more effective than the discretionary language, using the word "may," that characterizes much environmental law in Canada. To understand the fundamental importance of this seemingly minor difference in language, imagine the impact on government revenues if income tax laws used the phrase "may pay" instead of "must pay."

Another important factor contributing to the effectiveness of the federal and provincial laws is that both are backed by stiff penalties. For example, under BC's *Ozone Depleting Substances and Other Halocarbons Regulation*, fines range up to $200,000 per offence. Under the *Canadian Environmental Protection Act, 1999*, fines can be as high as $1 million and jail sentences can be up to five years.[34] Although their role has been relatively minor, municipal governments also deserve credit for passing bylaws regulating the use, recovery, and disposal of items containing ozone-depleting substances.[35]

Reductions in the Use of Ozone-Depleting Substances

The combination of federal and provincial regulations is working effectively to reduce Canada's impact on the ozone layer. In 1993 DuPont closed the world's largest CFC manufacturing facility, located in Canada.[36] By 1995 Canada had successfully eliminated the production of CFCs, halons, carbon tetrachloride, and methyl chloroform. Overall, Canadian production of ozone-depleting substances fell more than 95 percent between 1987 and 1996.[37] The federal auditor general reported in 1997 that "Canadian achievements compare favourably with those of other countries, in both influencing and implementing the international agenda."[38] The commissioner of the environment and sustainable development commended Environment Canada for showing "strong commitment and leadership, internationally and domestically, in developing policies and programs aimed at eliminating or reducing ozone-depleting substances."[39]

Globally, CFC production has dropped 88 percent from its peak in 1988, and atmospheric concentrations of some ozone-depleting substances have peaked and begun to decline.[40] Canada deserves additional credit for this international progress for two reasons. First, Canada played a key role in the development and evolution of the *Montreal Protocol*.[41] The chief negotiator of the various agreements on ozone-depleting substances for the United States, Richard Benedick, noted that Canada consistently pushed for "strong measures to protect the ozone layer" and exerted "disproportionate leverage on the course of events."[42] Second, Canada has contributed over US$30 million to the Multilateral Fund, to which industrialized nations, collectively, have now contributed over US$1.2 billion.[43] This fund plays a critical role in enabling developing countries to meet their obligations under the *Montreal Protocol*.

The United States also succeeded in meeting its international obligation to eliminate the production and consumption of ozone-depleting substances. The Americans used a combination of regulations, taxes, and an innovative market-based trading regime.[44] The *Ozone Protection and CFC Reduction Act* passed by Congress in 1989 imposed strict limits on the manufacture, use, and import of CFCs.[45] This law also established the Ozone Depleting Chemicals Tax, which targeted producers and importers of CFCs. This new tax raised over US$3 billion, some of which was used to develop CFC alternatives and promote new non-ozone-depleting technology.[46]

The Economic Benefits of Reducing Ozone Depletion

Did Canada, the United States, or the world pay a steep economic price for this environmental progress, as the chemical industry had warned? No. To the contrary, numerous studies show that reducing the use of ozone-depleting substances actually paid substantial economic dividends. Analyses by Environment Canada and the US EPA show that benefits outweighed costs by a ten-to-one ratio.[47] A comprehensive review of the American efforts to reduce ozone-depleting substances concluded, "Contrary to early predictions, meeting this *Protocol* goal did not severely disrupt the US economy, trigger massive job losses, or deny popular products or services to consumers. With considerable ingenuity, and aggressive investment in innovation, many US industries eliminated CFC use more quickly, at lower cost, or with greater environmental benefits than observers once predicted."[48]

In 1997 Environment Canada published a report concluding that the full implementation of the *Montreal Protocol* would provide the world with C$224 billion in net economic benefits (mainly from reduced damage to fisheries, agriculture, and materials). This figure does not include estimates of the economic benefits related to human health, which would push the total net benefits much higher. Full implementation of the *Protocol* will prevent an estimated 20 million cases of skin cancer, 129 million cases of cataracts, and 333,000 deaths.[49] To grasp the magnitude of the economic aspect of these health benefits, consider that in the United States alone, the government spends US$3.4 billion on 1.2 million cataract operations annually.[50]

The opponents of strong regulatory action to protect the ozone layer argued that substitutes for CFCs would likely be less safe and significantly more expensive.[51] These predictions proved to be false. Studies show that the switch from CFC-based propellants to substitutes reduced industry costs by as much as 80 percent, saving US businesses and consumers over US$1 billion. Cost savings have also been reported by former users of CFC-based solvents who switched to more environmentally benign alternatives.[52] Many corporations, such as AT&T and Nortel Networks, benefited from the elimination of ozone-depleting substances because regulatory changes forced them to critically reexamine their manufacturing processes. Nortel, the Canadian high-tech company, saved $50 million by eliminating the use of ozone-depleting substances in electronics manufacturing. Nortel vice-president Margaret Kerr noted that the changes "allowed us to reduce manufacturing defects, improve reliability, improve product performance, and reduce costs."[53]

Unfinished Business in Protecting the Ozone Layer

There continue to be several areas where Canada could improve its efforts to protect the ozone layer, including better enforcement of the regulations under the *Canadian Environmental Protection Act, 1999,* more consistent provincial regulations, the development of genuinely environmentally friendly substitutes for CFCs, and more expeditious programs to destroy ozone-depleting substances that are still in use.[54] A federal-provincial strategy is in place to address these issues, but the pace of implementation could be improved.[55]

Enforcement is a problem because there is a black market for CFCs now that they have been banned. New CFCs are smuggled or fraudulently described as recycled. Environment Canada admits that a lack of financial and human resources has caused it to adopt a "minimalist" approach to enforcement of environmental laws generally, including the ozone-depleting substances regulations.[56] Between 1989 and 1999 there were twenty-nine successful prosecutions for violations of Canada's various ozone-depleting substances regulations under the *Canadian Environmental Protection Act, 1999,* resulting in $393,600 in fines and one fifteen-month jail sentence.[57] In contrast, in the United States, there have been hundreds of charges and millions of dollars in fines related to illegal activities involving ozone-depleting chemicals.[58] The EPA formed a joint task force with the Internal Revenue Service, Department of Justice, and Customs Service to uncover illegal CFC imports. In one single case, the efforts of this task force resulted in a US$1 million fine, dwarfing a decade of Canadian enforcement efforts.[59]

A federal-provincial working group on ozone depletion recently undertook a comprehensive analysis of the various provincial and federal regulations. While concluding that the federal regulations are strong and consistent, the study found a high degree of variability among the provincial regulations.[60] The auditor general, the commissioner of the environment and sustainable development, and Friends of the Earth have all expressed concerns that the provincial regulations may be uneven and in some provinces, inadequate.[61] The inconsistency among provincial regulations could undermine Canada's efforts to be an international leader in protecting the ozone layer, and needs to be rectified.

Many ozone-depleting substances, such as CFCs and halons, are also powerful greenhouse gases, contributing to climate change. Thus eliminating ozone-depleting substances should have a minor positive effect on greenhouse gas emissions. This seemingly good news is tempered by the fact that some of the substitutes for ozone-depleting substances, such as hydrofluorocarbons (HFCs), are also powerful greenhouse gases. Greenpeace emphasizes, with good reason, that ozone-depleting substances should not be replaced with greenhouse gases. Greenpeace has developed a refrigeration technology called Greenfreeze using isobutane, which is neither an ozone-depleting chemical nor a greenhouse gas.[62] It should be a priority to find environmentally benign substitutes for ozone-depleting chemicals so as to avoid solving one global problem at the cost of exacerbating another.

Canadian consumption of HCFCs, a less harmful substitute for CFCs, increased 76 percent between 1986 and 1995. It should be noted that although HCFCs have only 2 to 5 percent of the ozone-depleting potential of CFCs, they still have a long-term impact on the ozone layer. Under the amended *Montreal Protocol*, HCFCs are to be phased out by 2020. In many European nations, consumption of CFCs has virtually reached zero. Europe has been more aggressive than Canada in eliminating them from current uses where they are stored and targeting them for destruction.[63]

Lessons Learned in Addressing Ozone Depletion

Given the success of Canada's efforts both at home and abroad to protect the ozone layer, it is useful to identify the reasons behind this progress. First, despite the scientific uncertainty about ozone depletion that existed in the early to mid-1980s, the risks made it important to implement the precautionary principle and take concrete remedial steps without waiting for scientific certainty. At the same time, extensive investments in scientific research produced regular improvements in our knowledge about ozone depletion, resulting in a positive feedback loop between scientists, the public, and lawmakers. Stronger science provided information that fuelled greater public concern, motivating politicians to address the issue and allocate further funds for scientific research.

The clear, firm schedules for reducing CFC production and use were integral to the international success in addressing ozone depletion. The well-publicized and ambitious targets motivated extensive investment in research and development for environmentally friendly alternatives to CFCs. The deadlines also made it obvious that nations would be held accountable. A failure to fulfill commitments could result in international embarrassment, a particularly humiliating prospect for nations like Canada with reputations for leadership in fighting ozone depletion.

Flexibility and transparency were strengths of both the *Montreal Protocol* and the Canadian laws that implemented it. The *Montreal Protocol* set clear targets without specifying how those targets would be achieved, giving governments and industry the freedom to find the most effective and efficient reduction strategies to meet the legal requirements. The Canadian government met repeatedly with concerned citizens and industry and held hearings about ozone depletion.[64] This openness, flexibility, and transparency encouraged a high degree of cooperation among government, scientists, the public, and industry.

The principle of shared but differentiated responsibility, which recognizes that countries at various stages of economic development face different challenges, also contributed to the success of the *Montreal Protocol*. The industrialized countries, which were the major producers and consumers of ozone-depleting substances, took responsibility for acting first. Developing countries were given extra time to phase out ozone-depleting substances as well as technical and financial assistance through the Multilateral Fund financed by the industrialized nations. As a result, developing countries are on track to fulfill their commitments.

The Canadian and American experiences in addressing ozone depletion indicate that:

- Regulations are an effective means of achieving environmental policy objectives.
- Economic costs and technological obstacles tend to be exaggerated by industry.
- Constant pressure from the public and environmental groups motivates governments and businesses to act.
- The benefits of solving environmental problems can exceed the costs, even using conventional economic analysis.
- Taxes are potentially powerful tools for environmental protection.
- Economic instruments, like permit trading programs, may achieve environmental goals with greater flexibility and at lower cost than regulations.
- Federal, provincial, and corporate leadership are important.
- Smart policies will drive technology innovation, increase net societal benefits, and bring compliance costs down.

Conclusion

The world's leading scientific experts agree that the international community's rapid response to ozone depletion prevented a horrible crisis. The doomsday scenario prophesied in 1990 by David Suzuki – that without a swift human response, by the year 2040 people in Australia would rarely venture outside their homes because of a skin cancer epidemic – was not far off the mark.[65] According to the WMO, the success of the *Montreal Protocol* can be measured by looking at "the world that was avoided ... Ozone depletion [in 2050] would be at least 50 percent at mid-latitudes in the Northern Hemisphere and 70 percent at mid-latitudes in the Southern Hemisphere, about ten times larger than today."[66] The consequences of ozone depletion on the order of 50 percent to 70 percent would have been devastating, including "a runaway increase" in skin cancer rates.[67] However, the latest global assessment of ozone depletion reveals that atmospheric concentrations of ozone-depleting substances peaked in the late 1990s.[68] Assuming that countries continue to comply with the *Montreal Protocol* and its various amendments, scientists anticipate that the ozone layer will repair itself by the mid to late twenty-first century.[69]

The *Montreal Protocol* is regarded as "the most successful attempt at protection of a global commons."[70] American diplomat Richard Benedick calls the *Montreal Protocol* a "forerunner of an evolving global diplomacy, through which nations accept common responsibility for stewardship of the planet."[71] Although the problem is not yet solved, in that less damaging, interim substitutes like HCFCs are still harmful to the ozone layer, the speed with which Canada and the world moved to address ozone depletion is genuinely impressive. The protection of the ozone layer is an inspiring success story, a beacon of hope and optimism showing that we can overcome seemingly insurmountable environmental challenges. Strong laws and regulations and innovative economic instruments were an integral part of achieving this success.

Unfortunately, there is a caveat to this optimism: there are growing scientific concerns that climate change may impair the ozone layer's ability to rebuild.[72] Recent research reveals that while greenhouse gas emissions have an overall warming effect on the lower layers of the atmosphere, they have a cooling effect higher up in the stratosphere, where colder temperatures exacerbate ozone destruction.[73] The implication of the emerging linkage between these two issues is that protection of the Earth's life-sustaining ozone layer depends not only on eliminating the use of ozone-depleting substances, but on addressing climate change as well.

> The Government of Canada addressed fiscal deficits,
> to avoid leaving a burden for future generations.
> Likewise, it would be irresponsible to leave an
> environmental deficit of climate disruptions and
> pollution for future Canadians.
> *Prime Minister Jean Chrétien, 2001*

Both ozone depletion and climate change pose serious threats to humanity and, more broadly, to the future of life on Earth. While there has been rapid progress, both domestically and internationally, in tackling the threat of ozone depletion, Canada continues to stumble badly in our efforts to confront climate change. Why? What explains our paralysis on global warming? Can the legal, economic, and policy lessons learned from successfully addressing ozone depletion be adapted in order to effectively reduce greenhouse gas emissions?

The Science of Climate Change

Climate change is caused by the increasing concentration of greenhouse gases in the atmosphere. Like a greenhouse, these gases trap the sun's heat (which ordinarily would be reflected back into space), resulting in warmer temperatures. Warmer temperatures also increase the rate of evaporation, resulting in more water vapour, which traps even more heat. Without the greenhouse effect, the Earth would be about 33 degrees Celsius colder, making it uninhabitable for most forms of life. However, as human activities send more greenhouse gases into the atmosphere, more heat is being trapped and the planet is growing progressively warmer.[1]

The overwhelming majority of the world's climate scientists agree that greenhouse gas emissions generated by human activities are altering the Earth's climate.[2] Only a handful of largely discredited scientists continue to deny the existence of ozone depletion and climate change.[3] As Andrew Weaver, the

Canada Research Chair in Atmospheric Science in the School of Earth and Ocean Sciences at the University of Victoria, states, "Those of us who work in the area of climate science are continually befuddled as to what the so-called debate on global warming is all about. There is really no scientific debate on the issue, only an artificial debate perpetuated by the media and certain corporate interests."[4] Scientists report that the level of carbon dioxide in the atmosphere remained relatively steady for the last ten thousand years at an average of about 260 parts per million (ppm) until recently. Since the beginning of the industrial age about two hundred years ago, the level of carbon dioxide in the atmosphere has risen to about 368 ppm today – a 42 percent increase. In concert with this increase in atmospheric carbon dioxide and other greenhouse gases, the global mean temperature has risen 0.6 degrees Celsius in the last hundred years, the most rapid increase in a thousand years.[5] The 1980s and 1990s were the warmest decades of the millennium.[6]

Climate scientists warn that a tripling of the preindustrial level of carbon dioxide is possible.[7] They expect that by the year 2100, the global climate will be between 1.4 and 5.8 degrees Celsius warmer. This will be the most rapid warming in ten thousand years, and represents a change that is roughly equal to the temperature difference between today's world and the last ice age, when much of Canada was beneath a thick sheet of ice.[8]

The Health and Environmental Impacts of Climate Change

Scientists report that "there is now ample evidence of the ecological impacts of recent climate change, from polar terrestrial to tropical marine environments."[9] Sea levels rose an average of 0.1 to 0.2 metres during the twentieth century and are projected to rise a full metre in the twenty-first century, jeopardizing the existence of low-lying island nations like Tuvalu. Snow and ice cover has decreased, with most glaciers retreating. Permafrost is thawing. Rivers and lakes are freezing later and melting earlier. Arctic sea ice has declined significantly in both extent and thickness. Precipitation patterns have changed. Extreme weather events, such as droughts, floods, heat waves, cyclones, and intense precipitation storms have increased in frequency and severity.[10] Scientists are already observing "lengthening of mid- to high-latitude growing seasons, poleward and altitudinal shifts of animal ranges, declines in some plant and animal populations, and earlier flowering of trees, emergence of insects, and egg-laying in birds."[11]

Anticipated future consequences of climate change vary widely from region to region, depend on many different variables, but are expected to be predominantly negative. Potential problems include reduced crop yields (particularly in tropical and subtropical regions where hunger is already a problem), more forest fires, more insect infestations, decreased water availability (particularly in areas already experiencing water shortages), increased incidence of diseases such as malaria, dengue, schistosomiasis, and cholera, more heat stress mortality, more extreme weather events, and increased energy required for cooling. Experts also expect significant damage to biological diversity caused mainly by habitat changes.[12] Human communities face increased risks of flooding, landslides, and other so-called natural disasters, with devastating environmental, economic, and social consequences.

Medical experts believe that climate change will cause "wide-ranging, mostly adverse consequences for human health."[13] Global warming worsens local air pollution problems, contributing to higher levels of smog and resulting in deaths, illnesses, and major economic losses.[14] Some diseases are expected to spread to areas where they do not currently occur.[15] A study in the British medical journal *The Lancet* estimates that 700,000 premature deaths will occur annually in the world by 2020 if climate change policies are not implemented.[16]

Potential benefits of climate change include increased crop yields in some midlatitude regions, increased timber supply in some forest regions, increased water availability in some places, fewer deaths in some regions due to milder winters, and less energy required for heating.[17]

The long-term effects of climate change are less certain. Scientists believe that temperature increases and rising sea levels will continue for centuries after atmospheric concentrations of carbon dioxide are stabilized. If greenhouse gas emissions continue to rise, more dramatic consequences are anticipated, such as the complete melting of the Greenland ice sheet – which could raise sea levels by up to seven metres – or the slowing of the ocean circulation system that transports warm water to the North Atlantic and gives Europe a hospitable climate. At the present time, the likelihood of such large-scale changes is thought to be low, although some scientists are concerned by the prospect of unpredictably rapid, nonlinear climate shifts.[18]

The Impacts of Climate Change on Canada

Because of our northern latitude, Canada will experience disproportionate consequences from climate change, with particularly profound implications for northern ecosystems and northern peoples. The Intergovernmental Panel on Climate Change warns that "climate change in polar regions is expected to be among the largest and most rapid of any region on the Earth, and will cause major physical, ecological, sociological and economic impacts, especially in the Arctic." It expects temperatures in the Arctic to rise by up to eight degrees Celsius by 2100.[19] Even Canada's arctic sovereignty is in jeopardy, as neither the United States nor Europe accepts Canadian jurisdiction over the Northwest Passage, a largely moot point until the ice melts and shipping becomes viable.[20]

Problems are already beginning to manifest themselves in the Canadian north. Malnourished polar bears provide a compelling and tragic early warning about climate change: changes in ice patterns have reduced some polar bears' ability to hunt for the seals that are a mainstay of their diet.[21] For Aboriginal people living in the far north, traditional indigenous lifestyles are being upset by changes in the distribution and abundance of wildlife species as well as by severe transportation difficulties caused by warmer weather. Melting permafrost will also cause "severe damage to buildings and transport infrastructure."[22] A Republican senator from Alaska, Ted Stevens, admits, "We face the problem of moving native villages that have been located along the Arctic and West Coast of Alaska for centuries. This is a creeping disaster."[23] Canadian communities in the Arctic may also face relocation.

Canadians working in climate-sensitive sectors such as fisheries, forestry, energy, and agriculture face mounting uncertainties. For example, wild salmon, which are sensitive to warmer temperatures, are in dire jeopardy on Canada's east and west coasts.[24] Reduced water availability on the prairies means that agricultural harvests could decline.[25] Unique ecosystems, including prairie wetlands, alpine tundra, and cold water ecosystems will be at risk, pushing some species toward extinction.[26]

The Canadian Public Health Association describes climate change as a major public health threat. For Canadians, one of the main effects of climate change will be more hot weather, resulting in more smog, more heat stress, and more premature deaths from air pollution.[27] Combined, these factors already cause between five thousand and sixteen thousand premature deaths in Canada annually.

On the other hand, some Canadians could potentially benefit from climate change. Environment Canada suggests that in some regions there could be "increased crop yields" and "certain forests could become more productive."[28] Health studies indicate that "in areas with relatively colder climates, an increase in ambient temperature could result in a decrease of cardiovascular mortality."[29] Overall, however, these speculative regional benefits pale in comparison to the negative consequences and uncertainties associated with climate change.

The Causes of Climate Change

The three main greenhouse gases produced by human activity are carbon dioxide, methane, and nitrous oxide. These gases also enter and leave the atmosphere through natural processes, resulting in climate stability when these sources and sinks are balanced. However, since the beginning of the Industrial Revolution, human activities have altered the natural balance by emitting vast quantities of greenhouse gases into the atmosphere. Since 1750, global atmospheric concentrations of carbon dioxide are up 31 percent, methane up 151 percent, and nitrous oxide up 17 percent. There is more carbon dioxide in the Earth's atmosphere today than there has been for twenty million years.[30]

In Canada 76 percent of our contribution to global warming comes from carbon dioxide emissions, produced primarily through the combustion of fossil fuels. Twelve percent is caused by methane, produced mainly by farms and landfill sites. Nitrous oxide, produced by the burning of fossil fuels and the use of fertilizers, accounts for 11 percent. Modern industrial chemicals such as CFCs, HFCs, per-fluorocarbons, and sulphur hexafluoride account for the other 1 percent. Greenhouse gas emissions in Canada break down by sector as follows:[31]

Transportation	25 percent
Fossil fuel production and distribution	19 percent
Electric power generation	17 percent
Agriculture	9 percent
Industrial energy use	8 percent
Miscellaneous industrial processes (cement, aluminum, iron, and steel)	7 percent
Residential buildings	6 percent
Commercial buildings	4 percent
Landfills	3 percent
Other	2 percent

Understanding the sources of Canada's greenhouse gas emissions is an essential first step in determining where attention and resources need to be focused in order to reduce these emissions. The fastest growth in Canadian emissions is from the energy and transportation sectors.[32]

The Evolution of International Concern about Climate Change

Although the suggestion that carbon emissions from human activities could influence the global climate dates back to 1827, global warming first reached public consciousness in the late 1980s, as scientists expressed growing concern about unusually warm temperatures and extreme weather events.[33] In 1988, Canada hosted the Global Conference on the Changing Atmosphere, which concluded with scientists calling for a 20 percent reduction of carbon emissions by 2005 and a long-term reduction of at least 50 percent in order to stabilize the climate. In response, the United Nations appointed the Intergovernmental Panel on Climate Change (IPCC) to assess the impacts of global warming. Over 2,500 leading scientists began working to investigate the science and assess the impacts of climate change. The IPCC's first report projected that a doubling of carbon dioxide concentrations in the atmosphere would result in temperatures increasing by up to 4.5 degrees Celsius by 2050.[34]

As early as 1990 Canada was undermining international efforts to limit greenhouse gas emissions. Publicly, the federal government promised to seek "a comprehensive international agreement on targets and schedules for the reduction of carbon dioxide and other greenhouse gas emissions."[35] Privately, a confidential briefing document prepared for Canadian delegates to a May 1990 meeting in Bergen, Norway, revealed that "Canada will not support expected proposals from the Nordic countries for targets and timetables on emission reductions."[36] Canada's early opposition was a sign of things to come.

Negotiations led to the *United Nations Framework Convention on Climate Change* in 1992, signed and ratified by 186 nations including Canada and the United States. The *Framework Convention* called for "stabilization of greenhouse gas concentrations in the atmosphere at a level that would prevent dangerous anthropogenic interference with the climate system," but did not establish any legally binding targets or timelines for reducing greenhouse gas emissions.[37]

The second report from the IPCC, published in 1995, concluded, "The balance of evidence suggests that there is a discernible human influence on global climate."[38] In response to growing public concern and stronger scientific evidence, the *Kyoto Protocol* was negotiated in December 1997. Under the terms of *Kyoto*, industrialized countries set specific targets and a timeline for reducing greenhouse gas emissions. However, *Kyoto* left questions unanswered by incorporating three "flexibility mechanisms" without specifying how they would be implemented: emissions trading among developed nations; joint implementation, meaning the financing of reductions in other developed countries; and the clean development mechanism, meaning financing reductions in developing countries. The flexibility mechanisms are intended to lead to more cost-effective emissions reductions by allowing industrialized nations to get credit for actions to reduce greenhouse gas emissions in other countries. Other unresolved issues involved the granting of credit for sinks (agricultural and forestry activities that result in the absorption of carbon dioxide), and the timing of commitments for emissions reductions in developing countries.

Further negotiations intended to finalize details on the implementation of the *Kyoto Protocol* took place in Buenos Aires (1998), Bonn (1999), and The Hague (2000). A group of industrial nations led by Canada, the United States, Australia, and Japan sought to exploit potential loopholes in *Kyoto* by maximizing emission reduction credits for selling nuclear reactors to developing countries, replacing old-growth forests with tree farms, and buying so-called hot air, meaning "unused" emissions from countries where economic collapse has reduced greenhouse gas emissions, like Russia.[39] The European Union and a number of small island nations attempted to restrict credit to actions that actually reduced greenhouse gas emissions. Canada was internationally humiliated at The Hague as environmental groups gave Canada five "fossil-of-the-day" awards for antienvironmental negotiating positions, concluding that Canada was the most obstructive of the 180 nations participating.[40]

In 2001 the IPCC released its third report on the science and impacts of climate change, stating that "there is new and stronger evidence that most of the warming observed over the last fifty years is attributable to human activities," and "anthropogenic climate change will persist for many centuries" even if greenhouse gas emissions are stabilized.[41] Although Canada continued to undermine the negotiations, detailed rules regarding implementation of *Kyoto* were finalized in 2001 in Morocco.[42] To reach agreement, Canada relinquished its insistence that credit be given for nuclear reactor sales to developing countries, but succeeded in getting generous credits for agricultural and forest sinks. As observers noted, "The final outcome suggests a remarkable level of intransigence amongst certain parties, most notably the Russian Federation, Japan and Canada, all of whom secured favourable deals as a precondition for their ratification."[43] The implementation of *Kyoto* suffered a serious blow when US president George W. Bush announced the United States would not support it. However, as of early 2003, more than one hundred nations had ratified *Kyoto*, including Canada. Although there are contrasting views on the efficacy of *Kyoto*, it is widely regarded as a first step toward the larger reductions needed to stabilize Earth's climate.[44]

Canada's Response to Climate Change

How has Canada responded to the challenge posed by climate change? What new laws and policies have been implemented, either federally or provincially, to reduce greenhouse gas emissions? What incentives and disincentives (i.e., carrots and sticks) or other economic policies have been created to reduce emissions of carbon dioxide, methane, and nitrous oxide, the three main greenhouse gases?

Canadian governments have repeatedly promised progress in addressing climate change. In 1990 Canada pledged to stabilize emissions of carbon dioxide and greenhouse gases at 1990 levels by the year 2000.[45] Canada repeated this promise in 1992 at the Rio Earth Summit when signing the *United Nations Framework Convention on Climate Change*. The Liberals confirmed this commitment in their Red Books in 1993 and 1997.[46] Then in December 1997, in Kyoto, Canada agreed to reduce greenhouse gas emissions to 6 percent *below* 1990 levels by 2008-12. After a heated national debate, Canada ratified the *Kyoto Protocol* in 2002. Ostensibly in order to meet our climate change commitments, Canada has produced a plethora of plans, strategies, and consultations since 1990, including:

- in 1990, a National Action Strategy on Global Warming
- from 1992 to 1994, a series of national consultations on climate change resulting in eighty-eight recommended actions
- in 1995, Canada's National Action Program on Climate Change
- in 1998, another series of national consultations as part of the National Climate Change Process, engaging 450 experts in fifteen round-table discussions
- in 2000, the First National Climate Change Business Plan, the National Implementation Strategy on Climate Change, the Federal-Provincial-Territorial Framework Agreement on Climate Change, and the Government of Canada Action Plan 2000 on Climate Change

- in 2002, a discussion paper outlining Canada's potential responses to growing greenhouse gas emissions, and the federal Climate Change Plan for Canada.[47]

Despite the abundance of action strategies, action programs, and action plans, Canada has taken few concrete actions to directly reduce greenhouse gas emissions. These plans and strategies sound good on a superficial level but lack teeth. The federal government candidly admits that "the bulk of the initiatives identified are voluntary in nature."[48] In 1994, the first multiyear, multi-stakeholder national consultation process on climate change recommended eighty-eight actions to federal and provincial governments.[49] A comprehensive study by the Pembina Institute concluded that by the year 2000, only one-third of these actions had been taken, almost all of which involved soft measures such as voluntary initiatives, education, or research.[50] Canadian governments avoided using the stronger tools at their disposal (laws, regulations, and such economic instruments as taxes and financial incentives) to reduce greenhouse gas emissions.[51] In 2002 the federal government continued to study concrete actions to reduce emissions, rather than implement them.

Do Voluntary Measures Produce Lower Greenhouse Gas Emissions?
Industry and provincial governments lobbied hard throughout the 1990s to convince Ottawa that voluntary programs were the best way to address climate change. Tom d'Aquino, president of the influential Canadian Council of Chief Executives (formerly known as the Business Council on National Issues) argued that "reliance on regulation and punitive measures by our governments will not work."[52] In 1995 Canada's minister of natural resources, Anne McLellan, announced that she was impressed by industry's willingness to voluntarily reduce greenhouse gas emissions and claimed that "legislation is often the least effective and most costly way to go."[53] Canadian governments capitulated to political pressure and relied on education and voluntary programs instead of laws, regulations, and economic instruments. Three of Canada's most prominent voluntary initiatives are a voluntary program to encourage industry to reduce greenhouse gas emissions, voluntary agreements with vehicle manufacturers to increase fuel efficiency, and a voluntary national building code.

The Voluntary Challenge and Registry Program
The flagship of Canada's voluntary emissions reduction program is the Voluntary Challenge and Registry Program. Begun in 1995, the program invites companies to report both their greenhouse gas emissions and the actions taken to reduce their emissions.[54] The theory is that companies will gain publicity and goodwill for being responsible corporate citizens. By the end of 1999,

980 companies had registered with the Voluntary Challenge and Registry Program. However, only 10 percent of the participating companies provided full information to the registry on their greenhouse gas emissions. Worse yet, "On average, emissions of companies in the program do not appear to be rising more slowly than companies outside the program." The Pembina Institute and others conclude that the "VCR has been wholly ineffective in helping Canada to meet its greenhouse gas emissions requirements."[55]

Voluntary Programs to Increase Fuel Efficiency

A second example of the inadequacy of voluntary programs involves the fuel efficiency of motor vehicles. In 1982 Canada enacted the *Motor Vehicle Fuel Consumption Standards Act* to impose mandatory fuel efficiency standards on vehicles.[56] Vehicle manufacturers strenuously objected to this law and successfully persuaded the government not to implement the *Act* but to rely on voluntary agreements instead. As a result, the average fuel efficiency of new vehicles in Canada has not improved since 1982.[57] In part because of soaring sales of trucks, minivans, and sport utility vehicles, the overall fuel efficiency of new vehicles sold in Canada worsened from 8.4 l/100 km to 9.5 l/100 km between 1986 and 1998.[58]

Despite twenty years of proven failure using voluntary agreements with vehicle makers, the federal government recently announced plans to phase in a "voluntary improvement in fuel efficiency" for motor vehicles.[59] Major improvements in fuel efficiency are possible with existing technology, at costs that can be recovered through savings on fuel costs.[60] Care must be taken to design new regulations that do not compromise passenger safety by widening the weight gap between large and small vehicles. Canada follows the United States when addressing fuel efficiency, and American standards are weak and plagued by loopholes.[61] Despite a new law in California restricting carbon dioxide emissions from vehicles, significant improvements to American fuel efficiency standards are unlikely in the short term, given President George W. Bush's lack of enthusiasm for conservation.[62]

Voluntary Programs for Energy-Efficient Homes

A third example of the lack of success of voluntary efforts to reduce Canadian greenhouse gas emissions involves a program started in 1982 to encourage the construction of energy-efficient homes, known as R-2000 homes. An R-2000 home reduces energy use and energy costs by 26 percent compared to conventional new home construction, provides superior air quality, reduces maintenance costs, and improves resale value, while costing only 4 to 6 percent more than the average new home.[63] Despite these attractive features and millions spent on promotion and education, fewer than ten thousand R-2000 homes have been built in Canada in the past twenty years, and only about 0.6 percent of recent housing starts involve R-2000 construction. Canada's latest

Climate Change Plan suggests that all homes built by 2010 should be R-2000, but is vague about how this will be accomplished.

Voluntary measures lack accountability. They are, by definition, unenforceable, like a politician's promise to eliminate the GST. Numerous experts conclude that "voluntary, educational and research measures are wholly insufficient to meet Canada's climate change challenge when they are not backed up by regulatory standards and positive financial incentives."[64]

Do Laws and Regulations Produce Lower Greenhouse Gas Emissions?

Despite international obligations and repeated promises, no controls on carbon dioxide emissions have been legislated by any Canadian government – federal, provincial, or territorial.[65] Some provinces, notably British Columbia and Ontario, introduced minor regulatory changes, including provincial energy efficiency standards.[66] Although both provinces also created mandatory vehicle inspection and maintenance programs in major urban areas, these programs have had a minimal effect on carbon dioxide emissions.[67] Ontario requires the mandatory capture of methane from landfills above a certain size and offers a fee-bate program where taxes on inefficient vehicles (i.e., gas guzzlers) are offset by rebates on fuel efficient vehicles.[68] Saskatchewan will require most gasoline sold in the province to be blended with ethanol by mid-2004, providing a boost to farmers while reducing carbon dioxide emissions.[69] A number of Canadian municipalities, led by Toronto, are implementing programs intended to reduce greenhouse gas emissions by 20 percent from 1990 levels. Toronto's municipal government has already achieved an impressive 67 percent decrease in emissions.[70]

Alberta has proposed a controversial law called the *Climate Change and Emissions Management Act* which is intended to reduce emissions intensity, or the amount of greenhouse gases released per unit of GDP, but which will not reduce total emissions.[71] In an interesting twist, the preamble to the proposed law describes carbon dioxide and methane as "natural resources," in an effort to assert the province's jurisdiction. Federal environment minister David Anderson dismissed the law, which relies on the same approach as US president George W. Bush's climate change policy, as being "as phony as a three-dollar bill."[72]

The only significant regulatory step taken by the federal government in the 1990s was the 1992 enactment of the *Energy Efficiency Act*, a law to increase the efficiency standards for thirty-three products, such as refrigerators, lights, and some kinds of motors.[73] The *Act* prohibits the import or interprovincial trade of products that do not meet prescribed standards. The law and associated regulations are clear, mandatory, and generally well-drafted. Failure to comply with the mandated energy-efficiency standards can result in fines of up to $200,000, and the government can seize the unlawful products.[74]

The products covered by the *Act* account for roughly 65 percent of residential energy use. According to Natural Resources Canada, the *Act* and regulations will reduce carbon dioxide emissions by 4 to 6 megatonnes by 2000 and 12 to 19 megatonnes by 2020 (the reductions increase over time as more older appliances and equipment are replaced).[75] To put these figures in context, Canada needs to reduce greenhouse gas emissions by roughly 240 megatonnes to meet its obligation under the *Kyoto Protocol*. Amendments made in 1999, extending the regulations to include lights, are expected to reduce carbon dioxide emissions by an additional 5.3 megatonnes per year (equivalent to the emissions of about one million cars).[76] The *Act* is reducing Canadian energy use, saving Canadians money, reducing greenhouse gas emissions, and protecting the environment. As of 2003, the latest fridges use 75 percent less energy than fridges made twenty years ago, and thus cause up to 75 percent less greenhouse gas emissions.[77] The *Act* is widely regarded as "the single action taken by Canada since 1990 that is likely to make the most significant contribution to greenhouse gas emission reduction."[78]

Given the apparent effectiveness of regulations, why does Ottawa focus on fridges and a handful of other household products? The products covered by the *Act* account for about 5 percent of Canada's greenhouse gas emissions, yet these are the only emission sources directly addressed by Canadian governments through regulations. What about coal-fired utilities, trucks, automobiles, sport utility vehicles, oil sands projects, cement plants, and other major contributors to Canada's total emissions? There are no regulatory limits on greenhouse gas emissions from the four sectors most responsible: transportation (25 percent of Canada's greenhouse gas emissions), fossil fuel development (19 percent), electricity generation (17 percent), and industrial activities (15 percent). In 1997, the federal government admitted that "the small number of regulatory measures accounts for a large percentage of the total impact" of its climate change initiatives.[79] Despite this candid assessment, Canada continues to rely heavily on voluntary measures.

The Results of Canadian Efforts to Reduce Greenhouse Gas Emissions

Despite a decade of solemn promises, international commitments, and impressive-sounding action plans to reduce Canada's contribution to global warming, Canadian greenhouse gas emissions rose 20 percent between 1990 and 2000.[80] At the dawn of the twenty-first century, Canadians continue to be among the world's leaders in per capita greenhouse gas emissions, generating 22.5 tonnes of greenhouse gases per person annually.[81] The global average is 3.8 tonnes of greenhouse gases per person annually, or about one-sixth the Canadian level.[82] Although Canada has 0.5 percent of the world's population, we produce approximately 2.2 percent of the world's greenhouse gas emissions. With 31 million people, Canada uses more energy and produces more greenhouse gas emissions than the entire continent of Africa, with its population of over 700 million.[83]

Canada's performance is getting worse, not better. The latest projections indicate that unless something dramatic happens in the next decade, Canada will be nowhere near meeting its commitment under *Kyoto*. Canadian emissions are already 20 percent above 1990 levels, and experts expect that emissions in 2010 will be at least 27 percent above 1990 levels instead of 6 percent below 1990 levels, as promised in Kyoto. By 2020, Canadian emissions could be 41 to 44 percent above 1990 levels.[84] The increases are due mainly to increased natural gas exports, oil, gas, and coal activities (especially oil sands development), electricity generation, increased transportation (both travel and freight), and the growth of Canada's population and economy. The new US National Energy Policy forecasts that in the next twenty years, American consumption of oil will rise 33 percent, natural gas more than 50 percent, and electricity demand by 45 percent, requiring 1,300 to 1,900 new power plants.[85] Canada's willingness to satisfy burgeoning American energy demands could badly compromise our ability to meet our climate change commitments.[86] Although the United States has not ratified *Kyoto*, American governments (federal and state) have taken more action to reduce greenhouse gas emissions than their Canadian counterparts.[87]

Reasons for Canada's Inaction
Canadian inaction on climate change is mainly due to vigorous opposition from corporations and provincial governments, particularly the fossil fuel industry and Alberta. The Canadian Council of Chief Executives, the Canadian Chamber of Commerce, and other industry groups formed the "Canadian Coalition for Responsible Environmental Solutions" to question the science of climate change, warn of economic doom, and dismiss public concerns as misguided.[88] Gwyn Morgan, CEO of EnCana, claimed that taking concrete steps to reduce greenhouse gas emissions "could spread a virulent virus which emaciates the livelihood and living standards of millions of Canadians."[89] The Canadian Coal Association warned that signing *Kyoto* would be "economic suicide."[90] The energy sector contributes 7 percent of Canada's GDP, produces $26 billion in exports, and directly employs 280,000 people.[91] Reducing greenhouse gas emissions will certainly require major changes to Canada's energy industry and overall economy, but it is hard to imagine that the impacts will amount to "trillions of dollars" of losses for Alberta alone, as suggested by Premier Ralph Klein.[92] Industry elsewhere is taking a different approach. Business executives attending the World Economic Forum 2000 in Davos, Switzerland, recognized climate change as "the greatest challenge facing the world at the beginning of the century."[93] Even British Petroleum and Shell openly acknowledge the reality of climate change and are investing billions of dollars in renewable energy.[94]

Climate change can be addressed practically and economically, such as by improving the energy efficiency of buildings, investing in renewable energy, promoting cogeneration, planting trees on marginal farmland, and expanding public transit, yet Canada has implemented few of these win-win solutions. It is also important to envision long-term solutions, from superior urban design to closed-loop industrial systems, and facilitate learning about future possibilities. Canada's two extensive national consultation processes on climate change prescribed many responses.[95] Respected research and advocacy organizations including the Pew Centre on Global Climate Change, the Pembina Institute, the American Council for an Energy Efficient Future, the World Wide Fund for Nature, the Union of Concerned Scientists, the Tellus Institute, the Rocky Mountain Institute, and the David Suzuki Foundation have published comprehensive reports outlining a range of regulatory and policy changes, financial incentives, and research and development priorities.[96] Canadian author Guy Dauncey published *Stormy Weather: 101 Solutions to Global Climate Change,* a book offering solutions at all levels from local to worldwide.[97] European nations are demonstrating leadership in cutting emissions by up to 25 percent through a variety of innovative means, while maintaining quality of life and economic prosperity. A European Union study estimates that Europe could create 900,000 new jobs by doubling production of renewable energy in the next ten years, while saving C$32 billion and 402 million tonnes of carbon dioxide emissions annually.[98]

In fact, expert opinion is divided over whether reducing greenhouse gas emissions will have negative or positive economic effects. At the pessimistic end of the spectrum, some studies suggest that the costs of complying with *Kyoto* for Canada will be between 0 and 3 percent of GDP by 2010 or, in absolute terms, up to $40 billion.[99] Although this figure sounds large, it means that total economic growth from 2000 to 2010 would be 26 percent instead of 30 percent. Conversely, studies by the World Resources Institute, the Royal Society of Canada, the US Department of Energy, the National Round Table on the Environment and the Economy, and the US National Academy of Sciences anticipate billions of dollars in economic benefits from reducing greenhouse gas emissions.[100] A statement signed by 2,800 economists from Canada and the United States (including eight Nobel laureates) declared, "Economic studies have found that there are many potential policies to reduce greenhouse gas emissions for which the total benefits outweigh the total costs."[101] As well, substantial costs, ranging from C$3.5 billion to $24.5 billion annually, will be incurred if Canada and the world fail to address climate change.[102]

Conclusion

Canada's record in responding to climate change, both internationally and domestically, is dismal. Emissions rose by 20 percent during the 1990s. Canada's commissioner on the environment and sustainable development criticized the federal government's lack of a clearly developed strategy for reducing emissions, lack of effective action, lack of accountability, failure to take a leadership role, failure to educate the public, refusal to impose a carbon tax, and heavy reliance on voluntary measures.[103] These criticisms apply with equal force to the provincial and territorial governments. In 2001, the commissioner observed that "the continuing rise in Canada's greenhouse gas emissions places the country on a path that is far from sustainable."[104]

Climate change is a signal to us that our society is harming the planet's climate control system, just as a high temperature indicates that an individual is ill. The longer we refuse to address the causes of the malady, the more difficult it will be to recover. Scientists expect that industrialized nations will have to reduce greenhouse gas emissions by more than 50 percent from 1990 levels in the long term in order to stabilize the climate.[105] Canada's commitment under *Kyoto* is a relatively modest first step toward resolving the problem, and even this commitment has been softened significantly.

To make progress in addressing climate change, Canadian governments need to adapt the strategies that successfully targeted ozone-depleting substances for elimination. Now that *Kyoto* is ratified, Canada should use effective tools including laws, regulations, improved standards, and innovative economic instruments, while aggressively investing in renewable energy, cogeneration, energy efficiency, public transit, and other proven emission reduction measures. There is no shortage of solutions to the challenge of climate change, only a shortage of social and political will. The protection of the Earth's ozone layer proves that humanity in general, and Canadians in particular, are capable of summoning the wisdom necessary to protect the planet for future generations. Because Canada's inaction on climate change threatens to undermine the progress in protecting the ozone layer, it is doubly important that Canadian governments, corporations, and citizens immediately take the steps necessary to reduce greenhouse gas emissions.

> Ontario's air quality has improved steadily since 1988.
> *Government of Ontario, 2001*

> Ontario's air quality is getting worse, not better.
> *Ontario Medical Association, 2001*

Do Canadians still need to worry about the health and environmental consequences of air pollution? Or have governments and industry responded in recent decades with an effective array of laws, policies, programs, and technological improvements such that air pollution ought no longer be a public concern? The answers to these questions are somewhat hazy. In recent decades Canada has made major strides in reducing several types of air pollution. Ambient levels of lead, one of the most toxic, health-damaging air pollutants, are down 95 percent since 1979.[1] Canadian emissions of sulphur dioxide, the main cause of acid rain, fell by 43 percent between 1980 and 1995.[2] New cars produce only a fraction of the nitrogen oxides, volatile organic compounds, and carbon monoxide of cars built in the early 1970s.[3] Ambient concentrations of benzene fell between 1995 and 2000.[4] Canada's National Pollutant Release Inventory showed a 12 percent decline in air releases from industrial sources between 1995 and 1998.[5] Most air quality objectives are met, most of the time, in most parts of the country.[6]

Yet despite this progress, air pollution causes between five thousand and sixteen thousand premature deaths in Canada annually. Even the low end of this range is higher than the annual death toll from breast cancer, prostate cancer, or motor vehicle accidents.[7] More than half of all Canadians are exposed to smog in concentrations that can adversely affect health. The three worst areas in Canada – the Windsor-Quebec City corridor, southern Atlantic region, and lower Fraser Valley, including Vancouver – continue to experience serious air quality problems, especially during the summer.[8] Medical research recently revealed that because of air pollution, a city resident faces the same risk of lung cancer as someone who lives with a smoker. Another new study establishes a connection between smog and heart disease.[9]

Partial progress in reducing air pollution must not, therefore, be used to downplay the urgent need for further action. Even in areas where Canada's performance on air pollution is improving, we continue to lag behind the majority of industrialized nations on many indicators. Canada still has among the highest per capita and total emissions of sulphur dioxide, nitrogen oxides, carbon dioxide, carbon monoxide, and volatile organic compounds in the OECD. Canadian industry pumps more than 100 million kilograms of toxic substances into the air annually, including more than 13 million kilograms of carcinogenic pollutants.[10]

Independent assessments of Canada's record in combating air pollution re-inforce the conclusion that while some gains have been made, much more remains to be done before Canadians can consistently breathe safe, clean air. According to the OECD, "There are still areas where air quality is inadequate for human health and ecosystems" because of lax pollution standards and inconsistent enforcement of environmental laws.[11] The World Economic Fo-rum also criticized the subpar effectiveness of Canada's air pollution regula-tions.[12] The federal commissioner of the environment and sustainable development said, "Risks to the public and environmental health are not be-ing managed effectively," and "While there have been downward trends in some of the common air pollutants, trends now appear to be leveling off or even increasing as improvements are slowly eroded."[13]

The Connection between Air Pollution and Energy Consumption
According to the Commission for Environmental Cooperation (CEC), the main reasons Canada is among the highest air pollution emitters in the world are high per capita consumption of energy and our dependence on fossil fuels.[14] Fossil fuels (coal, oil, and natural gas) provide roughly 80 percent of our en-ergy.[15] In part, our high consumption is because Canada is a large country with a cold climate. However, Canadians use energy very inefficiently, ranking twenty-eighth out of twenty-nine nations in the OECD, behind such coun-tries as Mexico, Turkey, and Poland.[16] Canada's energy use is divided as fol-lows: 39 percent industry, 27 percent transportation, and 34 percent agriculture, residential, commercial, and other. Of the energy used by industry, 70 percent is used in five sectors: pulp and paper, metal smelting, steel making, mining, and petrochemicals.[17] Canada's inefficient use of energy, like our inefficient use of water, results from the fact that the country enjoys abundant energy resources and thus prices are cheap. Energy prices in Canada are considerably lower than in most other industrialized nations.

The transportation sector, including both industry and individuals, is the largest single contributor to air pollution in Canada.[18] The number of motor vehicles doubled between 1970 and 1999.[19] Urban transit rides per person annually fell from 250 to less than 100 between 1950 and 1990. On an annual basis, Canadians travel further than residents of the other G8 countries. While this may be partially attributed to Canada's large size, "the largest proportion of the travel occurs within cities or the urban region surrounding cities, suggesting that low-density, spread out suburban development has also been a major factor."[20]

Types and Sources of Air Pollution in Canada

The five most common air pollutants are sulphur dioxide, nitrogen oxides, carbon monoxide, volatile organic compounds (VOCs), and particulate matter. These harmful substances combine and react to form other kinds of damaging air pollution. For example, nitrogen oxides and VOCs react with sunlight to form ground-level ozone. When ground-level ozone in turn mixes with particulate matter, smog results. Also of major concern are hazardous air pollutants or air toxics, including polycyclic aromatic hydrocarbons, heavy metals (e.g., lead, mercury, arsenic), and persistent organic pollutants (e.g., PCBs, pesticides).

Sulphur Dioxide

Sulphur dioxide comes mainly from metal smelting, fossil-fuel-fired power generation, upstream oil and gas activities, petroleum refining, and other industrial activities. Fossil fuel use causes the majority of sulphur dioxide emissions. As noted earlier, sulphur dioxide emissions fell 43 percent in Canada between 1980 and 1995, largely because of regulations that caused changes to industrial processes.

Nitrogen Oxides

About 90 percent of nitrogen oxide emissions come from the combustion of fossil fuels in motor vehicles, coal-fired electricity generation, and industrial processes. The replacement of nuclear reactors with coal-fired generating plants in Ontario and growing numbers of vehicles have increased nitrogen oxide emissions, while technological advances have decreased emissions. Overall, nitrogen oxide emissions in Canada remained fairly constant over the past twenty years.[21]

Acid Rain

Acid rain refers to any form of precipitation that is highly acidic because of emissions of sulphur dioxide or nitrogen oxides. The area of eastern Canada where levels of acid rain exceed the environment's assimilative capacity dropped more than 40 percent between 1991 and 1996, from 910,000 square kilometres to 540,000 square kilometres.[22] This improvement reflects reduced sulphur dioxide emissions in both Canada and the United States.

Volatile Organic Compounds

Volatile organic compounds are organic chemicals that readily evaporate at normal temperatures, cause adverse health effects when inhaled, and are precursors of smog. Emissions of VOCs result largely from fossil fuel combustion, as well as fuel evaporation, industrial processes, and products such as paints and solvents. Since 1980, Canada's emissions of VOCs have declined modestly.[23]

Ground-Level Ozone

Ground-level ozone, resulting from reactions between nitrogen oxides and VOCs, is "generally regarded as Canada's most serious urban air pollution problem."[24] Unlike most other air pollution indicators, levels of ground-level ozone climbed by 29 percent between 1979 and 1993 and continue to increase.[25] The increase is partially attributable to warmer summer temperatures caused by climate change.

Particulate Matter

Particulate matter includes airborne particles from a wide range of sources and is now divided into two classes – coarse and fine – with the latter having greater health impacts. Coarse particulates include dust and smoke from construction sites, agriculture, unpaved roads, and wood burning. Fine particulates are produced by the combustion of fossil fuels and wood; reactions involving sulphur dioxide, nitrogen oxides, and organic compounds; high-temperature industrial processes (smelters, steel mills); and solvent use. Industrial processes, transportation, and residential wood burning produce the majority of particulate matter in Canada.

Carbon Monoxide

Carbon monoxide is a colourless, odourless toxic gas produced by the combustion of fossil fuels. Most carbon monoxide emissions are caused by the transportation sector.

Hazardous Air Pollutants

Hazardous air pollutants (air toxics) are produced by a wide range of industrial activities and also by fossil fuel combustion. Concern about these toxic substances is heightened when they are persistent (meaning they take years or decades to break down or decompose in the environment) and bioaccumulative (concentrations of the substance build up in successively higher levels of the food chain). Hazardous air pollutants are not only produced in Canada but also transported by air currents from sources thousands of kilometres away, such as pesticides applied in Central or South America.

Indoor Air Pollution

While indoor air pollution is often overlooked, the fact that most Canadians spend over 80 percent of their time indoors means that exposure to air pollutants in residential and occupational settings often outweighs outdoor exposures. Indoor air pollution is caused by combustion (e.g., gas appliances), building materials, furnishings, human activities (e.g., smoking and painting), and radon, a naturally occurring radioactive gas that causes lung cancer.

The Health and Environmental Impacts of Air Pollution

There are many medical studies chronicling the health impacts of air pollution. Infants, children, people with illnesses, and the elderly are particularly vulnerable.[26] Various forms of air pollution affect the respiratory system, reduce the body's defences against infection, cause cancer, and exacerbate cardiovascular disease. Evidence of the extensive health impacts of air pollution in Canada today includes the following:

- The Ontario Medical Association reports that air pollution annually causes 1,900 premature deaths, 13,000 emergency room visits, 9,800 hospital admissions, and 47 million sick days.[27]
- The BC Medical Association estimates that 2,000 premature deaths occur in British Columbia each year as a result of air pollution.[28]
- Close to 8 percent of nontraumatic mortality in Canadian cities is attributed to air pollution.[29]
- In Ontario, 20 percent of hospital admissions for infants under the age of one for bronchitis, bronchiolitis, and pneumonia can be attributed to smog.[30]
- Elevated carbon monoxide levels result in increased rates of hospitalization for elderly patients with congestive heart disease.[31]
- Hospitalization of young children in Canada for asthma increased by 28 percent among boys and 18 percent among girls between 1980 and 1990.[32]
- High levels of contaminants are found in the breast milk of Inuit women.[33]

There is a corresponding body of work chronicling the enormous health benefits that would be generated by cleaning up Canada's air. Studies indicate that improving air quality in Vancouver alone would save 2,800 lives and prevent 33,000 hospital emergency room visits by 2020.[34] Environment Canada estimates that new federal standards in effect to reduce sulphur in gasoline will prevent 2,100 premature deaths, 6,800 emergency room visits, 3.3 million asthma symptom days, and 11 million acute respiratory symptom days between 2000 and 2020.[35] Tougher sulphur standards proposed for diesel fuel could avoid another 46 premature deaths, 33,700 restricted activity days, and 242,000 acute respiratory symptom days annually by 2020.[36]

It is worth noting that in developing countries, air quality is far worse than in Canada, with air pollution levels that are higher by an order of magnitude.

In these countries between 1.9 million and 2.8 million people die annually because of exposure to high concentrations of suspended particulate matter in the indoor air environment. An additional 500,000 deaths annually are due to particulate matter and sulphur dioxide in outdoor air.[37]

The environmental problems caused by air pollution include damage to crops, soils, forests, and other vegetation, damage to buildings, corrosion of metals, degradation of rubber and fabric, harm to wildlife, and impaired visibility (with potential impacts on quality of life and tourism). Acid rain causes extensive damage to lakes and streams, rendering freshwater habitat unsuitable for many aquatic species.[38] New studies indicate that acid rain also affects human health.[39]

The Economic Impacts of Air Pollution

Despite the progress made in recent decades, the economic costs of air pollution are still immense. Improving air quality in the Greater Vancouver Regional District would prevent $74 million in crop damage and reduced yields and result in a $1.6 billion benefit to the provincial economy annually. The Ontario Medical Association says air pollution costs Ontario citizens more than $1 billion a year in hospital admissions, emergency room visits, and absenteeism. Canada's commissioner of the environment and sustainable development estimates the health and other benefits of achieving the most stringent air quality standards at about $10 billion annually. Other government estimates of the health benefits from improving air quality in Canada range from $8 billion to $24 billion over twenty years.[40]

In light of the enormous anticipated benefits of cleaner air, one might reasonably ask why Canada is not moving more quickly in this direction. The answer is that these substantial health and environmental improvements may come at a significant cost. Canada's commissioner of the environment and sustainable development cites studies estimating the annual costs of reducing air pollution as between $968 million and $22 billion.[41] On the other hand, the expected costs of reducing pollution are consistently overstated, as were the costs of eliminating ozone-depleting chemicals. Studies have shown that "the economic impact of controlling airborne pollutants in the metals industry has been generally positive. The introduction of technologies that reduce sulphur dioxide emissions has generally improved productivity and reduced operating costs."[42] As Jim Lane, chair of the BC Medical Association Council on Health Promotion, concludes, "When we consider the high human cost of air pollution – more asthma, bronchitis, allergies, and premature death – the price of prevention seems low indeed."[43]

Laws and Policies Governing Air Pollution in Canada

Laws and policies intended to control air pollution can adopt four basic approaches: emission standards, ambient air quality standards, technology standards, and pollution prevention. Emission standards focus on the pollutants that are coming out of the end of the pipe, while ambient air quality standards focus on the state of the environment into which emissions are discharged. Technology standards prescribe specific devices or processes to minimize the release of air pollutants. When a government requires industry to meet standards for emissions, ambient air quality, or technology, this is referred to as "command and control" regulation. Pollution prevention, a more recent approach, emphasizes reducing or avoiding pollution through redesigning industrial processes, switching energy sources, or substituting materials.

At the federal, provincial, and territorial levels, Canada has emphasized emission standards, ambient air quality objectives, and, to a lesser extent, technology standards.[44] Generally, however, Canada relies on unenforceable air quality *objectives* instead of binding air quality *standards*. As law professor Jamie Benidickson points out, "Discharge standards have often been set without explicit linkages to overall objectives for environmental quality."[45] Permits to pollute from point sources add up. When nonpoint sources are piled on top, the result is often air pollution that exceeds the environment's assimilative capacity, creating health and environmental problems.

International Commitments

Ottawa represents Canada in international negotiations about air pollution, enacts and enforces national laws restricting air pollution, and attempts to encourage the provinces and territories to take effective action within the realm of their jurisdiction. Canada is bound by a number of regional treaties that limit our air emissions, such as the 1979 *United Nations Economic Commission for Europe Convention on Long Range Transport of Air Pollution*. Pursuant to protocols signed under this treaty, Canada agreed to reduce sulphur dioxide emissions (1985), decrease nitrogen oxide emissions (1988), and further reduce sulphur dioxide emissions (1994).[46] Canada also signed the 1991 *Canada-United States Air Quality Agreement* establishing emission reduction obligations for sulphur dioxide.[47] In 2000 the *Agreement* was extended to include nitrogen oxides and VOCs, the precursors of ground-level ozone and smog.[48]

Canada played a leadership role in the international negotiations aimed at phasing out the use of twelve persistent organic pollutants (POPs).[49] These toxic substances are a major concern to people living in the Arctic, who bear the brunt of the impacts despite never using any of the substances themselves.[50] In 2001 the terms of the *Stockholm Convention on Persistent Organic Pollutants* were finalized and Canada became the first country to ratify the agreement. Canada's early ratification was made easier by the fact that it had already eliminated the production and use of the twelve substances governed by the *Stockholm Convention*. However, there are other POPs not covered by the *Stockholm Convention* that pose a health and environmental threat to arctic people and ecosystems.[51]

Federal Laws Governing Air Pollution

The federal government plays a vital role in protecting Canada's people and ecosystems from air pollution. The single most important federal law governing air pollution is the *Canadian Environmental Protection Act, 1999 (CEPA)*. CEPA authorizes the federal government to establish national ambient air quality objectives, regulate motor vehicle emissions, set emissions standards for certain industries, maintain an inventory of pollution emissions, and regulate toxic substances. Other federal laws that play a lesser role in limiting air pollution include the *Canada Shipping Act* (pollution from ships), *Railway Safety Act,* and *Canada Transportation Act* (both addressing pollution from railways). There are no regulations governing indoor air quality, although guidelines do exist.[52]

Opinions about the strength of *CEPA* are deeply divided. *CEPA* was touted by the Canadian government as the toughest environmental legislation in the Western world when it was introduced in 1988.[53] However, when reviewing the law in 1995, Parliament's Standing Committee on Environment and Sustainable Development concluded that "*CEPA* has not effectively addressed Canada's pressing environmental problems."[54] In 1999 the federal commissioner of the environment and sustainable development compiled a disturbing catalogue of shortcomings in the implementation of *CEPA* including: unfulfilled commitments; the lack of rigour in existing voluntary initiatives; inadequate resources; failure to keep up with new health and environmental standards; inadequate tracking of releases of toxic substances into the environment; conflicting departmental priorities and agendas; poor interdepartmental coordination of research efforts; institutional and interdepartmental fragmentation; failure to apply the precautionary principle; incremental destruction as cumulative effects are overlooked; a "vexing lack of action"; and a "lack of emphasis on pollution prevention." The commissioner's audit concluded that the federal government is doing a poor job of protecting Canadians from the risks posed by pollution, as "cracks in the foundation threaten the federal government's ability to detect, understand and prevent the harmful effects of toxic substances on the health of Canadians and their environment."[55]

In 1999, after years of heated discussion, *CEPA* was amended. However, many improvements recommended by the Standing Committee on Environment and Sustainable Development were deleted at the last minute because of intense industry lobbying. Mark Winfield, an environmental lawyer, described the new *CEPA* as "a major step backwards in a number of key areas," including the imposition of cost-benefit analysis, mandatory consultation with provinces before the federal government acts, and weaker provisions for assessing the impacts of new biotechnology products.[56] The new *CEPA* allows the cabinet, not the ministers of health and environment, to determine whether to designate a substance as toxic. This may allow ministers with economic portfolios (who form a majority in cabinet) to dominate decision making about environmental protection.

National Ambient Air Quality Objectives

The revised *CEPA* enables the federal government to establish National Ambient Air Quality Objectives (NAAQOs). These objectives are intended to provide a measure of the safe amount or concentration of a contaminant in the air at a particular time as a result of the combined emissions of all sources. To date, NAAQOs have been set for only five substances: carbon monoxide, nitrogen oxides, sulphur dioxide, ozone, and particulates. Unfortunately, Canada's NAAQOs do not ensure even air quality across Canada because they are out of date and unenforceable. Canada's commissioner of the environment and sustainable development concluded in 2000 that "current national objectives for levels of ozone and total suspended particulates do not fully protect the health of Canadians."[57] The CEC observed that "the fact that the national ambient air objectives are guidelines rather than enforceable standards means that if these objectives are exceeded, no legal consequences follow."[58]

Regulating Toxic Substances

As discussed in Chapter 2.2, the *Canadian Environmental Protection Act, 1999* represents a move toward an ecologically sound approach to pollution. Intended to govern the elimination of particularly harmful toxic substances from our society, *CEPA* incorporates progressive principles like ecosystem management, pollution prevention, and the precautionary principle.

Only a handful of the major air pollutants in Canada have been designated as toxic under *CEPA*, including particulate matter, asbestos, mercury, lead, vinyl chloride, PCBs, and ozone-depleting substances. By comparison, the US *Clean Air Act Amendments* of 1990 cover 189 hazardous air pollutants.[59] However, as part of Canada's new clean air strategy (detailed below), more air pollutants may be added to *CEPA*'s list of toxic substances, including ozone, sulphur dioxide, nitrogen oxides, VOCs, and ammonia. The designation of these substances as toxic under *CEPA* could greatly increase the federal government's role in regulating air pollution in Canada.

Emissions Standards for Industries

Under *CEPA* the federal government has passed regulations establishing air emission standards for secondary lead smelters, chlor-alkali plants, asbestos mines and mills, and vinyl chloride manufacturing facilities.[60] These regulations have contributed to cleaner air in Canada, as the dramatic decrease in lead emissions demonstrates (although most of that reduction was due to the elimination of leaded gasoline).[61] A key drawback is that these standards apply to only a handful of Canadian industrial sectors. As more substances are designated as toxic under *CEPA*, more federal regulations will be enacted to apply to a broader range of industries. For example, proposed regulations will address emissions from copper smelters and zinc plants.[62]

Motor Vehicle Emissions

Originally regulated by the *Motor Vehicle Safety Act,* emission limits for motor vehicles imported into or manufactured in Canada are now governed by *CEPA.*[63] Historically, Canada has lagged behind the US in adopting stricter emission standards.[64] In 1990 the federal government promised to enact regulations that were as strong as the standards in California. However, in a move reminiscent of Canada's backpedalling on fuel efficiency standards, Ottawa chose to rely on a voluntary agreement with Canadian car manufacturers to reduce nitrogen oxide emissions.[65] In contrast, the American government regulated these emissions under the *Clean Air Act.* Stricter American vehicle emission standards are scheduled to come into force in 2004. As part of its new clean air initiative, Canada promises to move toward the new American standards.

Motor Vehicle Fuels

CEPA also allows Ottawa to regulate fuel content. Regulations have been passed addressing lead, benzene, sulphur, and contaminated fuel.[66] One of Canada's most compelling environmental success stories involves the elimination of lead from gasoline. Thousands of people were harmed by lead despite concerns expressed by medical experts when leaded gasoline was introduced in the 1920s.[67] Lead in gasoline was first regulated in Canada in 1974, with tighter rules imposed in 1987 before lead was eliminated in 1990. Benzene is a known carcinogen and was designated as a toxic substance under *CEPA* in 1994. In 1999 Canada passed a regulation reducing benzene emissions from vehicles – their major source – by about 20 percent at a cost of 0.2 to 0.4 cents per litre of gasoline.[68]

Until recently, Canada had one of the highest levels of sulphur in gasoline among industrialized nations, with an average of 343 parts per million (ppm) of sulphur, contributing to urban air pollution problems and acid rain. Levels of sulphur in gasoline refined in Ontario, which were kept secret by the oil industry until a lawsuit by environmental groups, were far above the Canadian average.[69] New regulations passed under *CEPA* dramatically reduce the average sulphur content of Canadian gasoline, to 150 ppm in 2002 and 30 ppm in 2005.[70] However, some loopholes remain. The regulations for diesel fuel used in on-road vehicles allow a much higher level of sulphur than is permitted for regular fuel. Worse yet, no regulations limit the sulphur content of diesel fuel for off-road vehicles (including boats, trains, tractors, and a range of recreational vehicles), which account for almost half of diesel fuel use in Canada.[71]

National Pollutant Release Inventory

The NPRI is a key tool in tracking industrial air pollution. Corporations must report, annually, their releases of specified toxic substances. Started in 1993, the NPRI has gradually improved as more substances and more sources of pollution are added to its coverage, which now includes 268 substances and over 2,500 facilities. The NPRI reveals trends and identifies problem industries and companies.

Although useful, the NPRI has several major limitations. The NPRI does not cover mobile sources (such as motor vehicles), small facilities, or nonpoint sources of pollution (agricultural and urban runoff). Many toxic substances are not covered by the NPRI, thresholds for reporting are quite high, companies may apply to have releases kept confidential, and the inventory relies on companies to estimate their own releases of pollutants. Little effort is made to confirm these estimates. An in-depth analysis of the NPRI published in 2001 revealed three weaknesses: overall reductions in releases were primarily due to legally compelled reductions in releases to surface water; the decrease in total releases was offset by an increase in the toxicity of waste streams; and Canadian manufacturers are more pollution-intense than their American counterparts.[72]

Toward Cleaner Air

In 2001 Environment Minister David Anderson pledged, "Clean air is my priority," as he unveiled an aggressive new strategy for reducing air pollution in Canada.[73] The new strategy promises more than $120 million in new spending; new regulations to gradually bring Canada's vehicle emission standards in line with those in the United States, beginning in the 2004 model year; new standards for diesel fuel used in trucks, buses, and construction and agricultural equipment; new standards for snow blowers, lawnmowers, chainsaws, and other small engines; programs to reduce nitrogen oxide and VOC emissions from industrial sectors; increased air quality monitoring; and an expansion of the NPRI.[74]

If these promises are fulfilled, Canada will make further progress toward the goal of clean air. Past experience, however, with ambitious but largely underfunded and underimplemented programs suggests that federal environmental promises should be viewed with a healthy degree of skepticism. The 1990 *Green Plan* promised an additional $3 billion of federal spending on environmental protection over five years. However, in part because of the recession in the early 1990s, more than 70 percent of the *Green Plan* money was never allocated to the environment.[75]

Provincial Regulation of Air Pollution

Because of the division of powers under Canada's *Constitution Act, 1867*, the provinces play an important role in protecting air quality. Most provinces control air pollution through a combination of air quality objectives, regulations targeting specific contaminants or industries, and permitting regimes. For example, Ontario sets ambient air quality objectives for twenty-three pollutants, and has a comprehensive air pollution regulation setting emission limits for over one hundred pollutants.[76] Other Ontario regulations restrict emissions from such specific sources as waste incinerators, iron foundries, asphalt facilities, and mobile PCB destruction facilities. Industrial operations must apply to the province for a permit that may set further limits on air pollution. There is also a regulation that exempts a wide range of air pollution sources from the other regulations.[77]

One of the most progressive air quality laws in Canada is New Brunswick's *Clean Air Act*, which is based on three ecologically progressive principles: polluter pays, pollution prevention, and the precautionary principle.[78] The *Act* provides for a significant public role in striving for cleaner air, with public notice required when pollution permits are applied for, public input into permitting decisions, and provision for members of the public to request investigations of alleged violations. Similar public participation rights exist in Ontario.[79] Nova Scotia's *Environment Act*, which regulates all forms of pollution, is also a strong provincial law. Penalties under pollution statutes are generally high, but severe cutbacks to enforcement capacity at both the federal and provincial levels make prosecutions rare.

The problems common to most provincial air pollution laws and policies include broad exemptions, incomplete coverage of contaminants, lack of distinctions based on relative level of harm (i.e., all contaminants are treated the same), and the encouragement of dilution and dispersal (e.g., through taller smokestacks) instead of pollution prevention. The terms of air pollution permits are determined in private negotiations between government and industry. Provincial air quality objectives are not legally binding and may or may not be used in setting emission limits. Monitoring and reporting requirements often vary widely. The result of this highly discretionary permitting system is uneven treatment between companies in the same industry, between different industries, and between different provinces.[80] Although progress has been made for some air pollutants, for others provincial legislation remains "sadly out of date."[81] For example, the burning of wood waste from mills in British Columbia releases high levels of particulate matter into the air of the communities where beehive burners are located. While these facilities have been prohibited in the United States for more than thirty years, they continue to harm human health in rural BC, while simultaneously wasting a potentially useful resource.[82]

Provinces also have laws and regulations addressing motor vehicle pollution. Most provinces mandate that pollution control devices, such as catalytic converters, must not be tampered with and must be maintained in good working condition. Most provinces also have legislated limits on the volatility of gasoline in order to reduce VOC emissions.[83] BC is a national leader in reducing pollution from motor vehicles with Canada's most progressive clean gasoline regulations and vehicle emission standards, modelled after those of California, the North American leader.[84]

Canada-Wide Standards for Air Pollution

Pursuant to a federal-provincial agreement to harmonize environmental laws, the Canadian Council of Ministers of the Environment has negotiated Canada-Wide Standards for several important air pollutants, including ozone and particulate matter. However, the use of the word "standards" is misleading. As the World Health Organization points out, an air quality standard is "a description of a level of air quality adopted by a regulatory authority as enforceable."[85] Because the Canada-Wide Standards are not enforceable, air pollution laws and regulations still vary widely from province to province. To add to the confusion, Quebec refused to sign the Canada-Wide Standards for particulate matter and ozone, arguing that it would independently determine its own environmental policy. The Canadian Institute for Environmental Law and Policy is highly critical of the Canada-Wide Standards because they are vague about means of implementation, have long timelines for action, reduce but do not eliminate pollution, and apply selectively to various industries.[86]

Municipal Regulation of Air Pollution

Provincial governments can empower local governments to pass air pollution bylaws. For example, BC's *Waste Management Act* allows the Greater Vancouver Regional District to address local pollution problems.[87] The Toronto Atmospheric Fund is an internationally renowned model for reducing municipal greenhouse gas emissions.[88] Municipalities can use licensing and zoning bylaws in an attempt to control air pollution. As well, by placing a priority on effective public transit systems, municipalities can contribute to reducing air pollution.

Strengths and Weaknesses of Canadian Air Pollution Laws

Canada's air pollution laws and policies have pros and cons. On the positive side, Canada is active in pursuing international agreements to reduce air pollution and has a good track record of fulfilling these commitments. Where the federal government plays a leadership role, as in eliminating lead, reducing acid rain, and requiring cleaner fuels and vehicle emissions, significant progress is possible. Environment Canada warns, however, "that we may be reaching the limits of technological fixes."[89] For example, gains achieved by lower vehicle emissions per kilometre are wiped out by growth in total kilometres travelled and consumer preferences for larger vehicles.

In terms of weaknesses, Canada's air pollution laws are inconsistent, plagued by discretion, and undermined by poor enforcement. Some important sources of air pollution fall through the cracks. Machines like airplanes, snowmobiles, chainsaws, lawnmowers, leaf blowers, weed eaters, and other gas-powered equipment are not covered by regulations. The National Ambient Air Quality Objectives and the Canada-Wide Standards share a common failing in that they "are not legally binding on politicians and bureaucrats. They merely represent targets or goals for pollution control efforts."[90] Ottawa has the power under *CEPA* to address sources of transboundary air pollution but has never used this power.[91] At the federal level, limited resources for enforcement means that only a handful of prosecutions have been pursued for violations of federal air pollution regulations.[92]

As is the case with water pollution, superior progress has been made in reducing air pollution from industrial point sources as opposed to diffuse sources, such as motor vehicles. The US EPA reports that 41 percent of air pollution is from mobile sources, 35 percent from small businesses, farms and other diffuse, nonpoint sources, and only 24 percent from large industrial sources.[93] In other words, nonpoint sources of air pollution are now the main problem. The strengths and weaknesses of Canadian air pollution laws and policies are demonstrated by the following case studies, which contrast Canada's progress on acid rain with Canada's paralysis on smog.

Acid Rain: A Case Study in Federal-Provincial Cooperation

Canadian efforts to control acid rain provide a positive example of the potential effectiveness of both international and federal-provincial cooperation. More than half of the acid rain in eastern Canada is caused by sources in the United States, which is why Canada cannot solve this problem on its own.[94] In 1985, the federal government and the provincial governments in Manitoba, Ontario, Quebec, New Brunswick, Nova Scotia, Newfoundland, and Prince Edward Island established the Eastern Canadian Acid Rain Program. The program's goal was to reduce sulphur dioxide emissions by 50 percent in the seven easternmost provinces, which was achieved by 1994.[95] The federal government contributed $150 million for pollution control technology, and the eastern provinces passed strong regulations targeting industrial sources of sulphur dioxide.[96]

Canada's strong steps and rapid progress placed pressure on the United States to make similar strides. International obligations also influenced the United States, including the *United Nations Economic Commission for Europe Convention on Long Range Transport of Air Pollution* and the 1991 *Canada-United States Air Quality Agreement*. After stalling throughout the 1980s, the United States passed amendments to the *Clean Air Act* in 1990, requiring major reductions in sulphur dioxide emissions by 2000 and even deeper cuts by 2010.[97]

Despite the encouraging progress in reducing emissions, during the 1990s only 33 percent of lakes in eastern Canada became less acidic, while 56 percent showed no improvement and 11 percent became more acidic. Scientists believe that "our current control programs for reducing Canadian and American sulphur dioxide emissions do not go far enough to protect many of our lakes and forests." To provide adequate protection for these areas, they estimate that US and Canadian emissions will have to be reduced by another 75 percent.[98] Both Canada and the United States plan further emission reductions. Eastern provinces, with the exception of Ontario, have agreed to cut sulphur dioxide emissions by 50 percent by 2010. Ontario will commit only to 50 percent cuts by 2015 unless the United States makes deeper cuts. In ongoing negotiations under the *Canada-United States Air Quality Agreement*, Canada "hopes to obtain a commitment from the U.S. for an SO_2 emission reduction of 50 percent or more."[99] Progress to date suggests that optimism about further reductions may be justified.

Smog: A Case Study in Federal and Provincial Inaction

For more than a decade, Canadian politicians have promised to tackle smog, the nation's most serious remaining air pollution problem. In the 1990 *Green Plan*, the federal government assured Canadians that "all of Canada's urban smog problems will be fully solved by 2005" with levels of smog "below the threshold of health effects."[100] That year the federal government and the provinces agreed to a joint management plan for nitrogen oxides and VOCs, the main precursors of smog. However, according to Environment Canada in 1999, "Recent studies have shown that every major Canadian urban centre has levels of ground-level ozone high enough to pose a health risk."[101] An audit by the commissioner of the environment and sustainable development concluded that the federal-provincial smog plan went "off the rails": funding was inadequate, targets were not met, the provinces failed to live up to their commitments, and the federal government relied excessively on ineffective voluntary programs.[102]

The federal and provincial governments are now belatedly moving forward on the smog front, with Ottawa's action plan *(Securing Cleaner Air for Canadians)*, new Canada-Wide Standards for Particulate Matter and Ozone, and the extension of the *Canada-United States Air Quality Agreement* to cover nitrogen oxides and VOCs. The jury is still out on whether these new programs will be more effective than their predecessors in addressing Canada's ongoing smog challenges.

Legal Protection for Clean Air in the United States

The US *Clean Air Act* was passed in 1963 and was strengthened in 1967, 1970, 1977, and 1990.[103] The *Act* requires the EPA to set standards that protect public health without regard to the costs of achieving those standards. The basic structure of the *Act* is that the federal government sets national standards and provides funding, while the states are responsible for implementation. Through the enactment and enforcement of legally binding ambient air quality standards, emission standards, and best available technology standards, American air has been significantly cleaned up. Emissions of particulate matter, sulphur dioxide, nitrogen oxides, carbon monoxide, and ozone declined by an average of 11.2 percent between 1970 and 1990.[104] The EPA estimates that over thirty years, the compliance costs of the *Act* are approximately US$500 billion, while benefits range from US$5.6 trillion to US$49.4 trillion. Annually, the *Act* prevents forty-five thousand deaths, thirteen thousand heart attacks, and seven thousand strokes.[105]

However, there is widespread, long-term noncompliance with the *Act*. Over fifty million Americans live in areas that frequently violate national standards for ozone, and an estimated sixty-four thousand premature deaths are caused annually by particulate matter.[106] Despite the *Act*, polluted air represents an estimated US$100 billion in health care costs in the United States annually. Ground-level ozone causes crop losses of US$2-3 billion and material damage of US$1 billion in the United States annually.[107] The majority of American air pollution comes from the transportation and power generation sectors. Part of the problem, as in Canada, is that "most air pollution control efforts ignore the land use component," meaning the planning and development of urban areas.[108] Experts conclude that "continuing sprawl development patterns defeat advances in motor vehicle control equipment."[109] There appears to be insufficient social and political will to pay the costs required to meet the *Act's* standards.

Conclusion

With respect to air pollution, Canada is like a runner at the halfway point of a marathon: while progress has been made, it would be premature to celebrate because the finish line remains distant. Renewed determination will be required for the more difficult kilometres that lie ahead. For a handful of high-profile substances, such as lead and sulphur dioxide, Canada has passed regulations and made substantial strides toward solving air pollution problems. Strong regulations spurred investment in better technology such as catalytic converters, improved fuel efficiency, new pollution control equipment, techniques to reduce flaring, vapour recovery systems, and cleaner burning fuels.[110] However, Canada has not yet recognized the cumulative and synergistic effects of global warming, ozone depletion, acid rain, and toxic air pollution. Taken together, these problems pose grave health and environmental threats.

Most Canadian air pollution, including most Canadian greenhouse gas emissions, is caused by the burning of fossil fuels. According to medical experts, for most of the fossil fuel-related pollutants, including ground-level ozone, smog, sulphur dioxide, nitrogen oxides, and particulate matter, "there is no safe level or threshold. That is, there is no level below which there are no adverse health outcomes."[111] These facts suggest that a key environmental priority for Canada must be finding ways to reduce our energy use and identify substitutes for fossil fuels. Clean, renewable energy sources like wind and solar power, which currently provide less than 1/10,000th of the energy consumed in Canada, must be developed.[112] Canadians must reduce kilometres travelled (through better land-use planning, urban design, or telecommuting), reduce emissions per kilometre (by adopting stricter standards for vehicle emissions, fuel content, and fuel efficiency), and switch to cleaner modes of transportation (such as rail, public transit, bicycles, and carpooling). There is reason for hope, because "Canadian governments and industry have demonstrated that they can tackle difficult problems of air pollution."[113] If Canadian governments live up to their commitments, Canada's air pollution problems should continue to diminish in the years ahead.

4 Land

> Canada is a nation built upon its natural capital.
> *World Wildlife Fund Canada, 2003*

The third area of environmental concern after air and water involves a broad range of issues affecting the land. Canada is the second-largest nation in the world after Russia, covering a land area of almost ten million square kilometres. With this prodigious size comes an incredible wealth of natural resources and a unique global responsibility. Canada has 10 percent of the world's forests, 25 percent of the world's wetlands, 20 percent of the world's fresh water, and 20 percent of the world's remaining wilderness.[1] This natural legacy is shared by only thirty-one million people (0.5 percent of the world's population), who live primarily in urban regions in a narrow band along the southern border of the nation.

Although Canada is sparsely populated, Canadians place heavy demands on the land. We are among the world's heaviest per. capita consumers of energy and water. In addition to consuming large amounts of domestic resources, Canada is the world's largest exporter of wood products, the world's largest producer of hydroelectricity, an exporter of large volumes of agricultural products, and one of the world's largest exporters of uranium, zinc, potash, aluminum, gold, lead, copper, gypsum, molybdenum, platinum, cadmium, titanium, asbestos, and other minerals and mineral products.[2]

Distinct law and policy regimes govern forestry, mining, land-use planning, oil and gas exploration and development, urban sprawl, waste management, agriculture, and development in the northern territories.[3] This book addresses a subset of the wide spectrum of environmental issues related to land and resources, focusing on the laws and policies that govern pesticide use, forest management, and environmental assessment. These three subjects cover some of the most contentious land-use debates in Canada. In recent years, each of these issues has been the focus of many new legal developments including both legislation and litigation.

Pesticide Regulation

The technological advances of the green revolution have produced dramatic increases in agricultural production. However, these gains have not come without environmental costs.[4] Industrial agriculture can cause far-reaching and long-lasting environmental damage through pesticide contamination, soil erosion, falling water tables, salinization, eutrophication, surface and groundwater contamination from fertilizers and manure, and the uncertain impacts of genetically modified organisms.[5] Regulating the environmental impacts of agriculture poses challenges for governments in Canada because farming takes place predominantly on privately owned land. Any regulations must be justified on the grounds that public health or environmental values are jeopardized or affected by agricultural activities. As a result, when grappling with environmental problems caused by agriculture Canada has generally avoided regulatory standards, preferring to use voluntary programs.[6]

Pesticides are an important exception because they pose a threat to human and environmental health. Accordingly, these chemicals are regulated by all levels of government in Canada: federal, provincial, and municipal. Governments claim that all pesticides approved for use in Canada are safe, and that Canada is an international leader in pesticide regulation. Are these claims accurate? Do Canadian laws governing pesticide use adequately protect Canadians' health and the environment?

Forest Management

Canada is internationally renowned as a forest superpower, for both environmental and economic reasons.[7] On the environmental side, Canada is home to 10 percent of the world's forests and more than one-quarter of the world's remaining primary or intact forests. Primary forests, meaning forests that have not been commercially logged, are of "critical importance" to the conservation of biodiversity.[8] Canada is also home to one-third of the world's boreal forest and one-quarter of the remaining coastal temperate rainforest. Although tropical rainforests receive more public attention, temperate rainforests (including those in British Columbia) are among the world's rarest forests, covering only 0.2 percent of the Earth's surface.[9] About two-thirds of Canada's 140,000 species of plants and animals rely on forests for habitat.[10] Most importantly, many ecological processes that occur in forests, such as the water cycle, the carbon cycle, and the nutrient cycle, are vital to making the Earth habitable for humans and other species. These complex interactions produce clean air and clean water, and moderate regional and global climates.

On the economic side, Canada is the world's largest exporter of forest products, ranking first in the world in newsprint (25 percent of global trade), second in softwood lumber (21 percent), and second in pulp (16 percent).[11] Forestry is described by those in the industry as Canada's "economic engine" and the "backbone" of Canada's economy.[12] In 2000 the forest industry contributed $20.8 billion to Canada's GDP. Over 370,000 Canadians are directly employed in the forest industry, while over three hundred Canadian communities depend largely on forestry.[13]

Forest management is the subject of an ongoing and highly charged debate in Canada. Environmental groups portray industrial logging as "disturbingly reminiscent of the cod fishery," because too many trees are cut too fast, with sloppy logging practices that threaten the biodiversity and ecological processes dependent on healthy forest ecosystems.[14] Government and industry claim that Canada is a world leader in sustainable forest management. All participants in the debate over forestry in Canada would probably agree that extensive changes have been made in the past decade to laws, regulations, and policies governing the use of Canadian forests. The hotly contested question is whether these regulatory changes have successfully transformed the forest industry in Canada into a model of sustainability, or whether the changes are more cosmetic than substantive.

Environmental Assessment

Environmental assessment laws are intended to place environmental protection on a level playing field with economic growth, producing the win-win outcome known as sustainable development. In theory, all proposed actions, both public and private, with the potential for significant environmental impacts should be subjected to this evaluative planning process in order to optimize decision making. While not an issue with high public prominence, environmental assessment has a surprisingly colourful and controversial history in Canada. The environmental assessment process prescribed by Canadian laws has been described as totalitarian, a boondoggle, a hoax, a paper tiger, a Trojan horse, and a nasty game. A seemingly straightforward planning process has evolved into a lightning rod for criticism, litigation, and debate about the nature of progress in the twenty-first century.

Legally binding environmental assessment processes are in force federally and in all provinces. Thousands of environmental assessments are conducted annually in Canada pursuant to these laws, but proposed projects are rarely turned down. Does the fact that 99.9 percent of the projects subject to environmental assessment are approved indicate that few environmentally harmful activities are ever proposed in Canada, or that environmental assessment is failing to stop projects that cause environmental degradation? Are Canada's environmental assessment laws and policies achieving an appropriate balance between economic and environmental considerations?

Canada is blessed by extraordinary natural wealth. Canadian governments and industry claim that Canada is a world leader in regulating pesticide use, sustainable forest management, and environmental assessment. Are these claims substantiated, either on paper, or more importantly, on the ground? Do Canadian laws governing pesticides, forests, and environmental assessment ensure that Canada's lands and resources are being managed in a sustainable manner?

> Pesticide residues can be found in the bodies of
> virtually all Canadians.
>
> *Dr. Kay Teschke, University of British Columbia,*
> *and Dr. Joe Thornton, University of Oregon*

> That Inuit mothers – far from the areas where
> Persistent Organic Pollutants are manufactured and
> used – have to think twice before breast-feeding their
> infants is surely a wakeup call to the world.
>
> *Sheila Watt-Cloutier, President, Inuit Circumpolar Conference*

Pesticides (including herbicides, insecticides, and fungicides) are chemicals intended for killing or controlling weeds, insects, fungi, rodents, and other plants or animals that are considered to be pests. Public concern about the health and environmental impacts of pesticides was galvanized by Rachel Carson's classic book *Silent Spring*, published in 1962. Today pesticides continue to arouse considerable anxiety among Canadians. A public opinion poll found that 70 percent of Canadians believe pesticides in food pose a high or moderate risk to their health.[1] Another poll found that 89 percent of Canadians support cutting pesticide use in half, even if it would result in less aesthetically pleasing and more costly fruits and vegetables.[2]

The main concerns about the use of pesticides include contamination of food, air, and water; threats to human health, particularly to children, farmers, and farm workers; and harm to wildlife, including fish, birds, and beneficial insects. Public anxiety about these problems is increased by the secretive nature of the pesticide industry, the government's reluctance to share information, and the fact that the studies upon which pesticide approvals are based are conducted by the companies themselves, suggesting a conflict of interest. In addition to health and environmental worries, another major concern is that pests develop resistance to pesticides, just as human pathogens develop resistance to antibiotics. There are now at least 500 insect pests, 270 weed species, and 150 plant diseases that are resistant to one or more pesticides. To make matters worse, many pesticides kill organisms that naturally control pest populations, leading farmers to rely more heavily on pesticides, and further exacerbating resistance problems.[3]

The federal government asserts that "a pesticide is accepted for use in Canada only if any human and environmental risks associated with the use of the product are acceptable."[4] The government of New Brunswick makes a similar claim, stating that "any pesticide used in Canada has passed an extensive health and environmental evaluation with wide safety margins."[5] Despite the government's confidence in its regulatory regime, comprehensive critiques of Canadian pesticide regulation have been published by the Law Reform Commission of Canada, the Standing Committee on Environment and Sustainable Development, the federal commissioner on the environment and sustainable development, and many academics.[6] The Canadian Environmental Law Association and the Ontario College of Family Physicians argue that "the health of Canadian children is at risk because of the inherent weaknesses of the Canadian regulatory system governing pesticides and the lack of capacity to implement existing laws and policies."[7] Critics describe the Pest Management Regulatory Agency as "a customer service department for the pesticides industry."[8] In 2002 the federal government responded to these concerns by overhauling the *Pest Control Products Act*.

The Use of Pesticides in Canada

Over seven thousand pesticide products containing 500 active ingredients are registered in Canada. Many of the pesticides in use today were approved decades ago. As the commissioner of the environment and sustainable development pointed out in 1999, "Of the 500 active ingredients contained in registered pesticides, over 300 were approved before 1981 and over 150 before 1960. Many pesticides were approved when the standards were much less stringent than they are today."[9] At least sixty pesticides approved for use in Canada, such as 2,4-D, lindane, atrazine, and carbofuran, have been banned by other countries (including Sweden, Finland, Denmark, the Netherlands, the UK, and the United States) because of health and environmental concerns.[10]

Agriculture accounts for approximately 90 percent of pesticide use in Canada, with domestic, garden, forestry, and industrial uses comprising the remaining 10 percent. Canadian pesticide sales in 1997 were estimated at $1.4 billion.[11] According to Statistics Canada, expenditures on agricultural pesticides rose 411.3 percent between 1970 and 1995. The area treated with herbicides in 1995 was 18 times larger than the area treated with herbicides in 1970, while the area treated with insecticides grew by 3.5 times during the same period. About three-quarters of croplands now receive treatment with pesticides.[12] Studies by Agriculture Canada report that a majority of farmers do not follow recommended practices for applying pesticides.[13] Depending on the method of application, as little as 1 percent of a pesticide will reach the intended target. As well, large amounts of pesticides are wasted because they are applied either before pests and diseases appear or to areas where pests and diseases are absent.[14]

In Ontario the most heavily used pesticide is metolachlor. Roughly 1.3 million kilograms of metolachlor was applied to Ontario crops, mainly soybeans, in 1998.[15] Little information on metolachlor is available from Canada's Pest Management Regulatory Agency (PMRA) or the Ontario Ministry of Agriculture, Food and Rural Affairs. In contrast, the US EPA provides the American public with extensive data on metolachlor and other pesticides. The EPA classifies metolachlor as a possible human carcinogen, highly toxic to fish, moderately persistent to persistent in soil, mobile to highly mobile in the environment, a threat to groundwater, and a suspected endocrine disruptor.[16]

Pesticide residues are frequently found in surface and ground water in Canada, in some cases exceeding recommended standards for drinking water.[17] However, for most Canadians the majority of pesticide exposure (80 to 95 percent) comes from consuming food.[18] Pesticide residues on fresh fruit and vegetables grown in Canada doubled between 1994 and 1998 while the percentage of domestic produce samples exceeding the maximum residue limits tripled during the same period. A remarkable 50 to 70 percent of the produce samples exceeding the maximum residue limits involved pesticides not approved for that particular crop.[19] The Canadian Food Inspection Agency claims that only 20 percent of the fruit and vegetable samples it tests have detectable pesticide residues, but this claim is dubious, given that the US EPA finds pesticide residues on 67 percent of produce samples.[20]

The Health Impacts of Pesticides

The health impacts of pesticides can be divided into two main categories: acute effects and chronic effects. Acute effects occur after heavy exposure and are well documented. Chronic effects develop in response to lower levels of exposure over longer periods of time. Because so many potential factors are involved, it is more challenging to conclusively prove a cause-and-effect relationship between pesticides and chronic health impacts.

The World Health Organization estimates there are about three million cases of acute pesticide poisoning in the world each year, largely in developing countries.[21] Statistics are not available in Canada, but in the United States, between ten thousand and twenty thousand physician-diagnosed injuries and illnesses are ascribed to pesticides annually.[22] Many of the people harmed by pesticides are farmers, farm workers, and children. According to the Canadian Association of Physicians for the Environment, presently acceptable levels of aldicarb on watermelons are such that a small child could easily consume enough of the pesticide to experience acute toxicity, including vomiting, seizures, and respiratory failure.[23]

In the past, the chronic effects of exposure were overlooked. There is still considerable uncertainty about the effects of recurrent exposure to low levels; cumulative, interactive, and long-term effects; effects on reproduction; and differential sensitivity according to factors such as people's age, gender, and size.[24] However, peer-reviewed medical and scientific studies have established links between pesticide exposure and various forms of cancer, birth defects, developmental abnormalities, neurological effects, reproductive effects, lung damage, and decreased immune function.[25] It is vital to understand that although pesticide residues in food and water occur at levels measured in parts per million or parts per billion, these very low levels may still be dangerous to human health and the environment.[26]

Scientific evidence is accumulating that some pesticides are among the chemicals that disrupt endocrine systems.[27] By mimicking hormones, endocrine-disrupting chemicals may harm the reproductive system, suppress the immune system, and impair normal development of intelligence. The damage may not be evident until years or even decades after exposure, posing a huge challenge to scientists and medical researchers. According to the Standing Committee on Environment and Sustainable Development, about 60 percent of the agricultural pesticides applied in Canada are known or suspected endocrine disruptors.[28]

Certain groups of Canadians are particularly vulnerable to health impacts from pesticides. Studies conducted by Health Canada indicate that farmers using pesticides may suffer from increased rates of fetal loss and an inability to conceive.[29] Inuit women in Canada's north suffer from high concentrations of pesticides in their breast milk, because persistent pesticides travel long distances to accumulate in the food chain and contaminate the Inuit's traditional food supply.[30] Infants and children are at greater risk from pesticides than are adults, particularly their neurological, behavioural, immune, hormonal, and reproductive systems. Infants and children ingest more pesticides relative to their body weight as they are exposed to pesticides at home, in public places, and through air, water, food, and behaviours such as eating dirt and putting hands in their mouths.[31]

The Environmental Impacts of Pesticides

Pesticides can have a devastating impact on wildlife and ecosystems. They can kill fish, birds, and other animals, contaminate aquatic ecosystems, and harm insects and invertebrates that perform valuable ecological services like pollination and natural pest control.[32] Residues from some widely used pesticides build up in the food chain through the processes of bioaccumulation and biomagnification. Recent studies link the agricultural pesticide atrazine, which is widely used in Canada, to sexual deformities in frogs.[33]

At least thirty pesticides registered for use in Canada are known to kill wild birds and mammals even when used as instructed.[34] Pesticides have been linked to major bird kills from BC to New Brunswick, reduced populations of Atlantic salmon, and fish kills in Prince Edward Island.[35] Studies by the Canadian Wildlife Service confirm that when the pesticide carbofuran is used by farmers, "kills of songbirds, small mammals, reptiles, and amphibians are common and unavoidable." In trials conducted by the manufacturer, carbofuran killed forty-five bird species.[36] Agriculture and Agri-Food Canada admits that "carbofuran has one of the highest recorded toxicities to birds of any insecticide registered for use in Canada."[37] While some uses of carbofuran were recently discontinued after years of pressure from environmental groups and wildlife biologists, other uses are still allowed in Canada.[38]

Many aquatic ecosystems in Canada suffer from pesticide contamination. A federal study of the Chibouet River in Quebec (a tributary of the St. Lawrence) found that between 1992 and 1998, concentrations of atrazine exceeded guidelines for the protection of aquatic life in 16 to 50 percent of the samples. Residues from seventeen other pesticides were found in the Chibouet River. The concerns raised by these results are magnified by "the possibility of still-unknown additive or synergistic effects on aquatic life." Other studies found 24 percent of small wetlands in Saskatchewan polluted by pesticides in excess of guidelines for protecting aquatic life, while 44 percent of Alberta streams and 51 percent of Alberta lakes contained pesticide residues (although within water quality guidelines for drinking water).[39] As well, while Canada has banned a handful of the most environmentally destructive pesticides, such as DDT, they remain in use in developing countries. More than half of the developing nations lack pesticide legislation.[40] Canada's arctic ecosystems and national parks in the Rocky Mountains continue to be contaminated by residues from the use of these pesticides thousands of kilometres to the south.[41]

Many questions about the ecological impacts of pesticides remain unanswered, because the required research has never been done. A major study conducted by the Canadian Wildlife Service found gaps in basic knowledge, a lack of research on subtle and long-term effects, and insufficient toxicological information.[42] Another government report states that "the bulk (about 70 percent) of pesticides used in Canada are herbicides, and there is almost no knowledge of their impact on potential non-target plant species, especially rare or endemic species."[43]

Alternatives to Pesticides

The main alternatives to pesticide use are organic agriculture, which uses no synthetic pesticides, and integrated pest management, which minimizes pesticide use.[44] Another possible means of reducing pesticide use is through bio-engineering resistance into plants, although there are widespread concerns about genetically modified organisms, particularly in relation to the food supply. Organic production in Canada is growing at 20 percent per year despite minimal government support.[45] Nevertheless, organic agriculture still comprises a tiny fraction of total agricultural production. In British Columbia, for example, the total area in organic production tripled between 1997 and 1999 but still covers only 0.5 percent of the agricultural land in the province.[46] Other nations are promoting organic farming much more aggressively: Austria has a goal of 20 percent organic production, while Denmark aims to triple organic production to 10 percent by 2003.[47] The main concerns about organic produce, which are hotly debated, are that yields will fall and food will become more expensive, potentially harming the diets of lower-income people.

Integrated pest management (IPM) is a strategy that emphasizes keeping fields and orchards healthy, monitoring carefully for signs of insects and disease, nurturing beneficial organisms, and avoiding pesticide use. More specifically, IPM combines biological pest control (introducing natural enemies or diseases of pest), cultural pest control (e.g., patterns of planting), genetic pest control (using pest-resistant varieties), and, as a last resort, chemical pest control (using the lowest quantity and toxicity possible).[48] A key element of IPM is the goal of reducing pesticide use. IPM offers long-term benefits such as less severe infestations and avoiding resistance problems caused by over-reliance on pesticides. US studies prove that IPM can lower costs while maintaining, and even improving, crop yield and quality. A program to reduce pesticide use on nine major crops in a fifteen-state area yielded a net increase of US$578 million to farmers.[49]

Only 2 percent of Canadian farmers use biological pest control methods.[50] Barriers to the implementation of IPM in Canada include powerful political and economic support for the status quo and resistance from farmers who are familiar with traditional pesticides and have invested heavily in machinery for applying them. IPM is more complex and labour intensive than chemical pest management, which does not require any understanding of ecosystems, ecological processes, or interactions between species.[51] Another obstacle is that "IPM strategies are intangible and not amenable to marketing, making them unattractive to private industry," whereas selling pesticides is a lucrative business.[52]

Laws and Policies Governing the Use of Pesticides in Canada

International Law

International law plays a modest but growing role in regulating pesticide use in Canada. Canada was the first nation to ratify the *Stockholm Convention on Persistent Organic Pollutants*, which bans a dozen toxic substances, including a handful of notorious pesticides.[53] If and when more pesticides are added to the list of banned substances under the *Stockholm Convention*, Canada will have to adjust its domestic laws and regulations to eliminate their use.

NAFTA also influences pesticide regulation in three ways: because the United States is the main export market for agricultural products from both Canada and Mexico; through the trilateral effort to harmonize pesticide laws and regulations; and because of corporate lawsuits under NAFTA's Chapter 11. The United States passed stringent pesticide legislation in 1996 called the *Food Quality Protection Act*. Regulatory changes under this *Act* could force Canada to make significant changes to laws and regulations governing pesticides in order to maintain access to American markets. A technical working group established pursuant to NAFTA is attempting to standardize pesticide regulations among Canada, the United States, and Mexico in order to facilitate free trade in agricultural products.

With respect to Chapter 11 of NAFTA, an American pesticide corporation, Crompton Co., is pursuing a claim for US$100 million in compensation based on Canada's decision to phase out some uses of lindane. In an earlier lawsuit using the Canadian court system, Crompton had failed to overturn the decision to phase out some lindane uses.[54] Lindane is a low-cost agricultural pesticide that was widely used in more than two dozen registered products in Canada. It is also a persistent organic pollutant, "acutely and chronically toxic to humans," a possible human carcinogen, and a neurotoxin with adverse impacts on reproduction, the immune system, and the liver. Until recently Canada was the sixth-largest user of lindane in the world.[55] However, if Crompton wins its Chapter 11 case under NAFTA, Canadian governments may be reluctant to ban pesticides in the future.

Federal Regulation of Pesticides

The main federal laws governing the use of pesticides in Canada are the *Pest Control Products Act (PCPA)* and the *Food and Drug Act*.[56] The *PCPA* was enacted in 1939, revised in 1969, and completely rewritten in 2002 after heavy criticism for failing to keep up with advances in scientific and medical knowledge. The new *PCPA* creates a modern system for the evaluation, registration, labelling, import, and export of pesticides. In essence, pesticides cannot be imported or sold in Canada unless they are registered and properly labelled. Pesticides are regulated by the PMRA, a government body that was moved from Agriculture Canada to Health Canada in 1995. The *Food and Drug Act* sets standards for pesticide residues in food.[57] The Canadian Food Inspection Agency is responsible for monitoring and testing food to ensure that pesticide residues are within legal limits.

Experts in environmental law confirm that the old *PCPA* lagged far behind legislation regulating other toxic chemicals.[58] The *PCPA* and its regulations were criticized for not considering multiple sources of exposure, total exposure, or cumulative effects; not assessing formulants (chemicals mixed with the active ingredients); not considering impacts on vulnerable groups, particularly infants and children; not requiring regular review and reevaluation or postregistration monitoring; not providing opportunities for public involvement; lacking a national compliance strategy; not requiring companies to report the results of new research indicating adverse effects; not including pesticide reduction as a goal; and not requiring the availability of less harmful substitutes to be considered in registration decisions. Professors Kathryn Harrison and George Hoberg add that in comparison to those of the United States, Canadian decisions about pesticides have been less clearly documented, rely on inconsistent standards of proof, and fail to "reflect contemporary understanding of the mechanisms of carcinogenesis."[59]

The old *PCPA*'s discretionary reevaluation system caused Canada to fall far behind other countries with major agriculture industries like the United States, UK, and Australia in reevaluating pesticides.[60] Reevaluation is vital because long-term toxic effects have been discovered for many pesticides once believed safe.[61] In 1986, Agriculture Canada promised to reevaluate 452 active ingredients of pesticides that were approved between 1926 and 1985.[62] This promise was never fulfilled. Canada's PMRA is finally beginning to reevaluate controversial pesticides, although budget shortfalls and a lack of political will have slowed the process. Seven pesticides have been voluntarily discontinued by pesticide companies to avoid regulatory action by the PMRA.[63] The new *PCPA* requires mandatory reevaluations at regular intervals – a great leap forward.

Another major criticism of regulation in Canada under the old *PCPA* involved lack of transparency, and the concomitant difficulty in obtaining information about pesticide use and risks. For example, the PMRA denied a request from the Inuit for copies of studies about the health impacts and risks of lindane, despite scientific studies showing that the Inuit were carrying disproportionately high levels of lindane in their body tissues. The PMRA claimed that it was precluded from disclosing pesticide data because the data are confidential business information.[64] The PMRA's claim overlooks the fact that while Canada's *Access to Information Act* protects confidential business information, it specifically excepts information about "public health, public safety, and the protection of the environment."[65] A government report suggested that the PMRA's refusal to release information about health impacts is legally incorrect.[66] Among the countries of the OECD, only Canada and the Slovak Republic do not routinely collect and publish information on pesticide sales.[67]

The veil of secrecy around pesticide information has been so tight that the PMRA refused to share information even with other federal agencies such as Environment Canada and the Department of Fisheries and Oceans.[68] As the Standing Committee on Environment and Sustainable Development noted in response to testimony from an emergency room physician who experienced difficulties in obtaining information required to treat children poisoned by pesticides, "It is essential that health care professionals have access to detailed toxicological information to be able to detect and treat cases of pesticide poisoning."[69] Ironically, much of the information that the PMRA refuses to disclose to Canadians is publicly available in the United States through the EPA.[70] The new *PCPA* provides much greater access to information about pesticides through the creation of a public registry.

Another source of concern is that most of the information relied upon by the PMRA comes from pesticide companies. This is like relying on the tobacco industry to provide data on the health risks of smoking.[71] Experts warn that "there is evidence that the assessments of pesticides and other chemicals have been seriously flawed" and in some cases even fraudulent.[72] Independent science and research is lacking. The PMRA also depends on fees from pesticide registrations for 30 percent of its budget, creating a perverse incentive to maintain or increase reliance on pesticides. Registration fees for new pesticides are much higher in Canada than in other industrialized nations, which may act as a disincentive to companies seeking registration for safer products.[73] The revised *PCPA* moves in the right direction by obligating companies to report evidence of the adverse effects of their pesticides.

The PMRA has no strategy to reduce the health and environmental risks of pesticide use. The commissioner of the environment and sustainable development points out that "the absence of a risk reduction strategy is striking in comparison with other countries."[74] The UK implemented such a strategy in 1985, and Sweden's program began in 1986. The PMRA established an alternative agriculture program focusing on IPM, but spends only 4 percent of its budget in this area.[75] The commissioner of the environment and sustainable development concluded in 1999 that the PMRA's IPM programs "lack focus and clear goals and are largely reactive" while the Canadian Environmental Law Association found that these programs "merely tinker with the status quo."[76]

There are also concerns about the enforcement of pesticide laws.[77] The federal government employs only forty-four officers across Canada to inspect farms, food processing plants, retail outlets, lawn care companies, exterminators, and other businesses that sell or use pesticides.[78] The maximum penalties in the old *PCPA* were far below the penalties provided in other environmental protection statutes such as the *Fisheries Act* and *Canadian Environmental Protection Act, 1999*. The new *PCPA*, with fines up to $1 million, is consistent with other federal environmental legislation.

In other areas of federal law and policy, pesticides received preferential treatment. For example, pesticides are exempt from the GST and exempt from Canada's National Pollutant Release Inventory.[79] Until the *PCPA* was revised in 2002, pesticides were also exempt from the federal *Hazardous Products Act*, which provides workers with information about the toxic substances that they encounter in the workplace. A report prepared for the Canadian Labour Congress concluded, "Workers and the public should have the same rights to know about pesticides as they have for other types of hazardous materials."[80] Information on pesticides must now be provided to workers who use them.

The federal government was aware of the weaknesses of the *PCPA* for many years but failed to act despite a report by the Law Reform Commission of Canada, public hearings, an interdepartmental review process, and extensive concerns about unjustifiable health and environmental impacts.[81] The commissioner of the environment and sustainable development described the government's track record on pesticides as full of "inaction and unfulfilled commitments."[82]

In 2002 Parliament passed a new and improved *Pest Control Products Act* that addresses most, but not all, of the weaknesses in the current law.[83] The new *PCPA* incorporates many of the recommendations made by critics of the old legislation and responds to public concerns in three key areas: prioritizing health and the environment, applying the precautionary principle, and facilitating public participation.[84] In addition to the improvements mentioned earlier, the public has new rights to appeal decisions, a precautionary approach to registration is required, protecting health is enshrined as the top priority, vulnerable populations like children and pregnant women receive special consideration, multiple pathways of exposure and cumulative effects will be considered, safe new pest control products can be fast-tracked, and pesticides banned in other OECD countries must undergo mandatory reevaluation.[85] Unfortunately, the new law fails to require the substitution of safer products for more harmful products, emphasize pollution prevention, establish specific targets or timelines for reducing pesticide use, ban cosmetic and nonessential uses of pesticides, make the precautionary principle govern all decisions, or emphasize IPM. While the new *PCPA* is a major improvement on paper, it remains to be seen whether its implementation will reduce the risks from pesticides in Canada.

The Provincial Role in Pesticide Regulation

All provinces have laws governing the sale, use, transportation, storage, and disposal of pesticides, as well as emergencies such as spills.[86] Detailed provisions are set out in regulations.[87] These provincial laws and regulations cover the use of pesticides in agriculture, forestry, commercial, and domestic applications. Sellers and users are generally required to obtain certificates and permits, which in some provinces involves mandatory education and training. However, many provinces, namely Alberta, British Columbia, Saskatchewan, Manitoba, New Brunswick, and Nova Scotia, exempt farmers from the rules governing pesticide use.[88] This is a major weakness given that 90 percent of Canadian pesticide use occurs in agriculture. Quebec, Ontario, Prince Edward Island, and Newfoundland and Labrador require farmers to become certified, and then exempt them from requiring permits to apply pesticides.

In general, provincial pesticide laws and regulations provide little additional protection for health and the environment beyond what is already provided by federal registration and labelling requirements. For example, prior to a major revision in 2002, Quebec's pesticide regulations were described by Professor Lorne Giroux as a "sophisticated system of exceptions, exemptions, and exclusions."[89] The same criticism applies to most of the other provinces and territories. Ontario is the only province that requires pesticides to be registered provincially, with a screening process like the federal government's.

In typical Canadian environmental law fashion, almost all provinces prohibit the application of pesticides in and around bodies of water, but the prohibition does not apply if a permit has been issued.[90] Laws prohibit pesticides from being used in a manner that causes an adverse effect, unless those adverse effects are expected.[91] In other words, if a pesticide is expected to kill birds, and birds die because of the application of the pesticide, no offence occurs. Most provincial statutes allow individual pesticides to be banned, but these provisions are rarely, if ever, used.[92] Finally, the maximum penalty provisions in provincial pesticide legislation vary dramatically, and in some provinces are extremely low. In Quebec, the maximum fine under the *Pesticide Control Act* is $60,000, while in Ontario, the maximum fine under the *Pesticides Act* is $10 million. In Saskatchewan, Manitoba, and PEI, the maximum fine is $1,000.

Provincial laws and regulations do have some strengths. Quebec's new *Pesticide Management Code* bans twenty-eight pesticides, prohibits the use of most pesticides on public and municipal green spaces, and plans to extend the ban to all private and commercial green space within three years. Nova Scotia and Quebec have provisions in their legislation referring to the importance of developing alternatives to pesticides.[93] Alberta has a provision that can be used to force an applicant for a licence to justify relying on pesticides if the government is aware of alternative pest control methods.[94] Unlike the federal regime, some provincial laws offer an opportunity for the public to become involved in pesticide decisions. For example, under BC's *Pesticide Control Act,* individuals can appeal any decision made under the *Act* to the province's Environmental Appeal Board. These provisions have been used extensively and have resulted in the cancellation of some pesticide permits and the imposition of additional restrictions on other permits.[95]

To their credit, some provinces have successfully used nonlegislated policies to reduce pesticide use and encourage IPM. In 1988 Ontario introduced a comprehensive program called Food Systems 2002, with goals of reducing pesticide use 50 percent by 2002, and saving over $100 million per year in chemical costs.[96] The program relied on a government-supported IPM program, investment in research and development of nonchemical approaches, education of farmers, and biotechnology advances in pest-resistant crop varieties. An Ontario survey indicated that the quantity of pesticides used in some agricultural applications fell 40 percent between 1980 and 1998, from 8.7 million kilograms to 5.2 million kilograms.[97] British Columbia also has a plan to reduce pesticide use 25 percent by using IPM.[98]

The Municipal Role in Pesticide Regulation
Until quite recently, there was uncertainty about the ability of local govern-

ments to regulate pesticide use.[99] This uncertainty was swept away by the Supreme Court of Canada in 2001 in a case involving the town of Hudson, Quebec.[100] Hudson's municipal government passed a bylaw prohibiting the use of pesticides for nonessential purposes. Pesticide companies challenged the bylaw, arguing that regulating pesticides was the responsibility of provincial and federal, not local, governments. The Supreme Court unanimously upheld the validity of the municipal bylaw, concluding that all levels of government, including municipalities, have important roles to play in environmental protection. The Court repeated the Brundtland Commission's exhortation that "local governments should be empowered to exceed, but not to lower, national norms" for environmental protection.[101]

The Supreme Court's rationale was that municipal governments are best positioned to respond to specific geographic conditions and local concerns. While municipalities, including Toronto and Halifax, can exercise only those powers delegated to them by the provinces, all provincial and territorial legislation allows municipalities to make bylaws for the general health and welfare of their citizens.[102] Quebec and Nova Scotia now have provincial legislation that explicitly authorizes municipalities to enact bylaws addressing local concerns about pesticides.[103]

The Supreme Court's decision has broad ramifications. Many Canadian municipalities, including Toronto and Halifax, have passed or are considering pesticide bylaws similar to Hudson's. There are at least thirty-seven such municipalities in Quebec alone.[104] Most of these bylaws target nonessential or cosmetic uses of pesticides, with exemptions common for agricultural activity and emergencies. Municipal pesticide bylaws often require public notice when spraying occurs, and warning signs in areas that have been treated. Victoria, Toronto, and Halifax have aggressively implemented IPM strategies and achieved reductions in pesticide use of greater than 95 percent.[105]

Another key element of the Hudson decision is that the Supreme Court explicitly endorsed the application of the precautionary principle. The Court relied upon the formulation of the precautionary principle from the *Bergen Ministerial Declaration on Sustainable Development*:

> Where there are threats of serious or irreversible damage, lack of full scientific certainty should not be used as a reason for postponing measures to prevent environmental degradation.[106]

According to several prominent environmental lawyers, the Hudson decision could have a profound impact on environmental law in Canada. In addition to incorporating the precautionary principle into Canadian law, the Hudson decision authorizes municipal governments to play a greater role in environmental regulation in the years ahead.[107]

The Regulation of Pesticides in the United States

Until Canada amended the *Pest Control Products Act* in 2002, the United States had much stricter laws governing pesticides than Canada. For many years the main laws in the United States were the *Federal Insecticide, Fungicide and Rodenticide Act* and the *Federal Food, Drug and Cosmetic Act*. Then in 1996 the United States passed the *Food Quality Protection Act (FQPA)* to strengthen laws governing pesticide use. The *FQPA* was enacted in response to a major scientific study by the National Research Council that concluded the previous regulatory scheme was placing infants and children at risk from pesticides.[108] The *FQPA* requires the EPA to assess aggregate exposure to pesticides from all sources, consider cumulative effects, provide an additional safety margin to protect infants and children, conduct an assessment of potential endocrine disruptors, increase public access to information, and reevaluate pesticides on an accelerated basis.[109] According to an independent watchdog, about one-third of the dietary risk posed by pesticides in the United States was eliminated in the first five years of the *Act's* operation.[110]

The United States is required to regularly reevaluate the safety of pesticides in use, whereas in Canada reevaluation was, until 2002, at the minister's discretion.[111] The result of the difference is that pesticides were consistently reevaluated in the United States and rarely reevaluated in Canada.[112] Legislation in the United States also requires manufacturers to inform the government when subsequent research or events reveal problems or adverse effects associated with a particular pesticide. Before 2002, Canada's *PCPA* had no similar requirement. The US EPA's Office of Pesticide Programs has a clear legislative mandate to put health and the environment first. The health-first approach was copied by Canada in the 2002 amendments to the *PCPA*, whereas previously Canada's PMRA attempted to balance economic and environmental priorities.[113]

Despite stronger US laws, agricultural pesticide use in the United States rose to 940 million pounds in 2000 from 900 million pounds in 1992. The General Accounting Office concludes that the American government efforts to promote IPM have demonstrated a lack of leadership, coordination, and management. The riskiest pesticides, as determined by the EPA, still account for more than 40 percent of total pesticide use in the United States.[114] Ironically, while insecticide use in the United States increased tenfold between 1945 and 1989, the proportion of crop losses caused by insects nearly doubled from 7 percent to 13 percent.[115]

As noted earlier, there are ten thousand to twenty thousand cases of pesticide poisoning annually in the United States, with between 2 percent and 5 percent of all poisoning deaths caused by pesticides.[116] In the United States, 67 percent of fresh fruits and vegetables sampled by the EPA contain residue from at least one pesticide, while 40 percent have multiple pesticide residues.[117]

Pesticide residues are also found in 49 percent of US milk supplies.[118] American corporations continue to export pesticides that are no longer legal for use in the United States to developing countries.[119]

International Leaders in Pesticide Regulation

Internationally, Denmark, Sweden, and the Netherlands are renowned as leaders in reducing risk from pesticides. These European nations have formulated national reduction strategies; imposed taxes on pesticides; established requirements that pesticides be sprayed only where there is an observed need; prohibited use in sensitive areas (e.g., near lakes); created mandatory education programs for users; provided economic support for organic agriculture; funded research on IPM; reevaluated pesticides registered years ago; and eliminated dozens of the most dangerous pesticides.[120] These strategies have been strikingly successful, with reductions in pesticide use ranging from 50 to 80 percent since the early 1990s.[121]

Denmark's Pesticides Action Program aimed at eliminating the use of the most dangerous 50 percent of active ingredients and reducing use of remaining pesticides by 50 percent. Swedish law incorporates a concept known as the substitution principle, which mandates prohibiting products when less hazardous substitutes are approved.[122] Sweden is striving to eliminate pesticides with "unacceptable characteristics," such as persistence, volatility, high acute toxicity, endocrine disruption, neurotoxicity, and carcinogenicity.[123] The decline in pesticide use has increased the economic health of the agricultural sectors in these European countries.[124] These policies offer successful models for Canada to emulate.

Conclusion

Clearly, Canadian pesticide laws and policies are less successful than those of the United States and Europe. Countries like Sweden, by aggressively promoting IPM and organic agriculture, have decreased pesticide use by up to 80 percent over the course of two decades, whereas use continues to rise in Canada.[125] The risks to human health and the environment are difficult to justify, given the availability of affordable, ecologically sound alternatives.[126] The federal government's amendments to the *Pest Control Products Act* and Quebec's new *Pesticide Management Code* are major steps in the right direction. However, Canada needs a consistent national approach to reducing the quantity and toxicity of pesticides used, and to eliminating those that are acutely toxic, persistent, volatile, endocrine disruptive, neurotoxic, and carcinogenic. As critics note, "The federal government's stated commitment to the well-being of Canadian children is hollow if it does not address the undeniable risks of current levels of pesticide exposure."[127] Many provincial laws also need to be modernized to reflect current scientific knowledge and the precautionary principle. As the Standing Committee on Environment and Sustainable Development states, "The use of pesticides must come to be regarded as a measure of last resort."[128]

The Supreme Court of Canada provided a ray of hope with the decision in the Hudson case. The Supreme Court not only solidified the role of municipalities in regulating pesticides and protecting the environment but also opened the door for Canadian governments at all levels to apply the precautionary principle. Consistently taking the precautionary approach would enable Canada to proactively avoid some environmental problems, rather than reacting to them after they have occurred.

> Despite its rich resource base and low population
> density, Canada's record of forest management is
> appalling.
>
> *Patricia Marchak, University of British Columbia*

> No better forestry is being generally practised
> anywhere in the world [than in Canada].
>
> *Adam Zimmerman, former CEO of Noranda Inc.*

Canada is home to a significant proportion of the world's remaining primary, frontier, and old-growth forests, while at the same time we lead the world in exports of forest products including pulp, newsprint, and lumber. The tension between the environmental and economic values of forests is at the heart of the ongoing controversy surrounding forest management in Canada. Canada's forests are not only important economically and environmentally, but are a vital element of Canadian culture. Canadians place a higher value on forests for environmental and ecological benefits than for industrial use. The majority of Canadians view the primary value of forests as protecting air, water, and soil, moderating the climate, and conserving habitat for fish and wildlife.[1]

Some key facts about Canadian forests are needed to frame the debate about forest management. Canada's forests are vast, which contributes to the cultural mythology that Canada has endless natural resources. Ontario's Ottawa Valley was once described as a region of "inexhaustible" pine forests with "timber enough here to supply the world for thousands of years."[2] Almost 45 percent of Canada's land, some 417 million hectares, is forested. About half of this forested area (234.5 million hectares) is considered commercially productive, while slightly more than a quarter (119 million hectares) is managed for timber purposes.

A remarkable 94 percent of Canadian forest land is publicly owned (71 percent by provincial governments and 23 percent by the federal government), leaving only 6 percent in private hands. Canada's high degree of public land ownership has positive implications for the regulation of Canadian forests because it is much more feasible, politically, to impose high environmental standards on public land than on private land. Nova Scotia, New Brunswick, and Prince Edward Island are anomalous in that substantial amounts of forest land are privately owned.[3] The predominance of public ownership in Canada contrasts with countries like the United States and Sweden, where roughly 70 percent of forest land is in private hands.[4] More than half (52 percent) of Canada's forest is licensed to be logged, while only 8 percent is protected in parks.[5]

A total of 193.2 million cubic metres was logged in Canada in 1999, the equivalent of about 4,830,000 logging trucks loaded with trees. To cut this volume of timber, slightly more than one million hectares was logged. The Canadian forest industry is concentrated in British Columbia, Quebec, and Ontario, and these three provinces account for more than 75 percent of the volume of trees logged in Canada annually. British Columbia has the highest rate of logging in terms of volume of timber harvested, while Quebec harvests the largest area. While a million hectares are logged annually, less than half this area of land is replanted or seeded, with the remainder left to regenerate naturally. Several million hectares of Canadian forest are affected by forest fires and insect infestations annually.[6] A relatively small area of forest, between 50,000 and 100,000 hectares annually, is converted to agricultural, urban, or other land uses.[7]

Are Canada's Forests Being Managed Sustainably?

According to the forest industry, "Canada is a world leader in forest conservation, protection, and sustainable use." The federal government echoes this claim, asserting that "Canada is viewed as a world leader in sustainability and in progressive, inclusive forest management." The provinces also claim to be leaders in sustainable forest management.[8] On the other hand, environmentalists, Aboriginal people, and a growing number of small communities are highly critical of forest management in Canada.[9] There is considerable evidence that Canadian forests are not being managed sustainably:

- At least 116 species in Canada that depend on forest habitat are endangered.[10]
- At least 142 salmon runs in British Columbia have already become extinct, and at least 600 more are on the verge of disappearing, partially due to logging.[11]
- Aboriginal languages are more likely to be extinct in watersheds with a significant degree of industrial development, primarily logging.[12]

- Governments and professional foresters acknowledge that current rates of logging are higher than can be sustained in the long term.[13]
- 90 percent of logging in Canada is still occurring in old-growth and primary forests, the intact forests with the highest biodiversity and wilderness values.[14]
- Almost 90 percent of logging in Canada is still done by clear-cutting.[15]
- About 90 percent of Canadian forest products are still commodities, including lumber, pulp, and newsprint.[16]
- Canada's huge boreal forest is "undergoing anthropogenic changes of unprecedented magnitude and rapidity, many of whose effects are potentially irreversible."[17]
- Some forest types, including Carolinian, Coastal Douglas fir, Aspen parkland, Acadian, and Columbian are heavily fragmented.[18]
- Watershed restoration programs costing billions of dollars are required to repair the damage caused by logging.[19]

Canada's forests are under pressure from other human activities besides logging, such as mining, oil and gas exploration and development, hydroelectricity production, and access roads associated with all of these industrial activities.[20] Forests are also harmed by climate change, ozone depletion, and acid rain. Climate change in particular is expected to result in "greater vulnerability of some forest species to insect infestations and disease [and] increased frequency and intensity of forest fires."[21]

The Evolution of Laws Governing the Management and Use of Canada's Forests

For more than a century, the laws and policies governing the use of Canada's forests focused on the extraction of commodities such as lumber, pulp, and newsprint.[22] Although fears of overexploitation have been expressed for decades, change was slow in coming because of the economic power of the forest industry and the seemingly inexhaustible forests. Public concern about mismanagement gradually mounted as environmental issues gained prominence in the late twentieth century. Environmentalists and Aboriginal people joined forces to criticize forest management and destructive practices. In the early 1990s, protests about clear-cutting and other logging activities in places such as BC's Clayoquot Sound, Alberta's boreal forests, Ontario's Temagami region, and New Brunswick's Christmas Mountains gained international prominence.[23] More than eight hundred protesters were arrested in Clayoquot Sound in 1993, while Bob Rae was arrested in Temagami for blocking a logging road the year before he became premier of Ontario.

Governments responded with a wide array of new legislation, new regulations, and new policies. The main thrust of these changes, according to government, is to move Canada toward sustainable forest management, defined as "maintaining and enhancing the long-term health of forest ecosystems, for the benefit of all living things both nationally and globally, while providing ecological, economic, social and cultural opportunities for the benefit of present and future generations."[24] The fundamental question addressed in this chapter is whether the changes have resulted in a rapid revolution in Canadian management and use of forests, incremental progress toward sustainable forest management, or cosmetic changes intended to assuage public concerns while having a minimal impact on the status quo.

This chapter focuses on the legal system's role in determining three key forestry questions. Have the new laws, regulations, and policies reduced the rate of logging to sustainable levels? Have forest practices improved, and to what extent are nontimber values like fish, wildlife, and water quality protected? Who has the right to cut forests on public land, and have these rights been reallocated in recent years?

The Federal Role in Governing the Conservation and Use of Forests

Environmental groups continue to insist that the federal government could play a role in establishing national standards. However, under Canada's *Constitution Act, 1867,* the provincial governments have exclusive responsibility for managing the use of forests.[25] In practice, the federal government's role is limited to conducting research, participating in international negotiations related to the conservation and use of forests, coordinating national forest strategies, and promoting Canadian forest products to foreign buyers.[26] Prior to the deficit-fighting budgets of the 1990s, Ottawa invested billions of dollars in provincial forests (primarily in reforestation efforts) through a series of federal-provincial agreements. These agreements were not replaced when they expired. The Canadian Forest Service saw its budget cut by 57 percent during the 1990s, severely limiting the federal government's research and reforestation programs.[27]

The federal environmental law that is most relevant to forests is the *Fisheries Act,* which prohibits damage to fish habitat or the deposit of harmful substances into fish-bearing waters. The federal government has been reluctant to enforce the *Fisheries Act* against logging companies that damage fish habitat because provinces object to federal interference in the development of provincial resources. For example, the federal Department of Fisheries and Oceans (DFO) recently criticized British Columbia's inadequate efforts to protect salmon habitat from the impacts of logging, but DFO has not taken any enforcement action.[28] The federal government's failure to enforce the *Fisheries Act* against logging companies is currently being investigated by the Commission for Environmental Cooperation in response to a complaint from environmental groups.[29]

The federal government coordinated the creation of a national forest strategy that produces reports extolling the virtues of Canadian forest management.[30]

Ottawa also pays for carefully orchestrated tours of forestry operations for foreign media and buyers of Canadian forest products. As a result, the federal government has been described by environmentalists as "a propaganda arm of Canada's forest industry."[31]

Canada supports efforts to negotiate a global treaty on forests, but these negotiations have not borne fruit. At the present time, international law experts admit that "only a patchwork of international agreements and arrangements address the multifarious causes of deforestation."[32] The Rio Earth Summit in 1992 produced only a nonbinding "Statement of Principles" on forests.[33] Canada wants stable rules governing trade in forest products but is "reluctant to commit to tough environmental standards imposed internationally."[34] Canada was criticized in 2002 for obstructing the progress of global negotiations at The Hague that were intended to foster an international forest treaty.[35]

Ottawa's efforts to resolve the chronic softwood lumber dispute with the United States have been unsuccessful. The United States continues to allege that Canadian provinces subsidize lumber production through low stumpage rates (royalties for logging on public land) and weak environmental standards. Although Ottawa, the provinces, and the Canadian forest industry strenuously deny the American charges, the dispute has resulted in quotas and duties on Canadian lumber exports to the United States for two decades.[36] Almost 80 percent of Canadian forest product exports are destined for the United States, so the softwood lumber dispute has major consequences for the Canadian industry. The dispute is unlikely to be resolved in the foreseeable future because Canadian forest management varies dramatically from American forest management, American timber producers have major political power, and the United States is implementing more protectionist trade policies.

Provincial Laws Governing Forest Use and Management

Because of amendments to Canada's Constitution in 1982, it is now beyond dispute that the provinces are primarily responsible for forest management.[37] It is challenging to generalize about the provincial laws governing the use of forests because each province has different types of natural forests, a distinct set of laws and regulations, and a different forest industry.[38] Forest management laws in Canada are described as "complex and sometimes arcane" and "contentious, complicated and confusing."[39] However, despite wide provincial variations, common themes emerge in terms of the effectiveness of forest laws in protecting environmental values.

Forestry legislation in British Columbia, Saskatchewan, Ontario, Quebec, Nova Scotia, and Newfoundland was modernized during the 1990s to respond to public concerns. Changes in these provincial laws reflect an evolution from a myopic focus on timber to recognition of a broader range of forest values.[40] Each of the new or amended laws enacted by these provinces states that sustainable development is a priority, and each provides innovative tools

for achieving sustainable forest management. Another useful legal development is that Saskatchewan, Manitoba, and Newfoundland and Labrador now
subject forest management plans to environmental assessment.[41] Ontario conducted an exhaustive environmental assessment of forest management that
produced extensive recommendations for improving forest policies and practices, and led to new legislation.[42]

British Columbia

Prior to 1994, when BC enacted the *Forest Practices Code,* rules governing logging in BC "were characterized by a weak or uncertain legal basis, substantial
regional variation, and weak enforcement."[43] The *Code* promised a revolution
in forest management, with strict, legally binding rules, improved protection
for wildlife, tough enforcement, and fines of up to $1 million. The provincial
government and the forest industry touted the *Code* as "the most comprehensive forestry law in the world."[44] More than twenty regulations under the *Code*
govern various aspects of forest management, and more than forty nonbinding
guidebooks recommend best practices for forest management. Unfortunately,
the strongest references to sustainable development and nontimber values are
in the *Code's* preamble. Preambles do not create legally binding obligations
and thus have limited legal utility, although they may be used in interpreting
other parts of legislation.[45]

Saskatchewan

In 1996 Saskatchewan enacted the *Forest Resources Management Act,* described
by the provincial government as "the most comprehensive, forward looking
forest management legislation in North America."[46] The innovative aspects of
the *Act* include a commitment to create a provincial forest accord every ten
years to outline broad principles to guide forest planning and management;
integrated land-use plans prepared regionally; independent audits of logging
company operations and land-use plans; extensive opportunities for public
participation; and an independent science advisory board. Saskatchewan has
been praised for its "more holistic and participatory approach to forest management," which recognizes "Aboriginal peoples, local communities, and the
general public as legitimate players in forestry policy-making."[47]

Ontario

In 1994 the government of Ontario introduced the *Crown Forest Sustainability
Act* to replace the old *Crown Timber Act.* The *CFSA* emphasizes sustainability
(defined as long-term forest health), maintaining ecological processes, and
conserving biological diversity. All forest management plans must comply with
the government's Forest Management Planning Manual, which outlines specific requirements for achieving sustainability. The provincewide environmental assessment of forest management published in 1994 also contains 115

terms and conditions that are legally binding on the Ministry of Natural Resources.[48]

Quebec

Quebec substantially amended its *Forest Act* in 1996 and again in 2001. The province also has extensive regulations governing forest practices.[49] This legislation includes strong language about preserving biodiversity and maintaining the function of forest ecosystems in global ecological cycles. Like BC, however, Quebec placed the strongest references to values other than timber in the legislation's preamble, deliberately reducing the legal impact of these provisions. The legislative changes made in 2001 allow (but do not require) the government to designate "exceptional forest ecosystems" where logging will be prohibited or subject to special restrictions. The changes also provide communities, especially Aboriginal communities, with a greater role in forest management. For example, Aboriginal communities can request that higher environmental standards be applied in their territory.[50]

Nova Scotia

Nova Scotia's *Forest Act* was updated in 1998 and now states that the principle of sustainable forest management forms the basis of all forest management programs in the province. It refers specifically to maintaining the diversity and stability of forest ecosystems.[51] Nova Scotia's legislation is unusual in that many of the regulations governing forest practices on public land apply equally on private land, whereas in most provinces the rules for logging on private land are much weaker.[52]

Newfoundland and Labrador

Newfoundland and Labrador's *Forestry Act,* amended in 1993 and 2001, requires that forest management plans be consistent with principles of sustainable development. In 1997, Newfoundland published a new twenty-year forest development plan that purported to reflect "a dramatic shift from a timber management approach to an ecosystem management approach."[53]

Provinces with Outdated Forest Legislation

Forestry legislation in New Brunswick, Alberta, Manitoba, and Prince Edward Island is silent on sustainable forest management, retaining an outdated emphasis on timber extraction to the exclusion of other values.[54] In comparison to the updated laws in the other provinces, these laws read like relics of a bygone era, although some are relatively recent. For example, Manitoba's *Forest Act* states that "timber cutting rights ... shall be granted in such manner and by such means as, in the opinion of the minister, secures the maximum benefit to the forest industry of the province."[55] In Alberta, the *Forest Act* ignores nontimber values, the minister "may make recommendations governing logging methods," and the maximum fine is $5,000.[56] Forest protection legislation in these provinces refers only to protecting forests from fires, not protecting forests from the damaging impacts of logging.[57] PEI deserves some credit for requiring that twenty-year management plans incorporate a hundred-year vision and for passing the *Public Forest Council Act* to explore the nonconsumptive and nontraditional uses of public forests.[58] In order to evaluate the practical impact of the new generation of provincial forest management laws, three critical issues will be reviewed: the rate of logging, the methods of logging (i.e., forest practices), and the allocation of licences or tenure for logging on public land.

Laws and Policies Governing the Rate of Logging

While most public attention focuses on the *method* of logging, particularly clear-cutting, the *rate* of logging is the single most important factor in determining the magnitude of environmental impacts. According to law professor Charles F. Wilkinson, "Nothing tells you more about timber domination than the level of the cut."[59]

Provincial governments establish the rate of logging (in cubic metres of timber) that will be allowed for a specific area or a specific licence on public land, a figure known as the allowable annual cut (AAC). The AAC serves as a maximum rate of logging, and in some provinces, like BC, also as a minimum rate of logging (intended to ensure social and economic stability). In Alberta and Ontario, companies set harvesting rates, subject to government approval.[60] The factors to be considered in determining the AAC are set out in forest legislation in some provinces (such as BC, Saskatchewan, and Newfoundland and Labrador).[61] In these provinces, criteria that must be considered in setting AACs include sustained yield; the capacity of mills; the social and economic objectives of the government; estimates of the extent of the forest landbase; the growth rate of trees; losses due to fire, insects, and disease; silvicultural investment; and constraints on timber harvesting resulting from the "use of the area for purposes other than timber production."[62] Laws in most provinces are silent on factors to be considered in setting the AAC, giving the government absolute discretion to set harvesting levels according to whatever criteria it deems relevant. In practice, however, the same factors are considered, whether specified in legislation or not.

The dominant factor in setting the rate of logging throughout Canada is a concept known as sustained yield, which refers to the maximum amount of timber that can be harvested annually in perpetuity. The concept of sustained yield is badly flawed from an ecological perspective because it places timber above all other forest values. Because sustainable forest management requires, at a minimum, a balancing of factors, experts conclude that "sustained yield and sustainable development are unquestionably in conflict."[63] To make matters worse, some provinces are logging at rates significantly *higher* than the sustained yield. This overcutting is justified on the basis that old-growth forests are "over-mature" or "decadent" and should be replaced by faster-growing younger forests in order to maximize the volume of timber produced.[64] From the industry and government perspective, "old-growth timber represents natural capital that is not earning a biological return but can be converted into financial capital for fueling economic growth."[65] In addition to environmental damage, overcutting undermines social and economic sustainability because of the inevitable "falldown," or decrease in logging when the old-growth forests are depleted.[66]

In British Columbia, a series of lawsuits by environmental groups in the 1990s challenged AAC decisions, arguing that the rate of logging was being set at levels too high to be sustained. In a case contesting the AAC for a tree farm licence in Clayoquot Sound, the Sierra Club argued that the word "sustained" should be given its ordinary meaning, meaning a level of harvest that does not decline over time. The government and MacMillan Bloedel argued that "sustained" referred to what could be sustained economically. The trial court agreed that sustained meant "maximizing social and economic benefits."[67] Before the BC Court of Appeal heard the Sierra Club's appeal of the lower court's decision, the government changed the wording of the relevant section of the *Forest Act,* making the appeal moot.[68] Subsequent lawsuits challenged the BC chief forester's refusal to consider environmental factors, such as areas set aside to protect spotted owls or areas designated as parks, when setting the AAC for the province.[69] A court overturned the chief forester's decision to ignore the designation of 324,000 hectares of new parks, but the chief forester reestablished the AAC at *exactly the same rate*.[70] These decisions illustrate one of the weaknesses of environmental litigation in Canada. Because setting the AAC under the *Forest Act* is a *discretionary* decision, "courts have consistently deferred to the chief forester's professional judgement and declined to apply a stringent standard of review."[71]

Unlike in Canada, court decisions in the United States have a major influence on improving forest management.[72] In the late 1980s and early 1990s, the US government's failure to fulfill its obligations under the *National Forest Management Act* and the *Endangered Species Act* was the subject of extensive litigation by environmental groups.[73] The court decisions prompted a move toward ecosystem management that resulted in a 55 percent reduction in the rate of logging in US National Forests since 1989.[74]

Changes in the Rate of Logging during the 1990s

None of the changes to provincial forestry laws in the 1990s directly affected the manner in which the AAC is determined. Nor did the many legislative changes that promised sustainable forest management lower the rate of logging in Canada. Various studies estimate that the rate of logging in Canada needs to decline by 10 to 25 percent in the boreal forests, and 30 to 40 percent on the coast of BC, to achieve sustainability objectives.[75] It is remarkable

that despite the new laws and policies promising sustainable forest management in many provinces, the rate of logging and the total area logged in Canada
annually increased rather than decreased during the 1990s. In fact, the rate of
logging in Canada reached an *all-time high* in 1999, the most recent year for
which statistics are available.[76] Studies of the AAC determination processes in
different provinces by academics and legal experts conclude that employment,
profitability, and government revenue from logging continue to dominate decision making about the rate of logging despite the increased prominence of
other forest values in recent years.[77]

The rate of logging increased to record high levels in Alberta, Manitoba,
Quebec, New Brunswick, and Nova Scotia during the late 1990s, a period
when, in theory, Canada made a dramatic shift toward sustainable forest management.[78] Nova Scotia's *Forest Act* explicitly sets a goal of doubling timber
production by 2025, while maintaining other values such as wildlife, water
quality, and recreation.[79] The rate of logging is stable in British Columbia,
Saskatchewan, and Newfoundland and Labrador, while it is declining in Ontario. The Ontario government projects that the rate of logging will decrease
for the next four decades, because of past overcutting.[80]

According to a recent book on forest policy in British Columbia, "Decisions
made when the sustained yield paradigm was established after the Second
World War set the province on a path that has been and will be extremely
difficult to reverse."[81] The BC government admitted in the early 1990s that
forests were being logged too quickly. According to the BC Ministry of Forests
in 1994, the rate of logging "could not remain at its current level, under existing management regimes, without risking steep reductions in future harvest
rates and severe impacts on the environment."[82] This statement was published
prior to the implementation of major provincial policy changes placing more
downward pressure on the rate of logging. The policy changes included the
Forest Practices Code, doubling of the amount of land in parks, a provincial
land-use planning process, the new BC treaty process intended to return lands
to First Nations, and a provincewide timber supply review. These policy changes
were expected to lower the AAC by an additional 20 percent during the 1990s.[83]
Instead, the AAC in British Columbia remained virtually unchanged throughout the decade, a testament to the rigidity of the status quo.[84] Although there
were some significant reductions in the rate of logging for southern and coastal
areas, these decreases were offset by increases in the northern and central
parts of the province. The BC forest industry is urging the provincial government to increase the AAC by more than 40 percent despite widespread recognition of the fact that the rate of logging in British Columbia is already above
the sustainable rate.[85]

Laws Governing Forest Practices

Rules governing forest practices vary widely from province to province, and are set out in a complex variety of legal instruments including laws, regulations, policies, guidelines, and logging licences. The purpose of these rules, in theory, is to minimize the environmental damage caused by logging and road building, and ensure that forests regenerate. Until very recently, there were few binding and enforceable legal constraints on the method of logging. For example, prior to the enactment of the *Forest Practices Code* in 1994, BC had no legislation governing forest practices. The following assessment looks at the *Forest Practices Code* and Ontario's *Crown Forest Sustainability Act,* two of the new generation of forestry laws that attempt to reconcile timber harvesting with ecosystem protection. As one of Canada's leading experts on forestry regulation notes, the "sudden shift from an earlier focus on timber management to sustainable management of all forest resources will, in order to become a reality, require more than a change in terminology."[86]

British Columbia's *Forest Practices Code*

Studies and audits of BC forest practices since 1995, when the *Code* came into force, reveal improvements in forest practices, but serious problems remain. The independent Forest Practices Board created in 1995 has conducted more than forty audits and investigations, concluding that there has been significant improvement in forest practices.[87] Clear-cuts, on average, are smaller in size.[88] The quality of roads has improved. Streams enjoy better protection than in the past. However, the Board reported "significant non-compliance" with *Code* requirements in more than half of its audits.[89] For example, nearly half of streams are misclassified or not identified by companies, resulting in substandard protection for riparian ecosystems.[90]

From the perspective of environmental protection, there are five main problems with the *Code*. First, section 45 of the *Code* illustrates the problem of symbolic language, and epitomizes some of the problems with environmental law in Canada.[91] Pursuant to section 45, forest practices that damage the environment are prohibited, *unless* a person or company has a plan or permit. Even if a person or company has a permit, it is unlawful to cause "significant damage" to the environment. However, "significant damage" is narrowly defined in an obscure regulation to mean "damage to a lake, stream, or other watercourse that results from the deposit of a petroleum product or a fluid used to service logging equipment."[92] The seemingly forceful language prohibiting "significant damage" to the environment is therefore largely meaningless.[93]

The second problem with the *Code* is that the provincial cabinet decided to restrict the law's impacts on the rate of logging to a maximum of 6 percent.[94] In other words, despite what the *Code* may say on paper, it has been interpreted and implemented so as to minimize changes to the rate of logging. The 6 percent cap on impacts was allocated to different elements of the *Code*.[95] Legal protection for streams must not restrict the rate of logging by more than 2.1 percent, while efforts to protect endangered species cannot reduce the rate of logging by more than 1 percent.[96] These arbitrary constraints were used to modify the regulations, guidebooks, and policies that spelled out in detail how the *Code* would be applied. In light of the government's own recognition that logging in British Columbia was at least 20 percent higher than the sustainable rate, the 6 percent cap on reductions due to the *Code* demonstrates the continued priority given to extracting timber from forests. As noted earlier, the overall rate of logging in BC is unchanged since the *Code* was enacted. Logging in BC continues to significantly affect ecological values, including species at risk such as salmon, spotted owls, mountain caribou, and marbled murrelets.[97]

The third problem with the *Code* is that bureaucrats have "an enormous amount of discretionary authority" to allow any activity that the *Code* seems to prohibit.[98] In this sense, the *Code* reflects a common characteristic of Canadian forest management laws.[99] For example, the *Code* promised to prohibit clear-cutting in a number of areas including steep sites with unstable terrain (to avoid landslides), critical wildlife habitat areas, streamside management zones, and old-growth management areas. In reality, clear-cutting continues not only to occur but to predominate in each of these areas because bureaucrats exercise their discretion to allow it.[100] District managers may authorize logging up to the banks of streams, clear-cutting on steep unstable slopes, and clear-cuts larger than the maximum set out in the *Code,* and *regularly* do so. Conversely, district managers may designate community watersheds for reduced levels of logging, sensitive areas for enhanced protection, and landscape units to increase protection for biodiversity, but *rarely* do so. Discretion is consistently exercised in ways that harm, rather than protect, the environment, because economic considerations are paramount.

Fourth, the *Code* has been undermined by a lack of implementation. Years after the *Code* became law, key tools for protecting biological diversity have never or rarely been used.[101] The independent Forest Practices Board views the failure to implement many of the *Code's* biodiversity and wildlife provisions as a serious problem.[102] The fifth problem is that enforcement of the *Code* has not lived up to expectations. As Professor George Hoberg points out, "Despite the much ballyhooed $1 million fines emphasized by the government when it introduced the FPC, no fine has come anywhere close to that maximum."[103] In fact, the Vancouver Public Library levies more fines for overdue books than the BC government imposes for unlawful logging.[104] Studies by BC's Ministry of Environment and the BC Government Employees Union found that increased enforcement was required to protect streams, old-growth forests, and wildlife habitat.[105]

While the *Code* has not lived up to environmental expectations, it has imposed major costs on the forest industry.[106] The government predicted that it would cost $250 million to $300 million annually. The cost of implementation was estimated by industry at between $840 million and $2.1 billion per year, although these estimates are flawed, and overestimate the *Code's* impact on logging costs.[107] Regardless of the exact costs, the forest industry has successfully lobbied for regulatory changes "to restore the competitiveness of the forest industry in B.C."[108]

Some changes were made to the *Code* in 1998 to address industry's concerns, such as cutting the number of plans required in half. Keith Moore, chair of the Forest Practices Board, warned that the proposed changes would "lead to a reduction in environmental standards and a loss of public confidence in the management of forest resources." He added that the changes "are unlikely to achieve the desired objective of streamlining and are more likely to create new problems in the long run."[109] Far more dramatic changes to the *Code* were made in 2002, with the stated purpose of reducing costs for the forest industry.[110] Government documents reveal that forest companies will be trusted to lead efforts to protect endangered species and conduct the timber supply review that sets the rate of logging.[111] Environmental lawyer Jessica Clogg warns that British Columbia may be "returning to a past era, where licensees logged on public land with less government and public oversight, and where fewer people questioned the priority given to timber extraction."[112]

Ontario's *Crown Forest Sustainability Act*

Ontario's *CFSA* also came into force in 1995, and at least on paper, "marked an important shift from the old *Crown Timber Act*, which made all values secondary to timber extraction."[113] Experts agreed that the extent of change in Ontario's forest practices would depend on the government's commitment to implementation.[114] Soon after the *CFSA* was passed, however, the provincial government changed; the Conservatives under Mike Harris were more interested in eliminating environmental regulations and cutting environment budgets than implementing and enforcing environmental laws. The budget of the Ontario Ministry of Natural Resources was cut by almost 50 percent, and enforcement responsibility was partially transferred to the forest industry to monitor itself.[115]

The *CFSA* required the minister of natural resources to create rules for protecting biodiversity and ensuring sustainable logging before approving any new forest management plans. For more than two years after the *CFSA* became law, forest management plans were approved even though the minister had not created the new rules for sustainable logging. As a result, the provincial government was sued by environmental groups for violating the *CFSA*. The Ontario Divisional Court found extensive violations of the new law and gave the government one year to ensure that forest management plans were revised to be sustainable. The court said that "the nature and quality of non-compliance is extreme ... The difficulty is not with individual foresters or planners, but with the institutional failure of the Ministry to appreciate and fulfill its legal obligations." The court concluded that the government's failure to obey its own law "undermines completely the object and purpose of the legislation and works serious prejudice to the public interest in the sustainability of the Crown forest for future generations."[116]

Since 1998 Ontario's forest industry has been responsible for conducting self-inspections to determine compliance with the *Crown Forest Sustainability Act,* with occasional monitoring by the Ministry of Natural Resources. An audit by Ontario's provincial auditor revealed that "ministry inspectors found significantly more violations than industry inspectors."[117] In fact, government inspections identified *five times* as many violations of the *CFSA* as industry self-inspections. The provincial auditor found that the rate of compliance with the *CFSA* fell from 87 percent in 1995-6, when the government enforced the law, to 75 percent in 1999-2000, when the forest industry enforced the law. Independent audits of Ontario forest practices have also identified extensive violations of rules intended to protect streams, wetlands, wildlife habitat, and other forest values.[118]

As in BC, the way in which government bureaucrats exercise their discretion has undermined effective forest management in Ontario. One of the terms of the 1994 provincial environmental assessment of forest management confined clear-cuts to a maximum of 260 hectares, except in limited circumstances where justified for biological or silvicultural reasons.[119] Yet the *average* clear-cut size in some Ontario forest management units is as high as 479 hectares, with the largest clear-cut measuring 2,924 hectares. The forest management plan for the Temagami area, approved in 1999, includes nineteen clear-cuts larger than 260 hectares.[120] Government proposals extending the maximum clear-cut size to 10,000 hectares, ostensibly to mimic natural disturbances like fires, were heavily criticized by scientists but continue to be advanced. Although clear-cutting may be appropriate in some forests in some circumstances, it cannot, from an ecological perspective, be equated with fire.[121]

Professors Jamie Lawson, Marcelo Levy, and L. Anders Sandberg conclude that changes in Ontario forest law and policy have been "more cosmetic than real." As a result, "the Ontario forest continues to be overcut ... and [there is a] continued degradation and decline of the wood supply."[122] Similarly, Professor Jeremy Wilson concludes that the potential of the *CFSA* has been "undercut by the Ontario government's continued emphasis on satisfying the industry's demands for fibre, as well as its sharp cuts to resource management staff levels."[123]

Overview of Changes in Canadian Forest Practices

Some improvements in forest practices have occurred in provinces that strengthened their forest laws and regulations in recent years.[124] An international evaluation found that "timber is still the central concern of forestry law in Canada, but [some] Canadian provinces have increased attention to the management of non-timber resources."[125] BC has seen a modest "shift toward greener forest practices."[126] Overall, however, progress toward sustainable forest management has been limited by poor implementation, excessive discretion exercised in ways that harm the environment, inadequate enforcement, and the continued dominance of economic, not ecological, considerations. The clearest indication of the modest rate of change is the fact that clear-cutting is still the dominant harvesting method in Canada: 89.3 percent of the volume of timber logged in 1999 was clear-cut.[127]

Sustainable forest management is more complex and demanding than timber management, yet provincial governments have cut staff and resources responsible for forests and environmental protection.[128] For example, Alberta increased the area of lands subject to long-term Forest Management Agreements from three million hectares in 1986 to nineteen million hectares in 1997 while reducing the provincial environment budget by more than 30 percent. British Columbia, Ontario, and Quebec, where the forest industry is concentrated, cut budgets and staff in environmental and resource management by 35 to 65 percent during the past decade. As a result, the scale of forest operations on public land in Canada threatens to outstrip the capacity of government agencies for hands-on management.[129] The lack of capacity is then used to justify turning responsibility for monitoring and enforcement over to forest companies, resulting in reduced levels of compliance with environmental laws and regulations.

Laws Governing the Allocation of Logging Rights

Most of the commercially valuable forests on public land in Canada were allocated to large companies many years ago.[130] Tenures were granted behind closed doors and corruption was prevalent.[131] About half of Canada's public forests are under tenure, ranging from 33 percent in Saskatchewan to almost 100 percent in Nova Scotia.[132] There are basically two main types of tenure in Canada, volume-based and area-based. A volume-based tenure gives the licensee the right to harvest a certain amount of timber over a specified period of time. An area-based tenure gives the licensee the right to harvest timber from a defined area of land. Area-based tenures are usually longer and more secure, involve more responsibility for planning and management, and encourage better stewardship.[133] There are also over 400,000 privately owned woodlots in Canada.

In recent decades the trend has been toward increasing corporate concentration of forest tenures. In British Columbia, seventeen large companies control nearly 70 percent of the AAC.[134] The theory when these licences were originally granted was that in exchange for valuable harvesting rights, companies would provide stable employment and a steady stream of government revenues. However, for several decades, rates of logging have been rising while employment levels in the forest industry have been falling.[135] Dissatisfaction with the environmental, social, and economic consequences of industrial forestry have resulted in growing support for greater local control over forest managements.[136]

For many years, royal commissions, provincial task forces, and others have called for the redistribution of forest tenures to communities, small businesses, and Aboriginal people.[137] Small steps in this direction have been taken through agreements with Aboriginal people and through community forestry pilot projects in BC and Ontario.[138] Although promising in terms of their potential for moving toward sustainable forest management, community forest programs in BC currently cover less than 0.1 percent of the province's forests.[139]

Provincial governments across Canada have been reluctant to address the demands for reallocating forest tenure. Relatively little unencumbered forest of commercial value is left to be allocated, and reallocation of existing tenures faces stiff political opposition from powerful interests satisfied with the current distribution. In addition, legitimate concerns exist about how much compensation would be payable to current licensees if their tenures were reallocated.[140] These concerns are deepened by Chapter 11 of NAFTA, which gives American forestry corporations additional rights and remedies in the event that their investments are affected by changes in government policy.[141]

At the other end of the spectrum, there is pressure to privatize forests that are currently owned by the Canadian public. Companies argue that there is inadequate security to justify investing in forests because of the short duration of licences and uncertainty as to whether licences will be renewed.[142] This industry argument is difficult to reconcile with the fact that all Canadian jurisdictions provide "perpetual" or "evergreen" licences, meaning licences have a fixed duration but are automatically renewed every five or ten years.[143] The public opposes privatization of public forests, as demonstrated by a recent proposal to provide MacMillan Bloedel (now Weyerhaeuser) with a small area of public land in BC as compensation for timber the company lost due to the creation of new parks.[144] Privatization does not necessarily require the outright sale of land, as Newfoundland's experience illustrates. Timber licences for 69 percent of the Crown land on the island of Newfoundland were given to pulp and paper companies through ninety-nine-year leases issued under the 1905 *Pulp and Paper Manufacturing Act* and the 1935 *Bowater Act*. Newfoundland and Labrador's financial and legal system treats this licensed land as private property.[145]

Numerous experts have observed that Canada's progress from timber management to ecosystem management is "hindered by the inflexibility of the current tenure system."[146] The forest industry opposes changes to the tenure system, and governments are constrained by past allocations. Despite considerable pressure for change, and despite the promotion of innovative alternatives to the status quo, changes in who has the right to harvest trees on public land in Canada have been minimal.[147]

Emerging Issues in Forest Management in Canada

Laws and policies governing the management and use of forests in Canada are subject to powerful and often conflicting pressures for reform. After decades of relative stability, the emergence of new actors and new sources of pressure made the 1990s a period of rapid change for laws and policies. These pressures do not appear to have abated, despite extensive changes to forest management laws in most provinces.

Aboriginal Influences on Laws Governing Forestry in Canada

One of the strongest pressures to change the existing system of forest management in Canada is the mounting legal strength of Aboriginal claims to the land and the forests. Aboriginal people from coast to coast are using negotiation, litigation, and direct action to regain control over the management of their traditional territories. More than a dozen treaties were signed in recent years establishing comanagement for natural resources, and in some cases reallocating forest tenures to Aboriginal people. For example, as part of the Nisga'a Final Agreement, the Nisga'a receive the right to a certain volume of timber and can pass forest laws, but must meet or beat BC laws.[148] In British Columbia, Nova Scotia, and New Brunswick, logging carried out by Aboriginal people on public land without authorization resulted in major controversies, court cases, and ongoing uncertainty about the extent of Aboriginal rights and the provincial governments' ability to manage the forests.[149] In Quebec the Cree used several high-profile forestry lawsuits as leverage in a successful effort to gain both an enhanced management role and an economic stake in logging activity in their territory.[150] The Algonquins of Barrière Lake negotiated a trilateral agreement with Canada and Quebec that gives the Algonquins considerable influence over forest management and requires sustainable forestry over ten thousand square kilometres.[151] In Newfoundland and Labrador the Innu have criticized the province's approach to forest management and advanced alternatives perceived to be ecologically and culturally more appropriate.[152] In BC, as a result of recent court decisions, First Nations must be consulted, and their interests accommodated, in forest management decisions.[153]

A recent federal law allows First Nations to create their own laws for logging on reserve lands, subject to the proviso that standards must be equal to or better than provincial standards.[154] Reserve lands, however, cover less than 1 percent of Canada. A more ambitious proposal from the National Aboriginal Forestry Association would allow First Nations to set the rules for logging on traditional lands, which cover a far larger area than reserves.[155] Recent legal developments in the field of Aboriginal rights, through both treaties and court decisions, signal a significant shift in access to, and control of, natural resources. Aboriginal people are assuming an increasing role in both forest management and participation in the economic benefits.[156] Traditional forms of tenure, with their focus solely on timber, do not equate with traditional Aboriginal values, leading to pressure for more holistic forms of forest tenure.[157] As treaty negotiations continue and cases work their way through the courts, more profound impacts on Canadian forest management can be anticipated.

International Pressures on Laws Governing Forest Management in Canada

Several important sources of pressure upon Canadian forest management come from beyond Canada's borders. In particular, "Canadian forest policy faces increased international scrutiny because of US-Canada forest trade disputes, international sustainable forestry initiatives, and international environmental groups' boycotts and certification campaigns."[158] These factors push Canadian forest management laws and policies in a more sustainable direction. The softwood lumber dispute provides an incentive for law and policy changes. Certification, which involves the independent verification of forest management practices against established standards, is a nonlegal development that may also have a major impact on forest practices in Canada. Canada has the largest area of certified forests in the world, with at least forty-four million hectares certified.[159] However, most of this certification is based on systems that lack widespread credibility. The certification program operated by the Forest Stewardship Council, favoured by environmental groups, has certified only a handful of Canadian forestry operations.[160] In recent years both environmental and Aboriginal groups have launched international campaigns to convince buyers of Canadian wood and paper products to take their business elsewhere.[161] Greenpeace has been particularly successful in convincing a number of major corporations to end their purchases of Canadian timber products because of unsustainable practices and the ongoing destruction of old-growth forests. These international market campaigns are ongoing.

On the other hand, international competition in the lumber, pulp, and newsprint markets has the opposite effect, placing downward pressure on environmental protection. The emergence of plantation forestry in such countries as Indonesia and Brazil poses a major challenge to Canada. These southern nations have advantages including faster growth of trees, lower labour costs, and lower environmental standards.[162] Canadian forest companies seek to reverse some of the regulatory changes made in recent years, using the argument that the Canadian forests products industry needs to lower costs in order to compete globally.[163] Experts believe that because of competition from other countries, the future of Canada's forest industry depends on innovation.[164]

Conclusion

> There is ample evidence to show that current forest
> use and management practices are destroying our
> legacy, that we are cutting too many trees over too
> large an area and that our forest policies have been ill
> advised. Yet, on paper at least, Canada has an enlight-
> ened, sustainable forest policy. Can these conflicting
> visions both be correct?
>
> *Senate Subcommittee on the Boreal Forest, 1999*

The answer to the Senate Subcommittee's question is yes, there is a contradiction between Canada's forest management laws, regulations, and policies and
the reality of what is happening to Canadian forests. On paper, forest management in Canada appears to have undergone a paradigm shift from a timber
focus to a more holistic approach that values ecological considerations like
biodiversity, water quality, and soil. On the ground there have been some modest
improvements in forest practices but this progress is limited. On three key
indicators, including the rate of logging, the predominance of clear-cutting,
and corporate concentration of tenures, there is little evidence of improvement. The US National Forests, where the rate of logging has fallen by 55
percent, illustrate the huge gap between genuinely sustainable forest management and the conventional forest management practised in most of Canada
today. Forestry experts conclude that despite the claims made by government
and industry, and the reforms of the past decade, Canada only pays "lip service to ecosystem management," "in all Canadian jurisdictions forests continue
to be managed primarily for commercial timber production," and there is still
a "gap between widely proclaimed principles of sustainable forest management and the reality of forest use and management."[165] Overall, government
and industry claims that Canada is a leader in sustainable forest management
are clearly unwarranted.

Canada's forests face an uncertain future. Laws and policies will continue to
evolve rapidly in the face of intense pressure from the softwood lumber dispute with the United States, the need to address constitutionally and judi-
cially recognized Aboriginal rights, increasing international competition from
nations with competitive advantages vis-à-vis Canada, and scientific and environmental pressure to protect biodiversity, ecosystem services, and some of
the last intact forests on Earth. Protecting and sustaining forests will also require finding solutions to climate change, acid rain, ozone depletion, and other
environmental challenges. Existing forest management laws in Canada, despite improvements, are incapable of addressing these demands.

> Environmental assessment has become a cynical,
> irrational, and highly discretionary process in Canada.
> What should be a coherent democratic filter for ensuring
> that ecological and economic follies do not destroy the
> country's natural riches or burden taxpayers with
> unexpected debts has become a labyrinth of political
> intrigue, bureaucratic vagueness and legal wrangling
> that neither saves money nor guarantees prudent
> resource use.
>
> *Andrew Nikiforuk, author and journalist*

According to government, environmental assessment (EA) is a success story in the realm of Canadian environmental law. The federal government's *Canadian Environmental Assessment Act (CEAA)* came into effect in 1995. The Canadian Environmental Assessment Agency claims that *CEAA* has "helped achieve sustainable development through the promotion of sound economic development while reducing adverse effects on our environment."[1] Every province also has its own legally binding EA process, and a harmonization agreement is in place to avoid duplication and overlap between the federal and provincial assessment processes. In 2000 Environment Minister David Anderson claimed that "Canada is recognized as a leader in the field."[2]

In contrast, everyone outside of government is brutally critical of Canadian EA. Industry loathes the process.[3] In a typical complaint, the Saskatchewan Mining Association criticizes EA as "overly complex, cumbersome, bureaucratic, time-consuming, costly, and subject to misuse by those whose desire is not to improve development but to stop it." Provincial governments resent the federal EA process, which they describe as "paternalistic" and a "federal intrusion into provincial jurisdiction." Quebec's minister of environment labelled *CEAA* "totalitarian."[4] The provinces argue that federal EA interferes with the development of provincial resources, causes costly delays, and duplicates effort without benefit.

At the other end of the spectrum, prominent scientists such as David Suzuki and David Schindler describe EA in Canada as "ludicrous" and a "boondoggle." Award-winning author and professor John Livingston decries EA as "a grandiloquent fraud, a hoax, and a con." Professor William Rees concludes, "The dominant project-oriented, one-shot, prediction-based approach is ecologically naive and wholly inappropriate for the requirements of sustainable development." Husain Sadar, director of Carleton University's Impact Assessment Centre, contradicts Environment Minister Anderson, arguing that "not a single country outside of Canada would call us a leader in environmental assessment anymore."[5] The striking divergence of opinion about EA in Canada has produced several dozen high-profile lawsuits and a flurry of academic articles. This chapter examines the theory of EA, the federal and provincial EA laws, and the court cases that have interpreted and shaped the laws.

The Theory of Environmental Assessment

Environmental assessment, as described by the Supreme Court of Canada, is "a planning tool that is now generally regarded as an integral component of sound decision-making."[6] EA involves gathering and evaluating information about the potential impacts of a proposed course of action, and integrating environmental and economic factors in order to produce sustainable development. In theory, EA "is important because it is one of the few institutionalized processes that we have developed to *prevent* environmental degradation."[7] Environmental lawyer Stephen Hazell argues that "environmental assessment is potentially the most powerful tool" to protect the environment.[8]

In the early years of EA, the focus was on individual physical projects. It is now understood that individually insignificant actions can be cumulatively significant, and that government policies and programs can cause widespread damage. Thus the World Commission on Environment and Development stressed the importance of applying EA more broadly, "not only to products and projects, but also to policies and programmes, especially major macroeconomic, finance, and sectoral policies that induce significant impacts on the environment."[9] The systematic process of addressing the environmental consequences of proposed policies, plans, and programs is known as strategic environmental assessment.

Experts in EA have identified a number of characteristics necessary for it to be effective. Ideally, EA laws and policies should:

- endorse sustainability as the primary purpose
- apply to all plans, decisions, and actions that may result in environmental impacts
- assess all potential impacts (environmental, economic, and social), including cumulative effects

- identify the best option, by evaluating needs and alternatives
- involve the public in an open and transparent process
- assign decision-making power to an independent agency or ensure that decisions are subject to review by an independent tribunal
- require monitoring of effects and provide effective enforcement options.

It is also important to acknowledge that EA is not a panacea for solving all environmental problems, but should form part of a broader land-use and planning regime. However, as environmental lawyer Steven Kennett points out, "Most governments in Canada have yet to establish the systems of public land law and integrated resource management that are required to ensure a logical progression of decision-making in support of sustainable development."[10] In the absence of land-use planning, disputes are more likely to arise about whether a proposed activity is appropriate in a specific location. As a result, EA in Canada is often placed in the difficult position of trying to address land-use issues that should be addressed on a broader geographic scale and with a longer timeline.

Environmental Assessment Laws in Canada
As is the case for many environmental subjects, constitutional responsibility for EA in Canada overlaps.[11] Federal EAs are required for projects involving federal land, federal funding, federal proponents, or certain federal permits. Provincial EAs primarily target major industrial developments occurring on provincial land or involving provincially managed natural resources. Occasionally a project or activity will trigger both provincial and federal EA laws, in which case there are procedures, described below, to harmonize the two processes. Both the federal and provincial processes will be evaluated, based on the key characteristics of effective EA described earlier, including the primary purpose of attaining sustainability, applying to a broad range of projects and policies, examining needs and alternatives, evaluating a wide range of potential impacts, involving the public, and providing an independent decision-making body.

Federal Environmental Assessment Law
The United States passed the world's first EA legislation in 1969.[12] In the early 1970s Canada decided to proceed by means of policy rather than passing a law, with the result that EA was a sporadic and unpredictable process. The high point of Canadian EA was the Mackenzie Valley Pipeline Inquiry conducted by Justice Thomas Berger in the mid-1970s.[13] Berger conducted extensive public hearings in the North before concluding that the pipeline would cause irreparable environmental harm, have negative social consequences, and provide limited economic benefits. Berger's inquiry was a model of excellence because it was undertaken before irrevocable decisions were made, public consultation was extensive and meaningful, the traditional knowledge

of Aboriginal people was given due respect, and the scope of the inquiry was broad-ranging but not infinite. The low point of EA in Canada, from a legal perspective, was probably the Mulroney government's decision to exempt Alcan's controversial Kemano Completion Project from assessment.[14]

The long history of Canadian EA is chronicled in detail elsewhere and need not be repeated here.[15] Suffice to say that the federal government refused to enact EA legislation until court decisions about the Rafferty-Alameda Dam in Saskatchewan and the Oldman Dam in Alberta revealed that the *Environmental Assessment and Review Process Guidelines Order* created by Ottawa in 1984 was, to the government's surprise, legally binding.[16] Largely in response to these court decisions, the *Canadian Environmental Assessment Act* was passed in 1992. Minister of Environment Robert de Cotret claimed that *CEAA* would be "more powerful in its impact on decision-making than any other environmental assessment legislation in the world."[17] Despite the minister's hyperbole, there was an extensive debate in legal and academic circles about whether *CEAA* improves upon or steps backward from the previous Guidelines Order.[18]

The Purposes of the *Canadian Environmental Assessment Act*
The purposes of *CEAA* include ensuring that environmental impacts are considered before actions are taken, encouraging actions that promote sustainable development, avoiding duplication, and providing opportunities for public participation.[19] Despite paying lip service to the concept of sustainable development, *CEAA* appears to be implemented in a manner that favours development over sustainability. According to the Canadian Environmental Assessment Agency, approximately twenty-five thousand projects were reviewed between 1995 and 2000. More than 99.9 percent of proposed projects were approved.[20]

The Application of the *Canadian Environmental Assessment Act*
CEAA applies when a physical project (e.g., a mine, a pipeline, or a dam) or an activity (e.g., low-level military training flights) is on federal land, receives federal funds, is carried out by the federal government, or requires certain federal permits. The federal permits that trigger the application of *CEAA* are listed in a regulation. Other regulations list specific physical activities that are covered by the *Act* and projects that are excluded because their environmental effects are regarded as insignificant.[21]

There have been few disputes about whether *CEAA* applies to a given project because for the most part the *Act* and its accompanying regulations are quite clear on this point. However, in 1996 Ottawa refused to conduct an EA of the sale of nuclear reactors to China despite having provided a $1.5 billion loan guarantee.[22] The federal government's refusal seems difficult to justify when compared to other overseas projects for which EAs have been completed under *CEAA*. Other projects in China for which the federal government conducted environmental screenings include a potato chip plant, a manufacturing plant for small bamboo articles, and a chicken hatchery. Small-scale foreign power projects that are much less problematic environmentally than nuclear reactors were also assessed by the federal government, including a bio-gas plant in Tanzania, a micro-hydroelectric power project in Sri Lanka, and a thermal power station in Senegal.[23]

One of the major shortcomings of the *Act* is that it does not apply to government policies, plans, and programs. The federal government has a separate, unenforceable policy for reviewing their environmental effects.[24] The drawbacks of this approach include the lack of transparency, the absence of a role for the public, and most importantly, the fact that it is largely ignored.[25] Another shortcoming of *CEAA* is its limited application to Crown corporations. The original *CEAA* was ambiguous about the obligations of Crown corporations to conduct EAs, with Ottawa insisting that they were exempt and environmental lawyers arguing that Ottawa was wrong.[26] Proposed amendments to *CEAA* in 2003 would clarify that the *Act* does *not* apply to Crown corporations unless government passes a regulation requiring Crown corporations to conduct EAs.[27] No such regulation exists at this time. ·

The Scope of the *Canadian Environmental Assessment Act*
Four different levels of EA are possible under *CEAA*: screenings, comprehensive studies, panel reviews, and mediation. Screenings provide the lowest level of scrutiny, but do require assessment of the environmental and cumulative effects of a project. The requirement to consider cumulative effects is important because evidence is increasing that the worst environmental damage may result from the combination of individually minor effects of multiple actions over time. Comprehensive studies must assess environmental and cumulative effects, plus additional factors including the purpose of a project, alternative means of carrying it out, and the need for a follow-up monitoring program. Projects that require comprehensive study are listed in a regulation.[28] Where a comprehensive study concludes that the environmental impacts of a proposed project require further study or that the project will cause significant adverse effects, or where there is public concern, the minister must refer the project to a review panel or mediator for further study. Changes to *CEAA* proposed in 2003 would eliminate the opportunity to upgrade a comprehensive study into a panel review. A panel review involves the appointment of independent experts to hold public hearings about a project and make recommendations to government. Mediation, available as an alternative to a review panel, must involve all interested parties in negotiating the outcome of an EA.

Over 99.9 percent of the twenty-five thousand federal EAs conducted between 1995 and 2000 were screenings. Only forty-six projects were subjected to comprehensive studies, only ten projects were reviewed by panels that held public hearings, and no projects were referred to mediation.[29] Environmental lawyer Stephen Hazell points out that "projects subject to screening are rarely found to have significant adverse environmental effects," projects are never stopped because of screenings, and follow-up programs are required for only about 5 percent of screened projects.[30] The federal government spends $40 million annually on EA.[31]

Public Participation under the *Canadian Environmental Assessment Act*

Public participation is vital to EA even though it may lengthen the process.[32] *CEAA* required the creation of a public registry to provide access to a wide range of EA documents, including details about every project subject to a federal assessment. The extent of public participation under *CEAA* depends on the type of EA being carried out. Public consultation is discretionary for screenings, with the decision made by the federal department responsible for a project. As a result, the public participates in only 10 to 15 percent of screenings.[33]

Public consultation is mandatory for comprehensive studies, although it is limited to receiving notice about a project and being given an opportunity to provide written comments. For review panels, the public has an opportunity to take part in public hearings by presenting evidence and questioning the proponent's experts. The federal government makes a limited amount of funding available to facilitate public participation in review panel hearings. The amount of participant funding in the first five years of *CEAA* totalled $840,046, or about 0.5 percent of total federal expenditure on EA during this period.

Independent Decision Making

In large part, *CEAA* relies on self-assessment, meaning the proponent of a project prepares the EA. The federal department in charge makes the decision about approving a project, even if the federal department itself is the proponent or has invested in the project. This system obviously creates potential conflicts of interest. A project can be approved if the EA finds no significant adverse impacts or if the EA finds that there are significant adverse impacts that can be "justified in the circumstances." The vague phrase "justified in the circumstances" gives the government broad discretion to approve environmentally damaging projects and contradicts the *Act*'s commitment to sustainable development. For example, the federal government allowed the Oldman Dam, the bridge to Prince Edward Island, and the expansion of the Toronto International Airport to proceed, against the recommendation of the EAs for the projects.[34] In 1993, the Liberals promised to "shift decision-making power to an independent Canadian Environmental Assessment Agency, subject to appeal to Cabinet."[35] This promise was never fulfilled.

Amendments to the *Canadian Environmental Assessment Act*

Amendments to *CEAA* were before Parliament in 2003 in an effort to improve the law. The three goals of the amendments were to make the process more certain, predictable, and timely; to increase the quality of EAs; and to provide more meaningful public consultation.[36] Critics observe that the amendments offer "gently positive" changes but do not address the fundamental flaws in the federal EA process.[37] In a related legislative change, Parliament amended the *Export Development Act* to preclude the application of *CEAA* to the Export Development Corporation. Although the EDC is now required by the *Export Development Act* to assess the environmental consequences of its actions, the process falls far short of what would be required by *CEAA*.[38]

Strengths and Weaknesses of the *Canadian Environmental Assessment Act*
In 1998 Canada's commissioner on the environment and sustainable development audited the federal EA process. The commissioner observed that not all projects are being assessed; many federal organizations such as Crown corporations are not required to conduct EAs; the policy requiring environmental review of departmental programs and policies is not being implemented; and important portions of projects are being excluded from EAs. In 77 out of 187 projects reviewed by the audit, "information on the existing environment was not provided or was too sketchy to allow a reader of the screening report to assess whether the assessment had considered all significant potential environmental effects." The commissioner concluded that "significant environmental consequences can be overlooked and environmental damage can occur as a result of some of the deficiencies that we have noted in the conduct of screenings."[39]

One of the fundamental flaws of *CEAA* is its discretionary nature. Provisions enabling the federal government to assess the impacts of projects with significant transboundary impacts are discretionary and have never been used.[40] Mediation is a promising alternative means of resolving EA controversies, but it is also discretionary and has never been used. Class screenings, which offer an efficient means of dealing with small projects that are similar and have a low likelihood of significant impacts, have only been used twice.[41] As noted above, the federal government has the discretion to approve a project even if the EA predicts significant adverse environmental impacts if "justified in the circumstances." Other weaknesses in *CEAA* include limited opportunities for public input, the lack of enforcement or offence provisions, the failure to require mandatory follow-up and monitoring, the potential conflict of interest created by self-assessment, and the lack of independent decision making.

On the positive side, federal review panels generally provide the most comprehensive EAs in Canada, although quality varies from panel to panel and only ten panels were appointed in the first six years that *CEAA* was in force.[42] Several recent panels have gone to great lengths to seriously address questions of sustainable development on a regional scale. For example, the Voisey's Bay Panel managed to engage the Innu and the Inuit in the EA process and made recommendations to address many Aboriginal concerns as well as social, economic, and environmental issues.[43]

Provincial Environmental Assessment Law

All of the provinces and territories have legislated EA processes, although the laws vary considerably.[44] For example, maximum fines for violating provincial EA laws range from $5,000 in Saskatchewan to $1 million in Manitoba and Newfoundland and Labrador. Some provincial laws are far weaker than *CEAA*, while others include innovative elements that surpass the federal legislation. Many provincial laws governing EA suffer from the same flaws that plague the federal process: narrow application, limited scope, excessive discretion, provisions that are never used, limited opportunities for public participation, and a lack of independent decision making. Some provincial assessment laws are distinguished from the federal process by the inclusion of legally binding timelines for the completion of EAs.[45] Despite promising the certainty sought by industry, in practice these timelines are regularly extended because of the time required to gather, analyze, and evaluate large amounts of information.

The Purpose of Provincial Environmental Assessment Laws

The purposes set out in provincial EA laws vary widely from province to province. Alberta, Manitoba, and Nova Scotia specifically prescribe sustainable development as one of the purposes set forth in their EA legislation. Nova Scotia's comprehensive *Environment Act,* which includes EA provisions, also endorses the precautionary principle, the polluter-pays principle, and pollution prevention. Like *CEAA*, provincial laws may mention sustainable development but development dominates. Few projects are ever turned down as a result of provincial EA processes. In BC every project that has completed the EA process has been approved. In Ontario only a handful of controversial proposals have been turned down. The Saskatchewan Environmental Assessment Review Commission examined 636 development proposals considered by the provincial Department of Environment and concluded that the process has not constrained economic activity.[46]

The Application of Provincial Environmental Assessment Laws

The breadth of application in the federal EA regimes differs strikingly from that of the provinces. Whereas at the federal level there are thousands of EAs annually, each province conducts a far smaller number of EAs – generally less than a hundred. For example, because of the narrow range of application of British Columbia's *Environmental Assessment Act,* only forty-one projects were reviewed in the first six years after the *Act* was passed. In Alberta, ten to twenty projects are reviewed annually. Each province lists the specific type and size of projects that will trigger EA. For example, new coal mines in BC are subject to EA if they produce more than 250,000 tonnes of coal per year. In Alberta, a sour gas processing plant that emits more than 2.8 tonnes of sulphur per day is subject to EA.[47] These kinds of thresholds may encourage government or industry to design projects that are slightly below the threshold in order to evade the EA process.

Major sectors of Canada's resource economy falling under provincial jurisdiction are exempt from EA. In Alberta, oil and gas exploration is exempt.[48] Each individual well may have limited impacts, but a regional field of wells, roads, gas plants, pipelines, and seismic lines can cause major ecological damage. In British Columbia, logging is exempt.[49] Again, while individual clear-cuts may have relatively minor effects, the cumulative impact of logging and road building can be severe. Across the prairies, agriculture is exempt. In Ontario, only government undertakings are subject to EA, and even they can be exempted. The private sector in Ontario is exempt unless the government specifically orders a project to undergo EA, which rarely occurs.[50]

Several provinces have provisions authorizing (though not requiring) strategic EA (of plans, policies, and programs) and class screenings. Because these provisions are predominantly discretionary, their use is rare. Ontario has conducted a handful of strategic EAs, including a provincewide review of forest management and a review of Ontario Hydro's 25-Year Energy Supply Plan. In Saskatchewan, a recent change to the law means that twenty-year forest management plans are subject to mandatory EA. The utility of class screenings is limited by the fact that so few projects and activities are covered by provincial EA laws.

The Scope of Provincial Environmental Assessment Laws

Provincial EA laws tend to have a narrower scope than *CEAA* in terms of the potential impacts that are examined. Some provincial laws focus strictly on environmental impacts, ignoring social, economic, and cultural impacts. Only Quebec, the Northwest Territories, and Alberta require the review of cumulative effects.[51] Only Alberta, Ontario, and Nova Scotia analyze the need for a project.[52] Alberta, Ontario, Quebec, Newfoundland and Labrador, and PEI require examination of alternatives. To its credit, Alberta's law specifically requires that the "no-go" alternative be considered, that is, the option of not proceeding with the project.[53] Nova Scotia requires consideration of alternatives only for larger projects.[54] The failure to require assessment of needs and alternatives is a major weakness of the laws in the remaining provinces, since examining needs and alternatives is integral to the EA process.

Public Participation under Provincial Environmental Assessment Laws

Public participation under provincial laws is weaker than under *CEAA*. In some provinces, such as Prince Edward Island, public participation depends on a discretionary decision by the minister. In most provinces, the role of the public is generally limited to being notified and given an opportunity to comment on a project. Public hearings are usually at the minister's discretion, with several exceptions. In Alberta the Energy and Utilities Board and the

Natural Resources Conservation Board may provide intervenor funding and hold public hearings before making recommendations to approve or reject a project. However, participation in EAs in Alberta is limited to those who can demonstrate that they will be "directly affected" by a project, a narrow legal category that excludes much of the public. In Ontario hearings may be held by the Environmental Review Tribunal. In Quebec the public can request a public hearing and the minister must hold a hearing unless the request is frivolous.[55]

Independent Decision Making

Under provincial EA laws, decisions about whether to approve projects are generally made by the minister of environment. In some circumstances, usually involving larger projects, the cabinet makes the decision.[56] Ontario, Nova Scotia, and Alberta are the only Canadian jurisdictions where decisions or recommendations on whether to approve projects are, in some cases, made by an independent tribunal following public hearings. In each of these provinces, the minister retains the right to override the recommendations of the expert panel.[57]

Recent Changes to Provincial EA Legislation

Recent amendments have weakened EA laws in Ontario and BC, former provincial leaders in EA. Changes to the Ontario *Environmental Assessment Act* in 1996 increased the discretionary powers of the minister of environment and have been heavily criticized for weakening the EA process and creating uncertainty.[58] In making the changes, the Harris government ignored the expert advice of the Environmental Assessment Advisory Committee, which was subsequently disbanded. The *Intervenor Funding Project Act,* an innovative experiment in facilitating public participation in EA, was repealed.[59] Environmental lawyers anticipate that EA in Ontario will become "increasingly ineffective as its full scope will apply to ever fewer proposals, the public will be less able to participate effectively, and decisions will be made in isolation from other decisions."[60]

BC's *Environmental Assessment Act* was rewritten in 2002, replacing one of the country's most progressive provincial EA laws with one of the weakest laws. Instead of a mandatory requirement to conduct an EA of any project, the discretion to conduct an EA now rests with a provincial bureaucrat. Strong provisions of the BC legislation that were eliminated include a purpose section emphasizing sustainability; requirements to examine cumulative effects, the need for a project, and alternatives to a project; and innovative public participation requirements, including a mandatory role for First Nations.[61] British Columbia had previously changed regulations to exempt many mines and other industrial projects from the application of the *Environmental Assessment Act*.[62]

Harmonization of Federal and Provincial EA Processes

Provincial governments and industry continue to complain about duplication and overlap between federal and provincial EA processes.[63] Yet in 1998, the federal and provincial governments signed the Canada-Wide Accord on Environmental Harmonization and a Sub-Agreement on Environmental Assessment. British Columbia, Alberta, Saskatchewan, and Manitoba have signed bilateral agreements with Ottawa to harmonize EA while the remaining provinces rely on informal arrangements to avoid duplication. The allegations of overlap and duplication are not supported by evidence. Only about eighty to one hundred projects per year are subject to both provincial and federal EA.[64] In an audit, Canada's commissioner of the environment and sustainable development found "more evidence of federal-provincial cooperation than of duplication of effort."[65] Despite extensive complaints from business, EA costs are generally less than 1 percent of project costs.[66]

Aboriginal People and Environmental Assessment

Adding another layer of complexity to federal and provincial laws governing EA is the fact that distinct EA mechanisms are being created through treaty settlements with Aboriginal people. For example, the Nisga'a Final Agreement enables the Nisga'a to create their own EA process, although federal or provincial laws will prevail in the case of conflict.[67] In Nunavut, the newly created Nunavut Impact Review Board is responsible for reviewing projects and making recommendations to the appropriate territorial or federal minister about whether a project should be approved.[68] The federal *Mackenzie Valley Resource Management Act,* which implements parts of the Gwich'in and Sahtu Dene treaties in the Northwest Territories, establishes a local EA board to assess development proposals and overrides the *Canadian Environmental Assessment Act.*[69]

These special arrangements have the potential to result in improved EA, but it is too early to determine whether that potential will be realized. Another promising development involving Aboriginal people is the trend toward incorporating traditional ecological knowledge into EA.[70] Like environmentalists, Aboriginal people are often dismayed by the prospect of unsustainable resource activities and projects. Industrial resource development often has a negative impact on the rights and lifestyles of Aboriginal people. As a result, they have challenged EA processes and decisions in the courts, with mixed results. The Cree of Northern Quebec, Taku River Tlingit, and Union of Nova Scotia Indians used litigation with considerable success. The Tsawwassen Indian Band, Cheslatta, Vuntut Gwitchin, and Naskapi-Montagnais Innu lost lawsuits.[71]

Environmental Assessment Litigation

Business and government have expressed grave concern about the number of

EAs that wind up tangled in litigation. These concerns are overstated. Only about thirty lawsuits arose from the first twenty-five thousand EAs conducted under *CEAA*, and a smaller number of lawsuits under provincial EA legislation. Many of these lawsuits involved large, high-profile projects. Most of the ten panel reviews conducted under *CEAA* between 1995 and 2001 were subject to legal challenges.[72] However, court decisions have played a critical role in shaping the EA process in Canada. Almost every year has seen one or two important EA cases decided by the courts.

In 1989 a Federal Court judge surprised federal and provincial governments by quashing a licence for the Rafferty-Alameda Dam on Saskatchewan's Souris River because Ottawa had failed to conduct an EA.[73] In 1992 the Supreme Court of Canada ruled that the federal government had failed to fulfill its legal obligation to conduct an EA of the controversial (and partially built) Oldman River Dam in Alberta.[74] The experts who conducted the court-ordered EA recommended that the dam not be completed, but their recommendations were ignored.[75] In 1993 environmentalists sued Parks Canada, challenging the piecemeal EA of the expansion of the Sunshine Village ski resort in Banff National Park.[76] The combination of the lawsuit and public pressure caused Parks Canada to reverse its position and order a full EA. Sunshine Village Corporation responded with a series of unsuccessful lawsuits in an attempt to evade the EA process, and eventually abandoned its expansion plans.[77]

In 1994 the Supreme Court of Canada ruled that the federal government had failed to fulfill its legal obligation to conduct a complete assessment of the environmental impacts of the Great Whale hydroelectric megaproject in northern Quebec.[78] The Court's decision, coupled with pressure from the Grand Council of the Crees, led to the project's cancellation. In 1995 the Federal Court ruled that an archaic Yukon mining law from 1898 (the *Yukon Quartz Mining Act)* overruled the Canadian EA regime.[79] In effect, the court decided that mineral exploration activities on public land in the Yukon could proceed without EA. In 1996 environmentalists lost a lawsuit challenging the EA of an oil pipeline in Alberta that bisected a rare area of native prairie.[80] The pipeline was built as planned. Also in 1996, the Sierra Club of Canada sued the federal government for refusing to conduct an EA of the sale of Candu nuclear reactors to China.[81] The reactors are now in operation, while the substantive issues raised by the litigation have yet to be determined by the Federal Court.

In 1997 a Federal Court judge blasted the federal government's efforts to duck EAs of projects that affect fish habitat, writing, "By making 'policy' not contemplated by the statutes, the DFO simply cannot immunize the Minister and DFO from judicial review, nor circumvent the environmental laws which they decline to obey."[82] Also in 1997, the Newfoundland Court of Appeal quashed permits for parts of the Voisey's Bay nickel project because the company was attempting to carry out its EA in a piecemeal fashion.[83] In 1998 an

Alberta environmental group won a lawsuit by arguing that a federal EA of a bridge was unduly narrow in scope and should have considered the road to which the bridge was attached and possibly the logging activities for which the road was being built.[84]

In 1999 the Federal Court of Appeal cancelled permits for an open-pit coal mine on the edge of Jasper National Park because of inadequacies in the EA.[85] The court held that the EA failed to consider critical information such as alternatives to open-pit mining and the cumulative effects of extensive mining and logging in the area. Environmentalists also lost three high-profile EA cases in 1999, involving a convention centre at Lake Louise in Banff National Park, road building and logging in Manitoba, and the Voisey's Bay mine/smelter proposal in Labrador.[86] In 2000 the Canadian Environmental Law Association failed in an effort to have a court strike down the national harmonization agreement on environmental protection, including the Sub-Agreement on Environmental Assessment.[87] Meanwhile, a group of local citizens in Ontario lost a lawsuit challenging the EA that approved a method of temporarily storing nuclear waste.[88] In 2001 the BC Supreme Court overturned the EA of a mine and access road, ruling that the government had failed to adequately address the issue of sustainability and other concerns raised by the Taku River Tlingit.[89]

Assessing EA Litigation in Canada

One of the main reasons there has been so much litigation about EA, in a relative sense, is that this is one of the few fields of environmental law in Canada where statutes impose some mandatory obligations on government. Environmental assessment laws, both federal and provincial, state that the government "shall" conduct EAs of certain projects, and "shall" consider certain factors in the course of these mandated assessments. A failure to obey these mandatory duties can be challenged in court.

The second reason underlying EA lawsuits is the ongoing conflict about what EA is intended to achieve. Environmental groups and Aboriginal people, who have filed most of the lawsuits to date, see EA as a forum for determining *whether* a particular project should proceed. In contrast, government and industry tend to view EA as a process to refine *how* a project will proceed in a manner that minimizes environmental impacts; they assume that the project will proceed because economic growth is paramount. An industry lawyer puts the issue plainly: "Few proponents are willing to risk the tens of millions of dollars in front-end costs associated with the project where the regulatory process, and thus the project's critical path, is fraught with uncertainty."[90] As a result of this fundamental conflict, EAs often turn into debates between competing worldviews that have no other arena in which they can be resolved.

Some court decisions have produced positive results for environmental protection by blocking environmentally damaging projects from proceeding.

However, the utility of using litigation to challenge EAs in Canada is limited because most of the mandatory requirements in federal and provincial EA statutes are procedural, not substantive. Courts will "jealously guard the process up to the point of the final decision to ensure that all procedural requirements have been rigorously complied with."[91] Thus lawsuits succeeded in cases where government refused to conduct an EA despite a legal obligation to do so.[92] Lawsuits also succeeded where legally required factors, such as cumulative effects, were completely ignored.[93]

On the other hand, Canadian courts are extremely reluctant to engage in substantive review of EA decisions. According to law professor Al Lucas, judicial review is "confined to the legality of decisions and will not extend to the substantive merits."[94] Lawsuits challenging the adequacy or substance of EAs have, for the most part, failed.[95] Industry emphatically rejects the idea that courts should engage in substantive review of government decisions.[96] Environmentalists respond that courts are the only forum available for appealing decisions that are factually wrong or based on false assumptions. The recent BC decision in favour of the Taku River Tlingit provides a rare example of a judge determining that the substantive contents of an EA were deficient, in that sustainability concerns were not adequately addressed.[97] Unfortunately, the requirement to consider sustainability was subsequently removed from the BC *Environmental Assessment Act*.

The most controversial EA cases involve situations where courts have been asked to determine whether governments correctly defined the scope of the project under review. In some cases, courts have ruled that government defined projects too narrowly, while other cases have upheld the government's determination of the scope of projects.[98] It seems appropriate for courts to subject government decisions about the scope of EA to careful scrutiny, given that the commissioner of the environment and sustainable development found over half of the federal departments reviewed "had leaned to a project scope more narrow than recommended."[99]

In the United States, courts have played an important role in supervising the substantive quality of EAs.[100] Such judicial activism does not exist in Canada and, from the perspective of industry and government, "would most certainly be perceived as an unwarranted intrusion into the administrative and regulatory realm of government."[101] Environmental groups and Aboriginal people, in contrast, would welcome any increase in the willingness of Canadian courts to scrutinize the substantive merits of EA decisions.

Conclusion

A tremendous gulf exists between the theory of EA and the reality of on-the-ground practices in Canada. A report prepared for the federal government concluded that the main weakness of EA in Canada is at the implementation stage.[102] Moreover, there is a contradiction between governments' stated goal of improving the quality of EA and government actions in weakening EA legislation and decreasing the staff, budgets, and resources of environmental departments. Canadian EA laws are hamstrung by the exclusion of many projects, activities, plans, and policies with significant environmental impacts. Provincial EA laws are weaker and narrower than *CEAA*. Other fundamental flaws include the unfulfilled commitment to sustainable development; the failure to consider needs, alternatives, and the full range of impacts; the lack of independent decision making; and inadequate opportunities for public participation.

Solutions for these weaknesses in Canadian EA have been proposed since the mid-1970s.[103] While procedural progress has been made, the substantive quality of EAs continues to be inadequate and the EA process is applied too narrowly. According to Professor William Rees, EA in Canada fails because of "the largely discretionary nature of the process as it is based essentially on voluntary self-assessment, the predominantly growth-oriented ideology of successive federal governments, the generally low political status of environmental issues, and an institutional framework that seems designed to circumvent political accountability."[104] Minor amendments to EA laws and policies, such as the proposed amendments to *CEAA*, will do little to address these deep-rooted systemic problems.

Perhaps because of its familiarity with the economic, social, and environmental devastation of the cod crisis, the Newfoundland Court of Appeal recognized the importance of *CEAA* and the Newfoundland *Environmental Assessment Act* in a recent decision:

> The regimes created by these statutes represent a public attempt to develop an appropriate response that takes account of the forces which threaten the existence of the environment. If the rights of future generations to the protection of the present integrity of the natural world are to be taken seriously, and not to be regarded as mere empty rhetoric, care must be taken in the interpretation and application of the legislation. Environmental laws must be construed against their commitment to future generations and against a recognition that, in addressing environmental issues, we often have imperfect knowledge as to the potential impact of activities on the environment. One must also be alert to the fact that governments, even strongly pro-environment ones, are subject to many countervailing social and economic forces, sometimes legitimate and sometimes not. Their agendas are often influenced by nonenvironmental considerations.
>
> The legislation, if it is to do its job, must therefore be applied in a manner that will counteract the ability of immediate collective economic and social forces to set their own environmental agendas. It

must be regarded as something more than a mere statement of lofty intent. It must be a blueprint for protective action.[105]

If EA in Canada was conducted with the rigour and integrity envisioned by the Newfoundland Court of Appeal, the problems would be largely solved. Unfortunately, the stubborn reluctance of industry and government to meet high standards means that controversy and litigation are destined to continue.

5 Biodiversity

> Biological diversity is the key to the maintenance of the world as we know it.
>
> *Professor E.O. Wilson, Harvard University*

> A comprehensive domestic framework for biodiversity issues remains largely undeveloped or unimplemented in most Canadian jurisdictions.
>
> *Ian Attridge, "Canadian Biodiversity and the Law"*

Biological diversity means the variety of life: the genetic, species, and ecosystem variability that differentiates Earth from every other planet in our solar system. Genetic diversity refers to the variety and variability of genes in a population, and enables organisms to adapt to changes in their surroundings and evolve in response to these changes. Species diversity is both a measure of the total number of species (species richness) and a measure of the relative abundance of species in an area (species evenness).[1] Ecosystem diversity describes the range of different biological communities, such as forests, wetlands, and prairies, which constitute the overall landscape. Ecological processes are an equally vital but often overlooked aspect of biodiversity. These are the mechanisms by which life functions, such as photosynthesis, nitrogen fixation, wildfire, and predation.

When scientists attempt to measure biodiversity, they generally focus on species richness (the number of species). About 1.75 million species have been identified to date, yet the most comprehensive global assessment ever undertaken estimated that there may be 13 to 14 million species on Earth.[2] Other estimates of global species richness range from 5 to 100 million species.[3] Fossil records suggest that in the past 500 million years there have been five waves of extinction when large numbers of species died out: 440 million years ago, 370 million years ago, 250 million years ago, 215 million years ago, and most recently, when the dinosaurs disappeared, 65 million years ago.[4] Preeminent scientists believe that humans are currently causing the sixth great extinction event in the history of life on Earth. On the other hand, skeptics argue that extinction is a natural process.[5] They are correct, to a degree. After all, 99 percent of the species that have ever lived are extinct.[6] However, what is abnormal is the current *rate* of extinction. Estimates of the current rate of extinction range from one hundred to ten thousand times greater than the normal rate.[7]

Given uncertainty about the overall number of species, the precise rate of extinctions is difficult to establish. However, there is compelling evidence that we are in the midst of an era of accelerated extinction as a direct result of human activities.[8] Between 1,500 and 2,000 species of birds have gone extinct in the last two thousand years. The World Conservation Union lists more than 11,000 species as critically endangered, including one in four mammal species and one in eight bird species. The US National Sciences Board warns that the total loss by 2020 could be as high as one-quarter of all species on Earth.[9] In the past, ecological recovery from episodes of mass extinction has taken five to ten million years.[10]

To what extent does the biodiversity crisis exist in Canada? There are myriad signs, at the ecosystem, species, and genetic levels, that all is not well. Some ecosystems in Canada are on the verge of disappearing. Coastal Douglas fir forest covers less than 1 percent of its original area. Less than 1 percent of tall-grass prairie is still in its native state. Ontario's Carolinian forest covers 3 percent of its previous range. British Columbia's Garry oak meadows occupy less than 5 percent of their historic area. Many of Canada's wetlands have disappeared, including 65 percent of Atlantic coastal marshes, 70 percent of southern Ontario wetlands, 71 percent of Prairie wetlands, and 80 percent of the Fraser River delta.[11]

In Canada there are 72,000 identified species, and scientists expect roughly the same number of as-yet-unknown species.[12] Canada's official list of species at risk records 431 species and populations (including twelve extinctions and twenty-one extirpations, i.e., species extinct in Canada but surviving elsewhere). This number is almost certainly an underestimate because very few species have actually been studied (see Chapter 5.2). At the genetic level, a telling example of loss is the extirpation of hundreds of salmon runs on both the Pacific and Atlantic coasts. The loss of these genetically unique populations weakens the overall gene pool of salmon.[13]

The loss of biodiversity is of tremendous concern for a variety of reasons. First, we have a moral obligation not to cause the extinction of other species.[14] Second, nature provides irreplaceable (albeit underappreciated) ecological services such as photosynthesis, the water cycle, carbon storage, pollination, and soil creation.[15] On a more utilitarian level, humans rely on biodiversity for food, clothing, shelter, and raw materials for medical, industrial, and commercial uses.[16] Biodiversity also offers recreational and aesthetic benefits: almost 90 percent of Canadians and millions of tourists participate in some form of wildlife-related activity each year. These activities generate billions of dollars of economic activity.[17]

Canadians care deeply about the diversity of life in this country. Wildlife are a cherished symbol of Canadian identity, from wild salmon, humming-birds, beavers, killer whales, maple trees, and loons to grizzly bears, caribou, wolves, songbirds, shorebirds, and butterflies. Wildlife are also essential to the cultural heritage of Canadians, particularly Aboriginal people. In 1992 Canada was the first industrialized nation to ratify the *United Nations Convention on Biological Diversity*. Three of the cornerstones of Canada's commitment to con-serve biodiversity pursuant to the *Convention* are to establish a national net-work of protected areas; to enact and enforce endangered species legislation; and to implement measures to protect marine biodiversity.[18] How does Cana-da's legal system fare in preserving our spectacular natural and cultural legacy?

Parks and Protected Areas

Canada's system of parks and protected areas includes national parks, provin-cial parks, wilderness areas, ecological reserves, territorial parks, and wildlife sanctuaries. Although Canada's network of protected areas covers 9.6 percent of the country, these parks are not immune to ecological problems caused by human activities both within and beyond park boundaries.[19] Recent evidence indicates that even Canada's national parks, widely acknowledged as our most stringently managed protected areas, are suffering severe environmental stresses.[20] Are Canadian laws and policies adequate to protect these natural wonders?

Endangered Species

Protecting endangered species is the biological equivalent of having emergency wards in hospitals. For close to a decade, federal and provincial governments have debated different architectural plans for building these biological emer-gency wards, but construction is barely under way. Canada passed federal endangered species legislation in 2002 after a decade of delay, but implemen-tation of the new *Species at Risk Act* has not yet begun.[21] Five provinces and territories still lack endangered species legislation. To make matters worse, despite overwhelming public opposition, Ottawa and the provinces are pro-ceeding with the ecological equivalent of two-tiered medicine. Endangered species receive dramatically different legal protection if they live on federal land or in federal waters than if they live on provincial lands and waters. Will this two-tiered legal approach protect Canada's species at risk?

Marine Biodiversity

Prior to the 1990s, little thought was given to the conservation of life in Cana-da's oceans. The seas were viewed as an endless storehouse of fish and other resources to be exploited. This cornucopian worldview came to a crashing halt with the collapse of cod stocks on the east coast. Has the federal government responded effectively to protect marine biodiversity, either by creating new laws and policies or by implementing and enforcing existing laws and policies?

Can our legal system stop the slide toward extinction facing many of Canada's ecosystems, species, and gene pools? Are the necessary tools in place to reverse today's pattern of decline so that Canadian biodiversity recovers and rebuilds to healthy levels? The following chapters attempt to answer these questions.

5.1 PARKS AND PROTECTED AREAS

From Gwaii Haanas, Banff, Head-Smashed-In Buffalo Jump, Cypress Hills, Riding Mountain, Algonquin, La Mauricie, Kouchibouguac, and Gros Morne, to Kluane, Vuntut, Tuktut Nogait, and Quttinirpaaq, Canada's national, provincial, and territorial parks are a source of tremendous pride. Over 70 percent of Canadians view national parks as icons of our national identity.[1] Former prime minister Pierre Trudeau described Canada's parks as "the greatest environmental treasures of the world."[2] Parks are where Canadians exercise restraint, putting nature's needs ahead of human demands. Parks are a soothing balm for our environmental guilt, for at least we have managed to preserve these priceless places and their extraordinary biological diversity as a lasting legacy for future generations.

Haven't we? Consider the following:

- With less than 10 percent of our country protected by 2003, Canada has broken repeated promises and failed to meet the international threshold of protecting a minimum of 12 percent of its land and waters.[3]
- Sixty other nations have protected a larger percentage of their territory than Canada.[4]
- In 2000 the Panel on Ecological Integrity in Canada's National Parks reported that thirty-eight out of thirty-nine national parks are suffering from severe ecological stress.[5]
- Hundreds of exotic species are displacing native species from Canadian parks.[6]
- Mining, logging, and oil and gas development continue to be permitted in parks in many provinces.[7]
- Governments continue to tamper with park boundaries, eliminating some parks and shrinking others.
- The United Nations warned that several of Canada's World Heritage Sites may have their status revoked if unconstrained development continues in and around the national parks within these sites.[8]

Viewed collectively, these examples indicate that Canada's legal system is failing to protect biological diversity in the very places where, at least in theory, protecting nature is the number-one priority.

Overview of Protected Areas Laws and Policies in Canada

While a plethora of protected area designations is employed by different governments, these designations generally fall into four categories: parks, wilderness areas, ecological reserves, and wildlife management areas. The laws governing these classes of protected areas vary among provinces and among different levels of government, but some broad characteristics of the protected area categories can be outlined. Parks (both provincial and national) often have a dual mandate of conservation and recreation. Wilderness areas are similar to parks but place more restrictions on commercial development and focus on nonmotorized recreation. Ecological reserves are usually smaller areas that conserve unique natural features or landscapes and have strict rules on permissible activities. Wildlife management areas protect specific species or ecosystems, but often allow a broader range of activities believed to be compatible with protecting wildlife.

More than one-third of the land protected in Canada is under federal jurisdiction, primarily in national parks, and to a lesser extent in national wildlife areas and migratory bird sanctuaries.[9] Legal experts agree that "the *National Parks Act* is the most progressive and ecologically conscious parks legislation in Canada."[10] The *Act* was strengthened in 1988 and again in 2000. Despite the strong legal framework, Canada's national parks continue to suffer severe ecological problems because of continuing commercial development within parks and destructive activities outside park boundaries.[11] The ongoing deterioration of ecological integrity in Canada's national parks contradicts the claim of some critics that the government is going too far in implementing stronger laws and policies for parks.[12]

Provincial and territorial governments manage two-thirds of Canada's protected lands. A recent assessment of provincial and territorial protected areas legislation gave passing grades only to Nova Scotia and Newfoundland and Labrador. Every other province and territory received Fs for their legislation, while Alberta and Ontario achieved the dubious distinction of an F-minus.[13] In the words of two academics, "Many provinces lack clear legislation and policy with respect to parks and protected areas. The consequence of this environmental limbo is a chaotic stream of ad hoc decisions and actions."[14] As a result, the degree of protection enjoyed by "protected areas" varies dramatically from province to province.

Three fundamental flaws inhibit the ability of Canada's legal system to protect biodiversity through parks and protected areas. First, the laws intended to protect these natural treasures, with several important exceptions, are grossly inadequate for such an important responsibility.[15] Relying on most current provincial and territorial park laws to protect biodiversity is like expecting a security firm's sticker in your window to protect your home: both give the appearance of protection without actually providing it. Second, Canada's parks are too few, too small, and too isolated to be able to protect biodiversity. These problems exist because economics, rather than ecology, dominates the process of identifying and selecting protected areas. Third, despite the Canadian pride and passion for these special places, parks are being starved of the funding necessary to ensure proper management.

Flawed Laws Governing Protected Areas

Scientific and public recognition of the biodiversity crisis dawned during the final decades of the twentieth century.[16] However, most Canadian laws governing protected areas were enacted during an earlier era and few jurisdictions have modernized their outdated legislation. For example, Ontario's *Provincial Parks Act* is largely unchanged from its 1954 version, while Ontario's *Wilderness Areas Act* dates from 1959.[17] As a result, "Ontario's protected areas legislation, particularly the *Provincial Parks Act,* has not kept pace with the emerging international emphasis on the ecological value of protected areas."[18] For years, environmental lawyers in Canada have advocated an overhaul of laws governing protected areas, with limited success.[19]

Most laws, from building codes to the Criminal Code, are updated periodically to reflect changes in values, technology, and knowledge. However, many laws governing protected areas in Canada fail to reflect either contemporary environmental values or modern ecological knowledge. A Parks Canada analysis of protected areas management in Canada observed that "in many cases, the objectives of the managing body do not even make reference to biodiversity."[20] Nova Scotia, Newfoundland and Labrador, and Manitoba are the only provinces whose protected areas legislation explicitly refers to conserving biodiversity. Similarly, none of the laws governing protected areas in Canada refer to the precautionary principle (with the sole exception of the federal *Oceans Act*).[21] Even some recent laws governing protected areas fail to reflect ecological principles and public values. The Yukon recently passed the disappointing *Parks and Land Certainty Act,* which allows industrial activities in parks. In 1999, Alberta unveiled a very regressive new law called the *Natural Heritage Act* but withdrew it in the face of strong public opposition.[22]

Laws governing the management of protected areas in Canada are generally characterized by the following weaknesses:

- Sections describing the purpose of protected areas are ambiguous and fail to make ecological integrity the top priority.
- Industrial resource activities such as logging and mining are not prohibited.
- Parks can be quickly and quietly eliminated or reduced in size.

- Management plans, and public participation in the development of these plans, are not required.
- Regular reports on the state of protected areas are not required.
- Broad, unfettered discretion is conferred upon the bureaucrats and politicians responsible for park management.

Each of these flaws will be examined in greater detail below.

Ambiguous Purpose

In recent years Canadian attitudes toward parks have evolved. Most Canadians believe that protecting nature, including wildlife, endangered species, and all aspects of biodiversity, should be the top priority in national parks, with recreation a distant second.[23] Environmental groups, such as the World Wildlife Fund and the Canadian Parks and Wilderness Society, agree, as do scientists.[24] Canadian governments at all levels also recognize that "the establishment of protected areas is an important element of Canada's effort to conserve biodiversity."[25] However, conservation is not the purpose for which many parks, and the laws governing their use, were originally created. For example, Banff, Canada's first national park, was created by Prime Minister John A. Macdonald in order to serve as a tourism drawing card and rest stop for the national railroad. Trains were eventually replaced by motor vehicles, but recreation remained the primary purpose for parks, with wildlife conservation a secondary goal.[26]

Despite the evolution of Canadian values, most protected areas legislation in Canada continues to embrace the two potentially conflicting purposes of conservation and recreation. The *Canada National Parks Act* illustrates the problem:

> 4. (1) The national parks of Canada are hereby dedicated to the people of Canada for their benefit, education and enjoyment, subject to the Act and the regulations, and the parks shall be maintained and made use of so as to leave them unimpaired for the enjoyment of future generations.[27]

For decades, this dual mandate (enjoy but leave unimpaired) resulted in excessive commercial development in some national parks, with Banff providing the most egregious example.[28] Recent amendments to the *Canada National Parks Act* failed to clarify the relative importance of conservation and use, which led the Federal Court to uphold the government's approval of a new highway through Wood Buffalo National Park despite ecological concerns.[29] In the realm of provincial legislation, only Nova Scotia's *Wilderness Areas Protection Act,* Quebec's *Parks Act,* Prince Edward Island's *Natural Areas Protection Act,* and Newfoundland and Labrador's *Wilderness and Ecological Reserves Act* are clear that conservation is the top priority.[30] In the Nova Scotia legislation, for example, recreation and scientific research are explicitly designated as "secondary" purposes. In the remaining provinces and territories, laws governing protected areas either fail to include an explicit purpose, prioritize recreation, or endorse the dual (and sometimes conflicting) purposes of recreation and conservation.

The ongoing failure to clarify that conservation is the number-one priority in *laws* governing protected areas causes serious problems. In British Columbia, despite a provincial *policy* stating unambiguously that "the preservation of park heritage values takes precedence over the provision of recreational opportunities," the government approved a major expansion of a ski resort in Cypress Provincial Park, allowing the logging of rare old-growth forests and the construction of a mountain-top restaurant. In a public review of the controversy, Bryan Williams, the former chief justice of BC's Supreme Court, concluded that the wording of the *Park Act* "creates a number of problems in determining the management priorities" and that "conservation may or may not be the primary purpose."[31] This is another example of the important distinction between law and policy. When a government breaks its own *law* it can be held accountable through the judicial system. However when a government violates its own *policy*, the only recourse is the court of public opinion.

Failure to Prohibit Industrial Activity

The second critical weakness of many laws governing protected areas in Canada is that these laws allow ecologically destructive activities such as logging, mining, oil and gas exploration, hydroelectric development, and industrial tourism. For example:

- Mining continues in an unprotected enclave in the heart of BC's Strathcona Provincial Park, and a logging road was built through the same park in 1999.[32]
- Exploration and drilling for oil and gas continues in Dinosaur Provincial Park and other protected areas in Alberta.
- Mineral exploration and mining continue in parks like Wapawekka Hills and Lac La Ronge in Saskatchewan.
- Logging continues to be allowed in Duck Mountain, Nopiming, Grass River, Whiteshell, and Clearwater Lake Provincial Parks in Manitoba, and in Algonquin Provincial Park in Ontario.
- Quebec removed legal protection for the Matamec Ecological Reserve in order to allow mining.[33]
- Nova Scotia allows mineral exploration and development in Moose River Provincial Park.[34]
- Newfoundland allowed a modern-day gold rush to continue during the process of establishing the Torngat Mountains National Park Reserve, resulting in over five hundred new mineral claims within the proposed park boundaries.

This extensive list of industrial activities in parks raises serious questions about the laws governing Canada's so-called protected areas. Until recently, even national parks were not immune to resource extraction. In 1964 Canada's National Parks Policy emphasized that industrial activities were no longer acceptable in national parks.[35] The 1979 National Parks Policy stated explicitly, "National parks are special areas which are protected by federal legislation from all forms of extractive resource use such as mining, forestry, agriculture, oil, gas and hydroelectric development, and sport hunting."[36] However, as pointed out earlier, such *policies* are not legally binding or enforceable.

Despite the National Parks Policy, clear-cut logging was allowed in Canada's national parks as recently as the early 1990s: Canadian Forest Products Ltd. was logging a fifty-thousand-hectare area of Wood Buffalo National Park (a UN World Heritage Site). Parks Canada Superintendent Doug Stewart admitted, "We're not supposed to be logging in a national park. That should be obvious."[37] However, the federal government defended the logging by arguing that it was bound by a twenty-one-year lease granted in 1983. In a groundbreaking lawsuit, the Canadian Parks and Wilderness Society sued Parks Canada for violating the *National Parks Act*. On the eve of the trial in 1992 Parks Canada capitulated, admitting that the contract with Canadian Forest Products was invalid and unauthorized by the provisions of the *Act*.[38] The logging stopped. Today, industrial resource extraction is prohibited indirectly through language in the *Act* requiring that ecological integrity be given top priority, and through a regulation limiting the use of natural resources within parks.[39]

The litigation about logging in Wood Buffalo was the first in a flurry of lawsuits involving commercial activities in and around national parks. Ski resort expansions, commercial whitewater rafting, the decommissioning of recreational airstrips, hotel expansions, commercial tours, an open-pit coal mine on the edge of Jasper National Park, the summer use of chair-lifts, new highways, and a convention centre in Banff have been the subject of legal battles.[40] All of the cases have focused more on the decision-making process employed by Parks Canada than on the substance of the decisions. Courts have yet to rule decisively on the nature of activities that will be allowed in national parks. Federal politicians responded to the barrage of litigation by attempting to strengthen the *Canada National Parks Act* in 2000. However, the first court case decided under the new *Act* ruled that the amendments were housekeeping changes rather than substantive changes.[41]

Quebec and Prince Edward Island are the only provinces whose protected areas legislation and regulations explicitly prohibit industrial resource extraction.[42] Ironically, these laws may have discouraged politicians in these provinces from creating parks, as Quebec and Prince Edward Island have the lowest percentages of land in protected areas in Canada.[43] Nova Scotia and

Newfoundland and Labrador prohibit new industrial activities but allow some existing activities to continue. A precedent-setting decision in 2001 by a Newfoundland court banned logging trucks from using roads through parks, on the basis that transporting timber was part of logging, which Newfoundland legislation prohibits in parks.[44] Laws in Alberta, Saskatchewan, Manitoba, Ontario, the Yukon, the Northwest Territories, and Nunavut allow industrial resource activity in some protected areas. For example, in Ontario the *Provincial Parks Act* allows mining, and the *Mining in Provincial Parks Regulation* identifies twenty-three parks where mining is permitted.

Protected Areas That Shrink or Disappear

Parks are more ephemeral than the public is led to believe. While environmental groups and politicians describe parks as "protected forever," laws provide far less certainty about the durability of park designations. Banff, Jasper, and Waterton Lakes National Parks were all much larger in the past.[45] Protected areas once covered 1.35 million square kilometres of the Northwest Territories (one-third of the entire territory) before being radically reduced.[46] British Columbia's Hamber Provincial Park used to be bigger than Banff and Jasper National Parks combined, protecting over a million hectares of mountains, lakes, and forests. In the early 1960s the provincial government was persuaded by industrial interests to reduce Hamber by 98 percent, leaving only twenty thousand hectares in the park. As timber, minerals, and fossil fuels are depleted elsewhere, the temptation to exploit resources within park boundaries has proven irresistible to some governments.

In 1986 Ontario quietly dropped Holiday Beach Provincial Park from the park system. British Columbia carved a chunk out of Silver Star Provincial Park for a developer in 1995. Prince Edward Island recently removed land from Brudenell River Provincial Park so a developer could build a golf course.[47] In 2002 a lawsuit stopped Newfoundland and Labrador from removing land from Windmill Bight Provincial Park for a golf course.[48] In 2001 the BC government eliminated the Southern Rocky Mountains Conservation Area and threatened to revoke the protected status of the Southern Chilcotin Mountains Park.[49]

A brief glimpse into the minutiae of the legal system is necessary to explain the ease with which governments can shrink or dismantle parks. Governments create laws and, pursuant to those laws, they can create regulations. Both laws and regulations have legal force, but there is a critical distinction in how laws and regulations are created. Laws must go through first, second, and third readings and accompanying debates in provincial legislatures or Parliament before coming into effect.[50] This is an open, public, and generally time-consuming process. In contrast, regulations can be created behind closed doors by federal and provincial cabinets, without public notice or debate.

Therefore it makes a big difference to the long-term security of a park whether its boundaries can be modified by an act of the legislature or by a regulation. National parks can be created by regulation but their boundaries can be modified only through legislation, giving them a relatively high degree of protection.[51] British Columbia, Nova Scotia, and Saskatchewan are the only provinces that require an act of the legislature to eliminate or diminish the size of a park or wilderness area.[52] In Quebec, Newfoundland and Labrador, and Manitoba, parks can be reduced or eliminated by regulation but only after meeting statutory public notice requirements.[53] However, in Alberta, Ontario, Prince Edward Island, New Brunswick, the Yukon, the Northwest Territories, and Nunavut, parks can be reduced in size or eliminated through regulations, making them vulnerable to the stroke of a politician's pen. In contrast, international standards suggest that protected areas should be reduced in size or eliminated only through legislation.[54]

Another category of parks is far weaker than those created by legislation or regulation. So-called press release parks are announced before legal steps are taken to formally create them. Such parks lack legal protection until a regulation is signed or an act is passed. Some national parks have been announced but are not yet protected by the *Canada National Parks Act*. In BC some "press release parks" on Vancouver Island were publicized years ago but still do not legally exist, leaving them vulnerable to continued industrial activity.

In 1999 Ontario set a dangerous precedent by creating "mobile" parks. On the face of it, the province's Lands for Life process created 378 new and expanded parks, adding about a million hectares to Ontario's park system.[55] However, in order to obtain the mining industry's approval, the Ontario government agreed that mineral exploration would be allowed to continue in some of the new parks. If a commercially valuable mineral deposit is found, mining will be allowed and the mined area will be returned "to the parks system when mining is finished."[56] The profoundly flawed philosophy underlying these mobile parks is that only land without economic value should be protected. Moreover, many of the parks announced in 1999 by the Ontario government are not yet legally protected.

The strongest legal protection that can be given to a park in Canada is inclusion in treaty and land claim settlements with Aboriginal people. Because treaties enjoy constitutional protection, and because changing the *Constitution Act* is a daunting task, parks included in these agreements will be extraordinarily difficult to reduce or eliminate. Most of the settlement agreements with northern Aboriginal people provide for national and territorial parks. For example, the Inuit land claim agreement confirms the establishment of Auyuittuq, Sirmilik, and Quttinirpaaq National Parks. Vuntut, Ivvavik, and Tombstone Parks were protected under the Yukon umbrella final agreement. The Nisga'a treaty in BC established Bear Glacier Provincial Park.[57]

Conversely, Aboriginal interests can hinder the establishment of protected areas. Several Aboriginal organizations have filed lawsuits contesting the creation of parks in their traditional territories. These lawsuits, from British Columbia to Labrador, have challenged the process for establishing the parks rather than the substance of the decisions. Courts have established that there is a duty on governments to consult with Aboriginal people, in a meaningful way, before making decisions about new parks.[58] As well, the final resolution of land claims agreements could potentially result in the removal of land from parks.[59]

Other Shortcomings of Protected Areas Legislation

Laws governing protected areas in Canada suffer from several other weaknesses. One problem, characteristic of Canadian environmental law, is that excessive discretion is given to politicians and bureaucrats. As one author observed, provincial park laws use loose language, provide bureaucrats with extremely broad powers that can be exercised in secret, and, in essence, preserve "the ancient discretionary power of the Queen over her lands."[60] Excessive discretion causes problems in two ways: when politicians or civil servants refuse to exercise it and when they exercise it improperly.

The first problem is demonstrated by the federal government's failure to designate wilderness areas in national parks. In 1988 the *National Parks Act* was amended to enable the formal designation of wilderness areas, which would entail strict restrictions on activities that "impair the wilderness character of the area." However, more than a decade passed before a single wilderness area was legally designated.[61] When a law uses discretionary language such as "may designate," the government cannot be forced to act.[62] To the federal government's credit, the most recent amendments to the *Canada National Parks Act* create a statutory deadline for the designation of wilderness areas identified in park management plans, thus alleviating this particular discretion problem.[63]

The second problem, improper exercise of discretion, can be seen throughout Canada's protected areas wherever governments allow ecologically destructive activities such as logging, mining, new highways, or the construction of convention centres. Discretionary language in a law means that government is not precluded from approving such activities, even though industrial development may contradict government policy. The improper exercise of discretion is extremely difficult to challenge because laws governing protected areas in Canada give governments the power to make such decisions without effective mechanisms to ensure accountability. Canadian courts tend to defer to the "expertise" of park bureaucrats when decisions are challenged in court.[64] This Canadian legal principle, known as judicial deference, means that courts will overturn only government decisions that are "patently unreasonable" or that involve a significant legal error. Evidence that a decision is wrong, or ecologically ill-advised, is not sufficient to ensure that a court will overturn the decision.

Another weakness of provincial and territorial legislation governing protected areas in Canada is that unlike the *Canada National Parks Act,* none of the laws require periodic reports on the state of the parks. Environmental lawyer Linda Nowlan observes that "the actual state of the ecological integrity of parks in BC is unknown since no comprehensive analysis has been carried out."[65] The same could be said of all provincial and territorial protected areas. Without this basic knowledge, it is difficult to evaluate the extent to which parks are protecting biodiversity.[66]

Only Newfoundland and Labrador, Nova Scotia, and the Yukon's legislation requires mandatory management planning for protected areas and public participation in the development of these plans. Manitoba requires management plans but not public participation.[67] All other provinces and territories lack legal requirements for either management plans or public participation in planning.

Ecological Problems Facing Canada's Protected Areas

From the perspective of conserving biological diversity, Canadian protected areas are often too small, too isolated, or located in the wrong places. The most damning evidence of this ecological inadequacy is that species are disappearing from protected areas. Scientific studies indicate that all of the national parks in western North America, including Banff and Jasper, are losing species.[68] In the east, Parks Canada admits that Point Pelee National Park has lost twenty-three species in the past century, Fundy National Park has lost twelve species, and Prince Edward Island National Park has lost nine species.[69]

The human activities around protected areas turn them into islands of natural habitat in a sea of highly modified landscapes. Scientists report that islands of habitat, whether surrounded by water or disturbed land, are particularly vulnerable to biodiversity losses. The smaller and more isolated an island is, the greater the susceptibility of species on that island to extinction.[70] Loss of habitat *within* islands (analogous to development within parks) exacerbates the problem.[71] The Panel on the Ecological Integrity of Canada's National Parks found that Parks Canada's ability to maintain the ecological integrity of national parks "is uncertain due to compromises in parks size, boundary configuration and adjacent land uses."[72] To avoid further loss of species from protected areas, Canada needs more and larger parks, buffer zones around parks, and greater connectivity between parks.[73]

In 2000 the World Wildlife Fund celebrated the fact that the amount of protected land in Canada had doubled since it launched its Endangered Spaces campaign in 1989. During the 1990s more than a thousand new parks, ecological reserves, and wilderness areas protected more than forty million hectares and doubled the land area protected in Canada. Governor General

Adrienne Clarkson described the campaign as an "important success" that produced "spectacular results."[74]

Despite this progress, almost every government in Canada violated its 1992 commitment to "complete Canada's networks of protected areas representative of Canada's land-based natural regions by the year 2000."[75] Only BC enacted a mandatory legislative requirement to protect land: a minimum of ten million hectares by 1 January 2000.[76] Not coincidentally, BC was the only province to fulfill its promise to protect at least 12 percent of its land base by 2000. No other province or territory has a legislative commitment to complete its protected areas system, and no other province or territory has protected 12 percent of its land base from all industrial development. BC's progress underscores the importance of using clear, legislated targets and timelines to achieve environmental protection objectives and ensure accountability.

During the 1993 federal election campaign, Jean Chrétien promised that the Liberals would accelerate the pace of national park creation and establish sixteen new parks by 2000.[77] As recently as 1998, the federal government assured the UN that it would fulfill "its commitment to complete the federal network of protected areas representative of Canada's land-based regions by the year 2000."[78] The federal government did not even come close to keeping its word, as thirteen out of thirty-nine national ecoregions still lack national parks.[79] Time is running out to protect areas in ecologically healthy condition in many regions of Canada. Back in 1989 Canada's auditor general warned, "There is a danger that opportunities to establish parks in some natural regions may disappear before the national parks system is complete."[80] Provinces and territories face similar pressures from ongoing development.

Compared to other countries, Canada has a surprisingly mediocre record on protected areas. According to the OECD, 9.6 percent of Canada enjoys some sort of protection. Not only does this fall far short of the international minimum threshold of 12 percent, this places Canada sixty-first in the world in terms of the percentage of land area protected.[81] Many other countries, including large nations and those less well-off economically than Canada, have protected a greater proportion of their geographic area, such as Australia, Germany, Costa Rica, Guatemala, Venezuela, Chile, Tanzania, Zimbabwe, and the Seychelles. The United States has protected 21.2 percent of its land.[82] The American national parks system protects ten million hectares more land than Canada's national parks system. When areas that lack effective legal protection (i.e., areas where logging, mining, and other forms of industrial activity may occur) are removed from the calculation, only 6.84 percent of Canada's land area was protected as of mid-2000.[83]

How much protected land is enough? Scientists are nearly unanimous that Canada's current goal of 12 percent is not sufficient to protect biodiversity or ecological processes. Estimates of the proportion of land that needs to be protected range from 25 percent to 75 percent, depending on a wide variety of factors.[84] A Parks Canada scientist agrees that "12 percent is a very conservative goal ... some researchers suggest that up to 35 percent protected areas with an equivalent area in complementary land uses" may be required to conserve biodiversity.[85]

Another reason existing protected areas are incapable of protecting biodiversity in Canada is that the wrong places are being protected. Decisions about which areas to protect are often based on economic rather than ecological factors. As one critic said, "The government banned hydro development where there were no rivers to dam, banned logging where there were no commercial forests, and banned mining where the mining industry indicated no valuable minerals were likely to be found."[86] The stormiest battles over new parks have involved areas of substantial economic value: copper in BC's Tatshenshini, gold in Nova Scotia's Jim Campbell's Barren, and old-growth forests in Clayoquot Sound, Gwaii Haanas, and Temagami.

A BC government study found that 61.2 percent of the area newly protected in BC from 1991 to 1996 was in the alpine and subalpine ecoregions (also referred to as "rock and ice").[87] Throughout Canada, biologically rich areas – such as old-growth forests, wetlands, estuaries, and prairies – tend to be underrepresented by parks.[88] In other words, the areas with the highest biodiversity value, which face the greatest threats from human activities, currently receive the least amount of protection.

Inadequate Resources

Despite Canadians' pride in parks, park agencies lack the financial resources necessary to protect biodiversity. At the federal level, Parks Canada has been extensively downsized since the 1980s. Staffing levels and budgets are down by at least 40 percent.[89] At the same time, there are more national parks, and changes to the *Canada National Parks Act* mean that Parks Canada should allocate more resources to protecting ecological integrity. In comparison, the budget of the US National Parks Service is four to five times larger than the Parks Canada budget although the American national park system is only 31 percent larger.[90]

The auditor general concluded in 1996 that further cuts to Parks Canada's budget would "seriously challenge" the agency's ability to preserve ecological integrity and ensure sustainable park use.[91] As author Rick Searle notes, "There is no doubt that recent budget cuts have greatly reduced Parks Canada's managerial effectiveness, especially in the areas of enforcement, research, and education."[92] The federal government responded to these concerns by restructuring the agency and forcing it to operate with a corporate philosophy and structure.[93] Although some benefits may accrue from a more businesslike approach to parks management, critics have attacked the changes, arguing that Parks Canada could be forced to treat revenue and profits as "more important than protecting ecological integrity."[94] Fortunately, the 2003 federal budget increases

Parks Canada's budget for both new park acquisition and management of existing parks.

While Parks Canada faces significant resource challenges, the problems faced by provincial parks departments are far worse. For example, to manage approximately half as many hectares as Parks Canada, British Columbia has less than one-tenth the park budget. Between 1977 and 2000, the amount of land protected in BC tripled, while the number of employees working for BC Parks fell by 10 percent. BC now has one field person for every five parks, and a budget of less than half of what it used to be.[95] In the past fifteen years in Ontario, while the area of parks has increased by 50 percent and the number of visits has increased by 60 percent, the parks management budget has declined by 62 percent.[96] Similar cutbacks are affecting provincial parks systems across Canada.

Conclusion

Placed in an international context, the scope and status of Canada's protected areas network is less impressive than many people believe, despite the magnificence of individual Canadian parks and the progress over the past decade in creating new parks. Not only has Canada set aside a smaller proportion of land than sixty other nations, but governments allow a range of ecologically destructive commercial and industrial activities within many Canadian protected areas. Existing legal tools are incapable of adequately protecting Canada's parks and their biological diversity.

Although legal experts from across the country have long advocated major reforms to laws governing protected areas, these pleas have also largely failed to move governments. Newfoundland and Labrador's *Wilderness and Ecological Reserves Act,* Nova Scotia's *Wilderness Areas Protection Act,* and the recently amended *Canada National Parks Act* are beacons of hope, lighting the way toward the legal protection Canada's protected areas deserve. These laws should serve as models, since many provinces and territories have expressed their commitment to improve parks legislation.[97] A blueprint for effective legislation, based on the best aspects of laws governing protected areas from throughout Canada, was published in 2002.[98] Of paramount importance are ending industrial resource extraction in parks and entrenching ecological integrity as the top priority for all park management decisions.

Parks cannot be expected to protect biodiversity by themselves. Instead, parks should function as core areas in a landscape where sustainable activities occupy the space between protected areas. Parks should provide representative ecological baselines for different ecosystems, so that the impacts of activities outside parks can be evaluated. As the Panel on the Ecological Integrity of Canada's National Parks concluded, "If Canadians cannot undertake the task of integrating various demands for development while protecting the ecological integrity of wild places, who in the world can?"[99]

5.2 ENDANGERED SPECIES

> Wildlife is an essential feature of life, and not
> only that, it is a treasured resource to be conserved,
> husbanded, protected and fostered, so it can continue
> to provide sustenance for the body and for the spirit
> in future ages as it has in past ages.
>
> *Mr. Justice Bourassa, Northwest Territories Territorial Court*

Canadians have a tremendous affinity for wildlife. Almost 90 percent of Canadians participate in nature-related activities such as bird watching and fishing, injecting $12 billion into Canada's economy every year.[1] Therefore it is not surprising that public opinion polls consistently show that more than 90 percent of Canadians support strong federal legislation to protect endangered species and their habitat.[2] The number of Canadians describing the loss of biodiversity as very serious and requiring urgent action has risen constantly, from 74 percent in 1996, to 77 percent in 1998, to 82 percent in 2000.[3] During the 1990s, more than 150,000 Canadians sent letters to the federal government urging the swift passage of an effective law to protect species at risk.[4]

Despite this incredible level of public support, Canada has been compared to a three-toed sloth and a "northern leopard frog on a cold spring morning" for moving so slowly to protect endangered species.[5] Canada was the first industrialized country to ratify the *United Nations Convention on Biological Diversity*. The *Convention* obligates the federal government to "develop or maintain necessary legislation and/or other regulatory provisions for the protection of threatened species and populations."[6] In 2002, a decade after signing the *Convention*, Canada finally passed the *Species at Risk Act*.

Canada's lack of progress in legally protecting species at risk is an international embarrassment.[7] Both Mexico and the United States have had strong laws in place for years.[8] Environmental groups from Mexico, the United States, and Canada filed a complaint with the Commission for Environmental Co-operation (CEC), set up pursuant to NAFTA, about Canada's failure to protect species at risk. The CEC, whose mandate is limited to investigating the failure to enforce environmental laws, found that it could not criticize Canada for failing to enforce its endangered species law because Canada had no law to enforce.[9] Canada's international reputation as an environmentally progressive nation is jeopardized by its ongoing reluctance to protect endangered species and their habitat.[10]

Others deny that Canada has a problem with endangered species and claim that legislation places an undue burden on business. Critics of the need for strong endangered species legislation cite the fact that only twelve species are known to have gone extinct since Europeans appeared in Canada.[11] This narrow perspective ignores the following facts:

- A species must be gone for at least fifty years before being confirmed as extinct, meaning that current figures on extinctions in Canada are an underestimate.
- Another 21 species have been extirpated from Canada.
- COSEWIC (Committee on the Status of Endangered Wildlife in Canada) has designated 398 more species as endangered, threatened, or of special concern.
- More than 600 species require immediate study to determine their status, according to COSEWIC.[12]
- A recent government study concluded that as many as one in three Canadian species is not secure.[13]
- Entire groups of species, such as arthropods, which make up a substantial proportion of Canada's 72,000 known species, have not yet been evaluated to determine if they are at risk.[14]
- Half of the species believed to live in Canada have not been scientifically identified, let alone studied or assessed, so there is no baseline for evaluating population declines.[15]

These facts confirm that Canada faces serious threats to its legacy of biological diversity, although we lack the knowledge to quantify the extent of the problem. While Canada commenced a comprehensive national geological survey in 1842, there has never been a national biological survey. In contrast, the United States began a national biological survey in 1993.[16] Canada's Biodiversity Convention Office admits that "Canada is still a long way from being able to produce a 'state of biodiversity' report that would provide a better understanding of the state of biodiversity in Canada."[17]

As with many other environmental issues in Canada, jurisdiction for protecting wildlife is divided between the federal and provincial governments.

The provincial record on providing legal protection for species at risk is only slightly better than the federal record. While more than half of the provinces and territories have legislation in place, these laws are largely inadequate, as the following analysis will demonstrate. Effective laws to protect endangered species must:

- designate species at risk based on scientific evidence
- prohibit harming or injuring species at risk
- protect the habitat of species at risk
- require recovery plans to be developed and implemented
- provide for effective enforcement, through both incentives and penalties.

The extent to which these criteria are fulfilled by laws and policies in Canada will be examined below.

Canada's *Species at Risk Act*

The first attempt to fulfill Canada's commitment under the *Convention on Biological Diversity* was Bill C-65, the *Canada Endangered Species Protection Act*. Introduced in 1996, Bill C-65 was widely criticized by scientists, environmental groups, provincial governments, and industry. A lawyer working for the Canadian Pulp and Paper Association described it as radical, drastic, extraordinary, extreme, and potentially disastrous.[18] Bill C-65 died on the order paper in 1997 when Prime Minister Chrétien called an early election. In 2000 Bill C-33, the *Species at Risk Act,* was introduced. Again the proposed law was attacked from all sides. Like its predecessor, Bill C-33 died on the order paper in 2000 when Prime Minister Chrétien called another early election.[19]

In 2001 the federal government introduced Bill C-5, the *Species at Risk Act,* with only minor revisions from Bill C-33. Bill C-5 prompted the same polarized reaction as the earlier bills. The David Suzuki Foundation's executive director, Jim Fulton, a former member of parliament, said, "Bill C-5 is a maze of phoney delays, short circuits, hand-offs, deception, Mickey Mouse science, false solutions and general sniveling. In its present form it should be thrown away. It is a tiny shadow to the US and Mexican laws and it reveals the Government of Canada as an international Pinocchio for signing the *Convention on Biological Diversity* and doing nothing at home."[20] At the other end of the spectrum, the Canadian Cattleman's Association, the Canadian Federation of Agriculture, the Fraser Institute, and the Western Stock Grower's Association warned that the law would be "disastrous" because it would force farmers and ranchers to "shoot, shovel, and shut up" if endangered species were found on their land.[21] Neither of these extreme perspectives is accurate. The following analysis seeks to clarify exactly how the *Act* will, or will not, protect endangered species.

The Scope of the *Species at Risk Act*

Canada's environment minister, David Anderson, claims that the *Act* "will protect habitat everywhere in Canada – not just on federal lands, not just on provincial Crown lands, but on private lands as well."[22] Unfortunately, Anderson's claim does not withstand scrutiny. The *Act* is extraordinarily narrow. It automatically protects designated species at risk in Canada only if the species is aquatic or lives on federal lands, not including federal land in the three northern territories.[23] Federal lands include national parks, military bases, Indian reserves, airports, and other federally owned areas. The *Act* generally does not apply to endangered species on provincial lands, private lands, or territorial lands in the Yukon, Northwest Territories, and Nunavut. In total, therefore, the *Act* applies to only about 5 percent of Canada's land area. In provinces where there is little federal land, such as British Columbia, the area covered by the *Act* is as low as 1 percent. The *Act* covers species in Canada's marine waters, which total roughly five million square kilometres, but provides less protection for aquatic habitat than existing provisions in the *Fisheries Act*.[24]

In theory, species at risk on provincial, territorial, and private land will be protected by provincial and territorial endangered species legislation, which is examined in detail later in this chapter. However, as international experts observe, "The effect of dividing populations and habitats by artificial jurisdictional boundaries is often to make the rational conservation and management of wild species very difficult."[25] Complex provisions in the *Act* enable, *but do not require*, the federal cabinet to extend the *Act*'s application to protect species and their critical habitat in both the provinces and the territories if, in the federal minister of environment's opinion, these jurisdictions lack effective legal protection for endangered species and their habitat.[26] These provisions, which rely on the proactive exercise of discretion by both the federal minister of environment and the federal cabinet, are known as the "national safety net" for species at risk. Given past experience with similar discretionary provisions in other federal environmental laws, the probability of the national safety net being implemented is low. Four other laws – the *Canada Wildlife Act,* the *Canadian Environmental Assessment Act,* the *Canada Water Act,* and the *Canadian Environmental Protection Act* – give the federal government the discretionary power to apply its authority on provincial lands or waters because of international or transboundary environmental concerns.[27] These discretionary powers have *never* been used.[28]

The federal government's rationale for the limited scope of the *Species at Risk Act* is that to go any further would be an unacceptable intrusion on provincial jurisdiction. This federal timidity dates back to the rise of the Quebec independence movement in the late 1960s and early 1970s. In the mid-1970s the federal government expressed reluctance about even generating a national list of endangered species for "fear of treading on the toes of the provinces."[29] A lawyer for the Department of Justice admitted that the *Act* was drafted to be as "deferential to provincial powers as possible."[30]

Under Canada's Constitution, provinces generally have jurisdiction over wildlife, except for migratory birds and aquatic species.[31] However, there are compelling constitutional arguments that the federal government could go much further to protect endangered species. Experts in constitutional law such as retired Supreme Court of Canada justice Gerard La Forest and Professor Dale Gibson have stated that the federal government has ample jurisdiction to protect *all* of Canada's species at risk, wherever these species are found, because endangered species are a national concern.[32] Gibson criticized the *Act* for taking "an unnecessarily narrow view of federal Constitutional powers."[33] The Canadian Bar Association also believes that the federal government has the constitutional authority "to enact broad endangered species legislation."[34]

The debate about constitutional jurisdiction has caused extensive delays in the passage and implementation of Canadian legislation to protect species at risk. As Canadian environment minister Sergio Marchi put it, "For too many years in this country when it has come to endangered species the time clock on the species has ticked while federal and provincial governments have bickered over the rock that the bird lands on. We argue: is it your rock, is it my rock and what do we do about it?"[35] Despite the narrow scope of the *Act,* some provincial governments (e.g., Quebec and Alberta) still perceive the law as an intrusion into their jurisdiction for managing wildlife. Unlike Canada's *Act,* with its narrow scope, the US *Endangered Species Act* applies on federal, state, and private land. The Mexican endangered species legislation also applies to all species, wherever they may be found.[36]

Scientific Listing Process

Under the *Species at Risk Act,* COSEWIC prepares a status report and classifies a species as extinct, extirpated, endangered, threatened, special concern, not at risk, or requiring further study.[37] The classification must be based on the best available scientific, community, and traditional Aboriginal knowledge. Geographically and genetically distinct populations, such as a specific salmon run, can also be listed, which is essential for preserving genetic diversity.[38] Although recommendations are made by scientists, the federal cabinet is responsible for deciding whether a species should be added, reclassified, or removed from the formal List of Species at Risk. Cabinet has ninety days to accept or reject the recommendations made by COSEWIC, after which in the absence of a cabinet decision to the contrary, the scientific recommendation automatically applies. If cabinet takes the extraordinary step of rejecting COSEWIC's scientific advice, it must publish its reasons for doing so in the public registry established by the *Act.*[39]

Giving the federal cabinet the ability to ignore expert scientific advice in deciding the status of an endangered species may undermine the *Act*. Almost two thousand scientists wrote to Prime Minister Chrétien before the *Act* was passed, warning that "Canada's endangered species are too imperiled, too close to extinction and too precious to be held hostage to lobbyists, political manipulation or simple ignorance."[40] When one considers the track record of provincial governments where legislation gives provincial cabinets the discretion to designate species as endangered, the gravity of this problem becomes obvious. Ontario's cabinet has designated only twenty-nine of the hundreds of known species at risk in that province.[41] Alberta's cabinet has designated twelve animals but no plants, although COSEWIC lists forty-three species at risk in the province.[42] Allowing the federal cabinet to decide which species will be protected raises the possibility that endangered species with low public profiles, such as insects, or species with large habitat requirements, such as grizzly bears, will not be formally designated for protection under the *Act*.

In contrast, listing decisions in the United States and Mexico are mandatory, on the basis of the best available scientific information.[43] Political, social, and economic considerations are not allowed to interfere. When these improper considerations do intervene, citizens concerned about endangered species can turn to the courts in an effort to overturn improperly made decisions.[44] At the very least, scientifically based listing decisions provide a basis for public education about the magnitude of the biodiversity problem, even if social and economic considerations subsequently lead politicians to provide suboptimal levels of protection for certain listed species.

Prohibiting Harm

The *Species at Risk Act* offers strong protection from direct harm to threatened and endangered species, but not species of special concern.[45] Unfortunately, this protection extends only to aquatic species, migratory birds, and species found on federal land.[46] A wide-ranging animal, such as a grizzly bear or mountain caribou, could be protected in a national park on one side of a mountain but targeted by hunters when it travelled to provincial land on the other side of the mountain. According to COSEWIC, more than 70 percent of Canada's species at risk either range or migrate into the United States.[47] Canada's lack of protection for these species is a concern to lawyers, scientists, and politicians in the United States, where large amounts of money are being spent on species, like bears, wolves, and caribou, that may cross the border into Canada and lose their legal protection.[48]

In limited circumstances, such as for scientific research, permits to harm a species at risk are available under the *Act*. A permit to conduct an activity that will incidentally harm a species at risk will be issued only if all reasonable alternatives have been explored, all feasible measures to reduce the impact are taken, and no threat is posed to the survival or recovery of the species.[49]

Protecting Habitat

The key to protecting species at risk is universally understood to be protecting their habitat.[50] In the words of Environment Minister David Anderson, a "federal law that does not adequately protect the critical habitat of an endangered species is a law of little value. Why? Simple. No habitat, no species. This is not a political argument, this is a biological fact. For 80 percent of all species, habitat is the critical feature of their recovery."[51] Despite Anderson's rhetoric, the weakest aspects of the *Act* are the provisions intended to protect habitat. Instead of automatically protecting the habitat of species at risk wherever they live, the *Act* protects only the "residence" of aquatic species and species living on federal lands.[52] Residence is a much narrower and more restrictive concept than habitat or even "critical habitat." To grasp the difference, imagine an endangered bird nesting in a tree in an old-growth forest on federal land. Under the *Act*, a logging company could leave that single tree standing in the middle of a large clear-cut and be in full compliance with the law. The *residence* would be intact, although the *habitat* would be destroyed. If the tree were on provincial land, the *Act* would not even apply.

Residence is a term unfamiliar to biologists or ecologists. Professor David Green, former chair of the Committee on the Status of Endangered Wildlife in Canada, stated, "at COSEWIC we deal with habitat. We don't talk about residence. We deal with habitat – critical habitat – and that's what we identify. We don't use the term residence at all, because we don't know what it means."[53] Similarly, Professor Geoff Scudder, of the University of British Columbia, said that the use of the term "residence" "is an attempt to avoid and circumvent using the word 'habitat.' It's biologically unacceptable. It doesn't mean a darn thing to a biologist and a scientist. The term 'residence' is nonsense."[54]

Habitat beyond the narrow concept of residence may be protected pursuant to the *Act* through the development of recovery strategies and action plans. The *Act* provides a mandatory process for protecting critical habitat in national parks (but not national park reserves), marine protected areas under the *Oceans Act* (but not marine protected areas under the *National Marine Conservation Areas Act*), national wildlife areas, and migratory bird sanctuaries.[55] Protecting critical habitat on provincial or territorial land is possible, but is at the discretion of the federal cabinet.[56] As environmental lawyer Stewart Elgie points out, "It would be difficult to design a more cumbersome, discretion-laden, and delay-prone process for protecting habitat."[57] In contrast to the uncertain protection for habitat provided by the *Species at Risk Act*, protecting critical habitat is *mandatory* under both American and Mexican endangered species legislation.

Recovery Plans

The *Act* involves a two-stage process: developing a recovery strategy for endangered and threatened species within one or two years of listing, respectively; and then preparing an action plan. Unfortunately, there is no time limit for completing or implementing the action plan.[58] Prior to the *Act,* recovery plans were prepared for fewer than one in ten Canadian species at risk because there was no legal obligation to prepare recovery plans and no legal deadline for completing them.[59] In this regard, the *Act* marks a significant step forward in efforts to protect endangered species and restore their populations to healthy levels.

Although recovery strategies and action plans must be prepared, significant infusions of new resources will be necessary to ensure their prompt and effective implementation. The Canadian government's 2000 budget indicated that $90 million would be dedicated to protecting endangered species over the next three years, with $45 million dedicated annually in subsequent years.[60] These sums, if they materialize, represent a major increase in Canadian spending on endangered species programs. Time will tell whether the government is willing to make the long-term investment necessary to bring endangered species back from the brink. The federal government has a track record of announcing major environmental programs and then failing to follow through with the resources required for implementation and enforcement.

Incentives, Penalties, and Enforcement

The UN's Global Biodiversity Assessment concluded that effective protection of endangered species requires a combination of carrots and sticks.[61] One of the more innovative and promising aspects of the *Species at Risk Act* is the recognition that positive incentives can play a major role in protecting species at risk. Many of Canada's endangered species hotspots are in southern Canada, where much of the land is privately owned. The *Act* specifically authorizes cooperative agreements with farmers and other landowners to conserve species at risk and their habitat. The federal government is also empowered to fund these cooperative ventures.[62] Other promising tools include stewardship action plans, land conservation easements, awards, and the ability to acquire land. A more controversial aspect of the *Act* is a provision, unprecedented in Canadian environmental law, enabling the payment of compensation to landowners who suffer economic losses as a result of the presence of endangered species on their land.[63] Environmentalists fear that the *Act's* compensation mechanism will import American legal doctrines about private property, and worry that endangered species will be held hostage by private interests seeking exorbitant levels of compensation. However, the fact that compensation is at the minister's discretion and available only for "extraordinary impacts" should limit the financial consequences of this provision.

In addition to the carrots offered by stewardship agreements and compensation, the *Act* also wields a large stick. The *Act* provides for fines of up to $1 million and jail terms of up to five years for breaking the law.[64] Concerned citizens can apply for an investigation if a violation of the *Act* is suspected, and the government is obligated to respond.[65] Despite Canada's poor record on enforcing environmental laws there is no mechanism built into the *Act* to allow the public to enforce the law when the government is unable or unwilling to do so. The failure to include such citizen enforcement provisions is a step backward from the proposed *Canada Endangered Species Protection Act,* is inconsistent with the approach adopted in the *Canadian Environmental Protection Act, 1999,* and contradicts the recommendations of the UN's Global Biodiversity Assessment.[66]

Conclusions about the *Species at Risk Act*

One of the surprising aspects of the *Act* is that it falls short of the recommendations made by several unusual alliances of environmental and industrial organizations. Prior to the introduction of the proposed *Canada Endangered Species Protection Act* in 1996, a Task Force on Endangered Species Conservation was created that included academic experts, the Mining Association of Canada, the Canadian Pulp and Paper Association, the Sierra Legal Defence Fund, the National Agriculture Environment Committee, and the Canadian Wildlife Federation. Many of the same organizations later formed the Species at Risk Working Group to provide recommendations on the *Species at Risk Act*. Both coalitions called for the legislation to include a science-based listing process and mandatory habitat protection, but the federal government ignored these recommendations.[67] The federal government also rejected many improvements recommended by the all-party Standing Committee on Environment and Sustainable Development.

Canada's *Species at Risk Act* represents a modest improvement over the status quo of not having any legislation, but falls far short of what is required to prevent extinction and ensure the full recovery of endangered species. The law is considerably weaker than either the US or Mexican endangered species laws. American lawyers who have examined the different legal regimes in North America for species at risk conclude that "habitat protection for threatened and endangered species is underdeveloped in Canada compared to the United States," with repercussions for the entire continent.[68] The narrow scope of the federal legislation means that much of the legal burden for protecting species at risk in Canada falls upon the provinces and territories.

Provincial and Territorial Endangered Species Legislation

In 1996 provincial and territorial governments signed the *National Accord for the Protection of Species at Risk,* pledging to establish "legislation and programs that provide for effective protection of species at risk throughout Canada."[69] The *National Accord* outlines fourteen specific commitments including independent assessments of the status of species, protection of habitat, timely implementation of recovery plans, and effective enforcement. By the end of 2002 eight provincial governments had endangered species legislation in place (Saskatchewan, Manitoba, Ontario, Quebec, New Brunswick, Nova Scotia,

Prince Edward Island, and Newfoundland and Labrador).[70] The remaining governments attempt to protect species at risk through laws primarily intended to regulate hunting and fishing.[71] These wildlife laws tend to ignore nongame animals, plants, invertebrates, and other lesser-known groups of species.

A 2001 report card from the Canadian Nature Federation awarded the following grades to the provinces and territories for their endangered species legislation and programs:[72]

Nova Scotia	C+	Quebec	D-
Manitoba	C	British Columbia	F
New Brunswick	C-	Newfoundland	F
Ontario	C-	Northwest Territories	F
Prince Edward Island	C-	Nunavut	F
Saskatchewan	D+	Yukon	F
Alberta	D-		

Newfoundland and Labrador would now receive a passing grade, in light of its new legislation.[73] Other provinces contest their grades, but without much substance to their arguments. In 2001 Ontario claimed that it had "the toughest and most comprehensive legislation in North America" for protecting wildlife and endangered species, but this claim is indefensible.[74] An internal report prepared for Ontario's Ministry of Natural Resources in 1993 identified numerous problems with the Ontario *Endangered Species Act* that have not been addressed.[75] Ontario's environmental commissioner warns that "species at risk are inadequately protected in Ontario because of a confusing blend of generally outmoded and ineffective laws and policies."[76] Saskatchewan also claims, erroneously, that its laws "ensure a high level of protection for species that are designated at risk."[77]

The dismal grades assigned to the provinces by the Canadian Nature Federation are supported by other critiques of provincial legislation prepared by environmental lawyers.[78] As well, an internal report prepared by the BC Ministry of Environment's chief of wildlife lists eighteen "holes" in BC's approach to protecting species at risk, concluding that BC deserved the F grade given to it by environmental groups.[79] The following examination of the five key elements of endangered species legislation illustrates the weaknesses of current provincial and territorial laws.

Scientific Listing Process

Without being designated as endangered, species enjoy no legal protection. Nova Scotia is the only jurisdiction in Canada where scientists, rather than politicians, are responsible for making this designation. All of the species listed by COSEWIC as "at risk" in Nova Scotia must be legally protected under that province's *Endangered Species Act*.[80] In every other province and territory, politicians are given the discretion to make decisions about whether species should be designated as endangered. When politicians are given this responsibility, they have failed. For a typical example, consider section 6 of BC's *Wildlife Act*, which gives the lieutenant governor in council (i.e., the provincial cabinet) the power, but not the duty, to list species as endangered:

> 6.(1) Where he considers that a species of wildlife is threatened with imminent extinction throughout all or a significant portion of its range in the Province owing to the action of man, the Lieutenant Governor in Council *may*, by regulation, designate the species as an endangered species.[81] (emphasis added)

The BC cabinet has designated only four out of more than 1,400 species identified as at risk by scientists with the province's Conservation Data Centre.[82] Prince Edward Island has not yet designated any species for protection. Newfoundland and Labrador deserves credit for listing all of the species identified as at risk by COSEWIC under that province's new legislation.[83] Nova Scotia and Manitoba are the only other provinces where more than half of the species listed by COSEWIC as nationally endangered are designated and protected by provincial legislation.[84]

Prohibiting Harm

Endangered species legislation in seven provinces, plus Saskatchewan's wildlife legislation, have reasonably strong provisions to protect listed species from direct harm. Although prohibiting killing or harming an endangered species is a basic step in conserving biodiversity, British Columbia, Alberta, the Yukon, the Northwest Territories, and Nunavut lack such legal provisions. With few exceptions, these provinces and territories preclude the hunting of designated endangered species, but are silent on the many other activities that harm species and their habitat. Other laws provide some protection for species at risk, but this protection is fragmented and largely inadequate, as internal government documents admit.[85] For example, regulations pursuant to BC's *Forest Practices Code* provide some additional protection from logging activities for some endangered species but are of limited effectiveness because of severe constraints on the implementation of the *Code* (see Chapter 4.2).

Protecting Habitat

Again, protecting habitat is a vital component of ensuring the protection and eventual recovery of species at risk. Laws in Manitoba, New Brunswick, Prince Edward Island, and Ontario provide mandatory habitat protection. It is worth noting that none of these provinces seems to have suffered economically from endangered species legislation. On the other hand, the lack of economic impact could be interpreted as evidence of a widespread failure to implement or enforce these laws.

In Nova Scotia, Saskatchewan, British Columbia, Newfoundland and Labrador, and Quebec, protecting habitat is a discretionary decision, with the predictable result that habitat is rarely protected. In British Columbia, where more than 1,400 species are at risk, critical habitat has been protected under the *Wildlife Act* for only one species.[86] Ironically, protecting habitat used to be mandatory in Quebec. However, when Quebec listed its first animal species (a fish called the copper redhorse), the Quebec government changed its endangered species law to make habitat protection discretionary.[87] The remaining provinces lack specific legal mechanisms for protecting endangered species habitat.

Recovery Plans
Nova Scotia and Newfoundland and Labrador are the only provinces where the government is under an obligation to prepare and implement recovery plans for all endangered and threatened species within specified time limits.[88] All other provinces either lack a legal requirement governing recovery plans or have a discretionary process. As a result, few provincial recovery plans have been implemented.

Incentives, Penalties, and Enforcement
None of the provinces have enforcement provisions as strong as the federal *Species at Risk Act*, although penalties are still significant. For example, New Brunswick's *Endangered Species Act* involves fines of up to $250,000 for individuals and $300,000 for corporations, while the maximum jail sentence is eighteen months.[89] Unfortunately, laws that are not enforced will fail to deter activities that harm endangered species and their habitat. As environmental lawyer Ian Attridge observes, "Enforcement has been almost non-existent."[90]

Weaknesses of Provincial and Territorial Legislation
The first obvious weakness is that five of Canada's provinces and territories lack endangered species legislation specifically intended to protect endangered species and their habitat. The second major problem is that only Nova Scotia has fulfilled the majority of the commitments enumerated in the 1996 *National Accord on the Protection of Species at Risk*. The third and perhaps most damaging criticism is that even in provinces where endangered species legislation has been in place for decades (e.g., Ontario, since 1971), the number of endangered species has not declined. This failure is due to the inadequacy of the laws, the refusal to list species at risk, the unwillingness to protect habitat, and the lack of resources allocated to enforcement.

The United States *Endangered Species Act*

Canada's legal approach to protecting species at risk has been heavily influenced by the US *Endangered Species Act (ESA),* initially passed in 1967 and strengthened in 1973.[91] The *ESA* is often referred to as the strongest environmental law in the world and has been described as "an extraordinary attempt at national self-restraint."[92] The *ESA* has been forcefully interpreted by American courts; the Supreme Court has ruled that "the plain language of the *Act,* buttressed by its legislative history, shows clearly that Congress viewed the value of endangered species as incalculable."[93] The law provides for mandatory listing based solely on scientific evidence, prohibition of harm regardless of where a species is located, mandatory habitat protection on federal, state, and private land, recovery plans within specified time limits, and enforcement by citizens if the government fails to apply the law. Nearly every state has enacted endangered species legislation and implemented programs supplementing the federal effort.[94]

Despite the strength of the *ESA,* opinion is split over its effectiveness.[95] Although the *ESA* is strong on paper, its implementation has been hampered by inadequate resources.[96] The most authoritative assessment of whether or not the law is working was carried out by the National Research Council in 1995. The study concluded that "the *Endangered Species Act* has successfully prevented some species from becoming extinct and slowed the decline of others" but that the success of the *Act* in achieving the recovery of species was more limited. Approximately half of the species covered by the *Act* either had stabilized or were improving.[97]

Part of Canada's reluctance to pass a strong federal law stems from the economic havoc ostensibly imposed on America by the *ESA.* According to its critics, "This type of legislation can have a devastating impact, particularly in resource communities. In the northwest U.S., they've had massive job losses without gaining much in conservation."[98] However, objective assessments refute the anecdotal evidence offered by opponents of endangered species legislation. The law is not as rigid as its critics suggest.[99] According to a study of over 120,000 projects by the US General Accounting Office, 99.9 percent of projects affecting endangered species were permitted to proceed.[100] Oregon, Washington, and Idaho, where "massive job losses" were supposedly caused by the *ESA,* are among the leading American states on most economic indicators, including job creation and per capita income.[101] The overall strength of the US economy in the years since 1973, when the *ESA* was strengthened, also undermines claims that the requirements of the *ESA* are a significant constraint on economic growth.[102]

Opponents of Canadian endangered species legislation exploited flawed economic arguments, based on misinformation about the American experience with the *ESA,* to delay and weaken federal and provincial legislation (see Chapter 9). The success of these opponents can be measured by the federal government's enactment of a law that is substantially weaker than comparable American and Mexican laws.

Conclusion

Both legal and scientific experts are unimpressed by Canada's efforts to protect endangered species. Environmental lawyer Ian Attridge concludes that despite modest improvements in recent years, Canada's wildlife laws "remain oriented towards the extractive use or taking of wildlife as a resource: hunting, trapping, and fishing."[103] Geoff Scudder believes that "the Canadian government seems set on a course that will not only fail to fulfill *Convention on Biological Diversity* requirements but will also fall far short of the desires of an overwhelming majority of Canadians."[104]

Canada's efforts to protect species at risk illustrate some of the fundamental problems with Canadian environmental law. There is a patchwork of provincial laws, with numerous gaps. Because of resource industry and provincial opposition, the federal government belatedly passed a weak law, thirty-five years after the United States first enacted endangered species legislation. The federal government has misled Canadians about the scope of the *Species at Risk Act*, claiming inaccurately that "the proposed Act will cover all wildlife species listed as being at risk nationally and their critical habitats."[105] Even the Senate expressed concerns about the weakness of the *Act*.[106] Both federal and provincial laws are rife with discretion, meaning that politicians cannot easily be held accountable for either refusing to exercise their discretion or improperly using it. The endangered species laws of Canada either ignore or contradict many of the basic principles of conservation biology, such as the need to address problems at the ecosystem level, the imperative of protecting habitat, the importance of ecological processes, the wisdom of a precautionary approach, and the importance of practising adaptive management.[107] These weaknesses illustrate the need for better communication between lawmakers and scientists.[108]

A scientific consensus is emerging that current approaches are not the most effective means of protecting biodiversity. The UN Global Biodiversity Assessment concluded, "Species, though important, may not be the best overall target for conservation. The ecosystem and its component communities which contain the species appear to be more appropriate targets for conservation, because they take into account explicitly the many ecological interactions between organisms and their biotic and abiotic natural environment."[109] Endangered species legislation is not a panacea but merely a tool in the much broader effort required to protect biological diversity. This effort must also include a more ecologically informed approach to land-use decisions, more and larger protected areas, more comprehensive environmental assessment, a national biological survey, greater public involvement, and more incentives for landowners and land users to protect endangered species and habitat. Additionally, adequate financial and human resources must be dedicated to implementing and enforcing these laws, policies, and programs.

At the end of the day, Canadians are more interested in whether endangered species are being adequately protected than in the legal niceties of how it happens. There is potential for rapid improvement because Nunavut, the Northwest Territories, the Yukon, Alberta, Ontario, and Manitoba have all expressed an intention to enact or improve endangered species laws. The federal *Act* will be reviewed by a public round table every two years and by a Parliamentary committee after five years.[110] These review processes will offer opportunities to strengthen the law. As E.O. Wilson concluded, "The one process ongoing in the 1990s that will take millions of years to correct is the loss of genetic and species diversity by the destruction of natural habitats. This is the folly that our descendants are least likely to forgive."[111]

5.3 MARINE BIODIVERSITY

> The oceans cover 70 percent of our planet, yet
> historically there has been little effort to preserve
> their ecological integrity.
>
> *Tim Parsons, Professor Emeritus, Department of Earth*
> *and Ocean Sciences, University of British Columbia*

Because of the immensity of the oceans, humans for many centuries regarded them as boundless warehouses of natural resources. This erroneous assumption wreaked havoc on the diversity and abundance of life in the seas. Globally, the volume of wild fish caught has increased almost 500 percent in the past fifty years.[1] As a result, 70 percent of the world's fisheries face serious difficulties due to overfishing.[2] The Living Planet Index, based on data for over a hundred marine species, documents an average decline of 35 percent in marine populations between 1970 and 1995.[3] Preeminent fisheries scientist Daniel Pauly examined forty-five years of UN data on 220 fish and invertebrate species from around the world and concluded that "continuation of present trends will lead to widespread fisheries collapses" and ultimately the breakdown of ecosystems. Pauly later conducted a similar study focusing on Canada and reached the same conclusion, describing both east and west coast fisheries as unsustainable.[4]

Marine Biodiversity in Canada

Canada's territorial seas include more than five million square kilometres of the Pacific, Atlantic, and Arctic Oceans. Canada also has the longest coastline of any nation in the world. One in four known species of animals, plants, and microbiota in Canada – roughly 17,750 species – is marine.[5] Despite popular icons such as killer whales, belugas, starfish, and sea otters, the diversity of life in Canada's oceans is largely unknown, out of sight and out of mind.

Yet even for landlocked Canadians, oceans are essential to well-being. Oceans provide food, medicines, industrial products, and tourism opportunities generating employment and economic activity worth $20 billion annually in Canada.[6] The fishing industry depends on healthy marine ecosystems, so that protecting biodiversity effectively protects fishers. Exciting new marine-based medical and industrial opportunities are being explored.[7] Most importantly, oceans provide irreplaceable ecological services, such as producing oxygen, absorbing carbon dioxide (the main gas causing global warming), regulating the climate, and recycling water.[8]

The importance of marine biodiversity continues to be overlooked. A recent assessment of Canadian biodiversity by the federal, provincial, and territorial governments examined over 1,600 species, yet only 3 percent of the species studied were marine.[9] Of the 431 species on Canada's list of endangered species, fewer than 40 are marine.[10] This is not an indication that marine ecosystems are healthier than terrestrial ecosystems but that marine species receive less scientific attention. Substantial numbers of marine species in Canada's oceans have never been identified, let alone studied.[11] Only a handful of Canadian marine species are known to have gone extinct, including the great auk (last seen in 1844), Labrador duck (1878), and the sea mink (1894). The marine species most recently designated as extinct, the eelgrass limpet, was last seen in 1929.

Despite the lack of recent documented extinctions, Canada's record on marine biodiversity is far from impressive. The total volume of fish caught in Canada fell 41 percent between 1990 and 2000. Atlantic salmon populations have fallen 85 percent since the 1960s.[12] The Department of Fisheries and Oceans (DFO) continues to permit the destructive practice of bottom dragging, described by some marine biologists as the aquatic equivalent of clear-cutting.[13] There are fewer than eighty killer whales remaining in the southern resident population near Vancouver Island, due to toxic pollution, decimated salmon populations, and commercial whale watching.[14] On Canada's west coast, fishing for ling cod and rockfish continues to be allowed by DFO despite scientific warnings and populations that are 95 percent lower than historic levels.[15] Canadian marine mismanagement is epitomized by the sad sagas of the Atlantic cod and Pacific salmon. There are many parallels between the two stories, including descriptions of past abundance that seem almost mythical, repeated but unheeded scientific warnings, political hubris, and swift population collapses.

Atlantic Cod

Explorer John Cabot said that the Grand Banks on Canada's east coast were so full of cod that the fish "could be taken not only with a net but in baskets let down with a stone."[16] From 1850 to 1960, the annual east coast cod catch averaged 200,000 tonnes. By 1970 the annual catch had quadrupled to 800,000 tonnes, largely because of the advent of the factory freezer trawler.[17] In 1977 Canada extended its authority to the two-hundred-mile offshore limit, in keeping with changes in international law, but Canadian trawlers simply took the place of foreign trawlers. The latter continued to fish heavily on the Grand Banks just beyond Canada's exclusive economic zone.

In the early 1990s the roof caved in. Federal fisheries ministers and bureaucrats with DFO were aware "as early as 1986 that the northern cod stock was less than half what they thought it would be."[18] Blind to all warnings, DFO continued to set fishing quotas far in excess of what scientists recommended. For example, in December 1988 DFO scientists advised Fisheries Minister Tom Siddon to set the 1989 quota at 125,000 tonnes. He set the quota at 235,000 tonnes. The 1992 quota set by Fisheries Minister John Crosbie was 185,000 tonnes despite the fact that all-out fishing in 1991 netted only 127,000 tonnes. Crosbie claimed "there was no advice indicating at this time that there should be any further reduction."[19] The Atlantic cod fishery was completely closed in July 1992. Cod had suffered a 97 to 99 percent reduction in biomass, and the consensus among scientists is that overfishing was the dominant cause of the cod's disappearance.[20] Carl Safina, an American fisheries expert, describes the collapse of Canada's cod fishery as "apocalyptic." Safina considers that "the international debacle in this region is the worst fishery management failure in the world."[21] From 1994 to 2000, over $2.6 billion in federal funds were allocated to restructuring and adjustment measures.[22]

The Canadian government never fully accepted responsibility for the cod collapse, blaming changes in ocean conditions and predation by seals, and claiming that DFO had "a stringent conservation regime."[23] DFO tried to prevent the Committee on the Status of Endangered Wildlife in Canada (COSEWIC) from placing Atlantic cod on the national list of species at risk, despite a scientific assessment concluding that cod should be designated as endangered.[24] Canada also fought attempts by the World Conservation Union to put Atlantic cod on the global red list of endangered species.[25] Atlantic cod remain on the global red list today, despite Canada's objections, and are listed as a species at risk within Canada. A decade after the closure of the fishery, Atlantic cod have not begun to recover.[26]

Pacific Salmon
Aboriginal oral history in British Columbia describes rivers so choked with salmon that people could walk across the water on their backs. Scientists estimate that in the nineteenth century, 120 to 160 million salmon would return to the Fraser River in a good year.[27] This extraordinary abundance of salmon returns has been decimated. Total salmon returns to BC rivers, although subject to natural fluctuations, are down by 80 to 90 percent since the turn of the century. For example, from 1.5 to 3 million sockeye salmon used to return to

Rivers Inlet; in the fall of 1999 fewer than 3,600 sockeye returned to spawn there.[28] The Yukon and BC have already lost at least 142 salmon runs, another 624 runs are on the brink of disappearing, and the status of thousands of other runs remains unknown because there are no resources to conduct inventories.[29] In a statement that echoes the government's denial of the cod collapse, Environment Canada claims that most Pacific salmon stocks "are in relatively good condition."[30]

In 1990 the federal government's *Green Plan* announced that the minister of fisheries and oceans would double the fish population in the Fraser River through stock rebuilding, protection of the habitat base, and the removal of migratory barriers. Scientists argue that a more appropriate target would be to restore the Fraser River salmon runs to historic levels, roughly ten times current populations.[31] Instead of restoring Pacific salmon populations during the early 1990s, however, Canada held the fish hostage in a dispute with the United States. The so-called salmon wars, fought over which country's fishers should harvest more fish, battered already depressed Pacific salmon populations. More than 80 percent of returning salmon were caught. In 1993 aggressive fishing came within hours of eliminating the huge Adams River run of sockeye salmon, which a public inquiry concluded would have had "devastating consequences for the Pacific fishery."[32] Overall, the commercial catch of Pacific salmon fell from forty million fish to ten million during the 1990s.[33]

Various experts were highly critical of DFO's mismanagement of salmon. Inquiries established in 1992 and 1994 to investigate the crisis identified budget cuts, information gaps, overly aggressive catch levels, and habitat loss as key factors in the demise of Pacific salmon.[34] Despite the many recommendations put forward in these reports, management changes were slow in coming. The auditor general's 1999 assessment of the Pacific salmon fishery concluded that the "fisheries management crisis has cast a cloud of uncertainty over the future of the salmon fisheries ... more stringent controls are needed in the short term to ensure that salmon survive."[35]

Environmental Laws to Protect Canada's Marine Biodiversity

Many human activities threaten the survival of marine biodiversity. According to marine experts, the five main threats are overexploitation (i.e., overfishing), loss of habitat, pollution, invasive species, and global atmospheric change (including climate change and ozone depletion).[36] Scientists believe that unless all five of these pressures are alleviated through effective laws and policies, the sustainability of Canada's fisheries is in grave doubt.[37]

From a legal perspective, protecting the diversity of life in Canada's marine waters is primarily a federal responsibility, one of the few environmental areas where constitutional jurisdiction is relatively clear. The *Constitution Act, 1867* explicitly assigns the federal government responsibility for "seacoast and inland fisheries." Even when activities on provincial land affect marine ecosystems,

Canadian courts have ruled repeatedly that Ottawa can intrude upon the provincial sphere of responsibility to the extent necessary to protect fish.[38]

The *Fisheries Act,* originally passed in 1868, is the federal government's primary law for conserving marine biodiversity. The *Act* is described by environmental lawyers as a "powerful weapon," "the strongest environmental law in Canada," and "the finest piece of environmental legislation in the country."[39] The *Act* prohibits damaging fish habitat, prohibits depositing harmful substances into water where fish live, allows the federal government to ensure adequate water flows in rivers and streams, and gives the federal government broad powers to control and regulate all types of fishing. Despite the *Act's* reputation as Canada's toughest environmental law, some of Canada's worst environmental disasters involve fisheries and oceans.

Addressing the Main Threats to Marine Biodiversity

Overexploitation

Overexploitation is widely regarded as the most important threat facing many marine species.[40] The federal government has "absolute discretion" under the *Fisheries Act* to issue fishing licences and regulate fishing activities.[41] All fishing for marine species requires a federal permit. Commercial fisheries are regulated through limits on boat licences, area closures, seasonal closures, equipment restrictions, and quotas.[42] Recreational marine fishing requires a federal licence and is regulated by daily or total catch limits and area closures.[43] Aboriginal fisheries are also subject to federal licensing and conservation regulations, despite the existence of constitutionally protected Aboriginal rights to fish.[44]

Motivated by the decline of cod and salmon, Canada played a key role in the negotiation of the 1995 international agreement to protect straddling fish stocks and highly migratory fish.[45] Canada has strong domestic legislation, the *Coastal Fisheries Protection Act,* which prohibits fishing by foreign vessels within Canada's territorial sea and on the high seas in areas where there are fish populations that range in and out of Canadian waters.

Despite the Atlantic cod and Pacific salmon debacles, DFO continues to allow unsustainable commercial and recreational fisheries, largely in response to political and economic pressure from the fisheries industry.[46] Bycatch (which includes unwanted species and fish that are too small) also contributes to overexploitation.[47] Canada's auditor general has reported, in blistering detail, on the management failures in the Atlantic groundfish, Atlantic shellfish, and Pacific salmon fisheries. With respect to Atlantic groundfish, the auditor general found "incomplete understanding of the biology of stocks," "limitations in the data," "excess harvesting capacity," and "unrecorded landings, misrecorded landings, dumping of bycatch and highgrading."[48] In his 1999 reports on Atlantic shellfish and Pacific salmon the auditor general noted the limited knowledge of ecological factors, limited scientific information, and lack of

enforcement capacity.[49] The auditor general revealed that shellfish management decisions contradicted scientific advice and that key conservation measures were dropped because of industry objections.[50]

The current regulation of groundfish in British Columbia reveals that DFO
continues to sanction overfishing. Management is hampered by a lack of basic
understanding about the ecology of marine species and ecosystems, a lack of
information about the stock status of many species, and a refusal to use a
precautionary approach in the face of scientific uncertainty. For example, an
assessment prepared by DFO scientists about canary rockfish, a species caught
by both commercial and sports fishers on the west coast, states that "stock
boundaries are unknown," "stock status is unknown," "future outlook is unknown," and "the stocks are probably close to maximum exploitation but actual status is unknown."[51]

Inadequate funding is a major problem for fisheries management. DFO's
entire Pacific region budget of $300 million amounts to less than half of what
the US government spends annually on salmon conservation initiatives on
the Columbia River.[52] More than 80 percent of DFO's budget in the Pacific
region is devoted to salmon, yet salmon make up only 15 percent of the total
catch by value and by volume.[53] The neglect of species and smaller stocks that
lack commercial importance poses a threat to biodiversity.[54] Resources are also
inadequate to stop the poaching of marine species. For example, poaching of
northern abalone, a species listed by COSEWIC as threatened, is estimated to
be occurring at higher levels than were ever legally permitted.[55] Canada's lengthy
coastline and huge territorial sea contribute to the difficulty of enforcement.
For the entire country, DFO has 644 fisheries officers (some of whom are
seasonal) to cover more than five million square kilometres of ocean and more
than 240,000 kilometres of coastline.

For over one hundred years, Canadian courts have ruled that the federal
government must "protect and preserve" Canada's fisheries.[56] A number of
lawsuits have attempted to force DFO to take a more conservative approach
to fisheries, with mixed success. In the early 1990s, concerned Newfoundland
fishers lost a case in Federal Court that tried to stop DFO from allowing bottom trawling in areas used by Atlantic cod for spawning. The fishers warned of
the imminent commercial extinction of cod and the devastation of hundreds
of coastal communities. However, the court ruled there was inadequate evidence of harm to cod.[57] On the other hand, the Inuit won a lawsuit challenging a 1997 DFO decision to increase the commercial catch of turbot.[58] Aboriginal
people in British Columbia filed several lawsuits during the 1990s in attempts
to reduce fishing of endangered coho salmon populations. The Neskonlith
First Nation was unsuccessful in court but its actions did pressure DFO to
exercise more caution in regulating coho salmon harvests in future years. Nevertheless, coho salmon from the BC interior were added to Canada's list of
species at risk in 2002.[59] In 2001 the Ecology Action Centre filed a lawsuit

against DFO seeking an environmental assessment of the destructive practice of bottom dragging on the east coast.[60] The mixed success of lawsuits seeking to conserve fish, despite DFO's history of errors, reflects the Canadian judiciary's tendency to defer to the expertise of government decision makers in matters concerning science and environmental policy.

Habitat Protection

The second major threat to marine biodiversity, destruction of habitat, is addressed by section 35(1) of the *Fisheries Act,* which states: "No person shall carry on any work or undertaking that results in the harmful alteration, disruption or destruction of fish habitat."[61] In characteristic Canadian environmental law fashion, the next section of the *Act,* section 35(2), allows DFO to grant permits for damage to fish habitat. In the past, DFO issued thousands of section 35(2) habitat destruction permits annually. That practice changed in the mid-1990s with the enactment of the *Canadian Environmental Assessment Act (CEAA),* which requires a federal environmental assessment every time a permit is granted under section 35(2).

In order to avoid the scrutiny provided by the environmental assessment process, DFO began issuing informal "letters of advice" and "referrals" indicating that fish habitat could be damaged without a permit or fear of prosecution. Because DFO avoided issuing a formal permit, *CEAA* was not triggered. A Federal Court judge criticized DFO's actions as "a transparent bureaucratic attempt at sheer evasion of binding statutory imperatives. It is neither cute nor smart, and this Court is not duped by it."[62] Despite this harsh judicial criticism, DFO continues to issue over ten thousand referrals and letters of advice while conducting fewer than four hundred environmental assessments annually. The number of screening-level environmental assessments conducted by DFO fell from over 12,000 in 1991-2 to 233 in 1995-6.[63]

Canada's auditor general observed in 2000 that DFO seldom follows up on projects after issuing letters of advice, although these projects often result in damage to fish habitat. As a result, DFO fails to monitor the cumulative impacts on fish habitat. The auditor general warned that "an accumulation of small habitat losses could result in a significant impact; indeed, such losses are probably the source of the slow net loss of habitat that is occurring."[64] Bill C-115, the amended *Fisheries Act* introduced in 1996, was supposed to establish national habitat protection standards for provinces with delegated responsibility for fish habitat. The law was never enacted.

Marine Protected Areas

Marine protected areas could play a vital role in conserving marine biodiversity by protecting habitat, maintaining or restoring ecosystems, permitting populations to recover, and increasing our knowledge and understanding of marine ecosystems. Although Canadian interest in marine protected areas dates back to the early 1970s, this interest blossomed in the 1990s because of "increased recognition that the world's marine and aquatic environments are considerably less healthy and are providing fewer ecosystem services than before humans began impacting these systems on a global scale."[65] Canada has many legal tools for establishing marine protected areas. Federally, the *Canada National Parks Act,* the *Oceans Act,* the *Canada Wildlife Act,* and the *National Marine Conservation Areas Act* all offer means of designating and managing areas where activities harmful to marine life could be limited. Several provinces with coastlines also have laws governing marine protected areas.[66]

Yet while the proportion of Canadian land protected from resource exploitation may seem low at 6.8 percent, the proportion of Canada's marine waters that enjoy similar protection is less than 0.1 percent.[67] Although approximately two hundred marine protected areas have been designated by various levels of government in Canada, fishing – the main threat to marine biodiversity – occurs in almost all of these so-called protected areas. There are only five extremely small exceptions, all located in British Columbia.[68] The bottom line, according to DFO scientists, is that "in the marine environment, there are virtually no areas at this time where all marine species and habitats are simultaneously protected through legislation."[69] Some scientists have estimated that at least 40 percent of the marine environment should be protected in order to take a truly precautionary approach.[70] Furthermore, it bears repeating that in light of DFO's limited resources, the creation of new laws is more easily accomplished than the effective implementation and enforcement of those laws.[71]

Pollution

A number of the marine species on COSEWIC's list of species at risk are endangered in part by pollution, including beluga whales, killer whales, harbour porpoises, and sea otters. Persistent organic pollutants (POPs) are particularly problematic in the marine context: they weaken reproductive success, suppress immune function, bioaccumulate upward through the marine food chain, and cause death. Killer whales and beluga whales exhibit extremely high levels of contamination, reflecting their position at the top of marine food webs.[72] Most of the pollution that affects marine species comes from sources on land. According to the World Conservation Union, "While the impacts of airborne and vessel sources are also significant, toxic chemicals, sewage, and agricultural runoff cause even more damage."[73]

The pollution provisions of the *Fisheries Act* are very strong, at least on paper. Section 36(3) prohibits the deposit of any "deleterious" substances into water where fish live.[74] Regulations authorize the discharge of effluent, meeting prescribed standards, from six major industries. Problems with the regulations include their narrow coverage (many industries and biological and chemical pollutants are omitted), the lack of emphasis on pollution prevention, and the grandfathering of older industrial operations.[75] Other Canadian laws play a significant but secondary role in protecting marine life from pollution. The *Canadian Environmental Protection Act, 1999* regulates some toxic substances and prohibits dumping substances at sea without a federal permit. The *Canada Shipping Act* and regulations govern certain forms of pollution – such as oil, sewage, and garbage – from ships. The *Arctic Waters Pollution Prevention Act* prohibits the deposit of any kind of waste in arctic waters unless authorized by regulation.[76]

However, the ability of these laws to protect marine ecosystems from pollution is undermined by the lack of effective enforcement. The pollution provisions of the *Fisheries Act* (s. 36) are enforced by Environment Canada, instead of DFO.[77] There are about ninety Environment Canada pollution enforcement personnel for the entire country, and these individuals are expected to enforce more than thirty laws and regulations. An internal study done by Environment Canada in 1993 concluded that at least three hundred staff would be required for effective enforcement. In 1998 Parliament's Standing Committee on Environment and Sustainable Development issued a scathing report on the enforcement of pollution laws in Canada, concluding that Environment Canada was failing to enforce the law because of inadequate resources and insufficient personnel. Provinces with responsibility for enforcing section 36 of the *Act* under federal-provincial agreements were equally ill-equipped to do the job.[78] For example, Ontario and Quebec devote no resources to enforcing the *Act* despite having signed agreements with Ottawa that they would do so.

A report for Environment Canada concluded that shipping companies on the east coast are dumping oily waste at sea because it is cheaper than properly disposing of it in a port, and the risk of being caught and prosecuted is low. The number of seabirds harmed by heavy fuel oil off Newfoundland's coast has risen steadily over the past fifteen years, yet only a few companies have been prosecuted and fines have been minimal.[79] There are similar concerns in British Columbia about pollution from cruise ships, which face stiff regulations in US waters but not in Canada.[80] Two convictions in 2002 for dumping oil produced record fines of $125,000, indicating growing awareness of this problem.[81]

Under the North American Agreement on Environmental Cooperation (the environmental side agreement to NAFTA), citizen groups have filed three submissions asserting that Canada is failing to adequately enforce the *Fisheries Act*. In the first case, the Commission for Environmental Cooperation (CEC) conducted an investigation and determined that Canada was failing to enforce the law against BC Hydro despite damage to fish habitat caused by BC Hydro's hydroelectric operations. The two ongoing cases involve allegations that Canada is failing to enforce the *Fisheries Act* against mines that are depositing deleterious substances into fish-bearing waters and against logging companies that are destroying salmon habitat.[82]

DFO is required, under the *Fisheries Act,* to publish annual reports describing the enforcement of the *Act*'s habitat and pollution provisions. From 1994 to 1998, DFO failed to publish its enforcement reports, covering up an embarrassing lack of action and violating the law in the process. Commercial fishers and environmental groups filed a lawsuit in 1998 to compel DFO to produce the overdue reports. The federal government responded to the lawsuit by blaming the delay on its inability to obtain information from provincial governments who were delegated responsibility for enforcement.[83]

In addition to inadequate resources, lack of political will hampers enforcement of pollution laws. Jobs and other economic factors are more important to federal and provincial governments than environmental protection. For example, law professor David VanderZwaag observes that "few prosecutions have occurred against pulp mills for pollution violations due to the fact that a majority of mills are located in relatively small communities where mills are the key employer."[84]

Invasive Species

The fourth main threat to marine biodiversity is invasive species, also called exotic or alien species. Invasive marine species can be introduced by accident (e.g., zebra mussels arriving in the ballast water of ships), on purpose (e.g., Atlantic salmon used in aquaculture operations in Pacific waters), or through migration (e.g., green crabs from Asia brought to the west coast of the United States are moving north into Canadian waters). Invasive species can outcompete and eradicate native species, alter predator-prey balances, and transmit new pathogens and diseases. There are over 160 alien species in the Great Lakes alone.[85]

Canada's present regulatory approach to preventing the introduction of invasive species is fragmented and ineffective. A number of federal departments, including Fisheries and Oceans Canada, Environment Canada, Agriculture Canada, Health Canada, and Canada Customs and Revenue are involved, using a variety of different regulations.[86] In contrast to the United States, where the *National Invasive Species Act* makes ballast water exchange mandatory for ships entering the Great Lakes, Canada relies on voluntary guidelines. Both the International Joint Commission and the Great Lakes Fishery Commission warn that Canada's approach puts the biodiversity of the Great Lakes at risk.[87] Fisheries and Oceans Canada admits that Canada needs "greater protection for Canadian environment and industries from introduction of exotic species."[88] The challenge posed by invasive species is expected to increase in the future as international trade and travel continue to grow.[89]

The use of exotic species for fish farming also may cause environmental damage. For example, farmed Atlantic salmon on the west coast pose a threat to native Pacific salmon. During the 1990s more than 345,000 Atlantic salmon escaped from BC salmon farms. Despite industry claims that they would be unable to reproduce in Pacific waters, Atlantic salmon are now present in at least seventy-nine BC rivers and streams. Canada's auditor general concludes that DFO "is not fully meeting its obligations under the *Fisheries Act* to protect wild Pacific salmon stocks and habitat from the effects of salmon farming in B.C."[90]

Global Atmospheric Change

The fifth major threat to marine biodiversity, global atmospheric change, includes both climate change and ozone depletion. Climate change causes major changes in habitat, in ocean circulation patterns, and in the geographic distribution of species – both predator and prey.[91] Some marine species, such as salmon and coral, are very sensitive to minor temperature variations.[92] Increased UV-B radiation resulting from ozone depletion harms phytoplankton, zooplankton, and picoplankton (the tiny organisms that play a vital role in marine food chains), as well as macroalgae, seagrasses, coral, and sea urchins. The Arctic Ocean is particularly vulnerable to the effects of both climate change and ozone depletion. Laws and policies governing fisheries and oceans are not intended to address these global problems (see Chapters 3.1 and 3.2).

Beacons of Hope for Canada's Marine Biodiversity

In 1996, Canada passed a new law called the *Oceans Act*, promising a new era of integrated, ecosystem-based management of Canada's marine regions. Under the *Act*, the minister of fisheries and oceans is responsible for developing a national strategy for Canada's coastal and marine ecosystems, in collaboration with provincial governments, Aboriginal organizations, and coastal communities. The *Oceans Act* requires that the national strategy be based on three pillars: sustainable development, the precautionary principle, and integrated management. Although the national strategy was published in 2002, its implementation has not yet begun.[93] Despite provisions in the *Oceans Act* for integrated management plans covering estuaries, coastal waters, and marine waters, none have been completed.[94] The *Oceans Act* also provides a mechanism for establishing marine protected areas. The first marine protected area under the *Oceans Act* was legally designated in 2003, seven years after the law was enacted.

Two more recent laws may provide additional tools for the conservation of marine biodiversity: the *Species at Risk Act* and the *National Marine Conservation Areas Act*. The *Species at Risk Act* may provide additional resources and address some threats to marine species, although the law suffers from some serious weaknesses (discussed in Chapter 5.2).[95] The *National Marine Conservation Areas Act* provides yet another tool for creating marine protected areas, but also suffers from significant flaws, such as allowing fishing in marine protected areas.[96] If some loopholes are closed and more resources are dedicated to marine conservation, these new laws could significantly improve protection for marine biodiversity in Canada.

During the 1990s, the Supreme Court of Canada made a number of decisions in cases about Aboriginal fishing rights. In each and every one of these decisions, from the *Sparrow* decision in 1990 to the *Marshall* decisions in 1999, Canada's highest court stated that conservation must be the overriding priority in fisheries management.[97] To use the court's own words, "The paramount regulatory objective is conservation."[98] The court also held that the conservation mandate goes beyond merely preventing extinction to include a positive duty to increase fish populations.[99] Although there is no language in the *Fisheries Act* suggesting that conservation is the overriding priority in fisheries management, the Supreme Court rulings are based on the irrefutable premise that unless conservation comes first, fisheries may be depleted, to the Canadian public's collective detriment.

The federal government claims that it has incorporated the Supreme Court of Canada's decisions into its fisheries management policies. According to Environment Canada, "Canada faced extraordinary social, economic and political costs when it made conservation the top priority in fisheries management decisions. In the wake of the collapse of Atlantic groundfish stocks and poor Pacific salmon returns, the Government of Canada resisted the pressure to compromise the future and has put in place measures that will ensure the sustainable management and exploitation of fisheries resources."[100] In reality, as the evidence in this chapter proves, Canada's progress in making conservation the top priority in fisheries management has been sporadic at best.

Conclusion

Among Canadian environmental laws, the area of marine biodiversity is anomalous because the requisite legislation exists to get the job done. The toolbox is full, but there is a shortage of carpenters and funds for construction. Despite strong laws and ecologically intelligent decisions from the Supreme Court of Canada, fisheries management continues to be skewed by social and political considerations like unemployment and elections. The Atlantic cod fishery was reopened briefly, and east coast turbot quotas were boosted, just before the federal election in June 1997, despite scientific advice to the contrary. It is little wonder that more than 60 percent of Canadians surveyed in 2001 by DFO believe Canada's oceans are poorly managed.[101]

Despite our history of mismanaging marine ecosystems, marine ecologists remain optimistic. As fisheries scientist Scott Wallace points out, "It's not like on land, where the wildlife are gone forever once you take away the habitat and build on it. In the ocean, the habitat is still there. It's just that the fish aren't."[102] Canada's goal for marine biodiversity must not be to merely protect and sustain today's depleted marine populations but rather to rebuild these ecosystems to their past diversity and abundance. As author Michael Harris concludes in *Lament for an Ocean*, "On paper we now have an excellent system. In practice we continue to make the same old mistakes."[103] Similarly, Professor David VanderZwaag says Canadian efforts to protect marine biodiversity "have largely remained at a conceptual level."[104] Strong laws alone cannot protect marine biodiversity unless they are rigorously enforced, and rigorous enforcement of Canada's marine protection laws will require a significant investment of resources.

PART TWO
Diagnosis

An investigation or analysis of the cause or nature
of a condition, situation, or problem.

6 Strengths and Weaknesses of Canadian Environmental Law and Policy

The examination, in Chapters 2 through 5, of Canadian laws and policies intended to conserve and protect water, air, land, and biodiversity reveals a number of recurring themes. Some explain Canada's progress in addressing specific environmental issues. Others identify debilitating, systemic weaknesses that have limited, and in some cases precluded, environmental progress. The balance of evidence indicates that weaknesses outnumber strengths by a sizeable margin, but delving into the reasons behind both successes and failures offers useful insights.

Examining areas where environmental progress has been made contributes vital information about the kinds of laws and policies that are effective. Highlighting progress also generates hope and optimism that further improvements are possible. The relentless negativity around environmental issues tends to cause apathy, cynicism, and a reluctance to make the changes needed to solve the problems. However, reflecting upon the weaknesses is necessary to provide guidance for better decision making in the future. Probing these systemic weaknesses reveals a deeper level of structural obstacles to future improvements in environmental law and policy in Canada. Finally, it is crucial to understand the root causes of environmental degradation so that laws and policies can target these root causes rather than merely treat their symptoms.

Canada's progress on environmental issues is often overlooked. Important lessons can be learned from our progress in reducing the use of ozone-depleting substances, acid rain, other air pollutants (such as lead, volatile organic compounds, and carbon monoxide), industrial water pollution, and municipal waste. Insights also can be gained by examining why strides have been made in recycling, protected areas, forest practices, and sewage treatment. The reasons for improvements in Canada's environmental record include international pressure, effective laws and regulations, intergovernmental cooperation driven by federal leadership, pressure from environmental groups and the public, progressive decisions from the Supreme Court of Canada, proactive steps taken by local governments, and the emulation of American environmental laws and policies.

On the negative side, there are systemic weaknesses that cause Canada's legal system to fail in vitally important areas: Canada is missing many basic environmental laws; existing laws are plagued by excessive discretion; laws and policies fail to reflect contemporary scientific knowledge; implementation and enforcement are undermined by inadequate resources; the public lacks opportunities for meaningful engagement; and governments rely upon an unduly narrow range of legal tools to address environmental problems. These problems in environmental law and policy are major contributors to Canada's poor environmental record relative to other industrialized nations.

Remedying these systemic weaknesses poses a daunting challenge. To make matters even more difficult, there are deeper societal obstacles to future improvements in environmental law and on-the-ground progress in protecting the environment. These underlying obstacles include ongoing constitutional uncertainty and the possibility of Quebec separation; the lack of separation of powers between the legislative and executive branches of government; the concentration of power in the offices of the prime minister and premiers; barriers to citizens seeking environmental justice through the courts; and most importantly, the ongoing subordination of environmental concerns to economic priorities, including trade liberalization.

In many ways, our approach to environmental problems is similar to our approach to health care problems. When medical problems arise, the health care system reacts, spending considerable time, money, and effort to treat the symptoms. Relatively little attention is paid to *preventive* medicine that targets the root causes of poor health by promoting a healthy diet, regular exercise, and a balanced lifestyle. Environmental law is also largely reactive, not proactive. When environmental problems arise, from oil spills to concerns about endangered species, environmental laws and policies are drafted and implemented to address symptoms rather than root causes. We struggle to mitigate the environmental impacts caused by fossil fuels instead of increasing energy efficiency or developing clean, renewable sources of energy. For health care and environmental law to achieve their ultimate objectives – a healthy population and a healthy environment – the *root causes* of poor health and environmental degradation must be clearly identified and addressed.

The following chapters analyze the reasons progress has been made on certain environmental issues, detail the systemic weaknesses in Canadian environmental law and policy that account for Canada's generally poor record, explain the major obstacles to positive environmental law and policy reforms, and identify the root causes of environmental degradation. This analysis sets the stage for Part Three, which prescribes the law and policy changes needed to improve Canada's environmental performance.

7 Reasons for Environmental Progress

> Our common future, that of every Canadian
> community, depends on a healthy environment.
> *Supreme Court of Canada, 2001*

When examining the causes of Canada's environmental progress, it is important to recognize that environmental law is a relatively new field. Thirty years ago, concepts such as "biological diversity," "ozone depletion," "climate change," and "endocrine disruptors" did not exist. As recently as 1970, Canada had no federal environment department, few laws or regulations governed air and water pollution, and maximum fines under Canada's strongest environmental law were $2,000.[1] The past three decades have seen a tremendous proliferation and strengthening of international, national, provincial, and local environmental laws and policies.

The surge in attention and resources dedicated to protecting the environment has produced a substantial amount of progress in recent decades. Sulphur dioxide emissions declined by almost 50 percent in eastern Canada. Production and use of ozone-depleting chemicals are down 95 percent. Lead emissions are down 95 percent. Emissions of other air pollutants, including nitrogen oxides, volatile organic compounds, and carbon monoxide, decreased between 10 and 50 percent in recent years. Water pollution from industrial sources declined, dramatically in some sectors. For example, the discharge of dioxins and furans from pulp and paper mills is down 99 percent. A higher percentage of Canadians is connected to sewage treatment plants, and the quality of sewage treatment is rising. Forest practices have improved modestly. Quantities of municipal waste have fallen by as much as 50 percent in some provinces, while recycling rates have risen rapidly. The area of Canada's land in parks and protected areas increased by more than forty million hectares during the 1990s. What factors are responsible for these advances in environmental protection? To what extent have environmental laws and policies contributed to this progress?

Strong Social, Political, and Economic Institutions

Compared to the majority of nations in the world, Canada has strong social, political, and economic institutions. Governments at all levels are democratically elected. Canadians enjoy many civil and political liberties ranging from freedom of expression to the right to "life, liberty and security of the person," enabling Canadians to speak out on environmental issues without fear of reprisal. Canadians, on average, enjoy high levels of literacy, high levels of post-secondary education, long (and lengthening) life expectancies, and increasing access to information (through freedom of information laws and the Internet). Civil society is strong and vocal. Canada's media, although subject to concerns about corporate concentration, enjoys freedom from political interference. The Canadian judiciary, although appointed by politicians, enjoys a high degree of independence because judges can be removed only for flagrant misbehaviour. Together, the foregoing factors contribute to Canada's perennial position at or near the top of the UN's Human Development Index and to Canada's high ranking on the World Economic Forum's Environmental Sustainability Index, which measures a nation's potential for achieving sustainability.[2]

Institutions designed specifically to improve Canada's environmental record also make a significant contribution, including the commissioner of the environment and sustainable development, the Standing Committee on Environment and Sustainable Development, the National Round Table on the Environment and the Economy, and the International Joint Commission. Some provinces have similar institutions, such as Ontario's environmental commissioner.

Canada also enjoys a level of economic wealth that facilitates increased efforts to protect the environment. A number of studies have demonstrated a correlation between increases in GDP and decreases in air and water pollution.[3] On the other hand, some environmental problems, such as greenhouse gas emissions, tend to worsen with rising affluence. Comprehensive analysis reveals that countries with similar levels of wealth have widely divergent environmental records. This finding leads experts to conclude that policy choices, not economic wealth, are the key factor in determining a nation's environmental performance.[4]

International Pressure

Because many environmental problems are global, the international response to them inevitably shapes Canada's response. International scientific bodies, international agreements, and international environmental groups have the ability to influence events in Canada. As well, advances in communication enable environmental laws, policies, and technologies to be disseminated rapidly from nation to nation.[5]

International Environmental Agreements

Canada is a party to over 230 international environmental agreements, ranging from well-known multilateral agreements such as the *United Nations Convention on Biological Diversity* to obscure treaties like the North Pacific Fur Seal treaty of 1911.[6] International environmental law is unusual in that there are no "police" available to enforce the law. Compliance relies instead on peer pressure among nations, public opinion, and fear of tarnishing a country's reputation. International environmental laws are characterized by weak language, committing nations to take action only "as far as possible and appropriate." Alberto Szekely, a former Mexican ambassador and member of the International Law Commission, wrote in reference to the *Convention on Biological Diversity* that "it would not be exaggerated to assert that the parties remain basically free to act depending only on their own, discretional criteria as to when it is *possible* and when it is *appropriate* to carry out the convention's provisions" (emphasis in original).[7] However, Canadian courts have ruled that the values enshrined in international law should be used to guide government decision making.[8]

Canada has demonstrated admirable international leadership on some environmental issues, contributing to such landmark agreements as the *Montreal Protocol on Substances That Deplete the Ozone Layer*, the *Stockholm Convention on Persistent Organic Pollutants*, the *UN Agreement on Straddling Fish Stocks and Highly Migratory Fish Stocks*, and the *1979 Convention on Long-Range Transboundary Air Pollution*. On each of these issues Canada not only led other nations, pushing the agenda in international negotiations, but also took steps to ensure consistency between its words and its actions.

Canada was motivated by self-interest in promoting effective, coordinated international action on these issues. Both ozone-depleting chemicals and POPs have disproportionately negative effects on Canada, because arctic people and ecosystems bear the brunt of these impacts. Canada's fisheries on both coasts have suffered as a result of foreign overfishing of straddling and migratory stocks (European catches of cod on the east coast and American interceptions of salmon on the west coast). Eastern Canada receives much of its air pollution from sources in the United States. Canada's leadership was also eased by the relatively modest domestic consequences of pursuing progress. For example, Canada had already banned the twelve POPs initially covered by the *Stockholm Convention*, making it painless for Canada to become the first nation to ratify the treaty.

Regardless of the motivation for its initial actions, once Canada garnered recognition as a leader on these international issues, expectations were generated, both at home and abroad, that motivated Canada to maintain its reputation by fulfilling its commitments. Canada also deserves credit for its role in negotiating the global land mines treaty and for supporting, at least to some extent, the Jubilee 2000 campaign to forgive the debt of the poorest developing nations.[9] Although these international initiatives are not generally considered environmental issues, progress in this sphere contributes significantly to sustainable development in the Third World.

Potential embarrassment is another intangible source of international pressure, illustrated by Canada's actions in the lead-up to the ten-year anniversary of the 1992 Earth Summit. In 1992 Canada had been the first industrialized nation to ratify the *Convention on Biological Diversity* and an early signatory of the *UN Framework Convention on Climate Change*. In 1997 at the Rio+5 meeting, Prime Minister Chrétien was embarrassed by Canada's failure to take effective domestic action on either biodiversity or climate change.[10] In an effort to avoid similar embarrassment at the Rio+10 meeting in South Africa in 2002, Canada announced the creation of new national parks, and promised to ratify the *Kyoto Protocol*.

The Commission for Environmental Cooperation

International pressure on Canada to improve its environmental record has also been generated, at least to a modest extent, by the North American Commission for Environmental Cooperation (CEC), established by the environmental side agreement to NAFTA.[11] Canadian citizen groups have filed submissions outlining Canada's failure to enforce environmental laws against pulp and paper mills, BC Hydro, Ontario Power Generation, mining companies, logging companies, and industrial hog farms.[12] The CEC has very circumscribed powers, limited to conducting an investigation that reports the facts about allegations of nonenforcement. The CEC cannot make recommendations or impose penalties.[13] Further limiting the CEC's powers is the fact that it is controlled by the environment ministers from Canada, Mexico, and the United States. The three ministers decide whether investigations should occur, what their scope will be, and whether the results will be made public.[14] Thus the CEC is subject to political manipulation, and there is no process for appealing decisions.

In a number of cases, the ministers have rejected or watered down CEC recommendations for investigations into Canada's failure to enforce its environmental laws. A recommended investigation into industrial hog farming in Quebec was rejected. Recommended investigations into the federal government's failure to enforce the *Fisheries Act* against the logging and mining industries were watered down to focus on a handful of isolated problems rather than pursuing systemic nonenforcement.[15] Canada is reputed to be the most obstructive of the three nations and has been the subject of the highest number of investigations for nonenforcement.[16] Indeed, Canada has been attempting to further weaken the CEC process because it may "shine an unwanted spotlight" on Canada's poor record of enforcing environmental laws.[17] Despite the weakness of the process, media scrutiny, public attention, and the ensuing political embarrassment appear to have spurred the federal government to undertake some enforcement activities.[18]

International Market Pressures

A different kind of international pressure is partially responsible for modest improvements in Canadian forest practices. Market campaigns, organized by environmental groups, generated concerns among buyers of Canadian forest products in Europe, the United States, and Japan.[19] The prospect of losing customers abroad caused forest companies to support the designation of new protected areas in biologically important locations and accept provincial regulatory improvements, such as BC's *Forest Practices Code*.[20] Similarly, the need to maintain access to American markets for Canadian agricultural products contributed to the recent strengthening of Canada's *Pest Control Products Act*.

Effective Laws and Regulations

Contrary to the Fraser Institute's belief that "the only good government regulation is no regulation at all,"[21] Canadians support regulations that protect public values like health and the environment. As the Supreme Court of Canada recognizes, "The realities and complexities of a modern industrial society, coupled with the very real need to protect all of society and particularly its vulnerable members, emphasize the critical importance of regulatory offences in Canada today. Our society simply could not function without extensive regulatory legislation."[22] Substantial progress on some environmental issues proves that Canada is capable of enacting, implementing, and enforcing effective environmental laws and regulations. These successful examples involve laws and regulations at the federal, provincial, and local levels, as well as co-operation between levels of government.

Ozone Depletion

In the areas where Canada has made environmental progress in recent decades, regulations have often been the most effective means of achieving those ends. For example, Canada used a combination of strong federal and provincial regulations to cut production of ozone-depleting substances by 95 percent within a decade. These regulations were comprehensive in scope, mandatory in nature, and strengthened regularly to reflect the progressive tightening of timelines under the *Montreal Protocol on Substances That Deplete the Ozone Layer*. Canada acted swiftly, despite dire industry warnings about economic impacts and a decline in the quality of life. Contrary to industry's predictions, the phasing out of CFCs and other ozone-depleting chemicals resulted in net economic benefits in addition to environmental benefits.

Energy Efficiency

On another global issue, climate change, Canada's overall record is very poor. However, federal and provincial energy-efficiency laws and regulations, such as Canada's *Energy Efficiency Act,* provide one bright spot. These regulations, mainly targeting household appliances and lights, are regarded as the most effective step taken by Canada to reduce greenhouse gas emissions.[23] Again, the language used in energy-efficiency legislation is mandatory, with clear requirements that must be achieved by a specific date.

Industrial Air and Water Pollution

For many years, a major Canadian environmental priority has been reducing industrial air and water pollution. Federal regulations targeted lead emissions from gasoline and smelters; effluent from petroleum refineries, pulp and paper mills, mines, and smelters; emissions from motor vehicles; and the content of fuels.[24] Provincial regulations targeted emissions from power-generating stations, pulp and paper mills, and other industrial sources of water and air pollution. Major reductions in effluent and emissions resulted from these regulations, as detailed in Chapters 2.2 and 3.3. Further reductions in pollution are anticipated as a result of recent federal regulations targeting sulphur and benzene in vehicle fuels.[25] The majority of these regulatory success stories involve efforts to curb pollution from industrial point sources. Canada is not alone in making progress in these areas, as "both water and air quality have been substantially improved in many jurisdictions over the past thirty years, due in large part to government regulation." Legal experts agree that regulations are "most effective in reducing pollution from single media, point sources."[26]

Laws Governing Forest Practices

New laws and regulations in some provinces, most notably British Columbia, Ontario, Saskatchewan, and Nova Scotia, target the timber industry. In many cases, unenforceable guidelines were converted into legally binding and enforceable laws and regulations. Because of these laws and regulations, Canadian forest practices, while far from perfect, cause less environmental damage than in the past.

The Costs of Effective Regulation

In each of these cases of successful regulation, the targeted industry objected to mandatory, binding regulations and standards, arguing that command-and-control regulations cost too much and achieve too little. Where governments hold firm and proceed with imposing and enforcing regulations, there is little evidence to suggest that the regulated industries are less competitive as a result of being held to higher environmental standards. In fact, stronger regulations may spur increases in productivity, efficiency, and competitiveness, while maintaining access to markets where environmental consciousness is rising.[27]

Overall, studies suggest that the total economic cost of making environmental progress in Canada over the past three decades was between 1 percent and 2 percent of GDP.[28] Even vocal critics of environmental protection admit that "most environmental initiatives of the past seemed expensive and questionable at the time and today every one of them appears a bargain in retrospect."[29]

General Characteristics of Effective Environmental Laws
An assessment of the laws and regulations that have contributed to environmental progress in Canada reveals that effective environmental laws share five common features:

1 clear jurisdiction or cooperation between different levels of government
2 clear, measurable, enforceable standards
3 mandatory language
4 effective compliance and enforcement mechanisms, including incentives and penalties
5 adequate resources for implementation and enforcement.[30]

These characteristics not only increase the effectiveness of laws and regulations, but also provide accountability, transparency, certainty, and fairness. Unfortunately, the majority of Canadian environmental laws do not reflect these characteristics, for reasons discussed in Chapters 8 and 9.

Federal-Provincial Cooperation

Although federal-provincial interactions on environmental issues are more often characterized by conflict than cooperation, when the two levels of government join forces, progress on difficult environmental issues is possible. For example, in response to the damage caused in eastern Canada by acid rain, the federal and provincial governments took complementary actions that reduced Canadian sulphur dioxide emissions by 43 percent (50 percent in eastern Canada) between 1985 and 1996. Canadian pressure contributed to the 1990 US *Clean Air Act* amendments that produced comparable reductions in American sulphur dioxide emissions.

Another encouraging example of cooperative federalism occurred when federal and provincial governments shared responsibility in addressing the problem of ozone depletion. The federal government took the lead in restricting the manufacture, use, sale, export, and import of ozone-depleting chemicals. Provincial governments took steps to address the release, recycling, and disposal of ozone-depleting chemicals. Through cooperation, the federal and provincial governments comprehensively addressed the problem without duplicating efforts or stepping on each other's toes. Unfortunately, despite efforts to promote harmonization and Canada-wide standards, such successful examples are rare. Failures are far more common, as Canada's experiences with the issues of smog, endangered species, drinking water, and climate change demonstrate.

Proactive Local Governments

Perhaps because many environmental problems make themselves felt at the local level, municipal governments have led successful efforts to improve Canada's record on sewage treatment, municipal waste, and recycling. Local governments have also demonstrated leadership on issues like pesticide use and climate change. Budget cuts at the federal and provincial levels have increased the importance of local governments in protecting the environment. For example, in British Columbia local governments have been given extended powers under the *Municipal Act,* responsibilities for contaminated sites, and new duties under the *Fish Protection Act.*[31]

Across the country, many communities made the improvement of sewage treatment a priority during the 1980s and 1990s. Municipal governments united, under the auspices of the Federation of Canadian Municipalities, to pressure provincial and federal governments to provide financial support for improving sewage treatment infrastructure. In response, billions of dollars were spent on upgrading sewage facilities in Canada during the 1990s. The percentage of urban Canadians served by secondary or tertiary sewage treatment rose from about 60 percent in 1990 to 78 percent in 2001, while 22 percent of urban Canadians still have only primary treatment (i.e., screening) or no treatment at all. Substantial investments of money and effort are generally a prerequisite to successfully addressing an environmental problem, whether it is the treatment of municipal sewage or reducing acid rain.

Because of the leadership of local governments, blue box and other recycling programs proliferated in Canada during the 1980s and 1990s, along with public awareness of the need to reduce household waste. Nova Scotia is Canada's leader in reducing solid waste, with municipal waste per capita down more than 50 percent during the 1990s. British Columbia decreased municipal waste per capita by 42 percent in the 1990s.[32] Leading Canadian municipalities include Edmonton, Ottawa, and many communities in Nova Scotia. Edmonton has achieved a 70 percent diversion rate (meaning only 30 percent of municipal waste goes to landfill sites) by promoting recycling and creating a municipal composting facility.[33] Toronto has pledged to achieve 100 percent diversion by 2010, which would make it a global leader.

Local governments are also responsible for progress on several environmental issues where federal and provincial governments have been reluctant to take effective action. Despite federal and provincial paralysis on climate change, a number of municipalities, led by Toronto, are implementing programs intended to reduce greenhouse gas emissions by at least 20 percent from 1990 levels.[34] This 20 percent target goes well beyond Canada's *Kyoto Protocol* commitment to reduce greenhouse gas emissions by 6 percent. In 2002, Toronto reported an extraordinary 67 percent decrease in greenhouse gas emissions.[35] The Federation of Canadian Municipalities operates a program called Partners for Climate Protection to assist communities interested in greenhouse gas reduction initiatives. Similarly, a number of municipalities (including Toronto, Halifax, and thirty-seven municipalities in Quebec) have passed bylaws restricting the use of pesticides.[36] Cities like Halifax, Toronto, and Victoria have reduced their use of pesticides by 95 percent. Some municipalities, faced with water shortages and rising infrastructure costs for dams, reservoirs, and water treatment plants, have implemented innovative conservation programs, saving both water and money.

Ultimately, however, municipalities are constrained by legal limits on their powers. Local governments are not explicitly assigned jurisdiction over any specific subjects under Canada's *Constitution Act, 1867*. Municipalities can take action only when explicitly authorized to do so by provincial governments. As the Supreme Court of Canada points out, "Municipalities may exercise only those powers expressly conferred by statute, those powers necessarily or fairly implied by the expressed power in the statute, and those indispensable powers essential and not merely convenient to the effectuation of the purposes of the corporation."[37] For example, when the city of Mississauga attempted to prevent a cement company from burning PCBs after the Ontario government approved the company's proposed activities, courts struck down the municipal bylaw. Similarly, BC courts have rejected attempts by local governments to regulate logging on private land because provincial regulations already govern logging.[38]

Despite these constraints on municipal action, the Supreme Court of Canada's *Hudson* decision in 2001, upholding a municipal role in pesticide regulation, suggests that local governments may have a larger future role in protecting the environment.[39] As the Supreme Court noted, local governments are better equipped with local knowledge, are able to reflect local environmental conditions, and are more accessible to citizens. Courts have already relied upon the *Hudson* case as a precedent in upholding local environmental bylaws that were challenged because they were stronger than provincial or federal laws.[40]

Progressive Decisions from the Supreme Court of Canada

Six times between 1988 and 2001, the Supreme Court of Canada was faced with a controversial case raising critical questions of environmental law. Six times the Court set precedents emphasizing the importance of environmental protection. The Supreme Court consistently supported environmental protection despite the fact that eight of its nine judges were replaced during the same period.

In 1988 the Court upheld the constitutionality of the federal *Ocean Dumping Control Act*. The Court ruled that because marine pollution is a matter of national and international concern, a federal regulatory role is appropriate, even for marine pollution that occurs in provincial waters.[41] In 1992 the Court ruled that the federal government had a legal obligation to conduct an environmental assessment of the impacts of the Oldman River Dam in Alberta. The opening words of the judgment stated, "The protection of the environment has become one of the major challenges of our time."[42] The Court's decision spurred the enactment of Canada's first national environmental assessment statute, the *Canadian Environmental Assessment Act*.

In 1994, in a case involving the proposed Great Whale hydroelectric megaproject in northern Quebec, a lower court suggested that an environmental assessment of the impacts of the transmission lines carrying electricity to the United States was sufficient and that the impacts of new dams need not be considered. The Supreme Court of Canada overruled the lower court, deciding that the federal government was obliged to examine the "overall environmental costs" of the project by conducting a comprehensive environmental assessment. Following the Court's decision, the Quebec government shelved the project.[43] Canadian Pacific Limited attempted to avoid conviction on pollution charges under Ontario's *Environmental Protection Act* in 1995 by arguing that the legislation was too vague. The Supreme Court of Canada rejected Canadian Pacific's arguments and upheld the constitutionality of the law, noting that environmental protection is a "fundamental value in Canadian society."[44]

In a 1997 prosecution against Hydro-Quebec for dumping PCBs into Quebec's St. Maurice River, the Supreme Court was asked to determine the constitutionality of the *Canadian Environmental Protection Act*'s provisions relating to PCBs. Hydro-Quebec argued that regulating local pollution fell solely within the provincial government's jurisdiction. The Supreme Court rejected Hydro-Quebec's argument, on the basis that the federal government has the constitutional authority to enact laws to protect public health under its criminal law power. The Court also noted that "measures to combat the evils of pollution" are directed toward "a public purpose of superordinate importance."[45]

In 2001 the Supreme Court of Canada upheld the validity of a municipal bylaw regulating pesticide use in the town of Hudson, Quebec.[46] Chemical companies argued that federal and provincial governments were solely responsible for addressing the risks posed by pesticides. The Court, however, ruled that all three levels of government have a role to play in environmental protection and explicitly endorsed the precautionary principle.

As well, in a series of cases about Aboriginal fishing rights during the 1990s, including the controversial *Marshall* decision, the Supreme Court of Canada repeatedly declared that conservation must be the overriding priority in all fisheries management decisions. As the Supreme Court observed, conservation is of "overwhelming importance to Canadian society."[47] These decisions signal dramatic, though not yet fully implemented, changes in Canadian management of fisheries and other natural resources.[48]

The Supreme Court of Canada's environmental enlightenment has important consequences, because its decisions set precedents that are binding on all other courts in Canada. For example, in a case involving the proposed Voisey's Bay nickel mine, the Newfoundland Court of Appeal issued one of the most strongly worded environmental judgments in Canadian legal history, quoting extensively from the Supreme Court of Canada's environmental decisions, referring to Rachel Carson's groundbreaking book *Silent Spring*, and emphasizing "the urgency of controlling the destruction of the Earth's environment."[49] In another case, the Manitoba Court of Appeal recognized that "damages will not compensate for a destroyed forest."[50] More broadly speaking, the Supreme Court is a beacon of leadership and moral authority in Canada. From time to time the Court is criticized for its judicial activism in criminal law cases or in cases involving the constitutional rights of Aboriginal people, homosexuals, and other minorities.[51] At the other end of the spectrum, the Court has been criticized for being unduly conservative.[52] Less ideological assessments suggest that the Court steadfastly strives to find balanced solutions and achieve justice rather than popularity.[53]

While it is encouraging that Canada's highest court has the wisdom and courage to stand up for the environment, the Supreme Court can only do so much. Only rarely do environmental cases make it onto the Court's docket, in part because of the huge demand on the Court and in part because of the weaknesses in Canadian environmental laws discussed in Chapter 8. Moreover, determined governments can, and do, find means of circumventing the Court's decisions. Alberta's Oldman Dam was built despite the fact that the court-ordered environmental assessment recommended cancellation of the project.[54] Quebec's Great Whale hydroelectric project may be revived.[55] Despite the Supreme Court's repeated support for a strong federal role in environmental protection, the federal government continues to interpret its jurisdiction very narrowly. Canada's *Species at Risk Act,* which protects only species and habitat on federal land, demonstrates Ottawa's timid approach. The narrow scope of the *Act* has been criticized by a retired Supreme Court of Canada judge.[56]

Public Pressure

Given the consistent results of polls demonstrating the strong environmental ethic of Canadians, governments appear to lag behind the public in their response to environmental problems. However, public pressure occasionally succeeds in putting environmental issues on the political agenda and generating enough momentum to overcome obstacles to action. There have been two major waves of public concern about the environment in Canada. The first occurred in the early 1970s, while the second was in the late 1980s and early 1990s. During these episodes of environmental salience, governments took a more aggressive approach to environmental issues, including the enactment of new laws. Unfortunately, these interludes of heightened environmental concern were followed by periods of government backsliding and failure to follow through on promises.[57]

Canada appears to be in the midst of a third wave of heightened environmental awareness, triggered by the Walkerton tragedy, consecutive record summers for smog in southern Ontario, and growing unease about climate change. In response, the federal government is rebuilding Environment Canada, has ratified *Kyoto* after a vociferous national debate, has enacted the *Species at Risk Act,* has passed new pesticide legislation, and is struggling to reduce air pollution. Most provincial governments have passed legislation banning bulk water exports, improved legal protection for endangered species, and strengthened laws governing drinking water.

In many cases, governments are forced to respond quickly to high-profile environmental crises that generate intense public and media pressure. Examples of this reactive style of governance include the federal PCB regulations passed after the St-Basile-le-Grand PCB fire in Quebec, the rapid international and domestic response to the discovery of the "hole" in the ozone layer, the enactment of the *Transportation of Dangerous Goods Act* following the Mississauga train derailment in 1979, the renewal of the offshore drilling moratorium on the west coast after the *Exxon Valdez* oil spill, and the strengthening of provincial drinking water laws and regulations in response to the Walkerton disaster. This disaster-response approach to environmental law and policy has many shortcomings. Extensive damage, which may be irreversible, is already done. Public confidence in government can be shaken. The costs of restoration and recovery are often much greater than the costs of prevention.[58]

There is no doubt that the Canadian public's top environmental interests – clean air and clean water – motivated the extensive federal and provincial regulations targeting industrial pollution. Public anxiety in the late 1990s led to the enactment of laws prohibiting bulk water exports. Similarly, widespread concern about the loss of old-growth forests, climaxing in controversial protests at Clayoquot Sound and Temagami, drove the enactment of forest practices legislation in BC and Ontario. Public concern about garbage inspired local governments to implement recycling programs and adopt strategies to reduce municipal waste. Another example of the positive impact of public pressure is Canada's progress in establishing parks and protected areas. The World Wildlife Fund and the Canadian Parks and Wilderness Society harnessed the public's attention with their Endangered Spaces campaign, beginning in 1989.[59] The goal of the campaign was to ensure the protection of representative examples of all Canadian ecosystems by the year 2000. All governments – federal, provincial, and territorial – endorsed this goal. Although most jurisdictions eventually fell short of fulfilling their commitments, more than forty million hectares (almost 100 million acres) of diverse and spectacular Canadian landscapes were protected during the 1990s in response to this well-executed environmental campaign.

Most of Canada's environmental laws and policies "bear the strong imprint of environmental organizations."[60] In particular, groups specializing in environmental law, such as the Canadian Environmental Law Association, Canadian Institute for Environmental Law and Policy, Sierra Legal Defence Fund, West Coast Environmental Law Association, Environmental Defence Canada, and Alberta's Environmental Law Centre, have made inroads into the policy-making arena that was previously restricted to government and industry. These public interest organizations are active in both environmental litigation and lobbying in their efforts to strengthen environmental laws and policies at all levels of government.

Public pressure is not always effective in motivating Canadian governments to act. Despite high levels of public concern and media attention focused on climate change, biodiversity, and smog, little progress has been made on these issues. In some cases, public pressure provokes only symbolic responses from government, such as Ontario's *Toughest Environmental Penalties Act,* a law that raises maximum fines for environmental offences in a province where enforcement of environmental laws has dropped dramatically since 1995.

The Influence of the United States

It is no surprise, given Canada's extensive geographic, economic, and cultural ties with the United States, that Canadian environmental law and policy is influenced by American environmental law and policy.[61] However, this pattern of policy emulation is a double-edged sword. Following the US approach to environmental law may be beneficial on issues where American standards are higher, such as drinking water or pesticides, but may hinder Canadian progress in areas where the United States is a laggard, such as greenhouse gas emissions and fuel efficiency standards for vehicles. Canadian environmental groups frequently highlight the weakness of Canada's laws and policies compared to the United States, however, when advocating changes to strengthen Canadian environmental law.[62]

The gap between the American passage of an environmental law and Canadian enactment of comparable legislation can often be measured in decades.[63] Nevertheless, Canada has eventually adopted American standards in areas such as energy efficiency, vehicle emissions, and fuel content. Canadian laws governing pesticides, toxic substances, and endangered species also tend to reflect American models, albeit with some important differences. The integration of the North American economy, through free trade and particularly NAFTA, has reinforced the trend toward convergence of Canadian and American environmental laws.

The complex relationship between Canada and the United States can work to the benefit of the environment in other ways as well. Canada was forced to address domestic sources of acid rain in order to exercise moral suasion on this issue vis-à-vis the United States in the 1980s. Once Canada had made progress in decreasing domestic sulphur dioxide emissions, the United States was under greater pressure to reduce its own emissions. Many Canadian environmental organizations are based on models that have been successful in the United States, from the Sierra Club to the Nature Conservancy. In the field of environmental law, Canada's Sierra Legal Defence Fund is directly patterned after the US Earthjustice Legal Defense Fund (formerly the Sierra Club Legal Defense Fund). Similarly, Environmental Defence Canada duplicates the approach taken by Environmental Defense in the United States. While emulating American environmental law and policy has contributed to Canada's environmental progress in recent decades, it also has negative consequences. The problems caused by Canada's emulation of American environmental law and policy will be explored in Chapter 10.

Conclusion: A Cautionary Note

Strong social and political institutions, economic wealth, international pressure, effective laws and regulations, federal-provincial cooperation, proactive local governments, progressive decisions by the Supreme Court of Canada, public pressure, and the emulation of American laws and policies have contributed to Canada's environmental progress. However, these factors do not always guarantee success. Despite these positive influences, Canada still has a poor environmental record compared to other industrialized nations.

Canada has resisted international pressure to reduce greenhouse gas emissions, increase foreign aid, stop exporting asbestos, take better care of its national parks, and strengthen protection for transboundary endangered species. In some cases where Canada has signed international agreements, such as the *Convention on Biological Diversity* or the *Kyoto Protocol*, Canadian commitments pursuant to these agreements remain unfulfilled. Seemingly strong Canadian laws to protect marine biodiversity and reduce toxic pollution have been largely ineffective. Plans for federal-provincial cooperation intended to solve Canada's smog problem and protect species at risk have produced little concrete action. Court decisions can be circumvented by governments intent on economic growth.

Nor is public concern a guarantee that an issue will be effectively addressed. Decades of public pressure for the clean-up of contaminated sites like the Sydney Tar Ponds have failed to produce significant progress. Canada has spent hundreds of millions of dollars on developing strategies to reduce greenhouse gas emissions but, because the money has been spent ineffectually, Canadian emissions continue to rise. Local governments, despite success in reducing waste and promoting recycling, have largely failed in other areas, such as restraining urban sprawl and developing effective public transit systems. While emulating American law and policy in some areas, Canadian governments have been reluctant to do so on other issues, such as contaminated sites and safe drinking water.

Nevertheless, the progress profiled in this chapter suggests that Canada could dramatically improve its environmental record by applying the lessons learned in addressing ozone depletion, acid rain, industrial water pollution, and municipal waste to such outstanding problems as smog, biodiversity, and climate change. To make further environmental progress on issues where strides have been made and to successfully address problems where Canada's record is poor will require overcoming the systemic weaknesses in Canadian environmental law and policy, which are examined in the following chapter.

8 Systemic Weaknesses

> Despite significant advances in Canada, including
> some progress in terms of the rehabilitation of
> particular sites and ecosystems, there can be no
> illusion about general success in bringing severe
> threats of continuing environmental risk under control.
> *Professor Jamie Benidickson,* Environmental Law

While it is encouraging to recognize that Canada has made progress in some
aspects of environmental protection, the reality is that on most environmental issues Canada is performing poorly. On seventeen of twenty-five environmental indicators, Canada is among the five worst nations in the OECD. The
failure of Canadian environmental laws and policies results, in large part, from
six systemic weaknesses. First, Canada still lacks a number of important environmental laws that are commonplace in other industrialized nations. Second, existing Canadian laws and regulations are undermined by excessive
discretion. Third, environmental laws and policies fail to reflect contemporary scientific knowledge and principles. Fourth, Canadian environmental law
suffers from inadequate resources for implementation and enforcement. Weak
implementation and enforcement are exacerbated by budget cuts, the
downloading of environmental responsibilities (from the federal government
to the provinces, and from provinces to municipalities), and excessive reliance
on voluntary initiatives. Fifth, the public has insufficient opportunities to
participate meaningfully in developing and enforcing environmental laws. Sixth,
Canadian governments rely on an unduly narrow range of law and policy
options in their efforts to protect the environment.

Missing Laws
Some of the most basic, rudimentary environmental laws enacted by other

nations are still absent in Canada. The most obvious comparison is between Canada and the United States. For example, at the federal level Canada has

- no enforceable national air quality standards
- no enforceable national water quality standards
- no national law guaranteeing safe drinking water
- no national law requiring the clean-up of contaminated sites
- no national law to protect wilderness areas outside of national parks
- no law to protect wild and scenic rivers
- no law guaranteeing citizens access to information about all of the types and sources of toxic pollution in their communities
- no comprehensive law to protect whales and other marine mammals
- no national law to protect wetlands
- no national hazardous waste law
- no law requiring sustainable fishing practices
- no law to address the threat of invasive exotic species
- no national forest management law.

In contrast, at the federal level the United States has, respectively, the *Clean Air Act,* the *Clean Water Act,* the *Safe Drinking Water Act,* the *Comprehensive Environmental Response, Compensation and Liability Act,* the *Wilderness Act,* the *Wild and Scenic Rivers Act,* the *Emergency Planning and Community Right-to-Know Act,* the *Marine Mammal Protection Act,* the *Emergency Wetland Resources Act,* the *Resource Conservation and Recovery Act,* the *Sustainable Fisheries Act,* the *National Invasive Species Act,* and the *National Forest Management Act.* While Canada has policies such as the National Ambient Air Quality Objectives, the Canadian Heritage Rivers program, and the Guidelines for Canadian Drinking Water Quality, *none of these policies have any legal effect.* These nonbinding policy mechanisms are clearly less effective than enforceable national legislation, regulations, and standards.[1]

This comparison is not meant to suggest that by merely passing a long list of laws Canada will solve its environmental woes, or that the United States is an ecological utopia. Nor is this comparison intended to suggest that the federal government bears full responsibility for environmental protection; Canada's Constitution places more power in provincial hands than the US Constitution gives to the states. Yet none of the gaps in Canada's federal environmental law identified above are adequately addressed by provincial laws. Some provinces have endangered species legislation while other provinces do not. Some provinces have safe drinking water laws while others do not. Some provinces have air quality standards while others do not. And so on. The result of these inconsistencies is that environmental standards vary widely among Canadian provinces and territories. The patchwork of provincial laws and policies is widely regarded as "a stumbling block to coordinated national action."[2] American states have more consistent environmental law regimes than Canadian provinces because they are responsible for meeting national standards established by federal environmental laws, and because the US government provides extensive funding to states for the purpose of environmental protection, which does not happen in Canada.

From time to time there have been unsuccessful efforts to fill some of the gaps in Canadian environmental law. Detailed proposals have been published by the Canadian Bar Association, the Law Reform Commission of Canada, academics, think tanks, and public interest environmental law organizations. In response, governments have promised laws but never introduced them, introduced laws but never passed them, and passed laws but never proclaimed them. Instead of moving forward, some provincial governments have begun to eliminate environmental laws and regulations.[3] In short, as an international assessment of environmental laws around the world concluded, in Canada "there exists no coherent or comprehensive legislative and regulatory scheme" to protect the environment.[4]

Filling the Gaps

To suggest that more laws and regulations are required to protect the environment runs counter to the prevailing political atmosphere in much of Canada, which is antagonistic to regulation. The situation in Canada is part of a global trend, as "regulators are in retreat, reluctant to argue for new or tougher regulation for fear of alienating either their political masters or influential business lobbies who are never reticent to suggest that such regulation will make them less competitive, or hasten their move to another jurisdiction."[5] This anti-regulatory attitude can have serious environmental consequences. The report of the Walkerton Inquiry identified the Ontario government's hostility toward regulation as a contributing factor in the contaminated water disaster.[6]

Canadian businesses complain about the allegedly onerous burden of environmental regulation, arguing that the market should be allowed to take the place of "regulatory red tape."[7] Although provincial governments in Alberta, Ontario, and British Columbia aggressively eliminated environmental regulations in response to these concerns, evidence suggests that the problem is illusory. A study conducted in 1999 revealed that Canada has the lowest business costs of all the countries in the G7. A seventy-five-country study by the World Bank concluded that Canada "throws up less red tape" than any other nation it examined.[8] Industries in Canada face fewer regulatory obstacles in the environmental field than their competitors in the United States.[9]

In any case, studies have not found that environmental policy reduces business competitiveness.[10] Strong, well-designed regulations can inspire technological innovation and enhance international competitiveness. The OECD and other economic experts agree that "environmental legislation can be a driver spurring technological changes that lead to efficiency and competitive advantages."[11] Strong air pollution standards helped make Germany a world leader in air pollution technology, while British environmental technology exports fell when Britain's standards lagged under Margaret Thatcher.[12] Canada's former finance minister, Paul Martin, supports the strategy of using environmental regulations to promote industrial competitiveness.[13] Numerous American studies have found that the states with the strongest environmental laws and policies enjoy the highest levels of economic growth and job creation.[14]

It seems that "couching the debate in terms of either regulation or deregulation kindles a spurious and sterile ideological divide, which inhibits attempts to find solutions containing the best of both approaches."[15] For some environmental problems, regulation has been very effective, as proven in Chapter 7. For other environmental problems, different law and policy solutions are required. The choice between more government and less government is a false choice. What Canada really needs is better governance, which will probably require more government intervention (including, though not necessarily limited to, more regulation) to achieve superior environmental protection.

Positive Signs

Despite industry opposition, Canada has recently shown signs that it may finally address some of the longstanding lacunae in its array of environmental laws. Federally, the long-awaited enactment of the *Species at Risk Act* and changes to the *Pest Control Products Act* in 2002, and the designation of major air pollutants as toxic substances under the *Canadian Environmental Protection Act, 1999,* represent steps in the right direction. At the provincial level, several provinces strengthened regulations for drinking water safety in response to the Walkerton disaster, efforts to limit acid rain through stronger regulations continue, and most provinces now prohibit bulk water exports.

There are still many holes to be filled before Canada's legal system can be said to comprehensively address threats to the environment. Moreover, whether new or existing laws and regulations passed by Canadian governments will be effective remains in doubt, as the following section explains.

Excessive Discretion

The second systemic weakness in Canadian environmental law is that the vast majority of laws and regulations are undermined by their broadly discretionary nature. Environmental laws are almost always drafted in such a way as to give Canadian governments the *power* to take action or meet specified standards but *no duty* to take action or meet those standards. Discretion is one of the defining characteristics of Canadian environmental law, as it pervades almost every law, regulation, and policy.[16] Seemingly insignificant differences in wording, such as using "may" instead of "must," transform potentially effective laws and regulations into paper tigers.

A prime example of the problem caused by discretionary powers in environmental law is provided by federal statutes that enable, but do not require, Ottawa to address cross-border issues where provincial actions are insufficient to address a problem. Such provisions are found in the *Canada Water Act, Canada Wildlife Act, Canadian Environmental Assessment Act,* and the *Canadian Environmental Protection Act, 1999.* These provisions have *never* been used, although they have existed for up to thirty years. The federal government has never used its discretionary power to require an environmental assessment of a project with international impacts, interprovincial impacts, or impacts on Aboriginal people. Nor has Ottawa ever used its discretionary power to address the sources of transboundary air or water pollution, or to protect wildlife at risk.[17]

There are many more examples of problematic discretion at the federal level. Under the *Canadian Environmental Assessment Act,* the federal government retains the discretion to approve a project even when experts determine that the project will have "significant adverse environmental effects." Over 99.9 percent of projects subject to federal environmental assessment are approved. The *Species at Risk Act* authorizes but does not require the federal government to establish a national safety net to protect endangered species and their habitat on provincial and private lands. Enforcement of environmental laws is also entirely discretionary, and not subject to judicial review.[18] In other words, the government cannot be forced to enforce the law. According to Professor George Hoberg, environmental laws in Canada "do not contain sufficient nondiscretionary, action-forcing language to justify judicial intervention."[19]

Provincial laws rendered ineffective by excessive discretion include endangered species legislation that enables but does not require the designation of species at risk, the protection of habitat, or the preparation of recovery plans. Because these provisions are discretionary, provincial laws do not protect most known endangered species, habitat is rarely protected, and recovery plans are rarely prepared. Provincial forest management laws give bureaucrats the discretion to approve logging beside streams, on steep slopes, and in areas that are important for drinking water or wildlife. As a result, logging commonly occurs right up to the banks of fish streams, on steep slopes subject to erosion, in community watersheds, and in critical wildlife habitat. Provincial drinking water laws give officials the power to protect drinking water sources but do not require the exercise of those powers. As a result, few sources of drinking water are protected. Provincial pollution laws allow discretion to be exercised in granting permits to pollute, resulting in unsafe air emissions and effluent discharges.

In its discretionary nature, the Canadian legal system differs markedly from the American legal system: Canadian environmental laws are "far more discretionary than comparable U.S. statutes."[20] For example, the US *Endangered Species Act* states that where there is scientific evidence that a species is endangered, the species *must* be listed under the *Act*. If government refuses to act, US citizens can use a variety of administrative and legal means to force government to comply with the law.[21] Accountability is built into the system, and is reinforced by the courts. In Canada, the listing of species is usually left to government discretion, so few species receive legal protection. If governments choose not to exercise their discretion, that is the end of the matter, because governments cannot be legally compelled to do so.[22] Excessive discretion thus profoundly limits the utility and efficacy of environmental legislation in Canada. The discretionary nature of Canadian environmental law dramatically reduces political accountability and undermines the judicial system's ability to act as a check on the exercise of bureaucratic decision making.

Beacons of Hope

The predominance of discretion in Canadian environmental laws may be starting to diminish. Some important provisions in recently enacted Canadian environmental legislation are mandatory rather than discretionary. For example, federal and provincial laws governing ozone-depleting chemicals and energy-efficient appliances use mandatory language. The *Canadian Environmental Protection Act, 1999* imposes a mandatory obligation on the federal government to enact regulations to address the threats posed by substances designated as toxic. Changes to the *Pest Control Products Act* require regular reevaluation of pesticides. The new *Canada National Parks Act* mandates the protection of ecological integrity and the designation of wilderness areas identified in park management plans. Saskatchewan's *Forest Resources Management Act* requires mandatory environmental assessment and auditing of forest management plans. However, the majority of Canadian environmental laws are still largely discretionary.

The Failure to Reflect Contemporary Science

The third systemic flaw running through Canadian environmental law and policy is the failure to incorporate contemporary scientific knowledge and principles. For example, laws governing endangered species, protected areas, and marine biodiversity do not reflect principles of conservation biology. The new *Species at Risk Act* protects "residences" rather than critical habitat. Laws governing parks and protected areas allow activities that are incompatible with the conservation of biodiversity, despite the role that these areas are intended to play in conserving nature. The new *National Marine Conservation Areas Act* allows fishing in marine protected areas, although fishing is the main threat to marine biodiversity. Increasing scientific awareness of the critical importance of the ecological services provided by water, forests, and other ecosystems is not yet reflected in environmental laws or policies.[23]

One of the most important scientific advances, ironically, is the recognition of how little humans understand about ecosystems, ecological processes, the relationship between chemicals and health, and other critical environmental issues. Only half of the species believed to live in Canada have been identified. The rate and severity of climate change, the rate of healing of the ozone layer, and the long-term health and environmental impacts of chemicals that disrupt endocrine systems are vital issues for which science offers no definitive answers. As a result, environmental law and policy must confront pervasive uncertainty. Two important scientific concepts – the precautionary principle and adaptive management – have emerged to respond to this uncertainty. However, neither of these concepts has been incorporated in a meaningful way into Canadian environmental laws and policies.

The Precautionary Principle

The precautionary principle requires that "where there are threats of serious or irreversible damage, lack of full scientific certainty should not be used as a reason for postponing measures to prevent environmental degradation." This principle is quickly becoming an established norm of international law.[24] Canadian environmental law is generally based on the opposite of the precautionary principle, in that conclusive scientific evidence of harm is necessary before steps will be taken to limit an activity or restrict the use of a particular substance.[25]

However, many notoriously dangerous chemicals were once deemed safe.[26] Paul Hermann Müller received the Nobel Prize in 1948 for his discovery that DDT is an efficient insecticide. Not until decades later was DDT banned in Canada after scientists identified the disastrous ecological effects of using DDT in agriculture. Other examples of past failures include chlorofluorocarbons (CFCs), regarded as wonder chemicals until scientists discovered their destructive impact on the ozone layer, and PCBs, used extensively in electrical applications before their harmful health and environmental effects became apparent. Back in the 1920s, Ethyl Corporation argued that there was no conclusive scientific proof that putting lead in gasoline would cause health impacts, although medical experts at the time expressed concern.[27] Decades passed before the scientific evidence and public outcry convinced governments to ban leaded gasoline. A precautionary approach could have prevented the tragic damage caused by these substances.

The stories of DDT, CFCs, PCBs, and lead cannot be dismissed as past mistakes that will not be repeated. In 2002 American scientists revealed that one of the most widely used pesticides in Canada and the United States, atrazine, has unexpected and devastating impacts on frogs at very low levels of exposure. Although exposed to atrazine at levels lower than existing standards for drinking water, frogs in lab tests and in the wild exhibited hermaphroditic characteristics – possessing both male and female sexual organs.[28] The implications of these findings for human health are unknown.

Canadian regulation of pesticides and toxic chemicals demonstrates the law's failure to apply the precautionary principle. All Canadians are living science experiments, with hundreds of synthetic chemicals present in our bodies.[29] More than 110,000 chemicals are in use globally, and approximately 1,000 new chemicals are added annually. Yet for most chemicals there are no long-term studies of their health and environmental impacts, no studies of the ways that they might interact in combination with other chemicals in the environment, and no studies of their cumulative impacts in addition to other environmental stressors. Despite these known knowledge gaps, Canada attempts to regulate single chemicals rather than the combination of chemicals that characterizes actual exposures. Because of industry pressure, Canada takes a reductionist approach whereby "every regulatory proposal is studied and contested for years until it theoretically provides acceptable public health protection from one chemical and one route of exposure."[30] Scientists argue that the "complexity of underlying biological and physical systems precludes a reductionist approach to management."[31]

The current approach of studying chemicals in isolation in an effort to find conclusive evidence of harm to health or the environment is expensive, difficult, and slow. Canada has fully evaluated only one hundred or so chemicals and designated only fifty-two substances as toxic under the *Canadian Environmental Protection Act, 1999*. The reevaluation process for pesticides continues to crawl along under the *Pest Control Products Act*. Although the total *volume* of releases of toxic chemicals in Canada appears to be stabilizing or declining, the *toxicity* of waste streams is increasing.[32] The overall goal of a precautionary approach should be to reduce risks to human health and the environment through pollution prevention.[33]

The controversy surrounding genetically modified organisms provides another example of Canada's failure to apply the precautionary principle.[34] Canada is one of the world's largest producers and exporters of genetically modified crops despite widespread public concern about the potential impacts.[35] Biotechnology in Canada is regulated under a tangled array of federal laws including the *Food and Drug Act, Fertilizers Act, Feeds Act, Seeds Act, Pest Control Products Act, Health of Animals Act, Fisheries Act,* and the *Canadian Environmental Protection Act, 1999*. The *Canadian Environmental Protection Act, 1999*, which is alone among these laws in incorporating the precautionary principle, applies only to biotechnology products *not covered by the other laws*. Lawyers warn that "it is questionable whether the current legislative and regulatory scheme is capable of preventing or mitigating any large-scale ecological disaster."[36] Government is supposed to be an "honest broker" but has been an "aggressive promoter" of plant biotechnology.[37] In short, the precautionary principle is not being used in Canada's regulatory approach to biotechnology.[38]

To make matters worse, Canada has argued against the precautionary principle in international forums, such as the World Trade Organization (WTO) and negotiations on the *Cartagena Protocol on Biosafety*.[39] When France banned asbestos imports because of health concerns, Canada challenged the French law in proceedings before the WTO. Although the WTO upheld the French ban, Canada continues to aggressively challenge other nations that attempt to ban asbestos, such as Chile.[40] Canada succeeded in persuading the WTO to overturn a European ban on Canadian beef produced with growth hormones, despite Europe's argument that its ban was a precautionary measure.[41]

Adaptive Management

Adaptive management recognizes the intrinsic variability of natural systems and the pervasive uncertainty inherent in regulating environmental issues.[42] Scientists are urging government and industry to practice adaptive management because it makes practical and effective links among science, policy, and law. In the legal context, adaptive management means adjusting laws and policies to reflect new knowledge and changing conditions. Canada's failure to incorporate the principles of adaptive management into the development of environmental laws and policies results in legislation that remains inflexible, even in light of ecological collapse.

Most areas of environmental law and policy would benefit greatly from adopting adaptive management. For example, the rate of logging in Canada should decline, in order to reflect our better understanding of the global and ecological values of forests. The designation of new protected areas should reflect improvements in our understanding of the size and representation required for marine areas, grasslands, old-growth forests, and large wilderness areas. Instead, relevant laws are not amended, bottom-dragging continues in sensitive ocean habitats despite evidence of habitat damage, pesticides are used in Canada that have been banned for health and environmental reasons in other nations, and point sources of pollution are emphasized when nonpoint sources now constitute the bulk of the problem. Adaptive management offers policy and law makers a framework that recognizes, simultaneously, that natural resource use is necessary but must be sustainable.

Signs of Hope

Some Canadian laws are beginning to reflect contemporary scientific principles. For example, the *Canada National Parks Act* and the *National Marine Conservation Areas Act* emphasize the importance of maintaining ecological integrity. More statutes are recognizing the meaning and value of biodiversity.[43] Several recently enacted or amended environmental laws in Canada tentatively incorporate the precautionary principle.[44] For example, the precautionary principle is specifically referred to in the *Species at Risk Act, Pest Control Products Act, Oceans Act, Canadian Environmental Protection Act, 1999,* New Brunswick's *Clean Air Act,* and Nova Scotia's *Environment Act.* In its 2001 decision confirming that municipalities have the power to regulate pesticides, the Supreme Court of Canada embraced the precautionary principle. Federal and provincial laws governing the use of ozone-depleting chemicals reflect both the precautionary principle (laws were passed before the science of ozone depletion was certain) and adaptive management (laws were repeatedly strengthened in response to new scientific knowledge).

Despite modest progress, many challenges remain in redesigning Canadian environmental laws and policies to incorporate the precautionary principle, adaptive management, and other scientific knowledge.[45] Science in Canada suffers from a chronic shortage of financial support. The National Round Table on the Environment and the Economy urged the federal government to invest heavily in research and "drastically increase government scientific capacity."[46] On the other hand, government control and manipulation of science can result in bad law and policy decisions, perhaps best illustrated by a series of fisheries management fiascoes.[47] Canada would be wise to make better use of the expertise of the Royal Society of Canada in shaping public policy on complex environmental issues, as the United States relies on the independent National Academy of Sciences.[48]

Inadequate Implementation and Enforcement

> It shall be unlawful, at any season, to hunt or kill buffalo for the mere motive of amusement or wanton destruction, or solely to secure their tongues, choice cuts or peltries.
>
> An Ordinance for the Protection of the Buffalo,
> *1877, Northwest Territories*

The fourth systemic weakness afflicting Canadian environmental law and policy is a failure to effectively implement and enforce the law, dating back to the nineteenth-century slaughter of the buffalo. On paper, Canada has many seemingly impressive environmental laws. In practice, key elements of these laws are rarely, if ever, implemented. For example, Canada has yet to develop a single ocean management plan under the *Oceans Act*. Until 2003 no marine protected areas had been formally designated under the *Canada National Parks Act, Oceans Act, Canada Wildlife Act,* or the *National Marine Conservation Areas Act*.[49] Provisions of the *Forest Practices Code* intended to protect biodiversity are not implemented, years after the law came into force. Environmental policies announced and promoted with great fanfare, such as Canada's *Green Plan*, the Canadian Biodiversity Strategy, and various climate change action plans, are never fully implemented.

Although the federal government candidly admits that "legislation and regulation are only as good as their enforcement," criticism of Canada's ongoing failure to enforce its environmental laws is widespread.[50] The OECD has repeatedly chided Canada for its lax environmental enforcement regime. In 1998 Parliament's Standing Committee on Environment and Sustainable

Development concluded, "Environment Canada and indeed some provinces are not enforcing environmental laws when they could and should. This failure to act is of deep concern."[51] The environmental group Friends of the Earth released a scathing report detailing ten years of "minimalist" enforcement by Environment Canada. In 1999 the *Globe and Mail* described Canada as the "promised land" for polluters because of a 78 percent drop in prosecution rates between 1992 and 1999. An audit by the commissioner of the environment and sustainable development concluded that "within existing budgets, departments are struggling to meet legislated responsibilities, policy commitments, and international obligations and, in many cases, are failing to do so."[52] Environment Canada itself admits that overall enforcement efforts are "falling short of fulfilling departmental responsibility, and ... not providing adequate protection to the public, the environment or wildlife."[53]

The following points illustrate the decline in the enforcement of environmental laws in Canada:

- Government reports acknowledge that hundreds of companies and municipalities regularly break environmental laws without being prosecuted.[54]
- Environment Canada identified over three thousand documented violations of federal laws by eastern Canadian pulp mills in recent years but conducted only seven prosecutions.[55]
- According to Ontario Ministry of Environment figures, in 2000 there were 1,900 violations of water pollution laws by two hundred corporations and municipalities, but only four charges laid.[56]
- The number of inspections carried out annually under the *Canadian Environmental Protection Act, 1999* fell during the 1990s from two thousand to seven hundred.[57]

Across Canada, major industrial polluters often break the law with impunity. During the 1990s large corporations like Alcan, Weyerhaeuser, Inco, Skeena Cellulose, Petro-Canada, and Ethyl Canada appeared repeatedly on provincial lists of companies in violation of pollution laws, yet were rarely prosecuted. All too often, governments interpret noncompliance "not as a sign that the company was breaking a law and that enforcement action was required but that the standards were too strict and accordingly should be renegotiated."[58] Law enforcement agencies are more likely to prosecute small companies or individuals despite the fact that their levels of pollution pale in comparison to major industrial polluters.[59]

American law professor Daniel Farber writes that "in all areas of law there are gaps between the 'law on the books' and the 'law in action' but in environmental law the gap is sometimes a chasm."[60] If there is a chasm between environmental laws and their enforcement in the United States, then in Canada there is a Grand Canyon. In 1998 the US Environmental Protection Agency

(EPA) used administrative actions to force companies to spend US$3.6 billion for environmental cleanups and pollution control equipment. That year the EPA's civil and criminal enforcement actions resulted in US$236.8 million in fines and 208 years of prison time.[61] In comparison, a decade (1989-99) of enforcing Canada's main pollution laws resulted in fines totalling $8,696,149.[62] In just one year, the EPA obtained more fines and jail sentences than authorities responsible for environmental enforcement in Canada have obtained in their *entire history*.[63] Three of the main reasons for Canada's failure to adequately implement and enforce environmental laws and policies have been budget cuts, the downloading of enforcement responsibilities to provinces (under the guise of harmonization), and excessive reliance on voluntary initiatives.

Cutbacks to Federal Environmental Budgets
The link is obvious between budget cutbacks in environmental departments and a declining ability to implement and enforce environmental laws. Governments in Canada engaged in an unprecedented downsizing of environmental departments in the 1990s, led by the federal government. In 1988 Environment Canada had a budget of $800 million, and the 1990 *Green Plan* promised to inject an additional $3 billion over five years. However, in part because of the recession in the early 1990s, more than 70 percent of the *Green Plan* money was never allocated to the environment.[64] By 1998 the budget for Environment Canada had fallen 30 percent to $550 million, more than $200 million of which was earmarked for weather forecasting.[65] In terms of personnel, in 1988 Environment Canada was the seventh-largest federal department; by 1998 it was the smallest.[66] Nationwide, Environment Canada had fewer than seventy enforcement officials in 1998. There was *one* Environment Canada enforcement officer in New Brunswick, a province with 750,000 people, a resource-based economy, numerous pulp and paper mills, and other heavy industry. The Pacific and Yukon region saw its operations and maintenance budget drop 72 percent in 1998 when temporary funding under the *Green Plan* expired.[67]

Other federal departments with environmental responsibilities suffered the same magnitude of cuts as Environment Canada. Between 1994-5 and 1998-9, the Department of Fisheries and Oceans budget was sliced by one-third, from $1.4 billion to $950 million, while staff cuts were roughly 40 percent.[68] The internationally renowned Great Lakes Laboratory for Fisheries and Aquatic Science, which studies the impacts of toxic substances on fish, suffered cuts ranging from 40 to 70 percent.[69] Parks Canada's budget and staff were cut by more than 40 percent. The Canadian Forest Service budget was cut by 57 percent.

In contrast, American spending and staffing levels for environmental protection have risen steadily since the 1970s.[70] The EPA's 2001 budget was US$8.3 billion, with US$400 million earmarked for enforcement.[71] The National Parks Service budgeted US$2.1 billion for 2000, the National Oceanic and Atmospheric Administration budget was US$2.6 billion, the Forest Service budget was US$3.5 billion, and the Fish and Wildlife Service budget was US$1.6 billion.[72] Compared to Canada, the United States spends at least twice as much per citizen on environmental protection. Unlike Canada's "kid gloves approach" to environmental crime, enforcement in the United States is getting tougher, with fines and jail sentences steadily rising over the past twenty years.[73]

To the federal government's credit, it has begun to rebuild Environment Canada, with the department's 2001 budget rising to $650 million.[74] Federal budgets from 2000 to 2003 began the process of reinvesting in environmental protection, with significant expenditures on climate change, clean air, and municipal infrastructure. The number of enforcement officers increased from fewer than 70 in 1998 to 93 in 2003. The 2003 budget, which Environment Minister David Anderson described as the "greenest budget in Canadian history," promised almost $3 billion in new spending over five years, primarily to address climate change.[75] However, there is still a long way to go before federal environmental departments have the resources needed to implement and enforce existing laws, let alone the new, stronger laws and policies required in many areas.

Provincial Cutbacks

The provinces followed the federal government's "leadership" in chopping environment departments. Newfoundland and Quebec led the way with cuts of 65 percent between 1994 and 1998: in Newfoundland the environment budget fell to $3.6 million from $10.6 million; the Quebec environment department's budget fell to $53 million from $151 million.[76] Spending on environmental protection in New Brunswick and Alberta fell by more than 30 percent in the same period, with Alberta's budget declining to $296 million from $405 million.[77] In Ontario, the Ministry of Environment budget fell to $165 million in 1998 from $290 million in 1995, a drop of 43 percent.[78] The BC Ministry of Environment budget was slashed by 35 percent between 1995 and 2000 and again by 30 to 35 percent in 2002.[79]

Ontario provides a compelling example of the tangible human and environmental costs of cutbacks in environmental spending and regulation. The Conservative government under Premier Mike Harris engaged in a dramatic campaign of deregulation, downsizing, privatization, and downloading of environmental responsibilities to municipalities. Ontario cut programs for reducing hazardous waste, funding public transit, promoting recycling, encouraging green industries, and enforcing wildlife conservation rules. The province weakened environmental laws governing pesticides, energy, wildlife, environmental assessment, and land-use planning. Ontario also eliminated mining and forestry regulations, privatized sewage treatment, and discontinued the

Ontario Round Table on the Environment and the Economy, the Advisory Committee on Environmental Standards, the Environmental Assessment Advisory Committee, and the Municipal-Industrial Strategy for Pollution Abatement Advisory Committee.[80] In the words of the Canadian Environmental Law Association, "Moving very quickly and with very little consultation the government dismantled thirty years worth of safeguards to protect the environment and conserve natural resources."[81]

In detailed annual reports, Ontario's independent environmental commissioner harshly criticized the Harris government's changes.[82] In 1996 the provincial auditor criticized the Ministry of Environment for inadequate tracking of hazardous waste, antiquated air pollution controls, and deficient monitoring of groundwater resources.[83] In 1998 the environmental commissioner urged the Ontario government to change its focus "from one of granting regulatory relief for polluters to improving its commitment to the environmental health of its residents and the natural environment." The next year, the environmental commissioner issued a three-hundred-page analysis concluding that "evidence of the deterioration of the province's environmental protection standards is widespread" and warning that laws and policies governing groundwater were inadequate.[84] In 2000 the provincial auditor concluded that the Ministry of Environment did not have satisfactory systems and procedures in place to administer approvals and enforce compliance with environmental legislation.[85]

As a result of budget cuts to environmental ministries and the weakening of regulations, Ontario is the most heavily polluted province, endured the Walkerton tragedy, and suffers significant health and environmental problems because of air pollution. Placing Ontario's forest companies in the position of policing themselves has resulted in far fewer violations being detected, as government audits find five times as many violations as the companies report. Despite the problems that have plagued Ontario, governments in British Columbia, Alberta, and other provinces are implementing similar environmental policies. It seems likely that the financial savings resulting from environmental cutbacks will be more than offset by increased health care, legal, and environmental costs.[86]

Harmonization Agreements

A second factor contributing to inadequate enforcement of Canadian environmental laws during the 1990s was the negotiation of so-called harmonization agreements between the federal and provincial governments. These agreements were ostensibly intended to reduce the overlap between environmental laws and policies at the two levels of government. In reality, harmonization was a euphemism for the devolution, or downloading, of responsibility from the federal government to provincial governments. Some provinces, such as Ontario and BC, in turn downloaded environmental responsibilities onto local governments and municipalities. Nationwide harmonization efforts in the 1990s grew out of a series of bilateral agreements between Ottawa and individual provinces dating back to the 1970s. These earlier agreements were sharply criticized by environmental lawyers as "a virtual abdication" of federal responsibility for environmental protection.[87]

Prior to the signing of the Canada-Wide Accord on Environmental Harmonization in 1998, Parliament's Standing Committee on Environment and Sustainable Development held hearings seeking evidence of overlap and duplication of federal and provincial environmental laws and regulations.[88] Despite extensive inquiries, the Committee could find *no evidence* of either duplication or overlap, and recommended that the federal government delay signing the Harmonization Accord until the Accord's implications could be more fully studied and evaluated. A 1995 report prepared for the Canadian Council of Ministers of the Environment examined the rationale for harmonization and concluded that "most overlap and duplication which existed has been addressed."[89] A study prepared for the Alberta government, a vocal advocate of harmonization, also failed to produce any evidence of costs associated with regulatory overlap or duplication.[90]

According to environmentalists, harmonization weakens environmental protection by reducing the federal role, tying Ottawa's hands, and leading to "lowest common denominator" outcomes.[91] Former Canadian environment minister Tom McMillan argued that "the record of provincial governments in this country in the environmental field is appalling when the federal government has devolved or delegated some of its authority."[92] The Canadian Bar Association also concluded that if harmonization proceeded, environmental protection would suffer.[93] Internal federal government documents confirmed that these concerns about harmonization were valid.[94]

Despite the warnings, the federal and provincial governments, with the exception of Quebec, moved forward with signing and implementing the harmonization agreements. A legal challenge brought by the Canadian Environmental Law Association, arguing that the federal government was unlawfully delegating authority to the provinces, was unsuccessful.[95] In 1999 the federal commissioner of the environment and sustainable development evaluated federal-provincial agreements regarding environmental protection. The commissioner found extensive problems common to all of the harmonization agreements, including:

- limited reference to environmental protection as an objective
- limited federal access to provincial information on enforcement
- no analysis of reductions in duplication
- no evaluation of the agreements' impact on environmental performance
- no audit provisions in the agreements
- no accounting for federal funds transferred to the provinces.

In conclusion, the commissioner warned that "if Environment Canada does not take corrective action, there is a risk that the environment could suffer as a result of deficiencies in both existing and future bilateral environmental agreements."[96]

Some of the predictions of harm arising from harmonization have already been compellingly borne out. After the federal government and Quebec signed a harmonization agreement assigning enforcement responsibilities to the provincial government, there were *no* prosecutions of pulp mills in Quebec despite 1,700 documented violations of the *Fisheries Act*. Similarly, Canada's auditor general observed lower levels of compliance with the *Fisheries Act* by industry when monitoring and enforcement of fish habitat provisions were downloaded to the provinces.[97]

In theory, reducing overlap and duplication between federal and provincial environmental laws is a laudable goal. Harmonization should be a process dedicated to negotiating, implementing, and enforcing mandatory national standards in all aspects of environmental protection. However, harmonization in Canada has been a subterfuge, because there is no evidence of duplication. The hidden agenda behind harmonization involved saving money and placating the provinces, with the result that the Canadian environment suffered.

Excessive Reliance on Voluntary Initiatives

The third factor implicated in the lack of adequate enforcement of Canadian environmental laws is that governments rely heavily on voluntary programs and industry self-regulation.[98] For example, instead of passing laws or regulations to govern greenhouse gas emissions, reduce smog, increase motor vehicle fuel efficiency, or require energy-efficient buildings, the federal government made voluntary agreements with industry. Advocates of voluntary agreements claim that they are more flexible and can achieve progress faster and more efficiently than regulations.[99] Critics argue that voluntary initiatives lack transparency and accountability, encourage free riders, undermine the role of government, maintain the status quo, have high administrative costs, and preempt more effective measures to protect the environment.[100]

Despite their promise, voluntary agreements in Canada have largely failed. Greenhouse gas emissions continue to rise despite the Voluntary Challenge and Registry Program. Smog alerts are more frequent despite voluntary efforts undertaken pursuant to the 1990 joint federal-provincial management plan. Overall motor vehicle fuel efficiency is getting worse, not better, despite a voluntary agreement between Ottawa and vehicle manufacturers. Only a tiny fraction of new homes are energy efficient despite the voluntary R-2000 standard. Reductions in toxic releases, which some industries have ascribed to voluntary programs, have in fact been compelled by regulations.[101] As the OECD concluded in 2000, Canadian "voluntary agreements have not proved up to the task of dealing with resource and environmental challenges."[102]

Numerous studies have examined the effectiveness of voluntary programs in achieving environmental objectives. A study conducted in 1996 surveyed 1,547 large corporations and institutions about factors motivating them to take action on environmental issues. Compliance with regulations was identified by 92 percent of corporations surveyed as an "important motivating factor." In second place, at 69 percent, was director and officer liability for environmental offences. Down at fifteenth place, with only 16 percent of corporations surveyed identifying them as an important motivating factor, were voluntary programs.[103] A report prepared by Environment Canada in 1998 also provides compelling evidence of the inadequacy of voluntary measures. The study looked at nineteen industrial sectors and found that sectors relying on voluntary measures and self-monitoring had a compliance rating of 60 percent, whereas industries subject to regulations, consistent inspections, and enforcement had a compliance rating of 94 percent. The study concluded, "Reliance on voluntary compliance was demonstrated to be ineffective in achieving even a marginally acceptable level of compliance."[104]

An audit of voluntary initiatives by the commissioner of the environment and sustainable development approved of these programs in theory but found them flawed in practice. Voluntary programs audited by the commissioner lacked clear goals and targets, standardized performance measures, clearly defined roles and responsibilities, consequences if objectives were not met, adequate reporting, and independent verification.[105] Canadian studies indicate that industry claims about the effectiveness of voluntary programs are exaggerated.[106] The evidence from the United States also suggests that voluntary initiatives produce little tangible environmental protection unless supported by legislation. As several American law professors point out, "Purely voluntary compliance cannot be expected within our social and economic institutions."[107]

Voluntary initiatives do have the *potential* to produce environmental results that go beyond regulatory requirements with less cost and less conflict. A group of Canadian business executives and environmentalists agreed in 1997 that in order to be successful and credible, voluntary programs should be developed in an open and participatory manner; be transparent in design and operation; be performance-based with specified goals, measurable objectives, and milestones; clearly specify rewards for good performance and the consequences of not meeting the goals; encourage flexibility and innovation in meeting goals; have prescribed monitoring and reporting requirements; include mechanisms for verifying performance; and encourage continual improvement.[108] If these ambitious requirements could be met, the concerns about the effectiveness of voluntary measures would largely be addressed.

The bottom line is that voluntary agreements should be used to supplement, not replace, regulations. As Professor Robert Gibson concludes in his book *Voluntary Initiatives*, "If designed carefully and adopted as contributing parts in a larger whole, [voluntary initiatives] could fill neglected niches and add to the diversity and integrity of a strong overall approach to environmental improvement."[109] However, others point out that "when a government is intent on deregulation, the policy instrument of voluntarism is inherently incapable of achieving its objectives."[110] In the current Canadian context, the increased reliance on voluntary measures is inappropriate, because the regulatory framework provides inadequate incentives in the form of either carrots or sticks.

Lack of Meaningful Opportunities for Public Participation or Enforcement
The fifth fundamental flaw of Canadian environmental law and policy is the lack of meaningful opportunities for public participation, including effective mechanisms for enforcement by the public. In 1990 the Canadian Bar Association (CBA) observed that greater public participation in environmental decision making would produce "fairer decision-making and better decisions" but that citizens are "either excluded from the process or treated as second-class citizens."[111] The CBA made nine recommendations to ensure greater democratization of environmental decision making, but none have been implemented.[112] Canadian environmental policy making is still described as "secretive and opaque, organized around negotiations that involve only a limited number of parties and are insulated from public scrutiny."[113] While access to information has increased in recent years, the public's role is still largely restricted to being notified of government decisions and provided with an opportunity to comment upon proposed decisions. This kind of limited input does not meet public expectations.[114] Even in the rare situations where the public has a more extensive role, as in public hearings either under the *Canadian Environmental Assessment Act* or before Parliament's Standing Committee on Environment and Sustainable Development, governments often ignore the public's input. For example, after public hearings about the *Species at Risk Act* and amendments to the *Canadian Environmental Protection Act,* the Standing Committee made extensive changes to the bills to reflect the concerns and expert evidence presented at the hearings. In both cases, the government reversed the majority of the changes made by the Standing Committee.

Professors Tony Dorcey and Timothy McDaniels observe that "relatively little progress has been made in enshrining public rights to participation in law in Canada (in contrast to the U.S.)." There were some interesting experiments during the 1990s, including Ontario's *Environmental Bill of Rights*, British Columbia's Commission on Resources and the Environment, and the Fraser Basin Council. However, "Enthusiasm across Canada for the new citizen involvement initiatives waned in the mid-nineties as governments at all levels became doubtful about their worth and as concerns about economic issues came to dominate their agendas."[115] A number of new public participation tools appear to have been designed to fail, in that the hurdles involved in using these tools render them toothless. For example, British Columbia's *Recall and Initiative Act* allows citizens to put forward proposals for provincial legislation if a sufficient number of voters' signatures are obtained, but high thresholds, short time periods, and complex rules make the legislation unworkable.[116] Overall, on the spectrum of public involvement ranging from nonparticipation to citizen control, the majority of environmental decision-making processes in Canada can still be characterized as allowing only token participation from the public.

An increasingly important exception to the rule of limited public participation in Canadian environmental policy making involves Aboriginal people. Recognition of their constitutional rights is forcing governments to engage in meaningful consultation or face legal challenges.[117] The trend in parts of the country, particularly in the northern territories, is to move toward comanagement of natural resources.[118] Comanagement means sharing the responsibility for decision making between government and Aboriginal people. Aboriginal involvement is expected to result in more sustainable decisions, because of traditional values and knowledge about local ecosystems. In the Supreme Court of Canada's landmark *Delgamuukw* decision, the Court stated that because of the special relationship between Aboriginal people and the land, there is an "inherent limit" on the kinds of activities that can take place on lands subject to Aboriginal title.[119] The Court used strip mining in a traditional hunting area and paving a burial site as examples of activities prohibited by the unique nature of Aboriginal title. At a minimum, comanagement systems represent an opportunity to innovate and diversify the range of institutions and approaches involved in environmental management in Canada.[120]

Citizen Enforcement Efforts

Another aspect of the lack of opportunities for meaningful public participation involves the difficulty faced by citizens and environmental groups seeking to enforce environmental laws when governments refuse to do so. Courts will not compel the government to enforce the law.[121] However, in a tradition of the legal system Canada inherited from England, individual citizens have the power to lay charges against a person or corporation that breaks the law. This type of legal proceeding is known as a private prosecution. The process is straightforward, but is subject to the supervision of the provincial attorney general, who can either allow such a prosecution to proceed or can intervene and take it over. If the attorney general takes over a private prosecution, he or she can either proceed with the case or drop the charges.[122]

The effectiveness of private prosecutions varies from province to province, depending on the provincial government's policy. The Ontario government has allowed numerous private prosecutions to proceed in recent years. For example, Kingston resident Janet Fletcher, assisted by lawyers from the Sierra

Legal Defence Fund, successfully prosecuted the city of Kingston for violating the *Fisheries Act,* resulting in a fine of $120,000.[123] A private prosecution against the city of Hamilton resulted in a guilty plea and fines of $450,000 under the *Ontario Water Resources Act* and the federal *Fisheries Act*.[124]

In contrast, Alberta, British Columbia, and Newfoundland have stonewalled citizen efforts to enforce the law. In Alberta, environmental activist Martha Kostuch laid a series of charges relating to the construction of the controversial Oldman Dam. In BC, lawyers with the Sierra Legal Defence Fund have laid numerous charges against forest companies and municipalities for violating the *Fisheries Act*. The provincial attorneys general took over *all* of these private prosecutions and dropped *all* of the charges before the cases went to trial.[125] Public efforts to enforce environment laws in Newfoundland when construction of a new hydroelectric project caused extensive damage were also unsuccessful.[126] Courts are extremely reluctant to review the reasons why an attorney general takes over a case and then drops the charges, leading to a dead-end for law enforcement. The government refuses to enforce the law and then blocks the public from enforcing the law. As author Jack Glenn observes, "The unfettered power of attorneys general, which the courts are not prepared to challenge and Parliament is not prepared to diminish, allows governments to sidestep their own laws."[127] Calls to reform the system so that private prosecutions function more effectively have been ignored.[128]

Because private prosecutions in Canada are undermined by the unconstrained ability of attorneys general to derail them, a new tool for public enforcement has been introduced. Several recently enacted environmental laws contain what are known as citizen suit provisions.[129] These provisions explicitly recognize the right of citizens to take law breakers to court in situations where the government refuses to enforce the law. Citizen suits have been successful in the United States in supplementing government enforcement action and in providing concerned citizens with a means of defending the environment.[130] A major advantage of citizen suits is that the standard of proof is based on the balance of probabilities, a much less onerous standard than beyond a reasonable doubt (which is the standard used in criminal and regulatory prosecutions).

Unfortunately, in Canada citizen suits are surrounded by a large degree of suspicion. Industry lobbyists warn of frivolous litigation, threats to corporate reputations, and economic chaos. When the federal government proposed including citizen suit provisions in its endangered species legislation, lawyers for the Canadian Pulp and Paper Association warned of a "flood of lawsuits," "rampant judicial second-guessing of federal ministers," and "potentially disastrous consequences."[131] These industry arguments are largely groundless. Procedural safeguards enshrined in the judicial system, such as cost rules and motions for summary judgment, provide adequate checks and balances to avoid frivolous cases or harassment. Citizen suits will result in fines or other penalties *only* if a citizen can prove that an environmental law has been broken. For law-abiding individuals and businesses, citizen suits should be no concern.

Despite the weak arguments against citizen suits, Canadian governments continue to capitulate to industry objections. Citizen suit provisions were dropped from the federal *Species at Risk Act,* even though Environment Minister Sergio Marchi assured the BC Forest Alliance (a timber industry lobby group) that these citizen suit provisions would be harmless. Marchi pointed out that citizen suit provisions in existing laws have "seldom, if ever, been exercised."[132] In fact, existing citizen suit provisions in Canadian environmental laws are so complex as to be unworkable. Citizens must jump through a series of hoops before being able to take court action. As a result, the citizen suit provisions that do exist, in Ontario, Quebec, the Yukon, the Northwest Territories, and in the *Canadian Environmental Protection Act, 1999* have *never* been used successfully.[133] Given the obstacles to private prosecutions and limited, unworkable citizen suit mechanisms, the public has no means of ensuring that environmental laws in Canada are enforced.

Canada's Narrow Approach to Solving Environmental Problems
The sixth systemic weakness in Canadian environmental law and policy is an excessively narrow approach to solving problems. Canada is paralyzed by a long-standing and intractable debate between two polar extremes: strict command-and-control environmental laws on one hand, and deregulation accompanied by voluntary measures on the other hand. Environmentalists advocate the former model while industry prefers the latter. This polarization breeds mistrust and sabotages efforts to create and implement more innovative laws and policies. Innovative tools such as economic instruments, producer responsibility programs, or environmental rights are rarely used. Canada continues to involve a limited number of parties (primarily government and industry) in developing and implementing environmental laws and policies, and uses policy tools in isolation rather than in combination. A one-size-fits-all philosophy continues to dominate, although the complexity of environmental challenges and the diversity of the regulated community demand a more nuanced approach.[134] Canada has been slow to react to changing circumstances and to learn from past experience.

Regulations may not always be the most efficient means of reaching environmental quality goals. As described in Chapter 7, regulations have been effective in achieving progress on a number of issues, particularly with respect to some industrial sources of air and water pollution. However, other environmental challenges, such as nonpoint source pollution and the protection of drinking water sources, have proven immune to conventional regulatory solutions. Certain areas where Canada's record is particularly poor, such as water and energy consumption, also do not lend themselves well to command-and-control regulation and have proven resistant to voluntary measures. To make progress on these issues, governments in Canada must employ a wider range of laws, regulations, programs, policies, and parties than they have to date. As Professors Gunningham, Grabosky, and Sinclair conclude in their book *Smart Regulation,* "Command and control regulation is not well-equipped to deal with diffuse, non-point and multi-media sources of pollution or with ever more complex and systemic environmental problems such as climate change and the loss of biodiversity, that demand far more sophisticated policy responses."[135]

Economic instruments and policies such as tax shifting, incentives, the removal of subsidies, and emissions trading can provide powerful incentives to change industry and individual behaviour.[136] Other economic instruments include taxes, charges, financial incentives, green loans, rebates, fee-bates, revolving loans, subsidies, full cost pricing, demand-side management (e.g., low-interest loans for energy-efficient building retrofits), buybacks of old, inefficient cars or appliances, liability instruments (e.g., financial responsibility for the rehabilitation of contaminated sites), and performance bonds.[137] These tools could be applied to redesigning the economic system so that incentives and disincentives are in the right places and capable of responding to changing circumstances.[138] Canada lags far behind most countries in using economic instruments to protect the environment.

For twenty-five years, reports and recommendations by Canadian academics, lawyers, and economists have extolled the potential virtues of economic instruments.[139] Yet as one academic observes, "For all practical purposes, nothing has been done. How many more reports will be commissioned, laboured over, submitted, and praised, only to be shelved by policy makers?"[140] The OECD also agrees that in Canada "there is a need to increase the use of economic instruments (for instance, charges on toxic emissions and waste, and disposal fees for products containing toxic substances) to reinforce the polluter-pays principle."[141] More detail on economic instruments and their effectiveness is provided in Chapter 13.

Implementing Broader Approaches

After years of delay, Canadian governments are beginning to experiment with a wider range of policy instruments. The *Canadian Environmental Protection Act, 1999* and several provincial laws explicitly authorize the use of economic instruments.[142] Environment Canada is using a cap-and-trade system to phase out methyl bromide, an ozone-depleting chemical. The federal government has endowed a number of funds with money to be used in research, climate change programs, and funding green municipal infrastructure.[143] The Toronto Atmospheric Fund is a municipal example of economic innovation. An endowment established in 1991 is used to finance projects that reduce greenhouse gas emissions, such as energy-efficiency upgrades to municipal buildings. BC has taken some tentative steps toward implementing programs to make producers responsible for a number of hazardous household items, from paint to batteries. Tax laws have been amended to encourage donations of ecologically sensitive land. Partnerships between environmental organizations and private landowners are being used to protect endangered species and their habitat. These examples suggest that Canada is belatedly beginning to adapt successful environmental law and policy tools from other countries to Canadian circumstances. Much more remains to be done.

Conclusion

This chapter identifies six critical weaknesses in Canadian environmental law and policy. Disturbingly, these systemic problems have been known for decades. Back in 1969 federal water quality laws were described as "a patchwork quilt" characterized by extensive "leeway" in granting permits to pollute.[144] In 1973 a book called *Canada's Environment: The Law on Trial* chronicled some of the same shortcomings of Canadian environmental law and policy described in this chapter.[145] In his 1980 book, *Environmental Regulation in Canada,* Andrew Thompson wrote that environmental law in Canada was hampered by a "lack of clearly stated goals and objectives and of will to obtain those that are stated, inadequate funding and staffing, inconsistent enforcement policies, and failure to inform or involve the public."[146] In 1990 environmental law in Canada was described as having a "history of regulations written and violated, of deadlines missed and rescheduled, of postponement and delay and exception."[147] These criticisms were echoed in 1990 reports from the Law Reform Commission of Canada and the Canadian Bar Association, and a report prepared for the National Round Table on the Environment and the Economy in 1992.[148] The problems persist today.

To remedy the systemic weaknesses in Canadian environmental law and policy outlined in this chapter is a daunting challenge. Considerable energy, resources, and ingenuity will be needed to enact new environmental laws and regulations, ensure the use of mandatory, binding language, incorporate contemporary scientific concepts like the precautionary principle and adaptive management, enforce laws vigorously, engage the public in decision making, and diversify the approach to solving environmental problems. Remedying these systemic weaknesses is made more difficult by a number of underlying institutional obstacles, which are explored in Chapter 9.

9 Obstacles to Further Progress

> I'm tired of hearing about trees.
>
> *Mr. Justice Low, BC Supreme Court, 1993*

For more than three decades, environmental problems have been a major concern for Canadians. Significant efforts have been made at every level – individual, community, corporate, and government – to improve Canada's environmental record. And yet, despite improvements in some areas, Canada's overall performance remains poor. As described in the preceding chapter, Canada's legal system is still plagued by systemic weaknesses. Why do these weaknesses persist?

The answer is that there are structural obstacles to further environmental progress, including, most importantly, the continued predominance of economic interests over environmental protection, international trade liberalization, unresolved constitutional problems, the lack of separation of powers between the legislative and executive branches of government, the extraordinary concentration of power in the prime minister's and premiers' offices, and barriers to an effective role for the courts. These obstacles impede efforts to strengthen Canadian environmental law and policy and, ultimately, to improve Canada's environmental record.

The Dominance of Economic Interests

Short-term economic considerations such as profits, competitiveness, and jobs are the main reasons that Canada is missing key environmental laws, that existing laws are flawed, and that laws are neither implemented nor enforced to the extent required to ensure environmental protection. Economic factors explain why many provincial laws allow industrial activities in parks and protected areas, why air pollution is tolerated at levels that cause thousands of premature deaths annually, why fishing is allowed in marine protected areas, why overcutting and clear-cutting are still prevalent in Canada's forests, why no laws have been passed to reduce greenhouse gas emissions, why the clean-up of contaminated sites is not required by law, why pesticides banned in other countries continue to be used in Canada, why environmental assessment laws favour development over sustainability, why laws do not protect the sources of Canadians' drinking water, why the habitat of endangered species lacks legal protection, and why laws are not enforced against known polluters.

The last two decades have seen a shift to the right in Canadian politics as governments have prioritized debt and deficit reduction, deregulation, privatization, downsizing, and free trade. Canadian governments, both federal and provincial, consider economic issues more important than environmental concerns, despite opinion polls suggesting that most Canadians would place environmental protection ahead of economic growth. The federal government's main concerns during the 1990s were eliminating the budget deficit, reducing the national debt, creating jobs, and maintaining national unity. This agenda, dominated by economic concerns, "resulted in major cuts to federal environmental science and regulatory capacity, a reluctance to challenge industry on environmental issues, and a desire to devolve as much activity to the provinces as possible."[1] At both federal and provincial levels of government, finance ministers have far greater influence than environment ministers. Economic portfolios dominate cabinets.[2]

Despite much ado about the "new economy," Canada still relies heavily on exports of natural resources, from softwood lumber, grain, and fish, to metals, minerals, natural gas, and petroleum products. Canada's eight largest exports are natural resource commodities.[3] The extraction of these natural resources accounts for a substantial proportion of the environmental damage in Canada. Economists have long warned that Canada is suffering both economically and environmentally because of excessive reliance on unprocessed exports of natural resources.[4] Studies indicate that governments will allow high levels of environmental degradation "in situations where the economic future of a community dependent on a particular resource industry is at stake."[5]

Over 80 percent of Canadian exports go to the United States. Indeed, Americans consume more Canadian forest products, more Canadian oil and gas, and more Canadian metals and minerals than do Canadians.[6] Because of the close economic relationship between the two countries, Canada is reluctant to implement environmental laws and policies that are perceived as potentially affecting Canadian industry's competitiveness vis-à-vis the United States. This reluctance is misguided for several reasons. According to the OECD, "The cost of compliance with environmental regulations has had little or no impact on the overall competitiveness of countries."[7] In fact, American industries generally face stricter environmental laws and policies than their Canadian counterparts. Weaker environmental regulations in Canada may limit Canadian access to American markets, as the softwood lumber dispute suggests.[8]

Industry's Influence on Environmental Law and Policy

Environmental regulation is described as "a classic case of diffuse benefits and concentrated costs."[9] In other words, the entire public reaps benefits from environmental protection, but regulated corporations and individuals bear the costs. The concentration of costs creates a defined group with a common interest in opposing the enactment, implementation, and enforcement of new or stronger environmental laws. Industry has far greater resources and power than environmental advocacy organizations.[10] Businesses own most media outlets and buy the lion's share of advertising. Industry can offer direct benefits to politicians in the form of campaign contributions, and indirect benefits by creating jobs and paying taxes. As a result, the majority of environmental laws and regulations in Canada are produced by negotiations between government and business in which the latter tends to have the upper hand.[11]

Industry has blocked and weakened many important environmental law and policy initiatives. For instance, objections from industry resulted in the watering down of the regulations for the *Canadian Environmental Assessment Act*.[12] Industry lobbying managed to delay the implementation of new standards for sulphur levels in gasoline.[13] One of the main reasons for the federal government's reluctance to make long-overdue changes to Canada's pesticide law was that the chemical industry opposed stricter regulation.[14] In effect, the government consistently puts the economic concerns of the private sector ahead of the need for public health protection.

Pressure applied by Canadian Pacific Hotels on the prime minister and the minister of Canadian heritage in 1996 resulted in the approval of a convention centre at Lake Louise despite public opposition, legal questions, and concerns over the environmental impact of additional commercial expansion in Banff National Park.[15] The forest industry played a major role in the weakening and eventual death of the proposed *Canada Endangered Species Protection Act* in 1997. According to an assessment of the history of the *Species at Risk Act*, the federal government's actions demonstrated a consistent bias in favour of business.[16] These examples are the tip of the iceberg. Every time government proposes a new or improved environmental law or policy, those with a vested interest in maintaining the status quo raise economic objections.

The Canadian Council of Chief Executives

The organization in Canada that plays the most powerful role in environmental law and policy development at the national level is not Greenpeace, but rather the Canadian Council of Chief Executives (CCCE, formerly the Business Council on National Issues). The CCCE is composed of 150 CEOs from Canada's largest corporations, is patterned after the US Business Roundtable, and is intended to protect corporations from public criticism and government intervention.[17] The member corporations of the CCCE have 1.3 million employees in Canada and over $2 trillion in assets. Because of this economic importance, the CCCE enjoys unparalleled access to, and influence with, the prime minister and federal cabinet ministers. Professor David Langille describes the CCCE as "a virtual shadow Cabinet."[18] The CCCE uses its political power to shape environmental laws and policies by opposing strict laws or regulations, opposing economic instruments such as energy or pollution taxes, and promoting voluntary initiatives as a panacea for solving environmental problems.

The Canadian Council of Chief Executives was responsible for the last-minute weakening of Bill C-32, the revised *Canadian Environmental Protection Act, 1999*. After Parliament's Standing Committee on Environment and Sustainable Development had strengthened Bill C-32, lobbying by the CCCE and other corporations led the government to overturn most of the Standing Committee's improvements.[19] The CEO of Alcan Aluminum wrote to Prime Minister Chrétien warning that the proposed law could result in the closure of all of Canada's aluminum smelters, including a smelter in the prime minister's Shawinigan riding.[20] This form of economic blackmail is a typical industry tactic. The chair of the Standing Committee, Liberal MP Charles Caccia, charged that the government had weakened the bill to please the chemical industry.[21]

The Canadian Council of Chief Executives also leads the lobbying efforts of Canadian corporations trying to dissuade the federal government from any effective steps to address climate change. To discourage government action, the CCCE warned that fulfilling Canada's promises to reduce greenhouse gas emissions under *Kyoto* would require either an end to Canadian agriculture and turning off the heat in 25 percent of Canadian homes, or taking all cars and 80 percent of commercial vehicles off the roads.[22] To date the CCCE has successfully persuaded the federal government to rely on voluntary programs to address climate change, programs that have failed to stop the Canadian growth in greenhouse gas emissions.

Further evidence of the extent of the influence of the CCCE, and industry generally, on environmental law and policy is that soon after his appointment as Canada's environment minister in August 1999, David Anderson telephoned at least ten major industry associations including the CCCE, the Canadian Chemical Producers' Association, the Mining Association of Canada, and the Canadian Pulp and Paper Association.[23] Within a week of his appointment, Anderson met with the CCCE. Briefing notes explain that one of Anderson's purposes for the meeting was to reassure the CCCE that, despite media coverage suggesting his appointment signalled a higher priority for environmental issues, "productivity continues to be the government's predominant theme."[24] The CCCE frequently meets with cabinet ministers and senior Environment Canada bureaucrats in order to push its agenda promoting voluntary programs and opposing regulation and economic instruments. In effect, the CCCE is lobbying for an environmental law and policy approach with a track record of failure, while blocking the use of laws and policies that have proven effective in protecting the environment.

Industry's Influence on Provincial Environmental Law and Policy
The predominance of economic considerations over environmental concerns is stronger at the provincial level. Provincial governments have jurisdiction over most natural resources and often rely heavily upon these industries for revenue and regional economic development. Professor Robert Paehlke argues that powerful resource industries, such as the oil and gas industry in Alberta, the forest industry in BC, and fisheries in the Maritimes, dominate provincial governments.[25] The BC forest industry's ability to minimize the on-the-ground impacts of government policy changes purporting to deliver sustainable forestry is well documented.[26] Resource industries and provincial governments enjoy a "symbiotic relationship," meaning that laws and policies favourable to industry are generally perceived as benefiting provinces as well.[27] Paehlke and other experts fear that provinces may engage in a "race to the bottom," lowering environmental standards in order to attract investment.[28] This theory is supported by the agenda of regulatory rollbacks, extensive cuts to environmental protection budgets, and the ensuing decrease in enforcement implemented by provincial governments in Alberta, Ontario, and British Columbia.

Labour Union Influence in Environmental Law and Policy
Industry is not always alone in blocking environmental initiatives. The economic interests of labour unions may also trump environmental concerns. The powerful loggers' union in British Columbia successfully derailed the provincial government's attempt to pass endangered species legislation and an environmental bill of rights in the mid-1990s.[29] Although drafted, published, and circulated for public comment, the proposed laws were never enacted. In a confidential letter, Environment Minister Moe Sihota informed the president of the loggers' union that, contrary to the government's public position, because of the concerns expressed by the union the government had no plans to enact endangered species legislation.[30] The loggers' union also contributed to the policy decisions that undermined the environmental protection potential of BC's *Forest Practices Code*.[31] On the other hand, unions deserve credit for supporting many environmental law initiatives, particularly those related to toxic substances and pollution.

Bureaucratic Inertia and Regulatory Capture
Another important reflection of the dominance of economic concerns involves the government agencies that are responsible for managing natural resources and regulating industry. Government departments that manage natural resources were originally established to ensure their orderly exploitation, which was perceived as vital to the economic growth that government values.[32] Environmental

protection is a relatively recent government priority and to some extent is still treated as an afterthought. Senior bureaucrats support the status quo and resist change, and bureaucratic inertia is a well-documented impediment to environmental protection.[33] Moreover, many senior environment bureaucrats are more concerned about protecting the government from environmental issues than protecting the environment. For example, deputy ministers of Environment Canada are appointed by, and report to, the prime minister. One of their primary duties is "blame avoidance," meaning minimizing the risk of backlash from the creation, implementation, or enforcement of environmental laws and policies.[34]

Government departments are also subject to regulatory capture, meaning that the corporations and individuals subject to environmental regulation become "clients" whose interests prevail over the broader public interest that the government is supposed to defend.[35] For example, the Department of Fisheries and Oceans, the agency in charge of protecting and restoring marine biodiversity, is also charged with maintaining an economically thriving fishing industry. The federal auditor general highlighted the conflict of interest between DFO's duty to protect and restore depleted wild salmon populations and DFO's active support for salmon farming, which threatens wild salmon.[36] Similarly, as one academic observes, "The instinct of Natural Resources Canada, urged on by Alberta and other key energy provinces, is to defend the oil and gas industry."[37] The Standing Committee on Environment and Sustainable Development found that enforcement officials with Environment Canada are "subject to undue managerial influence, particularly in so-called 'sensitive' situations, that is, where action is taken or being considered against influential economic entities."[38] The Standing Committee described the federal Pest Management Regulatory Agency as a captive agency, subservient to the pesticide and agriculture industries. The uncomfortably close relationship between the Canadian nuclear industry and its regulatory body (the Atomic Energy Control Board) also illustrates this problem.[39] Provincial resource and regulatory bodies, such as forest ministries, are also plagued by regulatory capture.

Economics Dominates International Environmental Negotiations

In the international environmental arena, where Canada was once a global leader, the 1990s saw a dramatic shift in the Canadian approach to environmental protection. Under Brian Mulroney, Canada led the development of international agreements such as the *Montreal Protocol on Substances That Deplete the Ozone Layer* and the *Convention on Biological Diversity*. With the election of the Chrétien government in 1993, Canada's domestic economic interests began to dominate.[40] Canada's negotiating stance on environmental issues now must be "consistent with Canada's competitive and trade goals."[41] Negotiations about greenhouse gas emissions exemplify the change in Canada's role from environmental leader to environmental laggard. As well, Canada's position in international talks about the *Cartagena Protocol* on genetically modified organisms was largely dictated by the Canadian agriculture industry.[42] Canada, along with the United States and Australia, has become one of the leading opponents of meaningful international agreements to address environmental issues.[43]

International Trade Liberalization

Another important aspect of the dominance of economic over environmental concerns involves international trade liberalization. Since the late 1980s, successive Canadian governments have aggressively pursued a series of trade and investment agreements that undermine existing environmental laws and policies. More ominously, these agreements limit prospects for new or improved environmental laws in the future.[44] As a report by the US Congress concluded, because of trade agreements "it is no longer possible for a country to create an appropriate environmental policy entirely on its own."[45] Of particular concern are NAFTA, the World Trade Organization, the Multilateral Agreement on Investment, the Free Trade Agreement of the Americas, and the General Agreement on Trade in Services.

The North American Free Trade Agreement

NAFTA came into force 1 January 1994, going well beyond the Canada-US Free Trade Agreement signed in 1988.[46] NAFTA's most environmentally problematic provision, is Chapter 11, the investor-state dispute resolution mechanism (see Chapter 2.4, this volume, for an examination of NAFTA's Chapter 11). Under Chapter 11, foreign corporations based in other NAFTA nations can sue governments for passing environmental laws that allegedly affect their investments through expropriation or actions "tantamount to expropriation." NAFTA thus gives foreign corporations unprecedented rights under international law – rights that were previously available only to nations.[47] Professor Luc Juillet describes NAFTA's Chapter 11 as "exceedingly generous to corporations."[48]

NAFTA is worded so broadly that it includes "virtual" expropriation: a corporation can claim that a law affects not property (the usual prerequisite for an expropriation claim), but the company's future profitability or opportunities for growth. Expropriation under NAFTA includes expropriation in its usual sense, "but also covert or incidental interference with the use of property which has the effect of depriving the owner, in whole or in significant part, of the use or reasonably-to-be expected economic benefit of property."[49] Thus an American logging company could seek compensation for new regulations that limit logging in a provincial park or restrict the use of clear-cutting. A study prepared by trade lawyer Howard Mann for the International Institute for Sustainable Development concluded that Chapter 11 of NAFTA goes far beyond what Canadian law considers expropriation that legally warrants compensation.[50] The fact that a law may be justified on environmental grounds makes no difference under NAFTA; the law can stand but the company is still entitled to compensation. As trade law expert Barry Appleton notes, "Governments make big mistakes. They make policies for reasons that are based on public governance – very legitimate – but they don't know what their international obligations are. As a result, when they run afoul of them, they are in a position where they have to pay compensation."[51]

The most notorious challenge to date under NAFTA's Chapter 11 involved the Canadian government's efforts to ban MMT, a gasoline additive containing the heavy metal manganese. There are health and environmental concerns about MMT, but no scientific consensus that MMT poses a significant health risk.[52] In 1997 Canada passed a law banning the import or interprovincial trade of MMT.[53] Because Health Canada concluded the health risks associated with MMT were negligible, the federal government could not ban MMT as a toxic substance under the *Canadian Environmental Protection Act,* but was forced to resort to using its power to regulate interprovincial trade. The American manufacturer of MMT, Ethyl Corp., filed a NAFTA lawsuit seeking C$250 million in compensation for harm to its business and reputation. Corporate lawsuits under NAFTA proceed in secret, and efforts by nongovernment organizations to intervene in the Ethyl case were rejected. In 1998 the government of Canada negotiated a settlement with Ethyl. Environment Minister Christine Stewart and Industry Minister John Manley apologized to Ethyl, promised that the ban on MMT would be lifted, stated that Health Canada found MMT poses no health risk, and agreed to pay Ethyl almost C$20 million in compensation.[54] The safety of MMT, which is now legally used in Canada, continues to be debated.

Canada lost a second Chapter 11 case brought by an American corporation after the federal government banned PCB exports.[55] In another ongoing NAFTA case, an American chemical company is seeking US$100 million in compensation from Canada because the federal government banned some uses of lindane, a pesticide banned in other nations because of health and environmental concerns.[56]

Although the provinces did not sign NAFTA, their laws are also subject to the agreement, as illustrated by Sun Belt Water's challenge of British Columbia's ban on water exports and a controversial case involving an American corporation called Metalclad. Metalclad sued Mexico because the state of San Luis Potosi refused to approve a landfill. Local authorities were concerned that the dump would pollute the local water supply. A NAFTA tribunal, interpreting expropriation very broadly, found that Metalclad's investment had been expropriated and ordered Mexico to pay Metalclad US$16,685,000.[57] A Canadian court upheld the decision, although it took note of the NAFTA tribunal's "extremely broad" interpretation of expropriation.[58]

The Chapter 11 lawsuits concluded thus far confirm earlier fears that NAFTA would be bad for the environment. The majority of the lawsuits filed by corporations under NAFTA's Chapter 11 investor protection provisions between 1994 and 2001 targeted environmental laws.[59] The uncertainty surrounding the scope of Chapter 11 has a chilling effect on new environmental laws, regulations, and policies. In other words, governments hesitate to enact new environmental laws because of fears that the laws *may* run afoul of NAFTA, resulting in expensive compensation claims by foreign corporations.

NAFTA also contributed to an unexpected 400 percent increase in hazardous waste imports from the United States into Canada. The CEC describes this jump as "a vivid example of what happens when domestic environmental policies are weakened at precisely the time that liberalization and open markets occur."[60] Most of the American hazardous waste was shipped to Ontario and Quebec, where loose regulations were eventually tightened.[61]

The World Trade Organization
The World Trade Organization (WTO) is an international trade body that enforces the General Agreement on Tariffs and Trade, the main global treaty governing trade between nations. Under WTO rules, environmental laws must be drafted so as to restrict trade as little as possible. The WTO has broad powers, and has repeatedly ruled against environmental laws that were alleged to interfere with free trade. Although the WTO does not have the power to actually strike down laws, it can effectively do so by requiring countries to pay large sums of compensation to other countries that suffer economic damage as a result of an impugned environmental law. Unlike NAFTA, the WTO dispute resolution mechanism is open only to nations, not corporations. Like NAFTA, the WTO process is conducted in complete secrecy, with no opportunities for public involvement.[62]

With only one exception, in each complaint to date targeting a nation's environmental laws, the WTO has ruled in favour of free trade and against environmental protection. For example, after a complaint from Mexico, an American law requiring tuna sold in the United States to be caught in dolphin-friendly nets was found to violate WTO rules.[63] In a case brought by Asian nations, an American law intended to protect endangered sea turtles being killed by shrimp fishing was found to violate WTO rules.[64] An American regulation under the *Clean Air Act* was successfully challenged by Venezuela and Brazil on the basis that it discriminated against foreign gasoline producers. The United States was ordered to pay US$150 million in compensation.[65]

Canada has used the WTO twice to attack the environmental laws of other countries. In an effort to promote Canadian beef exports, Canada challenged a European ban on hormone-fed beef.[66] Europeans are understandably cautious about beef in light of the mad cow epidemic that swept Great Britain. Canada also used the WTO to challenge a French ban on asbestos imports. In both of these cases, Canada argued *against* the precautionary principle, claiming that hormone-fed beef and asbestos should be considered safe until conclusive evidence proved them to be unsafe. In 1998 the WTO upheld Canada's challenge of the European beef ban. In 2000, for the first time, the WTO upheld a law intended to protect health and the environment by endorsing the French ban on asbestos.[67] Like NAFTA, the WTO not only has direct impacts on environmental laws, it also has a chilling effect on environmental laws not yet passed.

The Multilateral Agreement on Investment

Negotiated in secret during the late 1990s, the Multilateral Agreement on Investment (MAI) would have given multinational corporations the ability to challenge regulations in a broad range of sectors including the environment, culture, health care, and education. As details of the MAI emerged, concerned citizens, municipalities, Aboriginal organizations, and provincial governments fought to derail the negotiations. Although the government of Canada supported the MAI, Canadians played a leading role in opposing the deal, particularly the nonprofit Council of Canadians, led by Maude Barlow. Barry Appleton, the lawyer who represented Ethyl Corp. in its NAFTA case against Canada, admitted that his clients "like these agreements" but criticized the MAI as "very problematic" and "broader than NAFTA."[68] Ultimately, as a result of vocal protests from civil society, France withdrew from the negotiations and the MAI was scrapped.[69]

Ongoing Trade Liberalization Efforts

Despite the MAI's defeat and the unprecedented protests at the WTO meeting in Seattle in 1999, Canada continues to press for further trade liberalization. Canada is participating in ongoing negotiations for the Free Trade Agreement of the Americas and a global General Agreement on Trade in Services. Both of these prospective agreements are expected to further limit the ability of governments to take steps to protect the environment.[70]

Constitutional Problems

The Canadian Constitution's lack of clarity on environmental matters is often blamed for creating confusion about which level of government is primarily responsible for environmental protection. The Constitution provides "ample opportunities for ambiguity, redundancy, conflict, and evasion of responsibility."[71] Both provincial and federal governments use the Constitution's ambiguity to justify their reluctance to act, when the reality is that environmental authority overlaps.[72] For example, Ontario, with the worst pollution record in Canada, blames the federal government for refusing "to commit to tough national air quality and climate change standards for all provinces and territories."[73] The federal government in turn blames Ontario for not doing enough to reduce air pollution.[74] Provincial and federal governments have also clashed over constitutional responsibility for bulk water exports, environmental assessments, energy exports, endangered species, and climate change.

Although uncertainties do persist, the extent of the constitutional confusion is overstated. Experts in constitutional law, including Dale Gibson, Belzberg Fellow of Constitutional Studies at the University of Alberta, and retired Supreme Court of Canada justice Gerard La Forest, agree that the federal government has more power to protect the environment than it has exercised to date.[75] The Supreme Court of Canada has repeatedly supported a strong federal role in environmental protection.[76] Supreme Court decisions have identified marine pollution and the preservation of green space around Ottawa as issues of national concern and therefore subject to federal regulation.[77] As a federal report on protecting the ozone layer states, "The federal government is generally responsible for issues deemed to be in the national interest, and as such is responsible for implementing the provisions of the *Montreal Protocol*."[78] If marine pollution, green space around Ottawa, and ozone depletion are matters of national concern that justify federal regulation, then climate change, the loss of biological diversity, and safe drinking water could also be subject to federal laws. According to Professor Kathryn Harrison, "Constitutional uncertainty persists primarily because the federal government has taken a narrow view of its own powers."[79]

The Influence of Quebec

A major reason for the federal government's constitutional deference to the provinces is the fear of exacerbating federal-provincial tensions during a critical period for national unity.[80] Québécois nationalism and environmentalism emerged as political movements at around the same time: the FLQ crisis was simultaneous with the first Earth Day, and the proliferation of American environmental legislation in the 1970s coincided with the rise of René Lévesque and the separatist Parti Québécois. Since the ascendance of the sovereignty movement in Quebec, the federal government has been reluctant to assert its powers to protect the environment for fear that this would add fuel to the separatists' fire.

The prospect of Quebec separating from Canada has profoundly influenced environmental law in Canada for more than three decades. Quebec's fierce opposition to the *Canadian Environmental Protection Act* in 1987 led the federal government to incorporate the concept of equivalency, so that federal regulations would not apply in provinces with equal or stricter standards.[81] During debates about amendments to the *Canadian Environmental Protection Act* in 1998, Bloc Québécois MP Bernard Bigras attacked the federal government for "denying the right of the Quebec people to decide their own fate."[82] The federal government responded by adding mandatory consultation with the provinces before the federal government can take certain actions under the *Act*.

Industries in Quebec are particularly difficult for the federal government to regulate, for political and economic reasons. For example, "The power of the asbestos industry, and the close ties between the industry and the Quebec and Canadian governments, has created formidable obstacles to those favouring more stringent asbestos regulations."[83] As a result, US standards for asbestos are five times more stringent than Canadian standards, and Canada is the world's second-largest producer of asbestos.[84] The federal government is also reluctant to enforce federal environmental laws in Quebec, as demonstrated by the 1,700 recorded violations of the *Fisheries Act* by Quebec pulp and paper mills that failed to result in a single prosecution.

The Influence of Other Provinces

Pressure from other provincial governments urging Ottawa to decentralize powers also constrains the federal government's enthusiasm for environmental protection. Most provinces vehemently oppose the so-called threat of federal interference in the management of natural resources, fearing that a federal environmental law and policy role could limit economic activities. The pressure for decentralization is strengthened by a strong strain of political conservatism in western Canada that seeks to minimize Ottawa's role in all areas of government.[85] Provincial opposition contributes to the watering down of federal environmental laws and to the absence of legally binding national standards. Many provinces opposed the enactment of federal laws such as the *Canadian Environmental Protection Act, Canadian Environmental Assessment Act,* and the *Species at Risk Act.* A lawyer for the federal government candidly admitted that the narrow scope of the *Species at Risk Act* is a direct result of concern about alienating the provinces.[86]

The contentious environmental harmonization agreements are the product of three convergent forces: the possibility of Quebec separating, provincial pressure on the federal government to reduce its role in natural resource management, and the federal government's efforts to reduce the deficit. Harmonization was fast-tracked by Prime Minister Chrétien after the narrow federalist victory in the 1995 Quebec referendum. Numerous scholars and lawyers describe harmonization as a process through which the federal government has "abdicated" its environmental responsibilities.[87] In some areas that are clearly a federal responsibility, such as aquaculture or inland fisheries, it is difficult for Ottawa to refute this accusation.

At the end of the day, the Constitution provides a convenient smokescreen for both federal and provincial politicians seeking to avoid enacting, implementing, and enforcing environmental laws and policies. This constitutional buck-passing contributes to the spotty patchwork of laws, regulations, and policies ostensibly intended to protect Canadian air, water, land, and biodiversity. David Schindler accurately identifies the "tiresome, juvenile turf war between federal and provincial politicians" as a leading cause of environmental degradation.[88] Addressing Canada's environmental challenges will, as the Supreme Court of Canada recognizes, require a concerted effort by *all* levels of government.

The Lack of Separation of Powers in Canada

Chapter 8 explained in detail how Canadian environmental laws are characterized by discretion, enabling but not requiring governments to take actions that protect the environment. In contrast, in the United States, environmental laws are mandatory in nature, requiring governments to take specified actions and meet specified standards. This fundamental difference can be traced to the lack of separation of powers between the legislative and executive branches of government in Canada.

In the United States, power is divided between Congress (the legislative branch of government), which makes the laws, and the administration (i.e., the executive), which implements the laws. In practice, different political parties often rule the Congress and the administration. As a result of this separation of power, Congress writes and enacts laws that are mandatory, rather than discretionary, so that the administration is forced to obey congressional intent. For example, pollution laws enacted by Congress, such as the *Clean Air Act, Clean Water Act,* and *Safe Drinking Water Act,* create legally binding standards that the administration must meet. If these standards are not met, the government can be held accountable through the judicial system.

In Canada, both federally and provincially, there is no separation of powers. The cabinet effectively controls both the legislative and executive functions of government. As a result, Canadian environmental laws are drafted to provide maximum flexibility and a minimum of mandatory duties. In contrast to the US, with its legally enforceable standards for clean air, clean water, and safe drinking water, Canada has *flexible* national goals embodied by the National Ambient Air Quality Objectives, Guidelines for Canadian Drinking Water Quality, and the misnamed Canada-Wide Standards. There is no legal obligation upon either the federal or provincial governments to achieve these objectives, guidelines, and standards.

Advocates of the Canadian system argue that discretion allows the legal system to be more flexible. While this is true in theory, in practice Canada's overall environmental record shows that flexibility is almost invariably exercised to the detriment of the environment. The separation of powers results in uneven, inconsistent legal protection on vital issues like clean air, safe drinking water, and the protection of endangered species. Yet surely Canadians deserve equal environmental protection regardless of where they live. To achieve this equality will require overcoming the barrier posed by the separation of powers and implementing legally enforceable national standards on a range of environmental issues.

The Concentration of Power in the Prime Minister and Premiers

Every four years we elect a dictatorship.

Professor Chris Levy, University of Calgary Faculty of Law

The problems caused by the lack of separation of powers between branches of government in Canada are exacerbated by another flaw in the Canadian political system. As Professor Wesley Pue of the University of British Columbia observes, "An increasing concentration of power is transforming all 'Westminster-style democracies' into one-person prime-ministerial shows."[89] This trend is particularly strong in Canada. According to academics and journalists, more power is concentrated in the Canadian prime minister's office than in the leader of any other western democracy.[90] The reasons for the dramatic extent of this phenomenon in Canada are as follows:

• The Canadian political system lacks the checks and balances of the US system.
• Canada lacks the effective Parliamentary and party systems of Britain.
• Unlike Australia, Canada has no elected and independent second chamber.

As explained in the previous section, there is no separation of powers between the legislative and executive branches of government in Canada: the prime minister is the head of the civil service as well as the House of Commons. As a result, the prime minister is ultimately responsible for both the enactment and the administration or implementation of laws and policies. This is in marked contrast to the American system, where an independent, law-making Congress balances the president's executive power. The Canadian Senate, which is appointed by the prime minister rather than elected, generally does not provide effective oversight of the House of Commons.[91]

The prime minister appoints members of cabinet, judges, the governor general, the leaders of Crown corporations, senators, and ambassadors. Even Canada's ethics counsellor is appointed by, and reports to, the prime minister. As one lawyer and academic describes the situation, "The Prime Minister, in some respects at least, controls all three branches of government."[92] The prime minister's own website states, "The Prime Minister used to be described as 'the first among equals' in the Cabinet ... That is no longer so. He is now incomparably more powerful than any colleague."[93] Remarkably, even cabinet decisions are not necessarily determined by majority vote because "a strong prime minister, having listened to everyone's opinion, may simply announce that his view is the policy of the government, even if most, or all, the other ministers are opposed."[94] Another aspect of this concentration of power is that the prime minister's close advisors, although they are not elected and have low public profiles, wield tremendous influence. Author Jeffrey Simpson and former Liberal MP John Nunziata both suggest that Prime Minister Chrétien's advisors are more powerful than any cabinet minister.[95] Deputy ministers in all federal departments are also chosen by, and effectively work for, the prime minister.[96]

Moreover, a prime minister with a majority government wields total control over Parliament. Canada has a very strong tradition of party discipline, in part because any vote in the House of Commons may be viewed as a nonconfidence motion. Members of Parliament put loyalty to the party ahead of the opinions of their constituents, whereas members of the US Congress serve their electorate first and their party second. Backbenchers and maverick members of Parliament who refuse to follow the party line face harsh disciplinary action, including expulsion. For example, MP John Nunziata was expelled from the Liberal caucus in 1996 for voting against his party.

These observations apply equally to provincial politics and the role of premiers. There are no checks and balances, party discipline is strictly enforced, and there are no provincial senates. Like the prime minister, premiers control cabinet, the caucus, the legislature, and the civil service, as well as hundreds of appointments to provincial agencies, boards of Crown corporations, and other provincial bodies. In Ontario and Alberta under Premiers Mike Harris and Ralph Klein, large increases in the budget of the premiers' offices reflect increasing centralization of power.[97]

The Impacts of the Concentration of Power on Environmental Law and Policy

The concentration of power in the offices of the prime minister and provincial premiers affects environmental law and policy in three main ways. First, it is difficult for environmental issues to get priority because of the wide range of economic and social challenges confronting political leaders. Despite the heightened degree of environmental awareness in Canadian society, Canadians consistently base their votes on other issues (e.g., the economy and health care). Politicians understand that support for environmental protection is "a mile wide and an inch deep."[98] Prime ministers and premiers are acutely aware that their continued political success is far more likely to depend on the state of the economy than the state of the environment. Second, environmental initiatives are viewed by some politicians as lose-lose propositions.[99] Because environmental issues almost always involve vocal advocates on both sides, whatever action is taken will be loudly criticized. Third, access to prime ministers, premiers, and their top advisors is limited to very powerful members of society, who are usually opponents rather than proponents of environmental protection.[100]

Because so much power is concentrated in the prime minister and premiers, and because environmental laws and policies raise significant economic questions, the prime minister and premiers control the environmental law agenda. In 1997 and again in 2000, Prime Minister Chrétien called early federal elections, and important environmental laws died on the order paper when Parliament was dissolved. In 1997 the environmental laws that were abandoned were the *Canada Endangered Species Protection Act,* the revised *Canadian Environmental Protection Act,* the revised *Fisheries Act,* Bill C-96 implementing the *United Nations Convention on the Law of the Sea*, the *Nunavut Water Resources Act,* and the *Drinking Water Materials Safety Act*. Most of these laws have never been reintroduced. In 2000 the environmental laws that died on the order paper were the *Species at Risk Act,* the *National Marine Conservation Areas Act, An Act to Amend the International Boundary Treaty Waters Act,* and the *Foundation for Sustainable Development Technology Act.*

Prime Minister Chrétien pushed through the Canada-Wide Accord on Environmental Harmonization in 1998 despite opposition from his own environment minister, backbench MPs, the Standing Committee on Environment and Sustainable Development, environmental groups, and the Canadian Bar Association.[101] Despite similar opposition, the prime minister placated industry by forcing last-minute changes to weaken the *Canadian Environmental Protection Act, 1999* and the *Species at Risk Act*. In Alberta, Ontario, and more recently British Columbia, Premiers Klein, Harris, and Campbell have led dramatic reductions in environmental regulation and enforcement. The lack of effective checks and balances in the Canadian political system makes it difficult to effectively oppose decreases in environmental protection.

Occasionally the power of the prime minister or premiers works in favour of environmental protection. For example, in 1997 Prime Minister Chrétien was publicly embarrassed at the five-year follow-up meeting to the Rio Earth Summit. As a result, Chrétien ordered that Canada take a stronger stance than the United States during the negotiation of the *Kyoto Protocol*.[102] Canada's *Kyoto* commitment, to reduce greenhouse gas emissions by 6 percent between 1990 and 2010, is modestly better than the US commitment of a 5 percent reduction. Chrétien then used his power to ensure that Canada ratified *Kyoto* in 2002. Prime Minister Chrétien also deserves credit for the 2002 passage of the *Species at Risk Act, National Marine Conservation Act*, and *Pest Control Products Act*, in addition to significant funding increases for environmental priorities. These actions, in the final year of his mandate, represent a remarkable reversal of Chrétien's earlier record. In BC, Premier Mike Harcourt's personal commitment to environmental protection contributed to significant provincial law and policy improvements during the early 1990s. BC passed new laws including the *Environmental Assessment Act, Forest Practices Code of British Columbia Act, Water Protection Act,* contaminated sites legislation, tougher pulp and paper mill regulations, and regulations governing motor vehicle emissions and cleaner fuels. Harcourt's government also added millions of hectares of new protected areas, cancelled the ill-advised Kemano Completion Project, and created an environmental watchdog known as the Commission on Resources and the Environment.[103]

The OECD observes that for sustainable development to succeed, a strong political commitment "must come from the highest levels of government and be embraced by prime ministers as well as ministers of finance."[104] This strong political commitment is not yet consistent in Canada.

Barriers to an Effective Role for the Courts

Because of flaws in Canada's political system such as the lack of separation of powers and an ineffective Senate, the Canadian judicial system has a particularly important role in holding governments accountable. It is up to the courts to fill the void left by the Canadian political system's lack of effective checks and balances. Unfortunately, the judicial system's contribution to environmental protection in Canada is undermined by several factors, including a historical bias toward private rather than public interests, the absence of constitutional environmental rights, a lack of access to the courts, the high costs of litigation, judicial deference to government decision makers, and low penalties for environmental offences. Progress has been made on some of these issues in recent years, but major barriers remain.

Private Rights versus the Public Interest

The Canadian legal system is based mainly on the English common law system, which focuses on the *private* rights of parties. The emergence of a judicial role in protecting the *public* interest, sometimes at the expense of private interests, is a recent phenomenon.[105] Judicial recognition of the public interest in environmental protection was slow to develop in Canada but increased considerably in the 1990s. In 1973 an Ontario judge criticized environmental lawsuits by citizens as "ill-founded actions for the sake of using the courts as a vehicle for expounding philosophy."[106] In the 1980s a judge presiding over an environmental private prosecution in Ontario admitted a desire "to be back with my burglars and murderers."[107] In 1993 a judge involved in sentencing individuals for protesting at Clayoquot Sound in BC said, "I'm tired of hearing about trees."[108] One of clearest situations in which private and public interests clash is injunction applications by environmental groups to stop specific activities, such as the logging of a particular area or the building of a road. Courts must weigh the private interest in lost profits, economic impacts, and possible job losses against the public interest in environmental protection. Although judges have historically been reluctant to grant injunctions in these circumstances, the trend in recent years is toward environmental protection, in recognition of the irreparable nature of ecological damage.[109] Canadian courts, led by the Supreme Court of Canada, have become increasingly cognizant of the legitimate role and importance of public interest environmental litigation.

Environmental Rights

Constitutional recognition for rights is the strongest form of protection available under the Canadian legal system. Although citizens in many other countries, from Azerbaijan to Vanuatu, enjoy constitutional protection for environmental rights, Canadians do not. Canada's *Charter of Rights and Freedoms* contains no provision recognizing the right of Canadians to a clean, safe, and healthy environment. The closest provision is section 7 of the *Charter,* which protects Canadians' "right to life, liberty, and security of the person." Attempts to persuade courts to interpret this provision broadly, so as to include some form of environmental right, have not been successful.[110] A BC judge rejected arguments made by lawyers for a group of concerned residents that Canadians enjoy a right to safe drinking water.[111]

Residents of Ontario, Quebec, the Yukon, the Northwest Territories, and Nunavut enjoy limited statutory environmental rights because of recently enacted laws.[112] These environmental rights for the most part are procedural, not substantive. Statutory environmental rights are much weaker than constitutionally protected environmental rights. Apart from ensuring access to information and requiring public notification of changes to environmental laws and regulations, these laws have had minimal practical impact on environmental protection in Canada. For example, despite the *Environmental Bill of Rights* passed in 1993, Ontario is still Canada's most polluted province, the site of the Walkerton disaster, and a jurisdiction subject to dramatic reductions in environmental protection.

Access to Courts

Chapter 8 detailed the ineffectiveness of private prosecutions and citizen suits in protecting Canada's environment. Citizens can also go to court in an effort to overturn government decisions, a process known as judicial review. The first obstacle to judicial review is called standing, or the legal right to bring a case to court. Traditionally, a person needed a direct personal or property interest in order to gain standing. In recent years, however, courts have established a concept called public interest standing that allows citizens, environmental groups, and other organizations to bring lawsuits challenging government decisions.[113] As long as a citizen or group can demonstrate a genuine interest in a problem, raise a serious issue of law, and convince a judge that the issue would not otherwise be brought to court, then public interest standing will be granted.[114] Only in rare cases is public interest standing denied.[115] In some provinces, however, such as Alberta, standing is limited by some environmental laws to individuals who are "directly affected" by a project or activity.[116] This greatly restricts the public's ability to use the judicial system to hold governments accountable.

The High Costs of Litigation

The accessibility of the justice system under the concept of public interest standing is in danger of being undermined by the high cost of litigation.

Although there are now a number of nonprofit organizations offering free legal services (e.g., Sierra Legal Defence Fund, Canadian Environmental Law Association, Environmental Defence Canada, West Coast Environmental Law Association) and an increasing number of lawyers willing to work on a pro bono basis, demand still exceeds supply. A larger problem is that courts generally award costs against unsuccessful litigants, meaning the losing party in a lawsuit pays a portion of the winner's legal costs. These cost awards can be more than $100,000, making litigation prohibitively expensive for local citizens and smaller environmental groups.[117] Class actions, lawsuits brought on behalf of a group of individuals allegedly suffering similar damages, can also result in huge cost awards against unsuccessful plaintiffs, as two recent Ontario cases demonstrated.[118] Recent changes to the *Federal Court Rules* increased the likelihood that unsuccessful public interest litigants will be forced to pay costs.[119] There are compelling arguments that courts should create an exception to the costs rule for precedent-setting cases brought to advance the public interest, just as courts created an exception to the traditional rules of standing to enable public interest litigation.[120] To date, however, Canadian courts have refused to create an exception to the general costs rule for public interest litigants.

Judicial Reluctance to Engage in Substantive Review

Judicial review cases are based on two main considerations: did decision makers act "within their jurisdiction" (i.e., the parameters set out in the relevant law), and was their decision "reasonable"? Canadian courts are very deferential toward government decision makers, generally refusing to overturn decisions unless there is an "error of law" or the decision is "patently unreasonable." In practice, the doctrine of judicial deference can produce absurd results, as in a 1990 lawsuit intended to protect Atlantic cod where the court refused to critically examine federal fisheries management.[121] In the field of environmental law, Canadian courts focus on procedural matters, and are extremely reluctant to scrutinize the substantive factual issues. The consensus among legal experts is that "substantive review of legislative and administrative performance is highly atypical of the judiciary in Canada."[122]

Often courts will be satisfied if minimal procedural requirements are met by government decision makers, regardless of the extent or quality of substantive evidence to support the decision. In the late 1980s and early 1990s, Canadian courts made a series of relatively bold decisions forcing the federal government to conduct environmental assessments of major projects with impacts in federal areas of jurisdiction. However, since that time "courts have demonstrated reluctance ... to scrutinize those assessments with a high degree of intensity."[123] In a recent environmental assessment case, the Federal Court decided, "If there has been some consideration [of a factor, such as cumulative effects], it is irrelevant that there could have been further and better consideration."[124] Canadian courts are particularly reluctant to delve into the complex scientific questions raised in environmental cases. The same Federal Court decision stated, "It is not the function of this Court to identify and correct poor science." This is a familiar judicial position in environmental cases, yet in criminal cases courts are able to decipher expert evidence on complex scientific issues such as DNA testing, and in corporate cases courts untangle complicated business transactions.[125]

Low Penalties for Environmental Offences

Another problem is that, historically, penalties for environmental offences in Canada were extremely low. Several corporations convicted of violating the *Fisheries Act* for unlawfully discharging toxic effluent were fined $1.[126] According to author Michael Harris, among Canadian commercial fishers in the 1980s and early 1990s, "Fines had become so minimal, they were a standing joke in the industry, a minor cost of doing business."[127] Many federal and provincial environmental laws were amended at that time to provide stronger penalties. Stiff fines and jail sentences were intended to send a clear message that environmental offences will not be tolerated by Canadian society.[128] However, as Chapter 8 makes clear, environmental laws in Canada are not being rigorously enforced. Larger potential penalties have little deterrent effect where a law is not being enforced.[129]

Judicial awareness of the significance of environmental offences is increasing. During the 1990s, a Quebec company was fined $4 million for pollution offences, while a pulp and paper mill in Newfoundland was fined $750,000.[130] Some judges are making stronger pronouncements in environmental prosecutions, such as:

"Every act of degradation of the environment is cumulative and has to be addressed that way."[131]

"The message has got to go out there that infractions of the environmental legislation are not going to be tolerated."[132]

Pollution prevention "requires not only a change in technology but a change in mindset."[133]

Fines and jail sentences given to corporate directors and business leaders send a message to corporate Canada that violating environmental laws could have serious repercussions.[134] However, only a handful of individuals have ever received jail sentences in Canada for environmental offences.[135] Far more Canadians have been jailed for attempting to protect the environment than for damaging it. In the summer of 1993 alone over eight hundred people were arrested in the rainforest at Clayoquot Sound on Vancouver Island. Using mass trials, the courts handed out surprisingly harsh sentences ranging up to six months.[136] A grandmother, Betty Krawczyk, spent many months in jail for her part in various logging protests.[137] In contrast, four loggers who assaulted a group of environmentalists in British Columbia and deliberately destroyed evidence of the attack received no jail time but were sentenced to perform community service and take anger management courses.[138]

On a positive note, courts are beginning to use the creative sentencing provisions found in many modern environmental laws. These provisions enable courts to make a wide range of orders against parties convicted of environmental offences. Examples of creative sentences include orders to restore damaged habitat, contribute funds to universities for research, or undertake prescribed activities to prevent future pollution.

The Role of the Courts in the United States

In the United States, many of the barriers to an effective role for the courts have been lowered. Professors Kathryn Harrison and George Hoberg conclude that in the context of environmental law and policy, "Perhaps the most significant difference in the regulatory frameworks of the two countries is the pivotal role of the judiciary in the United States."[139] The United States has a more complete array of environmental laws, legally enforceable national standards, extensive opportunities for public involvement in decision making, and a judiciary with a history of activism. American courts are willing to evaluate the substantive merit of government decisions, even if it means delving into complex scientific evidence.[140] Courts in the United States have creatively modified ancient legal concepts, such as the public trust doctrine, to protect the environment.[141] Citizen suit provisions in almost all major American environmental statutes allow the public to assist government in enforcing environmental laws and are seen as "a critical aspect of democratization."[142] And finally, American courts impose very large sentences, both in terms of fines and jail time, on those who violate environmental laws.

The barriers to an effective role for the courts in Canada, combined with the absence of key laws, the lack of enforceable national standards, and the pervasiveness of discretion, make environmental litigation far less common in Canada than in the United States, and far less effective.[143] Environmental lawyers Elizabeth Swanson and Elaine Hughes conclude, "Litigation with the primary and immediate purpose of bringing a halt to unwanted development activity has not, for the most part, succeeded."[144] The systemic problems in Canada's environmental law system caused another author to bemoan the "absolute futility of looking to the courts to defend the environment from governments that wish to exploit its economic potential."[145] The bottom line is that in Canada, courts are unlikely to overturn government decisions in the area of environmental law and policy.[146]

Conclusion

This chapter describes a number of imposing obstacles that must be overcome to strengthen Canada's environmental laws and policies and improve Canada's environmental performance. First and foremost, economic considerations continue to dominate the enactment, implementation, and enforcement of environmental law and policy. Other hurdles to strengthening environmental law in Canada include constitutional problems, the ongoing threat of Quebec separation, the lack of separation of powers between the legislative and executive branches of government, the concentration of power in the prime minister and premiers, and barriers to an effective role for the courts. However, even if these hurdles could be successfully cleared, what would be the impact on Canada's environmental record? The next chapter addresses this question.

10 Root Causes of Environmental Degradation

> Environmental measures must anticipate, attack and prevent the causes of environmental degradation.
> *Supreme Court of Canada, 2001*

> There are a thousand hacking at the branches of evil to one who is striking at the root.
> *Henry David Thoreau*

What if Canada, despite the obstacles identified in the previous chapter, enacted a comprehensive set of new environmental laws? What if the new laws were mandatory instead of discretionary? What if the federal government overcame its constitutional timidity and imposed uniform national standards for air, water, land, and biodiversity, which the provinces and territories were obligated to meet? What if the federal and provincial governments doubled spending on environmental protection and enforcement? What if laws and policies were amended to facilitate increased public involvement in environmental policy making? What if citizens were given the right to enforce all of Canada's major environmental statutes, both federal and provincial? What if Canadian courts began to hand out consistently stiff sentences for environmental offences and to engage in substantive review of environmental decision making?

Canada could make all of these dramatic changes and still fail to achieve sustainability or a high degree of environmental protection. While these reforms would almost certainly result in substantial improvements to Canada's environmental record, ultimately they would neither solve our environmental problems nor ensure a sustainable future. This surprising conclusion is based on the experience of the United States, which offers profound challenges to conventional Canadian wisdom about environmental law and policy. The United States is living proof that a narrow, legalistic approach, relying on an exhaustive array of increasingly complex environmental laws and regulations to mitigate the impacts of growing energy and resource consumption, is insufficient to achieve sustainability.

The Failure of American Environmental Law and Policy

The United States has "the world's most extensive array of anti-pollution and conservation measures."[1] As noted in Chapter 8, the United States has enacted a comprehensive list of environmental laws that, as of yet, have no Canadian equivalents. Environmental laws in the United States are mandatory, detailed, and complex. Just three of the major American environmental laws, including regulations, total more than 11,500 pages.[2] The United States spends more money than any other nation on environmental protection; has mandatory national standards for clean air, clean water, safe drinking water, the rehabilitation of contaminated sites, forest management, and protecting endangered species; offers its citizens unparalleled opportunities to engage in enforcing environmental laws; has extensive checks and balances built into its political institutions; and has courts with a history of judicial activism and limited deference toward government decision makers.[3]

Despite this seemingly robust approach, American environmental law and policy is not producing the desired results. Americans have the largest per capita environmental impacts in the world.[4] The United States finished last in a comparison of the environmental records of the OECD nations.[5] According to the comprehensive Ecosystem Wellbeing Index, which examines fifty-one environmental indicators, the United States ranks 143rd out of 180 nations.[6] The United States has less than 5 percent of the world's population but produces 25 percent of global greenhouse gas emissions. Despite progress in reducing some types of industrial pollution, thousands of Americans die annually because of air and water pollution, while hundreds of thousands become ill. More than 1,200 species are listed as threatened or endangered under the US *Endangered Species Act* and a backlog of thousands more species, known to be endangered, is waiting to be listed. A recent statement released by senior officials at the Environmental Protection Agency confessed that "even if we had perfect compliance with all our authorities [environmental laws], we could not assure the reversal of disturbing environmental trends."[7]

An international assessment of the environmental laws and policies of industrialized nations concluded that while the United States was an innovator in environmental policy in the 1970s, the country is now plagued by "institutional rigidities," a "lack of political will," and a "refusal to take steps to solve global problems" like climate change and population growth.[8] American environmental law is described by lawyers as "immensely costly and technically confusing" and "a statutory and bureaucratic labyrinth."[9] American environmental law is also highly fragmented, taking a scientifically outdated pollutant-by-pollutant, medium-by-medium, species-by-species approach.[10] American law professor J.B. Ruhl concludes that "efforts to cling to a highly predictable, rule-habituated system of law undermine the adaptability of law to its changing subject matter."[11] The magnitude and complexity of economic activity overwhelms American efforts to mitigate, through the legal system, the impacts of the economy upon the environment. The US experience clearly refutes the idea that there is necessarily a positive correlation between economic growth and environmental protection.[12]

Three decades of American environmental laws and policies have managed to "reduce and even reverse some environmental damage, but only marginally to moderate the larger national and global forces of population growth, landscape transformation, natural resource use, and waste generation that define modern human history."[13] The ecological footprint of American society is increasing, and there is growing appreciation among American lawyers and academics that existing approaches are incapable of addressing these deeper problems.[14]

Canada: Following in American Footsteps

The foregoing critiques of American environmental law and policy are equally applicable to Canada. Despite American environmental law and policy's resounding failure to solve environmental problems, Canada continues to emulate the United States. NAFTA is contributing to this convergence.[15] Canadian environmental laws such as the *Canadian Environmental Assessment Act* and the *Energy Efficiency Act* are modelled after American legislation. Most of the solutions advanced for improving Canadian environmental law and policy are based on American laws, policies, and precedents. To protect endangered species, Canadian environmental lawyers advocated legislation similar to the US *Endangered Species Act*.[16] To reduce the health and environmental threats posed by pesticides, Canadian environmental lawyers championed numerous elements of the US *Food Quality Protection Act*.[17] Not surprisingly, Canada's *Species at Risk Act* and the new *Pest Control Products Act* incorporate many aspects of their American counterparts. To improve protection for Canadian drinking water, the US *Safe Drinking Water Act* and New Jersey's drinking water legislation are held up as models.[18] Canadian lawyers and judges also use American court decisions as precedents. For example, to interpret the *Canadian Environmental Assessment Act,* environmental lawyers rely on American court decisions interpreting the *National Environmental Policy Act*.[19] Like American laws, Canadian environmental laws are becoming far more complicated. The *Canadian Environmental Protection Act, 1999,* for example, is 150 pages long and has 343 sections, whereas the previous *Act* was 71 pages and had 139 sections. The new *Pest Control Products Act* is 70 pages and has 90 sections, while the old *PCPA* was 7 pages and had 13 sections.

As in the United States, despite thirty-plus years of sustained effort to protect the environment through increasingly detailed laws and policies, most indicators of environmental performance in Canada continue to worsen. Canada ranks second-last in the OECD on a range of twenty-five environmental indicators. On fifteen of them, Canada's performance has deteriorated over the past two decades. Other scientific assessments reinforce the conclusion that Canada is performing poorly on environmental issues. Canadians have the third-largest per capita environmental impacts in the world. According to the Ecosystem Wellbeing Index, Canada ranks 94th out of 180 nations. As the Commission for Environmental Cooperation (CEC) concludes, "On both a North American and a global scale, economic activity in Canada and the United States is exerting disproportionate environmental pressure."[20]

The fundamental problem with the American approach to protecting the environment, and by extension, the Canadian approach, is that the *root causes of environmental degradation are never addressed*. All of the effort is directed toward treating the *symptoms* of environmental harm, a strategy that may mask or mitigate the damage but will never prevent it. Canada, like the United States, attempts to protect the environment through an increasingly complex web of laws and regulations. These efforts focus on moderating the harmful impacts of human activities in industrial societies, without challenging the dominant paradigm of endless economic growth based on ever-increasing consumption of energy and resources. This approach is like a person diagnosed with lung cancer who begins taking medication and undergoing treatment but continues to smoke two packs of cigarettes per day. In neither situation is the cause of the problem being addressed.

Identifying the Root Causes of Environmental Degradation

Astronaut Marc Garneau was the first Canadian ever to fly in space, on the space shuttle *Challenger* in 1984. When asked what images he recalled from circling high above Earth, Garneau described three signs of environmental degradation: the bleeding of red soil from Madagascar's cleared forests into the Indian Ocean; the clouds of black smoke from forest fires burning in the Amazon; and the massive clear-cuts in British Columbia.[21] At first blush, all three images seem to relate to the environmental problem of deforestation. However, upon reflection, one realizes that their *root causes* are pressure from population growth (Madagascar), consumption (BC), or a combination of the two (the Amazon). In other words, the national and international growth in environmental degradation is caused by population growth and increasing consumption of resources.[22] Scientists express this as a simple mathematical formula:

$$\text{Human environmental impact} =$$
$$\text{Human population} \times \text{Consumption of energy and resources per capita}^{23}$$

In this equation, consumption includes two components: the energy and materials that are consumed, and the waste or pollution that is generated. In Canada and the United States, consumption is more problematic than population. As the CEC points out, North America's "prevailing emphasis on consumption – with high levels of waste, energy use, and greenhouse gas emissions – jeopardizes the capacity of natural resources and systems to support future generations."[24] Experts agree that without stabilization of both consumption (in industrialized nations) and population (in all countries), good health will remain elusive for many people, developing countries will find it impossible to escape poverty, and environmental degradation will continue to worsen.[25] At a fundamental level, laws and policies intended to protect the environment must directly address consumption and population, not merely their impacts.

All of Canada's environmental problems, from climate change to the loss of biodiversity, are more accurately described as *symptoms* of the real problem: excess consumption of energy and resources. Yet our environmental laws focus on treating the symptoms, not the causes, of the problems. Laws governing forest practices attempt to mitigate the damage caused by overcutting but fail to address the excessive demand for wood and paper that drives the unsustainable level of logging. Laws governing drinking water require chemical treatment of water but rarely protect the sources of drinking water from harmful land-use activities. Laws intended to limit air pollution rely on expensive technological solutions but ignore the unsustainable rate of fossil fuel use that causes air pollution. Laws to protect endangered species try to prevent extinction but fail to address the reasons why species are at risk in the first place, including excessive harvesting, the introduction of exotic species, and the loss of habitat, all caused by a wide range of human economic activities undertaken to facilitate consumption. This point is driven home by the fact that despite the strength of the US *Endangered Species Act,* only a handful of the thousands of endangered species have recovered sufficiently to be removed from the list of species at risk of extinction in the United States. The focus of environmental law needs to shift and address the root causes of environmental degradation.

The Concept of Limits

There is a critical reason why the root causes of environmental degradation must be addressed. According to astronaut Marc Garneau, "The planet is not as big as people think it is."[26] Although few humans will ever travel beyond Earth's atmosphere, anyone can share Garneau's understanding of the Earth's limits by looking at the remarkable photographs of this planet taken from outer space. Earth is a small, even fragile-looking planet relative to the immensity of the universe.

Scientists have identified three basic principles that must be respected in order to achieve an ecologically sustainable future and avoid irreversible environmental degradation. In simple terms, nature must not be subject to a systematic:

- buildup of materials extracted from the Earth's crust
- buildup of substances produced by society
- degradation of its diversity, productivity, or capacity for renewal.[27]

These three principles warrant further examination because they represent the scientific basis for rethinking Canadian environmental laws, policies, and institutions.

1   *Nature cannot withstand a systematic buildup of materials extracted from the Earth's crust.*
   As part of nature's cycles, substances flow from the Earth's crust to the ecosphere (the layer of earth, water, and sky where life occurs) through processes like erosion and volcanic eruptions. These substances are eventually reabsorbed into the crust through other processes, such as sedimentation. The first limit imposed by the finite nature of the Earth is that the natural flows of a given substance (e.g., carbon from decaying organic matter, forest fires, etc.) plus human-generated flows (e.g., carbon released from burning fossil fuels) must not exceed the planet's ability to assimilate that substance.

   Human activity can add to the natural flow of a substance so that total emissions exceed nature's absorption rates, and, as a result, the substance begins to accumulate. The ensuing disruption of natural cycles has environmental consequences. For example, increasing levels of carbon dioxide in the atmosphere due to the burning of fossil fuels disrupt the carbon cycle, contributing to climate change. Increasing levels of sulphur in the atmosphere from industrial activities contribute to acid rain. Increasing levels of heavy metals (e.g., lead, mercury, and cadmium) contaminate soil, poison wildlife, and threaten human health. Fulfilling the first condition of ecological sustainability will require Canada to reduce our dependence on fossil fuels, replace nonrenewable resources with renewable resources, substitute abundant minerals for scarce minerals, and use all mined materials as efficiently as possible.

2   *Nature cannot withstand a systematic buildup of anthropogenic substances.*
   Through advanced technology, humans are creating thousands of substances previously unknown on Earth. Nature has not evolved the capacity to assimilate many of these substances. Therefore, scientists conclude, the second natural limit is that society must not emit these substances at a rate that is faster than they are degraded into substances that can be incorporated into natural cycles.[28] Of particular concern are human-made substances that are persistent, bioaccumulative, or toxic at very low levels of exposure, such as CFCs, PCBs, many pesticides, and endocrine-disrupting chemicals. These human-made chemicals also pose challenges because of

the complexity of their interactions with each other and the potentially long period of time between the release of these substances into the environment and scientific recognition of their negative health and environmental impacts. CFCs, PCBs, DDT, and many pesticides were thought to be safe for decades before scientists identified their harmful effects and persistence. Human-made chemicals that do not break down in nature or break down only very slowly should be used with extreme caution, if at all. Fulfilling the second condition of ecological sustainability will require substituting abundant, natural, and biodegradable substances for persistent, unnatural substances, and using all substances produced by society as efficiently as possible.

3   *Nature cannot withstand a systematic deterioration of its diversity, productivity, or capacity for renewal.*
The third natural limit addresses the harvesting and manipulation of ecosystems. Harvesting includes activities like fishing, logging, hunting, and groundwater extraction. Manipulation includes displacing natural ecosystems (e.g., by building cities or roads), reshaping the structures of nature (e.g., by damming a river or replacing an old-growth forest with a plantation), and modifying natural processes (e.g., by breeding or genetic engineering).

Society depends upon the natural world for invaluable, irreplaceable goods and services including food, raw materials, energy, cultural inspiration, medicines, pest control, pollination, soil formation, waste disposal, climate regulation, flood prevention, and nutrient recycling.[29] In order to avoid impairing these vital ecosystem functions, the rate at which renewable resources are consumed must not exceed their rate of regeneration. Care must be taken to avoid reducing natural productivity, diversity, or resilience by manipulating ecosystems. Examples of such reductions include soil erosion, deforestation, the loss of species or genetic diversity to extinction, destruction of fresh water supplies, and the use of productive land for cities, roads, or landfill sites. Fulfilling the third condition of ecological sustainability will require using land, water, and all natural resources as efficiently as possible, and minimizing the modification of natural ecosystems.

Exceeding the Earth's Limits
The OECD, the UN, the World Resources Institute, the Union of Concerned Scientists, and many other respected organizations agree that humans are approaching or exceeding the three basic limits of the Earth.[30] Humanity is overloading the waste absorption capacity of the planet and approaching critical thresholds in the regenerative capability of renewable resources.[31] Anthropogenic emissions of many substances extracted from the Earth's crust are already

substantially higher than natural flows, exceeding the first limit. Since the beginning of the industrial age about two hundred years ago, the level of carbon dioxide in the atmosphere has risen by more than 40 percent. Contrary to earlier beliefs, scientists now understand that "for most elements, the assimilation capacity of the ecosphere is a more restrictive constraint on the use of these elements than the amount of resources available in the lithosphere [Earth's crust]."[32] For example, fears about running out of fossil fuels have been replaced by concerns about climate change caused by the accumulation of greenhouse gases in the atmosphere. Similarly, while there is plenty of lead left in the Earth's crust, the volume of lead already extracted by humans is roughly three hundred times nature's capacity to absorb this heavy metal.[33]

The depletion of the ozone layer by a handful of synthetic chemicals is probably the clearest example to date of the profound dangers of exceeding the second limit, Earth's assimilative capacity for human-made chemicals. Because of the twentieth-century use of ozone-depleting chemicals containing chlorine, chlorine levels in the atmosphere are now six times historic levels. The global biodiversity crisis, the depletion of fisheries, the poor condition of many freshwater ecosystems, and the loss of natural forests are evidence that society is exceeding the third limit, reducing the diversity and productivity of ecosystems.

Consumption

Few Canadians realize that "although each of us individually has an impact on the environment, our greatest impacts arise indirectly, through the broad economic activity required to meet our collective demands."[34] Canadian consumption of water provides a clear example. Individual Canadians drink about 2 litres of water daily, and use a daily total of 343 litres for all activities, from flushing toilets to watering gardens. But Canada uses 4,400 litres of water per person per day for various industrial, agricultural, municipal, and commercial purposes and another 8,800 litres per person per day to generate hydroelectricity. Thus, our collective impact on the environment, as part of Canada's industrial economy, is far greater than most Canadians realize. To accurately measure human consumption requires assessing energy and resources consumed at the four main stages of economic activity: resource extraction, industrial production, consumer behaviour, and waste generation. Scientists and economists are just beginning to assess the total use of resources by industrialized nations, a concept known as the total material requirement. More than half of the total material requirement of industrial economies consists of "hidden flows," meaning materials removed from the natural environment or disturbed in order to obtain natural resources or build infrastructure. Because these materials are never bought or sold, conventional economic measurements such as GDP do not include them.

A detailed assessment of energy and resource consumption in Germany, Japan, the Netherlands, and the United States revealed that these industrialized nations use from 45,000 kilograms per person (Japan) to 85,000 kilograms per person (United States) of energy and resources annually.[35] Given that Canadian consumption closely mirrors American consumption, this works out to 232 kilograms of materials per Canadian daily, or the equivalent of about forty-five full shopping bags. Lifetime statistics for consumption of energy and resources are equally incredible. The average Canadian will, in his or her lifetime:

- use 125,000,000 litres of water
- consume the equivalent of 600,000 cubic metres of natural gas, 1,100,000 kilograms of coal, or 575,000 litres of crude oil
- travel 700,000 kilometres in motor vehicles (seventeen times around the world at the equator)
- generate 40,000 kilograms of garbage
- produce 1,300,000 kilograms of greenhouse gases
- emit 7,000 kilograms of sulphur dioxides and 5,000 kilograms of nitrogen oxides
- require the use of more than 7,000 kilograms of pesticides and fertilizers.[36]

Canada's consumption has global impacts: it pollutes the atmosphere and the seas, and it consumes resources from other countries. For example, Canadian consumption of timber, produce, minerals, and other natural resources from tropical and subtropical nations places pressure on these hotspots of global biodiversity. Ironically, cutting back on the production of natural resources in Canada may worsen environmental problems elsewhere. For example, falling Canadian production of pulp and paper because of campaigns by environmentalists may benefit Canadian forests, but possibly at the expense of forests and endangered species in Indonesia, Brazil, or other nations with higher levels of biodiversity than Canada. From a global perspective, environmental gains in Canada may be pyrrhic victories, if unaccompanied by *overall reductions* in resource consumption.

Further economic growth, to the extent that it requires higher levels of energy and resource use in the industrialized world, will intensify today's environmental problems. Historically, economic growth has involved increasing resource use. As a result, even in areas where Canada is making progress, such as increasing energy efficiency, economic growth that depends on higher resource use is overwhelming the gains.[37] Although per capita energy use in Canada is declining, total energy use continues to rise, placing greater pressure on the environment.[38] The second law of thermodynamics, also called the law of entropy, is that whenever energy is used, disorder increases.[39] Therefore, "the cost of continuous economic growth is the increasing entropy or disordering of the ecosphere."[40] In other words, as society uses more energy and resources, waste, pollution, and environmental degradation increase. Thus Canada's current economic policies, seeking growth based on ever-greater consumption of energy and resources, will inevitably lead to worsening environmental degradation, despite the proliferation of well-intentioned environmental laws.

However, economic growth is not *necessarily* problematic, since economic growth does not *necessarily* require higher levels of resource use. In wealthy, industrialized countries like Canada, "the nature of growth must radically change in order to attain long-term sustainability."[41] Spending on solar, wind, or other forms of clean, renewable energy contributes to economic growth but reduces environmental harm associated with nonrenewable sources of energy. Economic growth stemming from the expansion of services may be less resource-intensive and therefore less environmentally damaging. The substitution of cleaner products for more toxic products, sales of low-emission vehicles, and pollution-reduction technologies may also result in economic growth that is positive from an environmental perspective. Different forms of economic growth are examined in Chapter 13.

Developing Countries

A crucial distinction must be drawn between industrialized and developing nations. Industrialized countries, with 20 percent of the world's population, consume over 80 percent of the world's natural resources.[42] Although the thirty OECD nations comprise only 18 percent of the world's population, their activities cause the majority of environmental damage.[43] The top 1 percent of the world's population enjoys an income equal to the total income of 57 percent of the world's population.[44] Income disparity is growing, both within nations and between nations.[45]

In developing nations, excess consumption of resources is not the problem. The poorest countries on Earth, also with 20 percent of the world's population, consume only 1.3 percent of the world's natural resources.[46] However, the social and economic challenges facing the developing world are daunting:

- 1 billion people lack access to clean water.
- 2.4 billion lack access to basic sanitation.
- 1.2 billion live on US$1 per day.
- 2.8 billion live on US$2 per day.
- 30,000 children under five die *daily* from preventable causes.[47]

Further economic growth and higher levels of resource consumption are urgently needed to meet basic human needs in the developing world. A major flaw of the Brundtland Report, which brought the imperative of sustainable development into global prominence, was that it called for an annual 6 percent increase in per capita income in poor countries and a 3 percent increase in wealthy countries.[48] By 2050, growth of 3 percent would mean per capita income of US$92,281 annually for Canadians, while growth at 6 percent would result in income of US$1,842 annually for the average Ethiopian.[49] Clearly economic growth in the developing world must be an overriding priority, and there should be a reallocation of wealth from rich countries to poor countries. Conventional economic growth in wealthy nations, by consuming more energy and resources, will aggravate today's environmental woes. However, population growth and poverty, not overconsumption, are the major obstacles to sustainable development in the developing world, making ecological, social, and economic progress difficult.

Population

> Be fruitful: multiply, fill the Earth and subdue it; have dominion over the fish of the sea, the birds of the air, and the domestic animals, and all the living things that crawl on the Earth.
> *Genesis 1:28*

Population has been an emotionally charged and controversial issue since the eighteenth century, when Reverend Thomas Malthus forecast an apocalyptic future in which human population growth outstripped the planet's capacity to produce food, resulting in mass starvation and a collapse of the human population. Noted environmentalists, such as Stanford biologist Paul Ehrlich, picked up where Malthus left off, publishing scenarios about exploding human populations. Ehrlich predicted massive famines would occur in the 1970s, in which "hundreds of millions of people are going to starve to death," the poor get poorer, and human population stabilizes at roughly two billion by the year 2050.[50]

The dire predictions of Malthus and Ehrlich were off the mark. However, economists who argue that there are no limits to human population growth are equally misguided. The Fraser Institute claims that "every human being on the face of the Earth could be housed in the state of Texas in one storey single family homes" and "the Earth is virtually empty, as anyone can attest who has taken an airplane ride and bothered to look out the window."[51] Economist Julian Simon maintained that the world has "the technology to feed, clothe and supply energy to an ever-growing population for the next 7 billion years."[52] These claims are absurd, as the following hypothetical population scenarios demonstrate:

1   If population growth continued at just 1 percent per year, the Earth's current population of 6.1 billion people would surpass 16 billion in less than one hundred years.
2   Ten thousand years ago there were roughly 5.7 million people. In 1995 there were 5.7 billion people, representing a thousandfold increase over a period of ten thousand years. If this level of growth occurred again in the next ten thousand years, there would be 5.7 trillion people (5,700,000,000,000). However, in the words of Joel Cohen, author of *How Many People Can the Earth Support?*:

> The total surface area of the Earth, including oceans, lakes, streams, icecaps, swamps, volcanoes, forests, highways, reservoirs and football fields, is 510 million square kilometres. With a population of 5.7 trillion, each person would be allotted a square area less than ten metres on a side. This area may be as commodious as a jail cell, but is incapable, on average over the oceans and continents of the Earth, of supporting a person with the food, water, clothing, fuel and physical and psychological amenities that distinguish people from ants or bacteria.[53]

3   If today's population of 6.1 billion people grew at just 1 percent a year (which is below current rates of population increase) for a thousand years, there would be over 126 trillion people (126,000,000,000,000), equal to 21,000 people for every person currently living.
4   If today's population of 6.1 billion people grew at just 1 percent a year for ten thousand years, there would be over 98.2 sexdecillion (98,200,000,000,000,000,000,000,000,000,000,000,000,000,000,000,000,000) people on Earth.[54]

These mathematical projections illustrate that continued population growth is untenable, even at very low rates of increase.

Current Population Growth Trends

The mathematics of population growth at the global level are simple. When births outnumber deaths, the population grows. The wider the margin between births and deaths, the faster the population grows. Falling death rates, in particular dramatic declines in infant mortality rates, fuelled this century's population explosion. Author Joel Cohen observes that the rate of population growth can be reduced only through fewer births or more deaths, and "hardly anyone favors more deaths."[55]

In 2000, the human population of the planet passed 6.1 billion.[56] Population projections from the UN forecast a world population ranging from 7.9 to 10.9 billion by 2050, with most of the variability caused by different assumptions about fertility rates (see Table 5).[57] The medium fertility projection anticipates a global population of 9.2 billion in 2050, an increase of roughly 50 percent from today's population.

Table 5

Global population growth

Year	Population	Number of years required to add a billion people
1804	1 billion	millions
1927	2 billion	123 years
1960	3 billion	33 years
1974	4 billion	14 years
1987	5 billion	13 years
1999	6 billion	12 years
2012	7 billion?	13 years?

Globally, population growth continues at 1.3 percent per year, meaning about 80 million people are added to the world's population annually.[58] Six countries account for half of this growth: India, China, Pakistan, Nigeria, Bangladesh, and Indonesia. The UN estimates that at least 90 percent of future population growth will occur in developing countries, which are expected to grow to 8.1 billion people by 2050 from 4.9 billion in 2000. In marked contrast, the population of developed nations will remain more or less constant at 1.2 billion. In the next fifty years, the poorest forty-eight nations on Earth will see their populations triple, to 1.8 billion people from 658 million. Even African nations ravaged by the AIDS virus are expecting major population growth in the decades ahead.

Despite these daunting projections, there is some good news about population growth. The global fertility rate has fallen to an average of 2.82 children per woman from 6 children per woman in the past thirty years. This decline is occurring on *all* continents.[59] Although fertility rates are declining across the world, there is still considerable population momentum. In other words, many young people in the developing world are reaching or approaching parenting ages. Over a billion people are currently between the ages of fifteen and twenty-four, and half of the world's population is under twenty-seven.[60] Just as the ozone problem worsened during the 1990s although humans were reducing the amount of ozone-depleting substances released into the atmosphere, so population will continue to spiral upward for decades to come despite decreasing fertility rates.

Population growth in the developing world is fuelled by a variety of factors including the desire for large families, unwanted fertility, and population momentum. In many parts of the developing world, large families are seen as a means of attaining economic security, as children can enter the workforce at a young age. High rates of infant and childhood mortality also encourage larger families. Unwanted fertility is a major problem in many countries. The UN estimates that there are 350 million couples of childbearing age who would like to practise family planning but lack access to safe and effective contraceptive methods and services.[61] Population momentum is a demographic reality resulting from the population boom in the late twentieth century.

The Unsustainability of Continued Population Growth

The growth of the world population poses serious threats to human health, socioeconomic development, and the environment.[62] Scientists believe that there are physical constraints on the sustainable size of the human population. In other words, "There is some limit – some threshold beyond which people would take up too much land, eat too much food, and produce too much waste for the Earth to support."[63] People are already using as much as half of the world's available fresh water. Water shortages are expected to affect between 2.4 billion and 3.2 billion people by 2025. Areas that are already experiencing serious water shortages, such as sub-Saharan Africa and the Middle East, are projecting high levels of population growth in the coming decades that will exacerbate water scarcity.[64] Rapid population growth is also anticipated in many regions where forests, cropland, and fisheries are already scarce.[65] Areas of high biological diversity are located in countries with large populations and high rates of population growth, particularly in Africa, Asia, and Latin America.[66] These biodiversity hotspots contain a disproportionate number of the world's plant and animal species, as up to half of the world's land species can be found on only 2 percent of the world's land area. Scientific studies indicate that humans are already consuming 32 to 40 percent of the planet's net primary productivity, raising ethical questions about our rights vis-à-vis the millions of other species on Earth.[67]

Food production is also a major concern, although not to the extent forecast by Malthus or Ehrlich. The good news with respect to food is that although the global population doubled between 1960 and 1999, *per capita* food production *increased* during this period.[68] The bad news is that over 800 million people are still chronically malnourished, although this figure is declining.[69] There are warning signs, such as soil erosion, loss of arable land, and depleted aquifers, that the Earth may not be able to sustain current levels of agricultural production.[70] World food production would have to double by 2025 to adequately feed the projected population of 8 billion.[71] One of the concerns about food is that half of the world's cereal grain production is fed to animals.[72] Another concern is that three-quarters of the world's fisheries are being exploited at unsustainable rates.[73]

The ramifications of continued population growth are deeply troubling, not just for environmental reasons but socially, economically, politically, culturally, and in terms of international security. Albert Einstein believed that "overpopulation in various countries has become a serious threat to the health of people and a grave obstacle to any attempt to organize peace on this planet."[74] In developing countries, rapid population growth aggravates environmental and social problems, increasing pressure on land, water, agriculture, infrastructure, education, and health care. Studies by Thomas Homer-Dixon demonstrate that environmental scarcity contributes to violent conflict, primarily within nations, and occasionally in the form of wars between nations.[75] Slowing the rate of population growth is therefore critical if future generations are to enjoy a reasonable quality of life. As Robert U. Ayres, one of the founders of industrial ecology, states, "It is unlikely that the other problems of the global environment can be solved if the world population is not stabilized."[76]

Conclusion

Leading conservation biologists suggest that society's number-one environmental priority should be to "encourage rapid stabilization, followed by decline, of the human population."[77] On the other hand, leading ecological economists suggest that "driven by an uncritical worship of economic growth, it seems that consumption by humans threatens to overwhelm the ecosphere."[78] As this chapter shows, neither of these perspectives accurately represents the whole picture, in that *both* population growth and increasing consumption must be addressed in order for environmental problems to be solved. For Canadians, it is "impossible for us to continue consuming at our current rate, and unthinkable that these rates of consumption could be extended to an expanding global population."[79]

In Canada, the United States, and the world, both population and consumption increased rapidly in the twentieth century. Globally, between 1900 and 2000, both population and per capita consumption quadrupled. Expert projections indicate that population growth and economic growth will continue for at least the first fifty years of the twenty-first century.[80] While the majority of projected population growth will occur in developing nations, the majority of economic growth is expected to occur in industrialized nations.[81] This economic growth, to the extent that it involves increases in resource consumption, will not only intensify environmental problems but will also worsen global inequality. By 2050, given projected rates of population and consumption growth, as many as fifteen planets like Earth would be needed to permit all humans to consume energy and resources at a rate equal to the average Canadian living in 2050.[82] Fifteen planets like Earth do not exist, which reinforces the urgency of addressing consumption and population, the underlying drivers of environmental degradation.

The track records of both Canada and the United States show that the conventional North American approach to environmental law and policy does not address consumption and population. As American lawyer Arnold W. Reitze observes, "The failure to understand the holistic interrelationship of environmental degradation to population and consumption has led to an over-reliance on environmental law."[83] Although improvements to conventional Canadian environmental laws and policies are obviously still necessary, and will ameliorate Canada's environmental record, different tools are required to address consumption and population. Achieving a sustainable future will require action in areas that until now have been viewed as beyond the scope of traditional environmental law and policy. For example, Natural Resources Canada identifies economic growth and population growth as *the main drivers* of increasing greenhouse gas emissions, but admits that these factors "are unlikely to be the subject of energy or environmental policy, programmes, or initiatives."[84] This entrenched attitude must change.

The evidence proves beyond a reasonable doubt that Canada is failing to adequately protect the environment. Although consumption and population have been identified as the root causes of the problem, the burning question remains: What are the laws, policies, and other actions that will successfully address consumption and population, enabling Canada to live within the Earth's limits, comply with the three scientific sustainability conditions, solve its vexing environmental challenges, and achieve the holy grail of a sustainable future?

PART THREE
Prescription

A course of action identified as necessary
for regaining or improving health.

11 New Directions for Canadian Environmental Law and Policy

> Can we move nations and people in the direction of sustainability? Such a move would be a modification of society comparable in scale to only two other changes: the Agricultural Revolution of the late Neolithic, and the Industrial Revolution of the past two centuries. These revolutions were gradual, spontaneous, and largely unconscious. This one will have to be a fully conscious operation, guided by the best foresight that science can provide. If we actually do it, the undertaking will be absolutely unique in humanity's stay on earth.
>
> *William D. Ruckelshaus, former head*
> *of the US Environmental Protection Agency*

To move in the direction of sustainability, Canada needs to remedy the systemic weaknesses in environmental law and policy identified in Chapter 8 *and* address the root causes of environmental degradation discussed in Chapter 10. The imperative of moving forward on both of these fronts can be illustrated by comparing criminal law and environmental law. Canada's *Criminal Code* is a comprehensive national law, consistent throughout the nation, across all provinces and territories. The *Criminal Code* is written in mandatory, legally binding language and it is rigorously enforced. The *Criminal Code* evolves to keep pace with contemporary Canadian values, prescribes punishment for those who violate the law, and deters undesirable behaviour. Criminal law has contributed to significant progress in reducing crime in Canada.[1] However, it is widely understood that crime cannot be eliminated without addressing the underlying causes of criminal behaviour – social and economic factors like poverty, lack of education, and child abuse. Effective criminal laws *and* efforts to address the root causes of crime, through changes in social and economic policy, are both necessary.

In contrast to criminal law, environmental law in Canada varies widely from province to province. Environmental law is predominantly discretionary, not mandatory, and enforcement is generally lax, although more people die from pollution in Canada every year than from homicides.[2] Environmental laws in Canada lag behind evolving Canadian values about the environment (as discussed in Chapter 1). Canada needs stronger, more consistent, and more effective (i.e., mandatory) environmental laws. Canada also needs to provide the financial and human resources necessary to enforce environmental laws. But Canadians must realize that just as crime problems cannot be solved with criminal laws, environmental problems cannot be solved solely with environmental laws. Other means, including changes in social and economic policy, must be used to address the root causes of environmental degradation.

Addressing the Systemic Weaknesses in Canadian Environmental Law and Policy

In order to make existing and future environmental laws more effective, Canada needs to address the systemic weaknesses identified in Chapter 8. There are many areas, identified in Chapters 2 through 5, where Canada needs new or improved environmental laws and policies at the federal or provincial level, including safe drinking water, water pollution, water use, climate change, air pollution, pesticides, forest management, environmental assessment, parks and protected areas, endangered species, the restoration of contaminated sites, energy efficiency, the protection of whales and other marine mammals, hazardous waste, and invasive species. Comprehensive, well-researched recommendations for new and improved laws to address most of these issues have already been published. For example, with respect to safe drinking water, the Sierra Legal Defence Fund has published recommendations for federal legislation, while the Canadian Environmental Law Association, Walkerton Inquiry, North Battleford Inquiry, West Coast Environmental Law Association, BC provincial health officer, BC Drinking Water Review Panel, and BC auditor general have published recommendations for provincial legislation. Many of the detailed law reform initiatives from the Canadian Bar Association's 1990 Sustainable Development Action Plan still await implementation.[3] The problem is not the lack of known legislative solutions but rather the failure to enact, implement, and enforce environmental laws and policies.

It is encouraging that the long-awaited modernization of the federal *Pest Control Products Act* drew extensively from recommendations published by the Law Reform Commission of Canada, the commissioner of the environment and sustainable development, the Canadian Association of Physicians for the Environment, the Standing Committee on Environment and Sustainable Development, the Canadian Environmental Law Association, and the Ontario College of Family Physicians. The enactment of the federal *Species at Risk Act,* the ratification of the *Kyoto Protocol,* and new measures addressing air pollution also suggest that the federal government may be emerging from a decade of inaction in the field of environmental legislation. At the provincial level, promising signs include the enactment of new or improved endangered species legislation in several provinces, stricter regulation of drinking water, stronger standards for hazardous waste disposal in Ontario and Quebec, and new laws prohibiting the bulk export of water.

The drafting of new laws and the amendment of existing laws should be guided by the five characteristics of effective legislation identified in Chapter 7: cooperation between different levels of government; clear, measurable, enforceable standards; mandatory language; effective compliance and enforcement mechanisms, including both incentives and penalties; and adequate resources for implementation and enforcement. Laws and regulations should include clear targets and timelines, which were critical to successful efforts to eliminate ozone-depleting substances, reduce acid rain, increase the energy efficiency of appliances, and increase parks and protected areas. Discretionary language in environmental laws and regulations should be replaced by mandatory language; three decades of experience have proven time and time again that politicians and bureaucrats will exercise their discretion to the environment's detriment. Similarly, all environmental laws and regulations should be revised to incorporate the precautionary principle as a key consideration in all decision making and to establish independent scientific advisory boards to monitor and report on the effectiveness of legislation in attaining the intended environmental benefits. The next generation of environmental laws and policies must embody a number of other established and emerging principles such as intergenerational equity, polluter pays, user pays, pollution prevention, full-cost accounting, life-cycle analysis, ecological design, and adaptive management.[4]

Budgets for environmental protection in Canada need to be increased, both federally and provincially, so that funds and staff are adequate to implement and enforce environmental laws and policies. To begin with, the extensive cuts to environmental departments that occurred throughout Canada in the past fifteen years must be reversed. The commitment of $3 billion to new environmental initiatives, made in the 2003 budget, will mark a major turning point if the funding materializes and is spent effectively. The Standing Committee on Environment and Sustainable Development believes that adequate enforcement of pollution laws would require *three to four times* the current level of enforcement staff and resources.[5] By applying the polluter-pays and user-pays principles, Canadian governments could generate more than enough revenue to cover increased environmental expenditures. Governments need to recognize that increased spending on environmental protection will pay social, economic, and environmental dividends in the long run. Stronger environmental laws will save money for the health care system, spur innovation, and increase people's quality of life.

Two major priorities for increasing public participation should be enacting a constitutionally protected right to a clean, safe, and healthy environment, and changing laws and policies to enable citizens to enforce environmental laws. First, because the Constitution not only symbolizes the nation's fundamental values but is the strongest law in Canada, enshrining the right to a clean environment in the Constitution would give citizens the most effective legal tool available to advance environmental protection.[6] The profound impact of entrenching rights in the Constitution is demonstrated by the gains made by Aboriginal people since 1982, when Aboriginal rights were protected by section 35 of the Constitution. It is anomalous that while many countries provide their citizens with constitutionally protected rights to a clean and healthy environment, Canada's Constitution is silent on this vital matter. Second, empowering citizens to enforce environmental laws when governments refuse to do so is also a crucial means of improving public participation, and has a track record of success in the United States. The Canadian public's right to conduct private prosecutions should be reaffirmed in all provinces and territories, and effective citizen enforcement provisions should be added to all new and existing environmental laws.

Implementing the foregoing recommendations would undoubtedly improve Canada's environmental record in many areas. However, solving environmental problems and achieving a sustainable future will require a new generation of laws and policies to address the root causes of environmental degradation – consumption and population growth – and to ensure compliance with the three scientific conditions for sustainability.

Promoting Sustainability

As discussed in Chapter 10, it is imperative that industrialized nations like Canada reduce the amount of pressure being placed on the Earth's natural systems by the excess consumption of resources. The challenge is to improve the quality of life while consuming fewer resources. Addressing this challenge requires a paradigm shift from the current approach to environmental law and policy, which takes increased consumption of resources as a given, necessary to provide further economic growth, but strives to mitigate the consequences. Some very fundamental questions need to be asked. Is economic growth an appropriate indicator for measuring human progress? Does economic growth necessarily require ever-higher levels of resource consumption? If not, what kinds of laws and policies will enable Canada to achieve economic growth and improve Canadians' quality of life, while concurrently reducing resource consumption and environmental damage?

Population growth is a global problem because humans are already close to or exceeding the Earth's ecological limits, yet everyone agrees that people in developing nations must increase consumption in order to achieve a better quality of life. The overwhelming majority of the projected population growth that will add an estimated three billion people in the next fifty years will take place in developing countries. What is Canada's role in addressing population growth in the developing world? How can Canada contribute to sustainable development and reducing poverty in the world's poorest countries? Does population growth need to be addressed in Canada as well?

Canada's search for sustainability poses daunting and complex challenges. The following chapters identify a new environmental role model for Canada, suggest laws, policies, and other means of reducing resource consumption, and outline Canada's potential contribution to addressing the global problems of population growth, poverty, and environmental degradation.

12 A New Role Model for Canada

"Would you tell me, please, which way I ought
to go from here?"
"That depends a good deal on where you want
to get to," said the Cat.
 "I don't much care where –" said Alice.
"Then it doesn't matter which way you go," said
the Cat.
                    Lewis Carroll, Alice's Adventures in Wonderland

Back in 1990, at the beginning of what David Suzuki and others labelled the
"turnaround decade," Canada outlined ambitious environmental aspirations
in *Canada's Green Plan for a Healthy Environment*.[1] The *Green Plan* pledged $3
billion in new funding for initiatives targeting clean air, clean water, endangered species, climate change, ozone depletion, new national parks, the Arctic, and better decision making. The *Green Plan* also promised new laws to
ensure safe drinking water and provide effective environmental assessment.
Lucien Bouchard, the federal environment minister at the time, claimed that
the government's goal was "to make Canada, by the year 2000, the industrial
world's most environmentally friendly country."[2] Most *Green Plan* promises
were never fulfilled, and the majority of the money never materialized. The
minor recession of the early 1990s, the defeat of the federal Progressive Conservatives by the Liberals, and the renewed threat of Quebec separation swept
environmental priorities off the government's radar screen. The year 2000
came and went. By any objective measure, Canada is still a long way from
achieving its goal of being "the industrial world's most environmentally friendly
country."

The Elusive Goal of Sustainable Development
Environmental law and policy in Canada today lacks the leadership and clear

direction embodied in the 1990 *Green Plan*. On paper, Canada endorses the goal of sustainable development as defined by the Brundtland Report: "development that meets the needs of the present without compromising the ability of future generations to meet their own needs."[3] This definition was adopted in the 1995 amendments to the federal *Auditor General Act,* which established the office of the commissioner of the environment and sustainable development. Although debate continues about the precise meaning of sustainable development, the concept has three critical components:

1   the *ecological* imperative – living within the Earth's physical limits
2   the *social* imperative – developing democratic systems of governance that enshrine and respect basic human rights
3   the *economic* imperative – ensuring that human needs and aspirations can be met worldwide.[4]

Unfortunately, Canada has no overall sustainable development strategy that reflects or incorporates these principles. Canada has no inspiring vision, no comprehensive set of goals, no measurable targets, no timeline, and no coherent plan for actually achieving a sustainable future.[5] The promising *Green Plan* was abandoned, and work toward preparing a new national sustainable development strategy was discontinued in the mid-1990s when political priorities shifted.[6] Canada's current environmental law and policy role model, the United States, also lacks a national sustainability strategy.[7]

Canada's Sustainable Development Strategies

Instead of an inspiring national vision, Canada has twenty-eight federal sustainable development strategies. Twenty-four federal departments and agencies are legally obligated to prepare sustainable development strategies and update them on a regular basis, while four Crown corporations do so voluntarily. This hodge-podge of plans provides different interpretations of what sustainable development means and how Canada ought to achieve it. Several provinces and territories, including Manitoba, Alberta, Ontario, the Yukon, and Newfoundland and Labrador also have sustainable development strategies.[8] In addition, Canada has the National Forest Strategy, the Canadian Biodiversity Strategy, the Federal Water Policy, Canada's Oceans Strategy, and several plans for climate change. There is no overarching, "big picture" strategy to guide the prioritization and implementation of these various strategies and ensure a coordinated, effective approach.

The piecemeal approach embodied by Canada's multiplicity of sustainable development strategies is doomed to failure by its lack of coherence and integration, a point made by Canada's commissioner of the environment and sustainable development. The commissioner, in a recent audit, identified two glaring weaknesses in the federal strategies. First, they "failed to establish the clear and measurable targets that are the key to the success or failure of the sustainable development strategy process." Second, "many strategies appear to represent less a commitment to change in order to promote sustainable development than a restatement of the status quo."[9] In 2001 the commissioner concluded, "After auditing 28 departments and agencies over three years, I am concerned that some departments view their sustainable development activities as a paper exercise rather than truly trying to make their activities more sustainable."[10]

It is telling that few, if any, of the twenty-eight sustainable development strategies published by Canadian departments and agencies discuss the Earth's ecological limits. Nothing in these strategies addresses the underlying causes of environmental degradation: excessive consumption of energy and resources in Canada, and population growth and poverty in the developing world. This absence indicates that Canada is unable to shake the notion that nature is a boundless cornucopia, with endless forests, endless water, endless oil and gas reserves, endless natural resources, and an infinite capacity to absorb our pollution and waste. Canada's vast size and incredible natural wealth still blind the nation to ecological reality.

A Different Approach: Europe Leads the Way

In comparison to Canada, European countries have adopted a much more holistic and inspiring approach to sustainable development. Indeed, European nations dominate international evaluations of environmental performance.[11] Sweden and the Netherlands in particular are globally renowned for their innovative leadership in pursuing ecological sustainability.[12] These European nations recognize that "at a minimum, sustainable development must not endanger the natural systems that support life on Earth: the atmosphere, the waters, the soils, and the living beings."[13] While Canada's international reputation as an environmentally friendly country has tarnished badly in recent years, Sweden and the Netherlands have continued to garner praise. The bold overall goal of both countries is to achieve ecological sustainability within a generation (i.e., by 2020-5).[14] More importantly, they are implementing the kinds of laws, policies, and actions necessary to attain their ambitious goals. Both have national sustainability strategies that establish measurable objectives and specific timelines for improvement. On a regular basis, Sweden and the Netherlands evaluate the extent to which sustainability objectives are being met, and adjust their laws and policies accordingly.

The latest version of the Dutch National Environmental Policy Plan targets overconsumption of resources, and emphasizes decoupling or delinking economic growth from resource use and pollution.[15] In other words, the Netherlands seeks an unconventional form of economic growth that is based on lower resource use and less pollution. Several nongovernmental organizations describe the Dutch plan as the world's most successful green plan. It is praised by the OECD as "comprehensive, action-oriented, and based on some of the most innovative and sophisticated analytical work in the world. There is much to learn from it for other countries."[16] Canada would do well to study the Dutch example, and also to learn from Sweden's experience of environmental planning, policy, and most importantly, progress.

Sweden: A Global Leader in Environmental Protection

> The use of resources in this part of the world must be reduced significantly if the Earth's ecosystems are to be capable of maintaining a growing population and if living standards are to be raised in the developing world.
>
> *Government of Sweden, 1999*

Both Sweden and Canada, northern industrialized nations with cold climates, are renowned for their universal medicare systems, dedication to global peace, and strength in winter sports. At a macro level, the economies of the two nations are also very similar. Although Canada's GDP is three times larger than Sweden's, both nations derive 27 percent of their GDP from industry, 70 percent from services, and 2 percent from agriculture.[17] Canada is dependent on the much larger US economy while Sweden has a similar relationship with Europe.

Sweden provides an inspiring role model for Canada and other industrialized nations aspiring toward sustainable development. Sweden earned the highest ranking for overall quality of life among 180 nations in a comprehensive study by the UN, the International Development Research Centre, and the World Conservation Union.[18] The study examined eighty-seven elements of sustainability in the areas of health and population, wealth, knowledge and culture, community, equity, land, air, water, biodiversity, and resource use. Sweden also finished first in the World Economic Forum's 2002 Environmental Performance Index, which evaluated nations' records on air, water, climate change, and land protection. The OECD has praised Sweden's "remarkable" environmental record.[19]

Internationally, Sweden strives to be "a driving force and a model of ecologically sustainable development."[20] Sweden was a leader in negotiations for international agreements that addressed ozone-depleting substances, acid rain, and persistent organic pollutants. In 2000 Sweden hosted a global meeting of environment ministers and led the negotiation of the *Malmö Declaration*, which calls on nations of the world to address the "alarming discrepancy between commitments and actions" on environmental issues and recognize that "special attention should be paid to unsustainable consumption patterns."[21] Sweden used its term as the president of the European Union (EU) to make environmental issues the number-one priority for the EU in 2001.

Nationally, the government of Sweden aims "to hand over to the next generation a society in which all the major environmental problems in our vicinity have been solved."[22] Unlike Canada, Sweden acknowledges that as a developed nation it must reduce its consumption of energy and resources while assisting developing nations to overcome poverty through economic growth.[23] Although Sweden still pursues economic growth, the nature of that growth will be fundamentally different in the future, as it will not be based on increased consumption of resources. The Swedish government defines ecological sustainability as incorporating three elements:

1   environmental protection: meaning that emissions of pollutants must not harm human health or exceed nature's capacity to absorb them
2   sustainable supplies: guaranteeing the long-term productive capacity of ecosystems by not using resources faster than nature can regenerate them and finding renewable substitutes for nonrenewable resources
3   efficient resource use: using energy and resources much more efficiently so as to reduce overall levels of consumption.[24]

Sweden's elements of ecological sustainability are clearly based upon the three ecological limits identified by scientists and described in Chapter 10. The Swedish government's recognition of the Earth's limits, and its understanding that laws and policies must be revised to incorporate ecological limits, mark a critical turning point in the search for a sustainable future. The recognition of limits is not only critical to rethinking societal goals, but also vital to educating the public about the need for substantial changes to laws, policies, institutions, societal priorities, and individual behaviour.

Based on the three elements of ecological sustainability, a Swedish law introduced in 1998 outlines fifteen general environmental quality goals including clean air, high-quality groundwater, flourishing wetlands, no eutrophication, natural acidification only, sustainable forests, a magnificent mountain landscape, a nontoxic environment, and a protective ozone layer.[25] A law introduced in 2001 sets concrete, measurable targets and timelines for each of these goals. For example, the general goal of a "nontoxic environment" means that the environment should be free from substances (e.g., mercury, cadmium) and manmade chemicals (e.g., PCBs, CFCs, DDT) that threaten human health or biological diversity. Targets for naturally occurring substances are set at background (i.e., natural) levels, while targets for harmful manmade substances are set at "close to zero." Sweden is engaged in an ambitious screening process to review thousands of potentially harmful manmade substances. Substances identified as toxic, persistent, carcinogenic, bioaccumulative, or endocrine disrupting will be either phased out or banned by the year 2010.[26]

Canada versus Sweden: A Comparison

On a head-to-head comparison of environmental records, Sweden outperforms Canada on most indicators. Both in total and on a per capita basis, Swedes generate less air pollution, provide superior sewage treatment, use less water and energy, use energy more efficiently, produce fewer greenhouse gas emissions, use a lower volume of pesticides, create less garbage, and donate a higher percentage of GDP as aid to promote sustainable development in poor countries.[27]

A nation's commitment to sustainable development can be quantified by examining the amount of money budgeted for environmental protection. Sweden already spends more than 3 percent of its GDP on environmental protection while Canada spends under 1 percent.[28] In the past decade, government environment budgets in Canada have been cut extensively. Although this trend has been reversed at the federal level, it is ongoing provincially, as the actions of the BC government demonstrate. In contrast, Sweden has consistently increased environment budgets in recent years. Sweden plans a major increase in spending on environmental protection between 2002 and 2004.[29]

The Reasons for Sweden's Environmental Success

As noted earlier, Sweden's environmental superiority over Canada comes despite close similarities between the two nations in terms of climate, economy, and standard of living. Environmental law and policy appears to be the primary determinant of the difference in performance between the two nations. For the most part, Canada has relied on a regulatory approach similar to that used in the United States. That is, Canadian governments use a combination of command-and-control laws and regulations and ineffective voluntary programs in an attempt to mitigate the environmental impacts of an industrial economy consuming ever-increasing amounts of energy and resources.

In comparison to Canada, Sweden has adopted a more holistic approach to sustainable development, using a variety of social, economic, and environmental tools designed to restructure its economy so as to place less pressure on the environment.[30] The OECD states, "In the past twenty-five years, Sweden has developed effective and often very innovative environmental policies."[31] Specifically, Sweden moved toward full-cost pricing of environmental goods and services by removing subsidies and implementing environmental taxes. Sweden introduced environmental taxes on waste, the sulphur content of fossil fuels, pesticides and artificial fertilizers, motor vehicles, carbon dioxide emissions, energy, and electricity. Sweden also used a combination of penalties and financial incentives to pursue improvements in efficiency, striving to use less energy and fewer resources while maintaining or improving quality of life. The laws and policies that produced Sweden's superior environmental performance vis-à-vis Canada contain crucial lessons for the future development of Canadian environmental law and policy.

Greenhouse Gas Emissions

Canada and Sweden both signed the *Framework Convention on Climate Change* in 1992, and initially pledged to stabilize greenhouse gas emissions at 1990 levels by the year 2000. Under the *Kyoto Protocol,* negotiated in 1997, Canada promised to reduce greenhouse gas emissions to 6 percent below 1990 levels by 2010, while Sweden committed to reduce them to 8 percent below 1990 levels by 2010. As of 1999, on a per capita basis, Swedes produced *less than half* the greenhouse gas emissions of Canadians. This is a striking divergence for two similarly situated northern industrial nations. Canadian greenhouse gas emissions, despite our international commitments, have increased by 20 percent since 1990. In contrast, Swedish greenhouse gas emissions stabilized between 1990 and 1999.[32]

Sweden used taxes as a key tool to reduce greenhouse gas emissions and increase energy efficiency.[33] Energy and carbon taxes were formulated to reflect the amount of environmental damage caused by different energy sources, then phased in gradually, so that businesses and consumers had time to adjust. These taxes raise roughly C$10 billion per year, and Sweden invests the proceeds in public transit, research and development, and promoting renewable sources of energy such as biomass. Energy generated by renewable sources like wood pellets and food waste now meets 15 percent of Sweden's energy requirements.[34] In an innovative program, the national government provides funding to local communities to implement leading-edge projects designed to reduce greenhouse gas emissions. For example, in the city of Lund, waste collected from the food-processing industry is used to generate methane, powering city buses that would otherwise burn diesel fuel.[35] Based on the success of Lund's experiment, by 2005 it will be unlawful throughout Sweden to dispose of food waste and other organic matter that can be collected and recycled into energy.[36] The program in Lund reduces carbon dioxide emissions, reduces garbage, and generates cleaner energy, thus reducing air pollution. Sweden, along with the UK, has now pledged to reduce greenhouse gas emissions by 60 percent by 2050 and is lobbying other European nations to make the same commitment.

Air Pollution

On a per capita basis, Canada produces more than eight times the Swedish level of sulphur dioxide emissions, and almost twice the Swedish level of nitrogen dioxide emissions. Sulphur dioxide and nitrogen oxides are two of the main pollutants involved in acid rain. While Canadian emissions of sulphur dioxide and nitrogen dioxide have fallen in recent decades, Swedish reductions in emissions of sulphur dioxide and nitrogen dioxide have been much larger.[37]

Sweden uses an innovative fee-bate system to reduce nitrogen oxide emissions from the energy industry. Energy companies are charged a fee for the volume of their nitrogen oxide emissions and then given a rebate based on the amount of energy they produce. This fee-bate system rewards the most efficient energy producers and provides an ongoing incentive for all companies to become more efficient.[38] Swedish nitrogen oxide emissions fell 35 percent in two years when the program was implemented.[39] To reduce sulphur dioxide emissions, Sweden combined regulations that required lower sulphur content in fuel with a tax on sulphur. The sulphur tax introduced in 1991 resulted in a reduction in the sulphur content of fuels to almost 40 percent *below* Swedish legal standards.[40] The tax encourages companies to continuously seek cost-effective ways to reduce sulphur content, because the lower the sulphur content, the less tax must be paid. A regulation, in contrast, that requires a maximum level of sulphur content provides a static target and no incentive for going beyond mere compliance.

Water Use

Sweden uses 310,000 litres of water per person per year, while Canada uses 1,600,000 litres per person per year, more than five times Swedish consumption. These figures do not include water diverted for purposes of generating hydroelectricity, which would increase the disparity in water use between Canada and Sweden. Since 1980 total water use in Canada has *increased* by 25.7 percent, while Sweden has *decreased* its total water use by 34 percent.[41]

Sweden has taken steps toward full-cost pricing for water by eliminating subsidies for water use. The price of water in Sweden is approximately four times the price of water in Canada, although the cost to consumers in Sweden is still only US$2.60 per thousand litres.[42] The main reason for Canadians' excessive use of water is that water in Canada is heavily subsidized, failing to reflect the infrastructure costs of dams, water treatment plants and distribution systems, the damage to aquatic ecosystems caused by human water use, or the value of the ecological services provided by water. In Canada many households and businesses pay a flat or declining rate for water, regardless of how much water they use. In Sweden almost all households and businesses are on water meters and therefore pay for every litre used, which encourages conservation. Sweden's substantial decrease in total water use during the past two decades of economic and population growth proves that it is socially, economically, and technologically feasible to use water far more efficiently.

Municipal Sewage Treatment

Some coastal areas, lakes, and beaches in eastern and western Canada are closed for fishing, swimming, or shellfish harvesting because of unsafe levels of fecal coliform bacteria from municipal sewage.[43] In contrast, many Swedish coastal areas that were once closed are now open, due to progress in reducing water pollution from sewage treatment plants. In fact, salmon fishing is now possible in the river running through Stockholm.[44]

In both Sweden and Canada, more than 90 percent of the urban population is served by connections to sewage treatment plants.[45] However, in terms of the quality of sewage treatment being provided, Sweden is far ahead. Three levels of sewage treatment – primary, secondary, and tertiary – provide progressively more effective treatment. In Sweden, 87 percent of the municipal population is served by tertiary treatment, the best available. In Canada, only 40 percent of the municipal population is served by tertiary treatment, 38 percent is served by secondary treatment, and 19 percent still have access only to crude primary treatment, the least effective form.

Sweden has allocated the necessary funds to improve its sewage treatment infrastructure. In part the funds were raised by removing subsidies for water and wastewater treatment, so that businesses and households pay the full cost of the services that are provided by government.[46] In Canada, municipal water prices are the lowest in the OECD. There is a major water infrastructure deficit in Canada, estimated to be in the tens of billions of dollars. As a result, large coastal cities like Victoria, Halifax, and St. John's still discharge raw, untreated sewage into the ocean.

Municipal Waste

Sweden and Canada spend billions annually to collect, transport, and dispose of municipal solid waste. However, Swedes generate 36 percent less municipal solid waste per person than do Canadians.[47] While municipal waste per capita in Canada declined slightly between 1980 and 1997, this decrease was more than offset by population growth so that the total amount of municipal waste in Canada rose by 17 percent. In contrast, Swedish levels of waste production are declining, both per capita and, more importantly, in total.[48]

Through a concept known as extended producer responsibility, Swedish law makes producers of goods responsible for the packaging and products that they produce, for the entire life cycle of the products.[49] Producers must either reuse or recycle their goods – even products as large and complex as cars are covered by the law. The effect of the law is that producers have an incentive to reduce environmental pressures throughout the entire life cycle of their products. Companies that use innovative designs and processes to make their products more durable and more easily recycled can gain a competitive advantage.[50] Sweden also has an ecocycle program, which includes regulations, to minimize the use of natural resources and the production of waste at all stages of a product's life. Different elements of the ecocycle program focus on reduction, reuse, and recycling. Recycling rates are much higher in Sweden than in Canada.[51]

Pesticide Use

Both Canada and Sweden generate 2 percent of their GDP through agriculture, although Canada has more arable land than Sweden. However, Canada uses five times the volume of pesticides per person that Sweden uses. The area of Canada treated with herbicides and insecticides in 1995 was far larger than the area treated in 1970. In stark contrast, Sweden decreased the volume of pesticides used by more than 80 percent since 1980 and now enjoys the lowest level of pesticide use in the OECD.[52]

Sweden achieved this remarkable reduction in pesticide use by implementing a national strategy: charging a special tax on pesticides; requiring that pesticides be sprayed only where there is an observed need; prohibiting pesticide use in sensitive areas (e.g., near lakes); providing mandatory education programs for users of pesticides; offering economic support for organic agriculture; funding research on alternatives to pesticide use; and reevaluating pesticides regularly.[53] Swedish law incorporates a concept known as the substitution principle, which mandates eliminating older products when less hazardous substitutes are approved.[54] Sweden is striving to eliminate pesticides with "unacceptable characteristics," such as persistence, volatility, high acute toxicity, endocrine disruption, neurotoxicity, and carcinogenicity.[55] As a result, Sweden has eliminated dozens of the most dangerous pesticides, including 2,4-D, atrazine, and lindane, that are still used in Canada.[56]

Official Development Assistance

Official development assistance (ODA), also known as foreign aid, plays a vital part in promoting sustainable development in poor countries. On a per capita basis, Sweden provides more than twice as much assistance to developing nations to facilitate sustainable development as Canada. Sweden contributes 0.71 percent of its GDP to ODA. Despite decades of promises to attain the internationally accepted threshold of 0.7 percent of GDP, Canada currently dedicates 0.22 percent of its GDP to ODA.[57] For more than twenty years, Sweden has consistently surpassed the threshold of 0.7 percent of GDP for ODA, while Canada has *never* met the target. Sweden recently revised its goal for ODA upward to 1.0 percent of GDP.[58] Meeting the 0.7 percent target for ODA is simply a matter of making foreign aid a priority for government spending. Sweden's actions live up to its words, while Canada's actions do not.

The Impact of Strong Environmental Laws and Policies on Sweden's Economy

Sweden's strong environmental laws and policies have had a negligible impact on the Swedish economy. Sweden has consistently applied the polluter-pays and user-pays principles. As a result, the OECD notes that in Sweden, "most of the costs of environmental protection are met by polluters and by users of environmental services." For example, the 80 percent reduction in pesticide use in Sweden was achieved at no net economic cost.[59] In Canada, the main objections to creating stronger environmental laws and policies, and to implementing the polluter-pays and user-pays principles, are based on economic arguments. Sweden's experience suggests that these arguments lack merit. By relying on a well-designed combination of regulations and economic instruments, intended to reduce society's environmental impact, Sweden has achieved the highest overall quality of life in the world.[60]

Conclusion: The Path Forward

Sweden has formulated and implemented an ambitious, innovative, and adaptive strategy for ecologically sustainable development, rooted in ecology and the precautionary principle. Canada, with its environmentally concerned public and unparalleled natural wealth, should be equally capable of charting and following a course toward sustainability. Canada should follow Sweden's exemplary environmental leadership, beginning by creating a national strategy aimed at achieving ecological sustainability within a generation. The goal of achieving ecological sustainability within twenty to twenty-five years is ambitious but appears to be attainable. As a starting point, Canada needs to acknowledge, as Sweden has done, that the Earth's resources are limited, and that Canadian consumption of resources must decline in order to achieve a sustainable future.

To be successful, Canada's national sustainability strategy must include clear objectives and timelines, and should be based on extensive national consultations with all Canadians. In light of the limited success of the Canadian Biodiversity Strategy, the 1987 Federal Water Policy, the National Forest Strategy, and various Canadian climate change strategies, the process of generating Canada's national sustainability strategy should be guided by a nongovernmental entity, such as the Royal Society of Canada or the National Round Table on the Environment and the Economy. In 2002 an international survey found that two-thirds of the sustainability experts polled believe that the most effective action governments could take would be to declare a time-specific generational objective for sustainable development with measurable milestones, like President Kennedy's objective of putting a man on the moon within a decade.[61]

Key components of a national sustainability strategy will be laws and policies designed to reduce Canadian consumption of energy and resources, achieve compliance with the three scientific conditions for sustainability, and contribute to the Third World's efforts to achieve sustainable development by slowing population growth and alleviating poverty. The next two chapters outline the changes to Canadian environmental law and policy required to begin addressing these issues.

13 Reducing Consumption

> The current overuse of natural resources, including
> energy resources, is probably one of the most profound
> challenges mankind has ever been confronted with.
> *Swedish Ministry of Environment, 2002*

> There is no getting around the fact that material
> consumption is at the heart of the sustainability crisis.
> *Professors Robert Woollard and William Rees*

In order to achieve ecological sustainability Canada must recognize, like Sweden, that energy and resource use in wealthy nations must be reduced if the Earth is to support a growing population and if living standards are to be raised in poor countries. For industrialized nations to reduce consumption and achieve ecological sustainability, two general types of actions are required: dematerialization and substitution.[1] Dematerialization refers to reductions in total material flows, such as using smaller volumes of water, gold, oil, and other natural resources. Achieving dematerialization requires increasing resource productivity and efficiency, while generating less waste. Substitution means changing the types of energy and resources used by society, such as replacing coal with wind energy or replacing chemical pesticides with biological pest control methods. Substitution entails substituting abundant materials for scarce materials, using renewable resources in place of nonrenewable resources, moving from an emphasis on commodities toward services, and replacing persistent, unnatural substances with natural, degradable substances. Dematerialization and substitution often overlap. For example, fossil fuel consumption can be reduced by using fossil fuels more efficiently and by replacing oil, gas, and coal with renewable forms of energy.

The challenge is to identify and implement laws and policies that reduce consumption and achieve dematerialization and substitution without reducing

Canadians' quality of life. Although specific products (e.g., computers, beverage cans) and companies (e.g., Interface) now use less energy and fewer resources, no nation has achieved dematerialization of its economy.[2] Some industrial nations, such as Sweden, the Netherlands, Japan, and Germany, have achieved decoupling, where consumption of energy and resources grows at a slower rate than the economy does.[3] While decoupling is a step in the right direction, it does not go far enough because the total consumption of energy and resources continues to grow, albeit more slowly, contrary to the ecological imperative that consumption in the industrialized world must decline. In the world's wealthiest nations, consumption of some resources has leveled off but total resource consumption is still growing.[4]

Profound social, economic, and environmental law and policy changes will be required, at both the individual and societal levels, to bring about reductions in consumption while maintaining or improving quality of life. Priorities will have to change, and the economy will have to be restructured to incorporate ecological limits. This chapter outlines fundamental changes in four main areas:

1   moving the goalposts by which society measures progress, that is, replacing the narrow goal of economic growth (measured by GDP) with a more holistic measure of societal development, such as the Genuine Progress Index
2   eliminating environmentally harmful subsidies to both corporations and individuals
3   shifting taxes onto resources, pollution, and waste, and away from employment, work, and investment
4   using innovative environmental laws and policies to pursue ambitious gains in energy efficiency and resource productivity, prevent pollution, replace harmful substances with safe substances, and replace goods with services.

Social Change

An infinite number of social actions, programs, and policies could be employed in pursuing the goal of reduced consumption. A comprehensive catalogue of social changes required to achieve sustainability, called Agenda 21, that includes actions intended to change consumption patterns, was published by the United Nations following the Earth Summit in 1992.[5] Countries like Sweden have attempted to implement Agenda 21 through local and national programs.[6] Governments can and should fund environmental education, publish accurate information about the state of the environment, promote social learning, invest in research to develop environmentally friendly policies, institutions, and technologies, provide training, create benchmarking programs (allowing companies, municipalities, and individuals to compare themselves with others), establish awards and recognition programs for sustainability innovations and behaviour, improve public access to information, and green government spending.[7] Outlining the nature and details of these social policies and instruments is beyond the scope of this book. However, achieving sustainability depends on social transformation to the same extent that economic and environmental changes are required. One fundamental social change that is necessary to reduce consumption and move Canada toward sustainability involves redefining Canada's notion of progress.

Redefining Progress

> Too much and too long, we seem to have surrendered community excellence and community values in the mere accumulation of things ... Gross National Product counts air pollution and cigarette advertising, and ambulances to clear our highways of carnage. It counts special locks for our doors, and jails for those who break them. It counts the destruction of our redwoods and the loss of our natural wonder in chaotic sprawl. It counts napalm and the cost of a nuclear warhead ...
> Yet the GNP does not allow for the health of our children, the quality of their education, or the joy of their play. It does not include the beauty of our poetry or the strength of our marriages; the intelligence of our public debate, or the integrity of our public officials. It measures neither our wit nor our courage; neither our wisdom nor our learning, neither our compassion nor our devotion to our country; it measures everything, in short, except that which makes life worthwhile.
> *Senator Robert F. Kennedy, 1968*

Economic growth, measured by increases in gross domestic product, is widely used as the leading indicator of whether our society is healthy, prosperous, and moving forward toward a better future. Similarly, for individuals the accumulation of material wealth is viewed as a sign of success, despite extensive evidence that material possessions fail to deliver happiness.[8] These goals, at both the collective and individual levels, clash directly with the ecological imperative of reducing consumption. For decades, environmentalists, politicians, international organizations, and even economists have questioned the wisdom of assessing the pace of human progress by measuring growth in GDP.[9] Economists admit that GDP is merely a yardstick of market activity, measuring the total number of dollars exchanged in society annually.[10] In many ways, GDP is wholly inadequate as a surrogate for determining our quality of life. First, GDP statistics "make no distinction between economic activity that contributes to well-being and that which causes harm."[11] Car accidents, earthquakes, robberies, oil spills, gambling, cancer, and war all cause economic growth (increases in GDP), but clearly cause declines in quality of life. Second, GDP ignores social and environmental values that are of great importance to society. GDP calculations do not measure household labour, volunteer efforts, the health of citizens, free time, the quality of education, inequalities in wealth distribution, natural resource depletion, or environmental damage. Assuming the things we measure and count are the things we value, then "if we do not count non-monetary and non-material assets, we effectively discount and devalue them."[12]

Although growth in GDP is used as an indicator of progress, conventional economic growth that relies on increased resource and energy consumption exacerbates environmental degradation and violates the scientific conditions of ecological sustainability. Higher rates of logging, new mines, overfishing, increases in oil and gas exploration and development, factory farms, land-use activities in watersheds that supply drinking water, and megaprojects like Alberta's tar sands, Newfoundland's offshore drilling, and Quebec's hydroelectric dams boost the GDP but cause extensive environmental harm. Critics warn that "traditional accounting methods inadvertently reinforce environmental deterioration, since cleaning up pollution appears as positive spending."[13] Because GDP is so widely accepted as measuring prosperity and progress, it influences laws, policies, and government decisions in ways that encourage increased consumption of energy and resources.

The GDP is also perverse in terms of how it treats environmental and social progress. A new car that costs the same amount as another new car but is twice as fuel-efficient may have a negative impact on GDP because of lower fuel costs. A new and improved building design that uses less material, incorporates recycled materials, and saves energy may reduce GDP. A factory that redesigns its manufacturing processes according to ecological principles and uses fewer toxic chemicals may reduce GDP. A farmer who phases out the use of pesticides may reduce GDP. Creating products that are designed for durability instead of obsolescence might decrease GDP. Carpooling, growing your own vegetables, borrowing books from libraries, reducing garbage, and conserving energy are among the many examples of environmentally positive activities that have negative impacts on GDP.

Contrary to conventional wisdom, slower economic growth, or even negative economic growth, as measured by stable or declining GDP, does not necessarily imply a reduced quality of life. Imagine a Canadian future where rates of crime, pollution, obesity, car accidents, and smoking decline. These developments would probably cause a drop in GDP (through lower costs to the justice system, lower health care costs, lower insurance premiums and insurance payouts, etc.), yet the quality of life in Canada would likely be higher. Despite all of the GDP's flaws, economists and politicians will continue using

GDP as a surrogate for progress until they have something better. The good news is that something better is now available.

Alternatives to GDP

New indicators are emerging that offer much more holistic and environmentally friendly assessments of trends in the quality of life than merely measuring economic activity. Some of these new approaches include the Index of Sustainable Economic Welfare, the Genuine Progress Index, the Wellbeing Index, the World Bank's Wealth of Nations, the UN's System of Integrated Environmental and Economic Accounts, and the Dashboard of Sustainability.[14] The Index of Sustainable Economic Welfare (ISEW) goes beyond GDP by incorporating such factors as income distribution, natural resource depletion, environmental damage, and the value of household labour. According to the ISEW, the United States experienced an increase in the overall quality of life in the 1950s and 1960s but the rate of progress slowed in the 1970s, and during the 1980s the United States actually saw a decline in the "true health of the economy."[15] This paints a dramatically different picture than the appearance of consistent economic growth depicted by the steady rise in American GDP.

The Genuine Progress Index (GPI), like the ISEW, synthesizes a range of economic, social, and environmental factors. The GPI incorporates educational attainment; the economic value of volunteer work, household work, and child care; air and water quality; health care; and leisure time. Between 1980 and 1998, the US GDP grew 38 percent while the GPI dropped 25 percent.[16] Evidence that the ISEW and the GPI provide a more accurate measure of quality of life or well-being than GDP comes from the UN, which reports that "the percentage of Americans calling themselves happy peaked in 1957 – even though consumption has more than doubled in the meantime."[17] Other studies confirm that American happiness is declining despite continued economic growth.[18]

The Pembina Institute created a GPI for Alberta and is working on similar indices for British Columbia and Ontario. In Alberta, the GPI incorporates fifty-one economic, social, and environmental indicators including crime, divorce, poverty, employment, water quality, and ecological footprints. Alberta's GPI reveals a gradual *decline* in the quality of life enjoyed by Albertans between 1961 and 1999, while the province's GDP *rose* by an average of 4.4 percent per year.[19] Similar research is under way to create a GPI in Nova Scotia. Preliminary reports on the economic value of civic and volunteer efforts, housework and child care; the costs of obesity, tobacco, and AIDS; income distribution; and the sustainability of forests and fisheries indicate that quality of life has also declined in Nova Scotia despite increases in the GDP.[20]

A Canadian expert on sustainable development, Robert Prescott-Allan, designed a sophisticated index that examines a range of eighty-seven social, economic, and environmental factors to determine a nation's progress toward sustainability. The Human Wellbeing Index measures the socioeconomic quality of life, the Ecosystem Wellbeing Index measures environmental health, and the Wellbeing Index combines both the human and ecological indices. The Wellbeing Index is even more comprehensive in scope than the GPI. The top nation in his 180-country study was Sweden, followed by Finland, Norway, Iceland, and Austria. Canada ranked very high (tenth) on the Human Wellbeing Index, which combines indicators of wealth, health, knowledge, community, and equity. However, Canada fared poorly (ninety-fourth) on the Ecosystem Wellbeing Index, which is based on indicators of land, air, water, biodiversity, and resource use.[21]

Moving Forward

Despite the availability of new indicators to measure societal progress, prosperity, and quality of life, Canada appears to be reluctant to relinquish its historical emphasis on GDP and conventional economic growth. Governments have promised, since the *Green Plan* in 1990, to develop new indicators that combine economic, social, and environmental factors.[22] In the 2000 budget, Finance Minister Paul Martin allocated almost $10 million to the development of natural capital accounts for Canada.[23] Natural capital accounts measure the negative environmental impacts of economic activities in the natural resource sectors, although they fail to include social considerations, unlike tools such as the GPI. Martin claimed that the development of natural capital accounts for Canada "could well have a greater impact on public policy than any other single measure we could introduce."[24] Whether this prediction comes true will depend on the indicators chosen and the extent to which they are incorporated in public discourse and government decision making. It is important that Canada begin to calculate factors such as total material requirements (the total volume of energy and resources used by society) so that progress toward dematerialization can be measured. Preliminary data on national total material requirements are available in such nations as Japan, Germany, and the Netherlands.[25] Unfortunately, total material requirements and similar indicators are not yet being contemplated for Canada.

The increasing prominence of alternatives to GDP that provide a more holistic picture of progress and quality of life could serve a vital educational role as well. Recent studies confirm that Canadians are more concerned about health care, education, the environment, and social programs than the economy.[26] However, economic growth still dominates the media, political priorities, and public discourse, to the detriment of the broader public interest in quality of life. More financial and human resources need to be invested in refining tools such as the GPI, the Wellbeing Index, or the ISEW, and the results of these studies should be widely communicated to Canadians. These comprehensive indicators of quality of life would provide a superior basis for creating laws and policies and making decisions to reduce consumption and achieve ecological sustainability. Broad public awareness about the GPI would contribute to the evolution of Canadian values away from today's emphasis on economic growth and material possessions toward a fuller, more encompassing focus on happiness, quality of life, and a sustainable future.

Economic Transformation

> The marketplace economy is the most pervasive and powerful social and political mechanism in modern governance.
> *American law professor Zygmunt Plater*

Actions intended to reduce consumption through social change, while necessary, are not sufficient to transform today's unsustainable Canadian consumption patterns. Because economic considerations play such a dominant role in contemporary society, the economy itself needs to be redesigned in order to reflect ecological realities and comply with the scientific conditions for sustainability. In a contemporary liberal democracy like Canada, the government cannot use command-and-control laws to order its citizens to consume less. As Canada's National Round Table on the Environment and the Economy (NRTEE) concludes, "It is much more likely that ten thousand small decisions, freely made each day, will sustain development than will the One Big Law flowing from government."[27] Individuals and businesses in Canada make billions of day-to-day consumption decisions in the marketplace primarily on the basis of economic considerations. In theory, Adam Smith's famed "invisible hand" ensures that the market and prices reflect all relevant information. In reality, economists readily admit that the market is a less-than-perfect mechanism. The market's flaws are particularly glaring in the environmental context, for two primary reasons: a failure to value nature adequately, and the related failure to internalize the costs of environmental harm. In the words of a former World Bank economist, "The way we undervalue natural capital services and fail to account for natural asset degradation often means we are impoverishing ourselves while imagining that our economies are growing."[28]

The market's first critical failure is that it radically undervalues natural capital and ecosystem services. Natural capital refers to ecological systems such as watersheds and wetlands as well as energy sources, minerals, forests, wildlife, plants, and fish. Natural capital provides a large array of benefits to humans, including food, medicine, materials for everything from clothing to houses, recreational opportunities, and cultural inspiration. Ecosystem services include life-supporting natural processes that clean the air, purify water, pollinate plants, absorb carbon dioxide, recycle nutrients, process wastes, prevent floods, control pests, and replenish the soil.[29] Ecological services are valued by the market at zero dollars and zero cents, in that nobody pays for pollination, the water cycle, natural flood control, and so on, yet the value of the *services* provided by ecosystems dwarfs the value of the *goods* they provide. Ecological economists have made preliminary efforts to quantify the value of the services provided by the Earth, which constitute a life support system for all living things. In 1997 a dozen experts estimated the value of ecological services at US$33 trillion per year.[30] Even this mind-boggling sum fails to reflect the reality that the value of ecological services is effectively infinite, because they are irreplaceable. The infinite value of ecological services was graphically illustrated by the failure of the US$200 million Biosphere 2 project, which was unable to provide adequate ecological services for eight people.[31]

The market's second fundamental flaw is that environmental damage and degradation are described as "externalities." Externalities, in economics, are factors that are excluded from consideration (not captured in prices) because of their complexity or insignificance. Climate change, extinction, and water pollution, for example, are viewed by economists as externalities arising from human economic activities. Therefore their costs are not integrated into the prices set by the market.

Because the market recognizes neither nature's value nor the cost of ecological damage, Canadians rarely pay the full or true costs of consuming and polluting. The prices Canadians pay for water, gasoline, electricity, garbage removal, and other goods and services are lower than the full costs of these goods and services. Artificially low prices encourage excessive, even profligate, use. This is simply human nature, as anyone who has dined at an all-you-can-eat buffet can attest. Low prices are a major reason why Canadians are among the world's leaders in water, energy, gasoline, and electricity consumption as well as greenhouse gas emissions. In the words of the NRTEE, "Sustainable development continues to be an uphill struggle because of the dissonance between the goal and the context in which we make everyday decisions."[32]

When the market fails, it is the government's job to protect the public interest by implementing laws and policies to correct these failures. Governments must adjust the erroneous signals that the market is conveying, signals falsely indicating that clean water is cheap, that gasoline is cheaper than bottled water, and that coal is cheaper than natural gas. Canada should follow the advice of the OECD, which "recommends the removal of environmentally harmful subsidies and a more systematic use of environmental taxes, charges, and other economic instruments to get the prices right."[33] The market-based policy solutions advanced by the OECD are intended to implement the user-pays and polluter-pays principles, by making resource users and polluters pay the full cost of consuming resources and generating pollution. A growing body of evidence, mainly from Europe, but also from the United States, indicates that "market mechanisms can achieve pollution reductions at dramatically lower costs than traditional command and control strategies."[34]

Restructuring the economy to reduce consumption and fulfill the three conditions of ecological sustainability will obviously require major changes to existing laws, policies, and institutions. The transformation will not happen overnight, because it requires a reversal of "200 years of policies in taxes, labor, industry, and trade meant to encourage extraction, depletion, and disposal."[35] Outlined below are recommended law and policy changes that will induce the dematerialization and substitution required to begin the process of economic transformation, reducing Canadian overconsumption of energy and resources and moving toward compliance with the scientific conditions of sustainability. These recommendations are not a replacement for the improvements to environmental law and policy described in Chapter 11, but a necessary complement. Restructuring the economy to incorporate ecological limits is critically important if Canada is genuinely committed to achieving sustainability. Ultimately, unless consumption is reduced, and unless the scientific conditions of sustainability are fulfilled, laws intended to ensure clean air and clean water, protect parks, conserve forests and fisheries, and save endangered species are destined to fail.

Smart Subsidies and Perverse Subsidies
Government subsidies are one of the major causes of market distortions, contributing to excessive consumption of resources, fostering pollution, waste, and inefficiency, and discouraging conservation. Subsidies involve a wide range of economic benefits conferred by governments upon individuals, companies, or industries to encourage certain activities. Not all subsidies are harmful. Many subsidies serve the public interest by overcoming cost or market disadvantages to achieve societal objectives. For example, public education and health care are subsidized in Canada so that all Canadians have access to these vital social services. From an environmental perspective there are smart subsidies, which are good for the environment, and perverse subsidies, which cause environmental harm.

Smart subsidies can protect the environment and save taxpayers money. For example, in Sweden and other European countries, governments provide tax incentives for sulphur-free fuel. The lower the sulphur content of fuel, the lower the fuel tax. The result is cleaner air, and health care savings reportedly outweigh the lower revenue from fuel taxes.[36] A potentially powerful use of smart subsidies is to promote the development and commercialization of new environmentally friendly technologies, such as hydrogen fuel cells, enabling companies to drive production costs down and compete with established, more environmentally damaging technologies. Renewable energy production is subsidized by Sweden, Denmark, and other nations because society benefits environmentally from reduced pollution and economically through health care savings and increased worker productivity. It is difficult for renewable energy to compete with established nonrenewable energy sources that received in the past, and in many cases continue to receive, large subsidies.[37] Government support may enable renewable energy companies to gain a competitive advantage, resulting in long-term economic benefits that outweigh the costs of the original subsidies. Denmark promotes wind energy through subsidies, tax credits, and accelerated depreciation of investments, which explains why Danish companies lead the world in wind power technology.[38] Other examples of environmentally smart subsidies include tax credits and other financial incentives for energy-efficient products, public transit, employer-provided transit passes, energy-efficiency retrofits for buildings, investments in renewable energy, organic agriculture, integrated pest management, alternative fuel vehicles, and land conservation. Innovative means of substituting services for commodities, such as leasing, sharing, and carpooling, also deserve government support. For example, in some Canadian cities "car clubs" give members access to vehicles for occasional use, thus reducing car ownership.[39]

Smart subsidies can be created through innovative legislative approaches as well as financial assistance. One outstanding example is legislated thresholds requiring automobile manufacturers to guarantee that a minimum percentage of vehicle sales meet designated standards for low or no emissions. California is playing a key role in the emergence of new vehicle technologies through such legislation. Other US states following its lead, although British Columbia is the only Canadian jurisdiction to adopt California's system.[40] A similar program could be applied to consumer goods, like light bulbs and appliances, as well as to industrial equipment like motors. For example, light bulb manufacturers could be required to produce a certain percentage of high-efficiency compact fluorescent lights. A second legislative example, known as a renewable portfolio standard, requires providers of electricity to guarantee that a minimum percentage of their electricity is produced from clean, renewable sources. This type of program has already been adopted in at least nine US states, three European countries, and Australia.[41]

On the other hand, perverse subsidies occur when governments subsidize environmentally destructive behaviour in such a way that Canadians are penalized twice.[42] First, Canadians pay the economic price of such subsidies as direct financial payments and tax credits. Second, Canadians bear the direct and indirect costs of ecological damage (e.g., degradation of natural resources, environmental restoration expenses, and increased health care costs). For example, provinces subsidize the logging of old-growth forests on public land by charging stumpage rates (i.e., royalties) that are below the market value of the timber, providing tax credits for logging equipment, paying road construction and maintenance costs, and promoting forest products on behalf of companies.[43] Taxpayers are out of pocket for the direct costs of these subsidies. The second level of costs includes the nonmonetary damages that logging causes to soil, salmon, streams, watersheds, and wildlife. Substantial indirect losses are incurred in other economic sectors including fisheries, tourism, and nontimber forest products. To add insult to injury, taxpayers, not logging companies, subsequently pay billions of dollars to restore damaged watersheds.[44]

Few Canadians realize the extent to which their governments subsidize a wide range of environmentally destructive activities. The price people pay to fill their gas tanks and heat their homes does not include the costs to the health system caused by air pollution; the cost of restoring wildlife habitat damaged by the exploration and development of fossil fuels; the indirect economic costs associated with illness caused by air pollution; or the costs of addressing the impacts of climate change. Canadians flush their toilets without considering the economic and environmental costs of diverting, storing, and treating what is in fact drinking water, the economic cost of treating the wastewater, or the environmental cost of dumping the wastewater back into nature. Industries discharge thousands of toxic chemicals into rivers, lakes, groundwater, the ocean, and the atmosphere either free or at a minimal cost. There are three kinds of environmentally harmful subsidies: resource subsidies, financial subsidies, and infrastructure subsidies.

Resource Subsidies

Resource subsidies involve giving away publicly owned resources or pricing publicly owned assets, such as forests, fish, or minerals, below market value. In Canada, resource subsidies are common in the context of mining, fishing, logging, grazing, and water rights. For example, many provinces collect no royalty payments for coal mined from public land.[45] Many provinces use cheap water and cheap energy as an incentive to attract industries such as aluminum smelters and pulp mills. Alberta gave more than $1.2 billion in subsidies to corporations to entice them to log Alberta's northern boreal forest.[46] In the fishing industry, no royalties are paid by fishers despite the fact that fish are a publicly owned resource.[47] Individuals, farmers, and businesses are generally allowed to use groundwater free of charge in Canada. All of these resource subsidies reduce or eliminate incentives to conserve, and contribute to overconsumption.

Financial Subsidies

Financial subsidies include direct payments, tax credits, and other economic incentives. Again these are common in Canada's natural resource industries: mining, fishing, logging, agriculture, and oil and gas development. For example, agricultural pesticides are exempt from the GST.[48] This subsidy effectively encourages farmers to use pesticides. The *Fisheries Prices Support Act* created a federal board to buy fish from commercial fishers at above market price in order to create a fair relationship between the returns from fishing and those from other occupations.[49] Until its repeal in 2002 this law contributed to overfishing. Coal, one of the dirtiest energy sources, is exempt from the federal excise tax, which applies only to fuels used for transportation. Even

Parliament's conservative Technical Committee on Business Taxation recognizes that giving a tax advantage to coal over cleaner energy sources is neither environmentally nor economically defensible.[50]

The OECD has criticized Canada because "direct subsidies and fiscal incentives to the energy industry continue to undermine efforts to improve energy efficiency."[51] Oil, coal, and gas companies enjoy a tax break called the Canadian Exploration Expense, which allows a 100 percent deduction of up to half of the capital costs related to exploration.[52] The most favourable tax treatment is given to investments in oil sands and offshore drilling.[53] In contrast, clean, renewable energy sources like solar and wind power receive a smaller tax break despite the expansion of the Canadian Renewable Energy and Conservation Expense.[54] The Liberals promised in their 1993 Red Book to give the renewable energy sector the same tax advantages enjoyed by the fossil fuel industry.[55] The promise remains unfulfilled, despite modest steps in the right direction.

Another form of financial subsidy occurs when governments pay the costs of cleaning up contaminated sites. Mining companies create toxic legacies that can cost taxpayers hundreds of millions of dollars to clean up.[56] In 1998 Canada's auditor general observed that the federal government "still does not have a comprehensive view of the potential risks to health, safety and the environment associated with its more than 5,000 contaminated federal sites."[57] In 2001 the federal government estimated that this liability could be as high as $30 billion.[58] The mining industry also benefits from multiyear tax holidays for new mine development, accelerated depreciation allowances for new mine equipment, and other financial subsidies.[59]

Individual Canadians also receive financial subsidies that harm the environment. In the winter of 2000-1, federal and provincial governments doled out $1.3 billion to consumers to offset the rising price of natural gas, reducing the incentive for Canadians to conserve energy.[60] The money could have been used more effectively to weatherproof homes and apartment buildings, making residences more energy efficient for the long term. Similarly, the price of gasoline in Canada is lower than in any OECD country except the United States. Gasoline prices in Europe are three to five times higher than gasoline prices in Canada.[61] As a result, Europeans tend to buy smaller, more fuel-efficient vehicles, rely on alternative forms of transportation, such as public transit or bicycles, and discourage urban sprawl. There is an established correlation between gas prices and per capita gasoline consumption.[62] In the words of Professor Owen Saunders, "Canadians have used energy with such profligacy because it has been cheap and readily available and this has been so because of conscious policy decisions – by both federal and provincial governments of all stripes – that energy should be cheap and readily available."[63]

Infrastructure Subsidies

Infrastructure subsidies occur when users of a service or a publicly owned asset pay less than the full costs of the facilities required to provide the service or build and maintain the asset. For example, Ontario provides reduced transmission rates for exported power, effectively subsidizing large coal and nuclear energy plants with excess capacity.[64] The OECD criticized Canada for charging water prices that are below the costs of water infrastructure. Studies show that per capita water consumption in Canada is 50 percent lower in areas where consumers are charged on the volume used, rather than on a flat or declining rate. Among OECD nations, "recent reductions in water use have been most pronounced in countries that have removed subsidies for water use and applied charges which better reflect the marginal costs of water."[65] However, in comparison to the rest of the OECD, "Canada seems to be moving quite slowly towards the goal of full cost pricing of public services."[66]

Another area that receives extensive infrastructure subsidies in Canada and the United States is the transportation sector.[67] For example, motor vehicle drivers in Vancouver receive an annual subsidy of $2,600 per car.[68] Costs not borne by drivers include the value of land used for roads and parking lots; road building and maintenance; health care necessitated by air pollution; traffic enforcement; economic losses associated with traffic jams; and medical treatment of accident victims.

Global Subsidies

Recent estimates of subsidies worldwide, from such sources as the UN, the International Monetary Fund (IMF), and the OECD, range from $700 billion to US$2 trillion annually.[69] In the thirty OECD nations, agricultural subsidies alone stood at US$327 billion in 2000.[70] The IMF estimates fossil fuel subsidies cost US$230 billion annually.[71] A substantial proportion of fishing, agriculture, energy, water, and transportation subsidies are perverse. For example, the Food and Agriculture Organization estimates that the global fishing industry is worth US$70 billion but costs $124 billion, suggesting a $54 billion subsidy annually. The World Bank estimates annual global fishing subsidies as somewhat lower, but still in the range of US$14 billion to $20 billion.[72] Overfishing encouraged by subsidies is the primary reason why 70 percent of the world's fisheries are depleted or overexploited.

Perverse Subsidies in Canada

The OECD recently stated that "incentives for natural resource development and use [in Canada] raise sustainability concerns."[73] Billions of dollars of federal and provincial subsidies in Canada may be contributing to excessive resource use and environmental degradation, including:

- subsidies to the forest industry of between $3 billion and $8 billion annually[74]
- subsidies to the mining industry of approximately $600 million annually[75]
- fishing subsidies of $553 million in 1997 and $694 million in 1996[76]
- agricultural subsidies of $5.6 billion in 2000[77]
- annual subsidies to the fossil fuel industry of $5.9 billion[78]
- transportation subsidies (air, marine, rail, and highway) from the federal government alone ranging from $600 million to $2 billion annually between 1995 and 2000[79]
- subsidies to the nuclear industry of $156.5 million in 2000.[80]

These huge figures indicate that Canada has extensive opportunities to change subsidy policies in ways that will save money, reduce the use of resources, decrease pollution, increase efficiency, and promote environmental protection. In 1996 the Standing Committee on Environment and Sustainable Development recommended identifying and eliminating federal subsidies that cause environmental damage. However, the federal government's response to the Standing Committee report was vague and evasive.[81]

Unfortunately, Canada has joined forces with the United States to undermine international efforts to reduce energy subsidies. Canada and the United States enjoy the lowest energy prices in the G8 because of extensive subsidies. An effort in 2001 by the other members of the G8 to reduce subsidies for fossil fuels, a move that would have reduced air pollution and helped address climate change, was blocked by the United States and Canada.[82]

Eliminating Perverse Subsidies in Canada
In Europe, implementation of the user-pays and polluter-pays principles has meant significant declines in the subsidization of some environmentally damaging activities.[83] In the United States, an unlikely coalition of fiscal conservatives and environmentalists was formed in 1994 to lobby Congress to reduce or eliminate environmentally destructive federal subsidies. In six years this coalition, known as Green Scissors, has successfully persuaded the US government to cut US$24 billion in wasteful, environmentally destructive spending.[84] Another US$50 billion is targeted for elimination. Government subsidies targeted by the Green Scissors Coalition include funding for nuclear energy and fossil fuel industries; giveaways of publicly owned natural capital for logging, mining, grazing, oil and gas development, and the production of hydroelectricity; and transportation subsidies.

Although no comparable coalition exists in Canada, the opportunities for reducing environmentally perverse subsidies are enormous. To the federal government's credit, it has ended direct financial support for energy megaprojects and taken some steps to level the playing field for renewable energy. For example, in 2000 Ottawa ended federal subsidies that exceeded $1 billion to two BC coal mines.[85] The vitriolic reaction of the Canadian public against proposed subsidies to National Hockey League teams in 2000 provides further evidence of the public's aversion to subsidies. If the public were informed about the extent of taxpayer subsidies contributing to environmental degradation, there might be similar opposition.

In order to accelerate the identification and elimination of environmentally destructive subsidies in Canada, independent task forces should be formed at both the federal and provincial levels. The task forces should have broad representation, including independent economists, personnel from the auditor general's office, and representatives from civil society. At a minimum, identifying and publicizing perverse subsidies would provide greater transparency and educate the public on this issue. These task forces would recommend both time-tables for the elimination of environmentally harmful subsidies and transition strategies for affected communities.[86] For example, a portion of the money saved by eliminating subsidies could be used to retrain displaced workers. There are some easy targets for eliminating environmentally perverse subsidies in Canada. The *Income Tax Act* should be amended so that fines and penalties for environmental offences are not tax-deductible expenses.[87] The GST exemption for pesticides should be removed. From the public's perspective, eliminating perverse subsidies will pay a double dividend by reducing government expenditures (or increasing government revenues) and reducing environmental harm.[88] By forcing prices to rise and reflect full environmental costs, ending perverse subsidies will also encourage dematerialization and substitution.

Ecological Tax Shifting

Taxes are one of the most potentially powerful tools at government's disposal when it comes to protecting the environment. The basic premise of ecological tax shifting is that instead of taxing employment, work, and investment, taxes should gradually be redirected toward resources, pollution, and waste.[89] Put simply, tax shifting means society should stop taxing activities it wants to encourage and start taxing activities it wants to discourage.[90] Environmental tax shifting is an economically efficient and cost-effective way to incorporate the user-pays and polluter-pays principles and to move toward ecological sustainability. Tax shifting begins to correct the market's failure to reflect the full costs of resource depletion and pollution, gets the market to send appropriate pricing signals, internalizes economic externalities, and encourages investment in new technology and efficiency.[91] For example, taxing sulphur content in fuels creates incentives to reduce the amount of sulphur, to reduce the use of the fuels, and to find cleaner substitutes. According to the OECD, "If properly conceived and implemented, green tax reforms can contribute to a real structural adjustment of economies" toward sustainability.[92] Professor William Rees believes that the most effective way to achieve a major increase in energy and material efficiency is through a sweeping overhaul of tax policy based on shifting toward environmental taxes.[93] Massachusetts Institute of

Technology economics professor Paul Krugman says "virtually every card-carrying economist" thinks pollution taxes are a good idea.[94] According to Parliament's Technical Committee on Business Taxation, replacing existing income, payroll, and investment taxes with environmental taxes "can improve incentives to invest and create jobs" as well as "stimulating innovation and technological change."[95]

Tax shifting can take two forms: imposing new environmental taxes or re-structuring existing taxes to reflect environmental goals. Potential environmental taxes include carbon taxes, which tax energy based on the amount of carbon dioxide released, and pollution taxes on the release of toxic substances. An existing tax that could be restructured to reflect environmental goals is Canada's federal fuel excise tax, which currently favours coal and diesel fuel over cleaner energy sources.[96] To reflect ecological impacts, excise taxes should be higher, not lower, for coal and diesel. Revenues raised by environmental taxes can be used to finance social programs, lower existing taxes (e.g., payroll and income taxes), improve environmental quality (e.g., by funding the clean-up of contaminated sites), or compensate affected workers and businesses.

Environmental Tax Shifting in Other Countries

European nations, and to a lesser extent the United States, are far ahead of Canada in implementing environmental tax shifting. After more than a decade of experience, the results in Europe are impressive. For example, carbon taxes address climate change in Norway, Sweden, Denmark, the United Kingdom, Finland, Switzerland, and the Netherlands.[97] As a result, Norway has reduced greenhouse gas emissions from some industrial sectors by more than 20 percent.[98] Sweden stabilized its greenhouse gas emissions between 1990 and 2000. Sweden raises more than US$1 billion per year from a carbon tax and roughly US$10 billion per year from energy taxes, which subsidize the development of renewable energy and public transit. Over the period from 1998 to 2002, Denmark gradually increased energy taxes, based on the carbon content of different energy sources.[99] The revenue generated will be used to reduce social security contributions and subsidize investment in new energy technology. The United Kingdom's Fossil Fuel Levy raises more than US$150 million per year to finance the development of renewable energy.[100] European nations are expected to fulfill or even surpass their commitments to reduce greenhouse gas emissions under the *Kyoto Protocol*.

As discussed in Chapter 12, Sweden now taxes waste, the sulphur content of fossil fuels, pesticides and artificial fertilizers, motor vehicles, and electricity. Similarly, Denmark introduced taxes on sulphur dioxide, natural gas, water, plastic and paper bags, chlorinated solvents, containers, disposable tableware, pesticides, and motor vehicles (based on weight and fuel efficiency).[101] Denmark also imposed special taxes on coal and heavy vehicles. A Danish tax on nonhazardous waste doubled the cost of using landfills and incineration, causing a 50 percent reduction in waste, a doubling of recycling rates, and an 82 percent rate of reuse for construction debris.[102] Ireland recently introduced a tax of 15 cents per plastic bag in retail outlets.

There are many other examples of progress achieved by environmental tax shifting.[103] Germany introduced environmental taxes on energy in 1999, accompanied by offsetting reductions to social security contributions. These energy taxes are gradually being increased.[104] Switzerland used environmental taxes on volatile organic compounds and sulphur dioxide to reduce emissions. The United States used taxes as part of its successful effort to eliminate ozone-depleting chemicals.[105] The OECD recommends that industrialized nations implement energy taxes based on the carbon content of various fuels and impose a tax on all chemical use in order to reflect the real costs of using these products and curb pollution.[106]

Moving Forward with Ecological Tax Shifting in Canada

Despite the success of tax shifting in other countries, Canada has virtually "no practical experience with environmental tax shifting."[107] One minor exception is Quebec's special tax on a dry-cleaning chemical called perchloroethylene, which is used to fund a tax credit on the purchase of more environmentally friendly dry-cleaning equipment.[108] In 2003, a proposal to impose a levy on tetrachloroethylene (another chemical used by the dry-cleaning industry) was rejected by the federal government despite industry support for the levy. Ottawa's rationale, that the *Canadian Environmental Protection Act, 1999* did not authorize such a levy, is legally questionable in light of the law's provisions governing economic instruments.[109] Since the late 1980s Canadian environmentalists have advocated unsuccessfully for the introduction of carbon taxes to reduce greenhouse gas emissions and air pollution.[110]

Canada's Standing Committee on Environment and Sustainable Development issued a report in 1995 calling upon the government to gather baseline information on reforming the tax system to create incentives for sustainable activities and disincentives for unsustainable activities.[111] The federal government accepted this recommendation. However, the commissioner of the environment and sustainable development reports that little, if any, progress in this direction has been made.[112] The biggest hurdle to environmental tax shifting will be overcoming public mistrust of government; Canadians are still angry about the imposition of the GST. Several trial balloons floated by Environment Minister David Anderson about potential gas-guzzler taxes (taxes on vehicles with poor fuel-efficiency ratings) were quickly shot down.[113] A proposal to fund public transit in Vancouver by using a modest vehicle tax (averaging $75 per vehicle annually) was also unsuccessful.

However, opinion polls suggest that Canadians would prefer to have environmental costs incorporated into prices, rather than paying higher income taxes.[114] Many economists argue that the key to gaining public acceptance of environmental taxes is ensuring that the taxes are revenue-neutral, meaning that new or increased taxes are offset by reductions in other taxes.[115] Other strategies to increase public acceptance of environmental tax shifting include recycling revenue within an industry, dedicating revenue to achieving specific environmental objectives, using funds to mitigate economic impacts for affected individuals and businesses, and educating the public.[116]

Tax shifting in Canada will require major amendments to tax laws, regulations, and policies at both the federal and provincial levels. Tax shifts must be well designed to ensure that they directly address environmental concerns, are within a particular government's jurisdiction, and will not have excessive economic or competitiveness consequences. Environmental taxes should be introduced incrementally, giving individuals, governments, and businesses time to adjust to the changes, and allowing time for fine-tuning. As well, environmental taxes must not unfairly burden certain segments of the population. Equity concerns can be addressed by tax credits, compensation payments, and free minimum allocations of resources like water.[117] Competitiveness concerns can be alleviated by pursuing international agreements on energy or pollution taxes, by recycling tax revenue within an industry, by using tax exemptions or tax refunds, and by making taxes conditional (i.e., applied only if industry does not meet agreed objectives, such as a 20 percent reduction in greenhouse gas emissions by 2010).[118] Based on European experiences to date, in order to be successful environmental tax shifting should supplement, not substitute for, regulation; and it should aim to change behaviour, not raise revenue. Three specific examples of potential environmental tax shifts for Canada are outlined below.

Pollution Taxes

Pollution taxes set a fee for each unit of pollution generated by a business or individual. These charges create an incentive to minimize pollution and allow the reduction to take place in the most cost-effective manner, rather than prescribing a specific approach through regulations. Many European countries have used pollution taxes to achieve significant pollution reductions. For example, the Netherlands used taxes to achieve a 72 to 99 percent reduction in various water pollutants.[119] If properly designed, pollution charges are capable of addressing nonpoint source pollution as well as point source pollution. This is important now that nonpoint source pollution is more problematic in Canada than point source pollution.

Canada's National Pollutant Release Inventory (NPRI) could be used as the basis for establishing a national system of pollution taxes, with higher taxes levied on more toxic, persistent, carcinogenic, or bioaccumulative substances.[120] The NPRI already tracks releases of more than 265 toxic substances, many of which are released into the environment at low or no cost to the polluter despite recognition that considerable health and ecological damages are caused. According to Parliament's Technical Committee on Business Taxation, "Canadian industries that perform least well in controlling emissions are those that have the greatest potential for causing environmental damage – refined petroleum and coal, chemicals, rubber and plastics, paper and allied products, and non-metallic minerals."[121] These industries could be targeted by pollution taxes. Using the NPRI as the basis for a national pollution tax would be consistent with the polluter-pays principle and would provide a substantial incentive for companies to reduce toxic releases (dematerialization), and switch to less ecologically harmful substances (substitution). Funds generated from pollution taxes could be used to clean up contaminated sites, address air pollution, water pollution, and climate change, or invest in developing cleaner technologies.

Restructuring the Federal Fuel Excise Tax

As noted earlier, the federal fuel excise tax is environmentally perverse in that it provides unwarranted advantages to coal and diesel. The rate of tax is ten cents per litre for gasoline and four cents per litre for diesel, while all other forms of energy are exempt. Parliament's Technical Committee on Business Taxation recommended restructuring the fuel excise tax as a more broadly based environmental tax based on the carbon content of various energy sources.[122] Restructuring the fuel excise tax as an energy tax would encourage businesses and consumers to substitute cleaner energy sources for dirty energy sources. The new energy tax should be raised over a period of years to reflect the high levels of health and environmental damage caused by air and water pollution.

Fee-Bates

Fee-bate programs impose fees for less efficient products and provide rebates for more efficient products.[123] As a result, fee-bates internalize environmental costs and subsidize environmentally friendly purchasing decisions. For example, in Ontario purchasers of fuel-efficient vehicles receive a rebate while purchasers of less efficient vehicles pay a surcharge. The theory behind this policy is sound, but the Ontario program has had limited effect, because "90 percent of cars are not subject to the surcharge or the subsidy; the maximum surcharge or subsidy is a small fraction of the purchase price; and most consumers only learn of the tax after they have decided to buy a car."[124] In British Columbia, a Ministry of Finance discussion paper on ways to reduce vehicle emissions identified fee-bates as a useful tool. The proposal was never implemented, although BC does offer a modest rebate to purchasers of low-emission hybrid vehicles. A more effective fee-bate program for vehicles would apply to all vehicles, be well publicized, and provide a sufficient financial cost or benefit to alter consumer behaviour.

Environmental Law and Policy Changes
In addition to policies intended to produce social change and economic restructuring, environmental laws also have a key role to play in promoting the
changes required to fulfill the three scientific conditions of sustainability. The
changes to environmental laws and policies outlined in Chapter 11, and the
social and economic changes recommended earlier in this chapter, will contribute to significant improvements in environmental protection. However,
environmental law in Canada also needs to embrace dematerialization and
substitution. A new generation of environmental laws is required to increase
resource productivity and efficiency, prevent pollution, replace scarce materials with abundant ones, replace nonrenewable with renewable resources, move
from an emphasis on commodities toward services, and replace persistent,
unnatural substances with nature-like, degradable substances.

Increasing Efficiency and Productivity
By aggressively pursuing increases in energy efficiency and resource productivity, Canadians could reduce consumption without reducing their standard
of living. For example, a car that is twice as efficient allows a person to travel
the same distance using half the resources, consequently causing half the environmental impact. Reducing the energy intensity of industry allows reductions in greenhouse gas emissions and air pollution with no decrease in
productivity. Japan increased its GDP by 81 percent between 1973 and 1991
without increasing its *total* use of energy.[125] We like to think of our society as
technologically advanced and fairly efficient, but in reality there is a surprising amount of room for improvement. Scientists calculate that the overall
energy efficiency of the Canadian and American economies ranges from 2.5
percent to 10 percent.[126] In other words, between 90 percent and 97.5 percent
of the energy generated is wasted. Ordinary light bulbs are a classic example,
as only 8 percent of the energy consumed by a bulb is used to produce light,
while the rest produces heat. Cars are another example: only about 1 percent
of the energy consumed is actually used to move the driver.[127] On the resource
side, scientist Robert Ayres estimates that 94 percent of the material extracted
for use in manufacturing goes to waste.[128]

   The surprising inefficiency of our modern economy presents us with a
tremendous opportunity to reduce consumption of energy and resources without reducing the amount of value or services provided. Scientists use the
phrases "factor four" and "factor ten" to describe future economies that are
four and ten times as efficient as today's economy.[129] In other words, a particular product or service will require one-quarter or one-tenth the amount
of energy and materials to provide the same level of performance. For Canada
to achieve a fourfold or tenfold increase in efficiency may seem unrealisti-
cally optimistic, yet many products, corporations, and industries have attained this goal.[130] According to the OECD, "It is relatively easy to identify

technical and organizational changes that can achieve 75 percent reductions in resource use or environmental impact."[131] The pursuit of tenfold efficiency gains is supported by visionary business leaders, corporations, environmentalists, and governments.[132]

According to scientists, there are four basic ways to raise the productivity of resources:

1   efficiency gains: more efficient use of a given material for a given function (e.g., a computer chip of the same size with ten times as much memory)
2   substitution: replacing a scarce or hazardous material with a more abundant, safer, more efficient material, or replacing a commodity with a service (e.g., lead pipes replaced by copper pipes, copper wire replaced by fibre optic cable)
3   repair, reuse, remanufacturing, and recycling: reducing the need for new materials, thus reducing the environmental damage and energy consumption associated with extracting and processing new materials (e.g., aluminum)
4   waste mining: using waste streams to provide a source of materials or energy (e.g., making fleece clothing from plastic bottles or generating energy from the methane released by landfills).[133]

These strategies can be driven by technological change, the quest for greater profits, or government policy. For example, in the computer industry, advances in microminiaturization are producing smaller computers with greater memory. In the household appliance sector, efficiency increases have been driven by a combination of regulations and incentive programs. Smart regulations can stimulate businesses to innovate, reduce energy and resource consumption, and develop cleaner, more efficient manufacturing processes. For example, regulations requiring the elimination of ozone-depleting chemicals led firms like AT&T and Nortel to reexamine their production processes, resulting in substantial cost savings and improved environmental protection. Pollution and waste are indicators of inefficiency – signs that energy and materials could be used more productively.

The Refrigerator: A Case Study of Increased Efficiency
As recently as 1975, the average North American refrigerator used 1,800 kilowatt hours (kWh) of energy per year. Today's refrigerators use roughly one-quarter of the energy and provide superior performance at a comparable price.[134] This dramatic decrease was spurred by regulations that set gradually higher standards. California passed a law requiring more efficient refrigerators in 1976. In the late 1980s the US government passed a regulation setting 900 kWh as the maximum for a standard refrigerator. Even higher efficiency standards were mandated to take effect in the United States in 1993. Fridge manufacturers balked, arguing that the technology did not exist and warning that consumers

would face much higher prices. In 1991 no large North American manufacturers made refrigerators that met the 1993 standards. Two years later, without a major price hike, all manufacturers were making fridges that met the new standards. Even tougher standards came into effect in the United States in 2001. Canada followed the American lead by setting progressively higher energy-efficiency standards for fridges, using regulations under the *Energy Efficiency Act*.

A new refrigerator, compared to a 1975 model, saves the equivalent of two and a half barrels of oil, 1,200 pounds of coal, or 13,000 cubic feet of natural gas every year.[135] The reduction in energy use pays multiple dividends. In Canada and the United States combined, energy-efficient fridges will save consumers billions of dollars. Increased efficiency also means cleaner air, because air pollution and greenhouse gas emissions caused by producing the energy to run fridges are reduced by about 75 percent. Remarkably, there is still further progress to be made. Refrigerators are available that use only 180 kWh per year, although not yet at competitive prices.[136] This represents one-tenth the energy of a standard 1975 fridge. In other words, in less than three decades, fridge manufacturers achieved a factor ten gain in efficiency.

Similar efficiency gains across all sectors of our industrial society would dramatically reduce our impact on the environment and save money. Natural Resources Canada estimates savings resulting from the *Energy Efficiency Act,* which covers approximately thirty household appliances, at $4.4 billion annually.[137] The American Council for an Energy Efficient Economy estimates that higher efficiency standards for household appliances would cost American consumers US$59 billion in higher prices, but would save them US$190 billion on their energy bills.[138]

Increasing Efficiency and Productivity in Canada

Canada needs a systematic effort to increase efficiency across all sectors of the economy, rather than in isolated sectors such as household appliances. A wide range of environmental laws and policies can be used to promote efficiency, substitution, recycling, remanufacturing, and waste mining. Governments can encourage greater efficiency and productivity with financial incentives, tax credits, or regulations that raise standards over time. Where softer approaches like voluntary agreements have proven ineffective, more coercive tools like taxes and regulations need to be used. For example, voluntary programs intended to increase fuel efficiency and promote the construction of energy-efficient buildings are proven failures and need to be replaced by regulations. The *Energy Efficiency Act* has worked well for household appliances and should be extended to vehicles, industry, and building construction. Regulations should set clear targets and rely upon gradual timelines, making it clear that continuous improvement is expected, as standards will rise at regular intervals. The R-2000 standard for energy-efficient buildings should be incorporated into federal and provincial building codes. With respect to the fuel efficiency of vehicles, existing technology could easily meet much stricter standards. Cars already available in Canada, like the Toyota Prius and the Honda Insight, are far more fuel efficient than most new vehicles. Efficiency standards would work for water and other natural resources as well as for energy. For example, Canadian building and plumbing codes should be amended to require low-volume toilets, showerheads, and faucets.

Certain segments of society will object, as they have in the past, claiming these steps cannot be taken without social and economic upheaval. Time will prove them wrong, again, and both society and the planet will come out ahead. However, there is one caveat about the potential environmental benefits of efficiency and productivity increases. First, savings enjoyed by consumers may translate into higher levels of energy and resource use. For example, someone who purchases a fuel-efficient vehicle and then drives additional distances will erode the efficiency gains. Studies indicate this so-called rebound effect is fairly minor.[139] Second, efficiency gains can be outweighed by increases in to-tal energy and resource use resulting from economic and population growth. For example, OECD countries are expected to increase energy efficiency by 20 percent between 2001 and 2020, yet total energy use in OECD countries is forecast to grow 35 percent by 2020.[140] Dematerialization requires more than efficiency gains.

Some specific environmental law and policy tools for fostering demateriali-zation and substitution are outlined in the following sections. What distin-guishes these tools from conventional environmental laws and regulations is that they promote continuous improvement; use incentives to motivate re-sponsible behaviour and going beyond compliance; focus on implementation and performance instead of process; decentralize decision making; make in-novation and efficiency priorities; rely on a broader range of participants; and emphasize flexibility.

Deposit-Refund Systems

Canadians are familiar with the deposit-refund system used for beverage con-tainers. Consumers pay a surcharge when purchasing a potentially polluting product and receive their money back when they return the item. Deposit-refund systems result in high rates of recycling and reuse. In the ten American states with laws requiring deposits on cans, 85 percent of aluminum cans are recycled. In the forty states without deposits, the rate of recycling for aluminum cans is only 50 percent.[141] In some jurisdictions, particularly in Europe, deposit-refund programs are being expanded to a broader range of items such as tires, batteries, paint cans, and even cars. In Norway over 90 percent of cars are brought to an approved site at end of life.[142] By promoting recycling, deposit-refund systems reduce waste, take pressure off virgin materials, and contribute to dematerialization.

Extended Product Responsibility

Germany passed a groundbreaking law in 1991, called the *Closed Substance Cycle and Waste Management Act,* that makes producers responsible for the packaging and products that they produce.[143] Producers must redesign their products so that all components can be either reused or recycled. Other countries, including Sweden and the Netherlands, have followed the German example. BC is a Canadian leader in implementing extended producer responsibility programs for products such as paint, pharmaceuticals, and pesticides.[144] Although BC's program is much narrower in scope than the European programs, it is a step in the right direction.

Pollution Prevention

Mandating pollution prevention is another policy that produces dematerialization and substitution, thus boosting productivity and efficiency. Pollution prevention is radically different from traditional Canadian approaches to pollution, which have emphasized end-of-the-pipe solutions and dilution. Pollution prevention involves reexamining extraction, production, and manufacturing processes to reduce and eliminate the release of harmful substances into the environment.[145] Pollution prevention slows resource depletion and reduces energy consumption; reduces costs by minimizing handling, storage, and treatment or disposal of waste; reduces societal costs related to cleaning up toxic sites; decreases health expenses caused by exposure to pollutants; and decreases risks of criminal and civil liability.[146]

After years of discussion, pollution prevention is making progress in North America. Twenty-three American states now have toxics use reduction laws that focus on reducing and eliminating chemical inputs instead of permitting certain levels of emissions.[147] In 2000 Canada's finance minister, Paul Martin, recognized that "we will need to abandon the very concept of waste" by shifting from a linear model, with waste as an end product, to a closed-loop system where no waste is generated.[148] Closed-loop industrial systems are patterned after the nutrient cycles of the biosphere.[149] The *Canadian Environmental Protection Act, 1999* and Nova Scotia's *Environment Act* embrace pollution prevention as a purpose although their specific provisions in this regard are weak. There are isolated examples of corporations pursuing innovative means of pollution prevention in Canada. Millar Western's Meadow Lake pulp and paper mill in Saskatchewan, built in 1993, has a closed-loop production process using no chlorine and producing no liquid effluent.[150]

Stronger laws and policies, in the form of either incentives or regulations, are necessary to make pollution prevention a more widespread practice in Canada. Like Sweden, Canada should be eliminating the production and use of toxic substances that cause cancer, accumulate in food chains, disrupt hormonal systems, or do not break down in nature. Laws governing chemicals, such as the *Canadian Environmental Protection Act, 1999* and the *Pest Control*

Products Act, should be amended to incorporate the substitution principle, so that harmful products must be phased out when safer alternatives become available. Canada's NPRI, which measures industrial pollution, could serve as the baseline for new incentives or regulations that require decreases in toxic releases over a prescribed period of time.

Eco-Labelling
Informational failures are a barrier to environmentally responsible behaviour. Eco-labelling provides consumers with information about the environmental costs of products, so that fully informed choices can be made. Just as there are warning labels on cigarettes and alcohol, there should be educational labels on products that are harmful or potentially harmful to the environment. Eco-labelling can be voluntary or mandatory, although based on experience with voluntary measures in other environmental sectors, mandatory programs are likely to be more effective. Eco-labelling can be operated by government or private interests. The American Energy Star program is a leading example of a voluntary eco-labelling program.[151] The Energy Star label is available to energy-efficient products, homes, and buildings that meet specified requirements. In the United States, it is mandatory for the federal government to purchase office equipment and appliances that meet Energy Star standards for efficiency. This requirement saves taxpayers billions of dollars in reduced energy bills and reduces environmental impacts.[152]

In Canada, eco-labelling has begun in the field of household appliances pursuant to the federal *Energy Efficiency Act*. As of 2000 the Environmental Choice Program involved 1,750 products in thirty-nine categories. The national eco-labelling program is privately operated; Canada is the only OECD nation whose eco-labelling program does not receive government funding.[153] Despite high levels of public support for mandatory labelling of food products containing genetically modified organisms, Canadian politicians have failed to enact a law to require such labelling. A private member's bill that would have required mandatory labelling was defeated in 2001.[154]

Cap-and-Trade Systems
Under cap-and-trade systems, also known as tradable permit systems, governments set limits on pollution for a company, an industry, a substance, or an area. Permits for a share of the pollution are then allocated or auctioned to companies and individuals. Finally, trading of permits between polluters is allowed. Companies whose emissions are lower than their permitted levels can sell the permits to other companies who are polluting above their permitted levels. All companies have an incentive to reduce pollution as efficiently as possible, and the market ensures that pollution is reduced at the lowest cost.

In the United States, a cap-and-trade program for sulphur dioxide emissions established in 1990 by amendments to the *Clean Air Act* proved to be a "terrific bargain."[155] Aimed at addressing the acid rain problems in eastern North America, the program produced at least US$12 billion in annual health benefits (the lowest estimate), which is four times the highest estimate of annual costs.[156] American sulphur dioxide emissions fell 50 percent from 1980 to 1995, to 39 percent below the maximum set by legislation. Many legal experts agree that "the acid rain program must be counted as a resounding success that has gone far to legitimize the use of market-based regulation of pollution."[157]

Not everyone is convinced of the merits of cap-and-trade systems. Some environmentalists are offended by the concept of providing industry with permits to pollute. This objection may be rooted in a failure to comprehend that at present, polluters already have licences authorizing pollution, but rarely pay for the privilege and thus have no reason to reduce emissions. Cap-and-trade systems improve on the status quo by setting enforceable limits on the total amount of pollution and creating an incentive to reduce releases to below legal limits (because surplus pollution credits can be sold). A legitimate concern is that a national trading system may result in inequitable outcomes because pollution becomes concentrated in a particular region or because one region may be more susceptible to harm due to ecological sensitivities.[158] These issues can and should be addressed in designing cap-and-trade systems.[159]

Canada has experimented only minimally with cap-and-trade systems. Canada set a limit for the use of methyl bromide (an ozone-depleting substance), allocated quotas, and allowed trading of quotas. The program is viewed as a success, as methyl bromide use declined ahead of schedule and alternatives were found at lower-than-expected costs.[160] Canada also has two experimental programs for trading greenhouse gas emissions, the Greenhouse Gas Emission Reduction Trading pilot (GERT) in British Columbia and the Pilot Emission Reduction Trading program (PERT) in the Windsor-Quebec corridor.[161] Because these programs are in their infancy it is difficult to evaluate their utility, although the federal government is counting on permit trading to make a significant contribution to achieving Canada's commitments under the *Kyoto Protocol*.

Mandatory Auditing

Another weakness of the market, often caused by incomplete information, is that individuals and corporations fail to make investments that produce both environmental and economic benefits. In order to overcome this failure, Denmark has made it mandatory for industry to implement any energy-efficiency measures that pay for themselves, through reduced energy costs, in less than four years. The four-year time span means that these measures produce a return on investment of at least 25 percent. Opportunities to increase energy efficiency are identified in energy audits provided by the Danish government.

As well, Denmark subsidizes some energy-efficiency investments that have a payback period longer than four years, which businesses would not otherwise undertake.[162]

In Canada, public utility companies have, from time to time, offered voluntary home inspection programs to identify the most cost-effective energy-efficiency renovations homeowners can make. These energy-efficiency programs should be expanded and made mandatory, particularly for major industrial energy consumers. Some provinces, such as Ontario and BC, have mandatory vehicle inspection and maintenance programs. In theory, these programs should ensure that vehicles meet efficiency and pollution standards. However, their effectiveness is limited by low thresholds, inconsistent standards, and extensive loopholes. A more promising approach, not yet implemented in Canada, involves accelerated retirement programs for the worst-polluting vehicles.[163]

Conclusion

Reducing consumption and moving toward compliance with the three conditions of ecological sustainability poses profound social, economic and environmental challenges. These challenges require governments to redesign social, economic, and environmental laws and policies. Environmental laws, on their own, are not capable of making sufficient changes. Canadian values and behaviour need to change. Our priorities as a society, and as individuals, must change. It is imperative that the economy be restructured to respect the value of natural capital and ecosystem services.

Reducing Canada's consumption of energy and resources through dematerialization and substitution will require leadership from government, businesses, and individuals. Governments themselves are among the largest consumers in industrialized economies. In Canada, roughly 20 percent of GDP involves government expenditure, and the federal government is the nation's largest employer.[164] Although Canada has repeatedly pledged to become a model of environmental excellence, efforts to "green" Canada's federal government have fallen far short of expectations.[165] Government needs to be a role model in pursuing dematerialization and substitution. Businesses also must change their ways. The corporate drive for short-term profits is often identified as a major impediment to improved environmental performance.[166] Although some corporations have made great strides in becoming sustainable, the majority of corporations have not. Law reform is needed to require corporations to pursue the "triple bottom line" of economic, social, and environmental responsibility. Finally, individuals must rethink present consumption patterns, and close the indefensible gap between Canadian words and Canadian actions. Despite their professed values, "too many Canadians who claim to be concerned about the environment are driving bigger and less efficient vehicles, building bigger homes, maintaining shopping habits that encourage environmental destruction."[167]

This chapter recommends replacing the narrow goal of increasing GDP with the broader goal of improving the overall quality of life, as measured by the Genuine Progress Index or a similar tool, eliminating environmentally perverse subsidies, implementing an ecological tax shift, and using a variety of laws and policies to bolster efficiency and productivity, reduce resource use, and prevent pollution. These recommendations, if implemented, would begin to move Canada toward ecological sustainability by addressing overconsumption, one of the root causes of environmental degradation. Although largely untested in Canada, these tools are proving successful elsewhere, particularly in northern Europe. Canada's role in addressing the other root cause of environmental degradation, overpopulation, is addressed in the next chapter.

14 Population Growth and Sustainable Development

As noted in Chapter 10, the world's population surpassed 6.1 billion in the year 2000. The unprecedented growth in human population during the past hundred years is a major contributor to the rate and magnitude of environmental degradation. Global population growth has slowed, but continues to add about 80 million people annually, so that the world's population is expected to surpass 9 billion people by 2050. Almost all population growth in the next fifty years will take place in the developing world, which already faces daunting social, economic, and environmental challenges.

Population growth will exacerbate the problems currently confronting developing countries.[1] From an environmental perspective, continued population growth will increase pressure on biodiversity, fisheries, forests, agricultural lands, and, perhaps most important, water. While the human population has tripled in the past seventy years, water use has increased sixfold.[2] As of the year 2000, 500 million people lived in water-stressed or water-scarce countries. By the year 2025, if current trends continue, 3 billion people will live in water-stressed or water-scarce countries. The UN concludes that "slower population growth in developing countries will contribute measurably to relieving environmental stress."[3]

Addressing poverty is also vital to sustainable development. Population growth and poverty in developing countries often combine to form a vicious circle in which rapid population growth prevents the kinds of social and economic development that would slow population growth.[4] It does so by outpacing infrastructure, harming the health of women and children, accelerating environmental degradation, and undermining social and political stability. Families increase the number of children in an effort to break free from poverty, but the ensuing population growth exceeds resources available for education, health care, and other social services, places stress on natural resources, and may depress wages due to surplus labour, thus worsening poverty. Alleviating poverty on a global scale is a complex challenge that will require an extensive effort including promoting sustainable development, facilitating democracy, upholding human rights, achieving gender equity, creating an equitable global trade regime, improving the lives of children, securing peace, and promoting food security. These goals are difficult to achieve in isolation. As the United Nations notes, "Efforts to slow down population growth, to achieve economic progress, to improve environmental protection, and to reduce unsustainable consumption and production patterns are mutually reinforcing."[5]

Wealthy industrialized countries like Canada have a critical role to play in helping developing nations overcome the challenges posed by rapid population growth and widespread poverty. This role has three aspects. First, Canada should provide international leadership in helping the developing world implement policies that will reduce the rate of population growth. Second, Canada should be a global leader in promoting sustainable development and alleviating poverty in developing countries. Third, there is a question whether Canada should be concerned about population growth nationally, as Canada's population has grown sixfold over the past century.

Addressing Global Population Growth

The steps required to reduce population growth in developing countries are straightforward, although not necessarily easy to implement. The consensus among 179 countries at the 1994 UN International Conference on Population and Development in Cairo identified the following priorities:

- improve access to quality family planning and other reproductive health services
- eliminate the gaps between boys' and girls' education
- reduce infant and maternal mortality
- improve the social, political, and economic status of women.[6]

The final point above, empowering women, is increasingly recognized as the single most important step in reducing population growth. Empowering women is not only a desirable goal in and of itself, but also results in progress toward many interwoven social, economic, and environmental objectives.[7]

Rapid progress on population issues can be achieved if the priorities identified at the Cairo Conference are vigorously pursued. In Thailand the average fertility level has fallen to 2.2 births per woman from 6.2 births per woman in less than thirty years. This progress is largely attributed to Thailand's National Family Planning Program, whereby eight thousand government facilities offer family planning and reproductive health advice.[8] Similarly, in Bangladesh, one of the world's most overpopulated countries, population growth fell to 1.6 percent from 3 percent in the past twenty-five years, largely due to improvements in family planning and growing use of contraceptives.[9]

Globally, the rate of population growth must be reduced to near zero in order to secure a sustainable future. As Joel Cohen, author of *How Many People*

Can the Earth Support?, concludes, "This is a simple mathematical fact, not subject to the whims of wars or elections or wish or chance. It is the one irrefutable proposition of demographic theory."[10] In most industrialized countries, fertility rates are already at or below the replacement rate for maintaining a stable population. For example, in Canada the average fertility level has fallen to 1.5 births per woman, well below the replacement level of 2.1 births.[11] Relatively small investments can achieve tremendous progress toward population sustainability.[12] Pursuing the priorities of the Cairo Conference will require an estimated US$17 billion annually. Developing countries agreed to shoulder two-thirds of this financial burden, while industrialized countries promised to pay the remaining one-third.

Canada's Role in Reducing Global Population Growth

Despite the vital importance of population issues, Canada has no official policy on global population growth. However, at the Cairo Conference in 1994, Canada promised to spend $200 million a year on population programs in developing countries.[13] This commitment involves targeting a portion of foreign aid money directly toward family planning and reproductive health. To date, Canada's promise has not been fulfilled. The Canadian International Development Agency and the Department of Foreign Affairs and International Trade indicate that Canada is spending $50 million annually on population and reproductive health programs, far short of its international commitment.[14] In fact, Canadian spending on population and reproductive health programs declined sharply in the early 1990s when Canada's economy endured a minor recession. Canada cut funding to the widely respected International Planned Parenthood Foundation by 50 percent between 1988 and 1997 and eliminated the population research program at the International Development Research Centre.[15]

Canada and the United States were the only industrialized countries to cut levels of spending on population assistance in the years following the Cairo Conference.[16] In contrast, such countries as Norway, Denmark, and the Netherlands have exceeded their commitments. Canada's international reputation suffered yet another blow because of this failure. As one expert observed, in a report prepared for the Canadian government, Canada's record on population assistance is "not a creditable record for a country that likes to depict itself as so earnestly committed to meeting the Third World's priority needs."[17]

There is some good news in terms of Canada's international efforts to address population growth, such as Canada's role in helping Bangladesh. Bangladesh provides an important illustration of family planning success and proves that economic progress is not necessarily a prerequisite to slowing population growth. Through the combined efforts of the Bangladesh Ministry of Health and Family Welfare, the World Bank, and the Canadian International Development Agency, Bangladesh managed to reduce its fertility rate to fewer than four children per woman from seven children, slowing the rate of population increase to 1.6 percent from 3 percent in the past twenty-five years. These results were achieved through investing in improved family planning and health services; increased education; reduced maternal mortality rates; and better nutrition for women and children.[18] More work remains to be done, because even at current growth rates, Bangladesh's population of 120 million will double in about forty years.

Experts believe that the decline in fertility rates in Southeast Asia was one of the main factors in the rapid social and economic progress achieved by nations like Thailand and South Korea (East Asia) during the latter part of the twentieth century.[19] From a global perspective, developing countries must be able to learn from the environmentally damaging mistakes of the industrialized nations as their economies grow. The Earth's ecosystems could not withstand the increased pressure that repeating the errors of industrialized countries would entail, so policies are needed that will enable the developing countries to "leapfrog" to growth patterns that are environmentally friendly.[20] Sustainable development is the key to achieving this goal. In order to avoid charges of hypocrisy and environmental imperialism from the South, the North must make a substantial commitment to facilitating this transition.

Addressing Poverty: Promoting Sustainable Development

In 2000 the global community established the Millennium Development Goals, setting ambitious, measurable objectives for improving the state of the world by the year 2015. The Millennium Development Goals include:

- attaining universal primary education
- halving world poverty
- halving world hunger
- reducing child mortality by two-thirds
- reducing maternal mortality by three-quarters
- halting and beginning to reverse the spread of HIV/AIDS and malaria
- eliminating the gender disparity in primary and secondary education
- halving the proportion of people without access to safe drinking water.[21]

The World Bank estimates that meeting the Millennium Development Goals will cost between US$40 billion and US$60 billion annually. Oxfam estimates that the cost may be as high as US$100 billion annually.[22] The worldwide understanding of the urgency of addressing poverty was illustrated by two parallel studies undertaken in 2002. A survey of thirty thousand people in thirty countries found that the number-one priority for the world should be alleviating poverty. A survey of three hundred experts in the field of sustainable development ranked only water higher than poverty as urgent global priorities.[23]

Canada, as a wealthy industrialized nation, has an important role to play in addressing poverty, promoting sustainable development in the developing world, and meeting the Millennium Development Goals. Three of the primary avenues for Canadian action include providing official development assistance (ODA), forgiving the debt of the world's poorest countries, and reducing trade barriers that harm developing nations. Canada can, and should, be a leader in encouraging other industrialized nations (particularly the United States) to prioritize, finance, and implement programs to reduce poverty and facilitate sustainable development.

Official Development Assistance
Back in the 1960s, Prime Minister Lester Pearson made a solemn promise, reflecting the compassionate nature and relative wealth of Canadians, that Canada would invest at least 0.7 percent of our GDP annually in assisting developing countries. Indeed, industrialized nations generally agree that 0.7 percent of GDP is a minimum threshold.[24] The Department of Foreign Affairs and International Trade says that ODA "is one of the clearest international expressions of Canadian values and culture – of Canadians' desire to help the less fortunate and of their strong sense of social justice."[25] ODA, or foreign aid, is intended to foster sustainable development. Developing countries often lack the financial resources to ensure basic human needs are met, provide social services like health care and education, build and maintain adequate infrastructure, generate economic opportunities, and prevent environmental degradation. Despite widespread recognition of the need to make more financial resources available to the world's poorest countries, the overall levels of aid provided by wealthy nations like Canada actually fell by about 20 percent during the 1990s.[26]

Prime ministers since Lester Pearson have repeated the promise to raise Canadian ODA to 0.7 percent of GDP but these promises have never been fulfilled. Brian Mulroney made the promise at the 1992 Earth Summit. Jean Chrétien reiterated it in the Liberal Red Book in 1993.[27] In fact, Canada spent a paltry 0.22 percent of our GDP on ODA in the year 2001. This dismal level of aid puts Canada nineteenth of the twenty-two donor nations of the OECD.[28] Canada lags far behind European nations like Denmark, Norway, the Netherlands, and Sweden that meet or exceed the international target; these countries provide double, triple, and even quadruple the level of Canadian foreign aid.[29] Canada's performance on this issue worsened throughout the 1990s. Canadian ODA as a percentage of GDP fell from 0.49 percent in 1991 to 0.22 percent in 2001.[30] In many other OECD nations (e.g., Austria, Denmark, Finland, Ireland, Italy, Luxembourg, Norway, Spain, and Switzerland), levels of ODA have increased in recent years.[31]

These are embarrassing facts, given that Canadians like to think of themselves as a compassionate and generous people. Canada's low level of ODA is another example of the gulf between Canadian values and the actions of our elected representatives. A glimmer of hope was provided by the federal budget in December 2001, when Finance Minister Paul Martin announced an increase in spending on ODA, targeting Afghanistan and Africa.[32] However, even this increase will not move Canada's level of official development assistance above 0.3 percent in the years 2001-4.[33] A further promise was made by Prime Minister Chrétien in 2002 to increase ODA by 8 percent annually for the next eight or nine years.[34] If the prime minister's commitment is fulfilled, Canada's level of foreign aid will still fall short of the target of 0.7 percent of GDP in 2012.

In addition to increasing the level of aid, it is also important for Canada to take a more focused approach to ODA. Canada's foreign aid program makes the reduction of poverty the overarching objective, with six broad priorities including meeting human needs, promoting gender equality, creating infrastructure, developing democracy and good governance, protecting the environment, and building a strong private sector.[35] These are sound goals. However, whereas countries like the Netherlands target 17 well-governed poor countries for aid, Canada currently distributes ODA to more than 130 countries.[36] World Bank studies show that aid is far more effective at improving key indicators like infant mortality and per capita income in countries with low levels of corruption.[37] By linking aid to respect for human rights, progress in eliminating corruption, and democratic governance, Canada could create incentives for poor countries to tackle corruption problems so that they become eligible for foreign aid. A recent study by the Canadian International Development Agency indicates that Canada may be moving in this direction.[38]

The final aspect of ODA where Canada could improve its practices involves the practice of tied aid, meaning aid that is conditional upon purchasing goods and services from Canadian suppliers. Studies have demonstrated that although tied aid benefits the Canadian economy, it hurts developing countries because the costs of goods and services procured under tied aid programs are 15 percent to 30 percent higher than costs on the open market.[39] Canada has one of the highest rates of tied aid among donor countries: 67 percent of Canada's bilateral aid is tied, and 90 percent of Canada's food aid is tied to the purchase of Canadian food.[40] Donor countries in the OECD have promised to reduce levels of tied aid, particularly to the world's poorest countries, but concrete actions have not yet been taken to fulfill these promises.[41] Reductions in tied aid must not be accompanied by reductions in the overall level of ODA.

Forgiving Third World Debt

Another major obstacle facing many developing nations is a heavy burden of debt owed to industrialized nations and to multilateral institutions like the World Bank and the International Monetary Fund (IMF). Total external debt in low- and middle-income countries grew from $1.5 trillion in 1990 to more than US$2.4 trillion in 2001.[42] Service payments on the debts of the world's poorest countries often exceed government spending on social services such as health care and education. In some countries, debt payments consume the majority of government revenues.[43]

At the close of the twentieth century a wide range of nongovernmental organizations conducted a high-profile effort, called Jubilee 2000, to encourage governments and multilateral institutions to cancel the debt of the world's poorest nations. Instead, governments, the World Bank, and the IMF created a program called the Heavily Indebted Poor Countries Debt Initiative. Under the Debt Initiative, countries must agree to undertake structural adjustment programs in exchange for debt relief. Structural adjustment programs involve increasing the participation of developing countries in the world economy by promoting export-oriented growth, privatizing state-owned industry, eliminating barriers to trade and investment, and reducing the role of government. Because of pressure from civil society's Jubilee 2000 campaign, the World Bank and the IMF implemented the Enhanced Heavily Indebted Poor Countries Debt Initiative (the Enhanced Debt Initiative) in 1999, providing faster, deeper debt relief tied not only to structural adjustment but also to a requirement that strategies for poverty reduction be created and implemented.[44]

The effectiveness of the Enhanced Debt Initiative in alleviating the burden of Third World debt has been widely questioned.[45] According to the World Bank, the benefits of the Enhanced Debt Initiative include reductions in total debt, decreased debt service costs, and increased social spending. The initiative is expected to reduce the debt of twenty-six countries by between 50 and 67 percent. However, the Enhanced Debt Initiative applies only to twenty-six countries, and even when complete, will leave these countries with sizeable debt loads.[46] Unless the poor nations achieve unprecedented economic growth and avoid social, economic, and environmental disruptions, their debt burdens are highly likely to become unsustainable again.[47] There are also serious concerns about the negative impacts of the structural adjustment programs imposed by the World Bank and IMF as a condition for receiving debt relief. While structural adjustment appears to raise GDP and average income, these gains come at a cost that includes worsening inequality, jeopardizing social stability, and increasing environmental degradation.[48] These trends move poor countries farther from the goal of sustainable development. Many organizations around the world involved in Jubilee 2000 continue to advocate the complete cancellation of the debt of the poorest countries in the world, without the extensive conditions imposed by the World Bank.

Canada is owed approximately $1.1 billion by seventeen heavily indebted poor countries. Pursuant to the Enhanced Debt Initiative, Canada has placed a moratorium on debt service payments from eleven countries that are improving governance and targeting poverty reduction.[49] To Canada's credit, Canada also forgave the debt owed by Bangladesh, a debt that stemmed from earlier development assistance in the form of loans rather than grants.[50] In the mid-1980s, Canada changed its development assistance policy so that it was exclusively composed of grants, rather than loans requiring repayment. Although Bangladesh owed Canada only $600,000, Canada has encouraged other nations to forgive debts stemming from the provision of foreign aid and to follow Canada's leadership in providing aid that does not require repayment.

Changes to International Trade Rules

The third main strategy available to increase the financial resources of developing nations involves changing international trade rules that currently operate to the detriment of poorer countries. International trade flows dwarf international development assistance in size. For this reason, increasing the participation of developing nations in trade is often identified as a potentially powerful means of achieving economic growth and reducing poverty. According to Oxfam, "If Africa, East Asia, South Asia, and Latin America were each to increase their share of world exports by one percent, the resulting gains in income could lift 128 million people out of poverty."[51] For Africa alone, a 1 percent increase in its share of world exports would generate about US$70 billion – approximately five times what the continent currently receives in aid. However, efforts by developing countries to participate in international trade face a number of obstacles. Some of these obstacles are internal, such as inadequate infrastructure, lack of skilled workers, corruption, and inadequate institutions. Some of the obstacles are external, and are created by wealthy industrialized nations including Canada.

The World Bank calculates that protectionism in rich countries "costs developing countries more than [US]$100 billion per year, twice the volume of aid from North to South."[52] Trade policies employed by wealthy countries that harm developing countries include import taxes, tariffs, subsidies, quotas, seasonal restrictions, and a range of other nontariff barriers. Tariffs in industrialized nations are much higher on labour-intensive goods and agricultural products, two of the primary exports of the poorest countries. The World Bank recommends that the priority in forthcoming international trade meetings be placed on a "development round" aimed at removing barriers facing developing nations.[53]

A recent study suggests that the benefits of Canada's ODA contributions to developing countries are outweighed by the costs of Canadian trade barriers that harm the nascent economies of these poorer nations. Canada places much higher import taxes on labour-intensive agricultural products, textiles, and clothing, policies that disadvantage the poorest countries with whom Canada trades. For example, for every dollar of Canadian aid to Bangladesh, Canadian trade barriers, particularly in the textile and clothing sectors, cost Bangladesh eight dollars.[54] Canadian trade barriers cost Haiti, the poorest country in the

Americas, $75 million annually, or twice the level of Canadian aid to this impoverished nation.[55] Canada imposes import taxes on processed foods that average three times as much as the import taxes on unprocessed foods, effectively discouraging developing countries from adding value to basic agricultural commodities. Canada ranks third on Oxfam's Double Standards Index "because of the wide gap between Canada's free trade rhetoric and protectionist practices that cause disproportionate harm to the poorest countries."[56] As the *Globe and Mail* concluded, "Giving with one hand and taking with the other, rich countries such as Canada are denying poor countries their best hope of escaping poverty."[57] It is encouraging that in 2003, Canada finally eliminated most of the tariffs and quotas affecting imports from the 47 poorest countries in the world.

Another trade agreement that harms the world's poorest nations is the World Trade Organization's *Agreement on Trade-Related Aspects of Intellectual Property Rights*, known as the TRIPS Agreement. A major concern in many developing nations, particularly in Africa, is affordable access to medicine. According to the World Health Organization, one million people in developing countries die from malaria because they do not have access to effective treatment, and thirty million people live with HIV without access to the drugs that could prolong their lives and reduce their suffering.[58] Protection for patented drugs under the TRIPS Agreement blocks developing countries' access to affordable generic drugs. People in African countries suffering from devastating problems with HIV/AIDS and other diseases are effectively denied medicine because patented drugs are prohibitively expensive and generic drugs are unavailable. Unfortunately, in international negotiations to resolve this problem, Canada is taking the side of pharmaceutical companies, who argue that their profitability and ability to develop new medicines depends on protecting their patent rights.[59]

Moving Forward
On the international front, Canada is failing to live up to its promises to assist developing countries with the battle against population growth and poverty. Canada should take the following steps to fulfill its international commitments to reducing population growth, eliminating poverty, and promoting sustainable development:

- legislate and fulfill the commitment, made at the Cairo Conference, to contribute $200 million annually to funding population programs in developing countries[60]
- restore funding to the International Planned Parenthood Foundation
- reinstate the population research program at the International Development Research Centre

- legislate a commitment, to be phased in over five years, to raise Canadian ODA to a minimum of 0.7 percent of GDP, increasing gradually to 1 percent of GDP by the end of the decade (as Sweden has done)
- reduce the amount of tied aid, particularly for the world's poorest countries
- completely cancel Canada's share of the debt of developing countries that meet certain conditions related to human rights, democracy, poverty reduction, and sustainable development
- remove all remaining trade barriers that have a disproportionately negative effect on poor countries, such as high tariffs on agricultural products
- ensure that trade agreements such as the *Agreement on Trade-Related Aspects of Intellectual Property Rights* are amended to meet the needs of developing countries for public health and access to affordable medicines, specifically generic drugs
- focus on transferring environmentally friendly technology and building human capital
- promote international action on population, poverty, and sustainable development through Canada's role in the UN, the G8, La Francophonie, and the Commonwealth.

While it is encouraging that Canada has recently announced that it will increase ODA, untie aid, and reduce quotas and duties targeting poor countries, the jury is out until concrete evidence of progress can be shown.[61]

Canada's Population

Is the current size of Canada's population problematic, from an environmental perspective? Does the current rate of population growth in Canada constitute an environmental concern? Both of these questions can be answered in the negative. One could argue that the size of Canada's population is important because the average Canadian has a disproportionate ecological impact on the planet, as a result of high levels of consumption and pollution.[62] Canadians have the third largest ecological footprint on Earth. According to the United Nations, "A child born in the industrial world adds more to pollution and consumption levels than do 30-50 children born in developing countries."[63] With a population of 31 million people, Canada produces more greenhouse gas emissions than the entire continent of Africa, with its 700 million people. However, these facts highlight the problem of *excessive consumption, not overpopulation*. Canada's population constitutes only 0.5 percent of the world's population. At more than one hundred times the area of Bangladesh, Canada has only one-quarter of the Bangladesh population. Canada is geographically larger than India or China, yet has less than one-thirtieth of the number of people of these populous nations, each of which has more than a billion residents. It is difficult to argue that Canada, with its huge size, small population, and incredible natural wealth is, in any sense, overpopulated at the current time.[64]

Is Canada's population growing too quickly? Some doomsayers warn that Canada faces "a dismal and crowded future brought about by massive immigration."[65] Like the rest of the world, Canada experienced a population boom in the twentieth century. In fact, Canadian population growth exceeded the global average, as Canada grew from 5.3 million people in 1901 to more than 31 million in 2001.[66] Although the rate of population growth has slowed in recent decades, Canada's population continues to grow by around 1 percent per year. At the current rate of growth, Canada's population will double, to over 60 million people, in seventy years. However, current rates of population growth in Canada are not expected to continue. Statistics Canada has modelled three scenarios for population growth – low, medium, and high – based on differing assumptions about fertility rates and net migration. Under the high-growth scenario, there will be 50 million Canadians by 2041. The medium-growth scenario produces a projection of 42 million and the low-growth estimate is 35 million.[67]

Population growth in Canada is the product of two factors: the rate by which births exceed deaths (known as the rate of natural increase), and the rate by which immigration exceeds emigration (known as net migration). At the present time, there are 11.8 births per thousand people in Canada annually and 7.3 deaths per thousand people, producing a modest natural increase in population.[68] However, according to Statistics Canada, the Canadian rate of natural increase will hit zero in 2020, because of the aging population and a declining average fertility rate.[69] From 2020 onward, net migration will determine whether Canada's population falls, stabilizes, or continues to increase.

Immigration and Population Growth in Canada

Immigration in Canada is governed by the *Immigration and Refugee Protection Act*, which requires the minister of immigration to set immigration targets on an annual basis. Canada planned to add 225,000 immigrants in 2001 and actually welcomed 250,000 immigrants. The federal government is "committed to gradually increasing the volume of immigrants to approximately 1 percent of the population," which means roughly 310,000 immigrants per year, based on current Canadian population figures.[70] If Canada increases its population by 1 percent annually through immigration, the Canadian population will double in about seventy years.

Canada has three main categories for prospective immigrants: refugees, applicants seeking to be reunited with their families, and economic immigrants (including skilled workers, investors, entrepreneurs, and the self-employed).[71] Canada is legally bound to comply with the *United Nations Convention and Protocol Relating to the Status of Refugees*, including an obligation to give a fair hearing to refugees seeking asylum. As a wealthy humanitarian nation Canada has a moral responsibility to provide a safe haven for some of the world's refugees. In fact, Canada is internationally renowned for our generous refugee policy. Canada also has a responsibility to contribute to resolving the root causes of conflicts that are creating refugees, through various programs aimed at fostering democracy, human rights, and sustainable development. There are equally obvious and compelling humanitarian reasons for reuniting families when some family members already live in Canada.

To some degree, the arguments for admitting skilled workers and investors are less persuasive, as Canada is motivated more by economic self-interest than by humanitarian concerns or the pursuit of social justice. Investors must have a net worth of $800,000 and must provide $400,000 to the receiver general for five years without interest. Entrepreneurs must create at least one new job for a Canadian citizen. Applicants in the self-employed category are individuals who intend to establish or purchase a business in Canada that will create an employment opportunity and will make a significant contribution to the economy or the cultural or artistic life of Canada.[72] The breakdown in the year 2001 was roughly 140,000 skilled workers and professionals, 15,000 business immigrants, 67,000 family members, and 28,000 refugees.[73]

Canada has a rich history and tradition of accepting immigrants, albeit scarred by regrettable incidents of racism. Immigration presents both daunting challenges and intriguing opportunities. Careful planning is needed to achieve political unity while maintaining cultural diversity, and to be inclusive without being assimilationist. Canada has been described as the world's most successful experiment in multiculturalism and a model for a global future of peace and harmony.[74] But many legitimate questions can be raised about immigration policy in Canada. Should immigrants be required to have a university education?[75] Should Canada recruit professionals from developing countries where their services are urgently needed?

In comparison with the political, social, economic, and cultural issues associated with immigration, concerns about the environmental impact of immigration to Canada are ill-conceived. Population growth is a global issue, and immigration does not directly affect global population growth. From a global perspective, immigration is neutral – increasing environmental pressure in one country and reducing environmental pressure in another country. The indirect effect of immigration to Canada may be to *reduce* the global rate of population growth, since Canadian families tend to be smaller than families in other countries. Immigrants may consume more resources in Canada than they would have consumed in their previous country of residence. However, in the words of Alan Durning, author of *How Much Is Enough?*, "Limiting the consumer life-style to those who have already attained it is not politically possible [or] morally defensible."[76]

Conclusion

Just as Canada was a leader in the campaigns to eliminate the use of land mines, ban persistent organic pollutants, and protect the stratospheric ozone layer, Canada should embrace a leadership role in tackling the international challenges of reducing population growth and promoting sustainable development. Canada's present record leaves much to be desired on funding for population programs, providing ODA, forgiving the debt of the world's poorest countries, and eliminating trade barriers that harm developing countries. To be a global leader in the field of sustainable development, Canada needs to fulfill its outstanding commitments and ensure that its actions live up to its words. If the ambitious Millennium Development Goals identified by the United Nations in 2000 are to be achieved, wealthy nations like Canada are going to have to dramatically increase their financial commitment to reducing poverty and creating a more just, democratic, and sustainable human society. It seems like a small price to pay for a markedly better world.

15 Conclusion

We must draw our standards from the natural world.
We must honour with the humility of the wise the
bounds of that natural world and the mystery which
lies beyond them, admitting that there is something
in the order of being which evidently exceeds all our
competence.

Vaclav Havel, President of the Czech Republic, 1993-2003

Sustainability is not a lofty ideal or an academic concept but rather an urgent imperative for humanity. In a sustainable future, air and water would be clean, so that no Canadian would ever think twice about going outside for a walk or drinking a glass of tap water. Food would be free from pesticide residues, antibiotics, and growth hormones. Air, water, and soil would be uncontaminated by toxic substances. In a sustainable future, it would be safe to swim in every Canadian river and lake, safe to eat fish wherever they were caught. A diverse range of clean, renewable sources harnessing the sun, the wind, water, and the heat of the Earth would provide energy.

A sustainable future would mean a global climate undisturbed by human activity. Canadians would no longer fear sunburn or cancer caused by damage to the ozone layer. Concerns about radiation from nuclear waste would be laid to rest. No one would have to worry about nature's extraordinary diversity diminishing at human hands. Endangered ecosystems and species at risk, from old-growth forests to beluga whales, would recover and thrive. In a sustainable future, Canadians would be confident that their children, grandchildren, and many more future generations would enjoy the same spectacular natural heritage and quality of life that Canadians enjoy today. A sustainable future is a powerful, appealing vision. Unfortunately, as this book reveals, the prospects of a sustainable future for Canadians appear to be growing dimmer, not brighter.

Examination

The federal government claims that Canada is "a world leader in sustainability."[1] This book's examination of the laws and policies intended to protect Canada's water, air, land, and biodiversity proves beyond a reasonable doubt that this claim is false. Canada is a world leader not in sustainability but in energy and water consumption, greenhouse gas emissions, and per capita environmental impact. More Canadians die every year from air pollution than from homicide. Canada's record on energy efficiency is among the worst in the industrialized world. Hundreds of communities, from British Columbia to Newfoundland, must boil their drinking water. One of the most widely used pesticides in Canada, atrazine, turns frogs into hermaphrodites when they are exposed to the pesticide at levels commonly found in Canadian drinking water. Killer whales on the west coast and beluga whales on the east coast are among the world's most toxic mammals because of industrial pollution. Mines operated by Canadian companies have left a legacy of contaminated sites not only in Canada but around the world, from Guyana to the Philippines. Canada's forests are being logged faster than ever. Stockpiles of nuclear waste are growing. More species are added to Canada's burgeoning list of endangered species every year. Climate-changing greenhouse gas emissions are up 20 percent since 1990. Thirty-eight of Canada's thirty-nine national parks face serious ecological problems. Atlantic cod are not recovering from decades of overfishing.

On the other hand, Canadian environmental law and policy evolved rapidly over the past three decades, producing significant progress on some environmental issues, including dramatic reductions in the production and use of ozone-depleting substances, reductions in garbage, improvements in municipal sewage treatment, rapid advances in energy efficiency for appliances, major declines in some types of industrial air and water pollution, and an increase in protected areas. In general, however, while some of Canada's environmental problems have been addressed, "other more complex and recalcitrant stresses have arisen that pose greater challenges."[2] For example, the compelling threat of ozone depletion was addressed, only to be replaced by the more abstract threat of climate change. Blatant pollution of air and water by industrial facilities has abated somewhat, but the invisible danger has grown from toxic substances capable of causing extensive health and environmental damage at extremely low levels, years into the future and thousands of kilometres from their point of release. On the majority of environmental indicators, Canada is moving away from, not toward, sustainability. Despite evidence from opinion polls indicating that Canadians value the environment highly, and despite Canada's incredible natural heritage, Canada lags behind most industrialized nations in environmental performance.

Diagnosis

On the issues where environmental progress has been made in Canada, the reasons include international pressure, effective laws and regulations, federal leadership, intergovernmental cooperation, pressure from environmental groups and the public, progressive decisions from the Supreme Court of Canada, proactive steps taken by local governments, and in some cases, the emulation of American environmental laws and policies. It is vital to acknowledge that gains have been made, and to build on these successes. It is equally important to understand the reasons for Canada's generally poor record relative to other industrialized nations. The Canadian system of environmental law is weak, inconsistent, narrow, unscientific, plagued by discretion, undermined by budget cuts, inadequate enforcement, and a lack of effective checks and balances, and subject to manipulation by society's most powerful interests. These critical environmental law and policy problems have been recognized for decades but never rectified.

Obstacles to environmental progress include the continuing priority given to economic growth over environmental protection, difficulties created by international trade liberalization, structural flaws in Canada's political system, and barriers limiting the effectiveness of judicial intervention. At a deeper level, the most fundamental roadblock to achieving a sustainable future is Canada's failure to acknowledge that there are physical limits to the amount of resources the Earth can provide and the amount of waste the Earth can assimilate. Because of these physical limits, continued economic growth, to the extent that it is based on an ever-increasing flow of energy and resources, is ecologically unsustainable in industrialized nations like Canada. While excess consumption is the root cause of environmental degradation in the industrialized world, continued population growth in the developing world exacerbates poverty, social problems, and environmental degradation. Canada has an important international role to play in addressing all of these threats to global sustainability.

Prescription

Achieving an ecologically sustainable future requires Canada to recognize that there are laws of nature, such as the laws of thermodynamics, which are immutable, irrevocable, written in stone. As Albert Einstein observed, "Everything that takes place is determined by laws of nature."[3] Despite humanity's prodigious ingenuity we cannot escape or repeal them.[4] These laws compel us to avoid subjecting nature to increasing concentrations of substances extracted from the Earth's crust, increasing concentrations of substances produced by society, or degradation of nature's productivity, resilience, or diversity. Canada needs to reconfigure its laws, institutions, and economy to reflect these ecological principles and, in particular, to recognize the fundamental reality that the Earth has limits.

As Canadian environmental law grapples with the emerging challenges of the twenty-first century, we find ourselves at a fork in the road, with the United

States and Sweden epitomizing the different directions we can take. On one hand, Canada can continue to follow the reactive American model, enacting increasingly complex laws and regulations in an effort to mitigate the environmental impacts of an energy- and resource-intensive industrial economy. The American experience, where the world's strongest environmental laws have failed to address the problems caused by constant economic and population growth, demonstrates that strong environmental laws are not sufficient to achieve sustainability, largely because they do not address the root causes of environmental degradation.

On the other hand, Canada could choose to change direction, following the trail blazed by Sweden and other European nations in implementing a more proactive and ecological vision of environmental law and policy. Instead of trying to accomplish the impossible task of limiting the environmental impacts of an economy that consumes growing volumes of energy and resources, Sweden is restructuring its economy to incorporate ecological limits and principles.

The choice for Canada is obvious, because only the ecological path taken by Sweden and other European nations can deliver the future that Canadians desire and that the planet requires. Achieving a sustainable future requires decreasing consumption of energy and natural resources in the industrialized world. Canada must implement policies that achieve dematerialization and substitution, maximize efficiency and productivity, substitute renewable resources for nonrenewable resources (especially fossil fuels), replace unnatural, persistent, environmentally harmful substances with natural, biodegradable, safe substances, and substitute knowledge and services for raw materials and commodities. Moving in the direction of sustainability also requires narrowing the gap between industrialized nations and the developing world by increasing official development assistance, forgiving debts, and reforming harmful trade policies. At the international level it is essential that the hegemony of free trade over environmental protection be reversed.

To move forward, Canada needs a national strategy containing targets, timelines, and tactics aimed at achieving sustainability within a generation. A new wave of social, economic, and environmental laws and policies, designed to ensure that Canada complies with the three scientific conditions of ecological sustainability, must be drafted and implemented. Canada needs to stop single-mindedly striving for economic growth and start pursuing more holistic, balanced societal goals, as measured by indices such as the Genuine Progress Index. Canadians need to focus on improving their quality of life rather than merely accumulating more material possessions. Ultimately, as David Suzuki and other environmental visionaries point out, "Sustainable living demands a fundamental shift in values."[5]

Urgency
The window of opportunity for making the many changes required to achieve

a sustainable future is closing. According to the best scientific evidence, species are becoming extinct every day, as the tapestry of life slowly unravels. Human demands on the planet are exceeding the Earth's limits. Scientists are increasingly concerned about the prospect of irreversible system "flips" that would result in nonlinear losses of ecosystem services.[6] In other words, scientists fear that human impacts on the Earth may cross unknown thresholds, after which catastrophic changes will occur that threaten our very existence. For example, climate change could disrupt the currents in the Atlantic Ocean that transport warm water northward and provide Europe with a temperate climate despite its northern latitude.[7] Renowned Canadian ecologist Buzz Holling warns that "surprise is inevitable" in complex systems perturbed by humans.[8] The prospect of catastrophic and surprising changes in global systems that are vital to supporting life on Earth increases the urgency of acting quickly and abiding by the precautionary principle. We need to avoid causing ecological catastrophes, not attempt to adapt to them or mitigate their impacts once they occur. Although complexity and uncertainty preclude us from foreseeing the path to sustainability with any degree of precision, we already know enough to move in the right direction.

Priorities

Canada's environmental challenges must be placed in a global context before wise decisions can be made about priorities. While Canadians unquestionably have an obligation to take better care of our own water, air, land, and biodiversity, the plight of other people and places demands our attention. More than two billion people lack access to safe sanitation and one billion people lack access to safe drinking water, causing millions of preventable deaths annually. Every year, air pollution causes hundreds of thousands of avoidable deaths in poorer countries. In light of these profoundly disturbing facts, Canada has an ethical duty to be a global leader in developing, promoting, and implementing solutions to these problems. Ultimately, our greatest contribution will be measured not in dollars, but in terms of international leadership. By making a concerted effort to address poverty, we could sow the seeds of a better future for the world's children and future generations to harvest.

Hope

> If people come to understand that support for sustainability-oriented policies will actually increase their personal well-being while enhancing their communities, then nothing can hold us back.
> *Professor William Rees, University of British Columbia*

The challenges that lie ahead in the struggle for a sustainable future are daunting in scope and scale, but humans have extraordinary problem-solving capacity. Humans succeeded in setting foot on the moon, a place that is 384,000 kilometres away. Humans succeeded in decoding the staggering complexity of the human genome. Humans reacted rapidly, collectively, to address the global threat of ozone depletion. These accomplishments suggest that we have the capacity to live on the Earth in a harmonious and genuinely sustainable manner. Sustainable solutions to today's problems exist, but in order to implement these solutions and fulfill our obligations to future generations we must summon unprecedented compassion and tap unused reservoirs of ingenuity. We need to demonstrate humility, not hubris; act on the basis of wisdom, not wishful thinking; and recognize that we are part of, not separate from, nature.

Canadians are stewards of substantial portions of the world's water, wetlands, forests, wildlife, and wilderness. Canadians are also one of the wealthiest and best-educated peoples in the history of the world. These facts impose an obligation on Canada to improve its environmental record. Only when our everyday actions live up to our aspirations will Canadian astronaut Roberta Bondar's vision of Canada as "the salvation of the whole planet" be possible. In light of our deep passion for nature and our unparalleled natural wealth, Canadians could, and should, help lead the world toward the holy grail of a sustainable future.

Notes

Preface
1 Lee (1993, 200).

1: Canada's Environmental Record
1 Duffy (1998); Angus (1997).
2 Environics International (1999).
3 Pynn (1999).
4 Statistics Canada (2000, 295); Baxter (2000).
5 Nevitte (1996).
6 On biological diversity, see Sierra Legal Defence Fund (2002e); on forests, see May (1998); on climate change, see Hornung (1998); on health and pesticides, see Canadian Environmental Law Association and the Ontario College of Family Physicians (2000); on water, see Christensen (2001); on mining, see Mining Watch Canada (2000); and on environmental assessment, see Nikiforuk (1997).
7 Suzuki and Gordon (1990, 3).
8 Environics International (1999).
9 UN Environment Program (2002); OECD (2001c); Union of Concerned Scientists (1992).
10 On forests and development, see Natural Resources Canada (2001b); on mining, see Natural Resources Canada (2002); on water, see Health Canada (1993); on pesticides, see Allan Rock, Minister of Health, Written Statement re Bill C-388, quoted in Swaigen (2001, 176); on assessment, see Canadian Environmental Assessment Agency (2000a, 3).
11 Jones, Fredricksen, and Wates (2002).
12 Jones (2000, A7).
13 Boyd (2001a).
14 The Slovak Republic joined the OECD in 2000, bringing the total number of member countries to thirty. The OECD's mandate is to help governments tackle the social, economic, and governance challenges associated with globalization.
15 Boyd (2001a).
16 Porter et al. (2000).
17 OECD (2000a).
18 OECD (2002b, 44).
19 OECD (1995a).
20 Wackernagel et al. (1999; 2002a).
21 Commissioner of the Environment and Sustainable Development (1998; 1999; 2000, 5; 2001b, 7; 2002).
22 Auditor General of Canada (2000b; 1999b; 1999c; 1998; 1997a; 1997c).
23 Prescott-Allan (2001).
24 World Economic Forum (2002). The Environmental Sustainability Index (ESI) covers a broad range of issues including traditional environmental indicators (water pollution, air pollution, etc.) and many unconventional indicators (child death rate from respiratory diseases, number of research and development scientists, number of scientific articles published, number of memberships in environmental groups, the extent of corruption, and the availability of

information). Some of the indicators are undermined by subjectivity and potential bias. For example, a limited survey of corporate executives is used to determine the stringency and consistency of environmental regulations. The ESI, as its authors admit, is a work in progress, evolving as feedback on its approach is received from other experts.

25 Environics International (2001).
26 OECD (1999b).
27 Commissioner of the Environment and Sustainable Development (1998).
28 Boyd (2001a).
29 Environics International (2001).
30 Canadian Press (1999).
31 Gherson (1998).
32 Scoffield (1999b).
33 Sinclair and Grieshaber-Otto (2002); McCarthy (2001).
34 For an excellent summary of the basic aspects of Canada's legal system, see Swaigen (1993).
35 Harrison (1995); Benidickson (2002).

2: Water

1 Scoffield (1998b).
2 The 6 percent figure is from Gleick (1993), while Environment Canada (1996c, 10-1) estimates 9 percent.
3 de Villiers (1999, 367-73).
4 OECD (1999b).
5 Postel, Daily, and Ehrlich (1996).
6 Environment Canada (1996c, 10-32).
7 Tate (1987, 63).
8 Environment Canada (2001g).
9 International Joint Commission (2000a).
10 Holmes (1999).
11 Environment Canada (1999e, 14).
12 Statistics Canada (2001d).
13 Van Der Leeden, Troise, and Todd (1990).
14 Environment Canada (1996c, 10-43).
15 Health Canada (1998a).
16 Linton (1997, 47).
17 Standing Committee on Environment and Sustainable Development (2000).
18 Nikiforuk (2000).
19 Pearse, Bertrand, and MacLaren (1985); Environment Canada (1987).

2.1: Drinking Water

1 Christensen (2001).
2 BC Provincial Health Officer (2001).
3 Health Canada (1995).
4 Health Canada (1997, 88).
5 Environment Canada (1996c, 12-17).
6 Auditor General of BC (1999).
7 Health Canada (1997).
8 Environment Canada (n.d.c).
9 Christensen (2001, 3).
10 Health Canada (1997, 85).
11 World Health Organization and UN Children's Fund (2000).
12 UN Environment Program (1997).
13 World Health Organization and United Nations Children's Fund (2000).
14 Barzilay, Weinberg, and Eley (1999); Guillette and Crain (2000).
15 O'Connor (2002a; 2002b); Laing (2002); Canadian Environmental Law Association (2001); Christensen (2001); BC Provincial Health Officer (2001); Auditor General of BC (1999); BC Drinking Water Review Panel (2002).
16 For example, Ontario's *Safe Drinking Water Act*, S.O. 2002, c. 32; Quebec's *Drinking Water Regulation*, c. Q-2, r. 4.1; Manitoba's *Drinking Water Safety Act*, C.C.S.M. D-101; and Saskatchewan's *Environmental Management and Protection Act*, S.S. 2002, c. E-10.21.
17 Schindler (2001, 21).

18   Christensen (2001, 17).
19   Shrybman (2000, 12).
20   Auditor General of BC (1999, 13).
21   See the City of New York website, <http://www.ci.nyc.ny.us/html/dep>.
22   For example, *Water Protection Act,* S.N.L. 2002, c. W-4.01, s. 39; Nova Scotia, *Environment Act,* S.N.S. 1994-95, c. 1, s. 106; *Clean Water Act,* S.N.B. 1989, c. C-6.1, s. 14, *Watershed Protected Area Designation Order,* N.B. Reg. 2001-83, *Water Classification Regulation,* N.B. Reg. 2002-13, and *Wellfield Protected Area Designation Order,* N.B. Reg. 2000-47; *Ontario Water Resources Act,* R.S.O. 1990, c. O-40, s. 33; Manitoba's *Protection of Water Sources Regulation,* Man. Reg. 326/88 under the *Public Health Act,* C.C.S.M. P-210, and *Sensitive Areas Regulation,* Man. Reg. 126/88 under the *Environment Act,* C.C.S.M. E-125.
23   *Watershed Protected Area Designation Order,* N.B. Reg. 2001-83.
24   *Public Water Supplies Regulation,* R.R.N.W.T. c. P-23, s. 8.
25   *Drinking Water Protection Act,* S.B.C. 2001, c. 9, s. 25.
26   Parfitt (2000).
27   Auditor General of BC (1999); BC Provincial Health Officer (2001).
28   For example see *Re: Gold Mountain Springs* (2002); Ontario's *Planning Act,* R.S.O. 1990, c. P-13.
29   Christensen (2001, 29-30).
30   Mills et al. (1998); Reif et al. (1996); Magnus et al. (1999).
31   Schindler (2001).
32   The Federation of Canadian Municipalities estimate is $16.5 billion <http://www.fcm.ca>. The Canadian Waste and Wastewater Association estimate is $88 billion <http://www.cwwa.org>. Environment Canada (1990a) suggests $100 billion.
33   *Drinking Water Materials Safety Act, 1996* (Bill C-76).
34   CBC, "Lead and Drinking Water," *Marketplace,* aired 27 March 2001; see <http://www.cbc.ca/marketplace>.
35   O'Connor (2002a).
36   *Safe Drinking Water Act,* S.O. 2002, c. 32; *Drinking Water Protection Regulation,* Ont. Reg. 459/00, ss. 5-14.
37   Health Canada (1997, 100).
38   *Ibid.*
39   Commissioner of the Environment and Sustainable Development (2001a, 117).
40   The Capital Regional District adds that "where appropriate" it uses the US EPA drinking water rules "on a voluntary basis" as "goals" <http://www.crd.bc.ca/water>.
41   Laing (2002, 28).
42   British Columbia *Drinking Water Protection Regulation,* B.C. Reg. 200/2003 addresses only fecal coliforms, total coliforms and E. Coli. B.C. Reg. 120/2001 required testing for more than eighty contaminants but was overturned by BC's new provincial government in September 2001.
43   Mittelstaedt (2002b).
44   Christensen (2001, 32-4).
45   O'Connor (2002a).
46   *Drinking Water Protection Regulation,* Ont. Reg. 459/00.
47   *Water Regulations,* 2002, c. E-10.21, Reg. 1.
48   Ironically, the communities most likely to provide voluntary drinking water reports are those with consistently excellent drinking water, such as Calgary (see <http://www.calgarywaterworks.com>).
49   O'Connor (2002a).
50   Laing (2002).
51   BC Ministry of Sustainable Resource Management (2002).
52   Canadian Press (2002).
53   Peritz (2001).
54   O'Connor (2002b).
55   Vigod and Wordsworth (1982, 92).
56   Environment Canada (1990a, 28, 35).
57   Health Canada (1997, 100).
58   *Drinking Water Materials Safety Act, 1996,* Bill C-76.
59   *An Act to Amend the Food and Drug Act (Clean drinking water),* Bill S-18 (2001).
60   *Safe Drinking Water Act,* 2002 S.O. 2002, c. 32, and *Drinking Water Protection Regulations,* Ont. Regs. 459/00, 505/01; Quebec's *Regulation respecting the quality of drinking water,* O.C. 647-2001;

Drinking Water Safety Act, S.M. 2002, c. 36, C.C.S.M. D-101; *Environmental Management and Protection Act,* S.S. 2002, c. E-10.21, and *Water Regulations,* 2002, c. E-10.21, Reg. 1; *Drinking Water Protection Act,* S.B.C. 2001, c. 9; Yukon Department of Renewable Resources (2001, 7).
61 *Red Mountain Residents and Property Owner's Association* v. *B.C. (Ministry of Forests)* (2000, 131).
62 Warburton et al. (1998).
63 Health Canada (1997, 82).
64 *Safe Drinking Water Act Amendments of 1996,* Public Law 104-182.
65 US Environmental Protection Agency (n.d.).
66 Christensen (2001, 34); see also DeMarco and Christensen (2002).
67 Christensen (2001, 34).
68 Canadian Environmental Law Association (2001, 14).
69 US Environmental Protection Agency (n.d.).
70 Olson (1998).
71 Bennett et al. (1987).
72 US Council on Environmental Quality (1996).
73 US Environmental Protection Agency (n.d.).
74 Hawken, Lovins, and Lovins (1999, 338).
75 US Environmental Protection Agency (n.d.).
76 *Ibid.*
77 US Environmental Protection Agency (n.d.).
78 The Hon. Chris Stockwell (2002), Second Reading Debate on Bill 195 (*Hansard,* 31 October 2002).

2.2 Water Pollution
1 Commission for Environmental Cooperation (1994, 19); Environment Canada (2001c, 14).
2 Environment Canada (1996c, 10-40).
3 BC Ministry of Environment, Land and Parks (2000, 31).
4 Environment Canada (1996c).
5 Environment Canada (2001c, 14).
6 Statistics Canada (2001d).
7 Schindler (1999; 2001).
8 Environment Canada (1996c, 11-62).
9 *Ibid.,* 10-54.
10 International Joint Commission (2000b).
11 Federal laws include the *Canadian Environmental Protection Act, 1999,* S.C. 1999, c. 33; *Fisheries Act,* R.S.C. 1985, c. F-14; *Canada Shipping Act,* R.S.C. 1985, c. s-9; *Canada Water Act,* R.S.C. 1985, c. C-11; and *Arctic Waters Pollution Prevention Act,* R.S.C. 1985, c. A-12. Provincial laws include *Waste Management Act,* R.S.B.C. 1996, c. 482; *Environmental Protection and Enhancement Act,* R.S.A. 2000, c. E-12; *Environmental Management and Protection Act,* S.S. 2002, c. E-10.21; *Environment Act,* C.C.S.M. c. E-125; *Ontario Water Resources Act,* R.S.O. 1990, c. O-40 and Ontario's *Environmental Protection Act,* R.S.O. 1990, c. E-19; *Environmental Quality Act,* R.S.Q. 1977, c. Q-2; *Environment Act,* S.N.S. 1994-95, c. 1; *Environmental Protection Act,* S.N. 2002, c. E-14.2; *Environmental Protection Act,* R.S.P.E.I. 1988, c. E-9; *Clean Environment Act,* R.S.N.B. 1973, c. C-6 and *Clean Water Act,* R.S.N.B. 1973, c. C-6.1; *Environmental Protection Act,* R.S.N.W.T. 1988, c. E-7; and *Environment Act,* S.Y. 1992, c. 5.
12 Although BC's *Waste Management Act* is being replaced by the *Environmental Management Act* in 2003 (Bill 57), the system is unchanged.
13 Canadian Council of Ministers of the Environment (1999).
14 Schrecker (2001); Hoberg (1997); VanderZwaag (1995, 424-5).
15 For example, *Chlor-Alkali Mercury Liquid Effluent Regulations,* C.R.C. 1978 c. 811.
16 For example, *Pulp and Paper Effluent Regulations,* SOR/92-269; *Phosphorous Concentration Regulations,* SOR/89-501.
17 Muldoon and Valiante (1989, 44).
18 Rueggeberg and Thompson (1985, 17).
19 Environmental Bureau of Investigation (2000, 52-3).
20 Task Force on Environmental Contaminants Legislation (1972).
21 *Canadian Environmental Protection Act, 1999,* S.C. 1999, c. 33, ss. 2(1)(a), 44, 54, 56-63, and 90; *Environment Act,* S.N.S. 1994-95, c. 1, ss. 2(b) and 8(2).
22 Environment Canada (2001c).
23 Estrin and Swaigen (1993).

24 The original *Phosphorous Concentration Control Regulations* were under the *Canada Water Act*, R.S.C. 1970, c. 5, 1st Supp.
25 Linton (1997, 118).
26 International Joint Commission (2000b).
27 For a good overview of efforts made to clean up the Great Lakes, see Sproule-Jones (2002).
28 International Joint Commission (2000b, 4).
29 Estrin and Swaigen (1993, 573).
30 Commissioner of the Environment and Sustainable Development (1999, 3-19; 2001b, 278).
31 Environment Canada (1998e).
32 Department of Fisheries and Oceans (1998, 3).
33 Environment Canada (1996c, 11-109).
34 *Ibid.*, 11-82; *Petroleum Refinery Effluent Regulations*, C.R.C. 1978, c. 828.
35 Environment Canada (1998b).
36 *Metal Mining Liquid Effluent Regulations*, C.R.C. 1978, c. 819; *Canadian Environmental Protection Act, 1999*, S.C. 1999, c. 33, Schedule 1, List of Toxic Substances.
37 Environment Canada (1998e, 26).
38 *Antisapstain Chemical Waste Control Regulation*, B.C. Reg. 300/90; Krahn (1998); Environment Canada (1998e).
39 Macdonald (1991, 239).
40 *Pulp and Paper Effluent Regulations*, SOR/92-269 *(Fisheries Act); Pulp and Paper Mill Effluent Chlorinated Dioxins and Furans Regulations*, SOR/92-267, as amended *(Canadian Environmental Protection Act, 1999); Pulp and Paper Mill Defoamer and Wood Chip Regulations*, SOR/92-282 *(Canadian Environmental Protection Act, 1999)*.
41 For example, *Pulp Mill and Pulp and Paper Mill Liquid Effluent Control Regulation*, B.C. Reg. 470/90.
42 Macdonald (1991).
43 *Fisheries Act*, R.S.C. 1985, c. F-14, s. 78; *Canadian Environmental Protection Act, 1999*, S.C. 1999, c. 33, s. 272(2); Environment Canada (1996c, 11-33).
44 Environment Canada (1998b; 1996c). These percentage decreases are based on pollution per tonne of production – if production increases, so does the amount of pollution. Thus to some extent these gains are overstated.
45 *Pulp and Paper Effluent Regulations*, SOR/92-269 *(Fisheries Act); Pulp and Paper Mill Defoamer and Wood Chip Regulations*, SOR/92-282; *Pulp and Paper Mill Effluent Chlorinated Dioxins and Furans Regulations*, SOR/92-267, as amended. Dioxins and furans are also regulated by the *Canadian Environmental Protection Act, 1999*, S.C. 1999, c. 33.
46 *Pulp Mill and Pulp and Paper Mill Liquid Effluent Control Regulation*, B.C. Reg. 470/90, as amended.
47 Leiss (2001, ch. 6).
48 Commission for Environmental Cooperation (2001b, 60).
49 Environment Canada (n.d.c).
50 Christie (2000).
51 *R. v. Corner Brook Pulp and Paper* (1997).
52 Krahn (1998).
53 Environment Canada (1999c), Summary 99-23.
54 Pearse and Quinn (1996, 330).
55 The Ontario government stopped publishing a list of polluters in 1996, ostensibly as a cost-cutting measure. The Sierra Legal Defence Fund obtains the data through Freedom of Information requests and publishes it. See Sierra Legal Defence Fund (2002f; 2001a; 2000; 1999).
56 Sierra Legal Defence Fund (1999).
57 National Pollutant Release Inventory (1999) at the NPRI home page, <http://www.ec.gc.ca>.
58 OECD (1999b).
59 Nova Scotia Department of Environment (1998, 36).
60 Environment Canada (2001g).
61 Environment Canada (1996c, 10-40).
62 Holmes (1999).
63 *Fisheries Act*, R.S.C. 1985, c. F-14, s. 36(3); Environment Canada and Quebec Ministry of Environment and Wildlife (1998).
64 Holmes (1999, 58-9).
65 Holmes (1999).
66 For further details on private prosecutions, see Chapter 8.

67 Holmes (1999).
68 Brower and Leon (1999, 219).
69 OECD (1995a, 203).
70 O'Connor (2002a).
71 OECD (1999b, 286).
72 Commissioner of the Environment and Sustainable Development (2001b).
73 Statistics Canada (2001d).
74 Auditor General of Quebec (1996).
75 Commissioner of the Environment and Sustainable Development (2001b).
76 *Ibid.*
77 Environmental Commissioner of Ontario (2000b, 9).
78 Ontario's *Environmental Protection Act,* R.S.O. 1990, c. E-19, ss. 6(2), 14(2), 15(2), and 91(4);
    see also BC's *Waste Management Act,* R.S.B.C. 1996, c. 482, and *Agricultural Waste Control
    Regulation,* B.C. Reg. 131/92, s. 2.
79 For example, *Ontario Farming and Food Production and Protection Act,* S.O. 1998, c. 1.
80 *Livestock Operations Act,* S.N.B. 1999, c. L-11.01; *Livestock Manure and Mortalities Regulation,*
    Man. Reg. 81/94; *An Act Respecting Agricultural Operations,* S.S. 1998, c. A-12.1; *Agriculture
    Operation Practices Act,* R.S.A. 2000, c. A-7; *Regulation on the reduction of pollution from agricultural
    sources* pursuant to the *Environmental Quality Act,* R.S.Q., 1994, c. Q-2.
81 *Nutrient Management Act,* S.O. 2002, c. 4.
82 See Citizen Submissions on Enforcement Matters at <http://www.cec.org>.
83 de Villiers (1999, 290).
84 Anderson (1990, 310).
85 Environment Canada (n.d.b).
86 Winfield and Swaigen (1993, 573).
87 West Coast Environmental Law Association (2001); Curran and Leung (2000).
88 Schindler (2001, 18).
89 Jackson (1997).
90 Muldoon and Valiante (1989).
91 Fraser Institute (1998, 7-8); Driscoll et al. (2001, 180); Environment Canada (1998a).
92 Linton (1997, 37); Environment Canada (1998a).
93 Selin and Hjelm (1999, 63).
94 US National Research Council (1999a); Colborn, Dumanoski, and Myers (1996).
95 International Joint Commission (1995, ch. 2); Colborn, Dumanoski, and Myers (1996).
96 *Canadian Environmental Protection Act, 1999,* S.C. 1999, c. 33, s. 2.
97 *Ibid.,* ss. 91-2.
98 *Ibid.,* s. 77(4). See also the *Persistence and Bioaccumulation Regulation,* SOR/2000-107.
99 US National Research Council (1996a).
100 Environment Canada (1996c, 13-4).
101 *Ibid.*
102 Roe and Pease (1998).
103 OECD (1995a, 203).
104 Environment Canada (1990a, 44); *Canadian Environmental Protection Act, 1999,* S.C. 1999,
     c. 33, Schedule 1, List of Toxic Substances.
105 Ruggiero (1999).
106 *Clean Water Act,* 33 U.S.C. 1251-376, s. 1329.
107 *Ibid.,* s. 1365.
108 US General Accounting Office (1999b); US Environmental Protection Agency (1996).
109 Commission for Environmental Cooperation (2001b, 28).
110 Flatt (1997); Johnson (1999); Berger (2000).
111 Muldoon and Valiante (1989, 99).

2.3: Water Use and Conservation
1 Van Der Leeden, Troise, and Todd (1990).
2 OECD (1999b).
3 Environment Canada's Freshwater website: <http://www.ec.gc.ca/water/index.htm>.
4 OECD (1999b).
5 *Ibid.;* breakdown is from Environment Canada's Freshwater website: <http://www.ec.gc.ca/
   water/index.htm>.
6 OECD (1999e, 18, 75).

7   Paper figures from the Forest Products Association of Canada at <http://www.fpac.ca>; steel figures and breakdown from Environment Canada's Freshwater website <http://www.ec.gc.ca/water>; manufacturing figures from Ryan (1997, 38, 51).
8   Environment Canada (2001g); OECD (1999b).
9   See "The Management of Water" at Environment Canada's Freshwater website: <http://www.ec.gc.ca/water/index.htm>.
10 *Friends of the Oldman River* v. *Minister of Transport*, [1992].
11 Linton (1997, 16).
12 Rosenberg et al. (1987).
13 Canadian National Committee of the International Commission on Large Dams (1991); Environment Canada (1996c, 10-43).
14 Drinkwater and Frank (1994).
15 World Commission on Dams (2000).
16 *Fisheries Act*, R.S.C. 1985, c. F-14, s. 22.
17 *B.C. Hydro and Power Authority* v. *Canada; Attorney General of Canada* v. *Aluminum Company of Canada* (1980).
18 Commission for Environmental Cooperation (2000).
19 *Friends of the Oldman River* v. *Minister of Transport*, [1992]; *Canadian Wildlife Federation* v. *Canada*, [1990]; *Quebec (Attorney General)* v. *Canada*, [1994]. Two of these dams were built despite the recommendations made in the environmental assessment process.
20 Sproule-Jones (2002).
21 International Joint Commission (2001a); *An Act to Amend the International Boundary Waters Treaty Act*, S.C. 2001, c. 40.
22 Percy (1988).
23 Postel (1997, 177).
24 Percy (1988, 31).
25 Lucas (1990).
26 *Fish Protection Act*, S.B.C. 1997, c. 21, ss. 6-7.
27 *Water Act*, R.S.A. 2000, c. W-3, ss. 81-3.
28 Rueggeberg and Thompson (1984, 11).
29 OECD (1999b; 2000a; 1995a; 1998c, 24).
30 Environment Canada (1996b).
31 Environment Canada (1998g).
32 OECD (1999d, 38).
33 *Ibid.*
34 *Ibid.*, 42; Tate and Lacelle (1995); Taylor (1999).
35 OECD (1999d).
36 *Ibid.*, 45.
37 The Municipal Water Use Database (MUD) is at <http://www.ec.gc.ca/water>.
38 OECD (1999d, 43).
39 Environment Canada (2001g).
40 Canadian Council of Ministers of the Environment (1994).
41 Environment Canada (2001f, 10).
42 The Municipal Water Use Database, at <http://www.ec.gc.ca/water>.
43 MacLaren (1985); Environment Canada (1990a).
44 Tate and Lacelle (1995).
45 Peritz (2001).
46 Canadian Council of Ministers of the Environment (1994).
47 OECD (1999e, 75; 1998c).
48 OECD (1999e, 23).
49 *Water Regulation*, B.C. Reg. 204/88, as amended.
50 See Coca-Cola's website, <http://www.dasani.com>.
51 OECD (1999a, 42).
52 *Sustainable Water and Sewage Systems Act*, 2002, Bill 175; BC Drinking Water Review Panel (2002).
53 OECD (1999d).
54 There is a national database of municipal conservation programs at <http://www.ec.gc.ca/water>.

55 For example, see *Water Conservation Plumbing Regulation,* B.C. Reg. 294/98.
56 *Waste Management Act Municipal Sewage Regulations,* B.C. Reg. 129/99.
57 Bell (2001); Capital Regional District website, <http://www.crd.bc.ca/water/>.
58 Environment Canada (1996c, 10-39).
59 Details available through the Water Efficiency Experiences Database at <http://www.cwwa.ca>.
60 Canadian Council of Ministers of the Environment (1994).
61 Postel (1997, 129).
62 Tate (1987, 65).
63 Postel (1997, 140).
64 Forest Products Association of Canada website, <http://www.fpac.ca>.
65 Linton (1997, 53).
66 Postel (1997, 144).
67 Tate, Renzetti, and Shaw (1992).
68 Pearse, Bertrand, and MacLaren (1985, 48).

2.4: Water Exports

 1 UN Economic and Social Council (1997).
 2 Vorosmarty et al. (2000).
 3 de Villiers (1999, 15). An opposing point of view comes from University of Toronto political scientist Thomas Homer-Dixon (1999), who believes environmental scarcity is one of a number of factors contributing to violent conflict, but rarely the sole factor.
 4 Jack (1999).
 5 Chrétien quoted in Morris (1999).
 6 Maude Barlow, fundraising letter for the Council of Canadians, 15 December 2000.
 7 Corcoran (1999).
 8 Premier John Hamm of Nova Scotia and Premier Roger Grimes of Newfoundland are both quoted in Canadian Press (2001b).
 9 See BC's *Water Protection Act* registrations at Land and Water British Columbia Inc.'s *Water Protection Act* information page, <http://www.lwbc.bc.ca/water>.
10 Pearse, Bertrand, and MacLaren (1985, 125).
11 OECD (1999b, 72).
12 Drinkwater and Frank (1994); Rosenberg et al. (1987).
13 Schindler (2001).
14 International Joint Commission (2000a).
15 Marq de Villiers, author of *Water,* claims there is no market for Canadian bulk water exports. Bill Turner, an American water trader, claims transporting Canadian water would be too expensive. See Toughill (2001).
16 Pearse, Bertrand, and MacLaren (1985, 129); International Joint Commission (2000a).
17 The cost of desalination is becoming increasingly competitive. For example, Tampa, Florida, is building a desalination plant to supplement that city's water supply. See <http://www.wateronline.com>.
18 See <http://www.globalwatercorporation.com>.
19 Barlow (1999).
20 Saunders (1990b, 199); Bocking (1987).
21 Barlow (1999, 20).
22 Environment Canada (1996c, 10-44); International Joint Commission (2000a).
23 *Snowcap Waters Limited and Sun Belt Water Inc. v. Minister of Environment* (1997).
24 Chow (1999).
25 See <http://www.dfait-maeci.gc.ca>.
26 Walker (1998).
27 "There's Plenty" (1999).
28 de Villiers (1999, 277).
29 Mittelstaedt (2001c).
30 Premier Grimes suggested that the $70 million in royalties from bulk water exports would be applied to free tuition for students at Memorial University of Newfoundland. Grimes should note that BC collected a total of $26,000 in fees and royalties from commercial bottlers for the rights to 4.9 billion litres of public water in 1998 *(Ibid.).*
31 Pearse, Bertrand, and MacLaren (1985).

32 Environment Canada (1987, 2, 19).
33 *Canada Water Preservation Act,* Bill C-156, 2d session, 33rd Parliament 1986-87-88. In 1995 and 1997, Kamloops Member of Parliament Nelson Riis introduced private member's bills, Bill C-202 and C-232, both called the *Canada Water Export Prohibition Act,* which never passed.
34 de Villiers (1999, 278-9).
35 Sterling quoted in Scoffield (1998a); Government of Newfoundland (1999).
36 Thompson (1987, 433).
37 International Joint Commission (2000a).
38 *An Act to Amend the International Boundary Waters Treaty Act,* S.C. 2001, c. 40.
39 *Water Protection Act,* R.S.B.C. 1996, c. 484; *Water Taking and Transfers Regulation,* Ont. Reg. 285/99, pursuant to *Ontario Water Resources Act; Water Resources Act,* S.N.L. 2002, c. W-4.01, s. 12(2); *Water Act,* R.S.A. 2000, c. W-3, s. 46; *Water Resources Conservation and Protection Act,* S.M. 2000, c. 72; *Water Resources Protection Act,* S.N.S. 2000, c. 10; Prince Edward Island's *An Act to Amend the Environmental Protection Act,* Bill 55, 2001; *Saskatchewan Watershed Authority Act,* S.S. 2002, c. S-35.02; and *Water Resources Preservation Act,* S.Q. 2001, c. 48.
40 *Water Resources Preservation Act,* S.Q. 2001, c. 48, s. 2(1).
41 *Water Act,* R.S.A. 2000, c. W-3, s. 46; *Water Resources Conservation and Protection Act,* S.M. 2000, c. 72, s. 3(3); *Water Resources Protection Act,* S.N.S. 2000, c. 10, s. 8(1)(a).
42 *North Red Deer Water Authorization Act,* S.A. 2002, c. N-3.5.
43 *Constitution Act, 1867,* ss. 91(2), 92(5).
44 Department of Foreign Affairs and International Trade (1999).
45 See "Bulk Water Removal: Questions and Answers," <http://www.dfait-maeci.gc.ca/can-am> (at Questions 26 and 27).
46 *North American Free Trade Agreement Implementation Act,* S.C. 1993, c. 44, s. 7.
47 Shrybman (1999b, 7).
48 Appleton (1994, 202).
49 Article 201, NAFTA.
50 *Harmonized Commodity Description and Coding System,* General Agreement on Tariffs and Trade, BISD, 34 Supp. 5 (1988) (L/6112, L/6222, and L/6292).
51 Appleton (1994, 201).
52 See "Bulk Water Removal: Questions and Answers," <http://www.dfait-maeci.gc.ca/can-am>.
53 Article 309.1 prohibits quantitative restrictions on exports. NAFTA also prohibits export taxes, duties, and charges that would have the same effect as a ban or quantitative restrictions (Article 313).
54 See NAFTA Article 2101(1) and GATT Article XX.
55 Appleton (1994, 204); Shrybman (1999a, 60-71).
56 Article 1102, NAFTA.
57 Council of Canadians (n.d.), "Fact Sheet #1: The Big Leak in Free Trade."
58 Natural Resources Canada (2001c).
59 Maude Barlow, fundraising letter to Council of Canadians members, 2 April 2001.
60 NAFTA, Article 1114.
61 Shrybman (1999a).
62 Appleton (1994).
63 Unpublished memo, "Options Paper for Canadian Council of Ministers of the Environment," 19 May 1999, quoted in Shrybman (1999b, 4).
64 See Barry Appleton's website on NAFTA (Examples of Disputes), <http://www.appletonlaw. com/3gExamples.htm>.
65 Saunders (1990b, 199).
66 Sinclair and Grieshaber-Otto (2002).
67 Jean Chrétien, *Hansard,* House of Commons Debates, 9 December 1998.
68 Fife (2001); MacKinnon and Clark (2001); Canadian Press (2001a).
69 McKenna and MacKinnon (2001).
70 Pearse, Bertrand, and MacLaren (1985, 125).
71 Day and Quinn (1992, 175).

3: Air
1 Pammett and Frizzell (1997).

2 Last, Trouton, and Pengelly (1998); Environment Canada's Clean Air website, <http://www.ec. gc.ca/air/introduction_e.cfm>; Ontario Medical Association (2000); BC Medical Association (2000).
3 Environment Canada (1991, 23-22).
4 Environment Canada (1998a, 1).
5 Arctic Monitoring and Assessment Program (1998b).
6 Commission for Environmental Cooperation (2001b, 28); Environment Canada (2001c, 47).
7 OECD (1999b; 1995a, 205).
8 Commission for Environmental Cooperation (2001b, 40, 122).
9 Environment Canada (1998a).
10 Statistics Canada (2000, 12).
11 Environment Canada (1996c, 16-8).
12 Boyd (2001a).

3.1: Ozone Depletion
1 Environment Canada (1996c, 15-19).
2 World Meteorological Organization (1998).
3 Environment Canada (1991, 23-9).
4 Environment Canada (1999g); World Meteorological Organization and UN Environment Program (1998).
5 Environment Canada (1999g, 1).
6 World Meteorological Organization and UN Environment Program (1998, x.)
7 de Gruijl and van der Leun (2000); World Meteorological Organization (1998).
8 Gallagher et al. (1990).
9 World Health Organization (1994).
10 World Meteorological Organization and UN Environment Program (1998); Schindler (2001).
11 Auditor General of Canada (1997b).
12 World Meteorological Organization and UN Environment Program (1998, xiii).
13 Kauffman (1997, 76).
14 Molina and Rowland (1974).
15 Makhijani and Gurney (1995, 218). See Canada's *Chlorofluorocarbon Regulations,* SOR/80-254.
16 Environment Canada (n.d.b, 17).
17 Ozone Trends Panel (1988); Stolarski (1988).
18 The precautionary principle is defined in the 1990 *Bergen Ministerial Declaration on Sustainable Development.*
19 Dotto and Schiff (1978, 180).
20 Manzer (1990).
21 Alliance quoted in Kauffman (1997, 81).
22 Block (1990, 172).
23 Maduro and Schauerhammer (1992).
24 Block (1990, 170).
25 Ozone Trends Panel (1988); Kauffman (1997, 74-96).
26 *Chorofluorocarbon Regulations 1989* (SOR/90-127) banned the use of CFCs as a propellant in hair sprays, deodorants, and antiperspirants. It was accompanied by *Ozone Depleting Substances Regulations, no. 1, Ozone Depleting Substances Regulations, no. 2, Ozone Depleting Substances Regulations, no. 3* (SOR/89-351, 29 June 1989, SOR/90-583, 28 August 1990, SOR/90-584, amended by the Canada Gazette Part I, 16 November 1991, 3743, and *Ozone Depleting Substances Regulations,* SOR/94-408. The latest regulation was passed in 1999: *Ozone Depleting Substances Regulations* (SOR/99-7).
27 *Ozone Depleting Substances Regulations,* SOR/99-7, s. 1.
28 *Ibid.*
29 Made (2000).
30 Cole and Grossman (1999).
31 *Environmental Protection Act,* R.S.O. 1990, c. E-19, ss. 56-9; *Ozone Depleting Substances General Regulation,* R.R.O. 1990, Reg. 356. See also *Ozone Depleting Substances and Other Halocarbons Regulation,* B.C. Reg. 387/99; *Ozone Depleting Substances and Halocarbon Regulation,* Alta. Reg. 181/00; *Environmental Management and Protection Act,* S.S. 2002, c. E-10.21; *Ozone Depleting Substances Act,* C.C.S.M., c. O-80, and *Ozone Depleting Substances Regulation,* Man. Reg. 103/

94; Quebec's *Regulation respecting ozone depleting substances*, O.C. 812-93; *Ozone Depleting Substances Regulation*, N.B. Reg. 97-132; *Ozone Layer Protection Regulations*, N.S. Reg. 54/95; *Ozone Depleting Substances and Replacement Regulations*, P.E.I. No. EC 619/94; *Ozone Depleting Substances Regulation*, Nfld. Reg. 120/97; Yukon's *Ozone Depleting Substances and other Halocarbons Regulations*, O.I.C. 2000/127.

32 Northwest Territories: Guideline for Ozone Depleting Substances, Yellowknife.
33 *Ozone Depleting Substances and Other Halocarbons Regulation*, B.C. Reg. 387/99.
34 For example, *Canadian Environmental Protection Act, 1999*, S.C. 1999, c. 33, ss. 272, 274.
35 For example, City of Toronto Bylaw No. 549-90.
36 Cook (1996, 34).
37 Statistics Canada (2000, 12); Environment Canada (1999g).
38 Auditor General of Canada (1997b, para. 27-131).
39 Commissioner of the Environment and Sustainable Development (2000, 9-5).
40 Environment Canada (1999g).
41 Auditor General of Canada (1997b, para. 27-3).
42 Benedick (1991, 7).
43 Auditor General of Canada (1997b).
44 Cook (1996).
45 *Clean Air Act*, Chapter VI, Stratospheric Ozone Protection, 42 U.S.C. 7671.
46 Hoerner (1995); Cook (1996, 40).
47 Barrett (2000); Smith et al. (1993); US Environmental Protection Agency (1993).
48 Cook (1996, 40); see also Hawken, Lovins, and Lovins (1999, 244).
49 ARC Applied Research Consultants (1997).
50 World Health Organization (1994).
51 Block (1990, 170).
52 Cook (1996, 15).
53 Kerr quoted in Environment Canada (1997a).
54 Commissioner of the Environment and Sustainable Development (2000, 9-16); Auditor General of Canada (1997b).
55 Canadian Council of Ministers of the Environment (2001).
56 Standing Committee on Environment and Sustainable Development (1998).
57 Friends of the Earth Canada (2000a).
58 See US Environmental Protection Agency's Ozone Depletion page, <http://www.epa.gov/docs/ozone>.
59 Environmental News Network (2001).
60 Environment Canada (2000a).
61 Auditor General of Canada (1997b); Commissioner of the Environment and Sustainable Development (2000, ch. 9); Friends of the Earth Canada (2000b).
62 Information on Greenfreeze technology at <http://www.greenpeace.org>.
63 Auditor General of Canada (1997b).
64 The Standing Committee on Environment and Sustainable Development held hearings about ozone depletion in 1990 (Deadly Releases: CFCs) and 1992 (Ozone Depletion: Acting Responsibly).
65 Suzuki and Gordon (1990, 29).
66 World Meteorological Organization (1998, 17).
67 Albritton and Kuijpers (1999, 21).
68 World Meteorological Organization (2002).
69 Montzka et al. (1999).
70 Kauffman (1997, 74).
71 Benedick (1991, 211).
72 World Meteorological Organization (1998); Shindell, Rind, and Lonergan (1998); Fergusson (2001).
73 Shindell, Rind, and Lonergan (1998).

3.2: Climate Change

1 McBean, Weaver, and Roulet (2001); Environment Canada (1996c, 15-4).
2 Intergovernmental Panel on Climate Change (1995); Intergovernmental Panel on Climate Change, Working Groups I and II (2001).

3 These scientists include S. Fred Singer, Richard S. Lindzen, Patrick Michaels, and Robert Balling. For samples of their writing, see Singer (1999) and Michaels and Balling (2000). See also <http://www.junkscience.com>. Their funding sources and a critique of their position on climate change are chronicled in detail in Gelbspan (1997).
4 Weaver (2001). For an example of the energy industry claim that there is a valid scientific debate about whether global warming is actually occurring, see Peterson (1999).
5 McBean, Weaver, and Roulet (2001).
6 Government of Canada (1999b).
7 Hengeveld (2000).
8 Intergovernmental Panel on Climate Change, Working Group I (2001, 16); Intergovernmental Panel on Climate Change (1996).
9 Walther et al. (2002, 389).
10 Intergovernmental Panel on Climate Change, Working Group I (2001).
11 Intergovernmental Panel on Climate Change, Working Group II (2001, 3).
12 *Ibid.;* Intergovernmental Panel on Climate Change, Working Group II (2001); Malcolm and Markham (2000).
13 Haines, McMichael, and Epstein (2000, 730).
14 World Health Organization (1996).
15 Epstein (2000; 1998).
16 Working Group on Public Health and Fossil-Fuel Combustion (1997).
17 Intergovernmental Panel on Climate Change, Working Group I (2001); Intergovernmental Panel on Climate Change, Working Group II (2001).
18 US National Research Council (2001).
19 Intergovernmental Panel on Climate Change, Working Group II (2001, 16).
20 Huebert (2001).
21 Norris, Rosentrater, and Eid (2002); Stirling, Lunn, and Iacozza (1999); Krajick (2001); David Suzuki Foundation (2001b, 4).
22 Intergovernmental Panel on Climate Change, Working Group II (2001, 13).
23 "Global Warming Threatens Alaskan Villages," Scripps Howard News Service, 5 May 2001. See the archive at <www.nandotimes.com>.
24 Taylor and Taylor (1998, 12-6); Pacific Fisheries Resource Conservation Council (1999).
25 Johnson and Hunter (1998, ii).
26 Intergovernmental Panel on Climate Change, Working Group II (2001).
27 Canadian Public Health Association (1999); Michael et al. (1996).
28 Environment Canada (1996c, 15-1).
29 Martens (1998, 151).
30 Intergovernmental Panel on Climate Change, Working Group I (2001).
31 Environment Canada (2001a).
32 Government of Canada (2002a).
33 Paterson (1996).
34 Intergovernmental Panel on Climate Change (1990).
35 Environment Canada (1990a, 111).
36 Suzuki and Gordon (1990, 212).
37 *United Nations Framework Convention on Climate Change*, Article 2.
38 Intergovernmental Panel on Climate Change (1995).
39 Rolfe (2000); David Suzuki Foundation (2000b).
40 Mitchell (2000a).
41 Intergovernmental Panel on Climate Change, Working Group I (2001, 10, 17).
42 Layton (2001).
43 International Institute for Sustainable Development (2001, 15).
44 Grubb (2000); Nordhaus (2000).
45 Environment Canada (1990a, 97).
46 Liberal Party of Canada (1993, 1997).
47 Canadian Council of Ministers of the Environment (1990); Measures Working Group for the Climate Change Task Group (1994); National Climate Change Process at <http://www.nccp.ca>; Government of Canada (1995; 2000a; 2000b; 2002a; 2002b).
48 Environment Canada (1997b, 35).
49 Measures Working Group for the Climate Change Task Group (1994).

50 Hornung and Bramley (2000).
51 Government of Canada (2000c); Hornung and Bramley (2000); Hornung (2000).
52 d'Aquino (1998).
53 McLellan quoted in Beauchesne (1995). Moe Sihota, BC's environment minister, responded by suggesting that Minister McLellan had her head stuck in the tar sands, referring to Alberta's massive crude oil projects.
54 For further information on the Voluntary Challenge and Registry Program, see <http://www.vcr-mvr.ca>.
55 Hornung and Bramley (2000, 1, 11); Bramley (2002a); Bachelder (1999).
56 The *Act*, passed by Parliament in 1982, was never proclaimed, meaning that although the law is on the books it is still not in force and has no legal effect.
57 Environment Canada (1998c).
58 Natural Resources Canada (2000c); Hornung (1998, 18).
59 Government of Canada (2000b, 5).
60 Sierra Legal Defence Fund (2002a).
61 For a critique of the American fuel efficiency standards, see *ibid.*
62 US Government (2001).
63 Hornung (1998).
64 Hornung and Bramley (2000, 6); Bachelder (1999); Bernstein and Gore (2001). For a detailed discussion of the pros and cons of voluntary measures to protect the environment, see Chapter 8.
65 Cotton and Lucas (2001, para. 2.66).
66 *Energy Efficiency Act*, R.S.B.C. 1996, c. 114; *Energy Efficiency Act*, R.S.O. 1990, c. E-17.
67 BC's Air Care program operates under the authority of ss. 45.1 to 45.3 of the *Motor Vehicle Act* and Division 40 of the *Motor Vehicle Act Regulations*, B.C. Reg. 26/58 (as amended). Ontario's Drive Clean program is set forth in Ont. Reg. 361/98 under the *Environmental Protection Act* and R.R.O. Reg. 628 under the *Highway Traffic Act*. For a critique of these programs, see Sierra Legal Defence Fund (2002a).
68 Methane capture at new landfill sites is required by s. 15 of Ont. Reg. 232/98 *(Landfill Sites)*. The Ontario Fuel Conservation Rebate/Charge program is listed in the OECD's environmental tax database, <http://www.oecd.org>.
69 *Ethanol Fuel Act*, S.S. 2002, c. E-11.1; *Ethanol Fuel (General) Regs.* E-11.1, Reg. 1.
70 Dauncey (2001, 96-7); Mittelstaedt (2002d). For information on the Toronto Atmospheric Fund, see <http://www.city.toronto.on.ca/taf>.
71 *Climate Change and Emissions Management Act*, 2003, Bill 37.
72 Anderson quoted in Mahoney and Chase (2002).
73 *Energy Efficiency Act*, S.C. 1992, c. 36; *Energy Efficiency Regulations*, SOR/94-651, as amended by SOR/95-173, SOR/95-522, SOR/97-529, and SOR/99-25.
74 *Energy Efficiency Act*, S.C. 1992, c. 36, s. 27.
75 Natural Resources Canada (1995b).
76 Natural Resources Canada (1999b).
77 Hawken, Lovins, and Lovins (1999, 105-6).
78 Hornung (1998, 66); Natural Resources Canada (1999a).
79 Environment Canada (1997b, 35).
80 Government of Canada (2002b).
81 Neitzert, Olsen, and Collas (1999).
82 US Energy Information Administration (1999).
83 Keating et al. (1997, 29).
84 Natural Resources Canada (1999a); David Suzuki Foundation (2001a).
85 US Government (2001).
86 David Suzuki Foundation (2001a).
87 Bramley (2002b).
88 Canadian Council of Chief Executives (2002). See also a letter to Prime Minister Chrétien from the Business Council on National Issues and the Canadian Chamber of Commerce, 28 September 2001, at <http://www.canadiansolution.com>.
89 Morgan (1998).
90 Bernstein and Gore (2001).
91 Natural Resources Canada (2000b).
92 Jeffs (2001). Klein's comments overlook the fact that Alberta's annual GDP is only $115 billion. For Klein's proposed solution to climate change, see Mahoney (2002).

93 Hornung and Bramley (2000).
94 Gelbspan (1997).
95 Measures Working Group for the Climate Change Task Group (1994).
96 Hornung (1998); Pape (1999); Torrie (2000). See also <http://www.climatechangesolutions.com> and <http://www.energyrevolution.com>.
97 Dauncey (2001).
98 European Commission (1997); For reductions in greenhouse gases produced by European nations see OECD (1999b, 53).
99 "An Assessment of the Economic and Environmental Implications for Canada of the *Kyoto Protocol*," <http://www.nccp.ca>. Intergovernmental Panel on Climate Change, Working Group II (2001).
100 Milko (1990); Royal Society of Canada, "Canadian Options for Greenhouse Gas Emission Reductions," quoted in Keating (1997); US Department of Energy (1997); McGuinty (2002).
101 Redefining Progress and David Suzuki Foundation (1997).
102 Chiotti and Urquizo (1999); Tol (1995). A David Suzuki Foundation report found that by instituting six measures to reduce greenhouse gas emissions, Canada would avoid $2.2 billion in health and environmental damage (David Suzuki Foundation 2000a).
103 Commissioner of the Environment and Sustainable Development (1998, 3-35).
104 Commissioner of the Environment and Sustainable Development (2001b, 7).
105 Keating (1997).

3.3: Air Pollution

1 Environment Canada (1996c, 16-8).
2 Environment Canada (1998a, 1).
3 Environment Canada (1996c, 11-93).
4 Environment Canada (2003).
5 Commission for Environmental Cooperation (2001b, 137).
6 Environment Canada (1996c, 12-13).
7 Commissioner of the Environment and Sustainable Development (2000, 4-14).
8 Estrin and Swaigen (1993); Environment Canada (1996c, 10-11, 12-14).
9 Pope et al. (2002); Brook et al. (2002).
10 Environment Canada (2001c, 14, 47).
11 OECD (1995a, 103); see also OECD (2000a).
12 Porter et al. (2000).
13 Commissioner of the Environment and Sustainable Development (2000, 4-21; 1999, 4-11).
14 Commission for Environmental Cooperation (2002b, 62).
15 Environment Canada (1996a).
16 OECD (1999b).
17 Environment Canada (1996a).
18 Environment Canada (2001e, 4).
19 OECD (1999b).
20 Environment Canada (1996c, 11-88).
21 OECD (1999b).
22 Environment Canada (1999a).
23 OECD (1999b).
24 Environment Canada (1996c, 12-14).
25 *Ibid.,* 12-13; Ontario Medical Association (2001).
26 Bascom (1996); Ontario Medical Association (1998); Stieb et al. (1995); Samet, Zeger, and Berhane (1995); Chance and Harmesen (1998); Raizenne (1998).
27 Ontario Medical Association (2000).
28 BC Medical Association (2000).
29 Burnett et al. (1998).
30 Burnett et al. (1994).
31 Last, Trouton, and Pengelly (1998).
32 Dales et al. (1994).
33 Dewailly et al. (1989).
34 BC Ministry of Environment, Land and Parks (1995, 5).
35 Sierra Legal Defence Fund (2002a).
36 Tollefson, Rhone, and Rolfe (2000, 60).

37 World Health Organization (1999).
38 Environment Canada (1998a).
39 Gerhardsson, Skerfving, and Oskarsson (1997).
40 BC Ministry of Environment, Land and Parks (1995); OMA cited by Environment Canada, Clean Air website <http://www.ec.gc.ca>; Commissioner of the Environment and Sustainable Development (2000, 4-17); Working Group on Public Health and Fossil-Fuel Combustion (1997); Health Canada (1997, 57).
41 Commissioner of the Environment and Sustainable Development (2000, 4-30).
42 Environment Canada (1996c, 11-64).
43 BC Medical Association (2000).
44 *Canadian Environmental Protection Act, 1999*, S.C. 1999, c. 33; *Waste Management Act*, R.S.B.C. 1996, c. 482; *Alberta Environmental Protection and Enhancement Act*, R.S.A. 2000, c. E-12; *Environmental Management and Protection Act*, S.S. 2002, c. E-10.21; *Environment Act*, C.C.S.M. c. E-125; *Environmental Protection Act*, R.S.O. 1990, c. E-19; *Environmental Quality Act*, R.S.Q., c. Q-2; *Clean Environment Act*, R.S.N.B. 1973, c. C-6, and *Clean Air Act*, S.N.B. 1997, c. C-5.2; *Environment Act*, S.N.S. 1994-95, c. 1; *Environmental Protection Act*, R.S.P.E.I. 1988, c. E-9; *Environmental Protection Act*, S.N. 2002, c. E-14.2; *Environmental Protection Act*, R.S.N.W.T. 1988, c. E-7; and *Environment Act*, S.Y. 1991, c. 5.
45 Benidickson (1997, 86).
46 Environment Canada (1996c, 11-63).
47 *Agreement Between the Government of Canada and the Government of the United States on Air Quality* (1991).
48 Reuters (2000).
49 The so-called dirty dozen are dioxins, furans, PCBs, aldrin, chlordane, dieldrin, DDT, endrin, heptachlor, hexachlorobenzene, mirex, and toxaphene.
50 Jensen, Adarer, and Shearer (1997); Arctic Monitoring and Assessment Program (1998a).
51 Arctic Monitoring and Assessment Program (2002).
52 Health Canada (1989).
53 Linton (1997, 126).
54 Standing Committee on Environment and Sustainable Development (1995, 32); see also Dwivedi et al. (2001, 64).
55 Commissioner of the Environment and Sustainable Development (1999, 4-14, 4-11).
56 Winfield quoted in Conrad (2000, 46).
57 Commissioner of the Environment and Sustainable Development (2000, 4-17).
58 Commission on Environmental Cooperation, "Environmental law summary," at <http://www.cec.org>.
59 Moyer and Francis (1992).
60 *Secondary Lead Smelter Release Regulations*, SOR/91-155; *Chlor-Alkali Mercury Release Regulations*, SOR/90-130; *Asbestos Mines and Mills Release Regulations*, SOR/90-341; and *Vinyl Chloride Release Regulations*, SOR/92-631.
61 *Lead-free Gasoline Regulations*, C.R.C. 408; *Leaded Gasoline Regulations*, C.R.C. 409.
62 *Canada Gazette*, Part I, 2 November 2002, Vol. 136, No. 44.
63 *Canadian Environmental Protection Act, 1999*, S.C. 1999, c. 33, ss. 149-65.
64 Tollefson, Rhone, and Rolfe (2000, 49).
65 *Canada Gazette*, Part I, Vol. 124, 17 February 1990, 560; Estrin and Swaigen (1993, 487).
66 *Canadian Environmental Protection Act, 1999*, S.C. 1999, c. 33, ss. 138-48; *Contaminated Fuel Regulations*, SOR/91-486; *Diesel Fuel Regulations*, SOR/97-110; *Benzene in Gasoline Regulations*, SOR/97-493; *Sulphur in Gasoline Regulations*, SOR/99-236.
67 Tollefson, Rhone, and Rolfe (2000, 33).
68 Environment Canada (1996c, 11-77).
69 Sierra Legal Defence Fund (2002a).
70 *Sulphur in Gasoline Regulations*, SOR/99-236.
71 *Diesel Fuel Regulations*, SOR/97-110; Tollefson, Rhone, and Rolfe (2000, 51).
72 Harrison and Antweiler (2001); see also Olewiler and Dawson (1998).
73 Anderson (2001).
74 Environment Canada (2001b; 2001e).
75 Environment Canada (1990a, 22); Stefanick and Wells (1998).
76 *Ambient Air Quality Criteria Regulation*, R.R.O. 1990, Reg. 337; *General Air Pollution Regulation*, R.R.O. 1990, Reg. 346.

77   See *Waste Incinerator Regulation,* Ont. Reg. 555/92; *Air Contaminants from Ferrous Foundries,* R.R.O. 1990, Reg. 336; *Hot Mix Asphalt Regulation,* R.R.O. 1990, Reg. 349; *Certificate of Approval Exemptions – Air,* Ont. Reg. 524/98.
78   *Clean Air Act,* S.N.B. 1997, c. C-5.2; *Air Quality Regulation,* N.B. Reg. 97-133.
79   *Environmental Bill of Rights, 1993,* S.O. 1993, c. 28.
80   Thompson (1980, 5).
81   Estrin and Swaigen (1993, 490).
82   Vedal (1995); Sierra Legal Defence Fund (1998a).
83   Environment Canada (1996c, 11-76). For example, see Ontario's *Gasoline Volatility Regulation,* Ont. Reg. 271/91.
84   *Cleaner Gasoline Regulations,* B.C. Reg. 498/95; *Motor Vehicle Emissions Reduction Regulation,* B.C. Reg. 517/95.
85   World Health Organization (1999).
86   Canadian Institute for Environmental Law and Policy (n.d.).
87   The Greater Vancouver Regional District passed *Air Pollution Control Bylaw* No. 603 and *Air Quality Management Bylaw* No. 725. See <http://www.gvrd.bc.ca>.
88   Air Quality Strategy Interdepartmental Working Group (2001).
89   Environment Canada (1996c, 11-93).
90   Tollefson, Rhone, and Rolfe (2000, 25).
91   *Canadian Environmental Protection Act, 1999,* S.C. 1999, c. 33, ss. 166-74.
92   Commission on Environmental Cooperation, "Environmental Law Summary," at <http://www.cec.org>.
93   US Environmental Protection Agency (1998).
94   Canadian Council of Ministers of the Environment (2000).
95   Environment Canada (1988; 1998a, 1).
96   Estrin and Swaigen (1993, 476). For example, see Ont. Reg. 660/85, 661/85, 662/85, and 663/85 regulating emissions from an Inco smelter, a Falconbridge smelter, Ontario Hydro's coal-fired power plants, and Algoma Steel's iron plant, respectively. Stricter limits on Ontario Power Generation Inc. (formerly Ontario Hydro) are included in Ont. Reg. 153/99.
97   *Clean Air Act,* 42 U.S.C. ss. 7401-626.
98   Environment Canada (1998a, 1-2).
99   Canadian Council of Ministers of the Environment (2000, 1).
100 Environment Canada (1990a, 12, 53).
101 Environment Canada (1999f).
102 Commissioner of the Environment and Sustainable Development (2000, 4-47-9).
103 Reitze (1999, 740).
104 US Council on Environmental Quality (1990).
105 US Environmental Protection Agency (1991); Davies and Mazurek (1998, 130).
106 Sunstein (1999); Schprentz (1996).
107 Hawken, Lovins, and Lovins (1999, 58); US Environmental Protection Agency (1997).
108 Reitze (1999, 693).
109 Richard E. Ayres (1998, 379).
110 Commissioner of the Environment and Sustainable Development (2000, 4-20, 21).
111 Last, Trouton, and Pengelly (1998, 26); see also World Health Organization (1999).
112 Environment Canada (1996a).
113 Commissioner of the Environment and Sustainable Development (2000, para. 4.60).

4: Land
1   Environment Canada (2001f).
2   Canadian Council of Forest Ministers (2002); Cranstone (2001); Natural Resources Canada (2002; 2001a; 2001c).
3   Franson, Lucas, and Milligan (2002).
4   Tilman et al. (2001, 281).
5   Evans (1998); Chambers et al. (2001).
6   Montpetit (2001, 275).
7   Hocking (1996).
8   Environment Canada (1997c); Bryant, Nielsen, and Tangley (1997); Hughes (1996, 117).
9   Bryant, Nielsen, and Tangley (1997); Environment Canada (1997c); Ecotrust, Pacific GIS, and Conservation International (1995).

10 Environment Canada (1997c).
11 Canadian Council of Forest Ministers (2002).
12 Garton (1997).
13 Natural Resources Canada (2001b, 24); Canadian Council of Forest Ministers (1998, viii).
14 May (1998, 37).

4.1: Pesticide Regulation

1 In contrast, only 30 percent of toxicology experts believe pesticides in food pose a high or moderate health risk (Slovic et al. 1995).
2 World Wildlife Fund (1996).
3 US General Accounting Office (2001, 4).
4 Allan Rock, minister of health, quoted in Swaigen (2001, 176).
5 Government of New Brunswick (2002).
6 Standing Committee on Environment and Sustainable Development (2000); Commissioner of the Environment and Sustainable Development (1999, ch. 3); Castrilli and Vigod (1987); Hughes (2001).
7 Canadian Environmental Law Association and the Ontario College of Family Physicians (2000, 351).
8 Cooper (1999a, 3).
9 Commissioner of the Environment and Sustainable Development (1999, 3-30).
10 It is far less common for Canada to ban a pesticide not banned in other countries. The pesticide alachlor is a controversial exception to this general rule. See OECD (1996a); Brunk, Haworth, and Lee (1991).
11 Standing Committee on Environment and Sustainable Development (2000).
12 Statistics Canada (2000, 99, 203).
13 Agriculture and Agri-Food Canada (1998).
14 *Ibid.;* McKinlay and Atkinson (1995).
15 Ontario Ministry of Agriculture, Food and Rural Affairs (1999).
16 US Environmental Protection Agency (1995). See the PMRA and Ontario Ministry of Agriculture, Food and Rural Affairs websites at <http://www.hc-sc.gc.ca/pmra-arla> and <http://www.gov.on.ca/OMAFRA>.
17 Standing Committee on Environment and Sustainable Development (2000).
18 Health Canada (1997, 106).
19 Neidert and Havelock (1998); Mitchell (1999).
20 Pest Management Regulatory Agency (n.d.).
21 World Health Organization (1990).
22 US General Accounting Office (2000).
23 Martin (1999).
24 These problems were reiterated by both the commissioner of the environment and sustainable development (1999) and Parliament's Standing Committee on Environment and Sustainable Development (2000).
25 Martin (1999); Canadian Environmental Law Association and the Ontario College of Family Physicians (2000); US National Research Council (1993); Repetto and Baliga (1996).
26 Dingle, Strahco, and Franklin (1997, 445).
27 Solomon and Schettler (2000); Colborn, Dumanoski, and Myers (1996).
28 Standing Committee on Environment and Sustainable Development (2000).
29 Health Canada (1998b); Wigle et al. (1990); Morrison et al. (1992).
30 Dewailly et al. (1993); Jensen, Adarer, and Shearer (1997).
31 US National Research Council (1993); Canadian Environmental Law Association and the Ontario College of Family Physicians (2000); Jackson (1995); Chance and Harmesen (1998).
32 Krieger (2001); Freemark and Boutin (1994).
33 Hayes et al. (2002); Dalton (2002).
34 Freemark and Boutin (1994).
35 Standing Committee on Environment and Sustainable Development (2000); Toughill (1999).
36 Mineau (1993, v).
37 Agriculture and Agri-Food Canada (1993).
38 Pest Management Regulatory Agency (1995).
39 Agriculture and Agri-Food Canada (2000, 54, 56).
40 Dingle, Strahco, and Franklin (1997).
41 Arctic Monitoring and Assessment Program (1998b); Blais et al. (1998).

42 Freemark and Boutin (1994).
43 Mineau and McLaughlin (1994, 82).
44 US National Research Council (1996b).
45 Standing Committee on Environment and Sustainable Development (2000).
46 BC Ministry of Environment, Land and Parks (2000, 19).
47 US Department of Agriculture (1999).
48 US National Research Council (1996b).
49 US General Accounting Office (2001; 2000); US National Research Council (1989).
50 Agriculture and Agri-Food Canada (1998).
51 McKinlay and Atkinson (1995).
52 Browne (1985, 33).
53 The *Stockholm Convention on Persistent Organic Pollutants* has its own website at <http://www.chem.unep.ch/sc>. See also UN Economic Commission for Europe 1998, *Aarhus Protocol on Persistent Organic Pollutants*, under the *Convention on Long-range Transboundary Air Pollution.*
54 *Crompton Co. v. Canada* (2001). See <http://www.dfait-maeci.gc.ca> for documents related to the NAFTA case between Crompton Co. and the Government of Canada.
55 National Round Table on the Environment and the Economy (2001a, 22).
56 *Pest Control Products Act,* S.C. 2002, c. 28, replaced *Pest Control Products Act,* R.S.C. 1985, c. P-9.
57 *Food and Drug Act,* R.S.C. 1985, c. F-27, s. 4; *Food and Drug Act Regulations,* C.R.C., c. 870, Part B, Division 15, Table II.
58 Estrin and Swaigen (1993).
59 Harrison and Hoberg (1994, 73).
60 Commissioner of the Environment and Sustainable Development (1999, 3-31).
61 Hall (1981).
62 Ombudsman of British Columbia (1988, 8).
63 Pest Management Regulatory Agency (2001); *Pest Control Product Regulations,* C.R.C. 1978, c. 1253, s. 16.
64 Fenge (1998); Commissioner of the Environment and Sustainable Development (1999).
65 *Access to Information Act,* R.S.C. 1985, c. A-1, s. 20(6).
66 Craig (2000).
67 Commissioner of the Environment and Sustainable Development (1999, 4-30).
68 *Ibid.*
69 Standing Committee on Environment and Sustainable Development (2000, para. 14.19).
70 US EPA. Office of Pesticide Programs <http://www.epa.gov/pesticides>.
71 See "DuPont Ordered" (2001). Dow Chemical was ordered to pay an Alberta farmer almost $400,000 for failing to warn him of pesticide dangers (O'Ferrall 1993).
72 Swaigen (2001, 179); see also Castrilli and Vigod (1987, 13).
73 Standing Committee on Environment and Sustainable Development (2000).
74 Commissioner of the Environment and Sustainable Development (1999, 4-27).
75 Standing Committee on Environment and Sustainable Development (2000).
76 Commissioner of the Environment and Sustainable Development (1999, para. 4.114); Canadian Environmental Law Association and the Ontario College of Family Physicians (2000, 343).
77 Swaigen (2001, 180).
78 Commissioner of the Environment and Sustainable Development (1999, 4-30).
79 Frechette (2000).
80 Davies (1998).
81 Castrilli and Vigod (1987, 130-1); Pesticide Registration Review Team (1990); Pest Management Secretariat (1994).
82 Commissioner of the Environment and Sustainable Development (1999, 3-31).
83 The major changes to the *PCPA* undermine the government's previous assertions that it was protecting Canadians from unacceptable risks (Pest Management Regulatory Agency 2000, s. 1.1).
84 Hughes (2001, 203).
85 Health Canada (2002).
86 *Pesticide Control Act,* R.S.B.C. 1996, c. 360; *Environmental Protection and Enhancement Act,* R.S.A. 2000, c. E-12; *Pest Control Products (Saskatchewan) Act,* R.S.S. 1978, c. P-8; *Pesticides and Fertilizers Control Act,* R.S.M. 1987, c. P-40; *Pesticides Act,* R.S.O. 1990, c. P-11; *Pesticides Act,* R.S.Q., c. P-9.3; *Pesticides Control Act,* S.N.B. 1973, c. P-8; *Environment Act,* S.N.S. 1994-95, c. 1; *Pesticides*

Control Act, R.S.P.E.I. 1988, c. P-4; *Environmental Protection Act*, S.N.L. 2002, c. E-14.2, ss. 32-44; *Pesticides Control Act*, S.Y. 1989, c. 20; *Pesticide Act*, R.S.N.W.T. 1988, c. P-4.

87 *Pesticide Sales, Handling, Use, and Application Regulation*, Alta. Reg. 24/97; *Pest Control Products Regulations*, Sask. Reg. c. P-8, Reg. 3; *Pesticides and Fertilizers Licence Regulation*, Man. Reg. 216/87; *Pesticide Regulation*, Man. Reg. 94/88; *Pesticide Act (General) Regulation*, R.R.O. 1990, Reg. 914 (as amended); *Regulation respecting permits and certificates for the sale and use of pesticides*, Quebec O.C. 305-97; *Pesticide Control Act Regulation*, N.B. Reg. 96-126; *Pesticide Regulations*, N.S. Reg. 61/95; *Pesticides, Prince Edward Island Regulations*, c. P-4; *Pesticide Regulations*, Y.T.O.I.C. 1994/125; *Pesticide Regulations*, R.R.N.W.T., c. P-2.

88 For example, *Pesticide Control Act Regulation*, B.C. Reg., 319/81 as amended, s. 10(2).

89 Giroux (1993, 207).

90 *Pesticides, Prince Edward Island Regulations*, c. P-4, s. 12(1)(a).

91 See Alberta's *Pesticide Sales, Handling, Use, and Application Regulation*, Alta. Reg. 24/97, s. 5(1), 5(2).

92 For example, in BC the minister can prohibit sale and use if "unreasonable adverse effect may result from use" (*Pesticide Control Act*, R.S.B.C. 1996, c. 360, s. 16).

93 *Pesticides Act*, R.S.Q., c. P-9.3, s. 8; *Environment Act*, S.N.S. 1994-95, c. 1, s. 81.

94 *Alberta Environmental Protection and Enhancement Act*, R.S.A. 2000, C. E-12, s. 164.

95 *Pesticide Control Act*, R.S.B.C. 1996, c. 360, s. 15; *Nisga'a Tribal Council* v. *British Columbia* (1988); *Canadian Earthcare Society* v. *British Columbia* (1988).

96 Environment Canada (1991).

97 Ontario Ministry of Agriculture, Food and Rural Affairs (1999).

98 BC Environment (1993).

99 Estrin and Swaigen (1993, 651).

100 *114957 Canada Ltée* v. *Hudson* (2001).

101 World Commission on Environment and Development (1987, 220).

102 For example, *Local Government Act*, R.S.B.C. 1996, c. 323, s. 249; *Municipal Government Act*, R.S.A. 2000, c. M-26, s. 7; *Municipal Act*, S.M. 1996, c. 58, C.C.S.M. c. M225, ss. 232-3; *Municipal Act*, R.S.O. 1990, c. M.45, s. 102; *Municipalities Act*, R.S.N.B., c. M-22, s. 190(2), First Schedule; *Municipal Government Act*, S.N.S. 1998, c. 18, s. 172; *Cities, Towns and Villages Act*, R.S.N.W.T. 1988, c. C-8, ss. 54 and 102; *Municipal Act*, R.S.Y. 1986, c. 119, s. 271.

103 *Municipal Government Act*, S.N.S. 1998, c. 18, ss. 172(j) and 533; *Cities and Towns Act*, R.S.Q., c. C-19, s. 463.1; *Municipal Code of Quebec*, R.S.Q., c. C-27.1, s. 550.1.

104 Swaigen (2001, 174).

105 Halifax Regional Municipal Council, 2000, Pesticide Bylaw P-800; see <http://region.halifax.ns.ca>. See also <http://www.city.victoria.bc.ca> and <http://www.city.toronto.on.ca/health/reduce_pesticide.htm>.

106 *Bergen Ministerial Declaration on Sustainable Development* (1990, para. 7).

107 Valiante (2002); Epstein (2001).

108 US National Research Council (1993b).

109 US EPA, Office of Pesticide Programs, "Regulating Pesticides (Laws)," <http://www.epa.gov/pesticides>.

110 Consumer Union of the United States (2001).

111 Compare the US *Federal Insecticide, Fungicide and Rodenticide Act*, 7 U.S.C. 136 et. seq., with the *Pest Control Product Act*, R.S.C. 1985, c. P-9.

112 Harrison and Hoberg (1994).

113 See, for example, Pest Management Regulatory Agency (1995).

114 US General Accounting Office (2001; 2000).

115 Briggs (1992).

116 Johnson and Ware (1990, 14-9, 10).

117 Cox (2001).

118 Dingle, Strahco, and Franklin (1997).

119 Harris (2000).

120 OECD (1995c); Wossink and Feitshans (2000).

121 OECD (1999b).

122 Shortle and Abler (2001, 159); Wahlstrom and Lundqvist (1993).

123 Andersson et al. (1990).

124 OECD (1996a).

125 *Ibid.*

126 Wargo (1996); Thornton (2000).
127 Canadian Environmental Law Association and the Ontario College of Family Physicians (2000, 318).
128 Standing Committee on Environment and Sustainable Development (2000).

4.2: Forest Management
1 Corporate Research Associates (1997).
2 Wildlands League (n.d., 1).
3 Clancy (2001).
4 Canadian Forest Service (1994, 91).
5 World Wildlife Fund Canada (1999a).
6 Canadian Council of Forest Ministers (2002).
7 Canadian Council of Forest Ministers (1997).
8 Forest Products Association of Canada (2001, 2); Natural Resources Canada (2001b, 1); Ontario Ministry of Natural Resources (2002); BC Ministry of Forests (n.d.).
9 Sierra Legal Defence Fund (2002b, 2002d); *Council of the Haida Nation v. B.C.* (2002).
10 Canadian Council of Forest Ministers (2000).
11 Slaney et al. (1996).
12 Ecotrust, Pacific GIS, and Conservation International (1995).
13 May (1998); BC Ministry of Forests (1994); Marchak (1999).
14 Environment Canada (1995b).
15 Canadian Council of Forest Ministers (2002).
16 Burda, Gale, and M'Gonigle (1997).
17 Alberta Environmental Protection (1998, 9).
18 Global Forest Watch (2000, 28-9).
19 Slaney and Martin (1997).
20 Global Forest Watch (2000).
21 Canadian Forest Service (1999).
22 Howlett (2001a); Ross (1995).
23 Pratt and Urquhart (1994); Swift (1983); May (1998); Sandberg (1993).
24 Canadian Council of Forest Ministers (1992a, 7).
25 La Forest (1969).
26 Howlett (2001c); *Department of Natural Resources Act,* S.C. 1994, c. 41.
27 Commissioner of the Environment and Sustainable Development (2000, 6-16).
28 Letter from Donna Petrachenko, director general Pacific Region, Department of Fisheries and Oceans, to Lee Doney, deputy minister, Ministry of Forests, 28 February 2000.
29 Commission for Environmental Cooperation (2001a).
30 Canadian Council of Forest Ministers (1997; 1998).
31 May (1998, 7); see also Greenpeace Canada (1997).
32 VanderZwaag and MacKinlay (1996, 36).
33 UN Conference on Environment and Sustainable Development (1992).
34 Bernstein and Cashore (2001b, 74).
35 Sierra Club of Canada (2002).
36 Bernstein and Cashore (2001b).
37 *Constitution Act, 1867,* s. 92A.
38 *Forest Act,* R.S.B.C. 1996, c. 157, and *Forest Practices Code of British Columbia Act,* R.S.B.C. 1996, c. 159; *Forest Act,* R.S.A. 2000, c. F-22; *Forest Resources Management Act,* S.S. 1996, c. F-19.1; *Forest Act,* C.C.S.M. c. F-150; *Crown Forest Sustainability Act,* 1994, S.O. 1994, c. 25; *Forest Act,* R.S.Q., c. F-4.1; *Crown Forests and Land Act,* S.N.B., c. 38.1; *Forest Act,* R.S.N.S. 1989, c. 179; *Forest Management Act,* R.S.P.E.I. 1988, c. F-14; *Forestry Act,* R.S.N.L. 1990, c. F-23; *Forest Management Act,* R.S.N.W.T. 1988, c. F-9.
39 Apsey et al. (2000, 29).
40 Ross (1997).
41 For example, *Manitoba Classes of Development Regulation,* Man. Reg. 164/88R.
42 Ontario Environmental Assessment Board (1994).
43 Hoberg (2001a, 355); *Forest Practices Code of British Columbia Act,* R.S.B.C. 1996, c. 159.
44 Quotations from BC premier Mike Harcourt in Greenpeace Canada (1997, 7, 11).
45 Cote (2000, 57-60); *Chetwynd Environmental Society v. B.C. (Minister of Forests)* (1995). See also Forest Alliance (n.d.).

46 Saskatchewan Environment and Resource Management (1999).
47 Urquhart (2001, 327, 340).
48 Ontario Environmental Assessment Board (1994).
49 *Forest Act*, R.S.Q. c. F-4.1, as amended by *Forest Act*, S.Q. 2001, c. 6; *Regulations respecting standards of forest management for forests in the domain of the State*, c. F-4.1, r. 1.001.1.
50 *Forest Act*, R.S.Q. c. F-4.1, as amended by *Forest Act*, S.Q. 2001, c. 6, s. 25.2.
51 *Forest Act*, R.S.N.S. 1989, c. 179, ss. 7, 10; *Forest Sustainability Regulations*, N.S. Reg. 148/2001; *Wildlife Habitat and Watercourses Protection Regulations*, N.S. Reg. 138/2001.
52 *Forest Act*, R.S.N.S. 1989, c. 179, s. 10A. In contrast, compare the *Forest Practices Code of British Columbia Act* with BC's weak *Private Land Forest Practices Regulation*, B.C. Reg. 318/99.
53 Clancy (2001, 228-9).
54 Moen (1990).
55 *Forest Act*, C.C.S.M. c. F-150, s. 11.
56 Alberta is also unique among Canadian jurisdictions in that licensees own the standing trees. In all other provinces and territories, governments retain ownership until the trees are cut down (*Forest Act*, R.S.A. 2000, c. F-22).
57 *Forest Protection Act*, R.S.N.W.T. 1988, c. F-10; *Forest and Prairie Protection Act*, R.S.A. 2000, c. F-19.
58 *Forest Management Act*, R.S.P.E.I. 1988, c. F-14; *Public Forest Council Act*, S.P.E.I. 2001, c. P-29.1.
59 Wilkinson (1997, 677-8); see also Seymour and Hunter (1999, 47).
60 Ontario is anomalous in that it sets the AAC according to an area to be harvested rather than a volume (*Crown Forest Sustainability Act*, 1994, S.O. 1994, c. 25).
61 *Forest Act*, R.S.B.C. 1996, c. 157, s. 8; Saskatchewan *Forest Resource Management Regulations*, c. F-19.1, Reg. 1, s. 5; *Forestry Act*, R.S.N.L. 1990, c. F-23, s. 9.
62 BC *Forest Act*, R.S.B.C. 1996, c. 157, s. 8.
63 Haley and Luckert (1995, 54); see also Dellert (1998).
64 For an excellent discussion of the history of the "liquidation-conversion" project in British Columbia, see Rayner (2001). See also Marchak (1999); May (1998).
65 Vincent and Clark (1992, 122).
66 Second-growth forests contain a significantly lower volume of timber than old-growth forests. See Marchak (1999); Rayner (2001).
67 *Sierra Club of Western Canada* v. *British Columbia* (1993).
68 *Sierra Club of Western Canada* v. *British Columbia* (1995).
69 *Western Canada Wilderness Committee* v. *British Columbia* (1996).
70 *Cariboo-Chilcotin Conservation Council* v. *British Columbia* (1997).
71 Rayner (2001, 144); see also Hoberg (1994).
72 Hoberg (1994; 2000).
73 *Seattle Audubon Society* v. *Evans; Seattle Audubon Society* v. *Mosely; Northern Spotted Owl et al.* v. *Hodel; Northern Spotted Owl* v. *Lujan*.
74 Wilkinson (1997); US General Accounting Office (1999a).
75 Williams, Duinker, and Bull (1997, 43); Senate Subcommittee on the Boreal Forest (1999).
76 Canadian Council of Forest Ministers (2002).
77 Rayner (2001); Ross (1995, 5); Lawson, Levy, and Sandberg (2001, 293).
78 Canadian Council of Forest Ministers (2002).
79 *Forest Act*, R.S.N.S. 1989, c. 179, ss. 2(g), 2(h).
80 Canadian Council of Forest Ministers (2002); Ontario Ministry of Natural Resources (2002, 25).
81 Cashore et al. (2001, 247).
82 BC Ministry of Forests (1994, ch. 9).
83 Forest Alliance (1995).
84 Rayner (2001); Marchak (1999).
85 Council of Forest Industries (1999).
86 Ross (1997, 119).
87 Moore (1999, para. 1.1.07).
88 Ironically, limiting the size of clear-cuts without reducing the rate of logging may increase ecological damage, as companies are forced to build more roads to access a larger number of dispersed, smaller clear-cuts.
89 Moore (1999, paras. 1.1.08-9).
90 BC Forest Practices Board (1998).

91 *Forest Practices Code of British Columbia Act,* R.S.B.C. 1996, c. 159, s. 45.
92 *Silviculture Practices Regulation,* B.C. Reg. 108/98, s. 30(2).
93 Only one company was penalized for violating section 45(3) in the first three years that the *Code* was in force (BC Ministry of Forests 1999).
94 For an insightful analysis of how the 6 percent cap came to be, see Hoberg (2001c).
95 BC Ministry of Forests (1996).
96 Haddock (1999).
97 BC Ministry of Environment, Land and Parks (2000); Pacific Fisheries Resource Conservation Council (2000); Sierra Legal Defence Fund (2002d).
98 Hoberg (2001a, 361); see also (1994, 9).
99 Ross (1995, 90).
100 Government of British Columbia (1993, 12); Sierra Legal Defence Fund (1998b; 1997a; 1997b; 1997c; 1996).
101 Haddock (1999); BC Ministry of Environment, Land and Parks (2000); Sierra Legal Defence Fund (1997c).
102 Forest Practices Board (1999); see also Moore (1999); Pynn (2000).
103 Hoberg (2001a, 366).
104 Global Forest Watch (2000, 81).
105 BC Ministry of Environment, Land and Parks (2001); BC Government Employees Union (1999).
106 Hoberg (2001a, 363).
107 KPMG Chartered Accountants (1997); Haley (1996). The KPMG study estimated increased logging costs based on interviews with forest company executives. The Haley study attributed $1.4 billion annually to the opportunity cost of a lower rate of logging caused by the *Code,* but the rate of logging in BC did not decline after the enactment of the *Code.*
108 Mancell (1999, p. 2.1.01).
109 Moore quoted in Palmer (1998).
110 *Forest and Range Practices Act,* S.B.C. 2002, c. 69; *Forest Statutes Amendment Act,* S.B.C. 2002, c. 45.
111 BC Ministry of Sustainable Resource Management (2002); BC Ministry of Forests (2002a).
112 Clogg (2001, 1).
113 Lawson, Levy, and Sandberg (2001, 297).
114 Swan (1994, 201).
115 Environmental Commissioner of Ontario (1998, 37).
116 *Algonquin Wildlands League* v. *Ontario* (1998), 197.
117 Ontario Provincial Auditor (2000, 222).
118 Sierra Legal Defence Fund (2002b); Sierra Legal Defence Fund and Wildlands League (2001; 2000; 1998); Environmental Commissioner of Ontario (1999).
119 Ontario Environmental Assessment Board (1994, condition 27, 439).
120 Ontario Ministry of Natural Resources (2002, 34; 1999).
121 Ontario Ministry of Natural Resources (2001a); Mittelstaedt (2001b); David Schindler, letter to Joe Churcher, Ontario Ministry of Natural Resources, 30 October 2001, on file with the author; McRae et al. (2001).
122 Lawson, Levy, and Sandberg (2001, 306); Environmental Commissioner of Ontario (1997, 37, 42).
123 Wilson (2001b, 115).
124 Moore (1999); Forest Practices Board (1999); Blue Ribbon Panel (1997); Independent Expert Evaluation Panel (2001).
125 Food and Agriculture Organization (1998, 80).
126 Hoberg (2001c, 61).
127 Canadian Council of Forest Ministers (2002).
128 Lindquist and Wellstead (2001, 424); Ross (1995, 343).
129 Howlett and Rayner (2001, 42).
130 Ross (1995, 17); Global Forest Watch (2000).
131 BC cabinet minister R. Sommers went to jail in 1958 for accepting a bribe in awarding a logging licence. See Ross (1995); Marchak (1995, 115).
132 Global Forest Watch (2000, 48).
133 Haley and Luckert (1990).
134 Marchak (1999).

135 M'Gonigle and Parfitt (1994, 22, 41, 83-93).
136 Egan et al. (2001, 38).
137 For example, BC Forest Resources Commission (1991).
138 Ross (1997, 15).
139 Hoberg (2001c).
140 Cohen and Radnoff (1998); Schwindt (1992); BC's *Protected Areas Forests Compensation Act,* S.B.C. 2002, c. 51.
141 Gale (1998).
142 Council of Forest Industries (1999).
143 For example, *Crown Forest Sustainability Act,* 1994, S.O. 1994, c. 25, s. 26; *Forest Resources Management Act,* S.S. 1996, c. F-19.1, s. 34.
144 Perry Commission (1999).
145 Canadian Council of Forest Ministers (2002).
146 Ross (1995, 317); See also BC Forest Resources Commission (1991).
147 M'Gonigle et al. (2001); Egan et al. (2001).
148 Nisga'a Final Agreement, ch. 5, para. 8 (*Nisga'a Final Agreement Act,* S.B.C. 1999, c. 2; *Nisga'a Final Agreement Act,* S.C. 2000, c. 7).
149 *R. v. Thomas Paul* (1997), (1998); Clancy (2001, 230).
150 Grand Council of the Crees (2002).
151 Trilateral Agreement between the Algonquins of Barrière Lake and Le Gouvernement du Québec (1991).
152 Clancy (2001).
153 *Council of the Haida Nation v. British Columbia* (2002); *Gitxsan and other First Nations v. British Columbia (Minister of Forests)* 2002 BCSC 1701 Tysoe, J.
154 *First Nations Land Management Act,* S.C. 1999, c. 24.
155 Curran and M'Gonigle (1999).
156 Lindquist and Wellstead (2001, 425); Doyle-Bedwell and Cohen (2001); Boyd and Williams-Davidson (2000).
157 Curran and M'Gonigle (1999).
158 Bernstein and Cashore (2001b, 84).
159 Natural Resources Canada (2001b, 78-9); Forest Products Association of Canada (2001).
160 Natural Resources Canada (2001b, 78-9).
161 Cashore et al. (2001, 255-6).
162 Marchak (1995).
163 Council of Forest Industries (1999).
164 Hayter and Holmes (2001, 152).
165 Wilson (2001b, 115); Howlett and Rayner (2001, 31); Ross (1995, 257).

4.3: Environmental Assessment

1   Canadian Environmental Assessment Agency (2000b; see also 1996).
2   Canadian Environmental Assessment Agency (2000a, 3).
3   Munn (1999).
4   Saskatchewan Mining Association (2000); "Provincial/Territorial Recommendations" (2001, 2); Seguin (1992).
5   Suzuki quoted in Elder (1992, 126); Schindler (1976); Livingston (1981, 33); Rees (1990, 132); Sadar quoted in Nikiforuk (1997, 3).
6   *Friends of the Oldman River v. Minister of Transport,* [1992].
7   Penney (1994, 268).
8   Hazell (1999).
9   World Commission on Environment and Development (1987, 222).
10 Kennett (1999, 6).
11 Mackenzie (1994); Hanebury (1999).
12 *National Environmental Protection Act,* 42 U.S.C. 4321 et seq.
13 Berger (1977).
14 *Kemano Completion Project Guidelines Order,* SOR/90-279. The Kemano Completion Project became embroiled in a series of lawsuits, was partially built, and then cancelled by the BC government after a belated series of public hearings in the mid-1990s.
15 See Northey (1994).
16 *Canadian Wildlife Federation v. Canada,* [1990]; *Friends of the Oldman River v. Minister of Transport,* [1992].

17 de Cotret quoted in Jeffery (1991, 1082).
18 *Ibid.*; Doelle (1994).
19 *Canadian Environmental Assessment Act,* S.C. 1992, c. 37, s. 4.
20 For example, in 1997-8, 5,042 out of 5,047 projects were approved. These statistics are based on the Agency's annual reports (Canadian Environmental Assessment Agency 1997; 1998; 1999).
21 *Law List Regulations,* SOR/94-163; *Inclusion List Regulations,* SOR/94-164; *Exclusion List Regulations,* SOR/94-316.
22 *Sierra Club of Canada* v. *Canada.* Section 5(1)(b) of the *Canadian Environmental Assessment Act* specifically states that an environmental assessment is required when the federal government "provides a guarantee for a loan."
23 Canadian Environmental Assessment Agency (n.d.).
24 Government of Canada (1999a).
25 Hazell and Benevides (1997).
26 *Canadian Environmental Assessment Act,* S.C. 1992, c. 37, s. 8; Hazell (1999, 123-4).
27 Bill C-9, *An Act to Amend the Canadian Environmental Assessment Act.*
28 *Comprehensive Study List Regulations,* SOR/94-229.
29 Canadian Environmental Assessment Agency (2000b).
30 Hazell (1999, 157).
31 Canadian Environmental Assessment Agency (2000b).
32 Tilleman (1995).
33 Canadian Environmental Assessment Agency (2000b, 26).
34 Hazell (1999, 152).
35 Liberal Party of Canada (1993, 64).
36 Canadian Environmental Assessment Agency (2001).
37 Robert B. Gibson (2001, 85).
38 *An Act to Amend the Export Development Corporation Act,* S.C. 2001, c. 33; Seck (2001).
39 Commissioner of the Environment and Sustainable Development (1998, 6-17).
40 Kennett (1995).
41 Canadian Environmental Assessment Agency (2000b, 26-7).
42 O'Reilly (1996).
43 Voisey's Bay Environmental Assessment Panel (1999); Gibson (2000).
44 Bill C-2, the *Yukon Environmental and Socioeconomic Assessment Act,* was enacted by Parliament on 18 March 2003. *Environment Assessment Act,* S.B.C. 2002, c. 43; *Environmental Protection and Enhancement Act,* R.S.A. 2000, c. E-12, ss. 37-57; *Environmental Assessment Act,* R.S.S. 1978, c. E-10.1; *Environment Act,* C.C.S.M. c. E-125; *Environment Assessment Act,* R.S.O. 1990, c. E-18; *Environmental Quality Act,* R.S.Q., Q-2, s. 31; *Regulation respecting environmental impact assessment and review,* R.R.Q. 1981, c. Q-2, r. 9; *Clean Environment Act,* R.S.N.B. 1973, c. C-6, and *Environmental Impact Assessment Regulation,* N.B. Reg. 87-83; *Environmental Protection Act,* R.S.P.E.I. 1988, c. E-9, s. 9; *Environment Act,* S.N.S. 1994-95, c. 1, and *Environmental Assessment Regulations,* N.S. Reg. 26/95; *Environmental Protection Act,* S.N. 2002, c. E-14.2, ss. 45-77, and *Environmental Assessment Regulations,* 2000, Nfld. Reg. 48/00.
45 For example, BC's *Prescribed Time Limits Regulation,* B.C. Reg. 372/2002. A report from Natural Resources Canada urged that the federal EA process should incorporate time limits so as to keep Canada competitive with Chile, as the Chilean mining industry apparently benefits from EA time limits (Standing Committee on Natural Resources 1996).
46 Saskatchewan Environmental Assessment Review Commission (1991).
47 *Reviewable Projects Regulation,* B.C. Reg. 370/2002; *Environmental Assessment (Mandatory and Exempted Activities) Regulation,* Alta. Reg. 111/93, Schedule 1(q).
48 *Environmental Assessment (Mandatory and Exempted Activities) Regulation,* Alta. Reg. 111/93, Schedule 2(e).
49 *Environment Assessment Act,* S.B.C. 2002, c. 43, s. 5(3).
50 The one exception is that all major waste projects (e.g., landfills, incinerators), whether public or private, are required to undergo EA (*Environmental Assessment Act,* R.S.O. 1990, c. E-18, s. 17.1; Valiante 1998).
51 For example, *Environmental Protection and Enhancement Act,* R.S.A. 2000, c. E-12, s. 47(d); *Mackenzie Valley Resource Management Act,* S.C. 1998, c. 25, s. 117(2)(a).
52 For example, *Environmental Protection and Enhancement Act,* R.S.A. 2000, c.E-12, s. 47(a).
53 *Ibid.,* s. 47(h).
54 *Environmental Assessment Regulations,* N.S. Reg. 26/95, s. 19.

55 For example, *Environmental Quality Act,* R.S.Q., Q-2, s. 31.3.
56 For example, *Environmental Assessment Act,* R.S.S. 1978, c. E-10.1, s. 15; *Environmental Quality Act,* R.S.Q., Q-2, s. 31(5)
57 For example, *Environment Assessment Act,* R.S.O. 1990, c. E-18, s. 11; *Environment Act,* S.N.S. 1994-95, c. 1, s. 40.
58 *Environmental Assessment and Consultation Improvement Act,* 1996, S.O. 1996, c. 27; Canadian Environmental Law Association (2002); Levy (2002).
59 *Intervenor Funding Project Act,* R.S.O. 1990, c. I-13.
60 Valiante (1998, 263-4).
61 *Environmental Assessment Act,* R.S.B.C. 1996, c. 119, ss. 20, 22, 30, 34.
62 For example, review thresholds for coal mines were raised from 100,000 tonnes of production per year to 250,000 tonnes (*Environmental Assessment Reviewable Projects Regulation,* B.C. Reg. 370/2002).
63 Provincial/Territorial Recommendations (2001).
64 Canadian Environmental Assessment Agency (2000b).
65 Commissioner of the Environment and Sustainable Development (1998, 6-23).
66 Sadler (1996a, 58).
67 Nisga'a Final Agreement, ch. 10; *Nisga'a Final Agreement Act,* S.B.C. 1999, c. 2.
68 *Agreement Between the Inuit of the Nunavut Settlement Area and Her Majesty the Queen in Right of Canada* (1993), article 12.
69 *Mackenzie Valley Resource Management Act,* S.C. 1998, c. 25, ss. 111-44.
70 Dene Cultural Institute (1995).
71 *Quebec (Attorney General)* v. *Canada,* [1994]; *Taku River Tlingit* v. *Ringstad* (2000), affirmed (2002); *Union of Nova Scotia Indians* v. *Canada* (1997); *Tsawwassen Indian Band* v. *Canada* (1998), affirmed (2001); *Cheslatta Carrier* v. *John Marczyk* (1998); *Vuntut Gwitchin* v. *Canada* (1998); *Naskapi-Montagnais Innu* v. *Canada,* [1990].
72 Litigation occurred in panel reviews for the Express Pipeline, Sable Gas, Voisey's Bay, Sunshine Village ski resort, Cheviot Coal Mine, and Red Hill Expressway projects.
73 *Canadian Wildlife Federation* v. *Canada,* [1990].
74 *Friends of the Oldman River* v. *Canada,* [1992].
75 Glenn (1999).
76 *Canadian Parks and Wilderness Society* v. *Superintendent of Banff National Park* (1994).
77 *Sunshine Village Corp.* v. *Superintendent of Banff National Park* (1996); *Sunshine Village Corp.* v. *Canada* (1995).
78 *Quebec (Attorney General)* v. *Canada,* [1994].
79 *Canadian Parks and Wilderness Society* v. *Canada (Minister of Indian Affairs and Northern Development)* (1994).
80 *Alberta Wilderness Association* v. *Express Pipelines Ltd.* (1996).
81 *Sierra Club of Canada* v. *Canada.*
82 *Friends of the West Country Association* v. *Canada* (1997).
83 *Labrador Inuit Association* v. *Newfoundland* (1997).
84 *Friends of the West Country Association* v. *Canada* (1999).
85 *Alberta Wilderness Association* v. *Canada* (1999).
86 *Bow Valley Naturalists Society* v. *Canada* (1999); *Manitoba Future Forest Alliance* v. *Canada* (1999); *Citizen's Mining Council* v. *Canada* (1999).
87 *Canadian Environmental Law Association* v. *Canada* (2000).
88 *Inverhuron and District Ratepayers Association* v. *Canada* (2000).
89 *Taku River Tlingit* v. *Ringstad* (2000), affirmed (2002).
90 Denstedt (1999, 53).
91 Carpenter (1999, 144).
92 *Canadian Wildlife Federation* v. *Canada,* [1990]; *Friends of the Oldman River* v. *Canada,* [1992].
93 *Alberta Wilderness Association* v. *Canada* (1999).
94 Lucas (1993, 194).
95 *Alberta Wilderness Association* v. *Express Pipelines Ltd.* (1996); *Inverhuron and District Ratepayers Association* v. *Canada* (2000).
96 Gilmour (1999).
97 *Taku River Tlingit* v. *Ringstad* (2000), affirmed (2002).
98 Examples of the former include *Quebec (Attorney General)* v. *Canada,* [1994]; *Friends of the West Country Association* v. *Canada (Minister of Fisheries and Oceans)* (1999, 2000). Examples of the

latter include *Manitoba Future Forest Alliance* v. *Canada* (1999); *Citizen's Mining Council* v. *Canada* (1999).
99 Commissioner of the Environment and Sustainable Development (1998, 6-16).
100 Robinson (1990).
101 Jeffery (1991, 1072).
102 Doyle and Sadler (1996).
103 Castrilli (1974); Rees (1991).
104 Rees (1990, 133).
105 *Labrador Inuit Association* v. *Newfoundland* (1997), 236.

5: Biodiversity
1 Krebs (1999).
2 Heywood and Watson (1995).
3 For a low estimate, see Dolphin and Quicke (2001). For a higher estimate, see Wilson (1992, 161).
4 Benton (1995).
5 Easterbrook (1995, 556-62); Jones and Fredricksen (1999).
6 May, Lawton, and Stork (1995); Tudge (2000); Raup (1992).
7 Heywood and Watson (1995).
8 Wilson (1992, 280); Levin (2001).
9 Ward (1994, 234); Heywood and Watson (1995, 198); World Conservation Union (2000); Bourdages (1996, 6); Ward (1994).
10 Jablonski (1995, 39).
11 Morrison and Turner (1994); Environment Canada (1996c, 3-11, 17-9); Mosquin (2000, 65); Linton (1997, 47).
12 Mosquin (2000).
13 Slaney et al. (1996); Environment Canada (1996c, 11-42).
14 Ehrenfeld (1988).
15 Daily (1997).
16 Chivian (2001).
17 Environment Canada (1996d).
18 Environment Canada (1995a).
19 OECD (1999b).
20 Panel on the Ecological Integrity of Canada's National Parks (2000); Auditor General of Canada (1996).
21 *Species at Risk Act,* S.C. 2002, c. 29.

5.1: Parks and Protected Areas
1 Panel on the Ecological Integrity of Canada's National Parks (2000, 1:9).
2 Trudeau (2000), Foreword.
3 Greene and Paine (1997).
4 *Ibid.*
5 Panel on the Ecological Integrity of Canada's National Parks (2000).
6 Searle (2000).
7 Boyd (2002c).
8 Struzik (1998).
9 See *Canada National Parks Act,* S.C. 2000, c. 32; *Canada Wildlife Act,* R.S.C. 1985, c. W-9, amended substantially by S.C. 1994, c. 23; *Migratory Birds Convention Act, 1994,* S.C. 1994, c. 22.
10 Eagles (1993b, 72).
11 Panel on the Ecological Integrity of Canada's National Parks (2000).
12 Le Roy and Cooper (2000).
13 Boyd (2002c).
14 Rollins and Dearden (1993, 294).
15 The exceptions are the *Canada National Parks Act,* S.C. 2000, c. 32; *Wilderness Areas Protection Act,* S.N.S. 1998, c. 27; and *Wilderness and Ecological Reserves Act,* R.S.N. 1990, c. W-9.
16 Wilson (1992).
17 Swaigen (2000).
18 McNamee (1993, 273).

19 Attridge (1996).
20 Stephenson (1994, 210).
21 *Oceans Act,* S.C. 1996, c. 31, s. 30(c).
22 See the brief by Alberta's Environmental Law Centre, "In Response to Bill 15: The Natural Heritage Act" at <http://www.elc.ab.ca>.
23 Bocking (2000). A poll by BC Parks found that over 80 percent of respondents said that the main reason for parks is to protect wildlife and wildlife habitat (BC Parks 1995).
24 Noss and Cooperrider (1994).
25 Environment Canada (1995a, 22-5); see also Environment Canada (1998d, 22).
26 Bella (1987).
27 *Canada National Parks Act,* S.C. 2000, c. 32, s. 4(1).
28 Banff-Bow Valley Task Force (1996).
29 *Canada National Parks Act,* S.C. 2000, c. 32, s. 8(2); *Canadian Parks and Wilderness Society* v. *Sheila Copps* (2001). The approval of the road was overturned in a separate decision on the basis that Parks Canada failed to adequately consult Aboriginal people; see *Mikisew Cree* v. *Sheila Copps* (2001).
30 *Wilderness Areas Protection Act,* S.N.S. 1998, c. 27, s. 2; *Parks Act,* R.S.Q. 1977, c. P-9; *Natural Areas Protection Act,* R.S.P.E.I. 1988, c. N-2; *Wilderness and Ecological Reserves Act,* R.S.N. 1990, c. W-9.
31 Williams (1995).
32 A lawsuit seeking to stop construction of the logging road was unsuccessful; see *Society of the Friends of Strathcona Park* v. *British Columbia* (1999).
33 World Wildlife Fund (1997, 38).
34 *Provincial Park Regulations,* N.S. Reg. 69/89, as amended, s. 20(2).
35 Searle (2000, 142).
36 Ministry of Environment (1979).
37 Sierra Legal Defence Fund (1992).
38 *Canadian Parks and Wilderness Society* v. *Superintendent of Wood Buffalo National Park* (1992).
39 *National Parks General Regulations,* SOR/78-213, as amended.
40 *Canadian Parks and Wilderness Society* v. *Superintendent of Banff National Park* (1994) and *Sunshine Village Corp.* v. *Superintendent, Banff National Park* (1996); *Young et al.* v. *Canada* (1999); *Bowen* v. *Canada,* [1998]; *Schwarz Hospitality Group Ltd.* v. *Canada* (2001); *Moresby Explorers Ltd. et al.* v. *Canada* (2001); *Alberta Wilderness Association* v. *Canada* (1999) and *Alberta Wilderness Association* v. *Cardinal River Coals Ltd.* (1999); *Peter G. White Mgmt.* v. *Canada* (1997); *Canadian Parks and Wilderness Society* v. *Sheila Copps* (2001), *Mikisew Cree* v. *Sheila Copps* (2001), and *Algonquin Wildlands League* v. *Northern Bruce Peninsula* (2000); *Bow Valley Naturalists Society* v. *Minister of Canadian Heritage* (1999), affirmed (2001).
41 *Canadian Parks and Wilderness Society* v. *Sheila Copps* (2001), paras. 49-50.
42 *Parks Act,* R.S.Q. c. P-9, s. 7; *Natural Areas Protection Act,* R.S.P.E.I. 1988, c. N-2, and *Natural Areas Protection Act Regulations* R.R.P.E.I. c. N-2, s. 3.
43 World Wildlife Fund Canada (2000).
44 *Newfoundland and Labrador Wildlife Federation* v. *Newfoundland* (2001).
45 Bella (1987).
46 Environment Canada (1991, 7-5).
47 McNamee (1993, 284); Hanna (1995); Federal Provincial Parks Council (2000).
48 *Protected Areas Association of Newfoundland and Labrador et al.* v. *Minister of Environment et al.* (2002) Supreme Court of Newfoundland and Labrador, Trial Division 2002 OIT No. 4357 (28 October 2002).
49 Pynn (2001); BC Ministry of Sustainable Resource Management (2001).
50 Federal laws must then repeat the same process in the Senate.
51 *Canada National Parks Act,* S.C. 2000, c. 32, ss. 5 and 7.
52 *Park Act,* R.S.B.C. 1996, c. 344, s. 5(6); *Wilderness Areas Protection Act,* S.N.S. 1998, c. 27, s. 11(5); *Parks Act,* S.S. 1986, c. P-1.1.
53 *Parks Act,* R.S.Q. 1977 c. P-9; *Wilderness and Ecological Reserves Act,* R.S.N. 1990, c. W-9; *Provincial Park Act,* S.M. 1993, c. P-20.
54 Lausche (1980, 31).
55 Partnership for Public Lands (1999).
56 Ontario Ministry of Northern Development and Mines (1999).

57 Tungavik Federation of Nunavut (1990); Morrison (1995, 18-26); See the Nisga'a Final Agreement (BC Ministry of Aboriginal Affairs, 1998). <http://www.aaf.gov.bc.ca/aaf/treaty/ nisgaa>.
58 *Makivik Corp. and Nunavik Inuit v. Canada* (1998).
59 *Canada National Parks Act,* S.C. 2000, c. 32, ss. 6(2) and 38.
60 Eagles (1993a, 72).
61 In 2000, wilderness areas in Banff, Jasper, Yoho, and Kootenay national parks were designated by *National Parks Wilderness Area Declaration Regulations,* SOR/2000-387.
62 Jones and de Villars (1999, 570-1).
63 *Canada National Parks Act,* S.C. 2000, c. 32, s. 14.
64 *Young et al. v. Canada* (1999); *Bow Valley Naturalists Society v. Minister of Canadian Heritage* (1999), affirmed (2001).
65 Nowlan (1996, 219).
66 Stephenson (1994, 202).
67 *Wilderness and Ecological Reserves Act,* R.S.N. 1990, c. W-9, ss. 15-16; *Wilderness Areas Protection Act,* S.N.S. 1998, c. 27, s. 15; *Parks and Land Certainty Act,* S.Y. 2001, c. 22, ss. 19, 21; *Provincial Park Act,* S.M. 1993, c. P-20, s. 11.
68 Newmark (1995; 1987).
69 Parks Canada (1998, 25).
70 MacArthur and Wilson (1967).
71 Quammen (1996).
72 Panel on the Ecological Integrity of Canada's National Parks (2000, 1:8-5).
73 Noss and Cooperrider (1994).
74 World Wildlife Fund Canada (2000, 1, i).
75 Canadian Council of Ministers of the Environment (1992, 299).
76 *Park Act,* R.S.B.C. 1996, c. 344, s. 5(2).
77 Hummel (1995, 39).
78 Environment Canada (1998d, 23).
79 World Wildlife Fund Canada (2000).
80 Auditor General of Canada (1989), Main Points, para. 11.3.
81 OECD (1999b); Greene and Paine (1997). The World Wildlife Fund ranks Canada thirty-third while the Panel on Ecological Integrity ranks Canada thirty-sixth (World Wildlife Fund Canada 2000, 6; Panel on the Ecological Integrity of Canada's National Parks 2000, 2:8-3).
82 Greene and Paine (1997); OECD (1999b).
83 World Wildlife Fund Canada (2000, 22).
84 Noss (1996); Sanjayan and Soule (1997).
85 Stephenson (1994, 204).
86 Turennes (2000).
87 BC Land Use Coordination Office (1996).
88 Scudder (2003).
89 Panel on the Ecological Integrity of Canada's National Parks (2000, 1:13); Searle (2000, ch. 2, 5).
90 Lowry (1994, 44, 90, 150).
91 Auditor General (1996, para. 31.31).
92 Searle (2000, 222).
93 *Parks Canada Agency Act,* S.C. 1998, c. 31.
94 Searle (2000, 96-112).
95 Peart (2001, 12, 8).
96 Lawson, Levy, and Sandberg (2001).
97 Federal Provincial Parks Council (2000).
98 Boyd (2002c).
99 Panel on the Ecological Integrity of Canada's National Parks (2000, 2:14-5).

5.2: Endangered Species
1 Environment Canada (1996d).
2 Pollara (1999).
3 Environics (2000).

4 Kate Smallwood, Canadian Endangered Species Coalition, personal communication, 4 December 2001.
5 McIlroy (1997b); see also Boyd (2000); Commissioner of the Environment and Sustainable Development (1998).
6 Environment Canada (1998d, i).
7 DePalma (1998); Kukowski (2000).
8 *General Law of Ecological Balance and Environmental Protection (Ley General del Equilibrio Ecológico y Protección al Ambiente)* and Official Mexican Standard NOM-059-ECOL-1994; *Endangered Species Act,* 16 U.S.C. 1531-44.
9 Mittelstaedt (1998).
10 Le Prestre and Stoett (2001, 213).
11 Jones and Fredricksen (1999).
12 Freedman et al. (2001).
13 Environment Canada (2000b).
14 Mosquin (2000).
15 Freedman et al. (2001).
16 US National Research Council (1993a).
17 Commissioner of the Environment and Sustainable Development (1998, 4-11, 12).
18 A. Keith Mitchell Q.C., letter to Jean-Pierre Martel, Canadian Pulp and Paper Association, 7 April 1997. On file with the author.
19 Amos, Harrison, and Hoberg (2001); Beazley and Boardman (2001).
20 Fulton (2001).
21 Jones and Fredricksen (1999, 19); Avram (1997).
22 Anderson quoted in Mittelstaedt (2002a).
23 *Species at Risk Act,* S.C. 2002, c. 29, ss. 32-4, 58-61.
24 Boyd and Wallace (2001).
25 de Klemm and Shine (1993, 73).
26 *Species at Risk Act,* S.C. 2002, c. 29, ss. 34-5, 58, 61.
27 *Canada Wildlife Act,* R.S.C. 1985, c. W-9, s. 12(b); *Canadian Environmental Assessment Act,* S.C. 1992, c. 37, ss. 46-7; *Canada Water Act,* R.S.C. 1985, c. C-11, ss. 6, 13; *Canadian Environmental Protection Act, 1999,* S.C. 1999, c. 33, s. 165.
28 Elgie (2001).
29 Bocking (2001, 127).
30 Dawson (2001).
31 Hogg (2000).
32 La Forest and Gibson (2000a; 2000b); Gibson (1996).
33 Dale Gibson (2001, 35).
34 Muir (2001).
35 Sergio Marchi, *Hansard,* House of Commons Debates, 31 October 1996, at 5961.
36 *Endangered Species Act,* 16 U.S.C. 1531; de Klemm and Shine (1993, 69).
37 *Species at Risk Act,* S.C. 2002, c. 29, ss. 14-25.
38 *Ibid.,* s. 2(1).
39 *Ibid.,* s. 27(1.2).
40 McIlroy (1999).
41 *Endangered Species Regulation,* R.R.O. Reg. 328.
42 *Wildlife Regulation,* Alta. Reg. 143/97 (amended to 151/01).
43 *Endangered Species Act,* 16 U.S.C. 1531; *General Law of Ecological Balance and Environmental Protection (Ley General del Equilibrio Ecológico y Protección al Ambiente),* NOM-059-ECOL-1994.
44 Yaffee (1994).
45 *Species at Risk Act,* S.C. 2002, c. 29, s. 32.
46 *Ibid.,* ss. 34-5.
47 Aniskowicz (1998).
48 Kukowski (2000); Ray and Ginsberg (1999).
49 *Species at Risk Act,* S.C. 2002, c. 29, s. 73.
50 Heywood and Watson (1995).
51 Anderson quoted in Canadian Nature Federation (2000).
52 *Species at Risk Act,* S.C. 2002, c. 29, s. 33.
53 Green (2001).
54 Scudder (2001).

55 *Species at Risk Act,* S.C. 2002, c. 29, s. 58.
56 *Ibid.,* ss. 58, 61.
57 Elgie (2001).
58 *Species at Risk Act,* S.C. 2002, c. 29, ss. 37-46, 50.
59 Freedman et al. (2001).
60 Amos, Harrison, and Hoberg (2001, 157).
61 Heywood and Watson (1995, 1045).
62 *Species at Risk Act,* S.C. 2002, c. 29, ss. 10-13.
63 *Ibid.,* s. 64.
64 *Ibid.,* s. 97.
65 *Ibid.,* s. 93.
66 Heywood and Watson (1995, 1046).
67 Species at Risk Working Group (1998).
68 Smith (2001, 522).
69 *National Accord for the Protection of Species at Risk.* See <http://www.ec.gc.ca/press/wild_b_e.htm>.
70 *Endangered Species Act,* C.C.S.M. c. E-111; *Endangered Species Act,* R.S.O. 1990, c. E-15 and *Fish and Wildlife Conservation Act,* S.O. 1997, c. 41; *An Act Respecting Threatened or Vulnerable Species,* R.S.Q. 1977, c. E-12.01, and *An Act Respecting the Conservation and Development of Wildlife,* R.S.Q. 1977, c. C-61.1; *Endangered Species Act,* S.N.B. 1996, c. E-9.101; *Endangered Species Act,* S.N.S. 1998, c. 11; *Wildlife Conservation Act,* S.P.E.I. c. W-4.1; *Endangered Species Act,* S.N. 2001, c. E-10.1.
71 *Wildlife Act,* R.S.B.C. 1996, c. 488; *Wildlife Act,* R.S.A. 2000, c. W-10; *Wildlife Act,* S.S. 1998, c. W-13.12, and *Wildlife Habitat Protection Act, 1998,* S.S. 1998, c. W-13.2; *Wildlife Act,* R.S.N.W.T. 1988, c. W-4; *Wildlife Act,* R.S.Y. 1986, c. 178.
72 Canadian Nature Federation (2001).
73 *Endangered Species Act,* S.N. 2001, c. E-10.1.
74 Ontario Ministry of Natural Resources (2001b).
75 Bowman and the Rare, Threatened and Endangered Species Task Force (1993).
76 Environmental Commissioner of Ontario (2000a, 48).
77 Environment Canada (1998f, 32).
78 Attridge (1996).
79 Jones (1997).
80 *Endangered Species Act,* S.N.S. 1998, c. 11, s. 10; *Species at Risk List Regulations,* N.S. Reg. 109/2000, as amended by N.S. Reg. 82/2001.
81 *Wildlife Act,* R.S.B.C. 1996, c. 488, s. 6(1).
82 *Wildlife Act Designation and Exemption Regulation,* B.C. Reg. 168/90, Schedules D and E; BC Ministry of Environment, Land and Parks (2000, 36).
83 *Endangered Species List Regulations,* N.L. Reg. 57/02.
84 Canadian Nature Federation (2001); Caccia (2001).
85 Jones (1997).
86 *Wildlife Management Areas Regulation No. 3 (Green Mountain Wildlife Management Area),* B.C. Reg. 183/91.
87 Canadian Nature Federation (2001).
88 *Endangered Species Act,* S.N.S. 1998, c. 11; *Endangered Species Act,* S.N. 2001, c. E-10.1.
89 *Provincial Offences Procedure Act,* R.S.N.B. c. P-22.1, ss. 56-70.
90 Attridge (1996).
91 *Endangered Species Act,* 16 U.S.C. 1531.
92 US National Research Council (1995, 1); Houck (1995, 702).
93 *T.V.A. v. Hill* (1978).
94 Kohm (1991, 38).
95 Lambert and Smith (1994); Helmy (2000); Babbitt (1994).
96 Kohm (1991).
97 US National Research Council (1995).
98 Forest Alliance (1996, 1).
99 Ruhl (1999a).
100 Houck (1993).
101 Power and Barrett (2001).
102 Houck (1993, 319).
103 Attridge (1996, 469).

104 Scudder (1999).
105 Environment Canada (n.d.a).
106 Senate Committee on Energy, the Environment and Natural Resources (2002).
107 Noss (1994).
108 McNeely (1999).
109 Heywood and Watson (1995, 258).
110 *Species at Risk Act*, S.C. 2002, c. 29, ss. 127, 129.
111 Wilson (1992, 280).

5.3: Marine Biodiversity
1   Groombridge and Jenkins (2000).
2   Food and Agriculture Organization (1999b).
3   Loh et al. (1999).
4   Pauly et al. (1998, 863); Pauly et al. (2001).
5   McAllister (2000).
6   Department of Fisheries and Oceans (2001b).
7   Benyus (1997); Chivian (2001).
8   Daily (1997).
9   Environment Canada (2000b).
10 See "Canadian Species at Risk," COSEWIC's website <http://www.cosewic.gc.ca>.
11 Mosquin, Whiting, and McAllister (1995).
12 See the Department of Fisheries and Oceans website for catch statistics, <http://www.dfo-mpo.gc.ca/communic/Statistics/landings/>; Environment Canada (1996c, 11-42).
13 Watling and Norse (1998). The impact of bottom trawling depends on the nature of the ocean floor. For example, coral is far more sensitive to disturbance than is sand (US National Academy of Sciences 2002).
14 Ford, Ellis, and Balcomb (2000).
15 Martell and Wallace (1998).
16 Kurlansky (1997, 48).
17 Berrill (1997, 112-17).
18 Harris (1998, 109).
19 Crosbie quoted *ibid.*, 141.
20 Fisheries Resource Conservation Council (1994); Hutchings and Myers (1994).
21 Safina (1998, 45).
22 Auditor General of Canada (1999a).
23 Environment Canada (1996c, 11-43).
24 Comeau (1997).
25 Harris (1998, 233).
26 Fu, Mohn, and Fanning (2001).
27 Northcote and Atagi (1997); Glavin (1996, 15).
28 Fisheries Renewal BC (2000).
29 Slaney et al. (1996).
30 Environment Canada (1996c, 3-1).
31 Environment Canada (1990a, 36); Walters (1998, 78).
32 Fraser (1994, xii).
33 Auditor General of Canada (1999c, para. 20.15).
34 Fraser (1994); Pearse (1992).
35 Auditor General of Canada (1999c, para. 20.1).
36 US National Research Council Committee on Biological Diversity (1995); Norse (1993).
37 Ryder and Scott (1994, 137).
38 *Constitution Act, 1867* (U.K.), s. 91(12); *R. v. Crown Zellerbach*, [1988]; *Fowler v. The Queen* (1980); *Northwest Falling Contractors Ltd. v. The Queen* (1980).
39 Estrin and Swaigen (1993, 522); Attridge (2000, 319).
40 US National Research Council Committee on Biological Diversity (1995).
41 *Fisheries Act*, R.S.C. 1985, c. F-14, ss. 7 and 43; *Comeau's Sea Foods Ltd. v. Canada* [1997].
42 For example, *Fishery (General) Regulations*, SOR/93-53; *Newfoundland Fishery Regulations*, SOR/78-443; *Pacific Fishery Regulations*, SOR/93-54.
43 For example, *BC Sport Fishing Regulations*, SOR/96-137.
44 *Aboriginal Communal Fishing Licences Regulations*, SOR/93-332; *R. v. Marshall*, [1999] and [1999].

45 *United Nations Agreement on Straddling Fish Stocks and Highly Migratory Fish Stocks.*
46 Auditor General of Canada (1997c, para. 14.3).
47 Glavin (1996, 64).
48 Auditor General of Canada (1997c, paras. 14.14, 14.33, 14.36).
49 Auditor General of Canada (1999b, paras. 4.52, 4.82; 1999c, paras. 20.21, 20.67).
50 Auditor General of Canada (1999b, paras. 4.50, 4.61; 2000c).
51 Department of Fisheries and Oceans (1999b). See also DFO (1999c).
52 Glavin (2001).
53 The 80 percent figure is from Baron (1998, 15). The 15 percent figure is from Department of
    Fisheries and Oceans (2001a).
54 Auditor General of Canada (2000a).
55 Wallace (1999).
56 *R. v. Robertson,* [1882].
57 *National Inshore Fisherman Association v. Canada,* [1990].
58 *Nunavut Tunngavik Inc. v. Canada* (1997) and (1998).
59 *Neskonlith Band v. Canada* (1997); see "Canadian Species at Risk" on the Species Listing page
    at <http://www.cosewic.gc.ca>.
60 *Ecology Action Centre v. Canada.*
61 *Fisheries Act,* R.S.C. 1985, c. F-14, s. 35(1).
62 *Friends of the West Country Association v. Canada* (1997), 141.
63 Department of Fisheries and Oceans (1999a); Juillet and Toner (1997, 185).
64 Auditor General of Canada (2000c, para. 28.50, 28.51).
65 Jamieson and Levings (2001, 138).
66 For example, in BC, the *Ecological Reserve Act,* R.S.B.C. 1996, c. 103; *Park Act,* R.S.B.C. 1996,
    c. 344; and *Wildlife Act,* R.S.B.C. 1996, c. 488.
67 Jamieson and Levings (2001, 142).
68 Jamieson and Lessard (2000).
69 Jamieson and Levings (2001).
70 Clark (1996).
71 Jamieson and Levings (2001).
72 Ross et al. (2000).
73 de Fontaubert, Downes, and Agardy (1996).
74 *Fisheries Act,* R.S.C. 1985, c. F-14, s. 36(3).
75 VanderZwaag (1995).
76 *Canadian Environmental Protection Act, 1999,* S.C. 1999, c. 33. s. 125; *Canada Shipping Act,*
    R.S.C. 1985, c. S-9, s. 656; *Arctic Waters Pollution Prevention Regulations,* C.R.C. 1978, c. 354;
    Arctic Shipping Pollution Prevention Regulations, C.R.C. 1978, c. 353.
77 Commissioner of the Environment and Sustainable Development (1999, 3-15).
78 Standing Committee on Environment and Sustainable Development (1998, paras. 153, 114).
79 Cox (2000).
80 Nowlan and Kwan (2001).
81 Transport Canada (2002).
82 See "Citizen Submissions on Enforcement Matters" at <http://www.cec.org>.
83 Lavoie (1998).
84 VanderZwaag (1995, 425).
85 de Fontaubert, Downes, and Agardy (1996); Enserink (1999); International Joint Commission
    (2002).
86 See, for example, the *Health of Animals Act,* S.C. 1990, c. 21; *Plant Protection Act,* S.C. 1990, c.
    22; and *Fish Health Protection Regulations,* C.R.C. 1978, c. 812.
87 International Joint Commission and Great Lakes Fishery Commission (1990).
88 Department of Fisheries and Oceans (2001b).
89 Kolar and Lodge (2001).
90 Auditor General of Canada (2000b, para. 30.1).
91 Intergovernmental Panel on Climate Change Working Group II (2001, 16).
92 Taylor and Taylor (1998, 12-6).
93 Department of Fisheries and Oceans (2002).
94 *Oceans Act,* S.C. 1996, c. 31, ss. 31-2.
95 Boyd and Wallace (2001).
96 Hughes (1992).

97   *R.* v. *Sparrow,* [1990]; *R.* v. *Gladstone,* [1996]; *R.* v. *Adams,* [1996]; *R.* v. *Cote,* [1996]; *R.* v. *Marshall,* [1999] and [1999].
98   *R.* v. *Marshall,* [1999] 3 S.C.R. 456, para. 57. See also *R.* v. *Marshall,* [1999] 3 S.C.R. 539, paras. 29 and 40.
99   *R.* v. *Nikal,* [1996].
100   Environment Canada (1999b).
101   Pollara (2001).
102   Wallace quoted in Baron (1998, 21).
103   Harris (1998, 288).
104   VanderZwaag (1995, 374).

7: Reasons for Environmental Progress
1   Systems Research Group (1969).
2   World Economic Forum (2002).
3   Pearse and Warford (1993); Rothman (1998).
4   Prescott-Allan (2001); World Economic Forum (2002).
5   Howlett (2001b, 319-20).
6   Commissioner of the Environment and Sustainable Development (1998, 2-25).
7   Szekely (1997, 237-8).
8   *Baker* v. *Canada,* [1999], para. 70.
9   Axworthy and Taylor (1998).
10   Bernstein and Gore (2001).
11   *North American Agreement on Environmental Cooperation.*
12   See <http://www.cec.org> for complete details of all citizen submissions: Ontario Logging, SEM-02-001; BC Logging, SEM-00-004; BC Hydro, SEM-97-001; BC Mining, SEM-98-004; Pulp and Paper, SEM-02-003; Ontario Power Generation, SEM-03-001.
13   Dwivedi et al. (2001, 198).
14   Knox (2001).
15   McKenna (2000).
16   Knox and McKenna (2000).
17   Tollefson (2002, 179).
18   Juillet (2001, 144).
19   Cashore et al. (2001, 255-6).
20   Bernstein and Cashore (2001a).
21   Block (2001).
22   *R.* v. *Wholesale Travel Group Inc.,* [1991], 233.
23   Hornung (1998, 66).
24   See the various regulations enacted pursuant to the *Fisheries Act* and the *Canadian Environmental Protection Act, 1999.*
25   *Sulphur in Gasoline Regulations,* SOR/99-236; *Benzene in Gasoline Regulations,* SOR/97-493.
26   Gunningham, Grabosky, and Sinclair (1998, 7, 43).
27   Porter and van der Linde (1995, 120).
28   Parson (2001, 13).
29   Easterbrook (1995, 210).
30   OECD (2001c); Duncan (1990b, 285).
31   Godsoe (1999).
32   Mitchell (2000b); BC Ministry of Environment, Land and Parks (2000). For information on Nova Scotia's successful waste reduction strategy, see "Solid Waste Resource Management Strategy" at <http://www.gov.ns.ca/enla/emc/wasteman/strasumm.htm>.
33   An organization called Target Zero Canada honours municipalities with excellent records in reducing waste. See <http://www.targetzerocanada.org>.
34   Dauncey (2001, 96-7). For information on the Toronto Atmospheric Fund, see <http://www.city.toronto.on.ca/taf>.
35   Mittelstaedt (2002d).
36   See the Responsible Pest Management Strategy developed by the Federation of Canadian Municipalities and Environment Canada at <http://www.pestinfo.ca>.
37   *114957 Canada Ltée* v. *Hudson* (2001), para. 18, citing *R.* v. *Sharma,* [1993], 668.
38   *Ontario* v. *Mississauga* (1981); *Denman Island Local Trust Committee* v. *4064 Investments Ltd.* (2000), affirmed (2001).

39 *Canada Ltée* v. *Hudson* (2001).
40 One such case involved a local bylaw limiting the number of livestock that could be raised on a single farm, and imposing restrictions on the handling of manure; see *Ben Gardiner Farms* v. *West Perth* (2002).
41 *R.* v. *Crown Zellerbach Canada Ltd.,* [1988].
42 *Friends of the Oldman River* v. *Canada,* [1992], 16-17.
43 *Quebec (Attorney General)* v. *Canada,* [1994]; Seguin, Gibbon, and Fraser (1994).
44 *Ontario* v. *Canadian Pacific Ltd.,* [1995], 1076.
45 *R.* v. *Hydro-Quebec,* [1997], 266-7.
46 *Canada Ltée* v. *Hudson* (2001), para. 31.
47 *R.* v. *Gladstone,* [1996], 775. See also *R.* v. *Sparrow,* [1990]; *R.* v. *Adams,* [1996]; *R.* v. *Van der Peet,* [1996]; *R.* v. *NTC Smokehouse,* [1996]; *R.* v. *Marshall,* [1999] and [1999].
48 Doyle-Bedwell and Cohen (2001).
49 *Labrador Inuit Association* v. *Newfoundland* (1997), 54.
50 *Caddy Lake Cottager's Association* v. *Florence-Nora Access Road Inc.* (1998), 324.
51 Morton and Knopff (1992).
52 Bushnell (1992).
53 Roach (2001); Howe and Russell (2001).
54 For a detailed history of the Oldman Dam debacle see Glenn (1999).
55 *Globe and Mail* (2001a).
56 La Forest and Gibson (2000a; 2000b).
57 Harrison (2000b, 75); Hoberg (1997, 385).
58 Schindler (1996).
59 Hummel (1995).
60 Wilson (2001a, 62).
61 Hoberg (1991); Harrison and Hoberg (1994).
62 For examples, see Christensen (2001), Canadian Environmental Law Association (2001), and Canadian Environmental Law Association and the Ontario College of Family Physicians (2000).
63 Hoberg (1997, 373).

8: Systemic Weaknesses

1   O'Connor (2002a); Harrison (2000b; 2001a).
2   VanNijnatten and Lambright (2001, 253).
3   For example, *Intervenor Funding Project Act,* R.S.O. 1990, c. I-13; *Commissioner on Resources and the Environment Act,* S.B.C. 1996, c. 59; *Public Participation Act,* S.B.C. 2001, c. 19, repealed by *Miscellaneous Statutes Amendment Act,* S.B.C. 2001, c. 32.
4   Handy and Hamilton (1996, 9).
5   Gunningham, Grabosky, and Sinclair (1998, 8).
6   O'Connor (2002a, 33).
7   Dewees (1993).
8   Scoffield (1999a); Dixon (2000).
9   Wolf (2001).
10 Hitchens (1999).
11 OECD (1993, 118). See also Porter and van der Linde (1995).
12 Porter (1990, 168).
13 Martin (1992).
14 Power and Barrett (2001). See also Gillies (1994); Kromm and Ernst (2000).
15 Gunningham, Grabosky, and Sinclair (1998, 9).
16 Schrecker (2001, 54); Hoberg (1997; 2001b, 176); Harrison and Hoberg (1994); Benidickson (1997, 5); Tilleman (1995, 397); Ross (1995, 90).
17 *Canadian Environmental Assessment Act,* S.C. 1992, c. 37, ss. 46-8; *Canadian Environmental Protection Act, 1999,* S.C. 1999, c. 33, ss. 166, 175; *Canada Wildlife Act,* R.S.C. 1985, c. W-9, s. 8.
18 Swanson and Hughes (1995, 111).
19 Hoberg (1994, 115).
20 Harrison (2001a, 140).
21 See *Seattle Audubon Society* v. *Evans; Seattle Audubon Society* v. *Mosely; Northern Spotted Owl et al.* v. *Hodel; Northern Spotted Owl* v. *Lujan; Administrative Procedures Act,* 5 U.S.C. 702.
22 Jones and de Villars (1999, 570-1).

23 Daily and Ellison (2002).
24 McIntyre and Mosedale (1997); Cameron and Abouchar (1996).
25 M'Gonigle et al. (1995).
26 European Environment Agency (2001).
27 Schettler et al. (1999).
28 Hayes et al. (2002).
29 Schettler et al. (1999); Thornton (2000).
30 Schettler et al. (1999, 308).
31 Ludwig, Hilborn, and Walters (1993).
32 Harrison and Antweiler (2001).
33 Leiss (2001, 199).
34 Leiss and Tyshenko (2001); Johnson (1996, 34).
35 Royal Society of Canada (2001); Commissioner of the Environment and Sustainable Development (2000, 6-24); US National Research Council (2002).
36 Mandrusiak (1999, 261).
37 Leiss (2001, ch. 2).
38 Barrett (2002); Royal Society of Canada (2001).
39 Shrybman (1999a, 84-5); Barrett (2002); Winfield (2000); Swenarchuk (2000).
40 Shrybman (1999a); Schiller (2001).
41 WTO Panel Report (1997); WTO Appellate Body Report (1998).
42 Walters (1986); Parson (2001).
43 See *Environment Act*, S.N.S. 1994-95, c. 1; *Endangered Species Act*, S.N.S. 1998, c. 11; *Wilderness Areas Protection Act*, S.N.S. 1998, c. 27; *Wilderness and Ecological Reserves Act*, R.S.N. 1990, c. W-9.
44 Abouchar (2001).
45 Moffet (1997); Freestone and Hey (1996); VanderZwaag (1998); Raffensperger and Tickner (1999).
46 National Round Table on the Environment and the Economy (2001a, 14); see also Science Council of Canada (1988, 18).
47 Leiss (2001, 180); Hutchings, Walters, and Haedrich (1997).
48 Schrecker (2001).
49 Canada announced the first MPA under the *Oceans Act* in March 2003. See *Endeavour Hydrothermal Vents Marine Protected Areas Regulations*, SOR/2003-87.
50 Environment Canada (1990a, 156).
51 OECD (2000a; 1995a); Standing Committee on Environment and Sustainable Development (1998, para. 114).
52 Friends of the Earth Canada (2001); Mittelstaedt (1999a; 1999b); Commissioner of the Environment and Sustainable Development (1999, 3-18).
53 Environment Canada (1999d).
54 For repeat offenders in British Columbia, see the annual "Non-compliance list" published by the Ministry of Water, Land and Air Protection, <http://wlapwww.gov.bc.ca/epd/epdnon>. For repeat offenders in Ontario, see Sierra Legal Defence Fund (2002f; 2001a; 2000; 1999).
55 Christie (2000).
56 Sierra Legal Defence Fund (2001a).
57 Benidickson (1997, 123).
58 Macdonald (1991, 181).
59 VanderZwaag (1995, 315-16).
60 Farber (1999).
61 US Environmental Protection Agency (1999).
62 Friends of the Earth Canada (2001).
63 Berger (1994, Sentencing tables).
64 Environment Canada (1990a, 22); Stefanick and Wells (1998).
65 Toner (1996).
66 Leiss (2001, 169).
67 Standing Committee on Environment and Sustainable Development (1998).
68 Harris (1998, 214).
69 Commissioner of the Environment and Sustainable Development (1999, 3-21).
70 US Office of Management and Budget (1998).
71 Natural Resources Defence Council (2001).

72 Fact sheets from US government websites: National Parks Service, <http://www.nps.gov>; National Oceanic and Atmospheric Administration, <http://www.noaa.gov>; Forest Service, <http://www.fs.fed.us>; Fish and Wildlife Service, <http://www.fws.gov>.
73 US Environmental Protection Agency (1999).
74 Government of Canada (2001).
75 Anderson (2003, 1).
76 McKay (1997); Canadian Institute for Business and the Environment (1997).
77 McKay (1997).
78 Muldoon and Nadarajah (1999, 54).
79 Boyd (1998; 2002a).
80 Clark and Yacoumidis (2000); Muldoon and Nadarajah (1999).
81 Cooper (1999b, 9).
82 Environmental Commissioner of Ontario (2000a; 1999; 1998; 1997; 1996).
83 Ontario Provincial Auditor (1996, ch. 3.09).
84 Environmental Commissioner of Ontario (1998, 4; 1999, 4, 35).
85 Ontario Provincial Auditor (2000, ch. 3).
86 West Coast Environmental Law Association (2002); Sierra Legal Defence Fund (2002c).
87 Huestis (1984).
88 Standing Committee on Environment and Sustainable Development (1997).
89 Canadian Institute for Environmental Law and Policy (1996).
90 Kennett, McKoy, and Yarranton (1996).
91 Ogan (2000).
92 McMillan quoted in Standing Committee on Environment and Sustainable Development (1993, 256).
93 National Environmental Law Section of the CBA (1996).
94 McIlroy (1997b).
95 *Canadian Environmental Law Association* v. *Canada (Minister of Environment)* (2000).
96 Commissioner of the Environment and Sustainable Development (1999, 5-22).
97 Auditor General of Canada (1999c, para. 28.79).
98 OECD (1999f, 93).
99 Moffet and Saxe (1998).
100 Harrison and Andrews (1998).
101 Harrison and Antweiler (2001); Harrison (2000a).
102 OECD (2000a, 17).
103 KPMG Chartered Accountants (1996).
104 Krahn (1998, 22).
105 Commissioner of the Environment and Sustainable Development (1999, ch. 4).
106 Harrison (2001b).
107 Menell and Stewart (1994, 531); see also US General Accounting Office (1997); Davies and Mazurek (1996).
108 New Directions Group (1997).
109 Gibson (1999, 239); see also Gunningham, Grabosky, and Sinclair (1998, 52).
110 Chang, MacDonald, and Wolfson (1998).
111 Gertler, Muldoon, and Valiante (1990, 79).
112 Andrews (2000).
113 Schrecker (2001, 32).
114 Shillington and Burns Consultants (1999).
115 Dorcey and McDaniels (2001, 264, 261).
116 *Initiative Petition Administration Regulation,* B.C. Reg. 70/95.
117 *Delgamuukw* v. *British Columbia,* [1997]; *R.* v. *Marshall,* [1999] and [1999]; *Council of the Haida Nation* v. *British Columbia* (2002). See Doyle-Bedwell and Cohen (2001).
118 *Mackenzie Valley Resource Management Act,* S.C. 1998, c. 25, and the *Nunavut Land Claims Agreement Act,* S.C. 1993, c. 28. See also Egan et al. (2001, 45-50).
119 *Delgamuukw* v. *British Columbia,* [1997].
120 For two innovative proposals based on Aboriginal comanagement, see Burda, Collier, and Evans (1999) and M'Gonigle et al. (2001).
121 Swanson and Hughes (1995, 111).
122 Duncan (1990a).
123 The conviction was overturned on appeal but is still before the courts; see *Fletcher* v. *Kingston* (1998).

124 *Hamilton (City)*, 18 September 2000 (unreported), described in Berger (1994).
125 For example, *Kostuch* v. *Kowalski* (1990); *Kostuch* v. *Kowalski* (1991); *Kostuch* v. *Kowalski* (1991); *Kostuch* v. *Alberta* (1992); *Kostuch* v. *Alberta*, [1996].
126 *Mitchell* v. *Canada (Attorney General)*, [1999].
127 Glenn (1999, 251).
128 Law Reform Commission of Canada (1986).
129 *Canadian Environmental Protection Act, 1999*, S.C. 1999, c. 33; *Environmental Bill of Rights, 1993*, S.O. 1993, c. 28; *Environmental Quality Act*, S.Q. 1994, c. Q-2; *Environment Act*, S.Y. 1991, c. 5; *Environmental Rights Act*, R.S.N.W.T. 1988 (Supp.) c. 83.
130 Morelli (1997).
131 A. Keith Mitchell, Farris, Vaughan, Wills & Murphy, letter to Jean-Pierre Martel, Canadian Pulp and Paper Association, 7 April 1997. On file with the author.
132 Sergio Marchi, letter to Jack Munro, chairman, Forest Alliance of BC, 21 March 1997. On file with the author.
133 VanNijnatten and Boardman (2001).
134 Gallon (1999, 250); Gunningham, Grabosky, and Sinclair (1998).
135 Gunningham, Grabosky, and Sinclair (1998, 7); see also Benidickson (1999).
136 Doern and Conway (1994); Nemetz (1986).
137 Panayatou (1994).
138 Wiener (1999).
139 Jutlah (1998); Rolfe and Nowlan (1993); Task Force on Economic Instruments (1994).
140 Leiss (2001, 172).
141 OECD (1995a, 17).
142 *Canadian Environmental Protection Act, 1999*, S.C. 1999, c. 33, ss. 322-7; *Environment Act*, S.N.S. 1994-95, c. 1, s. 15; *Environmental Protection and Enhancement Act*, R.S.A. 2000, c. E-12, s. 13.
143 *Canada Foundation for Sustainable Development Technology Act*, S.C. 2001, c. 23.
144 Systems Research Group (1969).
145 Morley (1973).
146 Thompson (1980, 5).
147 Dewees (1990, 145).
148 Webb (1990); Canadian Bar Association (1990); Doering et al. (1992).

9: Obstacles to Further Progress

 1 Juillet and Toner (1997, 194).
 2 Doern (2001, 116); Harrison (1995, 172).
 3 Canadian Global Almanac (2001).
 4 Porter (1991).
 5 Schrecker (2001, 36).
 6 Hoberg (2001b, 173); Natural Resources Canada (2001c; 2001b; 2001d).
 7 OECD (1993, 7).
 8 Bernstein and Cashore (2001a).
 9 Harrison (1996, 14).
10 Hessing and Howlett (1997, 220); Schrecker (1989).
11 Macdonald (2001, 66); Howlett (2001d, 34).
12 Harrison (1996, 157).
13 Sierra Legal Defence Fund (2002a).
14 Castrilli and Vigod (1987, 131).
15 Robert S. Demone, chairman, president and CEO of Canadian Pacific Hotels, letter to Sheila Copps, Minister of Canadian Heritage, 25 June 1996. On file with the author.
16 Amos, Harrison, and Hoberg (2001, 161).
17 Brooks and Stritch (1991, 211).
18 Langille (1987, 41).
19 Macdonald (2001, 81); Winsor (1999).
20 Jacobs (1999).
21 Eggerston (1999).
22 Gwyn Morgan, speech at the APEC CEO Summit, Vancouver, 21-4 November 1997.
23 Environment Canada, "Minister's Introductory Calls to Industry Associations," Briefing note, 5 August 1999. On file with the author.
24 Environment Canada, "Minister's meeting with Tom d'Aquino, Business Council on National Issues," Briefing note, 1. On file with the author.

25 Paehlke (2001, 86).
26 Cashore et al. (2001).
27 Harrison (1996, 176).
28 Paehlke (2001, 111-14).
29 Pifer (1997).
30 Moe Sihota, BC minister of environment, letter to Gerry Stoney, president IWA Canada, 13 February 1996. On file with the author.
31 Cashore et al. (2001).
32 Dale (2001, 98); Schrecker (2001, 40).
33 Rabe (1997); Doern and Conway (1994); Cashore et al. (2001).
34 Harrison (1996).
35 OECD (1999f, 31-7).
36 Auditor General of Canada (2000b).
37 Doern (2001, 116).
38 Standing Committee on Environment and Sustainable Development (1998, para. 96).
39 Leiss (2001, ch. 5).
40 Dwivedi et al. (2001, 216).
41 Boardman (2001, 225).
42 Winfield (2000); International Institute for Sustainable Development (2000a); Boardman (2001, 222).
43 Greenpeace International (2002).
44 Parson (2001, 359).
45 US Office of Technology Assessment (1994, 24).
46 Johnson and Beaulieu (1996).
47 Appleton (1994).
48 Juillet (2001, 141).
49 International Centre for Settlement of Investment Disputes (2000, para. 103).
50 Mann (2001).
51 Appleton (1998, 40).
52 Leiss (2001, 66-101); Schettler (1999).
53 *Manganese-based Fuel Additives Act,* S.C. 1997, c. 11.
54 Leiss (2001, 66-101).
55 Canada is appealing the tribunal decision, which determined Canada's ban on PCB exports violated NAFTA. See the NAFTA dispute resolution page, <http://www.dfait-maeci.gc.ca.>.
56 Chase (2001).
57 International Centre for Settlement of Investment Disputes (2000).
58 *United Mexican States* v. *Metalclad* (2001).
59 Mann (2001). See <http://www.naftaclaims.com>.
60 Commission for Environmental Cooperation (2002a, 14).
61 Castrilli (2002).
62 Shrybman (1999a).
63 World Trade Organization (1996). United States – Restrictions on Import of Tuna, GATT Doc. DS21/R, BISD (39th Supp.).
64 World Trade Organization (1998). United States – Import Prohibition of Certain Shrimp and Shrimp Products.
65 World Trade Organization (1996). United States – Standards for Reformulated and Conventional Gasoline.
66 World Trade Organization (1998). EC Measures Concerning Meat and Meat Products (Hormones).
67 World Trade Organization (2001). EC Measures Affecting Asbestos and Asbestos Containing Products.
68 Appleton (1998, 26, 37, 39).
69 Lalumière and Landau (1998); Drohan (1998).
70 Sinclair and Grieshaber-Otto (2002); Swenarchuk (2002); McCarthy (2001).
71 Parson (2001, 5).
72 Harrison (2001a, 125).
73 Ontario Ministry of Environment (2001).
74 VanNijnatten and Lambright (2001).
75 La Forest and Gibson (2000a; 2000b).
76 *Friends of the Oldman River* v. *Canada,* [1992]; *R.* v. *Hydro-Quebec,* [1997]; Valiante (2001, 19).

77 *R.* v. *Crown Zellerbach,* [1988]; *Munro* v. *National Capital Commission,* [1966].
78 Environment Canada (1997a, 13).
79 Harrison (1996, 54).
80 Juillet and Toner (1997, 180).
81 Harrison (1995, 129).
82 Bernard Bigras, *Hansard,* House of Commons Debates, 24 April 1998.
83 Harrison and Hoberg (1994, 149).
84 Hoberg (1991).
85 Paehlke (2001, 75).
86 Dawson (2001).
87 Harrison (1995, 175).
88 Schindler (2001, 21).
89 Pue (2000, 11).
90 Savoie (1999); Simpson (2001).
91 Hoy (1999).
92 Tilleman (1995, 394).
93 See the "Role of the Prime Minister" page, Prime Minister of Canada's website, <http://www.pm.gc.ca>.
94 Forsey (1991).
95 Simpson (2001); Cosh (1996).
96 Schrecker (2001, 39).
97 Taft (1997); Ralph, Regimbald, and St-Amand (1997).
98 Schrecker (2001, 35).
99 Harrison (1996).
100 Brooks and Stritch (1991).
101 Harrison (2001a, 131).
102 Stefanick and Wells (1998, 263).
103 Many of these advances have been weakened by subsequent governments.
104 OECD (2001e, 120).
105 Estrin and Swaigen (1993, 7).
106 *Green* v. *The Queen,* [1973].
107 Swaigen (1992, 204).
108 MacIsaac and Champagne (1994, 158).
109 Boyd (2001b).
110 *Operation Dismantle* v. *R.,* [1985]; *Energy Probe* v. *Canada* (1989).
111 *Red Mountain Residents* v. *B.C.* (2000).
112 *Environmental Bill of Rights, 1993,* S.O. 1993, c. 28; *Environmental Quality Act,* S.Q. 1994, c. Q-2; *Environment Act,* S.Y. 1991, c. 5; *Environmental Rights Act,* R.S.N.W.T. 1988 (Supp.), c. 83.
113 Elgie (1993).
114 *Finlay* v. *Canada,* [1986].
115 For a recent discussion of the principles of public interest standing, see *Sierra Club of Canada* v. *Minister of Finance,* [1999]. Examples of cases where public interest standing was denied include *Shiell* v. *Amok Ltd.* (1988) and *Shiell* v. *Canada* (1995).
116 *Kostuch* v. *Environmental Appeal Board* (1996).
117 *Palmer* v. *Stora Kopparbergs* (1983); *Reese* v. *Alberta* (1992); *Manitoba Future Forest Alliance* v. *Canada* (1999); *Inverhuron and District Ratepayers Association* v. *Canada* (2000).
118 *Pearson* v. *Inco* (2002); *Gariepy* v. *Shell Oil* (2002).
119 Under previous *Federal Court Rules* (C.R.C. 1978, c. 663), Rule 1618 limited cost awards in judicial review proceedings to cases where there were unusual circumstances, such as frivolous or vexatious proceedings. Under the new *Federal Court Rules* (SOR/98-106), Rule 400 gives courts complete discretion to award costs. Rule 400(3)(h) identifies one factor in the determination of cost awards as being "whether the public interest in having the proceeding litigated justifies a particular award of costs."
120 Tollefson (1995).
121 *National Inshore Fisherman Association* v. *Canada,* [1990].
122 Wood (2000, 197); see also Hessing and Howlett (1997, 208); Hoberg (2000).
123 Benidickson (1997, 187).
124 *Inverhuron and District Ratepayers Association* v. *Canada* (2000).

125 "It is not the role of the Court to become an academy of science to arbitrate conflicting scientific predictions" (J. Strayer, in *Vancouver Island Peace Society* v. *Canada*, [1992], 51). See also *Palmer* v. *Stora Kopparbergs* (1983).
126 *R.* v. *Cyanimid Canada Inc.* (1981); *R.* v. *McCain* (1984). McCain was actually fined $1 on each of eight separate counts upon which it was convicted, for a total fine of $8.
127 Harris (1998, 134).
128 Saxe (1990).
129 Ironically, after cutting back staff and funding for environmental enforcement, the Ontario government passed a law with potential fines of up to $6 million per day on a corporation's first offence and $10 million per day on subsequent offences (*Toughest Environmental Penalties Act, 2000*, S.O. 2000, c. 22).
130 *R.* v. *Tioxide Canada Inc.* (1993); *R.* v. *Corner Brook Pulp and Paper* (1997).
131 *R.* v. *Beaulieu* (2000), 103.
132 *R.* v. *Brunswick Electric Power Commission* (1991), 191.
133 *R.* v. *Canadian Pacific Forest Products Limited* (1991), 3.
134 *R.* v. *Bata Industries Ltd.* (1992), (1992).
135 Berger (1994).
136 *MacMillan Bloedel* v. *Sheila Simpson et al.* (1993).
137 *Interfor* v. *Paine and Krawczyk* (2001); Krawczyk (2002).
138 Canadian Press (2001c).
139 Harrison and Hoberg (1994, 13).
140 Hoberg (2000, 39-44).
141 *Sierra Club* v. *Department of Interior* (1974); *Sierra Club* v. *Department of Interior* (1975).
142 Wilkinson (1997, 659).
143 Hoberg (2001b, 176); Elgie (1993).
144 Swanson and Hughes (1995, 114).
145 Glenn (1999, 254).
146 Howlett (2001d, 34).

10: Root Causes of Environmental Degradation
1 Wolf (2000, 10283).
2 Plater (1999).
3 Rodgers (1994).
4 Wackernagel et al. (2002a).
5 Boyd (2001a).
6 Prescott-Allan (2001).
7 US EPA Ecosystem Protection Working Group (1994, 1).
8 Janicke and Weidner (1997, 25).
9 Wolf (2000, 10283).
10 Chertrow and Esty (1997).
11 Ruhl (1997, 1001; see also 1999b).
12 Rothman (1998); Prescott-Allan (2001).
13 Andrews (1999, 409).
14 Andrews (1999); Chertrow and Esty (1997); Shutkin (2000); Vig and Kraft (2000).
15 Juillet (2001).
16 Nowlan (1997).
17 McClenaghan and Cooper (2002).
18 Christensen (2001); Canadian Environmental Law Association (2001).
19 *Friends of the West Country Association* v. *Canada* (1999).
20 Commission for Environmental Cooperation (2002b, 86).
21 Marc Garneau, interview on CBC radio, Vancouver 690 AM, 28 November 2000.
22 Other academics identify different root causes including hierarchical power structures, capitalism, globalization, trade liberalization, and values (Merchant 1994).
23 Consumption per capita is generally represented by GDP per capita, although energy consumption is sometimes used as a surrogate (Goodland et al. 1991; Wackernagel and Rees 1996b; Homer-Dixon 2000, 53-4).
24 Commission for Environmental Cooperation (2002b, 86).
25 Spiedel (2000).

26 Marc Garneau, interview on CBC radio, Vancouver 690 AM, 28 November 2000.
27 Robert et al. (2002); Azar, Holmberg, and Lindgren (1996); Daly (1991).
28 Azar, Holmberg, and Lindgren (1996).
29 Daily (1997).
30 OECD (2001g); Vitousek et al. (1997); Holdren, Daily, and Ehrlich (1995); Arrow et al. (1996); Pauly and Christensen (1995); Wackernagel and Rees (1996).
31 Wackernagel et al. (2002b).
32 Holmberg, Robert, and Eriksson (1996).
33 Ayres (1992).
34 Barrett et al. (1987, 276).
35 Adriaanse et al. (1997); see also Naredo (2001).
36 Based on a life expectancy of seventy-eight years from Statistics Canada, and on OECD (1999b).
37 Commissioner of the Environment and Sustainable Development (2000, 4-29).
38 OECD (1999b).
39 Georgescu-Roegen (1971).
40 Rees (2000, 26).
41 R.U. Ayres (1998, 109).
42 UN Population Fund (2001).
43 OECD (2001g, 20).
44 Milanovic (2001).
45 World Trade Organization (2000).
46 UN Population Fund (2001).
47 UN Development Program (2001); World Bank (2001d).
48 World Commission on Environment and Development (1987, 50-1).
49 Ethiopia's gross national income (GNI) per capita in 1999 was US$100, while Canada's was US$21,050 (World Bank 2001c).
50 Ehrlich (1968); Ehrlich and Ehrlich (1990).
51 Block (1990, 304); see also Fraser Institute (2000).
52 Simon (1995, 131).
53 Cohen (1995, 105).
54 Julian Simon later claimed that he meant seven million years (Hardin 1998, 35-6).
55 Cohen (1995, 17).
56 UN Population Fund (2002).
57 *Ibid.;* Bongaarts and Bulatao (2000).
58 UN Population Fund (2002).
59 UN Population Fund (2001); Johnson (1994).
60 Bongaarts and Bulatao (2000).
61 UN Population Fund (2001).
62 Ahlburg (1996); US National Research Council (1994); Mazur (1994).
63 Union of Concerned Scientists (2000); see also Engelman (2000).
64 UN Population Fund (2001); Gardner-Outlaw and Engelman (1997).
65 Food and Agriculture Organization (2001); Gardner-Outlaw and Engelman (1999).
66 Cincotta and Engelman (2000).
67 Rojstaczer, Sterling, and Moore (2001); Pauly and Christensen (1995).
68 Evans (1998, 178).
69 Food and Agriculture Organization (1999a).
70 Worldwatch Institute (2002).
71 Food and Agriculture Organization (1999a).
72 Evans (1998).
73 Food and Agriculture Organization (1999b).
74 Einstein quoted in Blanshard (1984, 10).
75 Homer-Dixon (1999).
76 R.U. Ayres (1998).
77 Noss and Cooperrider (1994, 333); Tudge (2000).
78 Rees (2000, 23).
79 Woollard (2000, 7).
80 Homer-Dixon (2000, 53-4).
81 OECD (2001e).
82 The need for an additional fourteen planets like Earth is calculated by taking the number of Earths required for all current humans to consume at the rate of the average Canadian, five,

multiplying by 1.5 to represent population growth from today's 6 billion to 9 billion, and multiplying by 2, i.e., a doubling of per capita consumption by 2050.
83 Reitze (1997, 89).
84 Natural Resources Canada (1999a, 58).

11: New Directions for Canadian Environmental Law and Policy
1 Statistics Canada (2001b).
2 Statistics Canada (2001c).
3 Canadian Bar Association (1990).
4 Weiss (1989); Walters (1986); Raffensperger and Tickner (1999); McDonough (2002).
5 Standing Committee on Environment and Sustainable Development (1998).
6 Gibson (1988, 275).

12: A New Role Model for Canada
1 Environment Canada (1990a).
2 Environment Canada (1990b, 1).
3 World Commission on Environment and Development (1987).
4 Adapted from Dale (2001).
5 Clark, McKay, and Mitchell (2001).
6 Sadler (1996c).
7 US National Research Council (1999b).
8 *Sustainable Development Act,* 1998, C.C.S.M. c. S-270; *Environmental Protection and Enhancement Act,* R.S.A. 2000, c. E-12; *Environment Act,* S.Y. 1992, c. 5, and *Economic Development Act,* S.Y. 1992, c. 2.
9 For example, see Commissioner of the Environment and Sustainable Development (1998, para. 1.5); see also Swanson (1993).
10 Commissioner of the Environment and Sustainable Development (2001a, media release).
11 World Economic Forum (2002); Prescott-Allan (2001); Boyd (2001a).
12 Kenny and Meadowcroft (1999); Dalal-Clayton (1996); Janicke and Weidner (1997).
13 World Commission on Environment and Development (1987, 44-5).
14 Swedish Ministry of Environment (1998; 1999; 2001d); Netherlands Institute for Public Health and Environment (1999).
15 Netherlands Institute for Public Health and Environment (1999).
16 OECD (1995b, 2); see also Resource Renewal Institute (2000); de Jongh and Morisette (1998).
17 OECD (1999b).
18 Prescott-Allan (2001).
19 World Economic Forum (2002); OECD (1996b, 118).
20 Swedish Ministry of Environment (1998, 2).
21 *Malmö Declaration,* 31 May 2000, at the First Global Ministerial Environment Forum. See the United Nations Environment Programme's "Milestones" page at <http://www.unep.org>.
22 Swedish Ministry of the Environment (2001d).
23 Swedish Ministry of Environment (1998).
24 *Ibid.,* 3-4.
25 *Ibid.*
26 Swedish Ministry of the Environment (2001d).
27 Boyd (2001a; 2002b); OECD (2001d).
28 Swedish Ministry of the Environment (2001d).
29 Swedish Ministry of the Environment (2001b; 2000).
30 Swedish Ministry of Environment (1998; 2001d).
31 OECD (1996b, 172).
32 Swedish Ministry of Environment (2001c).
33 *Ibid.;* OECD (1996b).
34 Swedish Ministry of Environment (2001c).
35 Swedish Ministry of the Environment (2001a).
36 Swedish Ministry of Environment (2001c).
37 OECD (1999b).
38 Gale, Barg, and Gillies (1995).
39 Wise (2001).
40 OECD (1998a).
41 OECD (1999b).

42 OECD (1999d, 38).
43 Environment Canada (1996c, 10-54).
44 Lunquist (1995).
45 OECD (1999b).
46 Lunquist (1995).
47 Boyd (2002b).
48 OECD (1999b).
49 OECD (1996b).
50 Ackerman (1997, 105-22).
51 OECD (1999b).
52 *Ibid.*
53 Wossink and Feitshans (2000).
54 Wahlstrom and Lundqvist (1993).
55 Andersson et al. (1990).
56 Swedish National Chemicals Inspectorate (1998).
57 OECD (1999b; 2002a).
58 OECD (1999b; 1996b, 184).
59 OECD (1996b, 172, 175).
60 Prescott-Allan (2001).
61 World Bank and Environics International (2002).

13: Reducing Consumption

1 Robert et al. (2002).
2 Naredo (2001).
3 UN Development Program (1998, 81-2).
4 Adriaanse et al. (1997).
5 UN Conference on Environment and Sustainable Development (1992).
6 Nystrom (n.d.).
7 Orr (1992); US National Research Council (1999b).
8 Lane (2000); Wachtel (1989).
9 Nordhaus and Tobin (1972); Hawken, Lovins, and Lovins (1999, 61); Gore (1993, 85).
10 Daly and Cobb (1989).
11 Colman (2001, 70).
12 *Ibid.*, 71.
13 Commission for Environmental Cooperation (2002b, 8).
14 International Institute for Sustainable Development (2000b).
15 Daly and Cobb (1989, 505).
16 Cobb, Goodman, and Wackernagel (1999); Cobb, Halstead, and Rowe (1995).
17 UN Development Program (1998, 2).
18 Lane (2000).
19 Anielski et al. (2001).
20 See the website of GPI Atlantic, <http://www.gpiatlantic.org>.
21 Prescott-Allan (2001).
22 Environment Canada (1990c, 142).
23 National Round Table on the Environment and Economy (2002a).
24 National Round Table on the Environment and Economy (2001b).
25 Adriaanse et al. (1997).
26 Michalski (2000).
27 Kelly (1992, 9).
28 Goodland et al. (1991, 10).
29 Daily (1997).
30 Costanza et al. (1997).
31 Hawken, Lovins, and Lovins (1999, 5, 146-7).
32 National Round Table on the Environment and the Economy (2002b).
33 OECD (2001c, 24).
34 Yelin-Kiefer (2001).
35 Hawken, Lovins, and Lovins (1999, 319).
36 Sierra Legal Defence Fund (2002a, 22).
37 Commissioner of the Environment and Sustainable Development (2000, ch. 3); Natural Resources Canada (1996).

38 Hansen and Barg (1994, 8-9).
39 Oosterhuis (1999).
40 Jaccard, Nyboer, and Sadownik (2002); See *Motor Vehicle Emissions Reduction Regulation,* B.C. Reg. 517/95.
41 Jaccard, Nyboer, and Sadownik (2002).
42 Myers and Kent (2001); van Beers and de Moor (2001).
43 Sierra Legal Defence Fund (2001b).
44 Slaney and Martin (1997).
45 Environmental Mining Council of British Columbia (2001); Ryan (1995, 21, 29).
46 Urquhart (2001, 319); Hume (1992, 45).
47 Schwindt (1999).
48 Frechette (2000).
49 *Fisheries Prices Support Act,* R.S.C. 1985, c. F-23.
50 Technical Committee on Business Taxation (1998).
51 OECD (1995a, 148).
52 Natural Resources Canada (1996).
53 Commissioner of the Environment and Sustainable Development (2000, 3-20).
54 Natural Resources Canada (1996).
55 Liberal Party of Canada (1993).
56 Mining Watch Canada (2000).
57 Auditor General of Canada (1998, para. 28.245).
58 Government of Canada (2001, 1:24).
59 Young (2001).
60 Marshall (2002, 50).
61 OECD (1999b).
62 UN Development Program (1998, 95).
63 Saunders (1990a, 7).
64 Canadian Institute for Environmental Law and Policy (2002).
65 OECD (2001c, 22).
66 OECD (1995a, 131).
67 Litman (1995).
68 Tollefson, Rhone, and Rolfe (2000, 59).
69 UN Human Development Program (1998); de Moor (1997); Myers and Kent (2001).
70 OECD (2001a).
71 Larson and Shah (1992, 20).
72 Food and Agriculture Organization (1993); Milazzo (1998).
73 OECD (2000a, 17).
74 Sizer et al. (2000); Myers and Kent (2001).
75 Winfield et al. (2002).
76 OECD (2000c).
77 OECD (2001a).
78 Myers and Kent (2001, 85).
79 Transport Canada (2000).
80 Martin (2001).
81 Standing Committee on Environment and Sustainable Development (1996); Department of Finance (1996).
82 MacKinnon (2001).
83 Golub (1998); OECD (1995b; 1996b).
84 Friends of the Earth (2000).
85 Canadian Press (2000).
86 Marshall (2002).
87 The Supreme Court of Canada ruled that the *Income Tax Act* does not preclude businesses from treating fines as ordinary, tax-deductible business expenses (*65302 British Columbia Ltd. v. Canada,* [1999]).
88 OECD (2001e, 137).
89 Andersen and Sprenger (2000); Repetto et al. (1992).
90 Durning and Bauman (1998).
91 Olewiler (1990).
92 Barde (2000).
93 Rees (1995).

94   Krugman (1997).
95   Technical Committee on Business Taxation (1998, 5).
96   *Ibid.*
97   Cameron, Robertson, and Curnow (2001); Svendsen, Daugbjergand, and Pedersen (2001).
98   UN Development Program (1998, 95).
99   Barde (2000).
100 UN Development Program (1998).
101 Larsen (2000).
102 OECD (1998a); Hawken, Lovins, and Lovins (1999, 167).
103 The OECD maintains a comprehensive database of environmental taxes at its "Environmental Policies and Instruments" page; see <http://www.oecd.org/env/policies/taxes/index.htm>.
104 Schlegelmilch (2000).
105 Hoerner (1995).
106 OECD (2001c).
107 Olewiler (2000).
108 The Commission for Environmental Cooperation maintains a database of North American environmental laws. See "Environmental Law Summary" at <http://www.cec.org/compendium>.
109 *Tetrachloroethylene Regulations,* SOR/2003-79, *Canada Gazette,* Part II, Vol. 137, No. 6.
110 Hazell and Jessup (1989).
111 Standing Committee on Environment and Sustainable Development (1996).
112 Commissioner of the Environment and Sustainable Development (1998, 1-23).
113 Leblanc and Mahoney (1999); Duffy (2000).
114 Pammett and Frizzell (1997, 62-3).
115 Barde (2000).
116 OECD (2001g; 2001e).
117 OECD (2001g).
118 Barde (2000).
119 OECD (1998a).
120 Green Budget Coalition (2001).
121 Technical Committee on Business Taxation (1998, 9-10).
122 *Ibid.,* 9-15.
123 Taylor, Jaccard, and Olewiler (1999).
124 Tollefson, Rhone, and Rolfe (2000, 54); see also International Institute for Sustainable Development (1994, 10-11).
125 Goodland et al. (1991).
126 The 2.5 percent figure is from R.U. Ayres (1998); 10 percent is from Rosen (1992).
127 Hawken (2001).
128 Ayres (1989).
129 Lovins, Lovins, and von Weiszacker (1997).
130 Hawken, Lovins, and Lovins (1999).
131 OECD (1998a, 71).
132 Schmidheiny et al. (1992). See the Factor Ten Institute's website at <http://www.factor10.de>.
133 Adapted from R.U. Ayres (1998, 114-15).
134 Hawken, Lovins, and Lovins (1999, 105-6).
135 Hawken (1993, 196).
136 Hawken, Lovins, and Lovins (1999, 106).
137 Natural Resources Canada (2000a).
138 Brower and Leon (1999, 161).
139 Green (1992).
140 OECD (1998b; 2001c, 22).
141 Brower and Leon (1999, 158).
142 Cairncross (1992, 107).
143 Halpert (2001).
144 Ackerman (1997); Davis et al. (1997); Wylynko (1999). See BC's *Post-Consumer Paint Stewardship Program Regulation,* B.C. Reg. 200/94, and the *Post-Consumer Residual Stewardship Program Regulation,* B.C. Reg. 333/97.
145 Environment Canada (2001d).
146 Sandborn, Andrews, and Wylynko (1991).
147 Muldoon and Nadarajah (1999, 64).
148 Martin (2000).

149 Benyus (1997).
150 Christie (2000); see also Wylynko (1999).
151 See the US government's Energy Star website, <http://www.energystar.gov>.
152 Hawken, Lovins, and Lovins (1999, 276).
153 OECD (2000b, 65, 63).
154 *An Act to Amend the Food and Drugs Act*, 2001, Bill 287. Introduced in Parliament by Charles Caccia.
155 Cole and Grossman (1999, 887).
156 Brower and Leon (1999, 157).
157 Richard E. Ayres (1998, 380-1); see also Burtraw and Swift (1996).
158 Nash (2000).
159 OECD (2001f).
160 Made (2000).
161 Rolfe (1998).
162 Larsen (2000).
163 Kallen (2000).
164 OECD (2000b, 36).
165 Commissioner of the Environment and Sustainable Development (2000, ch. 2).
166 Gunningham, Grabosky, Sinclair (1998, 416); Yaron (2002).
167 Wilson (2001a, 62).

14: Population Growth and Sustainable Development

1 Homer-Dixon (1999).
2 Gardner-Outlaw and Engelman (1997).
3 UN Population Fund (2001, 2).
4 Birdsall, Kelley, and Sinding (2001); UN Population Fund (2002).
5 UN (1995, para. 3.14).
6 *Ibid.*
7 Sen (1994).
8 Bennett et al. (1990).
9 UN Population Fund (2001).
10 Cohen (1995, 154).
11 Statistics Canada (2000).
12 Johnson (1994).
13 Conly and De Silva (1999).
14 Canadian International Development Agency (2000).
15 Conly and De Silva (1999); Conly and Speidel (1993).
16 *Ibid.*
17 Shenstone (1997).
18 UN Population Fund (2001).
19 World Bank (1993).
20 UN Development Program (1998).
21 UN (2000). Millennium Declaration. Resolution of the General Assembly. A/55/L.2. See <http://www.developmentgoals.org>.
22 World Bank (2002b); Oxfam International (2002a).
23 World Bank and Environics International (2002).
24 International Monetary Fund and World Bank (2001).
25 Department of Foreign Affairs and International Trade (1995).
26 World Bank (2002a).
27 Liberal Party of Canada (1993).
28 OECD (2002a).
29 OECD (1999b).
30 OECD (2002a).
31 OECD (1999b).
32 Scoffield (2001).
33 Canadian Council for International Cooperation (2001).
34 Chrétien (2002).
35 Department of Foreign Affairs and International Trade (1995).
36 Goldfarb (2001).
37 World Bank (1998).

38 Canadian International Development Agency (2001).
39 Jepma (1991).
40 Canadian International Development Agency (2001).
41 OECD (2001b).
42 World Bank (2002a; 2002c).
43 Serieux (2001a); World Bank (1999; 2002c).
44 Andrews et al. (1999).
45 Serieux (2001b); World Bank (2001b); International Monetary Fund and World Bank (2001).
46 World Bank and International Monetary Fund (2002).
47 Serieux (2001b).
48 Reed (1996); Taylor and Pieper (1996).
49 Department of Finance (2002).
50 Department of Finance (1999).
51 Oxfam International (2002b, 5).
52 World Bank (2001a, 9).
53 *Ibid.*
54 Oxfam Canada (2001).
55 *Globe and Mail* (2001b).
56 Oxfam International (2002b).
57 *Globe and Mail* (2001b).
58 World Health Organization (2002).
59 Elliott and Bonin (2002).
60 Action Canada for Population and Development (2002).
61 OECD (2002a).
62 Spiedel (2000).
63 UN Development Program (1998, 4).
64 Ecological footprint analysis confirms that Canada is one of the few nations in the world with ecological capacity not fully appropriated by humans (Wackernagel et al. 1999; 2002a).
65 Salonius (1999, 1518). See also the website <http://www.canadafirst.net> for a fringe group opposed to immigration in Canada. The United States has a much more active public debate about limiting immigration based (ostensibly) on environmental concerns. More than forty environmental organizations are advocating a moratorium on immigration to the United States. See <http://www.balance.org> or <http://www.carryingcapacity.org>.
66 Statistics Canada (2001c).
67 Statistics Canada (2000).
68 Canadian Global Almanac (2001).
69 Statistics Canada (2000).
70 Citizenship and Immigration Canada (2001).
71 *Immigration and Refugee Protection Act,* S.C. 2001, c. 27. *Immigration and Refugee Protection Act Regulations,* 2002, SOR/2002-227.
72 *Immigration and Refugee Protection Act,* S.C. 2001, c. 27, s. 12. *Immigration and Refugee Protection Act Regulations,* SOR/2002-227.
73 Citizenship and Immigration Canada (2002).
74 Iyer (2001). For a contradictory perspective on Canadian multiculturalism, see Bissoondath (1994).
75 A phenomenal 40 percent of immigrants to Canada have university degrees, compared with 13 percent of Canadians. See Citizenship and Immigration Canada (2002, 9).
76 Durning (1994, 40).

15: Conclusion

1 Natural Resources Canada (2001b, 1).
2 Parson (2001, 13).
3 Einstein quoted in Dukas and Hoffman (1979).
4 Homer-Dixon (2000).
5 Suzuki and McConnell (1997, 214); Leopold (1966); Geisel (1971).
6 Scheffer et al. (2001).
7 US National Research Council (2001).
8 Holling (1994, 60).

References

Note: Internet sources are current as of March 2003.

Books, Articles, and Reports

Abouchar, Julie. 2001. "Implementation of the Precautionary Principle in Canada." In Tim O'Riordan, James Cameron, and Andrew Jordan, eds., *Reinterpreting the Precautionary Principle*, 235-67. London: Cameron May.

Ackerman, Frank. 1997. *Why Do We Recycle? Markets, Values, and Public Policy*. Washington, DC: Island Press.

Action Canada for Population and Development. 2002. *It's Time We Change the Fate of a Generation and Keep the Cairo Promise: 2001 Monitoring Report on Children and Adolescents.* Ottawa.

Adriaanse, A., S. Bringezu, A. Hammond, et al. 1997. *Resource Flows: The Material Basis of Industrial Economies.* Washington, DC: World Resources Institute, Wuppertal Institute, Netherlands Ministry of Housing, Spatial Planning, and Environment, and National Institute for Environmental Studies (Japan).

Agriculture and Agri-Food Canada. 2000. *The Health of Our Water: Toward Sustainable Agriculture in Canada.* Ottawa: Minister of Public Works and Government Services Canada.

–. 1998. *Manure, Fertilizer and Pesticide Management in Canada: Results of the 1995 Farm Inputs Management Survey.* Ottawa.

–. 1993. "Special Review of Carbofuran Insecticide: Effects on Avian Fauna and Value to Agriculture." Discussion Document D93-02. Ottawa.

Ahlburg, D.A. 1996. "Population Growth and Poverty." In D.A. Ahlburg, A.C. Kelley, and K.D. Mason, eds., *The Impact of Population Growth on Well-Being in Developing Countries.* New York: Springer–Verlag.

Air Quality Strategy Interdepartmental Working Group. 2001. "Moving Towards Cleaner Air: A Progress Report on the Air Quality Strategy for the City of Toronto." <http://www.city.toronto.on.ca/environment>.

Alberta Environment. 1996. *The Status of Alberta's Timber Supply.* Edmonton.

Alberta Environmental Protection. 1998. "The Final Frontier: Protecting Landscape and Biological Diversity within Alberta's Boreal Forest Natural Region." Protected Areas Report 13, March. Edmonton.

Albritton, Daniel L., and Lambert Kuijpers, eds. 1999. "Synthesis of the Reports of the Scientific, Environmental Effects, Technology and Economic Assessment Panels of the Montreal Protocol." Nairobi: United Nations Environment Program. <http://www.unep.ch/ozone>.

Amos, William, Kathryn Harrison, and George Hoberg. 2001. "In Search of a Minimum Winning Coalition: The Politics of Species at Risk Legislation in Canada." In Karen Beazley and Robert Boardman, eds., *The Politics of the Wild: Canada and Endangered Species.* Don Mills, ON: Oxford University Press.

Andersen, M., and R.U. Sprenger, eds. 2000. *Market-Based Instruments for Environmental Management.* Cheltenham, UK: Edward Elgar.

Anderson, David. 2003. Budget Speech 2003, House of Commons. (Speaking Notes). 26 February 2003. Ottawa.

–. 2001. "Speaking Notes." *Securing Cleaner Air for Canadians: Update 2001.* 19 February. <http://www.ec.gc.ca>.

–. 1990. "Tanker Traffic and Oil Spills." In Canadian Bar Association Committee on Sustainable Development, ed., *Sustainable Development in Canada: Options for Law Reform.* Ottawa: Canadian Bar Association.

Andersson, L., S. Gabring, J. Hammar et al. 1990. *Unacceptable Properties of a Pesticide.* Sweden: Chemicals Inspectorate.

Andrews, D., A.R. Boote, S.S. Rizavi et al. 1999. *Debt Relief for Low-Income Countries: The Enhanced HIPC Initiative.* Washington, DC: International Monetary Fund.

Andrews, Richard N.L. 1999. *Managing the Environment, Managing Ourselves: A History of American Environmental Policy.* New Haven: Yale University Press.

Andrews, William J. 2000. "Public Access to Environmental Justice: A Comment Ten Years After." In Leonard J. Griffiths and Patricia Houlihan, eds., *Sustainable Development in Canada: Into the Next Millenium.* Ottawa: Canadian Bar Association.

Angus, Ian. 1997. *A Border Within: National Identity, Cultural Plurality and Wilderness.* Montreal and Kingston: McGill-Queen's University Press.

Anielski, M., M. Griffiths, D. Pollock et al. 2001. *Alberta Sustainability Trends 2000: The Genuine Progress Index Report 1961 to 1999.* Drayton Valley, AB: Pembina Institute for Appropriate Development. <http://www.pembina.org>.

Aniskowicz, Theresa. 1998. *Cross-border Species Listed by COSEWIC.* Ottawa: Canadian Wildlife Service.

Appleby, Alan G. 1995. "Saskatchewan." In Monte Hummel, ed., *Protecting Canada's Endangered Spaces: An Owner's Manual.* Toronto: Key Porter.

Appleton, Barry. 1998. "Testimony." In BC Special Committee on the Multilateral Agreement on Investment, *Report of Proceedings (Hansard),* 29 September.

–. 1994. *Navigating NAFTA: A Concise User's Guide to the North American Free Trade Agreement.* Toronto: Carswell.

Apsey, M. et al. 2000. "The Perpetual Forest: Using Lessons from the Past to Sustain Canada's Forests in the Future." *Forestry Chronicle* 76: 29-53.

ARC Applied Research Consultants. 1997. *Global Benefits and Costs of the Montreal Protocol on Substances That Deplete the Ozone Layer.* Ottawa: Environment Canada.

Arctic Monitoring and Assessment Program. 2002. *Arctic Pollution 2002.* Oslo, Norway. <http://www.amap.no>.

–. 1998a. *AMAP Assessment Report: Arctic Pollution Issues.* Oslo, Norway.

–. 1998b. *Arctic Pollution Issues: A State of the Arctic Environment Report.* Oslo, Norway.

Arrow, K. et al. 1996. "Economic Growth, Carrying Capacity and the Environment." 6 *Ecological Applications* 13.

Attridge, Ian. 2000. "Canadian Biodiversity and the Law." In Stephen Bocking, ed., *Biodiversity in Canada: Ecology, Ideas and Action.* Peterborough: Broadview Press.

–, ed. 1996. *Biodiversity Law and Policy in Canada.* Toronto: Canadian Institute for Environmental Law and Policy.

Auditor General of BC. 1999. *Protecting Drinking Water Sources, 1998/99.* Report 5. Victoria.

Auditor General of Canada. 2000a. "Fisheries and Oceans Canada – Pacific Salmon: Sustainability of the Resource Base." Chapter 28 in *Report to Parliament.* Ottawa: Minister of Supply and Services. <http://www.oag-bvg.gc.ca>.

–. 2000b. "Fisheries and Oceans: The Effects of Salmon Farming in B.C. on the Management of Wild Salmon Stocks." Chapter 30 in *Report to Parliament.* Ottawa: Minister of Supply and Services. <http://www.oag-bvg.gc.ca>.

–. 2000c. "Follow-up of Recommendations in Previous Reports." Chapter 33 in *Report to Parliament.* Ottawa: Minister of Supply and Services.

–. 1999a. "The Atlantic Groundfish Strategy Followup." Chapter 8 in *Report to Parliament.* Ottawa: Minister of Supply and Services.

–. 1999b. "Managing Atlantic Shellfish in a Sustainable Manner." Chapter 4 in *Report to Parliament.* Ottawa: Minister of Supply and Services.

–. 1999c. "Pacific Salmon: Sustainability of the Fisheries." Chapter 20 in *Report to Parliament.* Ottawa: Minister of Supply and Services.

–. 1998. "Follow-up of Recommendations in Previous Reports." Chapter 28 in *Report to Parliament.* Ottawa: Minister of Supply and Services.

–. 1997a. "Control of the Trans-boundary Movement of Hazardous Waste." Chapter 4 in *Report to Parliament*. Ottawa: Minister of Supply and Services.

–. 1997b. "Ozone Protection: The Unfinished Journey." Chapter 27 in *Report to Parliament*. Ottawa: Minister of Supply and Services.

–. 1997c. "Sustainable Fisheries Framework: Atlantic Groundfish." Chapters 14, 15 in *Report to Parliament*. Ottawa: Minister of Supply and Services.

–. 1996. "Parks Canada: Preserving Canada's Natural Heritage." Chapter 31 in *Report to Parliament*. Ottawa: Minister of Supply and Services.

–. 1989. *Report to Parliament*. Ottawa: Minister of Supply and Services.

Auditor General of Quebec. 1996. *Rapport du Vérificateur-général à l'Assemblée nationale pour l'année 1995-96*, vol. 1, ch. 2. Quebec City.

Avram, J. 1997. "Endangered Species Overkill." *Alberta Report* 24: 6-9.

Axworthy, L., and S. Taylor. 1998. "A Ban for All Seasons: The Landmines Convention and Its Implications for Canadian Diplomacy." *International Journal* 53, 2 (Spring): 189-203.

Ayres, Richard E. 1998. "The 1990 Clean Air Amendments: Performance and Prospects." 13.2 *Natural Resources and Environment* 379.

Ayres, R.U., ed. 1998. *Eco-Restructuring: Implications for Sustainable Development*. New York: United Nations University Press.

–. 1992. "Toxic Heavy Metals: Materials Cycle Optimization." *Proceedings of the National Academy of Sciences* 89: 815-20.

–. 1989. *Technology and Environment*. Washington, DC: National Academy of Sciences.

Azar, C., J. Holmberg, and K. Lindgren. 1996. "Socio-ecological Indicators for Sustainability." *Ecological Economics* 18: 89-112.

Babbitt, Bruce. 1994. "The ESA and Takings: A Call for Innovation within the Terms of the Act." 24 *Environmental Law* 355.

Bachelder, Andrew. 1999. "Using Credit Trading to Reduce Greenhouse Gas Emissions." 9 *Journal of Environmental Law and Practice* 259.

Banff-Bow Valley Task Force. 1996. *Banff-Bow Valley: At the Crossroads*. Ottawa: Minister of Supply and Services.

Barde, Jean Philippe. 2000. "Green Tax Reform in OECD Countries: An Overview." In Environment Canada, ed., *Supporting a Sustainable Future: Making Dollars and Sense*. Conference proceedings. <http://www.ec.gc.ca/eco-n-ference/>.

Barlow, Maude. 1999. *Blue Gold: The Global Water Crisis and the Commodification of the World's Water Supply*. San Francisco: International Forum on Globalization.

Baron, Nancy. 1998. "The Straits of Georgia." *Georgia Straight*, 3-10 September, 19.

Barrett, Katherine. 2002. "Food Fights: Canadian Regulators Are under Pressure to Face the Uncertainties of Genetically Modified Food." *Alternatives Journal* 28(1): 28-33.

Barrett, M., S. Miles, H. Regier et al. 1987. "Potential Environmental Impacts of Changes in Population Size, Age and Geographic Distribution." 14.2 *Canadian Studies in Population* 261.

Barrett, Scott. 2000. "Montreal vs. Kyoto: International Cooperation and the Global Environment." In I. Kaul, L. Grunberg, and M.A. Stern, eds., *Global Public Goods: International Cooperation in the 21st Century*. New York: Oxford University Press.

Barzilay, Joshua I., Winkler G. Weinberg, and J. William Eley. 1999. *The Water We Drink: Water Quality and Its Effects on Health*. New Brunswick, NJ: Rutgers University Press.

Bascom, R., P.A. Bromberg, D.A. Costa et al. 1996. "State of the Art: Health Effects of Outdoor Air Pollution." *Am. J. Respir. Crit. Care Med.* 153: 3-50, 477-98.

Baxter, James. 2000. "Canadians Not Happy with Liberal Spending Priorities." *Edmonton Journal*, 7 October, E19.

BC Drinking Water Review Panel. 2002. *Final Report: Panel Review of BC's Drinking Water Protection Act*. Vancouver.

BC Environment. 1993. *Pesticide Management Program: A Strategic Five Year Plan*. Victoria.

BC Environmental Assessment Office. 2001. *Guide to the BC Environmental Assessment Process*. Victoria: Crown Publishing.

BC Forest Practices Board. 1998. *Forest Planning and Practices in Coastal Areas with Streams*. Victoria: Forest Practices Board.

BC Forest Resources Commission. 1991. *The Future of Our Forests*. Victoria: Queen's Printer.

BC Government Employees Union. 1999. *Environmental Protection in British Columbia*. Victoria.

BC Land Use Coordination Office. 1996. *Provincial Overview and Status Report*. Victoria.

BC Medical Association. 2000. "BC Doctors Speak out on Air Pollution." Press release, 29 May.

BC Ministry of Aboriginal Affairs. 1998. Nisga'a Final Agreement. Victoria.
BC Ministry of Environment, Land and Parks. 2001. *Evaluation of the Effectiveness of the FPC in Maintaining Environmental Values*. Victoria.
–. 2000. *Environmental Trends in British Columbia 2000*. Victoria.
–. 1997. *Depletion of the Stratospheric Ozone Layer: The Science, Impacts and Mitigation Measures*. Victoria.
–. 1995. *Clean Vehicles and Fuels for British Columbia: A Policy Paper*. Victoria.
–. n.d. *A Water Conservation Strategy for British Columbia*. Victoria.
BC Ministry of Forests. 2002a. *Discussion Paper on the Results-Based Forest Practices Code*. Victoria.
–. 2002b. *2002/03-2004/05 Service Plan Summary*. Victoria.
–. 1999. *The Annual Report of Compliance and Enforcement Statistics for the Forest Practices Code, 1997-1998*. Victoria.
–. 1996. *Forest Practices Code Timber Supply Analysis*. Victoria: Queen's Printer.
–. 1994. *Forest, Range, and Recreation Resource Analysis*. Victoria.
–. n.d. *Providing for the Future: Sustainable Forest Management in British Columbia*. Victoria: Queen's Printer.
BC Ministry of Sustainable Resource Management. 2002. *Service Plan 2002/03-2004/05*. Victoria.
–. 2001. *Southern Rocky Mountain Backgrounder*. 15 November.
BC Parks. 1995. *Public Views about BC Parks: Summary Report*. Victoria: Ministry of Environment, Land and Parks.
BC Provincial Health Officer. 2001. *Annual Report 2000 – Drinking Water Quality in BC: The Public Health Perspective*. Victoria: Ministry of Health.
Beauchesne, Eric. 1995. "Businesses Agree to Limit Emissions." *Halifax Daily News*, 28 September, 23.
Beazley, Karen, and Robert Boardman, eds. 2001. *The Politics of the Wild: Canada and Endangered Species*. Don Mills, ON: Oxford University Press.
Bell, Jeff. 2001. "Greater Victoria." *Victoria Times Colonist*, 6 July, B1.
Bella, L. 1987. *Parks for Profit*. Montreal: Harvest House.
Benedick, Richard E. 1991. *Ozone Diplomacy: New Directions in Safeguarding the Planet*. Cambridge: Harvard University Press.
Benidickson, Jamie. 2002. *Environmental Law*. 2d ed. Toronto: Irwin Law.
–. 1999. "Sustaining Old-growth Pineland in Ontario: Pathways to Reform." 9 *Journal of Environmental Law and Practice* 199.
–. 1997. *Environmental Law*. Toronto: Irwin Law.
Bennett, A., C. Frisen, P. Kamnuansilpa et al. 1990. *How Thailand's Family Planning Program Reached Replacement Level Fertility: Lessons Learned*. Population Technical Assistance Project, Occasional paper no. 4. Washington, DC: US Agency for International Development.
Bennett, J.V., et al. 1987. "Infectious and Parasitic Diseases." In R. Amler and H.B. Dull, eds., *Closing the Gap: The Burden of Unnecessary Illness*. Oxford: Oxford University Press.
Benton, M.J. 1995. "Diversification and Extinction in the History of Life." *Science* 268: 52-8.
Benyus, Janine. 1997. *Biomimicry: Innovation Inspired by Nature*. New York: William Morrow.
Berger, Emily A. 2000. "Standing at the Edge of a New Millenium: Ending a Decade of Erosion of the Citizen Suit Provision of the Clean Water Act." *Maryland Law Review* 59(4): 1371.
Berger, Stanley D. 1994. *The Prosecution and Defence of Environmental Offenses*. 2 vols. Toronto: Emond Montgomery.
Berger, T. 1977. *Northern Frontier, Northern Homeland: Report of the Mackenzie Valley Pipeline Inquiry*. 2 vols. Ottawa: Minister of Supply and Services.
Bernstein, Steven, and Benjamin Cashore. 2001a. "Globalization, Internationalization, and Liberal Environmentalism: Exploring Non-Domestic Sources of Influence on Canadian Environmental Policy." In Debora L. VanNijnatten and Robert Boardman, eds., *Canadian Environmental Policy: Context and Cases*, 212-32. 2d ed. Oxford: Oxford University Press.
–. 2001b. "The International-Domestic Nexus: The Effects of International Trade and Environmental Politics on the Canadian Forest Sector." In Michael Howlett, ed., *Canadian Forest Policy: Adapting to Change*. Toronto: University of Toronto Press.
Bernstein, Steven, and Christopher Gore. 2001. "Policy Implications of the Kyoto Protocol for Canada." *Isuma: Canadian Journal of Policy Research* 2(4): 26-36.
Berrill, Michael. 1997. *Plundered Seas: Can the World's Fish Be Saved?* Vancouver: Douglas and McIntyre.

Birdsall, Nancy, A.C. Kelley, and S.W. Sinding, eds. 2001. *Population Matters: Demographic Change, Economic Growth, and Poverty in the Developing World*. New York: Oxford University Press.

Bissoondath, Neil. 1994. *Selling Illusions: the cult of multiculturalism in Canada*. Toronto: Penguin.

Blais, J.M., D.W. Schindler, D. Muir et al. 1998. "Accumulation of Persistent Organochlorine Compounds in Mountains of Western Canada." *Nature* 395: 585-8.

Blanshard, Paul. 1984. *American Freedom and Catholic Power*. Boston: Beacon Press.

Block, Walter. 2001. "The Only Good Government Regulation Is No Regulation at All." *Vancouver Sun*, 16 May, A15.

–, ed. 1990. *Economics and the Environment: A Reconciliation*. Vancouver: Fraser Institute.

Blue Ribbon Panel. 1997. *National Forest Strategy Final Evaluation Report*. Ottawa: National Forest Strategy Coalition.

Boardman, Robert. 2001. "Milk and Potatoes Environmentalism: Canada and the Turbulent World of International Law." In Debora L. VanNijnatten and Robert Boardman, eds., *Canadian Environmental Policy: Context and Cases*, 190-211. 2d ed. Oxford: Oxford University Press.

Bocking, Richard C. 1987. "Canadian Water: A Commodity for Export?" In M.C. Healey and R.R. Wallace, eds., *Canadian Aquatic Resources*, 105-35. Canadian Bulletin of Fisheries and Aquatic Sciences 215. Ottawa: Department of Fisheries and Oceans.

Bocking, Stephen. 2001. "The Politics of Endangered Species: A Historical Perspective." In Karen Beazley and Robert Boardman, eds., *The Politics of the Wild: Canada and Endangered Species*. Don Mills, ON: Oxford University Press.

–. 2000. "The Background of Biodiversity: A Brief History of Canadians and Their Living Environment." In Stephen Bocking, ed., *Biodiversity in Canada: Ecology, Ideas, Action*, 3-30. Peterborough, ON: Broadview.

Bongaarts, John, and Rodolfo A. Bulatao, eds. 2000. *Beyond Six Billion: Forecasting the World's Population*. Washington, DC: National Academy Press.

Bourassa, Robert. 1985. *Power from the North*. Scarborough, ON: Prentice-Hall.

Bourdages, Jean-Luc. 1996. *Species at Risk in Canada*. Background Paper BP-417E. Ottawa: Library of Parliament.

Bowman, Irene, and the Rare, Threatened and Endangered Species Task Force. 1993. *An Agenda for Change: Species of Special Status in Ontario*. Toronto: Ministry of Natural Resources.

Boyd, David R. 2002a. "Beautiful B.C. Will Be Scarred by Cuts." *Victoria Times-Colonist*, 21 January, A9.

–. 2002b. *Canada vs. Sweden: An Environmental Face-off*. Victoria: Eco-Research Chair in Environmental Law and Policy. <http://www.enironmentalindicators.org>.

–. 2002c. *Wild by Law: A Report Card on Laws Governing Canada's Parks and Protected Areas, and a Blueprint for Making These Laws More Effective*. Victoria: POLIS Project on Ecological Governance.

–. 2001a. *Canada vs. the OECD: An Environmental Comparison*. Victoria: Eco-Research Chair of Environmental Law and Policy. <http://www.environmentalindicators.org>.

–. 2001b. "Seeing the Forest through the Trees: A Case Comment on *Algonquin Wildlands League* v. *Northern Bruce Peninsula* and Related Cases." 38 *Canadian Environmental Law Reports* (N.S.) 61.

–. 2000. "The Bear Necessities." *Vancouver Sun*, 11 February, A19.

–. 1998. *Betraying Our Trust: A Citizen's Guide to Environmental Rollbacks*. Vancouver: Sierra Legal Defence Fund.

Boyd, David R., and S. Wallace. 2001. *Sea Change: Strengthening Bill C-5, the* Species at Risk Act, *to Protect Marine Biodiversity*. Victoria: Eco-Research Chair in Environmental Law and Policy.

Boyd, David R., and T.L. Williams-Davidson. 2000. "Forest People: First Nations Lead the Way Toward a Sustainable Future." In Debra J. Salazar and Donald K. Alper, eds., *Sustaining the Forests of the Pacific Coast: Forging Truces in the War in the Woods*. Vancouver: UBC Press.

Bramley, Matthew. 2002a. *The Case for Kyoto: The Failure of Voluntary Corporate Action*. Drayton Valley, AB: Pembina Institute.

–. 2002b. *A Comparison of Current Government Action on Climate Change in the U.S. and Canada*. Toronto: Pembina/WWF.

Briggs, Shirley A. 1992. *Basic Guide to Pesticides: Their Characteristics and Hazards*. Washington, DC: Hemisphere Publishing.

Brook, Robert D., Jeffrey R. Brook, Bruce Urch et al. 2002. "Inhalation of Fine Particulate Air Pollution and Ozone Causes Acute Arterial Vasoconstriction in Healthy Adults." *Circulation* 105: 1534-6.

Brooks, Stephen, and Andrew Stritch. 1991. *Business and Government in Canada*. Scarborough, ON: Prentice Hall.

Brower, Michael, and Warren Leon. 1999. *The Consumer's Guide to Effective Environmental Choices: Practical Advice from the Union of Concerned Scientists*. New York: Three Rivers Press.

Browne, Jill A. 1985. *Pesticide Regulation in Canada: The Federal Registration Process and Its Development since 1927*. Edmonton: Alberta Law Foundation.

Brunk, Conrad G., L. Haworth, and B. Lee. 1991. *Value Assumptions in Risk Assessment: A Case Study of the Alachlor Controversy*. Waterloo, ON: Wilfrid Laurier University Press.

Bryant, Dirk, Daniel Nielsen, and Laura Tangley. 1997. *The Last Frontier Forests: Ecosystems and Economies on the Edge*. Washington, DC: World Resources Institute.

Burda, C., R. Collier, and B. Evans. 1999. *The Gitxsan Model: An Alternative to the Destruction of Forests, Salmon and the Gitxsan Land*. Victoria: University of Victoria Eco-Research Chair in Environmental Law and Policy.

Burda, C., F. Gale, and M. M'Gonigle. 1997. *Forests in Trust: Reforming British Columbia's Forest Tenure System for Ecosystem and Community Health*. Victoria: Eco-Research Chair in Environmental Law and Policy.

Burnett, R.T., et al. 1998. "The Effect of the Urban Ambient Air Pollution Mix on Daily Mortality Rates in 11 Canadian Cities." *Canadian Journal of Public Health* 89(3): 152-6.

Burnett, R.T., R.E. Dales, M.E. Raizenne et al. 1994. "Effects of Low Ambient Levels of Ozone and Sulphates on the Frequency of Respiratory Admissions to Ontario Hospitals." *Environmental Research* 65: 172-94.

Burtraw, Dallas, and Byron Swift. 1996. "A New Standard of Performance: An Analysis of the Clean Air Act's Acid Rain Program." 26 *Environmental Law Reporter* 10411.

Bushnell, Ian. 1992. *The Captive Court: A Study of the Supreme Court of Canada*. Montreal: McGill-Queen's University Press.

Caccia, Charles. 2001. Evidence, Standing Committee on the Environment and Sustainable Development. Hearings on Bill C-5, The *Species at Risk Act*, 31 May. <http://www.parl.gc.ca>.

Cairncross, Frances. 1992. *Costing the Earth: The Challenge for Governments, the Opportunities for Business*. Boston: Harvard Business School Press.

Cameron, James, and Julie Abouchar. 1996. "The Status of the Precautionary Principle in International Law." In David Freestone and Ellen Hey, eds., *The Precautionary Principle and International Law*. The Hague: Kluwer Law International.

Cameron, James, David J. Robertson, and Paul Curnow. 2001. "Legal and Regulatory Strategies for GHG Reductions – A Global Survey." *Natural Resources and Environment* 15, 3 (Winter): 176-212.

Canadian Bar Association. 1990. *Report of the CBA Committee on Sustainable Development: Options for Law Reform*. Ottawa.

Canadian Council for International Cooperation. 2001. Press release, 10 December.

Canadian Council of Chief Executives. 2002. "The Kyoto Protocol Revisited: A Responsible and Dynamic Alternative for Canada." <http://www.canadiansolution.com>.

Canadian Council of Forest Ministers. 2002. "Compendium of Canadian Forestry Statistics." <http://www.nfdp.ccfm.org>.

–. 2000. *National Status 2000: Criteria and Indicators of Sustainable Forest Management in Canada*. Ottawa: Natural Resources Canada.

–. 1998. *Sustainable Forests: A Canadian Commitment, National Forest Strategy, 1998-2003*. Ottawa: Natural Resources Canada.

–. 1997. *Criteria and Indicators of Sustainable Forest Management in Canada*. Technical report. Ottawa.

–. 1992a. *National Forest Strategy, 1992-1997*. Hull, QC: Canadian Forest Service.

–. 1992b. *Sustainable Forests: A Canadian Commitment*. Hull, QC: Canadian Forest Service.

Canadian Council of Ministers of the Environment. 2001. *Canada's Strategy to Accelerate the Phase-out of CFC and Halon Uses and Dispose of the Surplus Stocks*. Winnipeg. <http://www.ccme.ca>.

–. 2000. *2000 Annual Progress Report on the Canada-Wide Acid Rain Strategy for Post-2000*. Winnipeg.

–. 1999. *Canadian Environmental Quality Guidelines, 1999*. Winnipeg.

–. 1994. "National Action Plan to Encourage Municipal Water Use Efficiency." <http://www. ec.gc.ca/water>.
–. 1993. "A Statement of Commitment to Complete Canada's Network of Protected Areas." Appendix 1 in Philip Dearden and Rick Rollins, eds., *Parks and Protected Areas in Canada.* Toronto: Oxford University Press.
–. 1990. *National Action Strategy on Climate Change.* November. Winnipeg.
Canadian Environmental Assessment Agency. 2001. *Strengthening Environmental Assessment for Canadians.* Ottawa: Minister of Public Works and Government Services Canada.
–. 2000a. *Federal Environmental Assessment: Making a Difference.* Ottawa: Minister of Supply and Government Services Canada.
–. 2000b. *Review of the* Canadian Environmental Assessment Act: *A Discussion Paper for Public Consultation.* Ottawa: Minister of Public Works and Government Services Canada.
–. 1999. *Annual Report.* Ottawa: Minister of Public Works and Government Services.
–. 1998. *Annual Report.* Ottawa: Minister of Public Works and Government Services.
–. 1997. *Annual Report.* Ottawa: Minister of Public Works and Government Services.
–. 1996. *Environmental Assessment in Canada: Achievements, Challenges and Directions.* Ottawa: Minister of Supply and Services Canada.
–. n.d. "Federal Environmental Assessment Index." <http://www.ceaa.gc.ca>.
Canadian Environmental Law Association. 2002. *A Review of Environmental Assessment in Ontario.* Toronto.
–. 2001. *Tragedy on Tap.* Vol. 1. Toronto.
Canadian Environmental Law Association and the Ontario College of Family Physicians. 2000. *Environmental Standard Setting and Children's Health.* Toronto: Canadian Environmental Law Association.
Canadian Forest Service. 1999. *Climate Change and Canadian Forests.* Ottawa: Natural Resources Canada.
–. 1994. *The State of Canada's Forests, 1993.* Ottawa: Department of Natural Resources.
Canadian Global Almanac. 2001. Toronto: Global Press.
Canadian Institute for Business and the Environment. 1997. *Gallon Environment Letter,* 11 November.
Canadian Institute for Environmental Law and Policy. 2002. *Ensuring Green Power Supplies in Ontario: Responding to Perverse Subsidies and Other Market Inequities.* Toronto. <http://www. cielap.org>.
–. 1996. *The Environmental Management Framework Agreement – A Model for Dysfunctional Federalism?* Toronto.
–. n.d. *Canada-Wide Standards.* Toronto.
Canadian International Development Agency. 2001. *Strengthening Aid Effectiveness: New Approaches to Canada's International Assistance.* Ottawa.
–. 2000. "Population Fact Sheet." <http://www.acdi-cida.gc.ca>.
Canadian National Committee of the International Commission on Large Dams. 1991. *Register of Large Dams in Canada.*
Canadian Nature Federation. 2001. *2001 Species at Risk Report Card.* Toronto. <http://www. cnf.ca>.
–. 2000. "Endangered Species Report Card (2000)." <http://www.cnf.ca>.
Canadian Press. 2002. "$1 Billion for B.C. to Ensure Safe Water." *Vancouver Sun,* 19 June, A1.
–. 2001a. "Canada's Water Not for Sale: PM." *Toronto Star,* 19 July, 1.
–. 2001b. "Canada's Water Should Be Sold: Newfoundland Premier." *Toronto Star,* 13 May, A1.
–. 2001c. "Loggers Who Trashed Camp Get Probation." *Victoria Times-Colonist,* 5 January, A5.
–. 2000. "Ottawa to End Subsidies for 2 B.C. Mines." *Vancouver Sun,* 25 January, A1.
–. 1999. "Most Canadians Back Laws to Save Wildlife Even If Industry Cut." *Victoria Times-Colonist,* 26 May, A12.
Canadian Public Health Association. 1999. *Medical Post,* 23 March. <http://www.medicalpost. com>.
Carpenter, Sandy. 1999. "Status of the B.C. Environmental Assessment Process." In *Environmental Assessment of Natural Resource Projects,* 115-49. Toronto: Insight Press.
Carson, Rachel. 1962. *Silent Spring.* New York: Houghton Mifflin.
Cashore, Benjamin, George Hoberg, Michael Howlett et al. 2001. *In Search of Sustainability: British Columbia Forest Policy in the 1990s.* Vancouver: UBC Press.

Castrilli, J.F. 2002. "The New Ontario Hazardous Waste Regulations of 2000: Waste Identification and Protection of the Environment." 11 *Journal of Environmental Law and Practice* 285.

–. 1974. *Environmental Impact Assessment: The Law As It Is and As It Should Be.* Toronto: Canadian Environmental Law Association.

Castrilli, J.F., and Toby Vigod. 1987. *Pesticides in Canada: An Examination of Federal Law and Policy.* Ottawa: Law Reform Commission of Canada.

Catton, William. 1980. *Overshoot: The Ecological Basis of Revolutionary Change.* Urbana: University of Illinois Press.

Chambers, P.A., et al. 2001. *Nutrients and their Impact on the Canadian Environment.* Ottawa: Minister of Public Works and Government Services Canada.

Chance, G.W., and E. Harmesen. 1998. "Children Are Different: Environmental Contaminants and Children's Health." *Canadian Journal of Public Health* 89 (Supp. 1): 10-14.

Chang, E., D. MacDonald, and J. Wolfson. 1998. "Who Killed CIPSI?" *Alternatives Journal* 24(2): 20-5.

Chase, Steven. 2001. "Ottawa Faces Suit over Banned Pesticide." *Globe and Mail,* 11 December, B1, B6.

Chertrow, Marian R., and Daniel C. Esty. 1997. *Thinking Ecologically: The Next Generation of Environmental Policy.* New Haven: Yale University Press.

Chiotti, Quentin, and N. Urquizo. 1999. *The Relative Magnitude of the Impacts and Effects of Greenhouse Gas Related Emission Reductions.* Toronto: Environment Canada and Pollution Probe.

Chivian, Eric. 2001. "Species Loss and Ecosystem Disruption: The Implications for Human Health." *Canadian Medical Association Journal* 164(1): 66-9.

Chow, Wyng. 1999. "U.S. Firm Sues B.C. and Canada for Billions in Water Export Fight." *Vancouver Sun,* 23 October, A3.

Chrétien, Jean. 2002. Address to the Organization of African Unity and the United Nations Economic Commission for Africa. Addis Ababa, Ethiopia, 11 April.

Christensen, Randy. 2001. *Waterproof: Canada's Drinking Water Report Card.* Vancouver: Sierra Legal Defence Fund. <http://www.sierralegal.org>.

Christie, Elizabeth. 2000. *Pulping the Law: How Pulp Mills Are Ruining Canadian Waters with Impunity.* Toronto: Sierra Legal Defence Fund.

Cincotta, R.P., and R. Engelman. 2000. *Nature's Place: Human Population and the Future of Biological Diversity.* Washington, DC: Population Action International. <http://www.popact.org>.

Citizenship and Immigration Canada. 2002. Facts and Figures, 2001: Immigration Overview. Ottawa: Minister of Public Works and Government Services.

–. 2001. Press release, 8 February. <http://www.cic.gc.ca>.

Clancy, Peter. 2001. "Atlantic Canada: The Politics of Public and Private Forestry." In Michael Howlett, ed., *Canadian Forest Policy: Adapting to Change.* Toronto: University of Toronto Press.

Clark, C.W. 1996. "Marine Reserves and the Precautionary Management of Fisheries." *Ecological Applications* 6: 369-70.

Clark, Karen, Jennifer McKay, and Anne Mitchell. 2001. *Sustainable Development in Canada: A New Federal Plan.* Toronto: Canadian Institute for Environmental Law and Policy.

Clark, Karen, and James Yacoumidis. 2000. *Ontario's Environment and the Common Sense Revolution: A Fifth Year Report.* Toronto: Canadian Institute of Environmental Law and Policy. <http://www.cielap.org>.

Clogg, Jessica. 2001. "What's in Store for Forest Law and Policy?" *West Coast Environmental Law Association Newsletter* 26(5): 1.

Cobb, C., G.S. Goodman, and M. Wackernagel. 1999. *Why Bigger Isn't Better: The Genuine Progress Indicator – 1999 Update.* San Francisco: Redefining Progress.

Cobb, C., T. Halstead, and J. Rowe. 1995. "If the Economy Is Way Up, Why is America Down?" *Atlantic Monthly,* October, 3-15.

Cohen, David, and Brian Radnoff. 1998. "Regulation, Takings, Compensation, and the Environment: An Economic Perspective." In Chris Tollefson, ed., *The Wealth of Forests: Markets, Regulation, and Sustainable Forestry,* 299-341. Vancouver: UBC Press.

Cohen, Joel E. 1995. *How Many People Can the Earth Support?* New York: Norton.

Colborn, Theo, Dianne Dumanoski, and John P. Myers. 1996. *Our Stolen Future: Are We Threatening Our Fertility, Intelligence, and Survival? A Scientific Detective Story.* New York: Penguin.

Cole, Daniel H., and Peter Z. Grossman. 1999. "When Is Command and Control Efficient? Institutions, Technology and the Comparative Efficiency of Alternative Regulatory Regimes for Environmental Protection." 5 *Wisconsin Law Review* 887.

Colman, Ronald. 2001. "Measuring Real Progress." *Journal of Innovative Management* 7, 1 (Fall): 69-77.

Comeau, Pauline. 1997. "Report Calls Cod an Endangered Species." *Canadian Geographic,* July-August, pp. 18-22.

Commission for Environmental Cooperation. 2002a. "Free Trade and Environment: The Picture Becomes Clearer." <http://www.cec.org>.

–. 2002b. *The North American Mosaic: A State of the Environment Report.* Montreal.

–. 2001a. *BC Logging.* SEM-00-004. <http://www.cec.org>.

–. 2001b. *Taking Stock 1998: North American Pollutant Releases and Transfers Sourcebook.* Montreal.

–. 2000. *Final Factual Record Prepared in BC Hydro Case.* SEM-97-001. <http://www.cec.org>.

–. 1994. *Taking Stock: North American Pollutant Releases and Transfers, 1994.* Montreal.

Commissioner of the Environment and Sustainable Development. 2002. *Report to the House of Commons.* Ottawa: Minister of Public Works and Government Services.

–. 2001a. "Managing for Sustainable Development in Federal Departments." Press release, 2 October.

–. 2001b. *Report to the House of Commons.* Ottawa: Minister of Public Works and Government Services.

–. 2000. *Report to the House of Commons.* Ottawa: Minister of Public Works and Government Services.

–. 1999. *Report to the House of Commons.* Ottawa: Minister of Public Works and Government Services.

–. 1998. *Report to the House of Commons.* Ottawa: Minister of Public Works and Government Services.

Conly, S.R., and S. De Silva. 1999. *Paying Their Fair Share?: Donor Countries and International Population Assistance.* Washington, DC: Population Action International.

Conly, S.R., and J.J. Speidel. 1993. *Global Population Assistance: A Report Card on the Major Donor Countries.* Washington, DC: Population Action International.

Conrad, Monique. 2000. "The Canadian Environmental Protection Act." *Canadian Lawyer* 24, 1 (January): 46-9.

Consumers Union of the United States. 2001. *A Report Card for the EPA: Successes and Failures in Implementing the Food Quality Protection Act.* <http://www.consumersunion.org>.

Cook, Elizabeth, ed. 1996. *Ozone Protection in the United States: Elements of Success.* Washington, DC: World Resources Institute.

Cooper, K. 1999a. "Children at Risk: Exposure to Pesticides." *Intervenor* (Canadian Environmental Law Association) 24(4): 3.

–. 1999b. "An Updated Chronology of Changes in Ontario's Environmental Policy." *Intervenor* (Canadian Environmental Law Association) 24(1): 9-16.

Corcoran, Terence. 1999. "The Sheiks of Canadian Water." *National Post,* 11 February, C7.

Corporate Research Associates. 1997. *Tracking Survey of Canadians' Attitudes Toward National Resource Issues, 1997.* Ottawa: Natural Resources Canada.

Cosh, Colby. 1996. "The Elected Dictatorship: Can Parliament Be Made an Adequate Instrument of Democracy?" *Alberta Report,* 16 December.

Costanza, Robert, et al. 1997. "The Value of the World's Ecosystem Services and Natural Capital." 387 *Nature* 253.

Cote, Pierre-Andre. 2000. *The Interpretation of Legislation in Canada.* 3d ed. Scarborough, ON: Carswell.

Cotton, Roger, and Alastair R. Lucas. 2001. *Canadian Environmental Law.* Toronto: Butterworths.

Council of Forest Industries. 1999. *A Blueprint for Competitiveness: Five Ideas for Improving Public Policy Affecting the BC Forest Industry and the People, Businesses and Communities that Depend on It.* Vancouver.

Cox, Caroline. 2001. "Ten Reasons Not to Use Pesticides." 21.4 *Journal of Pesticide Reform* 2.

Cox, Kevin. 2000. "Seabirds Suffer in Oily Ground: Lax Laws Encourage Ships to Pollute the Sea, Report Says." *Globe and Mail,* 11 March, A1.

Craig, J. 2000. *Questions Regarding Access to Information Held by the Pest Management Regulatory Agency: The Federal* Access to Information Act *and the Common Law Duty of Confidentiality.* Parliamentary Research Branch, Library of Parliament, 26 January, Ottawa.

Cranstone, D. 2001. "Canada's Rank in World Mining." In *Canadian Minerals Yearbook.* Ottawa: Natural Resources Canada.

Curran, D., and May Leung. 2000. *Smart Growth: A Primer.* Victoria: Eco-Research Chair in Environmental Law and Policy.

Curran, D., and M. M'Gonigle. 1999. "Aboriginal Forestry: Community Management as Opportunity and Imperative." 37.4 *Osgoode Hall Law Journal* 711.

Daily, Gretchen. 1997. *Nature's Services: Societal Dependence on Nature's Ecosystems.* Washington, DC: Island Press.

Daily, Gretchen, and Katherine Ellison. 2002. *The New Economy of Nature.* Washington, DC: Island Press.

Dalal-Clayton, Barry. 1996. *Getting to Grips with Green Plans: National Level Experience in Industrial Countries.* London: Earthscan.

Dale, Ann. 2001. *At the Edge: Sustainable Development in the 21st Century.* Vancouver: UBC Press.

Dales, R.E., et al. 1994. "Prevalence of Childhood Asthma across Canada." *International Journal of Epidemiology* 23: 775-81.

Dalton, Rex. 2002. "Frogs Put in the Gender Blender by America's Favourite Herbicide." *Nature* 416: 665-6.

Daly, H.E. 1991. *Steady-State Economics.* Washington, DC: Island Press.

Daly, Herman E., and John B. Cobb, Jr. 1989. *For the Common Good: Redirecting the Economy Toward Community, the Environment and a Sustainable Future.* Boston: Beacon Press.

d'Aquino, Tom. 1998. "Punitive Measures Will Not Work." *Perspectives,* 18 May. <http://www.ceocouncil.ca>.

Dauncey, Guy. 2001. *Stormy Weather: 101 Solutions to Global Climate Change.* Gabriola Island, BC: New Society Publishers. <http://www.earthfuture.com/stormyweather>.

David Suzuki Foundation. 2001a. *Fueling the Climate Crisis: The Continental Energy Plan.* Vancouver. <http://www.davidsuzuki.org>.

–. 2001b. "Scientists Outline Severe Impacts." *Climate Chronicle,* Summer.

–. 2000a. *Clearing the Air: Air Quality Benefits of Reducing Greenhouse Gas Emissions in Canada.* Vancouver.

–. 2000b. *Negotiating the Climate: Canada and the International Politics of Global Warming.* Vancouver.

Davies, J.C., and J. Mazurek. 1998. *Pollution Control in the U.S.: Evaluating the System.* Washington, DC: Resources for the Future.

Davies, Katherine. 1998. *The Right to Know about Chemical Pesticides: A Discussion Paper.* Ottawa: Canadian Labour Congress.

Davies, T., and J. Mazurek. 1996. *Industry Incentives for Environmental Improvement: Evaluation of US Federal Initiatives.* Washington, DC: Global Environmental Management Initiative.

Davis, Gary A., et al. 1997. "Extended Product Responsibility: A Tool for a Sustainable Economy." *Environment* 39(7): 10-15, 36-8.

Dawson, Mary. 2001. Evidence, Standing Committee on Environment and Sustainable Development. Hearings on Bill C-5, The *Species at Risk Act,* 6 June. <http://www.parl.gc.ca>.

Day, J.C., and Frank Quinn. 1992. *Water Diversion and Export: Learning from Canadian Experience.* Waterloo, ON: Canadian Association of Geographers.

de Fontaubert, A.C., D.R. Downes, and T.S. Agardy. 1996. *Biodiversity in the Seas: Implementing the Convention on Biological Diversity in Marine and Coastal Habitats.* Gland, Switzerland: International Union for the Conservation of Nature.

de Gruijl, Frank R., and Jan C. van der Leun. 2000. "Environment and Health: Ozone Depletion and Ultraviolet Radiation." *Canadian Medical Association Journal* 163(7): 851-5.

de Jongh, Paul, and Laurie Morisette. 1998. *The Netherlands Approach to Environmental Policy Integration.* Washington, DC: Center for Strategic and International Studies.

de Klemm, Cyrille, and Clare Shine. 1993. *Biological Diversity Conservation and the Law.* Gland, Switzerland: International Union for the Conservation of Nature.

de Moor, A.P.G. 1997. *Perverse Incentives: Subsidies and Sustainable Development.* The Netherlands: Institute for Research on Public Expenditure.

De Sombre, Elizabeth R. 2000. "The Experience of the Montreal Protocol: Particularly Remarkable and Remarkably Particular." 19.1 *UCLA Journal of Environmental Law and Policy* 49.

de Villiers, Marq. 1999. *Water.* Toronto: Stoddart.

Dellert, Lois. 1998. "Sustained Yield: Why Has It Failed to Achieve Sustainability?" In Chris Tollefson, ed., *The Wealth of Forests: Markets, Regulation, and Sustainable Forestry.* Vancouver: UBC Press.

DeMarco, J., and R. Christensen. 2002. "Canada's Troubled Waters." *Globe and Mail*, 23 January, A17.

Dene Cultural Institute. 1995. "Traditional Ecological Knowledge and Environmental Assessment." In Pam Gaffield and Chad Gaffield, eds., *Consuming Canada: Readings in Environment History*. Mississauga, ON: Copp Clark Press.

Denstedt, Shawn H.T. 1999. "The Regulatory Context and Policy Approach to Environmental Assessment." In *Environmental Assessment of Natural Resource Projects*. Toronto: Insight Press.

DePalma, Anthony. 1998. "Canada No Safe Haven for Birds or Bears." *New York Times*, 13 March, A1.

Department of Finance. 2002. "Frequently Asked Questions – Debt Relief." <http://www.fin.gc.ca>.

–. 1999. "Canada Forgives Bangladesh's Debt." Press release, 9 December.

–. 1996. *The Federal Government Response to the Eighth Report of the Standing Committee on Environment and Sustainable Development, Keeping a Promise: Toward a Sustainable Budget*. Ottawa.

Department of Fisheries and Oceans. 2002. "Canada's Oceans Strategy: Our Oceans, Our Future." <http://www.dfo-mpo.gc.ca>.

–. 2001a. "B.C. Commercial Landings by Species in Round Weight and Value, 2000." <http://www.pac.dfo-mpo.gc.ca>.

–. 2001b. *Building Awareness and Capacity: An Action Plan for Continued Sustainable Development 2001-2003*. Ottawa.

–. 1999a. *Annual Report to Parliament on the Administration and Enforcement of the Fish Habitat Protection and Pollution Prevention Provisions of the* Fisheries Act *for the Period of April 1, 1997 to March 31, 1998*. Ottawa: Minister of Public Works and Government Services Canada.

–. 1999b. *Canary Rockfish*. DFO Science Stock Status Report A6-08.

–. 1999c. *Thornyheads (Shortspine and Longspine)*. DFO Science Stock Status Report A6-12.

–. 1998. *Review of the Fraser River Action Plan*. Ottawa.

Department of Foreign Affairs and International Trade. 1999. "Bulk Water Removal and International Trade Considerations." 16 November. <http://www.dfait-maeci.gc.ca>.

–. 1995. *Canada in the World: Canadian Foreign Policy Review*. Ottawa.

–. n.d. "Canada-U.S. Relations – Trade – Questions and Answers." <http://www.dfait-maeci.gc.ca>.

Dewailly, E., et al. 1993. "Inuit Exposure to Organochlorines through the Aquatic Food Chain in Arctic Canada." *Environmental Health Perspectives* 101: 618-20.

Dewailly, E., A. Nantel, J.P. Weber, and F. Meyer. 1989. "High Levels of PCBs in Breast Milk of Inuit Women from Arctic Quebec." *Bulletin of Environmental Contamination and Toxicology* 43(2): 641-6.

Dewees, Don. 1993. *Reducing the Burden of Environmental Regulation*. Discussion Paper 93-07. Kingston: Queen's University School of Policy Studies.

–. 1990. "The Regulation of Sulphur Dioxide in Ontario." In G. Bruce Doern, ed., *Getting it Green: Case Studies in Canadian Environmental Regulation*. Toronto: C.D. Howe Institute.

Dingle, P., A. Strahco, and P. Franklin. 1997. "Pesticide Residues in Food." In P. Cheremisinoff, ed., *Health and Toxicology*. Houston: Gulf Publishing.

Dixon, Guy. 2000. "Canada Tops for Least Amount of Red Tape: Study." *Globe and Mail*, 14 November, B9.

Doelle, Meinhard. 1994. "The *Canadian Environmental Assessment Act*: New Uncertainties but a Step in the Right Direction." 4 *Journal of Environmental Law and Practice* 59.

Doering, R., F. Bregha, D. Roberts et al. 1992. *Environmental Regulations and the Pulp and Paper Industry*. Ottawa: National Round Table on the Environment and the Economy.

Doern, G. Bruce. 2001. "Environment Canada as a Networked Institution." In Debora L. VanNijnatten and Robert Boardman, eds., *Canadian Environmental Policy: Context and Cases*. 2d ed. Oxford: Oxford University Press.

Doern, G. Bruce, and T. Conway. 1994. *The Greening of Canada: Federal Institutions and Decisions*. Toronto: University of Toronto Press.

Dolphin, K.P., and D.L.J. Quicke. 2001. "Estimating the Global Species Richness of Incompletely Described Taxa: An Example Using Parasitoid Wasps." *Biological Journal of the Linnaean Society* 73: 279-86.

Dorcey, Anthony H.J., and Timothy McDaniels. 2001. "Great Expectations, Mixed Results: Trends in Citizen Involvement in Canadian Environmental Governance." In Edward A. Parson, ed., *Governing the Environment: Persistent Challenges, Uncertain Innovations*. Toronto: University of Toronto Press.

Dotto, Lydia, and Harold Schiff. 1978. *The Ozone War.* Garden City, NY: Doubleday.

Doyle, Derek, and B. Sadler. 1996. *Environmental Assessment in Canada: Frameworks, Procedures and Attributes of Effectiveness.* Ottawa: Canadian Environmental Assessment Agency.

Doyle-Bedwell, P., and F.G. Cohen. 2001. "Aboriginal Peoples in Canada: Their Role in Shaping Environmental Trends in the Twenty-first Century." In Edward A. Parson, ed., *Governing the Environment: Persistent Challenges, Uncertain Innovations,* 169-206. Toronto: University of Toronto Press.

Drinkwater, K.F., and K.T. Frank. 1994. "Effects of River Regulation and Diversion on Marine Fish and Invertebrates." *Aquatic Conservation: Freshwater and Marine Ecosystems* 4: 135-51.

Driscoll, Charles T., et al. 2001. "Acidic Deposition in the Northeastern United States: Sources and Inputs, Ecosystem Effects, and Management Strategies." 51.3 *Bioscience* 180.

Drohan, Madelaine. 1998. "How the Net Killed the MAI." *Globe and Mail,* 29 April, A1.

Duffy, Andrew. 2000. "Anderson Opens Door to Green Taxes." *Ottawa Citizen,* 23 March, 3.

–. 1998. "Canadians Need 'Sense of Common Purpose': Mounties, CBC, Flag No Longer Unifying Symbols, Report Says." *Ottawa Citizen,* 3 May, A1.

Dukas, Helen, and Banesh Hoffman, eds. 1979. *Albert Einstein, The Human Side: New Glimpses from his Archives.* Princeton: Princeton University Press.

Duncan, Linda. 1990a. *Enforcing Environmental Law: A Guide to Private Prosecutions.* Edmonton: Environmental Law Centre.

–. 1990b. "The Rule of Law and Sustainable Development." In Canadian Bar Association Committee on Sustainable Development, ed., *Report of the Canadian Bar Association Committee on Sustainable Development in Canada: Options for Law Reform.* Ottawa: Canadian Bar Association.

"DuPont Ordered to Pay Damages of $78.3 Million in Benlate Case." 2001. *Wall Street Journal,* 13 August, B3.

Durning, Alan. 1994. "The Conundrum of Consumption." In Laurie Mazur, ed., *Beyond the Numbers: A Reader on Population, Consumption, and the Environment,* 40-7. Washington, DC: Island Press.

Durning, Alan T., and Yoram Bauman. 1998. *Tax Shift.* Seattle: Northwest Environment Watch.

Dwivedi, O.P., Patrick Kyba, Peter J. Stoett et al. 2001. *Sustainable Development and Canada: National and International Perspectives.* Peterborough, ON: Broadview Press.

Eagles, Paul F.J. 1993a. "Environmental Management in Parks." In Philip Dearden and Rick Rollins, eds., *Parks and Protected Areas in Canada.* Toronto: Oxford University Press.

–. 1993b. "Parks Legislation in Canada." In Philip Dearden and Rick Rollins, eds., *Parks and Protected Areas in Canada.* Toronto: Oxford University Press.

Easterbrook, Gregg. 1995. *A Moment on Earth: The Coming Age of Environmental Optimism.* New York: Viking.

Ecotrust, Pacific GIS, and Conservation International. 1995. *The Rain Forests of Home: An Atlas of People and Place.* Part 1, *Natural Forests and Native Languages of the Coastal Temperate Rain Forest.* Portland, OR: Ecotrust.

Egan, Brian, Lisa Ambus, Bryan Evans et al. 2001. *Where There's a Way, There's a Will.* Report 2, *Models of Community-Based Natural Resource Management.* Victoria: Eco-Research Chair in Environmental Law and Policy.

Eggerston, Laura. 1999. "Controversial Environment Bill Passed by House." *Toronto Star,* 2 June. News section.

Ehrenfeld, David. 1988. "Why Put a Value on Biodiversity?" In E.O. Wilson and F.M. Peters, eds., *Biodiversity,* 212-16. Washington, DC: National Academy Press.

Ehrlich, P.R., and A.H. Ehrlich. 1990. *The Population Explosion.* New York: Simon and Schuster.

Ehrlich, Paul. 1968. *The Population Bomb.* New York: Ballantine Books.

Elder, P.S. 1992. "Environmental and Sustainability Assessment." 2 *Journal of Environmental Law and Practice* 125.

Elgie, Stewart. 2001. Evidence, Standing Committee on Environment and Sustainable Development. Hearings on Bill C-5, The *Species at Risk Act,* 26 April, 7 June. <http://www.parl.gc.ca>.

–. 1993. "Environmental Groups and the Courts: 1970-1992." In G. Thompson, M.L. McConnell, and L. Huestis, eds., *Environmental Law and Business in Canada,* 185-224. Toronto: Canada Law Book.

Elliott, Richard, and Marie-Helene Bonin. 2002. *Patents, International Trade Law, and Access to Essential Medicines.* Ottawa: Médécins Sans Frontières. <http://www.aidslaw.ca>.

Engelman, Robert. 2000. *People in the Balance: Population and Natural Resources at the Turn of the Millennium.* Washington, DC: Population Action International.

Enserink, M. 1999. "Biological Invaders Sweep In." *Science* 285: 1834-6.

Environics. 2000. "Biodiversity Poll," conducted for the Canadian Nature Federation. <http://www.cnf.ca/wanted/poll_1.html>.

Environics International. 2001. *Canadian Environment Monitor.* 18 January. <http://www.environicsinternational.com>.

–. 1999. *Public Opinion and the Environment 1999: Biodiversity Issues.* Opinion poll conducted for Environment Canada. <http://www.ec.gc.ca>.

Environment Canada. 2003. *Environmental Signals: Headline Indicators 2003.* Ottawa: Minister of Public Works and Government Services.

–. 2001a. *Canada's Greenhouse Gas Emissions 1990-1999.* Ottawa. <http:// www.ec.gc.ca>.

–. 2001b. *The Government of Canada's Interim Plan 2001 on Particulate Matter and Ozone.* Ottawa: Minister of Public Works and Government Services.

–. 2001c. *National Pollutant Release Inventory, National Overview 1999.* Ottawa: Minister of Public Works and Government Services.

–. 2001d. *Pollution Prevention Planning Handbook.* Ottawa.

–. 2001e. *Providing Cleaner Air to Canadians.* Ottawa: Minister of Public Works and Government Services.

–. 2001f. *Tracking Key Environmental Issues.* Ottawa: Minister of Public Works and Government Services.

–. 2001g. *Urban Water Indicators: Municipal Water Use and Wastewater Treatment.* State of Environment Bulletin No. 2001-1.

–. 2000a. *Comparison of Ozone Depleting Substance Regulations in Canada: Regulatory Status as of December 31, 1999.* Ottawa.

–. 2000b. *Wild Species in Canada 2000: The General Status of Species in Canada.* Ottawa: Minister of Public Works and Government Services.

–. 1999a. *Acid Rain.* State of Environment Bulletin No. 99-3.

–. 1999b. *Canada's Oceans: Experiences and Practices.* Ottawa.

–. 1999c. *Compliance Report.* Ottawa.

–. 1999d. *National Enforcement Program Business Case.* Ottawa.

–. 1999e. *National Pollutant Release Inventory, National Overview 1998.* Ottawa: Minister of Public Works and Government Services.

–. 1999f. *Smog Fact Sheet.* Ottawa.

–. 1999g. *Stratospheric Ozone Depletion.* State of Environment Bulletin No. 99-2. Ottawa.

–. 1998a. *1997 Canadian Acid Rain Assessment.* Vol. 1, *Summary of Results.* Ottawa: Minister of Supply and Services Canada.

–. 1998b. *Canada and Freshwater: Experiences and Practices.* Ottawa.

–. 1998c. *Canadian Passenger Transportation.* State of Environment Bulletin No. 98-5. Ottawa.

–. 1998d. *Caring for Canada's Biodiversity: Canada's First National Report to the Conference of the Parties to the Convention on Biological Diversity.* Hull, QC: Ministry of Supply and Services Canada.

–. 1998e. *Fraser River Action Plan Final Report: Overview.* Ottawa: Public Works and Government Services.

–. 1998f. *Inventory of Initiatives. Caring for Canada's Biodiversity: Annex to Canada's First National Report to the Conference of the Parties to the Convention on Biological Diversity.* Ottawa: Public Works and Government Services.

–. 1998g. *Urban Water: Municipal Water Use and Wastewater Treatment.* State of Environment Bulletin No. 98-4. Ottawa.

–. 1997a. *The Right Choice at the Right Time: Highlights of the Global Benefits and Costs of the Montreal Protocol on Substances That Deplete the Ozone Layer.* Ottawa.

–. 1997b. *Second National Report on Climate Change: Actions under the United Nations Framework Convention on Climate Change.* Ottawa.

–. 1997c. *Sustaining Canada's Forests: Forest Biodiversity.* State of Environment Bulletin No. 97-1. Ottawa.

–. 1996a. *Energy Consumption.* State of Environment Bulletin No. 96-3.

414   *References*

–. 1996b. *Municipal Water Pricing Survey.* Ottawa: Minister of Public Works and Government Services.
–. 1996c. *Survey on the Importance of Wildlife to Canadians: A Federal-Provincial-Territorial Initiative.* Ottawa: Minister of Public Works and Government Services.
–. 1996d. *The State of Canada's Environment, 1996.* Ottawa: Minister of Public Works and Government Services.
–. 1995a. *Canadian Biodiversity Strategy: Canada's Response to the Convention on Biological Diversity.* Ottawa: Minister of Supply and Services Canada.
–. 1995b. *Sustaining Canada's Forests: Timber Harvesting.* State of the Environment Technical Supplement No. 95-4. Ottawa.
–. 1993. *A Global Partnership: Canada and the Conventions of the United Nations Conference on Environment and Development.* Ottawa.
–. 1991. *The State of Canada's Environment.* Ottawa: Government of Canada.
–. 1990a. *Canada's Green Plan for a Healthy Environment.* Ottawa: Minister of Supply and Services.
–. 1990b. *A Framework for Discussion on the Environment.* Ottawa: Minister of Supply and Services.
–. 1990c. *Sustainable Development Initiatives in Canada.* Ottawa: Government of Canada.
–. 1988. *Report of the Special Committee on Acid Rain.* Ottawa.
–. 1987. *Federal Water Policy.* Ottawa.
–. n.d.a. *Backgrounder: The Proposed* Species at Risk Act. Ottawa.
–. n.d.b. "The Ozone Primer." <http://www.ec.gc.ca/ozone>.
–. n.d.c. *Threats to Sources of Drinking Water and Aquatic Ecosystem Health in Canada.* Burlington, ON: National Water Research Institute.
Environment Canada and Quebec Ministry of Environment and Wildlife. 1998. "Evaluation of the Toxicity of Effluents from Municipal Wastewater Plants in Quebec." St. Lawrence Vision 2000 website, <http://www.slv2000.qc.gc.ca>, accessed August 2002.
Environmental Bureau of Investigation. 2000. *The Citizens Guide to Environmental Investigation and Private Prosecution.* Toronto: Earthscan Canada.
Environmental Commissioner of Ontario. 2000a. *Changing Perspectives: Annual Report 1999-2000.* Toronto.
–. 2000b. *The Protection of Ontario's Groundwater and Intensive Farming: Special Report to the Legislative Assembly of Ontario.* <http://www.eco.on.ca>.
–. 1999. *1998-99 Annual Report.* Toronto.
–. 1998. *Open Doors: Annual Report.* Toronto.
–. 1997. *Open Doors: Annual Report.* Toronto.
–. 1996. *Open Doors: Annual Report.* Toronto.
Environmental Mining Council of British Columbia. 2001. *Undermining Biodiversity.* Victoria.
Environmental News Network. 2001. "Ozone Smuggling." 12 April. <http://www.enn.com>.
Epstein, Howard. 2001. "Case Comment: *Spraytech* v. *Town of Hudson.*" 19 *M.P.L.R.* (3d) 56.
Epstein, Paul R. 2000. "Is Global Warming Harmful to Health?" *Scientific American* 282, 8 (August): 50.
–. 1998. "Biological and Physical Signs of Climate Change: Focus on Mosquito-borne Diseases." 79.3 *Bulletin of the American Meteorological Society* 409.
Estrin, David, and John Swaigen. 1993. *Environment on Trial: A Guide to Ontario Environmental Law and Policy.* Toronto: Emond Montgomery.
European Commission. 1997. *Energy for the Future: Renewable Sources of Energy.* European Commission White Paper. Brussels.
European Environment Agency. 2001. *Late Lessons from Early Warnings: The Precautionary Principle, 1896-2000.* Copenhagen.
Evans, L.T. 1998. *Feeding the Ten Billion: Plants and Population Growth.* Cambridge: Cambridge University Press.
Farber, Daniel A. 1999. "Taking Slippage Seriously: Noncompliance and Creative Compliance in Environmental Law." 23 *Harvard Environmental Law Review* 297.
Federal Provincial Parks Council. 2000. *Working Together: Parks and Protected Areas in Canada.* Ottawa: Parks Canada.
Fenge, Terry. 2000. "Indigenous People and Global POPs." *Northern Perspectives* 26(1): 8-14. <http://www.carc.org>.
–. 1998. "POPs in the Arctic: Turning Science into Policy." *Northern Perspectives* 25(2). <http://www.carc.org>.

Fergusson, Angus. 2001. *Ozone Depletion and Climate Change: Understanding the Linkages.* Ottawa: Environment Canada/Minister of Supply and Government Services.

Fife, Robert. 2001. "PM Reopens Water Trade Debate." *National Post,* 5 April, A1.

Fisheries Renewal BC. 2000. *Fisheries Renewal at Rivers Inlet, Backgrounder.* Victoria: Fisheries Renewal BC.

Fisheries Resource Conservation Council. 1994. *Conservation: Stay the Course.* Ottawa: Ministry of Supply and Services.

Flatt, Victor B. 1997. "A Dirty River Runs Through it: The Failure of Enforcement in the Clean Water Act." 25 *Boston College Environmental Affairs Law Review* 1.

Food and Agriculture Organization. 2001. *State of the World's Forests 2001.* Rome.

–. 1999a. *The State of Food Insecurity in the World.* Rome.

–. 1999b. *The State of World Fisheries and Aquaculture 1998.* Rome.

–. 1998. *Trends in Forestry Law in America and Asia.* Rome.

–. 1993. *Marine Fisheries and the Law of the Sea.* Rome.

Ford, John K.B., Graeme M. Ellis, and Kenneth C. Balcomb. 2000. *Killer Whales.* 2d ed. Vancouver: UBC Press.

Forest Alliance. 1996. "The Forest and the People." *Forest Alliance Newsletter* 5(12).

–. 1995. *Analysis of Recent British Columbia Government Forest Policy and Land Use Initiatives.* Vancouver: Price Waterhouse.

–. n.d. *Meeting the Challenge: Sustainability in B.C.'s Forests.* Vancouver. 8 pp.

Forest Practices Board. 1999. *Annual Report 1999.* Victoria.

Forest Products Association of Canada. 2001. *Forest Products and Practices: The Canadian Difference.* Montreal.

Forsey, Eugene A. 1991. *How Canadians Govern Themselves.* Ottawa: Minister of Canadian Heritage and the Minister of Public Works and Government Services Canada.

Franson, Robert T., Alastair R. Lucas, and John Milligan. 2002. *Canadian Environmental Law.* Toronto: Butterworths.

Fraser Institute. 2000. "The Environment is Improving – Eight Reasons to Celebrate the 30th Anniversary of Earth Day." Press release, 18 April. <http://www.fraserinstitute.ca>.

–. 1998. *Environmental Indicators for Canada and the United States.* Vancouver.

Fraser, John. 1994. *Fraser River Sockeye, 1994: Problems and Discrepancies.* Ottawa: Public Works and Government Services Canada.

Frechette, J.D. 2000. *Pesticides and the GST.* Ottawa: Library of Parliament, Parliamentary Research Branch.

Freedman, Bill, Lindsay Rodger, Peter Ewins, and David M. Green. 2001. "Species at Risk in Canada." In Karen Beazley and Robert Boardman, eds., *The Politics of the Wild: Canada and Endangered Species.* Don Mills, ON: Oxford University Press.

Freemark, K.E., and C. Boutin. 1994. *Impacts of Agricultural Herbicide Use on Terrestrial Wildlife: A Review with Special Reference to Canada.* Canadian Wildlife Service Technical Report No. 196. Ottawa: Minister of Supply and Services.

Freestone, D., and E. Hey, eds. 1996. *The Precautionary Principle and International Law: The Challenge of Implementation.* London: Kluwer Law International.

Friends of the Earth. 2000. *Green Scissors 2000: Cutting Wasteful and Environmentally Harmful Spending.* Washington, DC.

Friends of the Earth Canada. 2001. *Primary Environmental Care: An Assessment of Environment Canada's Delivery.* Vol. 2, *Ten Year Record of Environmental Prosecutions, 1989-1999.* Ottawa.

–. 2000a. *Environmental Enforcement: Ten Year Record of Environmental Prosecutions, 1989-1999.* Vol. 1. Ottawa. <http://www.foecanada.org>.

–. 2000b. *Ozone Protection Report Card.* Ottawa: Friends of the Earth.

Fu, Caihong, Robert Mohn, and L. Paul Fanning. 2001. "Why the Atlantic Cod *(Gadus Morhua)* Stock off Eastern Nova Scotia Has Not Recovered." *Canadian Journal of Fisheries and Aquatic Sciences* 58: 1613-23.

Fulton, Jim. 2001. Evidence, Standing Committee on Environment and Sustainable Development, Hearings on Bill C-5, The *Species at Risk Act,* 15 May. <http://www.parl.gc.ca>.

Gale, Fred. 1998. "Ecoforestry Bound: How International Trade Agreements Constrain the Adoption of an Ecosystem-based Approach to Forest Management." In Chris Tollefson, ed., *The Wealth of Forests: Markets, Regulation, and Sustainable Forestry,* 342-70. Vancouver: UBC Press.

Gale, Robert, Stephan Barg, and Alexander Gillies. 1995. *Green Budget Reform: An International Casebook of Leading Practices.* London: Earthscan.

Gallagher, P.R., B. Ma, D.I. McLean et al. 1990. "Trends in Basal Cell Carcinoma, Squamous Cell Carcinoma and Melanoma of the Skin from 1973 through 1987." 23 *Journal of the American Academy of Dermatology* 3.

Gallon, Gary. 1999. "A Five-Tier Approach to Effective Environmental Initiatives." In Robert B. Gibson, ed., *Voluntary Initiatives: The New Politics of Corporate Greening.* Peterborough, ON: Broadview Press.

Gardner-Outlaw, Tom, and R. Engelman. 1999. *Forest Futures: Population, Consumption, and Wood.* Washington, DC: Population Action International. <http://www.popact.org>.

–. 1997. *Sustaining Water, Easing Scarcity: Population and the Future of Renewable Water Supplies.* Washington, DC: Population Action International.

Garton, Billy. 1997. "The Timber Tenure System in B.C." In *Forestry Law: 1997 Update.* Vancouver: Continuing Legal Education Society of British Columbia.

Geisel, T.S. 1971. *The Lorax.* New York: Random House.

Gelbspan, Ross. 1997. *The Heat is On: The Climate Crisis, the Cover-up and the Prescription.* Reading, MA: Perseus.

Georgescu-Roegen, N. 1971. *The Entropy Law and the Economic Process.* Cambridge: Harvard University Press.

Gerhardsson, L., S. Skerfving, and A. Oskarsson. 1997. "Effects of Acid Precipitation on the Environment and on Human Health." In P. Cheremisinoff, ed., *Health and Toxicology,* 355-64. Houston: Gulf Publishing.

Gertler, Franklin, Paul Muldoon, and Marcia Valiante. 1990. "Public Access to Environmental Justice." In Canadian Bar Association Committee on Sustainable Development, ed., *Sustainable Development: Options for Law Reform.* Ottawa: Canadian Bar Association.

Gherson, Giles. 1998. "Canadians Reluctant to Pay for Expanded Involvement." *Edmonton Journal,* 25 April, A7.

Gibson, Dale. 2001. Evidence, Standing Committee on Environment and Sustainable Development. Hearings on Bill C-5, The *Species at Risk Act,* 26 April. <http://www.parl.gc.ca>.

–. 1996. Endangered Species and the Parliament of Canada, unpublished paper.

–. 1988. "Constitutional Entrenchment of Environmental Rights." In N. Duple, ed., *La droit à la qualité de l'environnement.* Montreal: Québec Amérique.

Gibson, Robert B. 2001. "The Major Deficiencies Remain: A Review of the Provisions and Limitations of Bill C-19, *An Act to Amend the Canadian Environmental Assessment Act.*" 11 *Journal of Environmental Law and Practice* 83.

–. 2000. "Favouring the Higher Test: Contribution to Sustainability as the Central Criterion for Reviews and Decisions Under the Canadian Environmental Assessment *Act.*" 10 *Journal of Environmental Law and Practice* 39.

–. 1999. "Voluntary Initiatives, Regulations, and Beyond." In Robert B. Gibson, ed., *Voluntary Initiatives: The New Politics of Corporate Greening,* 239-57. Peterborough, ON: Broadview Press.

–. 1992. "The New *Canadian Environmental Assessment Act*: Possible Responses to Its Main Deficiencies." 2 *Journal of Environmental Law and Practice* 223.

Gillies, A.M. 1994. *The Greening of Government Taxes and Subsidies, Where to Start: An Action Plan for Protecting the Environment and Reducing the Deficit.* Winnipeg: International Institute for Sustainable Development.

Gilmour, Bradley S. 1999. "The Moving Target of E.A. Requirements: The View from the Courts." In *Environmental Assessment of Natural Resource Projects,* 193-239. Toronto: Insight Press.

Giroux, Lorne. 1993. "Le droit environnemental québécois et les pesticides." In R. Cote, D. Russell, and D. VanderZwaag, eds., *Law and the Environment: Problems of Risk and Uncertainty,* 173-207. Montreal: Editions Themis.

Glavin, Terry. 2001. *The Conservation of Marine Biological Diversity and Species Abundance on Canada's West Coast: Institutional Impediments – Groundfish: A Case Study.* Victoria: Sierra Club of British Columbia.

–. 1996. *Dead Reckoning: Confronting the Crisis in Pacific Fisheries.* Vancouver: Greystone Books.

Gleick, Peter, ed. 1993. *Water in Crisis: A Guide to the World's Fresh Water Resources.* New York: Oxford University Press.

Glenn, Jack. 1999. *Once upon an Oldman: Special Interest Politics and the Oldman River Dam.* Vancouver: UBC Press.

Global Forest Watch. 2000. *Canada's Forests at a Crossroads: An Assessment in the Year 2000.* Washington, DC: World Resources Institute.

Globe and Mail. 2001a. Editorial, "The Cree's New Deal." 29 October, A12.

–. 2001b. Editorial, "Let trade walls tumble." 28 May, A12.

Godsoe, Craig. 1999. "The Increasing Importance in B.C. of Local Governments in Environmental Regulation." 9 *Journal of Environmental Law and Practice* 55.

Goldfarb, Danielle. 2001. *Who Gets CIDA Grants? Recipient Corruption and the Effectiveness of Development Aid.* Ottawa: C.D. Howe Institute. <http://www.cdhowe.org>.

Golub, Jonathan S. 1998. *New Instruments for Environmental Policy in the European Union.* London: Routledge.

Goodland, Robert, Herman Daly, Salah El Serafy, and Bernd von Droste. 1991. *Environmentally Sustainable Economic Development.* Paris: UNESCO.

Gore, Al. 1993. *Earth in the Balance.* Toronto: Penguin.

Government of British Columbia. 1993. *British Columbia's Forest Practices Code: Discussion Paper.* Victoria: Queen's Printer.

Government of Canada. 2002a. *Climate Change Plan for Canada.* Ottawa. <http://www.climatechange.gc.ca>.

–. 2002b. *A Discussion Paper on Canada's Contribution to Addressing Climate Change.* Ottawa.

–. 2001. *Public Accounts of Canada, 2000-2001.* Vol. 1. Ottawa: Minister of Public Works and Government Services.

–. 2000a. *First National Climate Change Business Plan.* Ottawa.

–. 2000b. *Government of Canada Action Plan 2000 on Climate Change.* Ottawa.

–. 2000c. *Taking Action on Climate Change: A Compendium of Canadian Initiatives.* Ottawa.

–. 1999a. *The 1999 Cabinet Directive on the Environmental Assessment of Policy.* Ottawa: Minister of Public Works and Government Services Canada.

–. 1999b. *Global Climate Change: It's about Our Environment, Our Economy, Our Future.* Ottawa.

–. 1995. *Canada's National Action Program on Climate Change.* Ottawa.

Government of New Brunswick. 2002. "Managing Pesticides and Their Application in New Brunswick." <http://www.gov.nb.ca>.

–. 1999. Press release, 1 October.

Grand Council of the Crees. 2002. Agreement Concerning a New Relationship Between Le Gouvernement du Québec and the Crees of Quebec. <http://www.gcc.ca>.

Green Budget Coalition. 2001. *Our Health, Our Economy, and Our Environment.* Ottawa.

Green, David. 2001. Evidence, Standing Committee on Environment and Sustainable Development. Hearings on Bill C-5, The *Species at Risk Act*, 26 April.

Green, David L. 1992. "Vehicle Use and Fuel Economy: How Big is the 'Rebound' Effect?" *Energy Journal* 13(1): 117-43.

Greene, Michael J.B., and James Paine. 1997. "State of the World's Protected Areas at the End of the Twentieth Century." Paper presented at the IUCN World Commission on Protected Areas Symposium, Protected Areas in the 21st Century: From Islands to Networks. Albany, Australia, 24-9 November. <http://www.unep-wcmc.org/protected_areas/albany.pdf>.

Greenpeace Canada. 1997. *Broken Promises: The Truth about What's Happening in B.C.'s Forests.* Vancouver: Greenpeace.

Greenpeace International. 2002. *Who to Blame Ten Years After Rio? The Role of the USA, Canada, and Australia in Undermining the Rio Agreements.* Amsterdam: Greenpeace International.

Groombridge, B., and M.D. Jenkins. 2000. *Global Biodiversity: Earth's Living Resources in the 21st Century.* Cambridge: World Conservation Press.

Grubb, Michael. 2000. "Governing the Global Commons: An Assessment of Kyoto." In Wilhelm Krull, ed., *Debates on Issues of Our Common Future,* 155-70. Germany: Velbruck Wissenschaft.

Guillette, Louis J., and D. Andrew Crain, eds. 2000. *Environmental Endocrine Disrupters: An Evolutionary Perspective.* New York: Taylor and Francis.

Gunningham, Neil, Peter Grabosky, and Darren Sinclair. 1998. *Smart Regulation: Designing Environmental Policy.* Oxford: Clarendon Press.

Haddock, Mark. 1995. *Forests on the Line: Comparing the Rules for Logging in British Columbia and Washington State.* Vancouver: Sierra Legal Defence Fund and Natural Resources Defense Council.

Haines, Andrew, Anthony J. McMichael, and Paul R. Epstein. 2000. "Environment and Human Health: Global Climate Change and Health." *Canadian Medical Association Journal* 163(6): 729-34.

Haley, David. 1996. "Paying the Piper: The Cost of the British Columbia Forest Practices Code." In *Working with the B.C. Forest Practices Code.* Toronto: Insight Press.

Haley, David, and Martin Luckert. 1995. "Policy Instruments for Sustainable Development in the B.C. Forestry Sector." In A. Scott, J. Robinson, and D. Cohen, eds., *Managing Natural Resources in British Columbia: Markets, Regulations, and Sustainable Development.* Vancouver: UBC Press.

–. 1990. *Forest Tenures in Canada: A Framework for Policy Analysis.* Ottawa: Minister of Supply and Services Canada.

Hall, Ross H. 1981. *A New Approach to Pest Control in Canada.* Canadian Environmental Advisory Council, Report No. 10. Ottawa: Environment Canada.

Halpert, Amy. 2001. "Germany's Solid Waste Disposal System: Shifting the Responsibility." 14 *Georgetown International Environmental Law Review* 135.

Handy, Francis J.F., and Douglas T. Hamilton. 1996. "Environmental Law of Canada." In Nicholas A. Robinson, ed., *Comparative Environmental Law and Regulation.* New York: Oceana Publications.

Hanebury, Judith. 1999. "Environmental Impact Assessment and the Constitution: The Never-Ending Story." 9 *Journal of Environmental Law and Practice* 169.

Hanna, Dawn. 1995. "Private Golf Course to Take Slice out of Provincial Park." *Vancouver Sun,* 22 December, B1-2.

Hansen, K.G., and S. Barg. 1994. *Making Budgets Green: Leading Practices in Taxation and Subsidy Reform.* Winnipeg: IISD.

Hardin, Garrett. 1998. *The Ostrich Factor: Our Population Myopia.* Oxford: Oxford University Press.

Harris, J. 2000. *Chemical Pesticide Markets, Health Risks and Residues.* New York: CABI Publishing.

Harris, Michael. 1998. *Lament for an Ocean, The Collapse of the Atlantic Cod Fishery: A True Crime Story.* Toronto: McClelland and Stewart.

Harrison, Kathryn. 2001a. "Federal-Provincial Relations and the Environment: Unilateralism, Collaboration and Rationalization." In Debora L. VanNijnatten and Robert Boardman, eds., *Canadian Environmental Policy: Context and Cases,* 123-44. 2d ed. Oxford: Oxford University Press.

–. 2001b. "Voluntarism and Environmental Governance." In Edward A. Parson, ed., *Governing the Environment: Persistent Challenges, Uncertain Innovations,* 207-46. Toronto: University of Toronto Press.

–. 2000a. Challenges in Evaluating Voluntary Environmental Programs. Paper prepared for National Academy of Sciences/National Research Council Workshop on Education, Information and Voluntary Measures in Environmental Protection, Washington, DC. 29-30 November.

–. 2000b. "The Origins of National Standards: Comparing Federal Government Involvement in Environmental Policy in Canada." In Patrick C. Fafard and Kathryn Harrison, eds., *Managing the Environmental Union: Intergovernmental Relations and Environmental Policy in Canada.* Montreal: McGill-Queen's University Press.

–. 1995. *Passing the Buck: Federalism and Canadian Environmental Policy.* Vancouver: UBC Press.

Harrison, Kathryn, and Richard N.L. Andrews. 1998. "Environmental Regulation and Business Self-Regulation." *Policy Sciences* 31: 177-97.

Harrison, Kathryn, and W. Antweiler. 2001. "Environmental Regulation vs. Environmental Information: A View from Canada's National Pollutant Release Inventory." <http://www.policy.ca>.

Harrison, Kathryn, and George Hoberg. 1994. *Risk, Science and Politics: Regulating Toxic Substances in Canada and the United States.* Montreal: McGill-Queen's University Press.

Hawken, Paul. 2001. "Beyond the 2 Percent Solution." *Watershed Sentinel,* June/July, 19.

–. 1993. *The Ecology of Commerce: A Declaration of Sustainability.* New York: Harper Collins.

Hawken, Paul, Amory Lovins, and L. Hunter Lovins. 1999. *Natural Capitalism: Creating the Next Industrial Revolution.* Boston: Little Brown and Company.

Hayes, T.B., et al. 2002. "Hermaphroditic, Demasculinized Frogs after Exposure to the Herbicide, Atrazine, at Low Ecologically Relevant Doses." *Proceedings of the National Academy of Sciences* (U.S.) 99: 5476-80.

Hayter, Roger, and John Holmes. 2001. "The Canadian Forest Industry: The Impacts of Globalization and Technological Change." In Michael Howlett, ed., *Canadian Forest Policy: Adapting to Change.* Toronto: University of Toronto Press.

Hazell, Stephen. 1999. *Canada v. The Environment: Federal Environmental Assessment 1984-1998.* Toronto: Canadian Environmental Defence Fund.

Hazell, Stephen, and Hugh Benevides. 1997. "Federal Strategic Environmental Assessment: Toward a Legal Framework." *J.E.L.P.* 7: 349.

Hazell, Stephen, and Philip Jessup. 1989. *Greenprint for Canada: A Federal Agenda for the Environment.* Ottawa: Greenprint for Canada Committee.

Health Canada. 2002. "A Comparison of the Proposed and Existing *Pest Control Products Acts*." <http://www.hc-sc.gc.ca>.

–. 1998a. *Health-Related Indicators for the Great Lakes Basin Population.* Ottawa: Minister of Public Works and Government Services.

–. 1998b. "Looking at Pesticides and Pregnancy: Ontario Farm Family Health Study." *Farm Family Health* 6(1).

–. 1997. *Health and Environment: Partners for Life.* Ottawa: Minister of Public Works and Government Services.

–. 1995. *Community Drinking Water and Sewage Treatment in First Nation Communities.* Ottawa.

–. 1993. *The Undiluted Truth about Drinking Water.* Ottawa.

–. 1989. *Exposure Guidelines for Residential Indoor Air Quality.* Ottawa: Minister of Supply and Services Canada.

Helmy, Eric. 2000. "Teeth for a Paper Tiger: Redressing the Deficiency of the Recovery Provisions of the Endangered Species Act." 30 *Environmental Law* 843.

Hengeveld, H. 2000. "The Science: Global Temperature is on the Rise and the Dangers are Real and Significant." *Alternatives* 26(2): 15-16.

Hessing, Melody, and Michael Howlett. 1997. *Canadian Natural Resource and Environmental Policy: Political Economy and Public Policy.* Vancouver: UBC Press.

Heywood, V.H., and R.T. Watson, eds. 1995. *Global Biodiversity Assessment.* Cambridge: Cambridge University Press/United Nations Environment Program.

Hitchens, D. 1999. "The Influence of Environmental Regulation on Company Competitiveness: A Review of the Literature and Some Case Study Evidence." In D. Hitchens, J. Clausen, and K. Fichter, eds., *International Environmental Management Benchmarks: Best Practice Experiences from America, Japan, and Europe,* 39-53. Berlin: Springer.

Hoberg, George. 2001a. "The British Columbia Forest Practices Code: Formalization and Its Effects." In Michael Howlett, ed., *Canadian Forest Policy: Adapting to Change.* Toronto: University of Toronto Press.

–. 2001b. "Canadian-American Environmental Relations: A Strategic Framework." In Debora L. VanNijnatten and Robert Boardman, eds., *Canadian Environmental Policy: Context and Cases.* 2d ed. Oxford: Oxford University Press.

–. 2001c. "The 6 Percent Solution: The Forest Practices Code." In B. Cashore, G. Hoberg, M. Howlett, J. Rayner, and J. Wilson, eds., *In Search of Sustainability: British Columbia Forest Policy in the 1990s.* Vancouver: UBC Press.

–. 2000. "How the Way We Make Policy Governs the Policy We Make." In Debra J. Salazar and Donald K. Alper, eds., *Sustaining the Forests of the Pacific Coast: Forging Truces in the War in the Woods,* 26-53. Vancouver: UBC Press.

–. 1997. "Governing the Environment: Comparing Canada and the United States." In K. Banting et al. eds., *Degrees of Freedom: Canada and the United States in a Changing World.* Montreal: McGill-Queen's University Press.

–. 1994. *Regulating Forestry: A Comparison of British Columbia and the U.S. Pacific Northwest.* Kingston: Queen's University School of Policy Studies.

–. 1991. "Sleeping with an Elephant: The American Influence on Canadian Environmental Policy." *Journal of Public Policy* 11: 107-32.

Hocking, Brian. 1996. "The Woods and the Trees: Catalytic Diplomacy and Canada's Trials as a Forestry Superpower." *Environmental Politics* 5(3): 448-75.

Hoerner, Andrew. 1999. *Green Taxes and their Policy Implications.* Washington, DC: Centre for Sustainable Economies.

–. 1995. "Tax Tools for Protecting the Atmosphere: The U.S. Ozone-depleting Chemicals Tax." In Robert Gale, Stephan Barg, and Alexander Gillies, eds., *Green Budget Reform: An International Casebook of Leading Practices,* 185-99. London: Earthscan.

Hogg, Peter W. 2000. *The Constitutional Law of Canada.* 4th ed. Don Mills, ON: Carswell.

Holdren, J., Gretchen Daily, and P.R. Ehrlich. 1995. "The Meaning of Sustainability: Biogeophysical Aspects." In M. Munasinghe and W. Shearer, eds., *Defining and Measuring Sustainability: The Biogeophysical Foundations.* Washington, DC: United Nations University.

Holling, C.S. 1994. "New Science and New Investments for a Sustainable Biosphere." In Ann-Marie Jansson, Monica Hammer, Carl Folke, and Robert Costanza, eds., *Investing in*

Natural Capital: The Ecological Economics Approach to Sustainability. Washington, DC: Island Press.

Holmberg, J., K.-H. Robert, K.-E. Eriksson. 1996. "Socio-ecological Principles for a Sustainable Society: Scientific Background and Swedish Experience." In R. Costanza et al., eds., *Getting Down to Earth: Practical Applications of Ecological Economics,* 17-48. Washington, DC: Island Press.

Holmes, Miranda. 1999. *Rating the Treatment Methods and Discharges of 21 Canadian Cities.* National Sewage Report Card Number Two. Vancouver: Sierra Legal Defence Fund.

Homer-Dixon, Thomas. 2000. *The Ingenuity Gap: Can We Solve the Problems of the Future?* Toronto: Random House of Canada.

–. 1999. *Environment, Scarcity and Violence.* Princeton, NJ: Princeton University Press.

Hornung, Robert. 2000. *Provincial Government Performance on Climate Change: 2000.* Drayton Valley, AB: Pembina Institute. <http://www.pembina.org>.

–. 1998. *Canadian Solutions: Practical and Affordable Steps to Fight Climate Change.* Vancouver: David Suzuki Foundation and Pembina Institute for Appropriate Development.

Hornung, Robert, and Matthew Bramley. 2000. *Five Years of Failure: Federal and Provincial Government Inaction on Climate Change.* Drayton Valley, AB: Pembina Institute.

Houck, Oliver. 1995. "Reflections on the Endangered Species Act." 25 *Environmental Law* 689.

–. 1993. "The Endangered Species Act and Its Implementation by the US Departments of Interior and Commerce." *University of Colorado Law Review* 64(2): 277-370.

Howe, Paul, and Peter H. Russell. 2001. *Judicial Power and Canadian Democracy.* Montreal: McGill-Queen's University Press.

Howlett, Michael, ed. 2001a. *Canadian Forest Policy: Adapting to Change.* Toronto: University of Toronto Press.

–. 2001b. "Complex Network Management and the Governance of the Environment: Prospects for Policy Change and Policy Stability over the Long Term." In Edward A. Parson, ed., *Governing the Environment: Persistent Challenges, Uncertain Innovations.* Toronto: University of Toronto Press.

–. 2001c. "The Federal Role in Canadian Forest Policy: From Territorial Landowner to International and Intergovernmental Coordinating Agent." In Michael Howlett, ed., *Canadian Forest Policy: Adapting to Change.* Toronto: University of Toronto Press.

–. 2001d. "Policy Instruments and Implementation Styles: The Evolution of Instrument Choice in Canadian Environmental Policy." In Debora L. VanNijnatten and Robert Boardman, eds., *Canadian Environmental Policy: Context and Cases.* 2d ed. Oxford: Oxford University Press.

Howlett, Michael, and Jeremy Rayner. 2001. "The Business and Government Nexus: Principal Elements and Dynamics of the Canadian Forest Policy Regime." In Michael Howlett, ed., *Canadian Forest Policy: Adapting to Change.* Toronto: University of Toronto Press.

Hoy, Claire. 1999. *Nice Work: The Continuing Scandal of Canada's Senate.* Toronto: McClelland and Stewart.

Huebert, Rob. 2001. "Climate Change and Canadian Sovereignty in the Northwest Passage." *Isuma: Canadian Journal of Policy Research* 2(4): 86-94.

Huestis, Lynn. 1984. *Policing Pollution: The Prosecution of Environmental Offenses.* Ottawa: Law Reform Commission of Canada.

Hughes, Elaine. 2001. "Pesticide Law Reform Initiatives: An Update." 10 *Journal of Environmental Law and Practice* 195.

–. 1996. "Forests, Forestry Practices, and the Living Environment." In D. VanderZwaag and P. Saunders, eds., *Global Forests and International Environmental Law,* 79-135. London: Kluwer Law International.

–. 1992. "Environmental Protection in National Marine Parks." 41 *University of New Brunswick Law Journal* 41.

Hume, Mark. 1992. *The Run of the River.* Vancouver: New Star.

Hummel, Monte, ed. 1995. *Protecting Canada's Endangered Spaces: An Owner's Manual.* Toronto: Key Porter.

Hutchings, J.A., and R.A. Myers. 1994. "What Can Be Learned from the Collapse of a Renewable Resource? Atlantic Cod, *Gadus Morhua* of Newfoundland and Labrador." *Canadian Journal of Fisheries and Aquatic Science* 51: 2126-46.

Hutchings, J.A., C. Walters, and R.L. Haedrich. 1997. "Is Scientific Inquiry Incompatible with Government Information Control?" *Canadian Journal of Fisheries and Aquatic Sciences* 54: 1198-210.

Independent Expert Evaluation Panel. 2001. *A Mid-term Evaluation of the National Forest Strategy (1998-2003), Sustainable Forests: A Canadian Commitment*. Ottawa: National Forest Strategy Coalition.

Intergovernmental Panel on Climate Change. 2001. *Climate Change 2001: Third Assessment Report of the Intergovernmental Panel on Climate Change*. Cambridge: Cambridge University Press.

–. 1996. *Second Assessment Report: The Science of Climate Change*. Cambridge: Cambridge University Press.

–. 1995. *Summary for Policymakers: Scientific Technical Analysis of Impacts, Adaptations and Mitigation of Climate Change*. Cambridge: Cambridge University Press.

–. 1990. *Scientific Assessment of Climate Change: Report of Working Group I*. Cambridge: Cambridge University Press.

Intergovernmental Panel on Climate Change, Working Group I. 2001. "Climate Change 2001: The Scientific Basis, A Summary for Policy Makers." <http://www.ipcc.ch>.

Intergovernmental Panel on Climate Change, Working Group II. 2001. "Climate Change 2001: Impacts, Adaptation and Vulnerability, A Summary for Policymakers."

International Institute for Sustainable Development. 2001. *Earth Negotiations Bulletin*. Vol. 12, No. 189. <http://www.iisd.ca>.

–. 2000a. *The Cartagena Protocol on Biosafety: An Analysis of Results*. Winnipeg.

–. 2000b. *Review Paper on Selected Capital-Based Sustainable Development Indicator Frameworks*. Ottawa: National Round Table on the Environment and the Economy.

–. 1994. *Making Budgets Green: Leading Practices in Taxation and Subsidy Reform*. Winnipeg.

International Joint Commission. 2002. "Eleventh Biennial Report on Great Lakes Water Quality." <http://www.ijc.org>.

–. 2000a. Protection of the Waters of the Great Lakes: Final Report to the Governments of Canada and the United States. <http://www.ijc.org>.

–. 2000b. Tenth Biennial Report on Great Lakes Water Quality. <http://www.ijc.org>.

–. 1995. Seventh Biennial Report 1995. <http://www.ijc.org>.

International Joint Commission and Great Lakes Fishery Commission. 1990. Exotic Species and the Shipping Industry: The Great Lakes-St. Lawrence Ecosystem at Risk. A Special Report to the Governments of the United States and Canada. <http://www.ijc.org>.

International Monetary Fund. 2001. *A Better World for All*. Paris.

International Monetary Fund and World Bank. 2001. Heavily Indebted Poor Countries: Progress Report. Washington.

Iyer, Pico. 2001. *Imagining Canada: An Outsider's Hope for a Global Future*. Toronto: Hart House, University of Toronto.

Jablonski, David. 1995. "Extinctions in the Fossil Record." In John H. Lawton and Robert M. May, eds., *Extinction Rates*. Oxford: Oxford University Press.

Jaccard, Mark, J. Nyboer, and B. Sadownik. 2002. *The Cost of Climate Policy*. Vancouver: UBC Press.

Jack, Ian. 1999. "Ottawa Wants to Ban Exporting of Bulk Water from Great Lakes." *National Post*, 18 August, A4.

Jackson, R.J. 1995. "The Hazards of Pesticides to Children." In Stuart M. Brooks et al., eds., *Environmental Medicine*, 377-82. St. Louis, MO: Mosby.

Jackson, T. A. 1997. "Long-range Atmospheric Transport of Mercury to Ecosystems, and the Importance of Anthropogenic Emissions: A Critical Review and Evaluation of the Published Evidence." *Environmental Review* 5: 99-120.

Jacobs, Donna. 1999. "How Industry Beat the Environmental Protection Act." *Ottawa Citizen*, 7 September, A1.

Jamieson, G.S., and J. Lessard. 2000. "Marine Protected Areas and Fishery Closures in British Columbia." Can. Spec. Publ. Fish. Aquat. Sci. No. 131.

Jamieson, Glen S., and C.O. Levings. 2001. "Marine Protected Areas in Canada: Implications for Both Conservation and Fisheries Management." *Canadian Journal of Fisheries and Aquatic Sciences* 58: 138-56.

Janicke, Martin, and Helmut Weidner, eds. 1997. *National Environmental Policies: A Comparative Study*. New York: Springer.

Jeffery, Michael I. 1991. "The New Canadian Environmental Assessment *Act* – Bill C-78: A Disappointing Response to Promised Reform." 36 *McGill Law Journal* 1070.

Jeffs, Allyson. 2001. "Damage Economy as Much as NEP, Klein Warns." *Edmonton Journal*, 24 July, A1.

Jensen, J., K. Adarer, and R. Shearer. 1997. *Canadian Arctic Contaminants Assessment Report.* Ottawa: Minister of Supply and Government Services.

Jepma, Catrinus. 1991. *The Tying of Aid.* Paris: Organization for Economic Cooperation and Development.

Johnson, Brian, and Fraser Hunter, eds. 1998. *Responding to Global Climate Change in the Prairies.* Vol. 3 of the Canada Country Study. Ottawa: Environment Canada.

Johnson, John M., and George W. Ware. 1990. *Pesticide Litigation Manual.* New York: Clark Boardman Company.

Johnson, Kristi. 1999. "The Mythical Giant: Clean Water Act Section 401 and Non-point Source Pollution." 29 *Environmental Law* 417.

Johnson, L. 1996. "Naked Lunch: Canada's Dismal Biotech Regs Are as Full of Holes as Swiss Cheese." 29 *This Magazine* 34.

Johnson, P.M., and A. Beaulieu. 1996. *The Environment and NAFTA: Understanding and Implementing the New Continental Law.* Washington: Island Press.

Johnson, Stanley P. 1994. *World Population – Turning the Tide: Three Decades of Progress.* The Hague: Kluwer Law International.

Jones, D.P., and A.S. de Villars. 1999. *Principles of Administrative Law.* 3d ed. Scarborough, ON: Carswell.

Jones, Greg. 1997. *Priority Issue: Endangered Species.* Victoria: Ministry of Environment, Land and Parks.

Jones, Laura. 2000. "Let's Not Ignore the Good News." *Calgary Herald,* 22 April, A7.

Jones, Laura, and Liv Fredricksen. 1999. *Crying Wolf: Public Policy on Endangered Species.* Vancouver: Fraser Institute.

Jones, Laura, Liv Fredricksen, and Tracy Wates. 2002. *Environmental Indicators.* 5th ed. Vancouver: Fraser Institute.

Juillet, Luc. 2001. "Regional Models of Environmental Governance." In Edward A. Parson, ed., *Governing the Environment: Persistent Challenges, Uncertain Innovations.* Toronto: University of Toronto Press.

Juillet, Luc, and Glen Toner. 1997. "From Great Leaps to Baby Steps: Environment and Sustainable Development Policy under the Liberals." In Gene Swimmer, ed., *How Ottawa Spends, 1997-98,* 179-209. Toronto: Oxford University Press.

Jutlah, Russell J. 1998. "Economic Instruments and Environmental Policy in Canada." 8 *Journal of Environmental Law and Practice* 323.

Kallen, R. 2000. "Components of a Model Accelerated Vehicle Retirement Program." Environmental Law and Policy Center website, <http://www.elpc.org>.

Kauffman, Joanne M. 1997. "Domestic and International Linkages in Global Environmental Politics: A Case Study of the Montreal Protocol." In Miranda A. Schreurs and Elizabeth C. Economy, eds., *The Internationalization of Environmental Protection.* Cambridge: Cambridge University Press.

Keating, Michael, et al. 1997. *Canada and the State of the Planet.* Oxford: Oxford University Press.

Kelly, Mike. 1992. *Market Correction: Economic Incentives for Sustainable Development.* Ottawa: National Round Table on the Environment and the Economy.

Kennedy, Robert F. 1993. "Recapturing America's Moral Vision (18 March 1968)." In *RFK: Collected Speeches.* New York: Viking Press.

Kennett, Steven A. 1999. *Towards a New Paradigm for Cumulative Effects Management.* Calgary: Canadian Institute of Resource Law.

–. 1995. "The *Canadian Environmental Assessment Act's* Transboundary Provisions: Trojan Horse or Paper Tiger?" 5 *Journal of Environmental Law and Practice* 263.

Kennett, S.A., E.J. McKoy, and G.C. Yarranton. 1996. *Overlapping Environmental Jurisdiction: A Selective Survey of Industry Perceptions and Costs.* Calgary: Canadian Institute for Resources Law.

Kenny, Michael, and James Meadowcroft, eds. 1999. *Planning Sustainability.* New York: Routledge.

Knox, John H. 2001. "A New Approach to Compliance with International Environmental Law: The Submissions Procedure of the NAFTA Environmental Commission." 28.1 *Ecology Law Quarterly* 1.

Knox, P., and B. McKenna. 2000. "NAFTA Partners' Environmental Deal at Risk, Groups Say." *Globe and Mail,* 27 April, A9.

Kohm, Kathryn A., ed. 1991. *Balancing on the Brink of Extinction: The Endangered Species Act and Lessons for the Future.* Washington, DC: Island Press.

Kolar, C.S., and D.M. Lodge. 2001. "Progress in Invasion Biology: Predicting Invaders." *Trends in Ecology and Evolution* 16(4): 199-203.

KPMG Chartered Accountants. 1997. *Financial State of the Forest Industry and Delivered Wood Costs.* Victoria: Ministry of Forests.

–. 1996. *Canadian Environmental Management Survey.* Toronto: KPMG.

Krahn, Peter K. 1998. *Enforcement vs. Voluntary Compliance: An Examination of the Strategic Enforcement Initiatives Implemented by the Pacific and Yukon Regional Office of Environment Canada, 1983 to 1998.* Vancouver: Environment Canada.

Krajick, Kevin. 2001. "Arctic Life on Thin Ice." *Science* 291, 19 January, 424-5.

Krawczyk, Betty. 2002. *Lock Me Up or Let Me Go: The Protests, Arrest, and Trial of an Environmental Activist and Grandmother.* Vancouver: Press Gang.

Krebs, C. 1999. *Ecological Methodology.* 2d ed. Menlo Park, CA: Benjamin/Cummings.

Krieger, Robert, ed. 2001. *Handbook of Pesticide Toxicology.* 2 vols. San Diego: Academic Press.

Kromm, Chris, and Keith Ernst. 2000. *Green and Gold 2000.* Durham, NC: Institute for Southern Studies.

Krugman, Paul. 1997. "Earth in the Balance Sheet: Economists Go for the Green." *Slate,* 18 April. <http://slate.msn.com>.

Kukowski, Leah. 2000. "Canada's Lack of Federal Endangered Species Legislation Attracting Attention from the United States." In *Colorado Journal of International Environmental Law and Policy Yearbook,* 89-101. Boulder, CO: University Press of Colorado.

Kurlansky, Mark. 1997. *Cod: A Biography of a Fish That Changed the World.* Toronto: Vintage Canada.

La Forest, G.V. 1969. *Natural Resources and Public Property under the Canadian Constitution.* Toronto: University of Toronto Press.

La Forest, Gerard, and Dale Gibson. 2000a. *Constitutional Authority for Federal Protection of Migratory Birds, Other Cross-border Species and their Habitat in Endangered Species Legislation.* Vancouver: Sierra Legal Defence Fund.

–. 2000b. *Federal Protection of Endangered Species and the Criminal Law Power.* Vancouver: Sierra Legal Defence Fund.

Laing, Robert D. 2002. Report of the Commission of Inquiry into matters relating to the public safety of the drinking water of the City of North Battleford, Saskatchewan. Regina.

Lalumière, C., and Jean-Pierre Landau. 1998. *Report on the Multilateral Agreement on Investment.* Paris: Ministry of the Economy, Finance and Industry.

Lambert, Thomas, and Robert J. Smith. 1994. *The* Endangered Species Act: *Time for Change.* St. Louis, MO: Washington University.

Lane, Robert E. 2000. *The Loss of Happiness in Market Democracies.* New Haven: Yale University Press.

Langille, David. 1987. "The BCNI and the Canadian State." *Studies in Political Economy* 24: 41-85.

Larsen, Hans. 2000. "Green Taxes: The Danish Experience." In Environment Canada, ed., *Supporting a Sustainable Future: Making Dollars and Sense.* Conference proceedings. <http://www.ec.gc.ca>.

Larson, Bjorn, and Anwar Shah. 1992. *Combating the Greenhouse Effect in Finance and Development.* Washington, DC: International Monetary Fund and International Bank for Reconstruction and Development.

Last, John, Konia Trouton, and David Pengelly. 1998. *Taking Our Breath Away: The Health Effects of Air Pollution and Climate Change.* Vancouver: David Suzuki Foundation.

Lausche, Barbara. 1980. *Guidelines for Protected Areas Legislation.* Gland, Switzerland: International Union for the Conservation of Nature.

Lavoie, Judith. 1998. "Fishermen's Union Joins Environmentalists in Suit against Anderson." *Victoria Times-Colonist,* 20 February, A2.

Law Reform Commission of Canada. 1986. *Private Prosecutions.* Criminal Law Working Paper No. 52. Ottawa.

Lawson, Jamie, Marcelo Levy, and L. Anders Sandberg. 2001. "'Perpetual Revenues and the Delights of the Primitive': Change, Continuity, and Forest Policy Regimes in Ontario." In Michael Howlett, ed., *Canadian Forest Policy: Adapting to Change.* Toronto: University of Toronto Press.

Layton, Jack. 2001. "Canada's Black Eye." *Globe and Mail,* 21 July, A13.

Le Prestre, Philippe, and Peter J. Stoett. 2001. "International Initiatives, Commitments and Disappointments: Canada, CITES, and the CBD." In Karen Beazley and Robert Boardman, eds., *The Politics of the Wild: Canada and Endangered Species*. Don Mills, ON: Oxford University Press.

Le Roy, Sylvia, and Barry Cooper. 2000. *Off Limits: How Radical Environmentalists Are Shutting Down Canada's National Parks*. Vancouver: Fraser Institute.

Leblanc, Daniel, and Jill Mahoney. 1999. "Anderson Wants Motorists to Change." *Globe and Mail*, 9 October, A14.

Lee, Kai. 1993. *Compass and Gyroscope: Integrating Science and Politics for the Environment*. Washington, DC: Island Press.

Leiss, William. 2001. *In the Chamber of Risks: Understanding Risk Controversies*. Montreal: McGill-Queen's University Press.

Leiss, William, and Michael Tyshenko. 2001. "Some Aspects of the 'New Biotechnology' and Its Regulation in Canada." In Debora L. VanNijnatten and Robert Boardman, eds., *Canadian Environmental Policy: Context and Cases*, 321-44. 2d ed. Oxford: Oxford University Press.

Leopold, Aldo. 1966. *A Sand County Almanac, with Essays on Conservation from Round River*. New York: Oxford University Press.

Levin, S.A., ed. 2001. *Encyclopedia of Biodiversity*. San Diego: Academic Press.

Levy, Alan D. 2002. "A Review of Environmental Assessment in Ontario." 11 *Journal of Environmental Law and Practice* 173.

Liberal Party of Canada. 1997. *Securing Our Future Together: Preparing Canada for the 21st Century*. Ottawa.

–. 1993. *Creating Opportunity: The Liberal Red Book for Canada*. Ottawa.

Lindquist, Evert, and Adam Wellstead. 2001. "Making Sense of Complexity: Advances and Gaps in Comprehending the Canadian Forest Policy Process." In Michael Howlett, ed., *Canadian Forest Policy: Adapting to Change*. Toronto: University of Toronto Press.

Linton, Jamie. 1997. *Beneath the Surface: The State of Water in Canada*. Ottawa: Canadian Wildlife Federation.

Litman, Todd. 1995. *Transportation Cost Analysis: Techniques, Estimates and Implications*. Victoria: Victoria Transport Policy Institute.

Livingston, John A. 1981. *The Fallacy of Wildlife Conservation*. Toronto: McClelland and Stewart.

Loh, J., J. Randers, A. MacGillivray et al. 1999. *Living Planet Report 1999*. Gland, Switzerland: World Wide Fund for Nature.

Lovins, Amory, L. Hunter Lovins, and Ernst von Weiszacker. 1997. *Factor Four: Doubling Wealth, Halving Resource Use: The New Report to the Club of Rome*. London: Earthscan Publications.

Lowry, William. 1994. *The Capacity for Wonder: Preserving National Parks*. Washington, DC: Brookings Institution.

Lucas, Alastair R. 1993. "Judicial Review of Environmental Assessment: Has the Federal Process Been Judicialized?" In Steven A. Kennett, ed., *Law and Process in Environmental Management*. Calgary: Canadian Institute of Resource Law.

–. 1990. *Security of Title in Canadian Water Rights*. Calgary: Canadian Institute for Resource Law.

Ludwig, Donald, Ray Hilborn, and Carl Walters. 1993. "Uncertainty, Resource Exploitation, and Conservation: Lessons from History." 260 *Science* 17.

Lunquist, Lennart J. 1995. "Municipal Sewage Treatment in Sweden: From Bans on Bathing to Schools of Salmon." In Martin Janicke and Helmut Weidner, eds., *Successful Environmental Policy: A Critical Evaluation of 24 Cases*. Berlin: Edition Sigma.

McAllister, Don E. 2000. "Biodiversity in Canadian Fresh and Marine Waters." In Stephen Bocking, ed., *Biodiversity in Canada: Ecology, Ideas, and Action*, 81-106. Toronto: Broadview Press.

MacArthur, R.H., and E.O. Wilson. 1967. *The Theory of Island Biogeography*. Princeton, NJ: Princeton University Press.

McBean, Gordon, Andrew Weaver, and Nigel Roulet. 2001. "The Science of Climate Change: What Do We Know?" *ISUMA: Canadian Journal of Policy Research* 2(4): 16-25.

McCarthy, Shawn. 2001. "Activists Promise FTAA Fight: Groups Do Not Oppose All Multilateral Trade but Say the New Deal Is 'NAFTA on Steroids.'" *Globe and Mail*, 20 April, A4.

McClenaghan, Theresa, and Kathleen Cooper. 2002. *Brief to the Parliamentary Standing Committee on Health Reviewing Bill C-53, Pest Control Products Act*. Toronto: Canadian Environmental Law Association.

Macdonald, Douglas. 2001. "The Business Response to Environmentalism." In Debora L. VanNijnatten and Robert Boardman, eds., *Canadian Environmental Policy: Context and Cases*. 2d ed. Oxford: Oxford University Press.

–. 1991. *The Politics of Pollution: Why Canadians Are Failing Their Environment.* Toronto: McClelland and Stewart.

McDonough, W. 2002. *Cradle to Cradle: Remaking the Way We Make Things.* New York: North Point Press.

McGuinty, David. 2002. "Climate Change: Treatment Is Affordable." *Globe and Mail,* 29 January, A15.

McIlroy, Anne. 1999. "Scientists Fear Bill on Endangered Species Will Repeat Mistakes." *Globe and Mail,* 24 February, A12.

–. 1998. "Green Just Not Ottawa's Colour." *Globe and Mail,* 27 May, A3.

–. 1997a. "Ottawa Aims to Beat U.S. with Long-term Green Plan." *Globe and Mail,* 4 November, A1.

–. 1997b. "Ottawa's Environmental Joy Ride." *Globe and Mail,* 4 October, D1-2.

McIntyre, O., and T. Mosedale. 1997. "The Precautionary Principle as a Norm of Customary International Law." 9 *Journal of Environmental Law* 221.

MacIsaac, Ron, and Anne Champagne. 1994. *Clayoquot Mass Trials: Defending the Rainforest.* Philadelphia: New Society Publishers.

McKay, Paul. 1997. "Environment Canada Told to Cut Staff, Spending: Impact Compounded by Provincial Cuts and Harmonization." *Ottawa Citizen,* 4 October, A1.

McKenna, Barrie. 2000. "Environmental Probes Derailed by NAFTA Nations." *Globe and Mail,* 18 May, A11.

McKenna, Barrie, and Mark MacKinnon. 2001. "Bush Eager for Talks on Canadian Water." *Globe and Mail,* 18 July, A1.

Mackenzie, James M. 1994. "The *Canadian Environmental Assessment Act*: A Constitutional Trojan Horse?" In *Environmental Assessments in British Columbia.* Toronto: Canadian Institute.

McKinlay, R.G., and D. Atkinson. 1995. *Integrated Crop Protection: Towards Sustainability.* Farnham, Surrey, UK: British Crop Protection Council.

MacKinnon, Mark. 2001. "Canada, U.S. Spoil G8 Plan to Curtail Fuel Subsidies." *Globe and Mail,* 13 July, A1, A4.

MacKinnon, Mark, and Campbell Clark. 2001. "Chrétien Lands in Hot Water." *Globe and Mail,* 15 May, A1.

MacLaren, J.W. 1985. *Municipal Waterworks and Wastewater Systems.* Research Paper No. 3. Ottawa: Inquiry on Federal Water Policy.

McNamee, Kevin. 1993. "Preserving Ontario's Natural Legacy." In David Estrin and John Swaigen, eds., *Environment on Trial: A Guide to Ontario Environmental Law and Policy.* Toronto: Emond Montgomery.

McNeely, Jeffrey A. 1999. "Strange Bedfellows: Why Science and Policy Don't Mesh and What Can Be Done About It." In Joel Cracraft and Francesca T. Grifo, eds., *The Living Planet in Crisis: Biodiversity Science and Policy,* 275-86. New York: Columbia University Press.

McRae, D.J., L.C. Duchesne, B. Freddman, T.J. Lynham, and S. Woodley. 2001. "Comparisons between Wildfire and Forest Harvesting and Their Implications in Forest Management." *Environmental Reviews* 9: 223-60.

Made, Bernard. 2000. "Experience Using Tradable Permits to Eliminate Methyl Bromide." In Environment Canada, ed., *Supporting a Sustainable Future: Making Dollars and Sense.* Conference proceedings. Was available at <http://www.ec.gc.ca/eco-n-ference>.

Maduro, R.A., and R. Schauerhammer. 1992. *The Holes in the Ozone Scare: The Scientific Evidence That the Sky Isn't Falling.* Washington, DC: 21st Century Science Associates.

Magnus, P., J.J.K. Jaakola, A. Skrondal et al. 1999. "Water Chlorination and Birth Defects." *Epidemiology* 10: 513-17.

Mahoney, J. 2002. "Klein on Cutting Smog: Just 'Quit Breathing.'" *Globe and Mail,* 27 February, A1, A6.

Mahoney, J., and S. Chase. 2002. "Klein Lays Kyoto Battle Groundwork." *Globe and Mail,* 20 November, A4.

Makhijani, Arjun, and Kevin R. Gurney. 1995. *Mending the Ozone Hole: Science, Technology and Policy.* Cambridge, MA: MIT Press.

Malcolm, Jay, and Adam Markham. 2000. *Global Warming and Terrestrial Biodiversity Decline.* Toronto: World Wildlife Fund International.

Mancell, Garry. 1999. "1998 Changes to the *Forest Practices Code.*" In *Forestry Law Conference 1999.* Vancouver: Continuing Legal Education Society of British Columbia.

Mancell, Garry, et al. 2001. *British Columbia Forestry Law: An Annotated Guide to the* Forest Practices Code *and* Forest Act. Aurora, ON: Canada Law Book.

Mandrusiak, Bradley. 1999. "Playing with Fire: The Premature Release of Genetically Engineered Plants into the Canadian Environment." 9 *Journal of Environmental Law and Practice* 259.

Mann, Howard. 2001. *Private Rights, Public Problems: A Guide to NAFTA's Chapter on Investor Rights.* Winnipeg: International Institute for Sustainable Development.

Manzer, L.E. 1990. "The CFC-Ozone Issue: Progress on the Development of Alternatives." *Science* 249: 31-5.

Marchak, M. Patricia. 1999. *Falldown: Forest Policy in British Columbia.* Vancouver: David Suzuki Foundation.

–. 1995. *Logging the Globe.* Montreal: McGill-Queen's University Press.

Marshall, Dale. 2002. *Making Kyoto Work: A Transition Strategy for Canadian Energy Workers.* Vancouver: Canadian Centre for Policy Alternatives.

Martell, S., and S. Wallace. 1998. "Estimating Historical Lingcod Biomass in the Strait of Georgia." In D. Pauly, T.J. Pitcher, and D. Preikshot, eds., *Back to the Future: Reconstructing the Strait of Georgia Ecosystem,* 45-8. Fisheries Centre Research Reports Vol. 6, No. 5. Vancouver: UBC Fisheries Centre.

Martens, Pim. 1998. *Health and Climate Change: Modelling the Impacts of Global Warming and Ozone Depletion.* London: Earthscan.

Martin, David H. 2001. "Canada Continues with Nuclear Folly." *Ottawa Citizen,* 21 June, A17.

Martin, Kelly (Canadian Association of Physicians for the Environment). 1999. Why Canadian Physicians Are Concerned about the Policies Regulating Pesticide Use. Presentation to the Standing Committee on Environment and Sustainable Development. <http://www.cape.ca>.

Martin, Paul. 2000. Speech to the Federation of Canadian Municipalities, London, ON, 5 June. <http://www.fin.gc.ca>, speech 2000-044.

–. 1992. *L'environnement: L'optique du Parti Liberal-Document de Travail.* Ottawa: Liberal Party of Canada.

May, Elizabeth. 1998. *At the Cutting Edge: The Crisis in Canada's Forests.* Toronto: Key Porter Books.

May, Robert M., John H. Lawton, and Nigel E. Stork. 1995. "Assessing Extinction Rates." In John H. Lawton and Robert M. May, eds., *Extinction Rates.* Oxford: Oxford University Press.

Mazur, L.A., ed. 1994. *Beyond the Numbers: A Reader on Population, Consumption and the Environment.* Washington, DC: Island Press.

Measures Working Group for the Climate Change Task Group of the National Air Issues Coordinating Committee. 1994. *Measures for Canada's National Action Program on Climate Change.* Final Report, June.

Menell, Peter S., and Richard B. Stewart. 1994. *Environmental Law and Policy.* Boston: Little, Brown.

Merchant, Carolyn. 1992. *Radical Ecology: The Search for a Livable World.* New York: Routledge.

M'Gonigle, M., et al. 1995. "Taking Uncertainty Seriously: From Permissive Regulation to Preventative Design in Environmental Decision-Making." 32 *Osgoode Hall Law Journal* 99.

M'Gonigle, Michael, Brian Egan, Lisa Ambus et al. 2001. *Where There's a Way, There's a Will.* Report 1, *Developing Sustainability through the Community Ecosystem Trust.* Victoria: Eco-Research Chair in Environmental Law and Policy.

M'Gonigle, Michael, and Ben Parfitt. 1994. *Forestopia: A Practical Guide to the New Forest Economy.* Madeira Park, BC: Harbour Publishing.

Michael, A.J., A. Haines, R. Sloof, and S. Kovat, eds. 1996. *Climate Change and Human Health.* Geneva: World Health Organization.

Michaels, Pat, and Robert Balling. 2000. *The Satanic Gases.* Washington, DC: Cato Institute.

Michalski, Joseph H. 2000. *Quality of Life Indicators Project: Preliminary Results – Public Dialogue.* Trent University: Canadian Policy Research Networks.

Milanovic, Branko. 2001. *World Income Inequality in the Second Half of the 20th Century.* World Bank Research Paper. Washington, DC: World Bank.

Milazzo, Matteo. 1998. *Subsidies in World Fisheries: A Reexamination.* Washington, DC: World Bank.

Milko, Robert. 1990. *Global Warming: Policies for Amelioration.* Research Branch of the Library of Parliament. Backgrounder, n. 221. Ottawa: Minister of Supply and Services.

Mills, C.J., R.J. Bull, K.P. Cantor, J. Reif, S.E. Hrudey, and P. Huston. 1998. "Health Risks of Drinking Water Chlorination Byproducts: Report of an Expert Working Group." *Chronic Diseases in Canada* 19: 91-102.

Mineau, Pierre. 1993. The Hazards of Carbofuran to Birds and Other Vertebrate Wildlife. Canadian Wildlife Service Technical Report No. 177. Ottawa: Minister of Supply and Services.

Mineau, Pierre, and Alison McLaughlin. 1994. "Effects of Agriculture on Biodiversity in Canada." In Biodiversity Science Assessment Team, *Biodiversity in Canada: A Science Assessment.* Ottawa: Minister of Supply and Services.

Mining Watch Canada. 2000. *Mining's Toxic Orphans: A Plan for Action on Federal Contaminated and Unsafe Mine Sites.* Ottawa: Mining Watch Canada.

Ministry of Environment (Parks Canada). 1979. *Parks Canada Policy.* Ottawa: Ministry of Supply and Services.

Mitchell, Alanna. 2000a. "Canada Called Environmental Dinosaur." *Globe and Mail,* 21 November, A6.

–. 2000b. "Waste Not: How Tricks from Tiny Holland Could Tame Canada's Garbage Beast." *Globe and Mail,* 18 November, F4-F5.

–. 1999. "Pesticide Residues on Canadian Produce Double." *Globe and Mail,* 24 May, A5.

Mittelstaedt, Martin. 2002a. "Canada Has Reneged on Rio Accord, Sierra Fund Says." *Globe and Mail,* 11 April, A8.

–. 2002b. "Ottawa Urged to Curb Solvent in Tap Water." *Globe and Mail,* 16 January, A9.

–. 2002c. "Smog Worst in Ontario History." *Globe and Mail,* 10 September, A11.

–. 2002d. "Toronto Emissions Decrease by 67 Per Cent." *Globe and Mail,* 13 February, A12.

–. 2001a. "Canada's Water for Sale on Net." *Globe and Mail,* 30 April, A4.

–. 2001b. "Clearcuts Likened to Natural Fires." *Globe and Mail,* 23 November, A9.

–. 2001c. "Don't Go with the Flow." *Globe and Mail,* 29 March.

–. 1999a. "Criminal Polluters Finding Canada the Promised Land." *Globe and Mail,* 23 March, A7.

–. 1999b. "Water Polluters Escaping Prosecution." *Globe and Mail,* 1 March, A1.

–. 1998. "A Safety Net for Threatened Species." *Globe and Mail,* 3 October, A1.

Moen, Andrea B. 1990. *Demystifying Forestry Law: An Alberta Analysis.* Edmonton: Environmental Law Centre.

Moffet, J. 1997. "Legislative Options for Implementing the Precautionary Principle." 7 *Journal of Environmental Law and Practice* 157.

Moffett, J., and F. Bregha. 1995. "The Role of Law Reform and the Promotion of Sustainable Development." 6 *Journal of Environmental Law and Practice* 1.

Moffet, J., and D. Saxe. 1998. "Canada." In *Voluntary Measures to Ensure Environmental Compliance,* 1-97. Montreal: Commission for Environmental Cooperation.

Molina, M.J., and F.S. Rowland. 1974. "Stratospheric Sink for Chlorofluoromethanes: Chlorine Atom Catalyzed Distribution of Ozone." *Nature* 249: 810-12.

Montpetit, Éric. 2001. "Sound Science and Moral Suasion, Not Regulation: Facing Difficult Decisions on Agricultural Non-Point Source Pollution." In Debora L. VanNijnatten and Robert Boardman, eds., *Canadian Environmental Policy: Context and Cases.* 2d ed. Oxford: Oxford University Press.

Montzka, S.A., et al. 1999. "Present and Future Trends in the Atmospheric Burden of Ozone-Depleting Halogens." 398 *Nature* 690.

Moore, Keith. 1999. "Audits and Investigations Conducted by the Forest Practices Board: A Report Card on the Code." In *Forestry Law Conference 1999.* Vancouver: Continuing Legal Education Society of BC.

Morelli, Lisa J. 1997. "Citizen Suit Enforcement of Environmental Laws in the United States: An Overview." *Environmental Liability* 5: 19-29.

Morgan, Gwyn. 1998. "Enough Hot Air on Kyoto." *Perspectives,* Spring. <http://www.ceocouncil.ca>.

Morley, C.G., ed. 1973. *Canada's Environment: The Law on Trial – Proceedings of an Environmental Law Conference.* Winnipeg: Manitoba Institute of Continuing Legal Education.

Morris, Chris. 1999. "Water Seen As Boiling Issue." *Telegram* (St. John's), 5 October, 6.

Morrison, H.I., et al. 1992. "Herbicides and Cancer." *Journal of the National Cancer Institute* 84(24): 1866-74.

Morrison, Jim. 1995. "Aboriginal Interests." In Monte Hummel, ed., *Protecting Canada's Endangered Spaces: An Owner's Manual,* 18-26. Toronto: Key Porter.

Morrison, K.E., and A.M. Turner. 1994. "Protected Areas in British Columbia: Maintaining Natural Diversity." In Lee E. Harding and Emily Macullum, eds., *Biodiversity in British Columbia: Our Changing Environment.* Vancouver: Ministry of Supply and Services.

Morton, F.L., and R. Knopff. 1992. *The Supreme Court as the Vanguard of the Intelligentsia: The Charter Movement As Post-Materialist Politics.* Calgary: University of Calgary, Research Unit for Socio-Legal Studies.

Mosquin, T. 2000. "Status and Trends in Canadian Biodiversity." In Stephen Bocking, ed., *Biodiversity in Canada: Ecology, Ideas and Action.* Peterborough: Broadview Press.

Mosquin, T., P.G. Whiting, and D.E. McAllister. 1995. *Canada's Biodiversity: The Variety of Its Life, Its Status, Economic Benefits, Conservation Costs and Unmet Needs.* Ottawa: Canadian Museum for Nature.

Moyer, Craig A., and Michael A. Francis. 1992. *Clean Air Act Handbook: A Practical Guide to Compliance.* 2d ed. Deerfield, IL: Clark, Boardman, Callaghan.

Muir, Magdalena. 2001. Evidence, Standing Committee on Environment and Sustainable Development. Hearings on Bill C-5, The *Species at Risk Act,* 26 April.

Muldoon, Paul, and Ramani Nadarajah. 1999. "A Sober Second Look." In Robert B. Gibson, ed., *Voluntary Initiatives: The New Politics of Corporate Greening.* Peterborough, ON: Broadview Press.

Muldoon, Paul, and Marcia Valiante. 1989. *Toxic Water Pollution in Canada: Regulatory Principles for Reduction and Elimination.* Calgary: Canadian Institute for Resource Law.

Munn, F.J. 1999. "Case Study: The Cheviot Coal Mine Regulatory Process." In *Environmental Assessment of Natural Resource Projects.* Toronto: Insight Press.

Myers, Norman, and Jennifer Kent. 2001. *Perverse Subsidies: How Tax Dollars Can Undercut the Environment and the Economy.* Washington, DC: Island Press.

Naredo, Jose Manuel. 2001. "Quantifying Natural Capital: Beyond Monetary Value." In M. Munasinghe et al., eds., *The Sustainability of Long-term Growth: Socioeconomic and Ecological Perspectives.* Cheltenham, UK: Edward Elgar Publishing.

Nash, J.R. 2000. "Too Much Market: Conflict Between Tradable Pollution Allowances and the Polluter Pays Principle." 24 *Harvard Environmental Law Review* 465.

National Environmental Law Section of the Canadian Bar Association. 1996. *Commentary on the Draft Environmental Management Framework Agreement.* Ottawa: Canadian Bar Association.

National Round Table on the Environment and the Economy. 2002a. *Environmental and Sustainable Development Indicators Initiative.* Progress Bulletin #3. Ottawa. <http://www.nrtee-trnee.ca>.

–. 2002b. *Toward a Canadian Agenda for Ecological Fiscal Reform: First Steps.* Ottawa.

–. 2001a. *Managing Potentially Toxic Substances in Canada: A State of the Debate Report.* Ottawa.

–. 2001b. NRTEE Indicators Overview for Stakeholder Workshop, 28 March. Ottawa.

Natural Resources Canada. 2002. *Canadian Mining Facts.* Ottawa. <http://www.oee.nrcan.gc.ca>.

–. 2001a. *Energy Factsheet: Electricity.* Ottawa.

–. 2001b. *The State of Canada's Forests 2000-2001, Sustainable Forestry: A Reality in Canada.* Ottawa.

–. 2001c. *Statistics and Facts on Energy.* Ottawa.

–. 2001d. *Statistics and Facts on Minerals and Metals.* Ottawa.

–. 2000a. *1999 Report on Implementation of Sustainable Development Strategy Action Plan.* Ottawa: Ministry of Supply and Services.

–. 2000b. *Energy in Canada, 2000.* Ottawa.

–. 2000c. *The State of Energy Efficiency in Canada.* Ottawa.

–. 1999a. *Canada's Emissions Outlook: An Update.* Ottawa.

–. 1999b. *Report to Parliament on the Administration and Enforcement of the Energy Efficiency Act, 1999.*

–. 1996. *The Level Playing Field: The Tax Treatment of Competing Energy Investments.* Ottawa: Natural Resources Canada.

–. 1995. *Report to Parliament on the Administration and Enforcement of the* Energy Efficiency Act, *1994-95.* Ottawa.

Natural Resources Defence Council. 2001. *The Bush Environmental Budget: Building a Bridge to the 19th Century.* Washington, DC.

Neidert, Eli, and Glenn Havelock. 1998. *Report on Levels and Incidences of Pesticide Residues in Selected Agricultural Food Commodities Available in Canada During 1994-1998.* Canadian Food Inspection Agency. Ottawa: Ministry of Supply and Services Canada.

Neitzert, F., K. Olsen, and P. Collas. 1999. *Canada's Greenhouse Gas Inventory: 1997 Emissions and Removals with Trends.* Ottawa: Environment Canada.

Nemetz, P.N. 1986. "Federal Environmental Regulation in Canada." *Natural Resources Journal* 26: 551-608.

Netherlands Institute for Public Health and Environment. 1999. "Where There's a Will There's a World: Sustainability and Quality of Life." Fourth National Environmental Policy Plan. <http://www.minvrom.nl>.

Nevitte, Neil. 1996. *The Decline of Deference: Canadian Value Change in Cross-national Perspective.* Peterborough, ON: Broadview Press.

New Directions Group. 1997. "Criteria and Principles for the Use of Voluntary or Non-regulatory Initiatives to Achieve Environmental Policy Objectives." In Robert B. Gibson, ed., *Voluntary Initiatives: The New Politics of Corporate Greening,* 229-38. Peterborough, ON: Broadview Press.

Newmark, William D. 1995. "Extinction of Mammalian Populations in Western North American National Parks." 9.3 *Conservation Biology* 518.

–. 1987. "Mammalian Extinctions in Western North American Parks: A Land Bridge Island Perspective." *Nature* 325: 430-2.

Nikiforuk, Andrew. 2000. "National Water Crisis Forecast." *Globe and Mail,* 7 June, A1.

–. 1997. *The Nasty Game: The Failure of Environmental Assessment in Canada.* Toronto: Walter and Duncan Gordon Foundation.

Nordhaus, William D. 2000. "Global Public Goods." In Wilhelm Krull, ed., *Debates on Issues of Our Common Future,* 143-54. Germany: Velbruck Wissenschaft.

Nordhaus, William, and James Tobin. 1972. "Is Growth Obsolete?" In *Economic Growth.* New York: Columbia University Press.

Norris, Stefan, Lynn Rosentrater, and Pal Martin Eid. 2002. *Polar Bears at Risk.* Gland, Switzerland: World Wide Fund for Nature.

Norse, Elliott A. 1993. *Global Marine Biological Diversity: A Strategy for Building Conservation into Decision-making.* Washington, DC: Island Press.

Northcote, T.G., and D.Y. Atagi. 1997. "Pacific Salmon Abundance Trends in the Fraser Watershed Compared with Other British Columbia Systems." In Deanna J. Stouder et al., eds., *Pacific Salmon and Their Ecosystems: Status and Future Options.* New York: Chapman and Hall.

Northey, Rodney. 1994. *The 1995 Annotated Canadian Environmental Assessment Act and EARP Guidelines Order.* Toronto: Carswell

Noss, Reed F. 1996. "Protected Areas: How Much Is Enough?" In R. Gerald Wright, ed., *National Parks and Protected Areas: Their Role in Environmental Protection.* Cambridge, MA: Blackwell Science.

–. 1994. "Some Principles of Conservation Biology As They Apply to Environmental Law." 69 *Chicago-Kent Law Review* 893.

Noss, Reed F., and Allen Y. Cooperrider. 1994. *Saving Nature's Legacy: Protecting and Restoring Biodiversity.* Washington, DC: Island Press.

Nova Scotia Department of Environment. 1998. "The State of the Nova Scotia Environment, 1998." Halifax.

Nowlan, Linda. 1997. *Protecting Endangered Species in Canada: Comments on Bill C-65, the Canada Endangered Species Protection Act.* Vancouver: West Coast Environmental Law Association.

–. 1996. "Biodiversity Law and Policy in British Columbia." In Ian Attridge, ed., *Biodiversity Law and Policy in Canada.* Toronto: Canadian Institute for Environmental Law and Policy.

Nowlan, Linda, and Ines Kwan. 2001. *Regulating Cruise Ship Pollution on the Pacific Coast of Canada.* Vancouver: West Coast Environmental Law Association.

Nystrom, Louise. (n.d.) *Living in Sweden: Between Tradition and Vision.* Karlskrona, Sweden: National Board of Housing, Building and Planning.

O'Connor, Dennis R. 2002a. *Report of the Walkerton Inquiry.* Part 2, *The Events of May 2000 and Related Issues.* Toronto: Queen's Printer.

–. 2002b. *Report of the Walkerton Inquiry.* Part 2, *A Strategy for Safe Drinking Water.* Toronto: Queen's Printer.

OECD (Organization for Economic Cooperation and Development). 2002a. *Development Assistance Committee Peer Review of Canada.* Paris. <http://www.oecd.org>.

–. 2002b. *Governance for Sustainable Development: Five OECD Case Studies.* Paris.

–. 2001a. *Agricultural Policies in OECD Countries: Monitoring and Evaluation 2001.* Paris.

–. 2001b. "Development Assistance Committee Reaches Agreement on Untying Aid to the Least Developed Countries." Press release, 14 April. Paris.

–. 2001c. *Environmental Outlook 2020.* Paris.

–. 2001d. *Key Environmental Indicators.* Paris.

–. 2001e. *Policies to Enhance Sustainable Development.* Paris.

–. 2001f. *Strategic Guidelines for the Design and Implementation of Domestic Transferable Permits.* Paris.

–. 2001g. *Sustainable Development: Critical Issues.* Paris: OECD.

–. 2000a. *Economic Survey of Canada.* Paris.

–. 2000b. *Greener Public Purchasing: Issues and Practical Solutions.* Paris.

–. 2000c. *Transition to Responsible Fisheries: Economic and Policy Implications.* Paris.

–. 1999a. *Agricultural Water Pricing in OECD Countries.* Paris.

–. 1999b. *Environmental Data Compendium, 1999.* Paris.

–. 1999c. *Environmental Indicators, 1999.* Paris.

–. 1999d. *Household Water Pricing in OECD Countries.* Paris.

–. 1999e. *Industrial Water Pricing in OECD Countries.* Paris.

–. 1999f. *Voluntary Approaches for Environmental Policy: An Assessment.* Paris.

–. 1998a. *Eco-efficiency.* Paris.

–. 1998b. *Towards Sustainable Consumption Patterns: A Report on Member Country Initiatives.* Paris.

–. 1998c. *Water Subsidies and the Environment.* Paris.

–. 1996a. *Agriculture, Pesticides and the Environment: Policy Options.* Paris.

–. 1996b. *Environmental Performance Review: Sweden.* Paris.

–. 1995a. *Environmental Performance Review: Canada.* Paris.

–. 1995b. *Environmental Performance Review: The Netherlands.* Paris.

–. 1995c. *Sustainable Agriculture: Concepts, Issues and Policies in OECD Countries.* Paris.

–. 1993. *Environmental Policies and Industrial Competitiveness.* Paris.

O'Ferrall, Brian. 1993. "Dow Chemical Found Liable for Herbicide Damage: *Van Oirschot* v. *Dow.*" 3 *J.E.L.P.* 214.

Ogan, Marshall. 2000. "An Evaluation of the Environmental Harmonization Initiative of the Canadian Council of Ministers of the Environment." 10 *J.E.L.P.* 15.

Olewiler, Nancy. 2000. "Tax-Shifting in Canada." In Environment Canada, ed., *Supporting a Sustainable Future: Making Dollars and Sense.* Conference proceedings. <http://www.ec.gc.ca>.

–. 1990. "The Case for Pollution Taxes." In G. Bruce Doern, ed., *Getting It Green: Case Studies in Canadian Environmental Regulation,* 188-208. Toronto: C.D. Howe Institute.

Olewiler, Nancy, and K. Dawson. 1998. *Analysis of National Pollutant Release Inventory Data on Toxic Emissions by Industry.* Working Paper 97-16. Ottawa: Department of Finance.

Olson, Eric D. 1998. "Implementation of the Safe Drinking Water Amendments of 1996." Testimony before the Subcommittee on Health and the Environment, Committee on Commerce, US House of Representatives, 8 October.

Ombudsman of British Columbia. 1988. *Pesticide Regulation in British Columbia.* Public Report No. 11. Victoria.

Ontario Environmental Assessment Board. 1994. *Environmental Assessment by the Ministry of Natural Resources for Timber Management on Crown Lands in Ontario.* No. EA 87-02. Toronto.

Ontario Medical Association. 2001. *Ontario's Air: Years of Stagnation.* Toronto. <http://www. oma.org>.

–. 2000. "The Illness Cost of Air Pollution." Toronto.

–. 1998. *Health Effects of Ground Level Ozone, Acid Aerosols and Particulate Matter.* Toronto.

Ontario Ministry of Agriculture, Food and Rural Affairs. 1999. *A Survey of Pesticide Use in Ontario, 1998.* Guelph.

Ontario Ministry of Environment. 2001. "Leading the Climate Change Challenge." Media backgrounder, 26 January. <http://www.ene.gov.on.ca>.

–. 2000. *Air Quality in Ontario: A Concise Report on the State of Air Quality in the Province of Ontario in 1998.* Toronto: Ministry of Environment.

Ontario Ministry of Natural Resources. 2002. *Ontario State of the Forest Report, 2001.* Toronto: Queen's Printer.

–. 2001a. *Draft Guideline for Natural Disturbance Emulation.* Toronto.

–. 2001b. "Ontario Protects Species at Risk under Law – Backgrounder" 27 April. Toronto.

–. 1999. *Forest Management Plan for Temagami Management Unit 1999-2019.* Toronto.

Ontario Ministry of Northern Development and Mines. 1999. "Hodgson Says Living Legacy Good News for Northern Ontario." Press release and backgrounder, 29 March. Toronto.

Ontario Provincial Auditor. 2000. *Special Report: Accountability and Value for Money.* Toronto.

–. 1996. *Annual Report.* Toronto.

Oosterhuis, Frans. 1999. "Reducing Environmental Harm from Products: More Than Selling Green Goods." In D. Hitchens, J. Clausen, and K. Fichter, eds., *International Environmental Management Benchmarks: Best Practices Experiences from America, Japan, and Europe*, 155-63. Berlin: Springer.

O'Reilly, Kevin. 1996. "Diamond Mining and the Demise of Environmental Assessment in the North." *Northern Perspectives* 24. <http://www.carc.org>.

Orr, David W. 1992. *Ecological Literacy: Education and the Transition to a Postmodern World*. Albany: State University of New York.

Oxfam Canada. 2001. *Rigged Trade and Not Much Aid: How Rich Countries Help to Keep the Less Developed Countries Poor*. Ottawa. <http://www.oxfam.ca>.

Oxfam International. 2002a. *Last Chance in Monterrey: Meeting the Challenge of Poverty Reduction*. London.

–. 2002b. Rigged Rules and Double Standards: Trade, Globalisation and the Fight against Poverty. London.

Pacific Fisheries Resource Conservation Council. 2000. *State of Salmon Conservation in the Central Coast Area*. Background Paper 2000/4. Vancouver. <http://www.fish.bc.ca>.

–. 1999. *Climate Change and Salmon Stocks*. Vancouver.

Paehlke, Robert. 2001. "Spatial Proportionality: Right-Sizing Environmental Decision-Making." In Edward A. Parson, ed., *Governing the Environment: Persistent Challenges, Uncertain Innovations*. Toronto: University of Toronto Press.

Palmer, Vaughn. 1998. "Zirnhelt Barks at Government's Forests Watchdog: Reduced Environmental Standards and a Loss of Public Confidence Are Cited by the Chair of the Forest Practices Board." *Vancouver Sun*, 16 April, A18.

Pammett, Jon, and Alan Frizzell. 1997. *Shades of Green: Environmental Attitudes in Canada and around the World*. Ottawa: Carleton University Press.

Panayatou, T. 1994. *Economic Instruments for Environmental Management and Sustainable Development*. Nairobi: United Nations Environment Program.

Panel on the Ecological Integrity of Canada's National Parks. 2000. *Unimpaired for Future Generations? Conserving Ecological Integrity with Canada's National Parks*. 2 vols. Ottawa: Minister of Public Works and Government Services.

Pape, Andrew. 1999. *Lost Opportunities: Canada and Renewable Energy*. Ottawa: Pembina Institute.

Parfitt, Ben. 2000. *Muddied Waters: The Case for Protecting Water Sources in B.C.* Vancouver: Sierra Legal Defence Fund. <http://www.sierralegal.org>.

Parks Canada. 1998. *State of the Parks 1997*. Ottawa: Minister of Public Works and Government Services.

Parson, Edward A. 2001. "Environmental Trends: A Challenge to Canadian Governance." In Edward A. Parson, ed., *Governing the Environment: Persistent Challenges, Uncertain Innovations*. Toronto: University of Toronto Press.

Parsons, Tim. 2001. "Survival, by Sea: An Eminent Scientist Ponders the Neglect with Which Humanity Treats a Resource Vital to Life on Earth." *Vancouver Sun*, 2 March, A19.

Partnership for Public Lands. 1999. *A New Way in the Woods: How Lands for Life Led to the Protection of Six Million Acres of Wilderness in Ontario*. Toronto.

Paterson, Matthew. 1996. *Global Warming and Global Politics*. London: Routledge.

Pauly, D., and V. Christensen. 1995. "Primary Production Required to Sustain Global Fisheries." *Nature* 374: 255-7.

Pauly, Daniel, V. Christensen, J. Dalsgaard et al. 1998. "Fishing down Marine Food Webs." *Science* 279: 860-3.

Pauly, Daniel, D. Preikshot, R. Froese et al. 2001. "Fishing down Canadian Aquatic Food Webs." *Canadian Journal of Fisheries and Aquatic Sciences* 58: 51-62.

Pearse, David W., and Jeremy J. Warford. 1993. *World without End: Economics, Environment and Sustainable Development*. Washington, DC: World Bank.

Pearse, Peter H. 1992. *Managing Salmon in the Fraser: Report to the Minister of Fisheries and Oceans on the Fraser River Salmon Investigation*. Ottawa: Department of Fisheries and Oceans.

Pearse, P.H., F. Bertrand, and J.W. MacLaren. 1985. *Currents of Change: Final Report of the Inquiry on Federal Water Policy*. Ottawa: Environment Canada.

Pearse, P.H., and Frank Quinn. 1996. "Recent Developments in Federal Water Policy: One Step Forward, Two Steps Back." *Canadian Water Resources Journal* 21(4): 329-40.

Peart, Bob. 2001. "Just the Facts – B.C. Parks Statistics and Figures." *Parks and Wilderness Quarterly* 12(4): 12.

Penney, Steven. 1994. "Assessing CEAA: Environmental Assessment Theory and the Canadian Environmental Assessment Act." 4 *J.E.L.P.* 243.

Percy, David R. 1988. *The Framework of Water Rights Legislation in Canada.* Calgary: Canadian Institute of Resources Law.

Peritz, Ingrid. 2001. "Tap-Water Standards Tightening in Quebec." *Globe and Mail,* 5 June, A4.

Perry Commission. 1999. *MacMillan Bloedel Parks Settlement Agreement Decision.* Victoria: Ministry of Forests.

Pest Management Regulatory Agency. 2001. *Update on the Re-evaluation of Organophosphate Pesticides.* Ottawa.

–. 2000. *Government Response to the Report of the House of Commons Standing Committee on the Environment and Sustainable Development.* Ottawa: Health Canada.

–. 1995. *Carbofuran.* Decision Document E95-05. Ottawa.

–. n.d. *Pesticides and Food: Fact Sheet.* Ottawa.

Pest Management Secretariat. 1994. *Government Proposal for the Pest Management Regulatory System.* Ottawa: Ministry of Supply and Services.

Pesticide Registration Review Team. 1990. *Recommendations for a Revised Federal Pest Management Regulatory System.* Ottawa: Agriculture Canada.

Peterson, Robert B. 1999. "The Real Consequences of Kyoto." *Perspectives,* Spring, <http://www.ceocouncil.ca>.

Picard, Andre. 2002. "Study Connects Smog to Illness." *Globe and Mail,* 12 March, A12.

Pifer, J. 1997. "Loggers Are an Endangered Species: Union Advice Thwarted NDP Plans for a Job-Killing Eco-bill." *British Columbia Report,* 16 June, 19.

Plater, Zygmunt J.B. 1999. "Environmental Law and Three Economies: Navigating a Sprawling Field of Study, Practice, and Social Governance in Which Everything Is Connected to Everything Else." 23 *Harvard Environmental Law Review* 359.

Pollara. 2001. "A Benchmark Survey of Public Opinion, 2001." Department of Fisheries and Oceans website, <http://www.dfo-mpo.gc.ca/communic/pollara>.

–. 1999. *Canadian Attitudes and Opinions toward Endangered Species.* Toronto: Pollara.

Pope, C. Arden, III, Richard T. Burnett, Michael J. Thun et al. 2002. "Lung Cancer, Cardiopulmonary Mortality, and Long-term Exposure to Fine Particulate Air Pollution." 287 *Journal of the American Medical Association* 1132.

Porter, Michael E. 1991. *Canada at the Crossroads: The Reality of a New Competitive Environment.* Ottawa: Business Council on National Issues and Government of Canada.

–. 1990. *The Competitive Advantage of Nations.* London: Macmillan Press.

Porter, Michael E., et al. 2000. *The Global Competitiveness Report 2000.* New York: Oxford University Press.

Porter, Michael E., and C. van der Linde. 1995. "Green and Competitive: Ending the Stalemate." *Harvard Business Review,* Sept.-Oct.: 120-34.

Postel, Sandra L. 1997. *Last Oasis: Facing Water Scarcity.* New York: W.W. Norton and Co.

Postel, S.L., G.C. Daily, and P.R. Ehrlich. 1996. "Human Appropriation of Renewable Fresh Water." *Science* 271: 785-8.

Power, Thomas M., and Richard N. Barrett. 2001. *Post-Cowboy Economics: Pay and Prosperity in the New American West.* Washington, DC: Island Press.

Pratt, Larry, and Ian Urquhart. 1994. *The Last Great Forest: Japanese Multinationals and Alberta's Northern Forests.* Edmonton: NeWest Press.

Prescott-Allan, Robert. 2001. *The Wellbeing of Nations: A Country-by-Country Index of Quality of Life and the Environment.* Washington, DC: Island Press.

"Provincial/Territorial Recommendations for Changes to the Provisions and Implementation of the Canadian Environmental Assessment Act." 2001. <http://www.eao.gov.bc.ca>/CEAA/background.htm>.

Pue, W. Wesley, ed. 2000. *Pepper in Our Eyes: The APEC Affair.* Vancouver: UBC Press.

Pynn, Larry. 2001. "South Chilcotin Park to Be Reviewed by Liberals: NDP's Protection for Spruce Lake Area Now in Question." *Vancouver Sun,* 8 August, A3.

–. 2000. "Study Says Logging Still Eco-Threat." *Vancouver Sun,* 17 April, A1.

–. 1999. "Environment Tops Poll of Canadians' Concerns: The High Ranking Given Pollution and Conservation Issues Is Being Attributed to an Improving Economy." *Vancouver Sun,* 20 September, A4.

Quammen, David. 1996. *The Song of the Dodo: Island Biogeography in an Age of Extinctions.* New York: Scribner.

Rabe, Barry. 1997. "The Politics of Sustainable Development: Impediments to Pollution Prevention and Policy Integration in Canada." *Canadian Public Administration* 40(3): 415-35.

Raffensperger, Carolyn, and Joel Tickner, eds. 1999. *Protecting Public Health and the Environment: Implementing the Precautionary Principle.* Washington, DC: Island Press.

Raizenne, M. 1998. "Air Pollution Exposures and Children's Health." *Canadian Journal of Public Health* 89, Supp. 1.

Ralph, Diana, André Régimbald, and Nérée St-Amand. 1997. *Open for Business: Closed to People: Mike Harris's Ontario.* Halifax: Fernwood Publishing.

Raup, David M. 1992. *Extinction: Bad Genes or Bad Luck.* New York: W.W. Norton.

Ray, Justina C., and Joshua R. Ginsberg. 1999. "Endangered Species Legislation beyond the Borders of the United States." *Conservation Biology* 13(5): 956-8.

Rayner, Jeremy. 2001. "Fine-tuning the Settings: The Timber Supply Review." In B. Cashore, G. Hoberg, M. Howlett, J. Rayner, and J. Wilson, eds., *In Search of Sustainability: British Columbia Forest Policy in the 1990s.* Vancouver: UBC Press.

Redefining Progress and David Suzuki Foundation. 1997. The Economists' Statement on Climate Change. San Francisco: Redefining Progress.

Reed, David. 1996. "Impacts of Structural Adjustment on the Sustainability of Developing Countries." In David Reed, ed., *Structural Adjustment, the Environment, and Sustainable Development.* London: Earthscan.

Rees, William E. 2000. "Ecological Footprints and the Pathology of Consumption." In Robert F. Woollard, and Aleck S. Ostry, eds., *Fatal Consumption: Rethinking Sustainable Development,* 21-51. Vancouver: UBC Press.

–. 1995. "More Jobs, Less Damage: A Framework for Sustainability, Growth and Employment." *Alternatives* 21(4): 24-30.

–. 1991. "EARP at the Crossroads: Environmental Assessment in Canada." *EIA Review* 1(4): 355-75.

–. 1990. "Economics, Ecology, and the Role of Environmental Assessment in Achieving Sustainable Development." In Peter Jacobs and Barry Sadler, eds., *Sustainable Development and Environmental Assessment: Perspectives on Planning for a Common Future.* Hull, QC: Canadian Environmental Assessment Research Council.

Reif, J.S., M.C. Hatch, M. Bracken et al. 1996. "Reproductive and Developmental Effects of Disinfection By-products in Drinking Water." *Environmental Health Perspectives* 104: 1056-61.

Reitze, Arnold W. 1999. "The Legislative History of U.S. Air Pollution Control." 36.3 *Houston Law Review* 679.

–. 1997. "Population, Consumption and Environmental Law." 12.2 *Natural Resources and Environment* 89.

Repetto, Robert C., and Sanjay S. Baliga. 1996. *Pesticides and the Immune System: The Public Health Risks.* Washington, DC: World Resources Institute.

Repetto, Robert, et al. 1992. *Green Fees: How a Tax Shift Can Work for the Environment and the Economy.* Washington, DC: World Resources Institute.

Resource Renewal Institute. 2000. *Update on National Environmental Policy Plan 4.* San Francisco: Resource Renewal Institute. <http://www.rri.org>.

Reuters. 2000. "Canada, U.S. Agree to Reduce Pollution." *Victoria Times-Colonist,* 8 December, A4.

Roach, Kent. 2001. *The Supreme Court on Trial: Judicial Activism or Democratic Dialogue.* Toronto: Irwin Law.

Robert, K.-H., B. Schmidt-Bleek, J. Aloisi de Larderel et al. 2002. "Strategic Sustainable Development – Selection, Design, and Synergies of Applied Tools." *Journal of Cleaner Production* 10: 197-214.

Robinson, Nicholas A. 1990. "A Legal Perspective on Sustainable Development." In J. Owen Saunders, ed., *The Path to Sustainable Development: A Role for Law in the Legal Challenge of Sustainable Development.* Calgary: Canadian Institute of Resource Law.

Rodgers, William. 1994. *Environmental Law.* St. Paul, MN: West Publishing.

Roe, David, and William S. Pease. 1998. "Toxic Ignorance." *Environmental Forum,* May-June, 26-7.

Rojstaczer, S., S.M. Sterling, and S.J. Moore. 2001. "Human Appropriation of Photosynthesis Products." 294 *Science* 2549.

Rolfe, Chris. 2000. *Negotiating the Climate Away: Report Card on Environmental Integrity of OECD Nations Climate Summit Negotiating Position.* Vancouver: West Coast Environmental Law Association.

–. 1998. *Turning Down the Heat: Emissions Trading and Canadian Implementation of the* Kyoto Protocol. Vancouver: West Coast Environmental Law Research Foundation.

Rolfe, Chris, and L. Nowlan. 1993. *Economic Instruments and the Environment: Selected Legal Issues.* Vancouver: West Coast Environmental Law Research Foundation.

Rollins, Rick, and Philip Dearden. 1993. "Challenges for the Future." In Philip Dearden and Rick Rollins, eds., *Parks and Protected Areas in Canada.* Toronto: Oxford University Press.

Rosen, M.A. 1992. "Evaluation of Energy Efficiency in Canada." *Energy* 17: 339-50.

Rosenberg, D.M., R.A. Bodaly, R.E. Hecky, et al. 1987. "The Environmental Assessment of Hydroelectric Impoundments and Diversions in Canada." In M.C. Healey and R.R. Wallace, eds., *Canadian Aquatic Resources,* 71-104. Canadian Bulletin of Fisheries and Aquatic Sciences 215. Ottawa: Department of Fisheries and Oceans.

Ross, Monique. 1997. *A History of Forest Legislation in Canada, 1867-1996.* Calgary: Canadian Institute for Resource Law.

–. 1995. *Forest Management in Canada.* Calgary: Canadian Institute for Resource Law.

Ross, P.S., G.M. Ellis, M.G. Ikonomou et al. 2000. "High PCB Concentrations in Free-ranging Pacific Killer Whales, *Orcinus Orca:* Effects of Age, Sex and Dietary Preference." *Marine Pollution Bulletin* 40: 504-15.

Rothman, D.S. 1998. "Environmental Kuznets curves." *Ecological Economics* 25: 177-94.

Royal Society of Canada. 2001. *Elements of Precaution: Recommendations for the Regulation of Food Biotechnology in Canada.* Ottawa.

Ruckelshaus, William D. 1989. "Towards a Sustainable World." *Scientific American* 261: 114-20.

Rueggeberg, Harriet, and Andrew R. Thompson. 1984. *Water Law in Canada: Report on a Workshop for the Inquiry on Federal Water Policy.* Vancouver: University of British Columbia.

Ruggiero, Jory. 1999. "Toward a Law of the Land: The *Clean Water Act* as a Mandate for the Implementation of an Ecosystem Approach to Land Management." 20 *Public Land and Resources Law Review* 31.

Ruhl, J.B. 1999a. "How to Kill Endangered Species Legally: The Nuts and Bolts of *Endangered Species Act* HCP Permits for Real Estate Development." 5 *Environmental Lawyer* 345-405.

–. 1999b. "Sustainable Development: A Five-Dimensional Algorithm for Environmental Law." 18 *Stanford Law Journal* 31.

–. 1997. "Thinking of Environmental Law as a Complex Adaptive System: How to Clean up the Environment by Making a Mess of Environmental Law." 34 *Houston Law Review* 933.

Ryan, John C. 1997. *Stuff: The Secret Lives of Everyday Things.* Seattle: Northwest Environment Watch.

–. 1995. *Hazardous Handouts: Taxpayer Subsidies to Environmental Degradation.* Seattle: Northwest Environment Watch.

Ryder, Richard B., and W.B. Scott. 1994. "Effects of Fishing on Biodiversity in Canadian Waters." In Biodiversity Science Assessment Team, *Biodiversity in Canada: A Science Assessment.* Ottawa: Minister of Supply and Services.

Sadler, B. 1996a. *Environmental Assessment in a Changing World: Evaluating Practice to Improve Performance.* Ottawa: Minister of Supply and Services Canada.

–. 1996b. *International Study of the Effectiveness of Environmental Assessment: Final Report.* Ottawa: Minister of Supply and Services.

–. 1996c. "Sustainability Strategies and Green Planning: Recent Canadian and International Experience." In Ann Dale and John B. Robinson, eds., *Achieving Sustainable Development.* Vancouver: UBC Press.

Safina, Carl. 1998. *Song for the Blue Ocean: Encounters along the World's Coasts and beneath the Seas.* New York: Henry Holt and Company.

Salonius, Peter. 1999. "Population Growth in the United States and Canada: A Role for Scientists." *Conservation Biology* 13(6): 1518-19.

Samet, J.M., S.L. Zeger, and K. Berhane. 1995. "The Association of Mortality and Particulate Air Pollution." In *Particulate Air Pollution and Daily Mortality, Replication and Validation of Selected Studies.* Phase 1 Report of the Particle Epidemiology Evaluation Project. Washington, DC: Health Effects Institute.

Sandberg, L. Anders. 1993. *Trouble in the Woods: Forest Policy and Social Conflict in Nova Scotia and New Brunswick.* Halifax: Gorsebrook Research Institute for Atlantic Canada Studies.

Sandborn, Calvin, William J. Andrews, and Brad Wylynko. 1991. *Preventing Toxic Pollution: Toward a British Columbia Strategy.* Vancouver: West Coast Environmental Law Research Foundation.

Sanjayan, M.A., and M.E. Soule. 1997. *Moving beyond Brundtland: The Conservation Value of British Columbia's 12 Percent Protected Strategy.* Vancouver: Greenpeace Canada.

Saskatchewan Environment and Resource Management. 1999. "Saskatchewan Leads North America with New Forest Legislation." Press release no. 99-244, 31 March. Regina.

Saskatchewan Environmental Assessment Review Commission. 1991. *Environmental Challenges.* Regina: Government of Saskatchewan.

Saskatchewan Mining Association. 2000. Submission for 5-Year Review of the Canadian Environmental Assessment Act. <http://www.saskmining.ca>.

Saunders, J. Owen. 1990a. "The Path to Sustainable Development: A Role for Law." In *The Legal Challenge of Sustainable Development: Essays from the Fourth Institute Conference on Natural Resources Law.* Calgary: Canadian Institute of Resource Law.

–. 1990b. "Water Diversions/Exports and Sustainable Development." In *Report of the Canadian Bar Association Committee on Sustainable Development in Canada: Options for Law Reform.* Ottawa: Canadian Bar Association.

Savoie, Donald. 1999. *Governing from the Centre: The Concentration of Power in Canadian Politics.* Toronto: University of Toronto Press.

Saxe, Dianne. 1990. *Environmental Offences: Corporate Responsibility and Executive Liability.* Aurora, ON: Canada Law Book.

Scheffer, Marten, Steve Carpenter, Jonathan A. Foley et al. 2001. "Catastrophic Shifts in Ecosystems." *Nature* 413: 591-6.

Schettler, Ted. 1999. "Manganese in Gasoline: A Case Study of the Need for Precautionary Action." In Carolyn Raffensperger and Joel Tickner, eds., *Protecting Public Health and the Environment: Implementing the Precautionary Principle,* 309-22. Washington, DC: Island Press.

Schettler, Ted, et al. 1999. *Generations at Risk: Reproductive Health and the Environment.* Cambridge, MA: MIT Press.

Schiller, Bill. 2001. "Chilean Ban to Boost Asbestos Woes." *Toronto Star,* 8 July, 9.

Schindler, David W. 2001. "The Cumulative Effects of Climate Warming and Other Human Stresses on Canadian Freshwaters in the New Millennium." *Canadian Journal of Fisheries and Aquatic Science* 58: 18-29.

–. 1999. "From Acid Rain to Toxic Snow." *Ambio* 28: 350-5.

–. 1996. "The Environment, Carrying Capacity and Economic Growth." 6 *Ecological Applications* 17.

–. 1976. "The Impact Assessment Boondoggle." 190 *Science* 509.

Schlegelmilch, Kai. 2000. "Ecological Tax Reform in Germany: Design and Experiences." In Environment Canada, ed., *Supporting a Sustainable Future: Making Dollars and Sense.* Conference proceedings. <http://www.ec.gc.ca>.

Schmidheiny, S., et al. 1992. *Changing Course: A Global Business Perspective on Development and the Environment.* Cambridge: MIT Press.

Schprentz, D.S. 1996. *Breath-taking: Premature Mortality Due to Particulate Air Pollution in 239 American Cities.* Washington, DC: Natural Resources Defense Council.

Schrecker, Ted. 2001. "Using Science in Environmental Policy: Can Canada Do Better?" In Edward A. Parson, ed., *Governing the Environment: Persistent Challenges, Uncertain Innovations.* Toronto: University of Toronto Press.

–. 1989. "Resisting Environmental Regulation: The Cryptic Pattern of Business-Government Relations." In R. Paehlke and D. Torgerson, eds., *Managing Leviathan: Environmental Politics and the Administrative State.* Peterborough, ON: Broadview.

Schwindt, Richard. 1999. "The Canadian Pacific Salmon Fishery: Issues in Resource and Community Stability." In John T. Pierce and Ann Dale, eds., *Communities, Development, and Sustainability across Canada,* 140-65. Vancouver: UBC Press.

–. 1992. *Report of the Commission of Inquiry into Compensation for the Taking of Resource Interests.* Victoria: Queen's Printer.

Science Council of Canada. 1988. *Environmental Peacekeepers: Science, Technology, and Sustainable Development in Canada.* Ottawa: Minister of Supply and Services.

Scoffield, Heather. 2001. "Federal Spending Will Jump by 9.4 Percent." *Globe and Mail,* 11 December, A1.

–. 1999a. "Canada Lowest of G7 in Business Costs." *Globe and Mail,* 11 March, B5.

–. 1999b. "Global Trade Raises Fears for Environment: Poll." *Globe and Mail,* 7 July, B6.

–. 1999c. "Ottawa Thought Debate Ended Five Years Ago." *Globe and Mail,* 11 February, A14.

–. 1998a. "Ottawa Seeks to Halt Water Exports." *Globe and Mail,* 5 May, A1.

–. 1998b. "Water, Water Everywhere: Not a Drop to Sell." *Globe and Mail,* 11 May, A1.

Scudder, Geoff. 2003. *Biodiversity Conservation and Protected Areas in British Columbia.* Vancouver: UBC Centre for Biodiversity Research.
–. 2001. Evidence, Standing Committee on Environment and Sustainable Development. Hearings on Bill C-5, The *Species at Risk Act,* 26 April.
–. 1999. "Endangered Species Protection in Canada." 13.5 *Conservation Biology* 965.
Searle, Rick. 2000. *Phantom Parks: The Struggle to Save Canada's National Parks.* Toronto: Key Porter.
Seck, Sara L. 2001. "Strengthening Environmental Assessment of Canadian Supported Mining Ventures in Developing Countries." 11 *J.E.L.P.* 1.
Seguin, Rheal. 1992. "Ottawa Accused of Totalitarianism." *Globe and Mail,* 18 March, A6.
Seguin, Rheal, Ann Gibbon, and Graham Fraser. 1994. "Quebec Shelves Great Whale Project." *Globe and Mail,* 19 November, A1.
Selin, Henrik, and Olof Hjelm. 1999. "The Role of Environmental Science and Politics in Identifying Persistent Organic Pollutants for International Regulatory Actions." *Environment Review* 7: 61-8.
Sen, Gita. 1994. "Women, Poverty and Population: Issues for the Concerned Environmentalist." In L. Arizpe, M.P. Store, and D.C. Major, eds., *Population and Environment: Rethinking the Debate.* San Francisco: Westview Press.
Senate Committee on Energy, the Environment and Natural Resources. 2002. Third Report on Bill C-5. Ottawa.
Senate Subcommittee on the Boreal Forest. 1999. *Competing Realities: The Boreal Forest At Risk.* Ottawa: Standing Senate Committee on Agriculture and Forestry.
Serieux, John E. 2001a. "Debt of the Poorest Countries: Anatomy of a Crisis Kept on Hold." *Canadian Journal of Development Studies* 21(2): 305-42.
–. 2001b. "The Enhanced HIPC Initiative and Poor Countries: Prospects for a Permanent Exit." *Canadian Journal of Development Studies* 21(2): 527-48.
Seymour, Robert, and M.L. Hunter. 1999. "Principles of Ecological Forestry." In M.L. Hunter, ed., *Maintaining Biodiversity in Forest Ecosystems.* Cambridge: Cambridge University Press.
Shenstone, Michael. 1997. World Population Growth and Movement: Towards the 21st Century. Paper prepared for the Department of Foreign Affairs and International Trade.
Shillington and Burns Consultants. 1999. *Background Study on Public Participation in Screening and Comprehensive Studies.* Ottawa: Canadian Environmental Assessment Agency.
Shindell, D.T., D. Rind, and P. Lonergan. 1998. "Increased Polar Stratospheric Losses and Delayed Eventual Recovery Owing to Increasing Greenhouse Gas Concentrations." *Nature* 392: 589-92.
Shortle, J.S., and D.J. Abler. 2001. *Environmental Policies for Agricultural Pollution Control.* New York: CABI Publishing.
Shrybman, Steven. 2000. *Safe to Drink.* Vancouver: West Coast Environmental Law Association. <http://www.wcel.org>.
–. 1999a. *A Citizen's Guide to the World Trade Organization.* Ottawa: Canadian Centre for Policy Alternatives.
–. 1999b. *A Legal Opinion Concerning Water Export Controls and Canadian Obligations under NAFTA and the WTO.* Vancouver: West Coast Environmental Law Research Foundation.
Shutkin, William A. 2000. *The Land That Could Be: Environmentalism and Democracy in the Twenty-first Century.* Cambridge, MA: MIT Press.
Sierra Club of Canada. 2002. *Rio Report Card.* Ottawa: Sierra Club. <http://www.sierraclub.ca>.
Sierra Legal Defence Fund. 2002a. *Canadian Regulation of Air Pollution from Motor Vehicles.* Toronto. <http://www.sierralegal.org>.
–. 2002b. *Clearing the Forest, Cutting the Rules.* Toronto: SLDF.
–. 2002c. *False Economy: The Hidden Future Costs of Cuts in Regulatory Services.* Vancouver.
–. 2002d. *Logging to Extinction: Last Stand of the Northern Spotted Owl.* Vancouver.
–. 2002e. *The Lost Decade: Canada's Conservation Track Record since Signing the 1992 Rio Convention on Biological Diversity.* Vancouver.
–. 2002f. *Polluter's Haven.* Toronto.
–. 2001a. *Ontario's 2000 Dirty Water Secrets: A Report on Ontario's Wastewater Violations in 2000.* Toronto.
–. 2001b. *Stumpage Sellout: How Forest Company Abuse of the Stumpage System Is Costing BC Taxpayers Millions of Dollars.* Vancouver.
–. 2000. *Ontario: Yours to Pollute: A Report on Ontario's Wastewater Violations.* Toronto.

–. 1999. *Who's Watching Our Waters? A Report on Who's Polluting and the Government That's Permitting It.* Toronto.

–. 1998a. *Beehive Burners: Putting Profits ahead of Human Health.* Vancouver.

–. 1998b. *British Columbia's Forestry Report Card, 1997-98.* Vancouver.

–. 1997a. *Going Downhill Fast: Landslides and the* Forest Practices Code. Vancouver.

–. 1997b. *Stream Protection under the* Code. Vancouver.

–. 1997c. *Wildlife at Risk: The Lack of Protection for Wildlife Biodiversity and Endangered Species under the* Forest Practices Code. Vancouver.

–. 1996. *British Columbia's Clearcut Code.* Vancouver.

–. 1992. "Keeping the Wood in Wood Buffalo." Newsletter No. 2, September.

Sierra Legal Defence Fund and Wildlands League. 2001. *Improving Practices, Reducing Harm: A Forestry Field Audit in the Lower Spanish Forest.* Toronto: SLDF.

–. 2000. *Grounds for Concern: An Audit of Compliance with Ontario Forest Protection Rules, Algonquin Park and the Magpie Forest.* Toronto: SLDF.

–. 1998. *Cutting around the Rules: The Algoma Highlands Pay the Price for Lax Enforcement of Logging Rules.* Toronto: SLDF.

Simon, Julian. 1995. "The State of Humanity: Steadily Improving." *Cato Policy Report* 17(5): 1, 10-11, 14-15.

Simpson, Jeffrey. 2001. *The Friendly Dictatorship.* Toronto: McClelland and Stewart.

Sinclair, Scott, and Jim Grieshaber-Otto. 2002. *Facing the Facts: A Guide to the GATS Debate.* Ottawa: Canadian Centre for Policy Alternatives.

Singer, S. Fred. 1999. *Hot Talk, Cold Science: Global Warming's Unfinished Debate.* Oakland, CA: Independent Institute.

Sizer, Nigel, et al. 2000. *Perverse Habits: The G-8 and Subsidies That Harm Forests and Economies.* Washington, DC: World Resources Institute.

Slaney, P.A., and A.D. Martin. 1997. "The Watershed Restoration Program of British Columbia: Accelerating Natural Recovery Processes." *Water Quality Research Journal of Canada* 33(2): 325-46.

Slaney, T.L., et al. 1996. "Status of Anadromous Salmon and Trout in British Columbia and Yukon." *American Fisheries Society* 21(10): 20-35.

Slovic, P., et al. 1995. "Intuitive Toxicology: Expert and Lay Judgements of Chemical Risks in Canada." *Risk Analysis* 15: 661-75.

Smith, D.A., et al. 1993. *Socio-Economic Assessment of Amendments to Regulations Related to Ozone Depleting Substances.* Ottawa: Environment Canada.

Smith, Karen L. 2001. "Habitat Protection for the New Millenium: An Analysis of Domestic and International Regimes in North America." *Georgetown International Environmental Law Review* 13(2): 509-61.

Solomon, Gina M., and Ted Schettler. 2000. "Endocrine Disruption and Potential Human Health Implications." *Canadian Medical Association Journal* 163(11): 1471-6.

Species at Risk Working Group. 1998. Conserving Species at Risk and Vulnerable Ecosystems: Proposals for Legislation and Programs. Unpublished briefing paper.

Spiedel, J.J. 2000. "Environment and Health: Population, Consumption and Human Health." *Canadian Medical Association Journal* 163(5): 551-6.

Sproule-Jones, Mark. 2002. *Restoration of the Great Lakes: Promises, Practices, and Performance.* Vancouver: UBC Press.

Standing Committee on Environment and Sustainable Development. 2000. *Pesticides: Making the Right Choice, for the Protection of Human Health and the Environment.* Ottawa: House of Commons.

–. 1998. *Enforcing Canada's Pollution Laws: The Public Interest Must Come First.* Ottawa: House of Commons.

–. 1997. *Harmonization and Environmental Protection: An Analysis of the Harmonization Initiative of the Canadian Council of Ministers of the Environment.* Ottawa: House of Commons.

–. 1996. *Keeping a Promise: Toward a Sustainable Budget.* Ottawa: Standing Committee.

–. 1995. *It's about Your Health: Towards Pollution Prevention.* Ottawa: Standing Committee.

–. 1993. *Our Planet ... Our Future.* Ottawa: House of Commons.

Standing Committee on Natural Resources. 1996. *Streamlining Environmental Assessment for Mining: Final Report.* Ottawa: House of Commons.

Statistics Canada. 2001a. *Canadian Crime Statistics.* No. 85-205-XIE. Ottawa: Minister of Public Works and Government Services. <http://www.statscan.ca>.

–. 2001b. *Canadian Statistics: Homicide Offences, Number and Rate.* CANSIM II, Table 253-7001.

–. 2001c. *Canadian Statistics: Population and Growth Components.* Ottawa.

–. 2001d. "A Geographical Profile of Manure Production in Canada." Ottawa.

–. 2000. *Human Activity and the Environment, 2000.* Ottawa: Minister of Public Works and Government Services Canada.

Stefanick, Lorna, and Kathleen Wells. 1998. "Staying the Course or Saving Face: Federal Environmental Policy Post-Rio." In Leslie A. Pal, ed., *How Ottawa Spends, 1998-99. Balancing Act: The Post-Deficit Mandate.* Toronto: Oxford University Press.

Stephenson, William. 1994. "Adequacy of Canada's Protected Areas Network." In Biodiversity Science Assessment Team, *Biodiversity in Canada: A Science Assessment.* Ottawa: Minister of Supply and Services.

Stieb, D.M., L.D. Pengelly, N. Arron et al. 1995. "Health Effects of Air Pollution in Canada: Expert Panel Findings for the Canadian Smog Advisory Program." *Canadian Respiratory Journal* 2(3): 155-60.

Stirling, Ian, Nicholas Lunn, and John Iacozza. 1999. "Long-term Trends in the Population Ecology of Polar Bears in Western Hudson Bay in Relation to Climate Change." *Arctic* 52(3): 294-306.

Stolarski, R.S. 1988. "The Antarctic Ozone Hole." *Scientific American* 258: 30-6.

Struzik, Ed. 1998. "UN Agency Asks Ottawa to Revoke OK for Cheviot: Heritage Site at Risk, It Says." *Edmonton Journal,* 19 March, A1.

Sunstein, Cass R. 1999. "Is the Clean Air Act Unconstitutional?" 98.2 *Michigan Law Review* 303.

Suzuki, David. 2001. "Our Environmental Shame." *Globe and Mail,* 21 March, A17.

Suzuki, David, and Anita Gordon. 1990. *It's a Matter of Survival.* Toronto: Stoddart.

Suzuki, David, and Amanda McConnell. 1997. *The Sacred Balance: Rediscovering Our Place in Nature.* Vancouver: Greystone Books.

Svendsen, G., C. Daugbjergand, and A. Pedersen. 2001. "Consumers, Industrialists and the Political Economy of Green Taxation: CO_2 Taxation in OECD." *Energy Policy* 29(6): 489-97.

Swaigen, John. 2001. "The Hudson Case: Municipal Powers to Regulate Pesticides Confirmed by Quebec Courts." 34 *C.E.L.R.* (N.S.) 162.

–. 2000. "Parks Legislation in Canada: A Comparison of the New *Canada National Parks Act* and Ontario's Existing *Provincial Parks Act.*" 10 *J.E.L.P.* 223.

–. 1993. "How the Legal System Works." In David Estrin and John Swaigen, eds., *Environment on Trial: A Guide to Ontario Environmental Law and Policy,* 3-20. 3d ed. Toronto: Emond Montgomery.

–. 1992. "The Role of Civil Courts in Resolving Risk and Uncertainty in Environmental Law." 2 *J.E.L.P.* 199.

Swan, Richard. 1994. "Legal Implications of the *Crown Forest Sustainability Act.*" In *Operating under Ontario's New* Crown Forest Sustainability Act. Toronto: Insight Press.

Swanson, Elizabeth. 1993. *Putting Sustainable Development to Work: Implementation through Law and Policy.* Edmonton: Environmental Law Centre.

Swanson, Elizabeth, and Elaine L. Hughes. 1995. *The Price of Pollution: Environmental Litigation in Canada.* Edmonton: Environmental Law Centre.

Swedish Ministry of Environment. 2002. *Stockholm Thirty Years On: Progress Achieved and Challenges ahead in International Environmental Cooperation.* Stockholm.

–. 2001a. "Local Climate Protection Measures in Sweden: Best Practices within the Local Investment Programmes." <http://www.miljo.regeringen.se>.

–. 2001b. Press release, 21 September.

–. 2001c. *The Swedish Environmental Objectives – Interim Targets and Action Strategies.* Government Bill 2000/01: 130.

–. 2001d. *Sweden's Third National Communication on Climate Change.* Stockholm.

–. 2000. *Sustainable Sweden: A Progress Report on Measures to Promote Ecologically Sustainable Development.* Government Communication 2000/01: 38.

–. 1999. *Sustainable Sweden: A Progress Report on Measures Promoting Ecologically Sustainable Development 1999/2000.*

–. 1998. *Environmental Quality Objectives Bill.* Government Bill 1997-98.

Swedish National Chemicals Inspectorate. 1998. "Chemical Products and Biotechnical Organisms Regulations (1998-8)." Appendices 5-8. <http://www.kemi.se>.

Swenarchuk, M. 2002. *From Global to Local: GATS Impacts on Canadian Municipalities.* Toronto: Canadian Environmental Law Association.

–. 2000. *The Cartagena Biosafety Protocol: Opportunities and Limitations.* Toronto: Canadian Environmental Law Association.

Swift, Jamie. 1983. *Cut and Run: The Assault on Canada's Forests.* Toronto: Between the Lines.

Systems Research Group. 1969. Canadian Legislation Relating to Environmental Quality Management. Toronto.

Szekely, Alberto. 1997. "Compliance with Environmental Treaties: The Empirical Evidence – A Commentary on the Softening of International Environmental Law." In *Proceedings of the American Society of International Law,* 237-8. New York: American Society of International Law.

Taft, Kevin. 1997. *Shredding the Public Interest: Ralph Klein and 25 Years of One-Party Government.* Edmonton: University of Alberta Press.

Task Force on Economic Instruments and Disincentives to Sound Environmental Practices. 1994. *Economic Instruments and Disincentives to Sound Environmental Practices: Final Report.* Ottawa: Department of Finance and Environment Canada.

Task Force on Environmental Contaminants Legislation. 1972. *Cross-Mission Report.* Ottawa: Government of Canada.

Tate, D.M. 1987. "Current and Projected Water Uses in Canada: 1981-2011." In M.C. Healey and R.R. Wallace, eds., *Canadian Aquatic Resources.* Canadian Bulletin of Fisheries and Aquatic Sciences 215. Ottawa: Department of Fisheries and Oceans.

Tate, D.M., and D.M. Lacelle. 1995. *Municipal Water Rates in Canada: Current Practices and Prices.* Ottawa: Environment Canada.

Tate, D.M., S. Renzetti, and H.A. Shaw. 1992. *Economic Instruments for Water Management: The Case for Industrial Water Pricing.* Ottawa: Environment Canada.

Taylor, Amy. 1999. "Ecological Tax Reform: Estimated Environmental and Employment Effects in British Columbia." Master's thesis, Simon Fraser University.

Taylor, A., M. Jaccard, and N. Olewiler. 1999. *Environmental Tax Shift: A Discussion Paper for British Columbians.* Victoria: Government of British Columbia.

Taylor, Eric, and Bill Taylor. 1998. *Responding to Global Climate Change in British Columbia and Yukon.* Vol. 1 of the Canada Country Study. Ottawa: Environment Canada.

Taylor, Lance, and Ute Pieper. 1996. *Reconciling Economic Reform and Sustainable Human Development: Social Consequences of Neo-Liberalism.* New York: UNDP.

Technical Committee on Business Taxation. 1998. "Taxes As User Charges: Environmental Taxes." Chapter 9 in *Report of the Technical Committee on Business Taxation.* Ottawa: Department of Finance.

Teschke, K., et al. 1992. *Organochlorine Pesticides and Polychlorinated Biphenyls in the Adipose Tissue of B.C. Residents.* Victoria: BC Environment.

"There's Plenty up North." 1999. *Economist,* 23 January, 26.

Thompson, Andrew R. 1987. "Who Controls the Aquatic Resources?" In M.C. Healey and R.R. Wallace, eds., *Canadian Aquatic Resources.* Canadian Bulletin of Fisheries and Aquatic Sciences 215. Ottawa: Department of Fisheries and Oceans.

–. 1980. *Environmental Regulation in Canada.* Vancouver: Westwater Research Centre.

Thornton, Joe. 2000. *Pandora's Poison: Chlorine, Health and a New Environmental Strategy.* Cambridge, MA: MIT Press, Appendix A.

Tilleman, William A. 1995. "Public Participation in the Environmental Assessment Process: A Comparative Study of Impact Assessment in Canada, the United States, and the European Community." 33 *Columbia Journal of Transnational Law* 337.

Tilman, David, et al. 2001. "Forecasting Agriculturally Driven Global Environmental Change." 292 *Science* 281.

Tol, R. 1995. "The Damage Costs of Climate Change: Towards More Comprehensive Calculations." 5 *Environmental and Resource Economics* 353-74.

Tollefson, Chris. 2002. "Games without Frontiers: Investor Claims and Citizen Submissions under the NAFTA Regime." 27 *Yale Journal of International Law* 141.

–. 1995. "When the Public Interest Loses: The Liability of Public Interest Litigants for Adverse Cost Awards." 29 *UBC Law Review* 303.

Tollefson, C., C. Rhone, and C. Rolfe. 2000. Cleanair.ca: A Citizen's Action Guide. Victoria: Environmental Law Centre.

Toner, Glen. 1996. "Environment Canada's Continuing Roller Coaster Ride." In Gene Swimmer, ed., *How Ottawa Spends 1996-97: Life under the Knife,* 99-132. Ottawa: Carleton University Press.

Torrie, Ralph. 2000. *Power Shift: Cool Solutions to Global Warming.* Vancouver: David Suzuki Foundation. <http://www.davidsuzuki.org>.

Toughill, Kelly. 2001. "Water Resistant: Newfoundland Wants to Sell Its Abundant Water." *Toronto Star,* 12 May, A1.

–. 1999. "The Summer the Rivers Died: Toxic Runoff from Potato Farms Is Poisoning PEI." *Toronto Star,* 11 October. First Edition.

Transport Canada. 2002. "Transport Minister Collenette Announces Another Record Penalty for Marine Pollution." Press release, 25 November. <http://www.tc.gc.ca>.

–. 2000. *Transportation in Canada 1999: Annual Report.* Ottawa: Minister of Public Works.

Trilateral Agreement between the Algonquins of Barrière Lake and Le Gouvernement du Québec and the Government of Canada. 1991. <http://www.barrierelake.ca>.

Trudeau, Pierre Elliott. 2000. "Foreword." In Roberta Bondar, *Passionate Vision: Discovering Canada's National Parks.* Vancouver: Douglas and McIntyre.

Tudge, Colin. 2000. *The Variety of Life: A Survey and a Celebration of All the Creatures That Have Ever Lived.* Oxford: Oxford University Press.

Tungavik Federation of Nunavut. 1990. *Agreement-in-Principle between the Inuit of the Nunavut Settlement Area and Her Majesty in Right of Canada.* Ottawa.

Turennes, Roger. 2000. "Conservation: The Filmon Legacy." <http://www.cpaws.org/chapters/mbeditorial.html>.

UN (United Nations). 1995. *International Conference on Population and Development Programme of Action.* Adopted at the International Conference on Population and Development, Cairo, 5-13 September. New York: UN.

UN Conference on Environment and Sustainable Development. 1992. *Agenda 21: Programme of Action for Sustainable Development.* New York: UN.

UN Development Program. 2001. *Human Development Report 2001: Making New Technologies Work for Human Development.* New York: Oxford University Press.

–. 1998. *Human Development Report 1998.* New York: Oxford University Press.

UN Economic and Social Council Commission on Sustainable Development. 1997. *Comprehensive Assessment of the Freshwater Resources of the World.* Geneva: World Meteorological Organization.

UN Environment Program. 2002. *Global Environmental Outlook.* 3d ed. New York: Earthscan.

–. 1997. *Global Environmental Outlook.* New York: Oxford University Press.

UN Population Fund. 2002. *People, Poverty, and Possibilities: Making Development Work for the Poor.* New York: UN. <http://www.unfpa.org>.

–. 2001. *The State of World Population 2001. Footprints and Milestones: Population and Environmental Change.* New York: UN.

Union of Concerned Scientists. 2000. "Population Briefing." <http://www.ucsusa.org>.

–. 1992. *World Scientists' Warning to Humanity.* Washington, DC.

Urquhart, Ian. 2001. "New Players, Same Game? Managing the Boreal Forest on Canada's Prairies." In Michael Howlett, ed., *Canadian Forest Policy: Adapting to Change.* Toronto: University of Toronto Press.

US Council on Environmental Quality. 1997. *Considering Cumulative Effects under the* National Environmental Policy Act. Washington, DC.

–. 1996. *Environmental Quality: The Twenty-fifth Anniversary Report of the Council on Environmental Quality.* Washington, DC.

–. 1990. *Environmental Quality: The Twentieth Annual Report of the Council on Environmental Quality.* Washington, DC.

US Department of Agriculture. 1999. *Agriculture, Environment, Sustainable Development: Facts and Figures.* Washington, DC.

US Department of Energy. 1997. "Scenarios of US Carbon Reductions: Potential Impacts." World Resources Institute website, <http://www.wri.org>.

US Energy Information Administration. 1999. World Carbon Dioxide Emissions, 1989-1998. Washington, DC.

US Environmental Protection Agency. 1999. Annual Report on Enforcement and Compliance Assurance Accomplishments in 1999. Washington, DC.

–. 1998. *Taking Toxics out of the Air.* Washington, DC.

–. 1997a. Ozone: Good Up High, Bad Nearby. Washington, DC.

–. 1997b. Water on Tap: A Consumer's Guide to the Nation's Drinking Water. Washington, DC.

–. 1996. National Water Quality Inventory: 1996. Report to Congress. Washington, DC.

–. 1995. *Reregistration Eligibility Decision: Metolachlor.* EPA-738-95-007. Washington, DC.

–. 1993. *Regulatory Impact Analysis: Protection of the Stratospheric Ozone Layer.* Washington, DC.

–. 1991. *The Benefits and Costs of the Clean Air Act, 1970-1990.* Washington, DC.

US EPA Ecosystem Protection Working Group. 1994. *Toward a Place-Driven Approach: The Edgewater Consensus on an EPA Strategy for Ecosystem Protection.* Washington, DC: EPA.

US General Accounting Office. 2001. *Agricultural Pesticides: Management Improvements Needed to Further Promote Integrated Pest Management.* GAO-01-815, 17 August. Washington, DC.

–. 2000. *Pesticides: Improvements Needed to Ensure the Safety of Farmworkers and Their Children.* RCED-00-40, 14 March. Washington, DC.

–. 1999a. *Forest Service Priorities: Evolving Mission Favors Resource Protection over Production.* Washington, DC.

–. 1999b. *Water Quality: Federal Role in Addressing and Contributing to Non-point Source Water Pollution.* Washington, DC.

–. 1997. *Global Warming: Information on the Results of Four of the EPA's Voluntary Climate Change Programs.* Washington, DC.

US Government. 2001. *National Energy Policy.* Washington, DC: White House.

US National Academy of Sciences. 2002. *Effects of Bottom Trawling and Dredging on Sea Floor Habitat.* Washington, DC: National Academy Press.

US National Research Council. 2002. *Environmental Effects of Transgenic Plants: The Scope and Adequacy of Regulation.* Washington, DC: National Academy Press.

–. 2001. *Abrupt Climate Change: Inevitable Surprises.* Washington, DC: National Academy of Sciences.

–. 1999a. *Hormonally Active Agents in the Environment.* Washington, DC: National Academy Press.

–. 1999b. *Our Common Journey: A Transition Toward Sustainability.* Washington, DC: National Academy Press.

–. 1996a. *Carcinogens and Anti-carcinogens in the Human Diet.* Washington, DC: National Academy Press.

–. 1996b. *Ecologically Based Pest Management: New Solutions for a New Century.* Washington, DC: National Academy Press.

–. 1995. *Science and the Endangered Species Act.* Washington, DC: National Academy Press.

–. 1994. *Population Summit of the World's Scientific Academies.* Washington, DC: National Academy Press.

–. 1993a. *A Biological Survey for the Nation.* Washington, DC: National Academy Press.

–. 1993b. *Pesticides in the Diets of Infants and Children.* Washington, DC: National Academy of Sciences.

–. 1989. *Alternative Agriculture.* Report of the NRC Committee on the Role of Alternative Farming Methods in Modern Production Agriculture. Washington, DC: National Academy Press.

US National Research Council Committee on Biological Diversity in Marine Ecosystems. 1995. *Understanding Marine Biodiversity: A Research Agenda for the Nation.* Washington, DC: National Academy Press.

US Office of Management and Budget. 1998. *Historical Tables, United States Government, Fiscal Year 1999.* Washington, DC: Government Printing Office.

US Office of Technology Assessment. 1994. *Trade and Environment: Conflicts and Opportunities.* Washington, DC: Government Printing Office.

Valiante, Marcia. 2002. "Turf War: Municipal Powers, the Regulation of Pesticides and the Hudson Decision." 11 *J.E.L.P.* 325.

–. 2001. "Legal Foundations of Canadian Environmental Policy: Underlining Our Values in a Shifting Landscape." In Debora L. VanNijnatten and Robert Boardman, eds., *Canadian Environmental Policy: Context and Cases.* 2d ed. Oxford: Oxford University Press.

–. 1998. "Evaluating Ontario's Environmental Assessment Reforms." 8 *J.E.L.P.* 215.

van Beers, Cees, and Andre de Moor. 2001. *Public Subsidies and Policy Failure: How Subsidies Distort the Natural Environment, Equity and Trade and How to Reform Them.* London: Edward Elgar.

Van Der Leeden, F., F.L. Troise, and D.K. Todd. 1990. *The Water Encyclopedia.* 2d ed. New York: Lewis Publishers.

VanderZwaag, David. 1998. "The Precautionary Principle in Environmental Law and Policy: Elusive Rhetoric and First Embraces." 8 *J.E.L.P.* 355.

–. 1995. *Canada and Marine Environmental Protection: Charting a Legal Course toward Sustainable Development*. London: Kluwer Law International.

VanderZwaag, David, and D. MacKinlay. 1996. "Towards a Global Forest Convention: Getting out of the Woods and Barking up the Right Tree." In Canadian Council on International Law, *Global Forests and International Environmental Law*. London: Kluwer Law International.

VanNijnatten, Debora L., and Robert Boardman, eds. 2001. *Canadian Environmental Policy: Context and Cases*. 2d ed. Oxford: Oxford University Press.

VanNijnatten, Debora L., and W. Henry Lambright. 2001. "Canadian Smog Policy in a Continental Context: Looking South for Stringency." In Debora L. VanNijnatten and Robert Boardman, eds., *Canadian Environmental Policy: Context and Cases*, 253-73. 2d ed. Oxford: Oxford University Press.

Vedal, Sverre. 1995. *Health Effects of Inhalable Particles: Implications for B.C.* Victoria: Ministry of Environment, Land and Parks.

Vig, Norman J., and Michael Kraft. 2000. *Environmental Policy: New Directions for the Twenty-first Century*. Washington, DC: Congressional Quarterly.

Vigod, Toby, and Anne Wordsworth. 1982. "Water Fit to Drink? The Need for a Safe Drinking Water Act in Canada." 11 *C.E.L.R.* 80.

Vincent, J., and Clark Binkley. 1992. "Forest Based Industrialization: A Dynamic Perspective." In N.P. Sharma, ed., *Managing the World's Forests: Looking for Balance Between Conservation and Development*. Dubuque, IA: Kendall Hunt Publishing.

Vitousek, Peter M., et al. 1997. "Human Domination of Earth's Ecosystems." 277 *Science* 494.

Voisey's Bay Environmental Assessment Panel. 1999. *Report of the Proposed Voisey's Bay Mine and Mill Project*. Ottawa: Minister of Public Works and Government Services Canada.

Vorosmarty, Charles J., Pamela Green, Joseph Salisbury et al. 2000. "Global Water Resources: Vulnerability from Climate Change and Population Growth." *Science* 289: 284-8.

Wachtel, Paul. 1989. *The Poverty of Affluence*. Gabriola Island, BC: New Society Publishers.

Wackernagel, M., et al. 2002a. *Ecological Footprint of Nations, November 2002 Update*. San Francisco: Redefining Progress. <http://www.redefiningprogress.org>.

–. 2002b. "Tracking the Ecological Overshoot of the Human Economy." In *Proceedings of the National Academy of Sciences* 99, 14 (June): 9926-71.

–. 1999. *Ranking the Ecological Footprint of Nations*. Costa Rica: Earth Council. <http://www.ecouncil.ac.cr/rio/focus/report/english/footprint/ranking.htm>.

Wackernagel, M., and W. Rees. 1996a. "Ecological Footprints and Appropriated Carrying Capacity: Measuring the Natural Capital Requirements of the Human Economy." In A.M. Jansson, M. Hammer, C. Folke, and R. Costanza, eds., *Investing in Natural Capital: The Ecological Economics Approach to Sustainability*. Washington, DC: Island Press.

–. 1996b. *Our Ecological Footprint: Reducing Human Impact on the Earth*. Philadelphia: New Society.

Wahlstrom, B., and B. Lundqvist. 1993. "Risk Reduction and Chemicals Control: Lessons from the Swedish Chemical Actions Program." In T. Jackson, ed., *Clean Production Strategies: Developing Preventive Environmental Management in the Industrial Economy*, 237-60. Ann Arbor, MI: Lewis Publishing.

Walker, Ruth. 1998. "Canada's Dry on Exporting Water." *Christian Science Monitor*, 15 June, 6.

Wallace, S.S. 1999. "Evaluating Three Forms of Reserves on Northern Abalone Populations in British Columbia, Canada." *Conservation Biology* 13: 882-7.

Walters, Carl. 1998. "Reconstructing the Strait of Georgia Ecosystem." In Daniel Pauly, Tony J. Pitcher, and Daniel Preikshot, eds., *UBC Fisheries Centre Research Reports* 6(5). Vancouver: UBC Fisheries Centre.

–. 1986. *Adaptive Management of Renewable Resources*. New York: Wiley.

Walther, G.W., E. Post, P. Convey et al. 2002. "Ecological Responses to Recent Climate Change." *Nature* 416: 389-95.

Warburton, Donald, et al. 1998. "A Further Review of the Microbiological Quality of Bottled Water Sold in Canada: 1992-1997 Survey Results." *International Journal of Food Microbiology* 39: 221-6.

Ward, Peter. 1994. *The End of Evolution: On Mass Extinctions and the Preservation of Biodiversity*. New York: Bantam.

Wargo, John. 1996. *Our Children's Toxic Legacy: How Science and Law Fail to Protect Us from Pesticides*. New Haven: Yale University Press.

Watling, Les, and Elliott A. Norse. 1998. "Disturbance of the Seabed by Mobile Fishing Gear: A Comparison to Forest Clearcutting." *Conservation Biology* 12(6): 1180-97.

Watson, R.T., Ozone Trends Panel. 1988. *Present State of Knowledge of the Upper Atmosphere.* National Aeronautics and Space Administration. Reference Publication 1208. 201 pp.

Weaver, Andrew. 2001. "Global Warming Debate Is a Puzzle." *Victoria Times-Colonist,* 8 February, A17.

Webb, Kernaghan. 1990. *Pollution Control in Canada: The Regulatory Approach in the 1990s.* Ottawa: Law Reform Commission of Canada.

Wedeles, C.L., D.C. Van Damme, and L. Sully. 1995. *Alternative Silvicultural Systems for Ontario's Boreal Mixed Woods.* Sault Ste. Marie, ON: Canadian Forest Service.

Weiss, Edith Brown. 1989. *In Fairness to Future Generations.* New York: Transnational Publishers.

Welch, D.W., Y. Ishida, and K. Nagasawa. 1998. "Thermal Limits and Ocean Migrations of Sockeye Salmon *(Oncorhyncus nerka):* Long-term Consequences of Global Warming." *Canadian Journal of Fish and Aquatic Sciences* 55: 937-48.

West Coast Environmental Law Association. 2002. *The B.C. Government: A One Year Environmental Review.* Vancouver. <http://www.wcel.org>.

–. 2001. *The Smart Growth Guide to Local Government Law and Advocacy.* Vancouver.

Wiener, J.B. 1999. "Global Environmental Regulation: Instrument Choice in Legal Context." 108 *Yale Law Journal* 677.

Wigle, D.T., et al. 1990. "Mortality Study of Canadian Male Farm Operators: Non-Hodgkin's Lymphoma Mortality and Agricultural Practices in Saskatchewan." *Journal of the National Cancer Institute* 82(7): 575-82.

Wildlands League. n.d. *The State of Ontario's Forests: Undercutting Our Natural Capital.* Toronto.

Wilkinson, Charles F. 1997. "The *National Forest Management Act:* The Twenty Years Behind, The Twenty Years Ahead." 68 *University of Colorado Law Review* 659.

Williams, Bryan. 1995. *Report of the Cypress Park Special Planning Commission.* Vancouver: Ministry of Environment, Land and Parks.

Williams, J., P. Duinker, and G. Bull. 1997. *Implications of Sustainable Forest Management for Global Fibre Supply.* Working Paper No. 3. Rome: Food and Agriculture Organization.

Wilson, E.O. 1992. *The Diversity of Life.* Cambridge: Harvard University Press.

Wilson, Jeremy. 2001a. "Continuity and Change in the Canadian Environmental Movement: Assessing the Effects of Institutionalization." In Debora L. VanNijnatten and Robert Boardman, eds., *Canadian Environmental Policy: Context and Cases.* 2d ed. Oxford: Oxford University Press.

–. 2001b. "Talking the Talk and Walking the Walk: Reflections on the Early Influence of Ecosystem Management Ideas." In Michael Howlett, ed., *Canadian Forest Policy: Adapting to Change.* Toronto: University of Toronto Press.

Winfield, Mark S. 2000. *Reflections on the Biosafety Protocol Negotiations in Montreal.* Toronto: Canadian Institute for Environmental Law and Policy.

Winfield, M., C. Coumans, J. Kuyek et al. 2002. *Looking beneath the Surface: An Assessment of the Value of Public Support for the Metal Mining Industry in Canada.* Ottawa: Pembina Institute.

Winfield, Mark, and John Swaigen. 1993. "Water." In *Environment on Trial: A Guide to Ontario Environmental Law and Policy.* Toronto: Emond Montgomery.

Winsor, Hugh. 1999. "Ex-Liberal Spearheads Industry's Campaign against Bill." *Globe and Mail,* 26 April, A4.

Wise, Timothy A. 2001. "Local and National Strategies." In Jonathan M. Harris, Timothy A. Wise, Kevin P. Gallagher, and Neva R. Goodwin, eds., *A Survey of Sustainable Development: Social and Economic Dimensions.* Washington, DC: Island Press.

Wolf, Michael Allan. 2000. "Environmental Law Slogans for the New Millennium." 30 *Environmental Law Reporter* 10283.

Wood, Paul M. 2000. *Biodiversity and Democracy: Rethinking Nature and Society.* Vancouver: UBC Press.

Woollard, Robert F. 2000. "Introduction: Fatal Consumption (When Too Much Is Not Enough)." In Robert F. Woollard and Aleck S. Ostry, eds., *Fatal Consumption: Rethinking Sustainable Development.* Vancouver: UBC Press.

Woollard, Robert, and William Rees. 1999. "Social Evolution and Urban Systems: Directions for Sustainability." In John T. Pierce and Ann Dale, eds., *Communities, Development, and Sustainability across Canada.* Vancouver: UBC Press.

Working Group on Public Health and Fossil-Fuel Combustion. 1997. "Short-term Improvements in Public Health from Global-Climate Policies on Fossil-Fuel Reduction." *The Lancet* 350(9088): 1341-8.

World Bank. 2002a. *Global Development Finance: Financing the Poorest Countries.* Washington, DC. <http://www.worldbank.org>.

–. 2002b. "World Bank Estimates Costs of Reaching the Millennium Development Goals at $40-$60 Billion Annually in Additional Aid." Press release, 20 February.

–. 2002c. *World Development Report 2002: Building Institutions for Markets.* Washington, DC.

–. 2001a. *Financial Impact of the Heavily Indebted Poor Countries Initiative: First 23 Country Studies.* Washington, DC.

–. 2001b. *Globalisation, Growth, and Poverty: Building an Inclusive World Economy.* Washington, DC.

–. 2001c. *World Development Indicators, 2001.* Washington, DC.

–. 2001d. *World Development Report 2000-2001: Attacking Poverty.* Washington, DC.

–. 1999. *World Development Report 1998-99.* Washington, DC.

–. 1998. *Assessing Aid: What Works, What Doesn't and Why.* World Bank Policy Research Report. New York: Oxford University Press.

–. 1993. *The East Asian Miracle.* Oxford: Oxford University Press.

World Bank and Environics International. 2002. "The Global Public's Agenda for the World Summit on Sustainable Development: Exclusive Release of Public Opinion and Expert Survey Findings." Press release, 31 January.

World Bank and International Monetary Fund. 2002. *Heavily Indebted Poor Countries Initiative – Status of Implementation.* Washington, DC: World Bank.

World Commission on Dams. 2000. *Dams and Development: A New Framework for Decision-making.* London: Earthscan. <http://www.dams.org>.

World Commission on Environment and Development. 1987. *Our Common Future.* Oxford: Oxford University Press.

World Conservation Union. 2000. *2000 IUCN Red List of Threatened Species.* Gland, Switzerland. <http://www.iucn.org>.

World Economic Forum. 2002. *2002 Environmental Sustainability Index.* Geneva.

World Health Organization. 2002. *Essential Drugs and Medicines Policy.* Geneva. <http://www.who.int>.

–. 1999. *Air Quality Guidelines.* Geneva.

–. 1996. *Climate Change and Human Health.* Geneva: WHO, World Meteorological Organization, United Nations Environmental Program.

–. 1994. *UV Radiation: An Authoritative Scientific Review of Environmental and Health Effects of UV, with Reference to Global Ozone Layer Depletion.* Geneva.

–. 1990. *Public Health Impact of Pesticides Used in Agriculture.* Geneva.

World Health Organization and United Nations Children's Fund. 2000. Global Water Supply and Sanitation Assessment, 2000. Geneva.

World Meteorological Organization. 2002. *Scientific Assessment of Ozone Depletion: 2002.* Geneva.

–. 1998. *Scientific Assessment of Ozone Depletion: 1998.* WMO Global Ozone Research and Monitoring Project Report No. 44. Geneva.

World Meteorological Organization and UN Environment Program. 1998. "Stratospheric Ozone Depletion: Environmental Effects 1998." <http://www.unep.ch/ozone>.

World Trade Organization. 2000. *Trade, Income Disparity, and Poverty.* Special Study No. 5. Geneva.

–. 1995. The Results of the Uruguay Round of Multilateral Trade Negotiations: The Legal Text. Geneva.

World Wildlife Fund Canada. 2000. *Endangered Spaces: The Wilderness Campaign That Changed the Canadian Landscape, 1989-2000.* Toronto. <http://www.wwfcanada.org>.

–. 1999a. *Canada's Commitment to Forest Protected Areas: A WWF Status Report.* Toronto.

–. 1999b. *The Problems with Pesticides: A Briefing Book for Parliamentarians.* Toronto.

–. 1997. *Endangered Spaces Progress Report: 1996-97.* Toronto.

Worldwatch Institute. 2002. *State of the World 2002.* Washington, DC: W.W. Norton and Company.

Wossink, Grada, and T.A. Feitshans. 2000. "Pesticide Policies in the European Union." 5 *Drake Journal of Agricultural Law* 223.

Wylynko, Bradley D. 1999. "Beyond Command and Control: A New Environmental Regulatory Strategy Links Voluntarism and Government Initiative." In Robert B. Gibson, ed., *Voluntary Initiatives: The New Politics of Corporate Greening,* 161-75. Peterborough, ON: Broadview Press.

Yaffee, Steven L. 1994. *The Wisdom of the Spotted Owl: Policy Lessons for a New Century.* Washington, DC: Island Press.

Yaron, Gil. 2002. *The Corporation Inside and Out.* Vancouver: Aurora Institute. <http://www. aurora.ca>.

Yelin-Kiefer, Jennifer. 2001. "Warming up to an International Greenhouse Gas Market: Lessons from the U.S. Acid Rain Experience." 20 *Stanford Environmental Law Journal* 221.

Young, Alan. 2001. *Mineral Development and Sustainability: Measuring Our Progress since Rio.* Victoria: Environmental Mining Council of British Columbia.

Yukon Department of Renewable Resources. 2001. *Yukon State of the Environment Interim Report 2000.* Whitehorse: Government of Yukon.

Zimmerman, Adam H. 1997. *Who's in Charge Here, Anyway? Reflections from a Life in Business.* Toronto: Stoddart.

Federal Laws and Regulations

Access to Information Act, R.S.C. 1985, c. A-1.

An Act to Amend the Export Development Corporation Act, S.C. 2001, c. 33.

An Act to Amend the International Boundary Waters Treaty Act, S.C. 2001, c. 40.

Arctic Waters Pollution Prevention Act, R.S.C. 1985, c. A-12.

Arctic Shipping Pollution Prevention Regulations, C.R.C. 1978, c. 353.

Arctic Waters Pollution Prevention Regulations, C.R.C. 1978, c. 354.

Auditor General Act, R.S.C. 1985, c. A-17.

Canada Foundation for Sustainable Development Technology Act, S.C. 2001, c. 23.

Canada National Parks Act, S.C. 2000, c. 32.

National Parks General Regulations, SOR/78-213.

National Parks Wilderness Area Declaration Regulations, SOR/2000-387.

Canada Shipping Act, R.S.C. 1985, c. S-9.

Canada Transportation Act, S.C. 1996, c. 10.

Canada Water Act, R.S.C. 1985, c. C-11.

Canada Wildlife Act, R.S.C. 1985, c. W-9, amended by S.C. 1994, c. 23.

Canadian Charter of Rights and Freedoms, Part I of the *Constitution Act, 1982,* being Schedule B to the *Canada Act 1982* (U.K.), 1982, c. 11.

Canadian Environmental Assessment Act, S.C. 1992, c. 37.

Comprehensive Study List Regulations, SOR/94-229.

Exclusion List Regulations, SOR/94-316.

Inclusion List Regulations, SOR/94-164.

Law List Regulations, SOR/94-163.

Canadian Environmental Protection Act, 1999, S.C. 1999, c. 33.

Asbestos Mines and Mills Release Regulations, SOR/90-341.

Benzene in Gasoline Regulations, SOR/97-493.

Chlor-Alkali Mercury Release Regulations, SOR/90-130.

Contaminated Fuel Regulations, SOR/91-486.

Diesel Fuel Regulations, SOR/97-110.

Leaded Gasoline Regulations, C.R.C. 409.

Lead-free Gasoline Regulations, C.R.C. 408.

Ozone Depleting Substances Regulations, SOR/99-7.

Persistence and Bioaccumulation Regulations, SOR/2000-107.

Phosphorous Concentration Regulations, SOR/89-501.

Pulp and Paper Mill Defoamer and Wood Chip Regulations, SOR/92-282.

Pulp and Paper Mill Effluent Chlorinated Dioxins and Furans Regulations, SOR/92-267.

Secondary Lead Smelter Release Regulations, SOR/91-155.

Sulphur in Gasoline Regulations, SOR/99-236.

Tetrachloroethylene Regulations, SOR/2003-79.

Vinyl Chloride Release Regulations, SOR/92-631.

Coastal Fisheries Protection Act, R.S.C. 1985, c. C-33.

Constitution Act, 1867 (U.K.), 30 & 31 Vict., c. 3, reprinted in R.S.C. 1985, App. II, No. 5.

Criminal Code, R.S.C. 1985, c. C-46.

Department of Natural Resources Act, S.C. 1994, c. 41.

Energy Efficiency Act, S.C. 1992, c. 36.

Energy Efficiency Regulations, SOR/94-651.

Environmental Assessment and Review Process Guidelines Order, SOR/84-467.

Federal Court Rules, C.R.C. 1978, c. 663.

Federal Court Rules, SOR/98-106.

First Nations Land Management Act, S.C. 1999, c. 24.
Fisheries Act, R.S.C. 1985, c. F-14.
  Aboriginal Communal Fishing Licences Regulations, SOR/93-332.
  BC Sport Fishing Regulations, SOR/96-137.
  Chlor-Alkali Mercury Liquid Effluent Regulations, C.R.C. 1978, c. 811.
  Fish Health Protection Regulations, C.R.C. 1978, c. 812.
  Fishery (General) Regulations, SOR/93-53.
  Metal Mining Liquid Effluent Regulations, C.R.C. 1978, c. 819.
  Newfoundland Fishery Regulations, SOR/78-443.
  Pacific Fishery Regulations, SOR/93-54.
  Petroleum Refinery Effluent Regulations, C.R.C. 1978, c. 828.
  Pulp and Paper Effluent Regulations, SOR/92-269.
Fisheries Prices Support Act, R.S.C. 1985, c. F-23.
Food and Drug Act, R.S.C. 1985, c. F-27.
  Food and Drug Act Regulations, C.R.C. 1978, c. 870.
Hazardous Products Act, R.S.C. 1985, c. H-3.
Health of Animals Act, S.C. 1990, c. 21.
Immigration and Refugee Protection Act, S.C. 2001, c. 27.
  Immigration and Refugee Protection Act Regulations, SOR/2002-227.
Income Tax Act, R.S.C. 1985 (5th Supp.), c. 1.
Kemano Completion Project Guidelines Order, SOR/90-279.
Mackenzie Valley Resource Management Act, S.C. 1998, c. 25.
Manganese-based Fuel Additives Act, S.C. 1997, c. 11.
Migratory Birds Convention Act, 1994, S.C. 1994, c. 22.
Motor Vehicle Fuel Consumption Standards Act, R.S.C. 1985, c. M-9 (not in force).
National Energy Board Act, R.S.C. 1985, c. N-7.
National Marine Conservation Areas Act, S.C. 2002, c. 18.
Navigable Waters Protection Act, R.S.C. 1985, c. N-22.
Nisga'a Final Agreement Act, S.C. 2000, c. 7.
North American Free Trade Agreement Implementation Act, S.C. 1993, c. 44.
Nunavut Land Claims Agreement Act, S.C. 1993, c. 28.
Oceans Act, S.C. 1996, c. 31.
  Endeavour Hydrothermal Vents Marine Protected Areas Regulations, SOR/2003-87.
Parks Canada Agency Act, S.C. 1998, c. 31.
Pest Control Products Act, S.C. 2002, c. 28.
  Pest Control Product Regulations, C.R.C. 1978, c. 1253.
Plant Protection Act, S.C. 1990, c. 22.
Railway Safety Act, R.S.C. 1985, c. R-4.2.
Species at Risk Act, S.C. 2002, c. 29.
Transportation of Dangerous Goods Act, R.S.C. 1985, c. T-19.
Yukon Environmental and Socioeconomic Assessment Act, S.C. 2003 (Bill C-2).

Provincial and Territorial Laws and Regulations

Alberta
Agriculture Operation Practices Act, R.S.A. 2000, c. A-7.
Environmental Protection and Enhancement Act, R.S.A. 2000, c. E-12.
  Environmental Assessment (Mandatory and Exempted Activities) Regulation, Alta. Reg. 111/93.
  Ozone Depleting Substances and Halocarbon Regulation, Alta. Reg. 181/00.
  Pesticide Sales, Handling, Use, and Application Regulation, Alta. Reg. 24/97.
Forest Act, R.S.A. 2000, c. F-22.
Forest and Prairie Protection Act, R.S.A. 2000, c. F-19.
Municipal Government Act, R.S.A. 2000, c. M-26.
North Red Deer Water Authorization Act, S.A. 2002, c. N-3.5.
Water Act, R.S.A. 2000, c. W-3.
Wildlife Act, R.S.A. 2000, c. W-10.
  Wildlife Regulation, Alta. Reg. 143/97 (amended to 151/01).

British Columbia
Drinking Water Protection Act, S.B.C. 2001, c. 9.
  Drinking Water Protection Regulation, B.C. Reg. 200/2003.

Ecological Reserve Act, R.S.B.C. 1996, c. 103.
Energy Efficiency Act, R.S.B.C. 1996, c. 114.
Environment Assessment Act, S.B.C. 2002, c. 43.
  Prescribed Time Limits Regulation, B.C. Reg. 372/2002.
  Reviewable Projects Regulation, B.C. Reg. 370/2002.
Fish Protection Act, S.B.C. 1997, c. 21, s. 6.
Forest Act, R.S.B.C. 1996, c. 157.
Forest and Range Practices Act, S.B.C. 2002, c. 69.
Forest Practices Code of British Columbia Act, R.S.B.C. 1996, c. 159.
  Operational Planning Regulation, B.C. Reg. 107/98.
  Private Land Forest Practices Regulation, B.C. Reg. 318/99.
  Silviculture Practices Regulation, B.C. Reg. 108/98.
  Timber Harvesting Practices Regulation, B.C. Reg. 109/98.
Forest Statutes Amendment Act, S.B.C. 2002, c. 45.
Local Government Act, R.S.B.C. 1996, c. 323.
  Water Conservation Plumbing Regulation, B.C. Reg. 294/98.
Motor Vehicle Act Regulations, B.C. Reg. 26/58.
Nisga'a Final Agreement Act, S.B.C. 1999, c. 2.
Park Act, R.S.B.C. 1996, c. 344.
Pesticide Control Act, R.S.B.C. 1996, c. 360.
  Pesticide Control Act Regulation, B.C. Reg. 319/81.
Protected Areas Forests Compensation Act, S.B.C. 2002, c. 51.
Recall and Initiative Act, R.S.B.C. 1996, c. 398.
  Initiative Petition Administration Regulation, B.C. Reg. 70/95.
Waste Management Act, R.S.B.C. 1996, c. 482.
  Agricultural Waste Control Regulation, B.C. Reg. 131/92.
  Antisapstain Chemical Waste Control Regulation, B.C. Reg. 300/90.
  Cleaner Gasoline Regulations, B.C. Reg. 498/95.
  Motor Vehicle Emissions Reduction Regulation, B.C. Reg. 517/95.
  Ozone Depleting Substances and Other Halocarbons Regulation, B.C. Reg. 387/99.
  Post-Consumer Paint Stewardship Program Regulation, B.C. Reg. 200/94.
  Post-Consumer Residual Stewardship Program Regulation, B.C. Reg. 333/97.
  Pulp Mill and Pulp and Paper Mill Liquid Effluent Control Regulation, B.C. Reg. 470/90.
  Waste Management Act Municipal Sewage Regulations, B.C. Reg. 129/99.
Water Protection Act, R.S.B.C. 1996, c. 484.
Water Regulation, B.C. Reg. 204/88.
Wildlife Act, R.S.B.C. 1996, c. 488.
  Wildlife Act Designation and Exemption Regulation, B.C. Reg. 168/90.
  Wildlife Management Areas Regulation No. 3 (Green Mountain Wildlife Management Area), B.C.
    Reg. 183/91.

Manitoba
Drinking Water Safety Act, C.C.S.M. D-101.
Endangered Species Act, C.C.S.M. E-111.
Environment Act, C.C.S.M. E-125.
  Livestock Manure and Mortalities Management Regulation, Man. Reg. 42/98.
  Manitoba Classes of Development Regulation, Man. Reg. 164/88.
  Sensitive Areas Regulation, Man. Reg. 126/88.
Forest Act, C.C.S.M. F-150.
Municipal Act, S.M. 1996, c. 58, C.C.S.M. M-225.
Ozone Depleting Substances Act, C.C.S.M. O-80.
  Ozone Depleting Substances Regulation, Man. Reg. 103/94.
Pesticides and Fertilizers Control Act, R.S.M. 1987, c. P-40.
  Pesticide Regulation, Man. Reg. 94/88.
  Pesticides and Fertilizers Licence Regulation, Man. Reg. 216/87.
Protection of Water Sources Regulation, Man. Reg. 326/88 under the *Public Health Act,* C.C.S.M.
    P-210.
Provincial Park Act, S.M. 1993, c. P-20.
Sustainable Development Act, 1998, C.C.S.M. S-270.
Water Resources Conservation and Protection Act, C.C.S.M. W-72.

New Brunswick
Clean Air Act, S.N.B. 1997, c. C-5.2.
  Air Quality Regulation, N.B. Reg. 97-133.
  Ozone Depleting Substances Regulation, N.B. Reg. 97-132.
Clean Environment Act, R.S.N.B. 1973, c. C-6.
  Environmental Impact Assessment Regulation, N.B. Reg. 87-83.
Clean Water Act, S.N.B. 1989, c. C-6.1.
  Water Classification Regulation, N.B. Reg. 2002-13.
  Watershed Protected Area Designation Order, N.B. Reg. 2001-83.
  Wellfield Protected Area Designation Order, N.B. Reg. 2000-47.
Crown Forests and Land Act, S.N.B. 1980, c. 38.1.
Endangered Species Act, S.N.B. 1996, c. E-9.101.
Livestock Operations Act, S.N.B. 1999, c. L-11.01.
Municipalities Act, R.S.N.B. 1973, c. M-22.
Pesticides Control Act, R.S.N.B. 1973, c. P-8.
  Pesticide Control Act Regulation, N.B. Reg. 96-126.
Provincial Offences Procedure Act, R.S.N.B. 1973, c. P-22.1.

Newfoundland and Labrador
Endangered Species Act, S.N. 2001, c. E-10.1.
  Endangered Species List Regulations, N.L. Reg. 57/02.
Environmental Protection Act, S.N.L. 2002, c. E-14.2.
  Environmental Assessment Regulations, 2000, Nfld. Reg. 48/00.
  Ozone Depleting Substances Regulation, Nfld. Reg. 120/97.
Forestry Act, R.S.N.L. 1990, c. F-23.
Water Resources Act, S.N.L. 2002, c. W-4.01.
Wilderness and Ecological Reserves Act, R.S.N.L. 1990, c. W-9.

Northwest Territories
Cities, Towns and Villages Act, R.S.N.W.T. 1988, c. C-8.
Environmental Protection Act, R.S.N.W.T. 1988, c. E-7.
Environmental Rights Act, R.S.N.W.T. 1988 (Supp.) c. 83.
Forest Management Act, R.S.N.W.T. 1988, c. F-9.
Forest Protection Act, R.S.N.W.T. 1988, c. F-10.
Pesticide Act, R.S.N.W.T. 1988, c. P-4.
  Pesticide Regulations, R.R.N.W.T. 1990, c. P-2.
Public Water Supplies Regulation, R.R.N.W.T. 1990, c. P-23.
Wildlife Act, R.S.N.W.T. 1988, c. W-4.

Nova Scotia
Endangered Species Act, S.N.S. 1998, c. 11.
  Species at Risk List Regulations, N.S. Reg. 109/2000, as amended by N.S. Reg. 82/2001.
Environment Act, S.N.S. 1994-95, c. 1.
  Environmental Assessment Regulations, N.S. Reg. 26/95.
  Ozone Layer Protection Regulations, N.S. Reg. 54/95.
  Pesticide Regulations, N.S. Reg. 61/95.
Forest Act, R.S.N.S. 1989, c. 179.
  Forest Sustainability Regulations, N.S. Reg. 148/2001.
  Wildlife Habitat and Watercourses Protection Regulations, N.S. Reg. 138/2001.
Municipal Government Act, S.N.S. 1998, c. 18.
Provincial Park Regulations, N.S. Reg. 69/89, as amended.
Water Resources Protection Act, S.N.S. 2000, c. 10.
Wilderness Areas Protection Act, S.N.S. 1998, c. 27.

Ontario
Crown Forest Sustainability Act, 1994, S.O. 1994, c. 25.
Endangered Species Act, R.S.O. 1990, c. E-15.
  Endangered Species Regulation, R.R.O. 1990, Reg. 328.
Energy Efficiency Act, R.S.O. 1990, c. E-17.
Environmental Assessment Act, R.S.O. 1990, c. E-18.
Environmental Assessment and Consultation Improvement Act, 1996, S.O. 1996, c. 27.

Environmental Bill of Rights, 1993, S.O. 1993, c. 28.
Environmental Protection Act, R.S.O. 1990, c. E-19.
  Air Contaminants from Ferrous Foundries, R.R.O. 1990, Reg. 336.
  Ambient Air Quality Criteria Regulation, R.R.O. 1990, Reg. 337.
  Certificate of Approval Exemptions – Air, Ont. Reg. 524/98.
  Environmental Protection Act Regulation, Ont. Reg. 361/98.
  Gasoline Volatility Regulation, Ont. Reg. 271/91.
  General Air Pollution Regulation, R.R.O. 1990, Reg. 346.
  Hot Mix Asphalt Regulation, R.R.O. 1990, Reg. 349.
  Landfill Sites, Ont. Reg. 232/98.
  Ozone Depleting Substances – General Regulation, R.R.O. 1990, Reg. 356.
  Waste Incinerator Regulation, Ont. Reg. 555/92.
Fish and Wildlife Conservation Act, S.O. 1997, c. 41.
Municipal Act, R.S.O. 1990, c. M-45.
Nutrient Management Act, S.O. 2002, c. 4.
Ontario Farming and Food Production and Protection Act, S.O. 1998, c. 1.
Ontario Water Resources Act, R.S.O. 1990, c. O-40.
  Drinking Water Protection Regulation – Larger Water Works, Ont. Reg. 459/00.
  Drinking Water Protection Regulation – Smaller Water Works, Ont. Reg. 505/00.
  Water Taking and Transfers Regulation, Ont. Reg. 285/99.
Pesticides Act, R.S.O. 1990, c. P-11.
  Pesticides Act (General) Regulation, R.R.O. 1990, Reg. 914.
Planning Act, R.S.O. 1990, c. P-13.
Provincial Parks Act, R.S.O. 1990, c. P-34.
  Mining in Provincial Parks Regulation, R.R.O. 1990, Reg. 954.
Safe Drinking Water Act, 2002, S.O. 2002, c. 32.
Sustainable Water and Sewage Systems Act, 2002, S.O. 2002, c. 29.
Toughest Environmental Penalties Act, 2000, S.O. 2000, c. 22.

Prince Edward Island
Environmental Protection Act, R.S.P.E.I. 1988, c. E-9.
  Ozone Depleting Substances and Replacement Regulations, P.E.I. No. EC 619/94.
Forest Management Act, R.S.P.E.I. 1988, c. F-14.
Natural Areas Protection Act, R.S.P.E.I. 1988, c. N-2.
  Natural Areas Protection Act Regulations, R.R.P.E.I., c. N-2.
Pesticides Control Act, R.S.P.E.I. 1988, c. P-4.
  Pesticides, Prince Edward Island Regulations, R.R.P.E.I., c. P-4.
Public Forest Council Act, S.P.E.I. 2001, c. P-29.1.
Wildlife Conservation Act, S.P.E.I. 1998, c. W-4.1.

Quebec
An Act Respecting the Conservation and Development of Wildlife, R.S.Q., c. C-61.1.
An Act Respecting Threatened or Vulnerable Species, R.S.Q., c. E-12.01.
Cities and Towns Act, R.S.Q., c. C-19.
Environmental Quality Act, R.S.Q., c. Q-2.
  Agricultural Operations Regulation, O.C. 695-2002.
  Regulation respecting environmental impact assessment and review, R.R.Q. 1981, c. Q-2, r. 9.
  Regulation respecting ozone depleting substances, O.C. 812-93.
  Regulation respecting the quality of drinking water, R.R.Q., c. Q-2, r. 4.1.
Forest Act, R.S.Q. c. F-4.1, as amended by *Forest Act*, S.Q. 2001, c. 6.
  Regulations respecting standards of forest management for forests in the domain of the State, O.C. 498-96.
Municipal Code of Quebec, R.S.Q., c. C-27.1.
Parks Act, R.S.Q., c. P-9.
Pesticides Act, R.S.Q., c. P-9.3.
  Pesticides Management Code, Gazette officielle du Québec, July 3, 2002, No. 27, p. 3548.
  Regulation respecting permits and certificates for the sale and use of pesticides, O.C. 305-97.
Water Resources Preservation Act, S.Q. 2001, c. 48.

Saskatchewan
An Act Respecting Agricultural Operations, S.S. 1998, c. A-12.1.

Environmental Assessment Act, R.S.S. 1978, c. E-10.1.
Environmental Management and Protection Act, S.S. 2002, c. E-10.21.
  Water Regulations, 2002, c. E-10.21, Reg. 1.
Ethanol Fuel Act, S.S. 2002, c. E-11.1.
  Ethanol Fuel (General) Regulations, E-11.1, Reg. 1.
Forest Resources Management Act. S.S. 1996, c. F-19.1.
  Forest Resource Management Regulations, c. F-19.1, Reg. 1, s. 5.
Parks Act, S.S. 1986, c. P-1.1.
Pest Control Products (Saskatchewan) Act, R.S.S. 1978, c. P-8.
  Pest Control Products Regulations, 1995, R.R.S., c. P-8, r. 3.
Watershed Authority Act, S.S. 2002, c. S-35.02.
Wildlife Act, 1998, S.S. 1998, c. W-13.12.
Wildlife Habitat Protection Act, S.S. 1998, c. W-13.2.

Yukon
Economic Development Act, S.Y. 1992, c. 2.
Environment Act, S.Y. 1991, c. 5.
  Yukon's *Ozone Depleting Substances and other Halocarbons Regulations*, O.I.C. 2000/127.
Municipal Act, R.S.Y. 1986, c. 119.
Parks and Land Certainty Act, S.Y. 2001, c. 22.
Pesticides Control Act, S.Y. 1989, c. 20.
  Pesticide Regulations, Y.T.O.I.C. 1994/125.
Wildlife Act, R.S.Y. 1986, c. 178.

United States
Administrative Procedures Act, 5 U.S.C. 702.
Clean Air Act, 42 U.S.C. 7401 et seq. (1970).
Clean Water Act (Federal Water Pollution Control Act), 33 U.S.C. 1251 et seq.
Comprehensive Environmental Response, Compensation and Liability Act of 1980 (the Superfund
  Act), 42 U.S.C. 9601 et seq. (1994 and Supp. III 1997).
Emergency Planning and Community Right-to-Know Act, 42 U.S.C. 11001 et seq. (1986).
Emergency Wetland Resources Act, 16 U.S.C. 3901 et seq.
Endangered Species Act of 1973, 16 U.S.C. 1531 et seq.
Federal Food, Drug and Cosmetic Act, 21 U.S.C. 301 et seq.
Federal Insecticide, Fungicide and Rodenticide Act, 7 U.S.C. 136 et seq.
Food Quality Protection Act of 1996, Public Law 104-170.
Marine Mammal Protection Act, 16 U.S.C. 1361 et seq.
National Environmental Protection Act, 42 U.S.C. 4321 et seq. (1969).
National Forest Management Act, 16 U.S.C. 1600 et seq.
National Invasive Species Act of 1996, 16 U.S.C. 4701 et seq.
Pollution Prevention Act of 1990, 42 U.S.C. 13101 et seq.
Resource Conservation and Recovery Act, 42 U.S.C. 6901 et seq. (1994 and Supp. IV 1998).
Safe Drinking Water Act, 42 U.S.C. 300 (1974).
Safe Drinking Water Act Amendments of 1996, Public Law 104-182.
Sustainable Fisheries Act reauthorized and amended as the *Magnuson-Stevens Fishery Conservation
  and Management Act*, 16 U.S.C. 1801 et seq.
Toxic Substances Control Act, 15 U.S.C. 2601 et seq. (1976).
Wild and Scenic Rivers Act of 1968, 16 U.S.C. 1271 et seq.
Wilderness Act, 16 U.S.C. 1131 et seq.

International Law
Agreement Between the Government of Canada and the Government of the United States on Air Quality,
  in force 13 March 1991, 30 I.L.M. 678.
Bergen Ministerial Declaration on Sustainable Development, 1990. 1 *Yearbook on International
  Environmental Law* 429: 4312.
Harmonized Commodity Description and Coding System, General Agreement on Tariffs and Trade,
  BISD, 34 Supp. 5 (1988) (L/6112, L/6222, and L/6292).
International Centre for Settlement of Investment Disputes. 2000. Award: Between Metalclad
  Corporation and the United Mexican States. Case No. ARB(AF)/97/1.

Montreal Protocol on Substances That Deplete the Ozone Layer, adopted and opened for signature 16 September 1987 and entered into force 1 January 1989, 26 I.L.M. 1541.

North American Agreement on Environmental Cooperation, 14 September 1993, 32 I.L.M. 1480.

North American Free Trade Agreement, 17 December 1992, 32 I.L.M. 605.

Stockholm Convention on Persistent Organic Pollutants, <http://www.chem.unep.ch/pops>.

United Nations. 2000. *Millennium Declaration.* Resolution of the General Assembly. A/55/L.2.

United Nations Agreement on Straddling Fish Stocks and Highly Migratory Fish Stocks, 8 September 1995, 34 I.L.M. 1542.

United Nations Conference on Environment and Sustainable Development. 1992. *Statement of Principles for a Global Consensus on the Management, Conservation, and Sustainable Development of all Types of Forests,* 31 I.L.M. 881.

United Nations Convention on Biological Diversity, 5 June 1992, 31 I.L.M. 818.

Cartagena Protocol on Biosafety, 29 January 2000, 39 I.L.M. 1027.

United Nations Economic Commission for Europe Convention on Long Range Transport of Air Pollution, 1979, 18 I.L.M. 1442.

United Nations Framework Convention on Climate Change, <http://www.unfccc.de>.

Kyoto Protocol, 11 December 1997, 37 I.L.M. 22.

Vienna Convention on the Protection of the Ozone Layer, 1987, 26 I.L.M. 1516.

World Trade Organization. 2001. European Communities – Measures Affecting Asbestos and Asbestos Containing Products, WT/DS135/AB/R, 12 March 2001. <http://www.wto.org>.

World Trade Organization. 1998. EC Measures Concerning Meat and Meat Products (Hormones) Complaint by Canada, WT/DS48/R/Can and WT/DS48/AB/R/1998.

World Trade Organization. 1998. United States – Import Prohibition of Certain Shrimp and Shrimp Products, WT/DS58/AB/R.

World Trade Organization. 1996. United States – Standards for Reformulated and Conventional Gasoline, WTO Doc. WT/DSR/R, 29 January 1996, 35 I.L.M. 274.

World Trade Organization. 1996. United States – Restrictions on Import of Tuna, GATT Doc. DS21/R, BISD (39th Supp.).

WTO Appellate Body Report. 1998. EC Measures Concerning Meat and Meat Products, WT/DS26/AB/R.

WTO Panel Report. 1997. EC Measures Concerning Meat and Meat Products, WT/DS26/R/USA.

Cases

114957 Canada Ltée (Spraytech, Société d'arrosage) v. *Hudson (Town)* (2001), 40 C.E.L.R. (N.S.) 1 (S.C.C.).

65302 British Columbia Ltd. v. *Canada,* [1999] 3 S.C.R. 804.

Alberta Wilderness Association v. *Canada (Minister of Fisheries and Oceans)* (1999), 29 C.E.L.R. (N.S.) 21 (F.C.A.).

Alberta Wilderness Association v. *Cardinal River Coals Ltd.* (1999), 30 C.E.L.R. (N.S.) 175 (F.C.T.D.).

Alberta Wilderness Association v. *Express Pipelines Ltd.* (1996), 47 D.L.R. (4th) 177 (F.C.A.).

Algonquin Wildlands League et al. v. *Northern Bruce Peninsula (Municipality)* (2000), 39 C.E.L.R. (N.S.) 53 (Ont. Sup. Ct.).

Algonquin Wildlands League v. *Ontario (Minister of Natural Resources)* (1998), 26 C.E.L.R. (N.S.) 163.

Attorney General of Canada v. *Aluminum Company of Canada* (1980), 115 D.L.R. (3d) 495 (B.C.S.C.).

Baker v. *Canada (Minister of Citizenship and Immigration),* [1999] 2 S.C.R. 817.

B.C. Hydro and Power Authority v. *Canada (Attorney General) and Minister of Fisheries and Oceans* (3 June 1998), T-1171-97 (F.C.T.D.), McGillis J.

Ben Gardiner Farms Inc. v. *West Perth (Township)* (2002), 43 C.E.L.R. (N.S.) 3 (Ont. Div. Ct.).

Bow Valley Naturalists Society et al. v. *Minister of Canadian Heritage* (1999), 32 C.E.L.R. (N.S.) 84 (F.C.T.D.), affirmed (2001), 37 C.E.L.R. (N.S.) 1 (F.C.A.).

Bowen v. *Canada (Attorney General) et al.,* [1998] 2 F.C. 395 (T.D.).

Caddy Lake Cottager's Association v. *Florence-Nora Access Road Inc.* (1998), 26 C.E.L.R. (N.S.) 322 (Man. C.A.).

Canadian Earthcare Society v. *British Columbia (E.A.B.)* (1988), 3 C.E.L.R. (N.S.) 55 (B.C.C.A.).
Canadian Environmental Law Association v. *Canada (Minister of the Environment)* (2000), 34 C.E.L.R. (N.S.) 159 (F.C.A.).
Canadian Parks and Wilderness Society v. *Canada (Minister of Indian Affairs and Northern Development)* (30 June 1994), (F.C.T.D.) [unreported].
Canadian Parks and Wilderness Society v. *Sheila Copps, Minister of Canadian Heritage* (16 October 2001), F.C.T. 1123, T-1066-01, Gibson J.
Canadian Parks and Wilderness Society v. *Superintendent of Banff National Park et al.* (1994), 69 F.T.R. 241 (T.D.).
Canadian Parks and Wilderness Society v. *Superintendent of Wood Buffalo National Park* (1992), 34 A.C.W.S. (3d) 618 (F.C.T.D.).
Canadian Wildlife Federation v. *Canada (Minister of Environment)*, [1989] 4 W.W.R. 526 (F.C.T.D.).
Canadian Wildlife Federation v. *Canada (Minister of Environment)*, [1990] 2 W.W.R. 69 (F.C.A.).
Cariboo-Chilcotin Conservation Council v. *British Columbia (Chief Forester)* (1997), Vancouver Registry No. A960948 (B.C.S.C.).
Cheslatta Carrier First Nation et al. v. *John Marczyk et al.* (1998), 3 C.N.L.R. 1 (B.C.S.C.).
Chetwynd Environmental Society v. *B.C. (Minister of Forests)* (1995), 13 B.C.L.R. (3d) 338 (S.C.).
Citizen's Mining Council of Newfoundland and Labrador Inc. v. *Canada (Minister of Environment)* (1999), 29 C.E.L.R. (N.S.) 117 (F.C.T.D.).
Comeau's Sea Foods Ltd. v. *Canada (Minister of Fisheries and Oceans)*, [1997] 1 S.C.R. 12.
Council of the Haida Nation v. *B.C. Minister of Forests and Weyerhaeuser* (22 February 2002), 0147 (B.C.C.A.).
Crompton Co. v. *Canada (Minister of Health)* (2001), 38 C.E.L.R. (N.S.) 248 (F.C.T.D.).
Delgamuukw v. *British Columbia*, [1997] 3 S.C.R. 1010.
Denman Island Local Trust Committee v. *4064 Investments Ltd.* (2000), 14 M.P.L.R. (3d) 29 (B.C.S.C.), affirmed (19 December 2001), 0736, (B.C.C.A.).
Ecology Action Centre v. *Canada (Minister of Fisheries and Oceans)*, Federal Court of Canada T-1179-01.
Energy Probe v. *Canada (Attorney General)* (1989), 68 O.R. (2d) 449 (C.A.).
Finlay v. *Canada (Minister of Finance)*, [1986] 2 S.C.R. 607.
Fletcher v. *Kingston (City)* (1998), 28 C.E.L.R. (N.S.) 229 (Ont. Ct. Prov. Div.).
Fowler v. *The Queen* (1980), 133 D.L.R. (3d) 513 (S.C.C.).
Friends of the Oldman River Society v. *Minister of Transport et al.*, [1992] 1 S.C.R. 3.
Friends of the West Country Association v. *Canada (Minister of Fisheries and Oceans)* (1997), 23 C.E.L.R. (N.S.) 135 (F.C.T.D.).
Friends of the West Country Association v. *Canada (Minister of Fisheries and Oceans)* (1999), 28 C.E.L.R. (N.S.) 97 (F.C.T.D.).
Friends of the West Country Association v. *Canada (Minister of Fisheries and Oceans)* (2000), 31 C.E.L.R. (N.S.) 239 (F.C.A.).
Gariepy v. *Shell Oil* (30 August 2002), (Ont. S.C.) [unreported], Nordheimer J.
Gitxsan and other First Nations v. *British Columbia (Minister of Forests)*, (2002) B.C.S.C. 1701, Tysoe J.
Green v. *The Queen in Right of the Province of Ontario*, [1973] 2 O.R. 396 (Ont. H.C.).
Interfor v. *Paine and Krawczyk* (25 January 2001), B.C.C.A. 48, C.A. 027708.
Inverhuron and District Ratepayers Association v. *Canada (Minister of Environment)* (2000), 34 C.E.L.R. (N.S.) 1 (F.C.T.D.), affirmed (2001), 39 C.E.L.R. (N.S.) 161 (F.C.A.).
Kostuch v. *Alberta (Attorney General)* (1992), 125 A.R. 214 (C.A.).
Kostuch v. *Alberta (Attorney General)* (1993), 143 A.R. 161 (Q.B.).
Kostuch v. *Alberta (Attorney General)*, [1996] 1 W.W.R. 292 (Alta. C.A.).
Kostuch v. *Environmental Appeal Board* (1996), 21 C.E.L.R. (N.S.) 257 (Alta. Q.B.).
Kostuch v. *Kowalski* (1990), 75 Alta.L.R. (2d) 110 (Prov. Ct.).
Kostuch v. *Kowalski* (1991), 78 Alta.L.R. (2d) 131(Prov. Ct.).
Kostuch v. *Kowalski* (1991), 81 Alta.L.R. (2d) 214 (Q.B.).
Krey v. *R.* (1982), 12 C.E.L.R. 105 (N.W.T. Terr. Ct.).
Labrador Inuit Association v. *Newfoundland (Minister of the Environment)* (1997), 25 C.E.L.R. (N.S.) 232 (Nfld. C.A.).
MacMillan Bloedel v. *Sheila Simpson et al.* (1993), 84 C.C.C. (3d) 559 (B.C.C.A.).
Makivik Corp. and Nunavik Inuit v. *Canada (Minister of Canadian Heritage)* (4 August 1998), T-545-97 (F.C.T.D.), Richard J.

Manitoba Future Forest Alliance v. *Canada (Minister of Environment)* (1999), 30 C.E.L.R. (N.S.) 1 (T.D.).

Mikisew Cree First Nation v. *Sheila Copps, Minister of Canadian Heritage* (20 December 2001), F.C.T. 1426, T-1141-01, Hansen J.

Mitchell v. *Canada (Attorney General)*, [1999] Newfoundland Supreme Court, Trial Division, 9 April 1999, Roberts J.

Moresby Explorers Ltd. et al. v. *Canada (Attorney General)* (2001), 40 C.E.L.R. (N.S.) 174 (F.C.T.D.).

Munro v. *National Capital Commission*, [1966] S.C.R. 663.

Naskapi-Montagnais Innu Association v. *Canada (Minister of National Defence)*, [1990] 3 F.C. 381 (T.D.).

National Inshore Fisherman Association v. *Canada (Minister of the Environment)*, [1990] 37 F.T.R. 230 (F.C.T.D.).

Neskonlith Band v. *Canada (Attorney General)* (8 August 1997), F.C. T-1497-97, Reed J., decision of MacKay J. dated 22 September 1997.

Newfoundland and Labrador Wildlife Federation v. *Newfoundland (Minister of Labour and Environment)* (2001), 38 C.E.L.R. (N.S.) 256 (Nfld. Sup. Ct. T.D.).

Nisga'a Tribal Council v. *British Columbia (E.A.B.)* (1988), 3 C.E.L.R. (N.S.) 91 (B.C.S.C.).

Northern Spotted Owl et al. v. *Hodel*, 716 F. Supp. 479 (U.S. Dist. Ct., 1988).

Northern Spotted Owl v. *Lujan*, 758 F. Supp. 621 (U.S. Dist. Ct., 1991).

Northwest Falling Contractors Ltd. v. *The Queen* (1980), 133 D.L.R. (3d) 1 (S.C.C.).

Nunavut Tunngavik Inc. v. *Canada (Minister of Fisheries and Oceans)* (1997), 149 D.L.R. (4th) 519 (F.C.T.D.).

Nunavut Tunngavik Inc. v. *Canada (Minister of Fisheries and Oceans)* (1998), 162 D.L.R. (4th) 625 (F.C.A.).

Ontario (Attorney-General) v. *Mississauga (City)* (1981), 10 C.E.L.R. 91 (Ont. C.A.).

Ontario v. *Canadian Pacific Ltd.*, [1995] 2 S.C.R. 1031.

Operation Dismantle v. *R.*, [1985] 1 S.C.R. 441.

Palmer v. *Stora Kopparbergs* (1983), 12 C.E.L.R. 157 (N.S.S.C. T.D.).

Pearson v. *Inco* (9 September 2002), (Ont. S.C.) [unreported], Nordheimer J.

Peter G. White Mgmt. Ltd. v. *Canada (Minister of Canadian Heritage)* (1997), 132 F.T.R. 89 (T.D.).

Protected Areas Association of Newfoundland and Labrador et al. v. *Minister of Environment et al.* (2002) Supreme Court of Newfoundland and Labrador, Trial Division 2002-0IT-No. 4357 (28 October 2002).

Quebec (Attorney General) v. *Canada (National Energy Board)*, [1994] 1 S.C.R. 159.

R. v. *Adams*, [1996] 3 S.C.R. 101.

R. v. *Bata Industries Ltd.* (1992), 14 O.R. (3d) 354 (Ont. Ct. Gen. Div.).

R. v. *Bata Industries Ltd.* (1992), 70 C.C.C. (3d) 394 (Ont. Ct. Prov. Div.).

R. v. *Beaulieu* (2000), 34 C.E.L.R. (N.S.) 100.

R. v. *Brunswick Electric Power Commission* (1991), 10 C.E.L.R. (N.S.) 184 (N.B. Prov. Ct.).

R. v. *Canadian Pacific Forest Products Limited* (12 June 1991), (B.C. Prov. Ct.) [unreported].

R. v. *Corner Brook Pulp and Paper* (1997), 22 C.E.L.R. (N.S.) 199.

R. v. *Cote*, [1996] 3 S.C.R. 139.

R. v. *Crown Zellerbach Canada Ltd.*, [1988] 1 S.C.R. 401.

R. v. *Cyanimid Canada Inc.* (1981), 3 F.P.R. 151 (Ont. Prov. Ct.).

R. v. *Gladstone*, [1996] 2 S.C.R. 723.

R. v. *Hydro-Quebec*, [1997] 3 S.C.R. 213.

R. v. *Kern* (20 February 2001), B.C.C.A. 174, C.A. 027698.

R. v. *McCain* (1984), 4 F.P.R. 300 (N.B. Prov. Ct.).

R. v. *Marshall*, [1999] 3 S.C.R. 456.

R. v. *Marshall*, [1999] 3 S.C.R. 533.

R. v. *Nikal*, [1996] 1 S.C.R. 1013.

R. v. *NTC Smokehouse*, [1996] 2 S.C.R. 672.

R. v. *Robertson*, [1882] 6 S.C.R. 52.

R. v. *Sharma*, [1993] 1 S.C.R. 650.

R. v. *Sparrow*, [1990] 1 S.C.R. 1075.

R. v. *Thomas Paul* (1997), 193 N.B.R. (2d) 231 (Q.B.), reversed, [1998] 3 C.N.L.R. 221 (N.B.C.A.).

R. v. Tioxide Canada Inc. (31 May 1993), File 765-72-000060-528 (Que. Crim. Ct.).

R. v. Van der Peet, [1996] 2 S.C.R. 507.

R. v. Wholesale Travel Inc., [1991] 3 S.C.R. 154.

Re: Gold Mountain Springs (2002), 44 C.E.L.R. (N.S.) 287 (Ont. Municipal Board).

Red Mountain Residents and Property Owner's Association v. B.C. (Ministry of Forests) (2000), 35 C.E.L.R. (N.S.) 127 (B.C.S.C.).

Reese v. Alberta (Minister of Forestry, Lands and Wildlife) (1992), 87 D.L.R. (4th) 1 (Alta. Q.B.).

Schwarz Hospitality Group Ltd. v. Canada (Minister of Canadian Heritage) (2001), 37 C.E.L.R. (N.S.) 295 (F.C.T.D.).

Seattle Audubon Society v. Evans, 771 F. Supp. 1081 (W.D. Wash., 1991), affirmed 952 F. 2d. 297 (9th Cir., 1991).

Seattle Audubon Society v. Mosely (U.S. Dist. Ct. W.D. Wash.), C92-479WD, 28 May 1992.

Shiell v. Amok Ltd. (1988), 27 Admin. L.R. 1 (Sask. Q.B.).

Shiell v. Canada (Atomic Energy Control Board) (1995), 33 Admin. L.R. (2d) 122 (F.C.T.D.).

Sierra Club of Canada v. Canada (Minister of Finance), T-85-97 (F.C.T.D.).

Sierra Club of Canada v. Minister of Finance, [1999] 2 F.C. 211 (T.D.).

Sierra Club of Western Canada v. British Columbia (Chief Forester) (1993), 22 Admin. L.R. (2d) 129 (B.C.S.C.).

Sierra Club of Western Canada v. British Columbia (Chief Forester) (1994), 117 D.L.R. (4th) (B.C.S.C.), affirmed (1995), 7 B.C.L.R. (3d) 375 (C.A.).

Sierra Club v. Department of Interior, 376 F. Supp. 90 (U.S. Dist. Ct., 1974).

Sierra Club v. Department of Interior, 398 F. Supp. 284 (U.S. Dist. Ct., 1975).

Snowcap Waters Limited and Sun Belt Water Inc. v. Minister of Environment et al. (15 April 1997), Docket No. S3013, B.C. Supreme Court, Bouck J.

Society of the Friends of Strathcona Park v. British Columbia (Minister of Environment, Land and Parks) (1999), 31 C.E.L.R. (N.S.) 274 (B.C.S.C.).

Sunshine Village Corp. v. Canada (Minister of Canadian Heritage) (1995), 98 F.T.R. 25 (T.D.), affirmed 199 N.R. 104 (C.A.).

Sunshine Village Corp. v. Superintendent, Banff National Park (1996), 20 C.E.L.R. (N.S.) 171 (F.C.A.). Leave to appeal to S.C.C. refused 209 N.R. 399n.

T.V.A. v. Hill, 437 U.S. 153 (1978).

Taku River Tlingit First Nation v. Ringstad et al. (2000), 77 B.C.L.R. (3d) 310 (B.C.S.C.), affirmed (2002), B.C.C.A. 59.

Tsawwassen Indian Band v. Canada (Minister of Finance) (1998), 27 C.E.L.R. (N.S.) 177 (T.D.), affirmed (2001), F.C.A. 57.

Union of Nova Scotia Indians v. Canada (Attorney General) (1997), 1 F.C. 325 (T.D.).

United Mexican States v. Metalclad Corporation (2001), 38 C.E.L.R. (N.S.) 284 (B.C.S.C.).

Vancouver Island Peace Society v. Canada, [1992] 3 F.C. 42 (T.D.).

Vuntut Gwitchin First Nation v. Canada (1998), 228 N.R. 128 (F.C.A.).

Western Canada Wilderness Committee v. British Columbia (Chief Forester) (1996), 62 A.C.W.S. (3d) 779 (B.C.S.C.), affirmed 158 D.L.R. (4th) 353 (B.C.C.A.).

Young et al. v. Canada (Attorney General) (1999), F.T.R. 100 (F.C.T.D.).

Index

David R. Boyd is an environmental lawyer, professor, writer, and activist. He is a Senior Associate with the University of Victoria's POLIS Project on Ecological Governance, an Adjunct Professor with Simon Fraser University's graduate Resource and Environmental Management program, and the former Executive Director of the Sierra Legal Defence Fund. He has represented clients such as Greenpeace and the Council of Canadians at all levels of court, including the Supreme Court of Canada.

Boyd is the editor of *Northern Wild: Best Contemporary Canadian Nature Writing* (Douglas & McIntyre, 2001) and the author of *Canada vs. The OECD: An Environmental Comparison,* and many other reports on environmental law and policy. His essays appear regularly in the *Globe and Mail* and other newspapers. His passions include hiking, biking, kayaking, river rafting, and running marathons.

Readers with comments or questions can contact David Boyd at drboyd@ uvic.ca. Updates on Canadian environmental law and policy will be provided at www.unnaturallaw.com.

Law and Society Series
W. Wesley Pue, General Editor

Gender in the Legal Profession: Fitting or Breaking the Mould
Joan Brockman

Regulating Lives: Historical Essays on the State, Society, the Individual, and the Law
Edited by John McLaren, Robert Menzies, and Dorothy E. Chunn

Taxing Choices: The Intersection of Class, Gender, Parenthood, and the Law
Rebecca Johnson

Collective Insecurity: The Liberian Crisis, Unilateralism, and Global Order
Ikechi Mgbeoji

Murdering Holiness: The Trials of Franz Creffield and George Mitchell
Jim Phillips and Rosemary Gartner

People and Place: Historical Influences on Legal Culture
Edited by Jonathan Swainger and Constance Backhouse